PSYCHOTHERAPY
An Australian Perspective

To students, for their passion for learning and their dedication in working with clients; and to clients, for their resilience and their courage to change.

PSYCHOTHERAPY
An Australian Perspective

Analise O'Donovan, Leanne Casey,
Marchiene van der Veen, and Mark Boschen

IP Communications
2013

IP Communications, Pty. Ltd.,
Level 1,
123 Camberwell Road,
East Hawthorn, Victoria, 3123,
Australia.

Phone: +61 3 9811 6818.
Fax: +61 3 9813 3979.
E-mail: ipcomm@bigpond.com
www.ipcommunications.com.au

ISBN: 978-0-9872905-1-9

National Library of Australia Cataloguing-in-publication data

Title: Psychotherapy: an Australian perspective/Analise O'Donovan ... [et al.].

ISBN: 9780987290519 (pbk.)

Notes: Includes bibliographical references and index.

Subjects: Psychotherapy—Australia

Other Authors/Contributors: O'Donovan, Analise.

Dewey Number: 616.8914

Edited by Gillespie & Cochrane, Pty. Ltd., Melbourne
Text design by Club Tractor Production Services, Melbourne
Typeset by Desktop Concepts Pty. Ltd., Melbourne
Cover design by Anne-Marie Reeves, Melbourne
Cover photograph: Albert Sulzer, Melbourne
Indexed by Mary Russell, Melbourne
Printed by BPA Print Group, Pty. Ltd., Melbourne

Contents

Authors

Associate Professor Analise O'Donovan is Deputy Head in the School of Applied Psychology at Griffith University, Mt Gravatt campus. She has had 17 years' experience training clinical postgraduate students as well as psychology undergraduate and honours students in a range of subjects, including psychopathology, psychotherapy, and practice skills. Analise was also Director of Clinical training Programs and Director of the Psychology Clinic at Griffith, Mt Gravatt campus, for a number of years. Analise has a particular passion for the practice of supervision, and has provided extensive training on effective supervision to supervisors and supervisees both nationally and internationally.

Dr Leanne Casey is Director of Clinical Psychology Programs at Griffith University, Mt Gravatt campus. She has had over 20 years' experience as a clinical psychologist, working in hospital, community, and private-practice settings. Clinical supervision has always been a highly-valued aspect of Leanne's professional practice, and since entering academia she has broadened her teaching interests to include counselling and psychotherapy training for both honours and postgraduate students. Her research interests are the use of technology in enhancing and disseminating psychological interventions, the therapeutic relationship, and change processes in psychotherapy.

Dr Marchiene van der Veen brings an international perspective, having worked as a clinical psychologist in South Africa, the United Kingdom, and more recently in Australia. Marchiene was Chair of the Queensland section of the Clinical College for a number of years. Currently, Marchiene runs a thriving private practice and has extensive experience in providing psychotherapeutic treatment to clients presenting with mental-health difficulties. Before establishing her private practice, Marchiene was Director of the Psychology Clinic at Griffith University. Throughout her career, Marchiene has been actively involved in the supervision and training of clinical postgraduate students and clinical psychologists. Marchiene's key interests are psychotherapeutic change processes, supervision, and ethical and effective psychological practice.

Dr Mark Boschen is a Senior Lecturer in Clinical Psychology at Griffith University. Mark specialises in the assessment and treatment of adult anxiety disorders, with a specific focus on treatment of obsessive-compulsive disorder. Mark maintains an active clinical practice in addition to his university research and teaching commitments, and is a regular presenter of workshops for the Australian Psychological Society on anxiety disorders, cognitive behaviour therapy, case formulation, and psychopharmacology.

Introduction

A range of books is available on psychotherapy. However, as educators, we struggled to find a book that incorporated the range of issues essential for practice by the early-career psychologist. Further, we could not find a book specific to the Australian setting. And, as you do when you can't find something, you do it yourself. The result is this text, intended to be used in the training of clinical psychologists. However, it may also be helpful for any practitioner who is working as a psychotherapist, as much of it is applicable to any work with clients seeking assistance with psychological issues.

We have had many discussions about what it was like to be an early-career clinical psychologist. All of us have vivid memories of seeing our first clients, and struggling to make sense of all the information they provided, trying to provide some structure, while building rapport, and hoping we were coming across as cool, calm, and collected, despite feeling quite nervous! The approach we present in this book is a culmination of many years of thinking about change, and of trying to instil fundamental practice knowledge in our students, while imparting our own sense of clinical psychology as a dynamic and ever-expanding discipline. We believe there is always scope to improve our knowledge and our ability to assist others—and we hope that you will adopt this attitude in your own practice.

Our goal is to provide coverage of the essential issues for effective and ethical practice as a psychologist in Australia. This text differs from most others; it addresses the broad range of topics important to practice, rather than focusing on a specific area, such as theoretical orientations, or microskills. Many excellent texts focus on these areas, which we recommend as additional reading. Instead, we started with the question: what issues confront psychologists as they begin to work with clients? As mentioned, we reminisced about our own early days of postgraduate training as being a mixture of uncertainty and doubt, and also of tremendous excitement about 'finally seeing clients' after all those years of academic training.

Over the years, we've also had the pleasure of working with many postgraduate students who were taking their own journey into clinical practice. To teach and supervise effectively, you need to be empathic, so we have tried to remain attuned to the experience of our students. Although there is variation among students, by and large their experience remains a mixture of enthusiasm, anxiety, doubts, and positive anticipation of the road ahead. We hope this book will enhance your enthusiasm and help to alleviate your concerns.

Much of the confusion and doubt that novice psychologists experience when working with clients is about trying to make sense of the often overwhelming stimuli. Students commence their professional-practice training after four years of university studies, which may have contained many mixed messages, such as: 'Be a

blank slate' *versus* 'The therapy relationship is really important—connect authenti-
cally with your client', *or* 'There are only some right ways to work with clients—and
you had better know the right theories and techniques' *versus* 'It's up to clients
whether they are motivated to change' or 'It's the therapist's responsibility to bring
about change'. An early-career psychologist has a head full of information—about
statistics, social psychology, personality theories, diagnosis, structures of the brain,
and so forth. How on earth do you sift through all this when your client is sitting in
front of you, waiting expectantly for you to take the lead and help them to overcome
their problems?

This book is intended to help you navigate your way through the ever-expanding
literature and opinion on psychological practice, and to assist you to become the
most competent and ethical practicing psychologist you can be. Although this book
is based on our best interpretation of current clinical knowledge and research, we
alert you to the one certainty about psychology—and psychotherapy in particular—
an enduring lack of certainty. Change in the literature is inevitable—but this should
be recognised as a positive, in fact as one of the great strengths of psychological
research. Continual attempts to improve the lot of our clients promote change in
what we know, and we develop knowledge and skills to address human suffering in
the best way possible.

Throughout this book we advocate an *approach* or *attitude to* therapy, rather than
a set of techniques or simple algorithms. Components of our approach include:

• In therapy, the client always comes first.
• The client has the capacity to change.
• As psychotherapists, we are accountable to our clients, the profession, society,
  and government to provide our best, professional services, and to make the best
  possible use of resources supplied by government or other organisations.
• As psychotherapists, at all times, we practise within the guidelines of the ethical
  code of conduct.
• Throughout our working lives, we must continue to learn, by keeping up to date
  with the literature, reflecting on our practice, seeking support when necessary,
  and learning from our clients. Complacency is not an option.
• A wide variety of views should be respected and carefully considered. As scientist–practitioners, we believe it is important to remain curious and open-minded,
  to explore knowledge about how we might best help clients, and if the evidence
  is substantial, to be open to changing clinical practice.

HOW THIS TEXT IS ORGANISED

Our text is arranged in four parts:

Part A: Foundations for professional psychological practice
This part provides the background for professional practice in psychology. The
chapter on the scientist–practitioner model reminds the reader of the most important aspects of this model, which remains the most recognised framework for

psychologists. The following chapter, on ethics, is vital for the profession of psychology. All psychologists, whether fully registered or not, must have a thorough understanding of ethics, and a commitment to behaving ethically at all times. Ethics goes across all theoretical and specialty boundaries. Our commitment to ethics allows our clients to know they will be safe.

Part B: Factors in psychological outcome

This part of the book starts with chapter 3, which presents our model for change in psychotherapy. Our model draws upon the factors identified in the psychotherapy-outcome literature related to client change, and provides a basis for thinking about and integrating what we know about effective treatment of clients.

Chapters 4 to 8 provide information on each major contributing factor in client outcome: client factors; therapist factors; the alliance; specific theories, rationales, and techniques; common factors. Chapter 9 is on the process and measurement of client outcome, and how it might be optimised. These chapters will provide a comprehensive overview of the factors considered to be important to clinical practice.

Part C: Psychotherapy process and practice

With knowledge of the key factors involved in change, how should a therapist proceed with a new client? Part C covers assessment, conceptualisation, treatment, and evaluation of outcome. The sequence of chapters follows the process a therapist would take with most clients. Part C starts with chapter 10, which introduces the therapist to practical issues in therapy delivery.

Chapter 11 considers the interpersonal and microskills required to interact with and establish rapport with a client. Certain therapist characteristics and skills assist in building a strong working alliance with clients, which is pivotal to treatment outcome. Throughout this book, we will stress how important it is for you to be effective interpersonally.

Chapter 12 provides information about intake assessments, gathering information about why a client presents for treatment, including getting a focus on his or her theory of change, presenting problems, strengths and vulnerabilities, previous treatment, and life situation. An accountable practitioner consistently evaluates the effectiveness of her or his practice; thus, we also discuss how to evaluate outcome and communicate findings to a client.

Chapter 13 looks at diagnosis to further determine type and range of problems. This enables conceptualisation, with use of psychological theory and knowledge of principles of behaviour, discussed in chapter 14. Based on the conceptualisation, the therapist will consider the most effective forms of treatment for the client.

Chapter 15 provides a brief overview of cultural, religious, and spiritual issues. Chapter 16 provides information on managing risk situations to ensure safety of clients.

Part D: Professional practice in the Australian context

The final part of this text is divided into three chapters. The need for professional training and development is the subject of chapter 17. Chapter 18 explains what supervision is, what you should expect from supervision, how to ensure you get most benefit from supervision, and what your role is in supervision. We conclude with a discussion in chapter 19 of therapist self-care.

OTHER FEATURES OF THIS BOOK

Each chapter will provide a list of reference books that we consider of great value to any clinician.

One of the most frequent comments we have had from trainees over the years has been that they would like to have examples of practice. It is rare that any of us get to see what other practitioners actually do with clients. In response to this need, this text provides a set of video vignettes, on YouTube, with links via the publisher's website, that illustrate many of the skills, techniques, process issues, and situations that are discussed.

We have used a range of terms in relation to individuals who provide treatment to individuals who require therapeutic interventions. In addition to *psychologist*, we have used *practitioner*, *therapist*, and *psychotherapist*. We have mostly used the term *client* to describe individuals who come to us for assistance. At times, we refer to *patients*. Mostly, this is because *patient* is more commonly used in the US, and much of the literature we discuss comes from the US. Some professionals are concerned about terms used to describe what they do, and there are legal restrictions around use of some terms.

Finally, our greatest hope is that you, our reader, will benefit from this book and find inspiration to do your best work with all your clients, to enable each to live a more productive and happier life.

Analise O'Donovan
Leanne Casey
Marchiene van der Veen
Mark Boschen

Acknowledgments

Of particular benefit for this book has been the direct involvement of a number of our postgraduate students. It was students' feedback that allowed us to know if we were on track or not. We would like to thank the following individuals for their assistance: Elisha Evans, Paul Finighan, Moana Harlen, Katherine Horrigan, Sam Minge, Angela Morgan, Anna Peck, Chris Pepping, Jacques Rizk, Emma Sanders, Brooke Stemm, Ea Stewart, Paula Stratton, and Ben Walters. It came as a surprise to us how considerable the task of editing, sorting out reference lists, preparing vignettes and so forth, is in getting a book ready. We would also like to thank our colleague, Sharon Dawe, for her invaluable contribution to the chapter on risk management, and Jeff Patrick, for his assistance with the figures and technical advice. All four of us would also like to thank our partners and families for their patience, cups of tea, and general support, while we spent too many weekends working on the book. We promise we'll make up for it!

One of the features of this book are the video vignettes, depicting a range of clinical situations. Throughout the text, we refer you to the vignettes, to enhance your learning and understanding of various situations, skills, problem solving, ethical issues, and so forth. We would like to thank those students and colleagues who participated in these vignettes: Briohny Cottler, Felicity Farmer, Danielle Faulks, Govind Krishnamoorthy, Alf Lizzio, Sam Minge, Angela Morgan, Brooke Stemm, and James Welch. We would also like to thank Kevin Judge, who managed to shepherd us through the process.

Video vignettes

Sixteen short video vignettes, on YouTube, with links via the publisher's website (www.ipcommunications.com.au), relate to issues discussed in the text. We have attempted to demonstrate scenarios that commonly cause the early-career practitioner some anxiety.

The vignettes are all role-play; the authors of the text are the actors, as well as a number of postgraduate clinical students in the GU program: Briohny Cottler, Danielle Faulks, Felicity Farmer, Govind Krishnamoorthy, Alf Lizzio, Sam Minge, Angela Morgan, Brooke Stemm, and James Welch. We thank each for his or her contribution.

In our text, in some of the exercises, a video vignette will be referred to. Here is a brief explanation of each of the vignettes.

Video 1: Discussing confidentiality
A number of issues need to be clarified at the beginning of a session with a new client. This vignette demonstrates a discussion with a new client focused on confidentiality.

> You always need to inform a client at the beginning of therapy about limits of confidentiality. However, would you always explain confidentiality to this extent to a client? Why?

Video 2: Therapy becomes a chat
This scene contains two vignettes that demonstrate different levels of self-disclosure by the therapist in response to the client's question. In the first scene, the therapist overdiscloses; as a result, therapeutic boundaries weaken. The session starts to resemble a chat between friends, rather than a therapy session. In the second scene, the therapist does a brief self-disclosure, but does not allow this to threaten therapeutic boundaries.

> Can you identify what it is that the therapist does in the second vignette that makes it more effective?

Video 3: Therapist being rigid
Two examples are provided of how a therapist responds to a client who has not done the homework agreed to in the session earlier. In the first scene, the therapist

appears to take the lack of homework personally, and gets upset with the client. The client becomes defensive, and a rupture is caused in the alliance. In the second vignette, the therapist remains non-defensive, and explores with the client the value of doing the homework, which results in a generally deeper understanding of the issues for the client. The importance of this example is not in whether clients should do homework or not, but how important it is that therapists remain non-attached to client choices about what they do regarding therapy; and most importantly, willing to explore clients' perspectives.

1   How would you manage your own behaviour to avoid being dogmatic in your work with clients?
2   Do you think there are situations in which it is appropriate for a therapist to insist on his or her suggestions being followed up by a client? If so, in what types of situations?

Video 4: Gifts from a client

A tricky issue is how to respond to gifts from clients. Some may say never accept a gift, but giving and receiving gifts can be used therapeutically, if managed well. In these vignettes, we depict a gift that is potentially problematic depending on how the therapist responds. In the first scene, the therapist is uncomfortable with the gift, and does not use the opportunity therapeutically. In fact, her response makes the gift problematic, and may send an inappropriate message to the client. In the second scene, the therapist uses the gift to enrich the therapeutic experience for the client, and ensures that the gift remains appropriate; there is no possibility of a boundary crossing.

1   This vignette depicts a fairly complex gift situation. However, some gifts given by clients will not be as loaded. How would you differentiate between gifts that are not problematic and those that must be carefully managed?
2   What does the *Code of Ethics* suggest about gifts from clients?

Video 5: Cross-cultural interview

You can expect to work with clients from a large range of different cultures. In this vignette, the client is from India, and the therapist has limited knowledge about his culture. However, the therapist manages to establish rapport and trust with the client and effectively lays the groundwork for therapy.

1   What are the essential components you can identify in this vignette that result in effective handling of cultural issues in therapy?
2   How can you ensure that you have skills and knowledge in working with clients from different cultures?

Video 6: Working with a distressed client

This vignette reveals a highly distressed client who is focused on her own feelings. The therapist is uncomfortable with the client's high level of emotional expression, and avoids engaging by sticking to facts, and even trying to get the client to move away from her emotions. The client initially escalates her emotion, to try to get the therapist to pay attention to her emotions, but in the end appears to give up.

1 What may be making it difficult for the therapist to cope with the client's level of emotional expression?
2 Why is it a problem if therapists are unwilling to tolerate high levels of emotion in clients?
3 What would you suggest to the therapist to improve this interaction?
4 How comfortable would you be working with such a distressed client?
5 How effective are your skills in dealing with strong emotions?

Video 7: Managing therapeutic boundaries in rural areas

Working in rural areas can often bring up boundary issues, as there is a greater likelihood of therapist and client having contact outside therapy than there is in larger centres. This vignette demonstrates a therapist managing this situation with a new client.

How well did the therapist discuss the issues with the client? Would you have any other suggestions for managing the situation?

Video 8: Working with a difficult client

This vignette provides another example of a client expressing strong emotion, in this case anger and resentment. The client is indignant because she feels she has been forced into therapy; she can be seen as a mandated client. The therapist does not avoid the client's emotion, and in fact encourages some exploration. The therapist does not become reactive to the client, common with an angry client, and does not tolerate inappropriate behavior. Instead, the therapist works to find ways for the client to manage her own affect.

1 What difficulties might you experience in managing an angry client? How might you work on, tackle, or approach these difficulties?
2 At what point do you think a client's behaviour is unacceptable, and you would need to take a time-out break in the session?

Video 9: Younger therapist working with an older client

Many new practitioners find themselves working with clients who are older than themselves. Can this work? In this vignette, the client raises his concern that the therapist is too young to understand him and relate to his problems. The therapist attempts to allay the client's concerns.

1   Do you think the client really felt at the end of this segment that the therapist understood him and that he really could relate to her?
2   What else could the therapist have done?
3   Are there some clients that you currently feel uncomfortable about working with? Why do you feel uncomfortable, and what can you do about it?

Scene 10: Interview with an adolescent
Establishing rapport with an adolescent client can require a different approach from that taken with an adult client. In this vignette, the therapist demonstrates how to form a bond with an adolescent client, exploring a wide range of topics, despite the client's initial reluctance; the client was brought in by her parents. Children and adolescents are rarely in therapy of their own accord; the therapist needs to demonstrate that therapy could be useful.

1   What issues might you need to bear in mind when working with children and adolescents?
2   How would you adapt to working with adolescents?
3   What skills do you have that would assist in working with young clients?

Scene 11: Therapist countertransference and supervision
There are two parts to this vignette. The first is a therapy session; the second part demonstrates a supervision session. The purpose of these vignettes is to illustrate the consequences of the therapist becoming emotionally reactive to material that a client raises. We all have our own issues; it is inevitable that therapy will bring up material that is difficult for us personally. This is a problem if left unrecognised and not managed. In the first scene, the therapist reacts personally to an issue raised by the client. In the second scene, the therapist receives supervision that explores the therapist's reaction, and encourages insight into the issue and consequences in therapy.

1   What are the potential consequences of the type of therapist reaction demonstrated in the first scene?
2   How might you manage your own issues to prevent them interfering in the therapy you do?
3   How would you respond to your supervisor raising these types of issues?

Video 12: Exploring feelings
The client has had a baby 6 weeks' previously and is upset that she is not as happy as she expected to be. The client is expressing negative feelings; at times, this can

create discomfort for a therapist. In this video, the therapist remains supportive of the client and encourages the client to explore her feelings.

> 1   If you were the therapist working with this client, what would your goals be?
> 2   What do you think the client's goals are?
> 3   What microskills does the therapist use and how effective are they in assisting the client?

Video 13: Ending a session on time

There are two parts to this vignette. It demonstrates a client not wanting to end the session, despite being cued by the therapist that it is time to finish. This is a common, and at times difficult, situation for therapists to manage. In the first scene, the therapist does not manage the situation very well. However, in the second scene, the therapist is more effective.

> 1   What does the therapist do in the second scene that demonstrates more effective management of this issue?
> 2   Do you think it is important to always end sessions at the agreed time? Why?
> 3   What would prevent you from finishing a session on time? What could you do to be more effective with endings?

Video 14: Assessment feedback

Providing feedback on test results requires understanding of the results and an ability to communicate them in a manner that the client can readily understand, and in a way that is therapeutic for the client.

> 1   What skills do you require to provide effective feedback of assessment results?
> 2   Why is it important to be competent in providing feedback on results?

Video 15: Suicide risk assessment

One of the biggest anxieties for early therapists (and experienced ones) is that a client may be suicidal. This vignette demonstrates a psychologist doing an assessment with a depressed young man. At the end, the psychologist debriefs about the role-play.

> 1   What thoughts and feelings might a therapist in this situation be attempting to manage in him- or herself? Why is it important for the therapist to manage these thoughts and feelings effectively?

2   How will you manage your own reactions when doing a suicide risk assessment?

3   What should you do if you feel out of your depth doing a suicide risk assessment?

4   How effective was this assessment? Do you think the psychologist made the correct decisions?

5   How well do you think the psychologist managed the client's distress?

6   How confident do you feel at the moment about doing a risk assessment? What would assist you to feel more confident?

Video 16: Working with a client in a domestic violence situation.

In this vignette, the therapist explores the extent of aggressive behaviour in a relationship with the husband of a couple. The wife has threatened to leave the marriage unless her husband seeks treatment. The client does not initially recognise that there is a problem, and uses minimisation and denial to play down the seriousness and consequences of the behaviour. The vignette demonstrates the therapist attempting to remain focused, non-judgmentally but persistently, on the alleged violence in the relationship.

1   What do you think is the intended consequence of the therapist remaining focused on this issue with the client?

2   What were your reactions to watching this vignette?

3   How would you have managed this situation?

Note to viewers of videos

In these videos, all characters, 'therapists' and 'clients', are played by actors, and scenarios are fictitious; any resemblance to a real person, living or dead, is purely coincidental.

Scenarios are designed and offered for the sole purpose of facilitating the education and training of helping-professionals; they cannot be used to guide the treatment of an individual client. Clinical management, including assessment of risk, and health and safety issues relating to any clinical context, remains the responsibility of the relevant clinician, in the context of policies and procedures of the clinician's governing agency.

Part A

Foundations for professional psychological practice

Chapter 1

The scientist–practitioner model

INTRODUCTION

The scientist–practitioner model is regarded as the cornerstone of training and practice in clinical psychology in Australia. Development of the scientist–practitioner model is often traced to the famous Boulder conference, held in Boulder, Colorado, in 1949. However, the origins of this model stretch back to Hippocrates, who first articulated the precept 'do no harm' (later translated into Latin as *'Primum non nocere'* by the Greek physician, Galen). The Hippocratic Oath, traditionally taken by doctors as they commence their careers, provides further foundation for the scientist–practitioner model: 'I will use my power … to the best of my ability and judgment; I will abstain from harming or wrongdoing any man by it.'

The scientist–practitioner model recognises the immense responsibility and trust that our clients place in us to provide them with the most optimal and effective range of treatments and services available. However, adoption of the scientist–practitioner model has not proven straightforward. In this chapter, we look at the strengths and limitations of the model, and examine ways in which professional practice as a psychologist is optimised as individual practitioners translate principles into clinical practice. To understand the importance of the scientist-practitioner model in the work of a psychologist, it is useful to reflect on what is meant by professional practice as a psychologist.

PROFESSIONAL PRACTICE

It is common for people who decide to train as psychologists to report that their decision to become a psychologist is motivated by their desire to 'help people'. This is a laudable aim, but, to a greater or lesser extent, many people have a desire to help others, and there are many ways to realise this aim. Becoming a psychologist certainly involves committing to helping others, but it carries with it the expectation that this help will occur in the context of a professional relationship and be based on a thorough understanding of psychology as a discipline. To illustrate this point, consider two scenarios and reflect on how you might respond.

Scenario 1.1

A friend comes to see you. She has recently broken up with her partner and is also having difficulties at work. She is having problems sleeping, and seems overwhelmed by the demands of her two children. She is feeling hopeless about her situation, and, in particular, is worrying that she will never find another partner.

Scenario 1.2

A client is referred to you. She has recently broken up with her partner and is also having difficulties at work. She is having problems sleeping, and seems overwhelmed by the demands of her two children. She is feeling hopeless about her situation, and, in particular, is worrying that she will never find another partner.

Exercise 1.1

For each scenario, ask yourself:
1   How would you help this person?
2   What would influence your decision about how you could help?

One of the keys to professional practice is to recognise that there would and should be a difference in how you respond. As a friend, you may offer to help mind the children, agree with her that her partner was a 'no-hoper', and suggest she joins you on a weekend away. As a psychologist, none of these responses would be appropriate or desirable. You may certainly explore with her ways in which she may enlist the support of her friends, but your work with her will be guided by psychological principles and be based on a clear understanding that this is a professional rather than a personal relationship.

Does this mean that a psychologist should act like a cold automaton with a client and hide all his or her personality? Of course not—as we discuss in chapter 6, the relationship between psychologist and client is optimally a warm and responsive one, in which the psychologist is willing to engage with the client genuinely and empathetically. It is wise to remember, though, that while there are many people who are potential 'friends' for a client, when a client comes to see a psychologist, the client rightfully anticipates that the assistance he or she receives will be based on professional expertise and knowledge. This professional expertise and knowledge depends on an understanding of the scientist–practitioner model, and a commitment to practising as a psychologist in accordance with the tenets of this model.

Definition and development

The scientist–practitioner model rests on the concept that psychologists should be trained as both scientists *and* practitioners. The 'scientist' role of psychologists is threefold: as a consumer of research findings that inform how they assess and treat their clients; as an evaluator of their clinical interventions; and as a researcher, who undertakes research in their own treatment setting for sharing with the broader professional community (Hayes et al., 1999).

The 'practitioner' role of psychologists has been less well defined, but implicitly involves the broad range of assessment and treatment skills that psychologists bring to their work, with knowledge and attitudes that guide sensitive and ethical application of these skills. These roles of 'scientist' and 'practitioner' should be inextricably linked in the work of psychologists, as they address the following fundamental questions:

- 'How can I best assess and treat my clients?'
- 'Am I effectively assessing and treating my clients?'
- 'How can I best assist others in the profession to effectively assess and treat their clients?'

Although a number of influential psychologists had earlier argued for a joint approach—notably the 1947 Report of the Committee on Training in Clinical Psychology, widely known as the Shakow Report—it was at the Boulder Conference that the idea of psychologists embodying the roles of both scientist and practitioner was firmly endorsed (Raimy, 1950). This conference brought together a range of stakeholders, from academic and clinical settings, to address the fundamental issue of how psychologists should be trained, and to identify the key elements in the training and professional identity of psychologists. Australian endorsement of the scientist–practitioner model occurred at Melbourne's La Trobe University in 1977 (Kenneth & Montgomery, 1977). Support for the concept that psychologists should be trained as both scientists and practitioners rested on the following assumptions:

- psychologists should engage in research and practice—and preferably both—to allow development of skills and interest
- the need for psychologists to engage in continuous development of the knowledge base regarding effective interventions means that research should be regarded as vital to the profession
- psychology training programs attract high-quality applicants who are able to undertake both roles
- direct clinical contact alerts psychologists to important issues that need to be investigated systematically
- there is a symbiotic relationship between effective psychological practice and funding for research, in that research provides the basis for effective practice and effective practice demonstrates the worth of continued research funding (Hayes, et al., 1999).

THE SCIENTIST-PRACTIONER MODEL AND THE STATUS OF PSYCHOLOGY

In many ways, the current status of psychology as a profession, and acceptance of psychological interventions, supports the wisdom of adopting the scientist–practitioner model. From their beginnings as experimentalists and psychometricians, psychologists have assumed a central role in the provision of mental-health services (Martin & Birnbrauer, 1996). Psychologists are now responsible for psychometric assessment, developing and administering psychological-treatment programs, providing consultation for administrative and organisational elements, and designing and implementing research programs. This expanded role rests largely on the vast amount of research that has been conducted into providing effective interventions over the last 50 years.

There is now strong evidence to support the efficacy of psychological interventions in treating anxiety, depression, bulimia nervosa, and marital discord, and accumulating evidence to suggest the utility of psychological interventions in the areas of substance abuse, binge eating disorder, chronic pain, sexual dysfunction, borderline personality disorder, and childhood anxiety (Nathan & Gorman, 2007). These findings are based predominantly on the commitment of psychologists to adopting a scientific approach to determining which treatments work for which client groups.

Such developments in the evidence base for psychological interventions have been critical to acceptance of the profession, particularly in view of wider concerns regarding accountability in the health arena. A strong influence here has been the push towards evidence-based practice, exemplified by the efforts of bodies such as the Cochrane Collaboration, an online library that publishes regular updates and reviews of evidence-based practice in health care. In part, this push towards evidence-based practice has been motivated by increasing concerns regarding health expenditure, as well as broader concerns regarding the importance of ensuring that individuals receive optimal care (Hickie et al., 2007). In Australia, the success of this approach—development of an evidence base—has resulted in an historic move to enable individuals who receive psychological services for mental-health concerns to receive rebates under the Better Access to Mental Health Care initiative, approved by the federal government in November 2006 (Hickie & McGorry, 2007). This has taken place in the context of increasing awareness of the economics of health expenditure (Hickie et al., 2007).

Findings from psychological research have also altered the way in which some clinicians view their approach to practice. An example of this is research on common factors in psychotherapy. Considerable research has been conducted on the effectiveness of various theoretical approaches, with an underlying assumption that techniques of a particular paradigm are responsible for change. However, recent research has revealed that techniques can account for approximately 15 per cent of client improvements, with 'common factors' (therapeutic relationship, expectancy, client-, and extra-therapeutic events) accounting for a substantial proportion of change (Lambert & Asay, 2004). This has resulted in many practitioners reevaluating the emphasis they place on different aspects of their clinical work. Although the scientist-practitioner model may sound laudable in principle, many people who choose to train as psychologists can experience a sense of frustration or disillusionment at the emphasis on research in their training. But embracing the scientist-practitioner approach has distinct advantages for both clients and practising psychologists.

ADVANTAGES TO CLIENTS

Imagine for a moment that you are in the position of a client. It may be that you have been experiencing problems for a long time, or have recently had a series of crises—or both. The impact of these factors has been to place you in a state of psychological distress so severe that you are willing to seek assistance. But who do you seek assistance from? How will you know the person you seek assistance from can be trusted to give you the best possible help?

Certainly, the first step that affords some measure of protection is seeking services from a qualified psychologist. It is this kind of service that the Australian Psychological Society (APS) performs by providing a database of qualified psychologists, endorsing training standards, and reviewing training programs on a regular basis. Similarly, mandatory continuing professional development introduced by the APS is meant to provide a formal mechanism to ensure that psychologists remain up to date with developments in the field. The APS also makes provision for clients to make complaints and express concerns about their treatment to relevant regulatory bodies (clients can also make complaints to registration boards—see chapter 2). Although these measures provide some protection, much of the responsibility for ensuring optimal professional service rests in the hands of individual psychologists.

While it would be desirable to be able to assume that all psychologists embrace this responsibility, consistently provide optimal treatment, and implement best practice, this may be a challenging goal to achieve. Failure to provide optimal treatment may be prompted by unethical behaviour (see chapter 2) or therapist factors (see chapter 5). A more subtle influence on the quality of treatment provided concerns the capacity of psychologists to be critical consumers of the research literature and the often unacknowledged impact of information-processing factors.

'But I know what works with my clients'

As Lilienfeld and colleagues (2003) document, there have been a number of instances where assessment and/or treatment practices were adopted without sufficient research basis, and yet adherents maintained them long past when it was known they did not work. An example of this is *critical incident stress debriefing*, which has been widely implemented despite a paucity of reliable studies to support the effectiveness of group approaches to debriefing (Devilly & Cotton, 2004).

There are three potential harms from adopting techniques that are not empirically supported:

- *direct harm:* either physical or psychological harm caused to the client through the intervention
- *opportunity cost:* receiving the treatment prevents the client from receiving a treatment that may be more effective

- *impact on the profession:* the use of unsubstantiated treatment erodes the scientific foundations of clinical psychology.

Why do psychologists do what they do?

Therapy is a demanding practice. The psychologist needs to listen attentively, provide empathic and accurate responses, monitor process, conceptualise, develop and test hypotheses, assess risk, and make treatment decisions in any given session, which is likely to be characterised by emotional intensity or distress. As Tracey and Rounds (1999) note, there is a vast array of information that the psychologist needs to process. As a consequence, clinical decision-making can be influenced by a number of shortcuts in reasoning, or heuristics, that individuals typically adopt in such situations.

As Tversky and Kahneman (2005) describe, clinicians may adopt a number of heuristics to guide them through the maze of information that confronts them, which can bias their clinical decision-making. These are:

- *representativeness:* the extent to which something matches relevant categories; that is, assuming that the client is 'representative' of a certain group, or her or his symptoms are representative of a diagnostic category, and ignoring other, contradictory, information or symptoms
- *availability:* decision-making is influenced by information that is most easily brought to mind. This may be influenced by the following factors:
  - *exposure:* if many of a therapist's previous clients presented with depressive symptoms, the therapist may be inclined to view a new client from this perspective
  - *mood:* there is ample evidence to suggest that recall of information and decision-making can be unduly influenced by mood
  - *imaginability:* what is plausible, rather than what is probable; for example, potentially adverse outcomes may not be considered if the therapist does not believe them to be possible
  - *anchoring:* the tendency to allow initial information and impressions to be used as a basis for subsequent decision-making. At its most basic, this would result in the therapist forming lasting impressions of a client on an insufficient basis, and using observations from the first session to inform conceptualisations and treatment plans when disconfirming evidence may be available.

The effect of such biases is made even more problematic when we think of the clinical context again. Psychologists and mental-health practitioners are in a position of power (Szasz, 1972) legitimised by society, and they are, for the most part, dealing with clients who are in an inherently vulnerable position, where they are likely to accept uncritically the view of the 'expert' they trust.

Clinicians can rely too much on their memory, and on their own idiosyncratic processing of information, and the manner in which clinicians interpret and present this to clients is accepted unquestioningly. Adoption of the scientist–practitioner model, while not foolproof in eliminating bias, can increase the likelihood of scientific and objective clinical decision-making in all aspects of clinical practice, from diagnostic decisions to choice of treatment intervention.

ADVANTAGES FOR THERAPISTS

Adoption of the scientist–practitioner model also has advantages for therapists.

Enhancement of clinical outcomes

There is growing evidence that evaluating practice systematically can lead to enhanced client outcomes. While this can be a confronting practice, there can be considerable advantages for the therapist, in reducing client dropout and increasing client satisfaction. Patient-focused research introduced by Howard and colleagues (1996) focuses on monitoring an individual client's progress over the course of therapy. Being more aware of unfolding outcome allows the therapist to collaborate more clearly with the client, and to make corrections or modifications to the therapeutic approach more quickly.

Coping with uncertainty

Capacity to cope with uncertainty is a vital skill in psychological practice. By its nature, psychological practice involves dealing with complex and at times ambiguous information and knowledge. Over 20 years ago, estimates were that approximately 400 therapeutic techniques existed (Kazdin, 1986) and close to 200 therapy models (Henrink, 1980). Today, these figures have substantially increased, with practising psychologists having a vast number of treatment approaches from which to choose (Lambert, 2004); most have varying degrees of empirical support to be considered (Chambless et al., 1998). Furthermore, controversies can arise surrounding how, and if, these empirically supported therapies are identified (Chambless, 2001). Adopting a scientist–practitioner approach to psychological practice, by remaining aware of the treatment-outcome literature, can help guide the therapist through this maze.

Yet, even the existence of treatment approaches that have demonstrated benefit for particular clients or disorders does not mean the end of uncertainty. Although psychologists bring expert knowledge to understanding the client, it is not possible to *know* exactly what the best explanation for the client's difficulties is, nor to predict whether treatment will be effective. The scientist–practitioner model recommends that psychologists use a hypothesis-testing approach to clinical work. A hypothesis is a possible or tentative explanation for phenomena, and ways in which a hypothesis can be tested form the basis for most scientific research.

Similarly, in psychological practice, we are confronted with the phenomena of a client and his or her difficulties. Thus, psychologists form hypotheses—possible explanations—then seek to test and evaluate these in their interventions. An important aspect of this approach is that it assumes that the psychologist must respond to the evidence (for example, evidence that treatment is not assisting the client) and modify their approach accordingly. Given the potential for heuristics to bias information-processing, adopting a hypothesis-testing process also helps to reduce the likelihood of bias influencing decision-making, and to increase therapist objectivity. The hypothesis-testing approach assists with conceptualisation of the client's issues, and consideration of alternative explanations for presenting symptoms and response to treatment. This approach can facilitate development of the observing self of therapists, allowing them to step back from emotive aspects of clinical work, maintain boundaries, and increase awareness of potential countertransference. It also helps to ensure that treatment plans are evaluated and modified to ensure optimal outcome for clients. Chapters 14 (case conceptualisation) and 12 (outcome assessment) will deal with this process in more detail.

Adherence to ethical practice

Finally, it is the ethical duty of clinicians to provide the most effective treatment for clients—skills in the critical evaluation of the empirical literature on efficacy studies, and knowledge of which treatments may be contraindicated for some clients or presenting problems, are vital to ethical practice. It is also incumbent upon psychologists to evaluate routinely the impact of their interventions with clients. These ethical duties are best carried out through adherence to the scientist–practitioner model.

APPLICATION OF THE MODEL

There has been debate among practising clinicians about the extent to which multi-site random controlled trials can provide information that is relevant for individual clients. This is partly because of the practice of excluding participants with comorbidity or other extraneous issues that tend to be the rule rather than the exception in real-world practice. The published results may not necessarily provide guidelines in working with non-compliance, or other challenges in implementing the treatment. Standardised treatment manuals are criticised for lacking flexibility, and being tailored to a conceptualisation of a disorder rather than to the client as a person.

Central to this debate is the issue of efficacy versus effectiveness. *Efficacy studies* are large, randomly controlled trials using standardised manuals, objective assessment, and homogeneous client groups, with minimal comorbidity. *Effectiveness studies* focus on the success of the treatment in real-world clinical settings, for clients with comorbidity and complex and multifaceted problems. These are the domains of the practising clinician, and are vital to the development of psychological practice; an empirically validated treatment that does not transfer to the general population is of limited use.

Although it may not be feasible to conduct RCTs in routine practice, the practising clinician does have research options. Two that will be briefly described here are the *case study* and the *single-case research design*. As Kazdin (2003) has noted, the individual case study is of great value to psychology. A case study can allow the study of disorders that may be of lower prevalence, and not amenable to large-scale research. Case studies can also provide valuable information on exceptions to commonly-held theories.

Characteristics of the case study
- Intensive study of an individual, group, family, or institution
- Focus on complexity and anecdotal narratives rather than on quantitative data
- Focus on nuances of the case: the client, the presenting problem, the therapeutic relationship, challenges in treatment
- Can be useful in developing therapy techniques and hypotheses regarding clinical issues.

Single-case research design

As Kazdin (2003) explains, this design (also known as an N = 1 study) does not necessarily mean that only one participant is studied; it refers to empirical research where there is no control or comparison group, which makes research more feasible in an applied setting. Clients serve as their own controls; the question is to determine whether the client's behaviour changes in relation to his or her own baseline (pre-treatment) scores, rather than in relation to a comparison or control group.

Features of single-case designs

- *Continuous assessment:* multiple observations prior to and during the intervention (for example, BDI scores, frequency of behaviours)
- *Baseline assessment:* collection of data during the baseline phase, prior to intervention. This is used to predict behaviour for the immediate future, as if the intervention were not to occur
- *Typical statistical analysis is not used:* rather, data is examined by visual inspection. Changes in means over phases of the intervention, changes in slope, and latency of change are assessed.

While case studies and single-case research designs may lack the rigour of large-scale RCTs, they do serve an important purpose in clinical psychology, and provide an avenue for the clinician to work within the scientist–practitioner model. Kazdin (2003) provides a comprehensive description of case studies and single-case designs.

CRITICISMS OF THE MODEL

While the scientist–practitioner model is the dominant paradigm in clinical psychology training and practice, it is not without its critics. The most commonly asserted criticism rests on the observation that the vast majority of clinicians who are trained in the scientist–practitioner model do not regularly conduct research, and that even fewer publish. This observation has prompted the question whether it is realistic to provide training in both scientist and practitioner roles, when most graduates will adopt one role only—typically, they become practitioners rather than researchers (Gelso, 1993). Rather than discarding the model on this basis, it is important to recognise that, while many psychologists will have no direct involvement in research after training, research findings can and should remain the basis of their practice. Our understanding of effective treatments is constantly being updated on the basis of research, and it is essential that practising psychologists remain aware of these developments, to provide optimal treatment for clients.

A related issue is whether the practising psychologist works in a setting that is conducive to research. In many non-academic settings, time, resources, incentives, and encouragement to participate in research may be lacking. A survey of Australian psychologists revealed that only 20 per cent of clinical psychologists engaged in research, 88 per cent indicated that incentives for research were minimal or nonexistent, and 50 per cent did not regard publication to be related to promotion (Martin, 1989). As academic institutions provide opportunities and reward research publication, it is not surprising that most research occurs in university psychology departments. Again, this may reflect the shortcomings of non-academic settings, rather than the model, and points to the need for psychologists to actively engage in dialogue regarding the importance of research in non-academic settings.

A further criticism is that the scientist–practitioner model does not—or is reluctant to—acknowledge the value for psychological practice of knowledge that has not been accumulated through the consumption of scientific literature, such as knowledge based on life experience, cultural understanding, or personal insights into human nature (O'Gorman, 2001). Supporters of the model would argue that the 'practitioner' aspect of the model incorporates such acknowledgment. Indeed, the growing body of research that endorses the value of the therapeutic alliance (explored further in chapter 6) demonstrates that the therapist's interpersonal and relationship skills are essential components of effective practice.

Conclusion

Despite criticisms and controversies, the scientist–practitioner model continues to be the most widely used and influential format for training and practice in clinical psychology. Other disciplines have incorporated the model, including counselling and educational psychology. In an era of increased accountability, continued adherence to the scientist–practitioner model is critical for the practising clinician. Psychologists will increasingly be called upon to document outcomes, and to provide evidence of

Practice implications

1 Continue to seek ongoing professional development opportunities throughout your career (such as attendance at workshops, professional supervision, and peer supervision groups).
2 Identify ways in which you can remain up to date with developments in the field (through journal clubs, membership of professional organisations, affiliation with universities, and use of online professional forums).
3 Be prepared to undertake periodic literature searches to update your knowledge of current approaches to assessment and treatment of specific disorders, particularly when a client presents with a disorder you have not worked with recently.
4 Conduct systematic assessment of clients and identify ways of embedding ongoing evaluation of progress (through self-report measures or objective assessment) into management of cases.
5 Adopt a hypothesis-testing approach to clinical work, and always be prepared to consider alternative explanations for presenting symptoms, client behaviour, and outcome.
6 Try to be aware of personal biases in gathering and interpreting clinical data, and take steps to avoid allowing these biases to dominate your conclusions.
7 Be alert to opportunities to initiate or become involved in research in your clinical setting. This may occur informally (through program evaluation) or more formally (through becoming involved in a research project).

the effectiveness of their practice. Researchers involved in large clinical trials are enhancing the relevance of their research to clinicians by considering and reporting the clinical significance of findings, along with statistical significance (Hayes et al., 1999). The scientific community is also appreciating the value of case study and single-case design research. Thus, the importance of the scientist–practitioner model is growing, and methods of implementing the model are becoming more accessible to practising clinicians. These developments will help towards 'bridging the gap' between research and practice, and provide movement toward realisation of the ideal for training and practice envisioned at the Boulder Conference.

Recommended reading
Hayes, S. C., Barlow, D, H., & Nelson-Gray, R. O. (1999). *The Scientist Practitioner: Research and Accountability in the Age of Managed Care* (2nd edn). Boston: Allyn & Bacon.

Chapter 2

Ethics and ethical practice

INTRODUCTION

This chapter provides an overview of ethical psychological practice. It discusses what ethical practice is and its importance to various facets of practice. By the end of the chapter, you will have an awareness of common ethical dilemmas and the process of ethical decision-making. Some specific areas from the *Code of Ethics* (2007) identified as common and/or challenging in clinical practice will be covered. You are strongly encouraged to do further reading and to view relevant scenarios on the videos. Ethical issues are common in practice and maintaining professional development in ethics is essential.

ETHICS AND THE REQUIREMENT FOR ETHICS

All our relationships with others, whether with our families, friends, or colleagues, tend to follow certain implicit and/or explicit rules. Usually, we have expectations about how interactions should occur. When these rules or expectations are broken or not met, we can experience conflict, disappointment, or hurt. This occurs particularly when rules and expectations are implicit, unclear, or have not been discussed. You may be able to recall occasions in your life where this has been the case and you have felt confused and/or hurt as a result.

The relationship between client and psychologist is a professional one. A difference in power exists by virtue of it being a contractual arrangement: the client goes to the psychologist for psychological assistance and pays fees. The client expects that the psychologist will conduct him- or herself professionally and that what will be done will be of help. But how do we determine what behaviours are helpful, professional, correct, or incorrect? This is where ethics comes into play. Ethics refers to the study of values, principles, morals, and assumptions of conduct that help us to know what is right or wrong conduct (Bersoff, 2008). Ethics refers to the rules of behaviour that govern provision of psychological services. If we did not have rules of conduct, each psychologist would need to rely on his or her own judgment of what is right and wrong in his or her behaviour with clients. There would be no consistency in the field regarding professional conduct, given that we have different histories and values. We therefore have a code of conduct or ethics that promotes professional practice by providing standards, guidelines, and expectations for psychologists' professional behaviour, with the aim of protecting recipients of psychological services, the integrity of the profession, and how it is perceived. A code provides psychologists with guidance on what is expected from them and a basis to help explain professional decision-making and conduct.

In psychology, codes of conduct and ethics came into existence in the mid twentieth century, much later than in medicine. The American Medical Association established a code of ethics and an ethics committee in the mid nineteenth century. Development of a code in psychology was hotly debated in the 1940s and 1950s in the USA after a committee on ethical behaviour was established in 1938 (Pope & Vetter, 1992). In the process of developing a code, a number of issues and concerns were raised that are still relevant today. One concern was that some individuals might use a code to excuse perhaps unprofessional behaviour. There was concern that statements made in codes are often stated in general terms, and can be ambiguous, open to interpretation, and subject to clinical judgment. In addition, because of the complexity of human interactions and situations, different principles or statements in codes, which sometimes conflict with each other, could be applied simultaneously. Professional conduct and expectations are not static constructs, but are subject to social and political influences and pressures. It is helpful to be aware of these ongoing social and political influences as you develop ethical awareness and practice.

A number of forces and factors, which may be contradictory, need to be considered when deciding the best course of action in clinical practice. Along with the professional code of practice, there are also the psychologist's own moral principles and values, clinical and cultural factors, and workplace rules and policies to consider. In Australia, we need to take into account federal, state, and case law, and other requirements set out by the Psychology Board of Australia and the *Health Practitioner Regulation National Law Act*.

Australian psychologists are bound by the Australian Psychological Society's *Code of Ethics*, the most recent version of which was published in 2007. It was first developed in 1949, has been reviewed approximately every 10 years (Code of Ethics, 2007), and has been adopted by the Psychology Board of Australia. Other relevant codes of ethics are the British Psychological Society's *Code of Ethics and Conduct* (BPS, 2009) and the American Psychological Association's *Ethical Principles of Psychologists and Code of Conduct* (2010). These codes tend to be similar in nature, but specific to their respective cultures.

THE AUSTRALIAN PSYCHOLOGICAL SOCIETY'S CODE OF ETHICS

This *Code* consists of three general principles, which reflect the basic values and standards of the profession. Basic standards of behaviours listed under each principle are outlined, indicating to psychologists the minimum behaviours expected in order to adhere to the overarching principle. In addition, the Australian Psychological Society has produced guidelines to help psychologists follow the principles and standards, and to provide guidance on ambiguous or complex situations. Every psychologist should have a copy of and be familiar with the *Code* because 'lack of awareness or misunderstanding of an ethical standard is not itself a defence to an allegation of unethical conduct' (Code of Ethics, 2007, p. 10).

The *Code* and its related *Guidelines* get updated and amended, so keep abreast with what is current. It is useful to think of the *Code* in terms of a flow chart (see Figure 2.1). When faced with a dilemma, you can either start at the guidelines or the standards, but when these do not provide sufficient guidance or answers, refer to the underlying principle from which the guidelines and standards are derived.

Principles

Standards

Guidelines

Figure 2.1   Recommended ethical decision-making process depicted as a flow chart

As the *Code* is often phrased in legal terms, take note of definitions of terms used; doing this will help clarify what is referred to. For example, a *party or parties receiving a psychological service* can refer to a client but also to a supervisee (Code of Ethics, 2007). Thus, psychologists need to keep the *Code* of ethical conduct in mind when supervising.

General ethical principles

The three general principles of the APS *Code of Ethics* (2007) are:

- General principle A: Respect for the rights and dignity of people and peoples
- General principle B: Propriety
- General principle C: Integrity.

The first principle focuses on the values of the profession. The second principle covers what services a psychologist provides and how the psychologist provides them. The third principle focuses on a psychologist's position of trust and power and promotes professional behaviour.

General principle A: Respect for the rights and dignity of people and peoples

Principle A covers areas such as promoting a person's right to diversity, culture, confidentiality, and equity. It addresses standards of behaviours related to justice, respect, informed consent, privacy, confidentiality, and collection and release of information.

Respect

Psychologists are required to respect their clients and their colleagues. For instance, when a psychologist hears something about another psychologist's professional behaviour or approach they may not agree with, the psychologist is required to respond in a manner that is respectful and not harmful or derogatory. A client might complain about what his or her previous psychologist may or may not have done. Although it might be tempting to agree with the client about the other psychologist's lack of competence, and assure the client that you are much better, this response would be considered unethical under the *Code*:

> A.2.1. In the course of their *conduct, psychologists*:
> (b) do not behave in a manner that, having regard to the context, may reasonably be perceived as coercive or demeaning.
>
> A.2.3. When *psychologists* have cause to disagree with a colleague in psychology or another profession on professional issues they refrain from making intemperate criticism.
>
> (Code of Ethics, 2007, p. 12)

You might ask, what exactly is 'intemperate criticism', and what is considered 'coercive or demeaning'? This is an example of how statements in codes can be ambiguous and open to interpretation. The context in which you receive information about another psychologist also needs to be taken into account, particularly when you are receiving information about someone at second hand. Perhaps the client has a tendency to negate any experience he may have had, thus telling you that his previous psychologist was incompetent, whereas the psychologist may have acted professionally and competently. People's perceptions of events are just that—perceptions, not necessarily facts—and this needs to be taken into account when making ethical decisions. Often, the psychologist will see things differently. It is imperative that you show respect, verbally and nonverbally, even when you might (dis)agree strongly with the client's views.

The requirement for mandatory notifications stipulated by *The Health Practitioner Regulation National Law Act* 2009 is of relevance here. According to the *Act*, a psychologist would be required to report certain behaviours of a colleague, employee, or student to the Australian Health Practitioner Regulation Agency (AHPRA). Reportable behaviours include practising under the influence of drugs or alcohol and sexual misconduct, and placing the 'public at risk of substantial harm' through impairment and/or 'departure from accepted professional standards' (Guidelines for Mandatory Notifications, 2010, p. 2). The Psychology Board of Australia Guidelines explain that there would need to be 'direct knowledge or observations of the behaviour' (p. 2) for a notification to occur, and that this needs to be done in good faith. This is in line with the *Code of Ethics*' (2007) Standard of Respect and 'C.7.3. *Psychologists* do not lodge, or endorse the lodging, of trivial, vexatious or unsubstantiated ethical complaints against colleagues' (p. 30), and reaffirms the need to take into account the validity and factual nature of information about others that you may receive.

Informed consent

A client needs to be informed about and understand the service he or she is going to receive. This requirement means providing information on the nature of the treatment or intervention, its purpose, length, risks involved, effectiveness, and other treatments that may be available. Inherent is the need to determine whether the person is able to provide consent—this may not be possible for a young child or some-one with cognitive impairment. If the person is not able to provide informed consent, consideration needs to be given to who (such as a parent or guardian) has legal authority to provide consent for the person. In a survey of therapists, Somberg and colleagues (1993) found that 25 per cent of therapists did not discuss potential risks of therapy, and just over half (52 per cent) did not discuss treatment length, indicating that therapists may not manage consent as well as they are ethically required to.

Explaining the process of therapy to a client, and what might happen, can be difficult, in particular in psychodynamic psychotherapy, because every therapeutic relationship is unique and has an experiential nature. But some other approaches (such as cognitive behavioural psychotherapy) may be easier to explain, being more structured and discernable (Goddard et al., 2008).

The manner in which information is provided to a client is important. The aim would not be to scare the client about potential risks to such an extent that he declines further psychological treatment, but to let him know that therapy may, for example, result in him initially feeling worse, result in changes in the way he relates to others, and that it may impact, possibly in unexpected ways, on his current relationships. When utilising particular interventions, such as graded exposure, it would be important to let the client know that he is likely to experience initially increased levels of anxiety.

Hypnosis is another intervention that requires clear discussion about processes and potential risks. Hypnosis involves altered states of consciousness and sugges-tion, and psychologists need to be particularly mindful of the potential for harm or misuse (Yapko, 2003). There are specific guidelines (see APS website) for use and teaching of hypnosis, which highlight the requirement to clarify and discuss the nature of the intervention, what is involved, and possible outcomes.

All interventions have potential for harm if used irresponsibly or inappropri-ately. This fact highlights the need for competence, a standard that falls under the ethical principle of propriety, described below. Given the ever-evolving nature of therapy, interventions used will change over the course of treatment. Obtaining consent is not a one-off event, but something that may need to be sought fre-quently, as interventions are adapted to the changing needs of the client.

Exercise 2.1

Reflect on how you would obtain consent in a manner that is respectful and provides infor-mation related to the intervention you plan.

  View Videos 1, 5 and 7. How do you think these relate to consent, what was done well, and what would you do differently?

Confidentiality and privacy

Dealing with confidentiality issues in practice can be perplexing. Some consider confidentiality to be the most important ethical standard, and essential for relationships to be therapeutic. An American survey of 697 psychologists (Pope & Vetter, 1992) showed that the ethical decisions psychologists struggled with most were those surrounding confidentiality (for example, whether to break confidentiality or not), followed by those around maintaining appropriate boundaries, and finally those related to payment. This fits with our own clinical experience of ethical dilemmas. According to the *Code*, psychologists should 'take reasonable steps' to protect clients' confidentiality.

In the *Code*, privacy and confidentiality are separate standards. McMahon (2006) explains that confidentiality relates to the expectation within the relationship that information told in confidence will go no further. Privacy relates to the type of information that is normally collected to provide the service. According to the *Code*, only information relevant to the service should be collected. A psychologist would not ask a client how much her car cost her; asking this would be considered an invasion of privacy. There may, of course, be occasions when it might be relevant to ask such a question, when problem-solving with a client whose difficulties relate to high debt. If a client chooses to tell the psychologist that he has driven his mother's car without permission, then he, under confidentiality, would expect that information not to be divulged.

To complicate matters further, psychologists should be aware of privacy legislation, both federal and state, that applies to them in their work settings. These laws can be found by accessing government websites; they relate to what information can be kept and how, in addition to how it can be released. This also relates to record keeping, which falls under the ethical principle of propriety.

In clinical practice, the following questions often arise.

1   When and how do you discuss confidentiality and its limitations?

It is usually good practice to explain the process of confidentiality and its limitations when a client first comes to see you, at the beginning of the first session, before the client begins to tell you about her or his life. This explanation can be provided in different ways. The client can be provided with a consent form in which the limitations of confidentiality are detailed. It is still important, however, to talk through confidentiality, as the client might not have read the form or understood what it means in practice (and it is important not to assume that the client has). Individuals with symptoms such as depression may also find it hard to concentrate on reading, and may say they have read and understood it when they haven't. Some clients may be eager to talk or feel compelled to talk because they feel anxious. These clients may enter the consulting room and immediately launch into their story, before you have had a chance to inform them of confidentiality. Such clients may disclose information assuming that what they disclose will be held in confidence. This is a situation where the psychologist needs to use micro-counselling skills (discussed in chapter 11), to intervene in such a way that the client feels heard but is provided with information on confidentiality.

It is essential to explain what confidentiality means in practice and in which situations confidentiality will be broken. For example: 'Confidentiality means that what we talk about in this room goes no further. In other words, I can't talk to anyone else about what we discuss without your consent. There are, however, some situations where, even if you didn't want me to, I may have to disclose information to someone else. For instance, there may be a legal requirement for me to disclose information (say, if your files are subpoenaed), or when there is concern for your safety or someone else's. Usually I would discuss this with you, if this were to happen. Do you have any questions or concerns about this?'

In addition, a discussion needs to occur about what the process will be if confidentiality is broken. If letters need to be written to doctors, as required when, for example, clients are referred under Medicare, or if information needs to be provided to third parties, this needs to be declared at the outset. Finally, check with clients if they have any questions or concerns regarding confidentiality. It is much easier to resolve issues at the beginning of therapy than to deal with misunderstandings at a later stage.

Breaking confidentiality can be a stressful process, and knowing that you have discussed this possibility with a client before can ease the stress for the client and for you.

2   How does confidentiality apply when working with children?

According to the latest Australian Psychological Society's (APS) *Guidelines on Confidentiality* (2008) and the APS *Guidelines for Working with Young People* (2009), confidentiality with younger persons is related to their ability to provide informed consent and their ability to understand the limitations of confidentiality. The age of the child is a factor in this, as is the attitude of the psychologist toward confidentiality. Some psychologists might believe that parents have the right to all information regarding their child's welfare; others may believe that children have a right to confidentiality, and will only disclose what they think is pertinent for the parents to know. However, if a young person is able to provide informed consent, information should only be disclosed with the consent of the young person, with the exception of situations where there is clear risk to the child or teenager (see chapter 16). Teenagers can be particularly sensitive to issues surrounding confidentiality, especially if they are experiencing conflict with parents. Video 10 shows that establishing rapport with an adolescent who is reluctant to engage requires specific skills, but also highlights that it is vital to discuss what confidentiality means, and its limits, to both the younger person and to her or his parents or legal guardians (*informed consent*). Being clear about what will be discussed with whom and how—with the child/adolescent present or not—will encourage transparency in the process and help clarify for the client what she or he can or can't expect.

Discussion of confidentiality with a child of three will be very different from discussion with an adolescent who is 17 years old. Usually, it is when you are working with children aged between approximately 8 and 13–14 years old that clinical judgment surrounding capacity to understand confidentiality and consent is necessary, because young people of the same age can vary markedly in level of maturity and ability to understand.

Determining whether a young person can understand the psychological service, its risks and benefits, the impact of (not) receiving the service, and understanding the limits of confidentiality, are all 'part of the process of obtaining informed consent' (Symons, 2009). State laws regarding confidentiality also need to be taken into account. In some states, for example, there is a legal requirement for psychologists to report sexual abuse; in other states there is not, it being left to a psychologist's discretion whether to report sexual abuse, unless the workplace has clear policies on the issue.

At the age of 15, young people can have their own Medicare card, and can obtain medical services without the consent of parents (McMahon, 2006).

Confidentiality can be particularly complex when providing a service to a young person whose parents are separated. Knowledge and familiarity with the *Code of Ethics*, the relevant ethical guidelines, and legal requirements, is essential to help you navigate these potentially difficult situations. For instance, if you are contacted by the 'other' parent, information can not be disclosed to the non-presenting parent without the consent of the young person and the parent or guardian who has arranged the service.

3 How do you address confidentiality when working with couples and/or families?

The process and limitations of confidentiality can be complex when working with more than one person, for example, with a couple or a family. It is not such an issue if the couple or family members are always seen together, but becomes trickier if individuals are seen separately. One partner of a couple may, for example, tell you something that is not known to the other. The question then is not whether you can or can't disclose this information to the other party, but what you have explained to the couple about what information will be kept confidential, and what has been agreed upon as the limits of confidentiality.

Decisions around confidentiality may be determined by the psychologist's particular approach. Some psychologists are forthright, stating that all information will be discussed openly and transparently within the family; others will state that only information pertinent to the couple's or family's relationships will be disclosed. Information that qualifies as pertinent will then need to be determined by the psychologist and the individual, where possible. If information is considered to be pertinent to the relationship—as when a partner discloses that he is having an affair—it is usually helpful to discuss what the partner would feel comfortable disclosing, and encourage him to do the disclosing.

4 When is it acceptable or indicated to break confidentiality (disclose information without the client's consent)?

According to the *Code*, there are three occasions when a psychologist may break confidentiality.

First, when there is a legal obligation to do so, such as when a psychologist is subpoenaed by a court of law, or if a state law requires disclosure of information (for example, mandatory reporting of a crime or sexual abuse). Laws vary from state to state in Australia; find out about the laws in your state. Certain work settings may also have policies and/or legal obligations about disclosure; you need to provide information to clients about these from the outset.

Second, disclosure can occur 'if there is an immediate and specified risk of harm to an identifiable person or persons that can be averted only by disclosing information' (Code of Ethics, 2007, p. 15). You will need to determine if there is imminent and specific risk, and then judge what information needs to be disclosed and to whom, and whether this will avert the risk. When making this decision, a supervisor or trusted colleague can help you think through the process. Currently, there is no legal duty to divulge confidential information when a person is considered a risk to others (Kampf et al., 2008), but ethically there is the expectation that we should prevent harm where possible. For more on risk assessment, see chapter 16. The guidelines that are helpful with regard to this standard are:

Australian Psychological Society (2005). *Guidelines for Working with People Who Pose a High Risk of Harming Others.* Melbourne: Australian Psychological Society.

Australian Psychological Society (2004). *Guidelines Relating to Suicidal Clients.* Melbourne: Australian Psychological Society.

Australian Psychological Society (2010). *Guidelines on Reporting Abuse and Neglect, and Criminal Activity.* Melbourne: Australian Psychological Society.

Third, the Code allows for psychologists to discuss confidential information in supervision, collegial consultation, and training, as long as the information is masked in such a way that the client could not be identified.

5   How do you tell clients that you are going to break confidentiality?

Once you have decided that breaking confidentiality is required, you have two options. The first, and preferred, option is to inform the client first. This step can be taken by reminding the client of the limits of confidentiality, explaining the purpose of talking to someone else, and what you are going to say. It is helpful to explain what might happen next, and provide the client with the opportunity to ask questions and to express concerns. If possible, reveal the information to a third party with the client present. For instance, when a client has been assessed as being at risk of suicide, talk to the client's partner about a safety plan, bringing the partner into the session or speaking to him or her on the speaker phone with the client present.

If there is concern that the psychologist may be at risk if the client is informed that confidentiality will be broken, what information is provided, how it is provided, and to whom needs to be carefully considered. It is always vital to safeguard your own safety, even if this may mean that the relationship is harmed. It is difficult to remain empathic in a relationship if the client has harmed you physically or if you are no longer alive. Level of risk will determine what course of action you might take, as well as the setting in which you work.

6   When are you more likely to break confidentiality unintentionally?

Even with the best intentions, psychologists may break confidentiality when they don't mean to. Some situations may make you vulnerable to disclosing information without thinking. These include being tired and overworked, working in a context where discussing clients is the norm, or where there are covert pressures to reveal information, being used to discussing or debriefing with colleagues, or receiving unexpected requests for information.

Consider, for example, this situation. You are at the end of the day, and a trusted colleague phones, wanting to discuss one of your supervisees with you. Your colleague states that she has permission from the supervisee to talk to you. If you are tired and not really focused, you may want to help and to discuss the supervisee or client without really stopping and thinking. Because you do not have consent from the client yourself, this would be unethical; you would breach the *Code*. What this example highlights is that psychologists need to be mindful at all times of their ethical responsibility, and the contexts in which they are most vulnerable to not behaving ethically.

Legitimate discussion of clients in group supervision or in class situations in training settings may create an environment where discussion of clients is the norm. Students then might continue to discuss clients and what they have learned when outside of these specific contexts (over coffee, for example), becoming complacent about the process. The danger is that, if overheard, there is a risk of divulging confidential information to third parties. We will illustrate with an actual event. Two colleagues continued to discuss a client in general terms, without names, while having a tea break. Another person overheard the conversation, knew the client, and was able to identify the client from the little information the two colleagues discussed. You can imagine the discomfort when this person suddenly said, 'Are you talking about X; how is she?'

7   When is it acceptable to discuss confidential information?
Discussing confidential information is acceptable only in the situations described under question 4 above, or with the person's consent. It is not ethical to discuss clients with family members or your partner or friends. Helpful questions to ask yourself are: 'If I were a client, what would I expect from my psychologist in terms of what I tell her? Would I feel comfortable if I knew that she discussed my situation with her partner, even without giving particulars?'

Exercise 2.2

View Videos 1, 7, 8, and 15. What do you think the issues are with regard to confidentiality, and would you do anything differently?

General principle B: Propriety
This principle refers to psychologists acting in the best interests of their clients, the public, and the profession. It focuses on what psychologists do when providing psychological services, and covers 14 standards of behaviour, such as competence, record keeping, responsibility, psychological assessments, and standards related to the processes of providing services.

Competence and professional responsibility
Psychologists should work within their areas of knowledge and skills, and are expected to seek supervision and consultation to maintain competence. In addition, psychologists are expected to continually monitor their competence and ability to

provide psychological services. Sometimes psychologists may experience financial or external demands to provide services over and above what they can manage realistically. Ongoing supervision, as well as monitoring one's own mental heath and burnout levels, will assist with this. Supervision and burnout are discussed in chapters 18 and 19.

Psychologists are also required to be competent to work with Aboriginal and Torres Strait Islander people. The ethical guidelines for working with Aboriginal and Torres Strait Islander people state that psychologists need to have an awareness of research that is relevant to working with Indigenous Australians, and that they must take into account factors such as ethnicity and culture when working with, and making professional judgments about, Indigenous clients (APS, 2008). It is important that psychologists acknowledge and respect the value systems of Indigenous clients. Similarly, psychologists need to be aware of their own beliefs and values, and the impact these can have on the therapeutic process. For a more detailed discussion of cultural competence, see chapter 15.

In the context of competence, the issue of responsibility is relevant. Whose responsibility it is that clients get better in therapy? What are the respective responsibilities of therapist and client within the process? A major issue for all therapists, and in particular for early-career therapists, is finding a balance between taking too much or too little responsibility for clients. Again, the best place to start understanding what the responsibilities of a psychologist are towards a client is with the *Code of Ethics* (2007). The professional responsibilities of every psychologist are highlighted by the *Code* (2007, p. 20):

> B.3. *Psychologists* provide *psychological services* in a responsible manner. Having regard to the nature of the *psychological services* they are providing, *psychologists*:
> (a) act with the care and skill expected of a competent psychologist;
> (b) take responsibility for the reasonably foreseeable consequences of their *conduct*;
> (c) take reasonable steps to prevent harm occurring as a result of their *conduct*;
> (d) provide a *psychological service* only for the period when those services are necessary to the client;
> (e) are personally responsible for the professional decisions they make;
> (f) take reasonable steps to ensure that their services and products are used appropriately and responsibly;
> (g) are aware of, and take steps to establish and maintain proper professional boundaries with *clients* and colleagues; and
> (h) regularly review the contractual arrangements with *clients* and, where circumstances change, make relevant modifications as necessary with the informed consent of the *client*.

In practice, this standard means that psychologists should be aware of and take responsibility for providing competent services to all clients. Psychologists should be aware of how many clients they can see in a day, and be present and competent with each, putting reasonable effort into the process. Naturally, there will be days when you are feeling unwell, and not at your best. It is, however, your responsibility to cut your workload, if you find that clients later in the day are not getting your proper attention because you are tired.

Engaging in reflective practice, supervision, and good self-care can help to ensure that you are aware of and reflect on the possible consequences of your behaviour (point (b)). This means being aware of any personal issues that could have a negative impact on therapy, taking responsibility to resolve these, and to not practise if impaired.

Often useful questions to keep asking yourself are:

- Is this in the best interests of the client?
- Am I doing everything reasonable and to the best of my ability to prevent harm?
- Is what I am doing effective, and what evidence am I using to determine this? (Using multiple sources of evidence is usually helpful here: questionnaires, objective changes, reports from others.)

The *Code of Ethics* does not outline the responsibilities of clients, but it is useful to reflect on this. There are two people involved in a therapeutic relationship, the client and the therapist–psychologist. Both client and psychologist have input into the relationship, and have responsibilities within the relationship (see chapter 6). It is usually not helpful for the psychologist–therapist to take on too much responsibility (for example, to feel solely responsible for what happens); in fact, feeling overly responsible can actually work against working competently. It is useful for psychologists to have a list of reasonable expectations about clients' responsibilities. In our view, psychologists might expect that clients:

- *treat the therapist with basic civility within our cultural norms.* Clients need to recognise that therapists have the same rights as other individuals in the community, and are to be treated with respect. Therapists have the right to request such treatment from clients. Any form of verbal abuse or behaviour from the client that is deemed offensive is unacceptable. There are steps a therapist can take if a client is being verbally abusive. The therapist could respectfully express that the client's behaviour is inappropriate and request that he or she should be treated with respect. The therapist should explain that the session will be terminated if the behaviour continues, and that this may prevent any further service from being offered. It is essential that therapists ensure their own safety by ending interactions and, if appropriate, calling for assistance if the client is threatening or acting violently
- *be honest with the therapist and give feedback about what is effective or not effective in treatment.* This is an ideal, and may not be an achievable task for some clients, at least not initially. For many, being assertive with others, particularly individuals they see as authority figures, is difficult. Nevertheless, therapists should attempt to create a 'culture of openness and feedback' within the therapeutic relationship
- *attempt to make best use of therapy, and to work collaboratively with the therapist as far as possible.* Of course, if the therapy is poor, this cannot be expected of clients. In addition, there may be reasons why a client will be resistant to treatment; managing resistance will be part of the treatment.

Exercise 2.3

1   Do you think clients have responsibilities in addition to those listed above? If so, what are they?
2   If you don't think clients have responsibilities, what does this mean for therapy? Does this mean that outcome solely rests with the therapist?

Reflecting on and discussing in supervision what we are *not* responsible for is also part of being professionally competent and responsible. Being aware of and taking responsibility for foreseeable consequences of *your* conduct is not equivalent to being responsible for the actual conduct and emotions of a client.

New therapists often worry about being responsible for clients' emotions, fearing that they will upset clients and be the 'cause' of negative emotion; this fear can lead to them not acting in ways that are helpful to clients. Having a good understanding of what is happening for clients (see chapter 14) is essential in determining helpful and unhelpful interventions and clarifying responsibilities.

Another major concern for new therapists is that clients will harm themselves, attempt suicide, or complete suicide. We do have an ethical duty of care to protect our clients from harm from themselves or others to the best of our ability. At times, this involves conducting thorough risk assessments and implementing safety plans, and sometimes even breaking confidentiality. It is stressful work. A sense of responsibility for clients' safety is a double-edged sword. On the one hand, it motivates therapists to do the best they can to prevent harm to their clients. On the other hand, therapists can blame themselves and feel guilty if, despite their best efforts, clients hurt themselves.

Exercise 2.4

What else do you think therapists are *not* responsible for in providing psychological services?

Professional boundaries
Part of being professionally responsible for what you do is having appropriate professional boundaries (point (g)). Boundaries can be viewed as the limits around behaviours. Some behaviours fall within these limits, some fall outside. There are two types of boundary issues, boundary crossings and boundary violations. Glass (2003) states that 'boundary crossings relate to the therapist's attempts to enhance the treatment, while boundary violations, which more grossly breach the patient's physical and or psychological subjective space, often do so in the service of the therapist's interests' (p. 432).

Good questions to ask when faced with a boundary dilemma are, 'What is in the client's best interests?', and 'Am I doing this to make me feel better, or is this going to be helpful to the client?' Let's look at the issue of self-disclosure. There are different views, depending on a psychologist's theoretical orientation, as to whether self-disclosure is considered acceptable within a therapeutic relationship. An example of a boundary-crossing self-disclosure would be when a psychologist reveals something about himself as a way of validating the client or normalising the client' experience. He might, for example, share that he too experiences anxiety in new situations. If a psychologist were to talk at length about all the problems he has had with anxiety, and the impact it has had on his life, the self-disclosure would be a boundary violation.

Exercise 2.5

View Video 2, scene 1. How well do you think the therapist managed self-disclosure, and what type of boundary violation would you say it was, if any? Then watch scene 2 of this video.

Establishing a sexual relationship with a client is a clear boundary violation. Standards regarding sexual relationships with clients and/or persons close to clients fall under the principle of integrity, but cross over into propriety too. Establishing a sexual relationship with a current client, or any behaviour that can be considered sexually inappropriate, is prohibited, and a reportable behaviour (Psychology Board of Australia, 2010). This may include establishing a sexual relationship with someone who is close to the client (such as the parent of a child client). Establishing a sexual relationship with a former client is problematic, and can be deemed misconduct; it would be the responsibility of the psychologist to show that she or he is not in any way exploiting the vulnerability of the client, regardless of how much time may have elapsed since the psychologist last saw the client.

The matter of touching a client non-sexually (as with a hug) is one of the most debated issues in therapy. Some hold the view that any touch must be avoided at all costs; others deem that it may be appropriate in certain circumstances. Psychologists from different theoretical orientations often have differing opinions on touch. Yalom (2001) encourages the use of appropriate physical touch; he argues that it demonstrates a more human and individualised approach. Holub and Lee (1990) suggest that psychodynamic therapists may be less approving of non-erotic hugging and touch. According to the APS Ethical Guidelines (2008) relating to procedures and assessments that involve contact between psychologist and client, physical contact can constitute a boundary violation. McMahon (2006) recommends that psychologists document the motivation or rationale for physical contact, and discusses how important it is that contact is non-exploitative, culturally sensitive, and done not for the psychologist's own satisfaction but for the benefit of the client.

Another boundary crossing, which could lead to a boundary violation, might be accepting a gift. The guidelines for managing professional boundaries and multiple relationships (APS, 2008) state that, 'Psychologists ordinarily refrain from accepting goods or other non-monetary remuneration from clients in return for psychological services because such arrangements create inherent potential for conflict and exploitation within the professional relationship' (p. 94).

Does this mean that accepting a gift such as a bunch of flowers at the end of therapy would be inappropriate? Remember the question, What is in the client's best interests? Refusing a gift from a client who is trying to show her appreciation of your help may be hurtful and detrimental to the client. The work you have done together may have had a major impact on the person's life, and that person is show-ing that she values the work and the relationship with a token. Refusing that token might be viewed as demeaning the work and its value, which would go against the ethical standard of respect, and may undo some of the good work. This is a nice example of how making ethical judgments is a constant process.

If a client starts giving gifts during therapy, or gifts of great value, this is unlikely to be in the client's best interests, as it may have a negative impact on the relation-ship. The onus is on the psychologist to show non-exploitation (integrity); this may be difficult if a client has (say) left all his or her worldly goods to you. Employers may have more specific policies than the *Code* and guidelines with regard to receiv-ing gifts. It may, for example, be that a psychologist is unable to accept a gift, but that the employing organisation can. For instance, a bunch of flowers could be put in a communal area.

Exercise 2.6

View Video 4, scene 1. How well do you think the therapist managed this 'gift' situation? What would you do differently? Then watch scene 2 and the debrief of this scene.

Although boundary crossings may not initially be harmful, they may lead to increased crossings and possible violations; psychologists need to know and ques-tion the potential results of their behaviours.

Termination of psychological services

The *Code of Ethics* states that '*psychologists* terminate their *psychological services* with a *client*, if it is reasonably clear that the client is not benefiting from their services' (APS, 2007, p. 23). Termination is also appropriate when a client has achieved relief from symptoms, and has achieved many of his or her goals of therapy. Regardless of reason for termination, the *Code* emphasises the importance of carefully managing this process.

Here are four common termination scenarios.

1   When therapy time is unlimited

Indications that it may be time to terminate therapy when time is unlimited are when clients:

- have achieved significant relief from symptoms
- can respond more flexibly to their current situation
- have made promising changes in their lives and are working toward further change.

In addition to ongoing formal measurement of client progress (see chapters 9 and 12), good indicators that changes have taken place include when the client reports that he or she feels better and can respond in more adaptive ways, and when the client responds consistently to the therapist in new ways, and does not reenact maladaptive patterns. Another good indicator is when significant others in the client's life give feedback that the client is behaving differently. Termination tends to occur naturally, and clients leave with greater self-efficacy and the ability to manage their lives more successfully.

2   When therapy time is limited

When therapy time is limited (such as in situations where the therapist is in a short-term placement, or when the number of sessions is limited), it is particularly important to manage termination well, as the following issues can arise:

- termination can be experienced as harmful, and may evoke blaming and distancing from a client, resulting in feelings of guilt in the therapist. This can particularly be the case with clients who have abandonment issues.
- termination can prompt powerful emotional reactions in both client and therapist. Either or both may deny or avoid dealing with the topic, which is not therapeutic. Teyber (2006) suggests the most important guideline for negotiating a successful termination is to acknowledge unambiguously the reality of the ending.

Teyber (2006) provides the following suggestions for making the termination process therapeutic. Termination needs to be discussed at a number of points in treatment, for instance, at the beginning, during the course of treatment, and towards the end (say, during the last three or four sessions). This provides opportunities to discuss and work through any issues (both negative and positive emotions) regarding the ending of therapy, and complies with the standard of 'respect' and 'consent'. A mutually agreed date can be helpful, as the ending is then unlikely to be a surprise. It is also helpful to acknowledge any work that may not have been done because time has been limited, and to acknowledge and process the client's feelings regarding termination. It is important to end the therapy as agreed, as ambiguous endings, or continuation of therapy because the client presents with a new crisis, can reinforce unhelpful patterns from the client's past and tend to be non-therapeutic.

3   When the client needs to return

It may be appropriate and beneficial if clients can return if they need further treatment. At a university psychology clinic, clients can return to the 'holding environment' of the clinic, but not see the same therapist. In private practice, clients may return to the same therapist, if they feel they need further psychological work, or booster sessions to help them stay on track and maintain the changes they may have made. Clients grow at different rates, and may benefit hugely from time to consolidate therapy. Some benefit from return for an emotional 'tune-up' when needed, or if a different problem arises. But an option to return should not be used to avoid termination.

Exercise 2.7

1   What has been your most and least successful termination with a client and why?
2   What difficulties have you experienced in terminating individual sessions (for example, with clients who find ways of trying to extend session time), and what might be occurring in these situations?
3   Reflect on your own issues related to endings, such as feelings of guilt, and not wanting to let people down, tolerate unfinished work, or say goodbye.

4   When the client needs referral to another service
There are a number of situations when it is advisable and indicated to refer a client to another service or therapist–psychologist:

- the psychologist may not have the expertise to manage the client's presenting problems
- a good working alliance between client and therapist is not able to be established (for example, when there are insurmountable value differences between therapist and client)
- the client's issues trigger such strong reactions from the therapist that this interferes with the therapist's ability to provide effective treatment (for example, the therapist has just gone through a divorce and is still too upset to deal with couples in crisis)
- the therapist is over-booked and cannot effectively work with the current caseload.

Whenever a therapist's ability to provide effective treatment to a client is obstructed, it is the therapist's ethical duty to deal with the obstacle quickly or refer the client on in a timely manner. This can be difficult to recognise and implement with a client who has been in treatment a long time and shows little or no change. Continued monitoring of outcome (see chapter 12) and supervision can help to determine what might be in the best interests of the client. Complacency and failure to address these issues are not in the best interests of the client.

Record keeping
The *Code* states that '*Psychologists* make and keep adequate records' (Code of Ethics, 2007, p. 19). What does 'adequate records' mean? The answer to this question will depend on the context in which you work, the requirements of your employer, legal requirements, and personal preference. Ask a number of psychologists working in the same setting how they write their notes and they may all provide slightly

different answers. There are, however, basic requirements that need to be adhered to in terms of retention, control of, provision of, and content of records. Read *Guidelines on Record Keeping* (APS, 2004) for more detailed information, but also become familiar with your state laws regarding records, privacy laws, and if employed, the policies regarding records of your employer.

It is vital to keep in mind that other people, including clients, may read the notes; make sure that what you write is respectful, nonjudgmental, and accurate. The guidelines state that notes should have enough detail so that another psychologist would be able to continue the interventions. You could die, retire, move away, or become ill. Furthermore, records could be used in court, or to back up and give an account of actions taken in the event of a complaint or adverse event, such as a death. Record keeping should protect confidentiality, where possible, and not be used to the detriment of the client.

Records need to be kept for a number of years, how many being specified by laws in each state and the APS. The APS requires that records of adults and children be kept for a minimum of seven years, and for children at least until they are 25 years old (which therefore may be longer than seven years). Some states require that records be kept for 10 years; it is advisable to check. Given that records are confidential, they need to be stored securely. Every reasonable action has to be taken to secure them. Leaving records unattended in a car may not be wise, as cars get stolen.

Psychological assessments

Complaints have often been made about psychological reports related to assessments. The Psychologists Board of Queensland, for example, received seven complaints (the highest number of complaints) in 2004–05 about reports being inadequate or inaccurate (Psychologists Board of Queensland, Registrant Update, April 2006). The accuracy and validity of reports is particularly important in forensic settings. The *Code* states that '*Psychologists* report assessment results appropriately and accurately in language that the recipient can understand' (Code of Ethics, 2007, p. 25). Thinking through the purpose of the assessment and report, and who is going to read it, is essential.

General principle C: Integrity

This principle highlights that psychologists are in positions of power and trust, and promotes professional and honest behaviour. Its standards cover areas such as reputable behaviour, communication, conflict of interest, non-exploitation, authorship, financial arrangements, and ethics investigations and concerns.

Reputable behaviour

This standard focuses on preventing psychologists from behaving in ways that will impair their ability to practice or bring the profession into disrepute. Psychologists need to be aware that they need to behave professionally and in socially-acceptable ways even in their private lives. Behaving in questionable ways outside of the work environment (such as driving under the influence of alcohol and being charged) may therefore be considered unethical, as it could bring the profession into disrepute. Psychologists also need to be careful about what they present and communicate in the public domain, such as in social networks like Facebook. Essentially, a psychologist is always viewed as being a representative of the profession; it is important not to behave in any way that could be perceived as putting the profession at risk of being perceived in a negative way.

Conflict of interest

Multiple relationships can cause conflicts of interest and boundary violations. Providing therapy to two members of the same family can lead to confusion and confidentiality issues. Seeing someone you know from a social setting for therapy can be confusing for both client and psychologist, leading to blurring of boundaries and expectations of behaviour.

Multiple relationships are hard to avoid in areas outside of cities, given that there may be no other psychologist who can be referred to. A survey conducted in the US of 447 urban and non-urban psychologists (Helbok et al., 2006) showed that rural and small-town practitioners were more likely than urban practitioners to have and struggle with multiple relationships, in addition to being highly visible in the community. A psychologist could have business dealings with a client or family of a client (such as a client who is manager of the only bank in town). Another example might be that a psychologist's children are in the same football team as the children of a client. Being more visible in rural communities may have advantages and disadvantages. People might feel more comfortable seeking help because they know something about the psychologist, but this could work against them seeking help if the impression is negative.

To manage unavoidable multiple relationships, ascertain whether the other relationship will in any way inhibit the client's or your own responses, and whether this will be detrimental to the client (Schank & Skovholt, 2006). The key is to cause the least amount of harm possible.

Also vital is to obtain informed consent. This process would involve discussing the different contexts in which psychologist and client might come into contact, how meeting in different contexts may have an impact on therapy, and how they might manage these situations. To prevent difficulties arising in multiple relationships, obtain support and supervision, and remain aware of ethical requirements and possible responses within the community.

Another difficulty associated with working in small and usually underresourced communities is that the psychologist might be asked to work in an area in which she or he may have little knowledge. This issue falls under the standard of competence. One approach might be to not provide a service—but what if providing no service might result in increased harm? Informed consent, seeking supervision, and being aware of what is ethically appropriate are essential in these situations.

Supervision can also be problematic in a small community. A psychologist might supervise a person, teach and evaluate that person's academic work, and employ the person as a research assistant. Some psychologists will supervise or be supervised by a colleague. It is imperative that both parties are mindful of the potential hazards and that clear contracts are made to prevent exploitation. For more on supervision see chapter 18.

Exercise 2.8

View Video 7. How well do you think the therapist addressed the issue of dual relationships? Is there anything that you would do differently or add?

ETHICS AND THE MEDICARE BENEFITS SCHEDULE (MBS)

In Australia, clients can receive Medicare benefits for a number of psychological services provided by an approved psychologist (for example, clients with mental-health difficulties, autistic-spectrum difficulties, and/or chronic physical conditions with complex-care needs). Psychologists need to be familiar with the requirements of these schemes, eligibility criteria, and the relevant processes. Psychologists working under these schemes may experience ethical dilemmas and conflicts of interest:

- a client may require more sessions than the scheme allows and be unable to fund further sessions
- determining how much information is appropriate to provide to referring agents
- managing the conflict between high demand for services and being able to provide the best possible service.
  Ethical and legal breaches may be:
- receiving payment in a manner that contravenes the legislation (for example, by getting the client to pay the gap while bulk billing)
- providing services in which the psychologist may not be competent
- seeing a client who does not meet eligibility criteria (for example, a client who has been under the Mental Health Care Plan but who does not appear to have mental-health difficulties). Ethically and legally, the psychologist would not be able to continue to see this client under this scheme
- incorrectly claiming a Medicare item.

WHEN THERE ARE ETHICAL CONCERNS

The *Code of Ethics* (2007) and the Australian Health Practitioner Regulation Agency provide standards and guidelines for what needs to occur when there are concerns about a psychologist's practice. Earlier in this chapter, we noted the behaviours for which there is mandatory reporting; you are encouraged to read the *Guidelines for Mandatory Notifications* (Psychology Board of Australia, 2010). If you have concerns about a psychologist's behaviour that fall outside the mandatory notification requirements, the *Code of Ethics* (2007) notes that the first step is to approach the psychologist and discuss the concerns. If you become aware of concerns through a third party, encourage the third party to take appropriate action, such as making a complaint to the Australian Health Practitioner Regulation Agency and, if appropriate, the APS.

It is important to be familiar with complaints procedures and processes. These can be obtained from the Psychology Board of Australia's website. Usually, complaints are made in writing, and the Board will, if it deems the complaint requires action, write to the psychologist for a response. The nature of complaints can vary, including dissatisfaction with outcomes, inappropriate professional conduct, breaches of confidentiality, or sexual relationships. A useful chapter to read is:

Wignenfield Hammond, S. & Freckelton, I. (2006). Being the subject of a complaint to a regulatory board. In Morrissey, S. & Reddy, P. *Ethics and Professional Practice for Psychologists*. Sydney: Thomson, 150–62.

PRACTICE IMPLICATIONS AND ETHICAL DECISION-MAKING

Ethical issues are inherent in everything a psychologist does, and psychologists need to be constantly aware of ethical requirements and expectations. We may be aware of the obvious ethical standards (such as not having sex with a client), but the more subtle and unexpected dilemmas may prove most challenging or difficult to resolve. The following guidelines may be helpful in promoting ethical awareness and practice:

- be alert to ethical issues
- be familiar with the current *Code of Ethics*, and where to find information on ethical issues
- frequently ask, what is in the best interests of the client?
- does the benefit of the decided-on action outweigh the harm?
- what are the possible effects of the decided-on action for the client, the psychologist, the community, other clients, and the profession?
- keep your ethical knowledge current
- learn from your mistakes, and be open to self-reflection and feedback
- be professional and responsible
- utilise supervision regularly to monitor your ethical practice.

When faced with a dilemma, the following process may be helpful:

1 Identify the ethical issue (for example, to report something or not)
2 Go to the current *Code* and relevant resources, such as the *Guidelines*
3 Explore possible courses of action and their outcomes
4 Consult with a trusted colleague and/or supervisor
5 Consult with the relevant professional board or professional society (that is, the APS)
6 Keep a record of the decision-making process and actions
7 Implement the action decided on
8 Review and reflect on outcomes, and adjust as required.

The questionnaire in table 2.1 may be helpful for monitoring how you are managing ethically, and whether you are at risk of behaving unethically. We recommend that

Table 2.1   Ethics at risk test for therapists

The following is designed to allow you to assess your ethics as a therapist. Please answer the following questions honestly, then add up your score and compare the total with the key at the end of the test.

		No = 0 Yes = 1
1	Is it true you have never taken an academic course on ethics?	
2	Are you familiar with the relevant parts of the APS code of ethics?	
3	Do you think the ethics code interferes somewhat with the quality of your work?	
4	Do you feel sexually attracted to any of your present clients?	
5	Do you fantasise about kissing or touching a present client?	
6	Do you comment to a present client how attractive he or she is or make positive remarks about his or her body?	
7	Are you tempted to ask out an ex-client even though less than two years has passed since termination?	
8	Do you commonly take off your jewellery, remove shoes, loosen your tie, or become more informal during therapy sessions?	
9	Has a present client given you an expensive gift or frequently given you inexpensive gifts?	
10	Are you stimulated by a current client's description of sexual behaviour or thoughts?	
11	Are you in the midst of a difficult personal or family crisis yourself?	
12	During the past six months, have you seen clients while you were hung over or under the influence of drugs, even if only a little?	
13	Do you feel manipulated by a current client such that you are wary of him or her or are angry and frustrated by him or her?	
14	Have you avoided seeing a client because of intense emotional reactions?	
15	Have you, in the previous six months, avoided disclosing important information concerning a client for fear of the potential consequences?	
16	Have you wanted to talk to a colleague about a current case but feared doing so would show your lack of skill or lead to an undesirable outcome for yourself?	
17	Are you aware of a potential breach of the ethics code by a colleague or supervisee or supervisor that you have not reported?	
18	Are you behind on case notes?	
19	Do you talk about clients with other clients or gossip about clients with colleagues?	
20	Have you experienced sexual attraction toward a supervisee or supervisor?	

Total score:
0   Excellent. You are nearly risk free.
1–3   Review your practice. Read and follow the Ethics Code.
4–6   Review your practice for problem areas. Consider needed changes.
7–8   Consult a supervisor. You are engaging in high-risk behaviour.
9+   You are probably harming your clients and/or yourself. Seek therapy and supervision. Come to terms with your situation by making immediate changes.

Source: Campbell (2000). Ethics at risk test for therapists. Questionnaire (published with permission of the author)

you complete this on a regular basis. After all, being alert to a need to make changes to your practice is easier than having to deal with the consequences of unethical practice.

Exercise 2.9

When reviewing the various scenarios on the videos, try to identify the relevant ethical principles and standards that relate to that segment.

CONCLUSION

This chapter has provided a brief overview of some of the ethical issues related to practising as a psychologist. Ethical principles help clarify what is appropriate and professional conduct. But, as noted throughout this chapter, ethical principles and standards are not static or always clear cut. Practising ethically requires frequent reflection, continuous updating of knowledge, and questioning of practice. Nothing a psychologist does is devoid of ethics, and you are encouraged to do more reading on ethical issues, and to always keep ethics in mind when practising and when reading the rest of this book.

Recommended reading
Australian Psychological Society. (2007). *Code of Ethics*. Melbourne: author.
All the APS Ethical Guidelines.
Bersoff, D. (2008). *Ethical Conflicts in Psychology* (4th edn). Washington, DC: American Psychological Association.
Davidson, G. (2002). Dealing with subpoenas: advice for APS psychologists. *Inpsych*, 24, 31, 33, 35.
Kampf, A., McSherry, B., Thomas, S., & Abrahams, H. (2008). Psychologists' perceptions of legal and ethical requirements for breaching confidentiality. *Australian Psychologist*, 43 (3), 1940–1204.
Morrisey, S. & Reddy, P. (2006). *Ethics and Professional Practice for Psychologists*. Sydney: Thomson.

Recommended websites
<www.psychology.org.au>
<www.psychologyboard.gov.au>

Part B

Factors in psychological outcome

Chapter 3

Factors in change

Introduction

Psychotherapy is effective in bringing about psychological change for most clients. The focus of this chapter is on understanding what factors influence client change. There has been debate between proponents of evidence-based treatments that focus on techniques and those who focus on process issues, such as the therapeutic relationship. Our position is that a range of factors is critical to effective outcome, and that an effective practitioner will attend to all mechanisms that may contribute to client change. In this chapter, we present a model for change, to provide a framework for conceptualisation, treatment planning, and evaluation of psychological practice, irrespective of theoretical orientation or the client's presenting problems.

Psychotherapy effectiveness

One thing we can be sure of: psychotherapy works. Psychotherapy has been found to be very successful, with effect sizes ranging from .75 to .85 (Wampold, 2001). For a long time we have known that psychotherapy is effective. Ever since Eysenck, in 1952, suggested that psychotherapy was ineffective, and, worse still, more likely to harm, research has repeatedly demonstrated, from the earliest meta-analysis by Smith and Glass (1977), that treated individuals, on average, do about 80 per cent better than those untreated (Wampold, 2007). The focus of inquiry, thus, becomes what is it about this process of working through problems with a therapist that seems to help most people to feel better, and to increase healthy functioning in their lives. The psychotherapeutic-outcome literature is replete with claims that one therapy is more effective than others for particular psychological disorders, or that there are no differences between therapies because common factors alone are responsible for therapeutic outcome. The result of such claims is that the literature can be daunting and confusing for even experienced psychologists as they try to incorporate scientific knowledge into their practices. The risk is that many psychologists may deal with the confusion by ignoring the literature altogether, resulting in practice that is not informed by science. The aim of this chapter is to present a balanced picture of the relative contributions of each of the factors that influence psychotherapeutic outcome, to assist psychologists to make informed choices about their practice. Understanding that each factor may contribute to outcome provides a rationale for the conceptual model presented later in the chapter.

Exercise 3.1

Before reading any further, reflect on your thoughts about the components of therapy that you believe help clients with their problems, enhance their wellbeing, and improve their functioning.

COMPONENTS OF PSYCHOTHERAPY CHANGE

For over a century, psychologists have debated the essential elements in therapy. For decades, this debate focused on determining which psychological theory (and concomitant techniques) best explained clients' difficulties (Norcross & Goldfried, 2005). More recently, there has been a shift away from focusing on which theory is most effective to whether 'specific factors' (techniques or procedures specific to a theory) or 'nonspecific or common factors' (processes common to all effective therapies) matter more. More broadly, the debate centres on whether it is theory-specific techniques or common factors, such as the therapeutic relationship, that bring about client change. However, Castonguay and Grosse Holtforth (2005) have referred to this debate as posing a 'false dichotomy', because it implies an either–or approach to the role that specific or common factors play in outcome. Such an approach, they argue, is 'both logically flawed and empirically untenable' (Castonguay & Grosse Holtforth, 2005, 199); it is more likely to be complex interplay between a range of specific and common factors that determines therapeutic outcome. To understand this conclusion, it is helpful to review the psychotherapy-outcome research that informs practice to date.

EMPIRICALLY SUPPORTED TREATMENTS (ESTs)

One of the most concerted attempts to guarantee effective treatments for clients was the creation of the Division 12 (American Psychological Association) Task Force on the Promotion and Dissemination of Psychological Procedures (Chambless et al., 1998). The focus of the Division 12 Task Force was to determine which treatments were most effective for which disorders. To attempt this, and in response to societal and professional demands that therapists be more accountable, the focus of much of the therapeutic field moved towards attempting to identify *empirically validated treatments* (EVTs), or, as they were later called, *empirically supported treatments* (ESTs) (Castonguay & Beutler, 2006). For a psychological treatment to be considered an EST, its effects need to be demonstrated in two separate *randomised controlled trials* (RCTs), and it needs to be shown to be more effective than placebo or a no-treatment-control group. This emphasis on empirical demonstration led to a flurry of RCTs that resulted in treatment manuals and books describing 'treatments that work' (e.g. Nathan & Gorman, 2002).

This focus on identifying effective treatments needs to be understood in the broader health-care context, with increasing demands for accountability. Psychology needed to provide evidence that its treatments worked, given the emphasis on treatment effectiveness in the medical world. Despite criticisms of the EST movement, without it there would likely still be lack of widespread support for psychological treatments. Psychology-treatment research, using RCTs, provided evidence that psychology had much to offer, and could be used in combination with medical treatments, or, in many cases, be equivalent or superior to pharmaceutical intervention. It is also likely that, without the EST movement, psychological interventions would not have had notable increases in financial support, such as Managed Care in the USA, and Medicare in Australia. Although some have argued that introduction of managed funding for psychological interventions has been one of the worst things that has occurred in the history of psychology (Hubble et al., 2010), it has allowed more individuals to benefit from psychological interventions.

Criticisms of EST

Despite its contribution, the work of the Division 12 Task Force was criticised by some in the psychotherapeutic field, who argued that focus on specific factors in ESTs ignored important issues, such as the impact of the therapeutic alliance on outcome (e.g. Beutler & Castonguay, 2006). There have also been concerns raised about validity of findings based on RCTs; individuals present with many issues, not just with discrete symptoms that indicate a diagnosis (the basis for manuals used in RCTs) (Kazdin, 2008). It has been argued that, because of strict inclusion–exclusion criteria for participants in trials, results may not be useful in everyday clinical practice, where clients often present with comorbidity (Kazdin, 2008).

Other issues raised concerned the reliance on demonstrating statistical significance in many RCTs, which is of limited utility; it does not provide information regarding the size of change or any description of variability within the sample group. More meaningful measures of clinical change require use of clinical significance testing, which we consider in chapter 14. However, the most important criticism of the EST movement concerned its neglect of common factors.

COMMON FACTORS

Recognising the limitations of ESTs, another Task Force was constituted under Division 29 (Psychotherapy) to focus on common factors that affected psychotherapeutic outcome (Norcross, 2002). It is important to grasp the empirical base that underpins the common-factors approach. Many researchers have noted that, despite the lengthy history of the comparative-outcome literature, it has been difficult to demonstrate consistently and systematically the effectiveness of one therapeutic approach over another (Smith & Glass, 1977; Smith et al., 1980; Shapiro & Shapiro, 1982; Stiles et al., 1986; Elkin et al., 1989; Wampold et al., 1997; Hubble et al., 1999;

Wampold, 2001; Luborsky et al., 2002; Wampold et al., 2002; Lambert & Ogles 2004). In 1936, Rosenzweig headed his seminal article with a quote from Lewis Carroll's *Alice in Wonderland*: 'Everyone has won, so all shall have prizes'. That was the Dodo bird's verdict after judging an animal race; 'Dodo bird verdict' came to symbolise the outcome-equivalence phenomenon in psychotherapy (Luborsky et al., 1975).

Criticisms of common factors
Despite the plethora of meta-analyses in support of the Dodo bird verdict, there remains debate about its validity. The most common criticisms of the Dodo bird verdict are that the meta-analyses were methodologically flawed (Chambless, 2002; Craighead et al., 2005), that it was a mistake to compare psychotherapies across all disorders (De Rubeis et al., 2005), and that specificity has indeed been demonstrated for some presenting problems, such as panic disorder, obsessive-compulsive disorder, post-traumatic stress disorder, and social phobia (De Rubeis et al., 2005), and for specific populations, such as behavioural strategies for children (Chambless, 2002).

Other researchers acknowledged the Dodo bird verdict's existence, but suggested alternative explanations for common factors; one was that different schools of therapy had different mechanisms of change leading to comparative outcomes (Hill, 1995; De Rubeis et al., 2005). Lambert and Ogles (2004) proposed three possible explanations for the Dodo bird verdict. First, there may be common factors operating across therapies. Second, therapies may achieve similar outcomes, but through different mechanisms of change. Third, differential outcomes do occur, but are not detected through current research methodologies.

Mechanisms of change

To make sense of this debate between specific and common factors, mechanisms of change is a useful concept (Kazdin, 2006). Mechanisms of change refers to the components of psychotherapy treatment that predict client outcome. Components most commonly hypothesised to be mechanisms of change are the strategy or technique related to a specific theoretical model, the therapeutic alliance, therapist factors, and client factors. Understanding which aspect of treatment is the 'active ingredient'—which aspect actually results in client change—is obviously of great importance. To just say, for example, that cognitive behaviour therapy (CBT) is an efficacious treatment for bulimia (Thackwray et al., 1993) is useful information, but it does not tell us exactly which aspects of the treatment are responsible for change. Is it mostly the behavioural components, or challenging thoughts, or perhaps components common to more than one therapy? Knowing which aspects are most *active* enables the design of more effective interventions (Kazdin, 2007).

Importance of various factors
Castonguay and Beutler (2006) have argued that, although the work of the two task forces had been valuable in establishing factors that are implicated in psychotherapeutic outcome, the result has been an ever larger gap between those who empha-

sise the role of theory and technique (Division 12), and those who emphasise the interpersonal relationship between therapist and client (Division 29), as the mechanism for change. Castonguay and Beutler argue that this gap ignores findings that suggest that only between 1–8 per cent of variance in outcome is attributable to treatment type (Luborsky et al., 2002; Norcross, 2002; McKay et al., 2006), whereas more variance is attributable to the alliance, at least 5–12 per cent (Horvath & Bedi, 2002; Norcross, 2002), and to the therapist, 5–17 per cent (Crits-Christoph et al., 1991; Lutz et al., 2007; Wampold & Brown, 2005). Wampold (2001) has argued that more than 70 per cent of client outcome due to therapy can be accounted for by factors common to all therapies, and only 8 per cent to factors specific to one theory. These statistics help us to make sense of the debate, as they indicate that all factors related to client outcome matter, even though we don't know exactly how much they matter, and that to ensure best outcome for our clients we should develop knowledge and skills in all areas.

Such complexity demonstrates a need to retain flexibility and a scientific attitude towards the psychotherapeutic-outcome research, because it is clear there is no one answer. This is being increasingly recognised in the literature, with pleas from eminent researchers and practitioners for a move away from the dichotomous approach to specific or common factors (Samstag, 2002; Castonguay & Grosse Holtforth, 2005; Craighead et al., 2005). The dichotomous approach presupposes that specific and common factors are independent of each other, which is illogical, unhelpful, and divisive.

We endorse the position that common and specific factors are synergistic and interactive, and to prioritise one over the other is a 'false dichotomy' (Castonguay & Grosse Holtforth, 2005) that does not reflect the dynamic and interactive process that is psychotherapy. We have based this book on the premise that all factors indicated in the literature (client factors, therapist factors, relationship and common factors, and theory-specific factors) can contribute to client outcome. Accordingly, the effective psychotherapist must be knowledgeable about all factors, and committed to doing his or her best to acquire the knowledge, skills, and values that will enhance his or her ability to assist clients to better outcomes. We adopt this premise because it is the most pragmatic and defensible position at this point. Adopting a scientific attitude means remaining open and respectful towards new evidence and being ready to acknowledge our own biases. We recommend this attitude as the healthiest position a scientist–practitioner can take to ensure that we always act in our client's best interests.

In summary, there has been evolution within the psychotherapy field from a focus on theory-based specific factors to agreement that both specific and common factors influence therapeutic outcome. More specifically, there is some agreement that the factors that primarily impact on therapy are:

- factors specific to the treatment modality or theory, particularly those related to technical skills, such as behavioural activation
- common factors, which are the facilitative conditions in treatment not specific to any particular treatment modality, thus literally 'common' to all therapies, such as the therapeutic alliance or experiential exposure

- client factors, such as the stage of readiness of the client to engage in treatment, and level of functionality
- therapist factors, especially empathic ability, warmth and listening skills, and ability to instil hope.

A GENERIC MODEL FOR PRACTICE

At this point, you may be wondering, how on earth do I put all this together and make sense of all these views and evidence when actually working with clients? We have asked ourselves this question, in relation to our own practice, and in how we train new psychotherapists. There are few black-and-white answers regarding human behaviour and change—and anyone who suggests that he or she has the sole answer should be viewed with scepticism. However, we all need a framework for practice, and part of our purpose is to provide the beginning psychologist with a model for how to discern significant content from peripheral information, to focus on what is in the client's best interests. Norcross and colleagues (2006) end their book on evidence-based practices with this: 'Debate and dialogue we should, but let's keep our eye on the goal: happier and healthier people' (p. 406). And this is our aim with this text: to describe the central debates, and to assist in synthesising the psychotherapy-outcome literature, while keeping in mind our primary goal, to help people with difficulties find a way to having a happier, more functional and fulfilling life.

The work of a number of eminent researchers on psychotherapy outcome is of importance to any practitioner—see the list of recommended readings at the end of this chapter. Drawing on the work of these and other researchers, as well as on our own clinical practice, we suggest the following guidelines for conducting effective psychotherapy:

- The client always comes first in treatment.
- Each client is an individual, no two clients are the same, consequently, the therapist needs to adapt to each client for optimal outcome.
- The therapist is a key player in the success of therapy.
- Procedures or techniques should be based on the best available evidence from systematic research, and psychologists need to be accountable in this regard.
- Effective therapists need to be mindful of all factors that have an impact on outcome, including their own skills and knowledge, theories, and techniques, the alliance, and, of course, client factors. A focus on one factor will inhibit effective treatment.
- The quality of the relationship/alliance between client and therapist will, in most cases, have a great impact on client outcome.
- There needs to be a rationale or explanation for a client's problem that makes sense to the client and that he or she accepts.
- To achieve change, there needs to be a set of actions or interventions that are consistent with this shared rationale.
- If a client is not responding to treatment, or the presenting issues are outside the scope of specific research outcomes, the therapist needs to base treatment on the best science-based principles that relate to the problems.

- The therapist needs to be responsible for monitoring client progress, and to be comfortable in addressing lack of progress collaboratively with the client.
- Therapists need to evaluate their practice continually, formally through reliable measures, and informally through reflection, to maintain the highest standards of client care.

Figure 3.1 incorporates all these points. It illustrates the respective roles of therapist and client, and their contributions to the three critical elements of therapeutic change: building an alliance; providing a viable explanation for a client's problems; and providing a set of activities to be undertaken by therapist and client that are consistent with the explanation. Through the client's acceptance of the explanation, it is argued, the client's response-expectancy changes (increasing hope), the client's self-efficacy increases (leading to increased participation in the therapeutic process), and the working alliance is enhanced. As a result, the client is more likely to engage in explanation-consistent activities, leading to change. Figure 3.1 is drawn from Wampold's (2007) review of the outcome literature. For a full discussion of the work Wampold reviewed, and a more extensive discussion of the basis for this model of change, see chapter 8.

The model takes into account factors that are pre-therapeutic in nature, factors that therapist and client bring to therapy, factors that come into play during therapy, and post-therapy factors. In the model, the arrows indicate that pre-therapy factors contribute to therapy factors, which, in turn, contribute to post-therapy outcome factors. Each of these is described briefly below, with more complete discussion in later chapters.

Pre-therapy
The client
It may seem so obvious, but we can forget that therapy is really about the client. Possibly because much of our focus, as therapist, is on getting it 'right', and the anxiety and preoccupation that can result, the client can sometimes take second place; of course, this can interfere with client outcome. Numerous client factors will have an impact on the process and outcome of treatment, including the presenting problem, the client's ability (or lack of ability) to develop a therapeutic relationship, the client's support network, and the client's health, unresolved issues, and defences. Each client presents with a unique set of characteristics; it is important to remember this and to adapt rationale and treatment to fit with the needs of the individual.

During therapy, there will also be events in the client's life outside of therapy that will have an impact on outcome. In figure 3.1, the arrow from client to elements of treatment indicates that the client plays a central role in all aspects of treatment. Chapter 4 focuses on client factors. Please note: figure 3.1 presents the client as an individual. The 'client' also represents a 'couple', 'family', or 'group'.

The therapist
Our model indicates the dual nature of therapist factors: therapist characteristics that tend to be stable and the skills and techniques that the therapist brings to therapy. The two aspects of the therapist are interwoven in the way therapists work with clients; this is reflected in the model by the arrow from therapist to the critical elements of

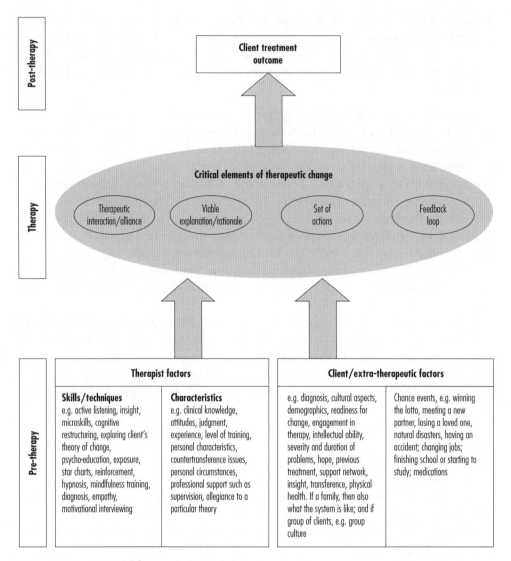

Figure 3.1 A model for psychological change

therapy. In short, the model reflects the need for the therapist to have clinical knowledge that has breadth and depth, an attitude that incorporates respect for the client and for the science of psychology, flexibility and openness, a sense of ongoing learning and growth, and allegiance to a theory, or theories, of psychological therapy.

As there is currently no definitive evidence that one theory, with its techniques and interventions, is superior in predicting client outcome, we believe that considering the collective range of psychotherapeutic theories and techniques is the most useful approach. We have thus taken an atheoretical approach, by incorporating all the techniques a therapist can use that have demonstrated effectiveness into one group. This is not to suggest that a therapist should not have one theory with which he or she is familiar and finds useful for conceptualising. It does suggest that the therapist needs to be aware of the range of theories and techniques, with the deciding factors:

a what fits best with the client's theory of change (Duncan & Miller, 2000)—what makes most sense to the client, and what will the client respond to; and

b what are the procedures and techniques based on the best available evidence from systematic research?

For our purpose, *technique* is defined as 'a practical method, skill or art applied to a particular task' (Collins Dictionary, p. 872). These techniques, and those discussed in chapters 7 and 8, are related to a range of psychotherapy theories and other methods commonly used in psychotherapy. We have included, for example, assessment and diagnosis as methods, because they are essential, particularly to providing a client with a rationale. Thus, a technique can be thought of as any method or skill that will achieve any of the critical elements.

Although different techniques might be used to achieve different elements, the same technique might be used to achieve all critical elements. For example, empathy is required to: (a) build an alliance and maintain it, as it assists the client to recognise that the therapist understands and cares about him or her; (b) come up with a viable explanation, as empathy will assist in understanding the client's problems and worldview, thus making sure that the rationale is plausible to the client; and (c) assist the client to take action, as empathy will be useful when the client gets stuck, or feels demoralised, and will assist in continuing to motivate change.

It is not useful to discount techniques because they do not 'belong' to the theory or rationale the therapist subscribes to: (a) most techniques are common to most theories; and (b) the most important decision is what technique or techniques would be most useful with a particular client, at a particular time, to achieve one or more of the critical elements. Again, the therapist needs to keep the goal in mind and adapt, trying different techniques, bearing in mind the importance of being responsive to the client's needs. *Responsive* is the term used by Stiles and colleagues (1998) to describe behaviour that is 'influenced by the emerging context, including emerging perceptions of others' characteristics and behaviour' (p. 440). To behave responsively, the therapist must continually monitor the client's problems, capacity, and state, with the clear knowledge that no two clients are the same.

Therapist factors that contribute to effective therapeutic outcomes will be discussed more fully in chapter 5.

The therapy process

Depicted in the model (figure 3.1) are the three critical elements of therapeutic change: the *therapeutic interaction/alliance*, a *viable explanation/rationale*, and an *explanation-consistent set of actions*. In developing this model, a challenge has been how best to represent the range of techniques and processes used in treatment without getting bogged down trying to discriminate between specific techniques/processes and common techniques/processes. Psychologists need to be familiar with the range of theoretical approaches and empirically-demonstrated common factors, to have a platform from which to build therapeutic alliances, to provide viable explanations/

rationales, and to develop explanation-consistent sets of actions. Each critical element of therapeutic change is described briefly below, with chapters 7 and 8 exploring theoretical approaches and common factors.

The alliance

A strong alliance is a significant predictor of successful client outcome, and is the basis for providing an explanation the client can accept and effective treatment. Building a therapeutic alliance that enables a client to accept that the therapist is trustworthy and is listening is essential. 'If the patient feels understood and ascertains that the therapist will work diligently on his or her behalf, then the probability of accepting the explanation of psychotherapy and the concomitant treatment is increased' (Wampold, 2007, p. 864). The range of microskills is essential to effective alliance building and practice generally, and should be practised and used competently by all therapists.

Many other techniques or abilities, such as empathy, are also essential. Research indicates that it is not which interventions and processes are used that is important, but how they are used (Wampold, 2007). Given that the alliance has been described as the quintessential common factor, it is described more fully in chapter 6.

The rationale

Clients require an adaptive explanation or conceptualisation of their difficulties that is different from their previous maladaptive explanation. Adaptive explanations assist in therapeutic outcome through instilling belief in the client that change is possible, influencing the working alliance, and leading to action via increased self-mastery and self-efficacy. One of the most challenging ideas that Wampold (2007), among others (e.g. Frank & Frank, 1991), has put forward is that the objective truth of an explanation given to clients for their problems is irrelevant to outcome. What matters is not the 'scientific' truth of the explanation, but whether the client accepts it. In fact, we don't know all about what causes mental disorders. As Wampold suggests, 'What is critical to psychotherapy is understanding the patient's explanation and modifying it to be more adaptive' (2007, p. 863). Thus, the client needs to accept the therapist's rationale and corresponding set of activities. Acceptance by the client is contingent on the rationale fitting with his or her own theory of change (Duncan et al., 2004) or explanation for their problems. Again to quote Wampold (2007), 'Effective explanations in psychotherapy must be different from presently held explanations for a patient's troubles but not sufficiently discrepant from the patient's intuitive notions of mental functioning to be rejected' (p. 864). The therapist needs to carefully monitor how the client responds to his or her explanations, and adapt the rationale if necessary.

This suggestion will be quite appalling to therapists who believe they have the 'truth' of what causes problems, and that therapy is a didactic process in which the client has to accept the rationale provided and do as he or she is told to improve. Our model does not suggest that the therapist cannot hold on to her or his preferred theory and techniques; if a theoretical rationale and concomitant techniques make sense to you and your client, then use it. However, if your client does not 'buy' the rationale, and does not accept the treatment, you need to adapt. Rigid adherence by a therapist to a set of techniques or theory is inimical to good client outcome (Castonguay et al., 1996).

To provide a rationale, the therapist needs knowledge of a range of areas. To rely on one theory is a bit like the old story of the blind men touching the elephant: each touched a different part of the elephant and had a completely different idea of what the whole elephant looked like. At the same time, not everything will apply to all clients, and parsimony in developing a rationale is important in order not to overwhelm the client (or the therapist!) with too many options. A comprehensive rationale may need to include a number of theories or types of psychological knowledge, primarily:

- the biological basis of behaviour, including temperament and genetic, inherited qualities
- personality traits
- the nature-versus-nurture debate
- psychological theories, including psychodynamic, Jungian, behavioural, cognitive, experiential, humanistic, and family systems, and theories that include variations on the basics, such as cognitive behavioural therapy (CBT), acceptance and commitment therapy (ACT), and dialectical behaviour therapy (DBT)
- developmental theories, including attachment theory.

Chapters 7 and 8 provide information about dominant theoretical approaches and common factors. Separation is to facilitate comprehension; it does not reflect the artificial splitting of theoretical approaches and common factors, which has been the bane of psychotherapeutic-outcome research in the past 20 years.

Explanation-consistent actions and interventions

To achieve client goals in therapy, there must be a set of explanation-consistent actions and interventions. Once a client has an alternative understanding of his difficulties, it is more likely that he will have an expectation that such difficulties can be ameliorated by treatment that is consistent with the explanation. Such sets of actions and interventions are likely to be theory specific for therapists; a cognitive therapist may help clients to think differently about their world, a behaviour therapist may suggest engaging in more pleasurable and meaningful activities. For a successful therapeutic outcome, the important thing is that there is a therapeutic structure and focus that is consistent with the rationale accepted by the client (Beutler & Castonguay, 2006), but that the structure is not rigidly adhered to by the therapist. A serious risk of rigidly sticking to a particular theoretical treatment protocol is lack of adaptation to client needs (e.g. Castongauy et al., 1996). Within the suggested framework, if a method or skill is not of use to a particular client, don't waste time with it; at a minimum, it will negatively affect the alliance, at worst, it will harm the client. For example, if exposure is ineffective, or worse, possibly harmful for a traumatised client at a specific time, don't use it just because you are supposed to be following a manual. Instead, revisit the client's understanding of the purpose of this procedure, reconsider the state the client is in, and postpone implementation, or consider alternative strategies to achieve the therapeutic objectives. The most obvious way to determine whether a client is benefiting from actions and interventions is checking with him at the end of a session, as well as undertaking ongoing outcome measurement.

Feedback loop
The fourth element of treatment is collecting feedback on how it is going, and using this to improve intervention session by session, to ensure that the client is moving forward rather than being held up, with no change, or getting worse. In chapter 9, how a therapist can enhance client-outcome gains by using consistent and regular feedback is outlined.

Client outcomes

Optimal client outcome is the goal of psychotherapy. A client enters treatment to get assistance with a range of problems he or she is trying to deal with. Usually clients come into therapy having exhausted all avenues they can pursue themselves to solve their problems, to make sense of their lives, and to increase their wellbeing. They require a therapist to assist them to reach their goals by helping them move beyond where they have got stuck. Factors that predict outcome will be discussed in chapters 4 to 8, specific and common factors. Chapter 9 focuses generally on client outcome, and outlines differing views regarding outcome goals appropriate to therapy, number of sessions required for optimal outcome, factors resulting in premature dropout, when outcome is harmful to a client, and how the therapist can enhance client-outcome gains. Chapter 12 will discuss methods and measures for assessing outcome.

Practice implications

Our model (figure 3.1) is intended to provide a blueprint for you to use in conceptualising your clinical cases, deciding on an intervention, and evaluating outcome, irrespective of client presentation, diagnosis, or your theoretical framework.

Conclusion

Despite the complexity of the psychotherapeutic-outcome literature, a number of factors contribute to client outcome, and rigidly focusing on one factor is inimical to effective psychotherapy. Our intention with the model we present is to provide a road map for navigating the variables related to client outcome in a way that is consistent with the scientist–practitioner model. We urge you to find your own style of working with clients that is grounded in the scientist–practitioner model and ethical-practice guidelines, and gives priority to client needs and goals. We recommend the approach described succinctly by Norcross and colleagues (2006): 'Our bias is towards informed pluralism. We oppose zealots on both sides; we champion moderation in the middle. Our most cherished value is to give full voice to the field's differences through respectful discourse' (p. 8).

Recommended reading

Castonguay, L. G. & Beutler, L. E. (eds) (2006). *Principles of Therapeutic Change That Work*. New York: Oxford University Press.

Duncan, B. L., Miller, S. D., Wampold, B. E., & Hubble, M. A. (eds). (2010). *The Heart and Soul of Change* (2nd edn). Washington, DC: American Psychological Association.

Frank, J. D. & Frank, J. B. (1991). *Persuasion and Healing: A Comparative Study Of Psychotherapy* (3rd edn). Baltimore: Johns Hopkins University Press.

Lambert, M. (2004). *Bergin and Garfield's Handbook of Psychotherapy and Behavior Change* (5th edn). New York: John Wiley. This book incorporates best-known research about psychotherapy and client outcomes, containing the views of important thinkers in psychotherapy, including Aaron Beck, Larry Beutler, Leslie Greenberg, Steven Hollon, Alan Kazdin, Benjamin Ogles, and David Orlinsky.

Nathan, P. E. & Gorman, J. M. (eds) (2002). *Treatments that Work* (2nd edn). New York: Oxford University Press.

Norcross, J. C. (ed.) (2011). *Psychotherapy Relationships that Work: Evidence-Based Responsiveness* (2nd edn). New York: Oxford University Press.

Norcross, J. C., Beutler, L. E., & Levant, R. F. (eds) (2006). *Evidence-Based Practices in Mental Health: Debate and Dialogue on the Fundamental Questions*. Washington, DC: American Psychological Association.

Norcross, J. C. & Goldfried, M. R. (eds) (2005). *Handbook of Psychotherapy Integration* (2nd edn). New York: Oxford University Press.

Wampold, B. E. (2001). *The Great Psychotherapy Debate: Models, Methods and Findings*. Mahwah: Lawrence Erlbaum Associates Inc.

Wampold, B. E. (2010). *The Basics of Psychotherapy. An Introduction to Theory and Practice*. Washington DC: American Psychological Association.

Chapter 4

Client variables

INTRODUCTION

This chapter is intended to provide you with an understanding of how factors specific to clients can have an impact on therapy outcome. Therapy would not exist without clients and their presenting concerns, but the role that client factors play in therapy is often overlooked (Bohart & Tallman, 2010). Although it is important to consider the impact of therapist and technique factors in therapy outcome, understanding the influence of the client is equally if not more important. Research indicates that approximately 25–40 per cent of the outcome of psychotherapy can be attributed to factors related to the client and extra-therapeutic factors (e.g. Asay & Lambert, 1999; Norcross & Lambert, 2005). If therapists are to assist clients in the most effective way possible, understanding how individual client variables can influence the therapeutic venture is essential. Some of the most important client factors include severity of symptoms, client beliefs and attitudes regarding change, including expectations of change, client interpersonal skills and ways of relating to others, demographic and social factors, and client strengths and resources. Further, the effectiveness of therapy largely depends on how involved a client is in treatment; the therapist needs to ensure there is a strong alliance with the client, and needs to encourage the client to be engaged in treatment.

CLIENT FACTORS AND EXTRATHERAPEUTIC ASPECTS

When clinicians refer to *client factors*, what exactly do we mean? Client factors are aspects or characteristics of a client (or group of clients) that can significantly affect progression and outcome of therapy. Extra-therapeutic factors are those that result in improved functioning for clients outside of the impact of therapy, and are specific to the individual client (Asay & Lambert, 1999). Hubble and colleagues (2010) suggest that these factors include client readiness for change, socio-economic status, motivation, level of functioning before treatment, strengths, supports, and chance life events, such as meeting a new partner, having an accident, or winning lotto.

Not only can client variables be used to understand the likely outcome of therapy, but they may also help a clinician to decide on techniques that might be useful for an individual client. Despite often working from a particular therapeutic orientation, at some point most practitioners have realised that not every client responds effectively to the same techniques, and that no two clients present in exactly the same way, with the same history, life stressors, symptoms, or symptom severity. Every client is unique, whether or not he or she shares similarities in diagnosis or life circumstances. It is important that therapists recognise that each client's experience is different, and that this will have an impact on therapeutic outcome. Let's look at an example.

Case study 4.1: Joe and Andrew

Joe presents to therapy because he is feeling depressed. Joe has never experienced depressive symptoms, and reports no history of depression in his family. He has had a relatively stable life until six months ago, when he was made redundant from his job as a stockbroker. Since that time, Joe's mood has become progressively worse, and he is often irritable and frustrated with his family. Joe's relationship with his wife has suffered, and she has threatened to leave him if he does not seek psychological help. Joe has never seen a therapist before, and does not feel convinced that therapy can help him. Over the past few months, Joe has also lost weight because of a decrease in his appetite, and has had trouble staying asleep at night. He reports that he experiences fleeting thoughts of suicide. Although Joe's wife is supportive of him attending therapy, he feels resentful that she has threatened to leave to make him attend. Joe's parents are concerned for him and have moved from interstate to be closer to him, and he has several friends who visit him weekly.

Andrew also reports that he is feeling depressed, and would like help to 'get my life together'. However, unlike Joe, Andrew has a long history of depression, personally and within his family. As a child, Andrew moved between foster homes and had few friends. Andrew is now morbidly obese, and eats more than usual when he feels particularly down. He spends much of his day sleeping, and rarely leaves the house. Andrew completed school until year 10, and for the last 10 years has had difficulty maintaining employment. Andrew is lonely, single, and has always struggled to keep a girlfriend. Andrew has a history of suicidal ideation, and two years ago was admitted to hospital after taking an overdose of pain medication. This time, Andrew presented to therapy because he is sick of feeling depressed and would like to make a change in his life for the better. He has had extensive contact with mental-health services, but previously felt that he wasn't ready to make a change. Andrew now thinks the time is right, and believes therapy is the key to helping him overcome his depression.

Exercise 4.1

Before reading any further, try to identify specific client factors which have the potential to influence the outcome of therapy for both Joe and Andrew. Based on the details provided, who do you think would have most the successful outcome in therapy?

Attempting this exercise, you might gain a sense of the difficulty that researchers and clinicians can face when attempting to identify which types of clients experience most improvement in therapy, and why. As you can see, at face value, two clients presenting with the same diagnostic concern (depression) could be predicted to have the same therapeutic outcome. However, by considering other factors, such as each client's reasons for coming to therapy, his motivation to change, his expectations of therapy, severity of symptoms, social-support system, and psychiatric history, we see the potential for two different therapeutic processes, including approaches to treatment and outcomes.

If client characteristics were overlooked, as they often are in practice, a therapist may have attempted to work in the same way with Joe and Andrew, with the result that they may not have benefited equally. Practitioners should consider individual characteristics and circumstances in their work with clients rather than taking into account only therapist and technique factors known to be effective. To achieve best outcome for clients, we need to consider which treatment is best for whom, under what circumstances. To illustrate the importance of client factors in the therapeutic process, we will revisit Joe and Andrew's cases throughout this chapter.

What do we know about client factors? Despite the lack of attention they often receive in psychological discourse and practice, the list of possible client influences is considerable, with 175 having been identified (Beutler, 1991). These range from biological factors to environmental and demographic factors, individual personality traits, attitudes, and expectations, and factors such as symptom type, severity, and diagnosis. They include factors internal (such as attitudes and beliefs) and external (such as environmental conditions) to the client, static factors (such as age, gender, and intelligence), those which are more variable (such as level of motivation), and factors that are psychological (such as personality traits) or biological (such as increased cortisol levels) in nature (Clarkin & Levy, 2004). Factors that have been consistently identified as important can be categorised as factors related to (a) client presenting problem and diagnosis; (b) client beliefs and attitudes; (c) interpersonal factors; and (d) social and demographic factors. Let's now look at each of these categories in detail.

Client problem or diagnosis

The importance of client presenting problem or diagnosis to outcome has been researched extensively. Although some therapists would argue that too much focus is placed on diagnosis in the treatment of individuals, it makes sense that this has received copious research. After all, to be effective, therapy needs to be targeted to the client's presenting concern; without such a match, positive outcomes would be difficult to achieve (Lambert, 2004). One of the most common diagnostic templates used by therapists today is the Diagnostic and Statistical Manual of Mental Disorders. There is copious research on the usefulness of the DSM diagnostic system, some criticising it for its promotion of the medical model, and others arguing that it is a necessary part of the evolution of psychology. This issue is further discussed in chapter 13. Here, we will summarise the current state of research on aspects of client presenting problems.

Three factors relating to the presenting concern of the client appear to play a role in outcome of treatment: (1) severity of symptoms at presentation; (2) the client's premorbid level of functioning and adaptability; and (3) the existence and severity of comorbid conditions, including personality vulnerabilities.

Severity of symptoms

Clients who do not experience considerable improvement following psychotherapy are often those with severe and entrenched problems (Petry et al., 2000). In a large multisite study, severely depressed individuals who suffered significant impairments in functioning responded best to medication in combination with psychosocial interventions, in comparison to those individuals with less severe symptoms who improved significantly without medication (Elkin et al., 1995). However, Shapiro and colleagues (1994) found little difference in treatment outcome across symptom severity in their depressed sample. They did, however, find that more severely depressed individuals had significantly more positive outcomes if they received sixteen rather than eight sessions of therapy. Research also indicates that the more severe a client's symptoms are, the more room there may be for significant improvement in symptoms (Norcross & Lambert, 2005).

Case study 4.1 (continued)

Andrew's symptomatology would perhaps be more severe than **Joe's** at presentation. Considering the chronicity of his symptoms and his poor history of treatment response, we might expect that he would score high on a measure of general distress. If, for example, the measure of outcome used with both clients was the Outcome Questionnaire 45 (OQ45, Lambert et al., 1996), a score over 63 indicates clinically significant distress, and the higher the score, the higher the distress. Assume that Andrew started therapy with a score of 125, but following therapy, his score was 80. Andrew's score is still within the clinically distressed range, but he has achieved notable gains from therapy. Conversely, let's suppose Joe began therapy with a score of 69, indicating a much lower level of distress than Andrew's, even though it still falls within the clinical range. After therapy, Joe scored 51, moving him out of the clinical range of distress. Joe's therapy might be considered more successful than Andrew's, given that he is no longer clinically distressed. However, as illustrated here, individuals with greater levels of distress at presentation often have more scope for improvement, and Andrew's life changed considerably, despite him still being in a clinical range.

Premorbid functioning and adaptability

In determining therapeutic outcome, the extent to which symptoms have an impact on the client's life is also important. The client's level of functioning before seeking treatment needs to be assessed. Clients with a higher level of functional impairment (including social, cognitive, and work impairment) tend to have poorer prognosis across a range of disorders (Gitlin et al., 1995; McLellan et al., 1983), and clients with better psychological health before seeking treatment tend to achieve more in therapy than those who have poor premorbid psychological health (Luborsky et al., 1980).

Case study 4.1 (continued)

These findings make sense: clients who have managed better in the past have a better chance of managing better in the future. If we again illustrate using **Joe** and **Andrew**, Joe reports a higher level of premorbid functioning than Andrew. Joe reports consistently experiencing positive relationships, working full time for many years, and having no history of psychopathology; Joe's premorbid functioning was high. Andrew reports always struggling in relationships, work, and with mood; his premorbid functioning is likely to be assessed as low. A likely difference between Andrew and Joe is that Joe has possessed the skills to function effectively socially and at work. Andrew has had limited opportunities to develop such skills, and functions poorly in these areas. Therefore, if we consider the factor of premorbid functioning alone, we might expect that Joe would experience more positive outcomes from therapy than Andrew; the skills he already possesses would enable him to better engage and apply the material covered in therapy. However, the picture is never as clear as this, and many factors interact to determine client outcome.

Comorbidity and personality disorders

Another factor is complexity of the client diagnosis, including comorbid conditions and personality vulnerabilities. Most research examining outcomes for clients with comorbid personality disorders indicates poorer response to treatment (e.g. Greenberg et al., 1995; Burns & Nolen-Hoeksema, 1992) and greater risk of premature dropout from therapy.

Let's illustrate: let's liken psychotherapy to a 100-metre sprint. Two individuals are taking part, and their aim is to reach the finish line (recovery from symptoms or problems). Both start at the same point, but bring different histories to the race. Runner 1 has always run well, whereas runner 2 has never run well, is unsure whether he can make it, and is overweight. It is likely that runner 2 will take longer to finish than runner 1, if he manages to get there at all.

In figure 4.1, person A has greater symptom severity and lower premorbid functioning than person B. X indicates the ideal outcome of psychotherapy: high level of functioning and low level of symptoms. Clearly, A has a lot further to go, and may not reach X or become symptom free.

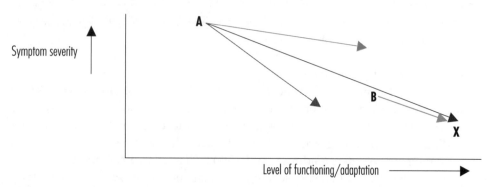

Figure 4.1   Influence of symptom severity and level of functioning on client change

One would expect that if person A's pattern of functioning, relating, and ability to adapt is inflexible and difficult to change, which is common in individuals diagnosed with a personality disorder, his progress would be more difficult. Research supports this, showing that individuals who suffer from depression and a personality disorder do not tend to do as well after psychotherapeutic treatment as those with depression but no personality disorder (McDermut & Zimmerman, 1998), particularly if the comorbid personality disorder is borderline personality disorder or obsessive-compulsive personality disorder (Burns & Nolen-Hoeksema, 1992; Wells et al., 1992; Mohr, 1995). Type of presenting problem and type of personality disorder also appears to play a role, with some studies showing that clients who have social phobia and an avoidant, schizotypal, or borderline personality disorder do not do so well. In addition, having both an eating disorder and a personality disorder is linked to poorer outcome (Clarkin & Levy, 2004).

Such findings are important for treatment planning, and therapists need to assess both psychological and personality symptomatology to appraise a client's level of functioning. If personality vulnerabilities exist, it is important that the therapist sets more modest goals for therapy, and tries to address the difficulties inherent in therapy with individuals with these symptoms, such as early dropout and alliance difficulties.

Practice implications

1   Severity and extent of comorbid symptoms will tend to have an impact on treatment.
2   Treatment may take longer and require a greater number of types of interventions, the more severe or comorbid the client presentation is.
3   The process of treatment, particularly the therapeutic alliance, may be more complex, particularly if there are comorbid personality issues.
4   Supervision is thus of particular importance in these cases.

Client beliefs and attitudes

How the therapist perceived progression of therapy has been considered more influential on outcome than perception of the client (Bohart & Tallman, 1999). The client's interpretation of the therapeutic process was often viewed as distorted by his or her pathology, or tainted by his or her biases and dysfunctional interaction style. In more recent years, research has indicated that the opposite is true. Various studies have indicated that the client's perception of therapist empathy, the therapeutic relationship, and the therapeutic process more strongly correlate with therapy outcome than do therapist perceptions (Bohart et al., 2002; Zuroff et al., 2000). Clients who perceive their therapist as more empathic, and therapy as more positive, are more likely to make significant gains during therapy. Because of this, it is imperative that therapists attempt to understand the client's perception of therapy, to ensure the best chance of a positive outcome. It can be a tricky undertaking; clients are not always forthright with their opinions and perspectives on the therapeutic process and the therapist. Interpersonal communication is something with which many clients struggle, and discussing their opinions, good and bad, can be threatening. However, if a therapist understands a client's concerns that can have an impact on therapeutic outcome, these issues can be raised and addressed.

Client perceptions, beliefs, and attitudes to therapy that have received considerable research attention include client expectations of therapy, client motivation to engage in therapy, client theory of change, self-efficacy for change, and psychological mindedness. Each of these will now be addressed in more depth.

Client motivation

When clients come to therapy, it is important to consider why they have come: what motivated them to seek therapeutic assistance? Have they come by choice or because they have been mandated? What are they hoping to gain from therapy? Such questions can help a therapist to determine how motivated a client is to change and to engage in the therapeutic process. Clients who are motivated to change and engage in therapy are more likely to complete assigned tasks and apply skills learnt to everyday life. They are also more likely to experience positive outcomes in therapy than clients who do not share this same level of motivation.

Client motivation to change is often conceptualised using Prochaska and DiClemente's (1983) 'stages of change' model. Prochaska and Di Clemente identify five stages of change from research on smoking cessation; each of these stages is readily applicable across the range of therapeutic approaches. The five stages are:

1 *Pre-contemplation:* the person generally does not think about making changes. It may be that he has tried to make changes unsuccessfully in the past and/or is not aware that change is possible or required
2 *Contemplation:* the person is thinking about change and the possible benefits and costs associated with it, but tends to be ambivalent about implementing it
3 *Preparation:* the person has decided that he wants to change, and begins taking steps to prepare
4 *Action stage:* the person is making specific adjustments to his behaviour with the goal of making significant changes
5 *Maintenance:* the person has made changes to behaviours and is working on continuing with the new behaviours, trying not to revert to old (familiar) patterns; he is working to maintain changes achieved in the action stage.

Findings are mixed regarding the efficaciousness of this model. Some research suggests that the model is a better predictor of outcome than type and severity of presenting concerns (e.g., Clarkin & Levy, 2004; Prochaska et al., 1993). However, Gollwitzer (1993) and Heckhausen (1991) suggest that a two-phase motivational-volitional model is better than the stage model in explaining behaviour change.

Another criticism is that focusing on stages of change distracts from looking at processes in change (Armitage, 2009). As with all change models, it is important that you consider advantages and disadvantages: how effective will it be with clients?

Reasons for presenting to therapy

Clients' reasons for seeking psychotherapy, their expectations of what will be involved, and what they hope it will provide, are factors that are likely to have a strong influence on the process and outcome of therapy; they are important factors for therapists to assess. There are numerous reasons why clients present for therapy. Commonly, people seek psychotherapy when they are experiencing some form of distress, with the hope that talking to someone will make them feel better. Often they do not understand how the process will work.

Some clients come to therapy with the belief that the therapist will 'do something to me', like a medical doctor prescribing a medication when the client feels ill. This expectation may result in the client approaching therapy in a passive manner. Other clients may understand that, to feel better, they will need to take an active role in the process. Naturally, this perception of how 'feeling better' will come about will influence the process, the working alliance, and the outcome.

Some clients will not have come to the decision that they need psychotherapy themselves. It may be that, because of their behaviour or level of expressed distress, other people (a partner, family member, or a court) may feel that they need help. They may be encouraged to seek psychotherapy or given an ultimatum ('if you don't see someone, I will leave you!', or when psychotherapy is an alternative to prison). Such clients may not feel they require psychotherapy, or agree that they have difficulties. Thus, the motivation for psychotherapy is not internal but driven by others. Assessing a client's motivation, and trying to work with it from the outset, is therefore paramount; otherwise, the therapist could find him- or herself in a situation in which the client consistently attends appointments but may not feel the need to contribute.

Some clients will present because they are feeling stuck. They may have tried many different things to improve their life, and how they feel, but nothing seems to change. As a result, they may not feel hopeful about the therapeutic process, doubting that it will be helpful for them. Also, because they feel they have already tried everything, they may adopt a passive role in the process. Alternatively, they may view psychotherapy as their last chance, putting all their hopes into it, and possibly putting undue pressure on themselves and the therapist to achieve change quickly. Exploring the client's 'stuckness', particularly what it means to them and their expectations, is important.

Some clients will not know what they want from therapy. They may just feel it is a good idea, perhaps having been encouraged by others to attend, or referred by someone. They may not understand what is going on for them, and may be confused. Exploring their difficulties, without necessarily setting immediate goals, would be quite helpful, as clients are unable to change what they cannot understand.

Some clients will present because they want to grow psychologically. These clients may be clear on what they want and what they hope to achieve from therapy.

Child clients may have no concept of why they are being seen. Usually, parents, relatives, or school will decide that a child will attend psychotherapy. A child may have no expectations about what is going to happen, or their expectations may be related to what they have been told and/or past experiences. For example, a child who has frequently been told she is 'no good', and needs to be punished, may expect that she will be punished and 'told off'. The child may believe that she is at fault for all the problems in her family, or that it is everyone else's fault. Motivations and expectations can be complex and varied.

Exercise 4.2

Watch Video 10, for an example of establishing rapport with an adolescent.

Everyone who presents has different circumstances and histories that influence motivations for and expectations of therapy.

It may be useful to consider the existential view that one of the dilemmas all humans face is that we would like freedom (freedom to do what we would like, or freedom from suffering), but for the degree of freedom we can have, we have to take an equal amount of responsibility in our lives (e.g. Yalom, 1989). Much human suffering, and lack of change in therapy, appears to be a result of clients resisting taking responsibility for their 'freedom' from suffering. Some want the therapist to provide a 'magic bullet' that will take away their symptoms without the client having to put in effort. Some are reluctant to take responsibility for change, because it is more rewarding to blame others, and may see it as 'unfair' that they have to take responsibility for change when it is someone else's 'fault'. Some clients do not want to be 'free', as their suffering has become so entrenched in their identity that they have become attached to it, defining themselves as trapped rather than free. They have little motivation to take responsibility for change.

It can be disheartening for a therapist to try to help a client who will not take any or enough responsibility for change, especially when the therapist can see how much better off the client would be if he or she did. Often, in an attempt to help the client, a practitioner will try to take responsibility for the client. In these situations, remember the light bulb joke: 'How many psychologists does it take to change a light bulb? Only one, but the bulb must really want to change'.

Practice implications

1 Carefully assess a client's motivation for coming to therapy, as this will be important in treatment planning.
2 You may need to use some initial motivational-interviewing techniques with clients who are not sufficiently motivated.
3 Some clients may not have the required motivation for treatment at that particular time, and the therapist may need to suggest an alternative referral, or for the client to return at a later date, when he or she is ready for change. It is important, though, that you do not confuse ineffective practice with low client motivation, so you need to discuss these cases with your supervisor.

Client expectations

Research has suggested that what clients expect from therapy can play an important role in their psychological recovery. Whisman (1993), reviewing mediators and moderators of change in the cognitive treatment of depression, found that clients who displayed a positive expectation of help, and a willingness to master new strategies for coping (essentially by completing homework tasks), were more likely to experience a positive outcome in therapy than clients who weren't. Similarly, in a study of panic disorder, client variables of negative attitude toward the treatment offered was independently associated with early dropout (Grilo et al., 1998). Hence, it is essential that therapists are aware of clients' expectations at the beginning of therapy, so they can be addressed, if not in line with what therapy can offer.

Commonly, clients who terminate therapy prematurely were more likely to expect specific advice, and were passive rather than involved in therapy (Grilo et al., 1998). Their expectation of therapy—that the therapist would solve their problems—was unrealistic. Therapists tend to expect that clients will be active participants in the process, and put effort into helping themselves; the therapist would act as a facilitator for the client making the change. The more unrealistic a client's expectations, the less likely it is that he or she will remain in therapy, because of dissatisfaction. It's important to note that few clients expect to be in therapy long term (Duncan et al., 2010). Given that, for some clients, long-term treatment will be needed for a positive outcome, there will be differences in expectations of length of treatment between therapist and client.

Expectations are likely to play a role in how willing clients are to form a strong alliance with the therapist, which requires a shared expectation of what therapy may achieve. It is thus important to address clients' expectations and work towards shared expectations. One aspect of understanding expectations is to enquire about previous therapy, and what occurred there. A client who has had a number of attempts at therapy, mostly unsuccessful, may have lower expectations than someone who has never tried therapy. A previous, helpful, experience of therapy will encourage positive expectations.

Client beliefs about change

Clients usually enter therapy for a purpose, with their main goal to feel better. Clients often have some idea what they need and want from therapy, and what needs to be done to lead to positive change. The client's specific ideas about the cause of her or his complaints, and how resolution can be achieved, is often referred to as the client's *theory of change (TOC)* (Held, 1991). Each client comes to therapy with his or her own 'theory' of what brings about change. We need to understand this theory, as it will impact on the effectiveness of treatment.

For decades, it has been recognised that similarity in client and therapist beliefs about the causes and treatment of client difficulties is vital for successful therapeutic outcome (Frank & Frank, 1991). Exploring and acknowledging the client's TOC, and aligning therapy, fosters a positive relationship between therapist and client, and is likely to increase client participation, which ultimately increases positive outcomes (Duncan & Monyihan, 1994). Research has supported the importance of the client's TOC in therapy, indicating that clients whose beliefs about the cause of their problems are congruent with the therapist's beliefs had greater expectations for change, greater levels of positive change, and greater levels of satisfaction with the therapeutic process, than did clients whose beliefs were incongruent (Duncan & Miller, 2000; Worthington & Atkinson, 1996; Hayes & Wall, 1998), with some research indicating that congruent therapist and client TOC decreases the likelihood of premature termination (Tracey, 1988).

Considering this research, it is important that therapists understand clients' TOC. However, because many clinicians work from a particular therapeutic orientation, their own models of change often take precedence over clients' (Duncan & Miller, 2000). This means that clients' perceptions of their quandary, and what is needed to change, are often dismissed, ignored, or overlooked. The detrimental effect that this can have on client expectations of therapy, motivation to participate, and, ultimately, therapeutic success, is substantial. It is essential that therapists practise flexibility in conceptualising client problems, and be open to applying models that are congruent with or can be made to fit with the client's TOC (Held, 1991).

To understand the client's TOC (Duncan & Miller, 2000), the therapist:

- inquires directly about the client's goals and ideas about change
- listens for or inquires about the client's usual method of change
- listens for or inquires about the client's previous attempts at a solution
- inquires about what his or her own role should be.

It is suggested that the following questions, posed to a client early in therapy, will be useful (e.g. Duncan & Miller, 2000; Teyber, 2006; Teyber & McClure, 2010). You may not need to ask all of them, and some are similar, but find those that will fit your own style:

- What did you (hope/wish/think) would be different as a result of coming here?
- What did you want to change about your (life/problem/etc)?
- What would, minimally, change in your life for you to consider our work together a success?
- What do you think would be helpful for us to do?
- What ideas do you have about what needs to happen for improvement to occur?
- Many people have a pretty good hunch about what is causing a problem, and what will resolve it. Do you have a theory of how change is going to happen here?
- How does change usually happen in your life? What causes change to occur in your life?
- What do you do to initiate change (if anything)?
- What do others do to initiate or facilitate change in your life?
- What is the usual order of the change process?
- What events usually precede or occur during or after the change?
- What have you tried to help the problem so far? Did it help? How did it help? Why did it not help?

This approach is based on a fundamental belief that clients have a set of 'theories' or ideas about their problems and have tried to help themselves. It is a respectful attitude that recognises clients' capacities to be active participants in their own change; clients are not expected to rely on the therapist to tell them what their problem is and what to do about it.

Exercise 4.3

What effect do you think asking questions such as these may have on:
1 the therapeutic alliance?
2 the client's level of engagement or hope for change?
3 the client's level of responsibility for change?
4 the effectiveness of treatment in bringing about change?

Clients' beliefs in their ability to change

Not only are clients' beliefs about what *needs* to be done important to therapeutic outcome, but so are their beliefs about what *can* be done. How the client appraises his or her circumstances, and the likelihood of achieving change, can have a significant impact on the process and outcome of therapy (Peterson & Stunkard, 1992). This type of client appraisal is often referred to as the client's level of *self-efficacy*, a concept developed by Albert Bandura, and defined as 'a person's belief that they can master a specific situation in a specific context' (Thompson & Wierson, 2000). The client's degree of self-efficacy can influence how he or she approaches the psychotherapeutic process and the process of change. For example, if a client were asked to keep a diary of her thoughts every time she felt angry, but doubted her ability to do this in a way that would result in positive change, the client would be unlikely to complete the task. On the other hand, if the client felt confident that she could adequately keep a diary of thoughts, which would help her experience positive change in therapy, it is highly likely that she would be motivated to engage in this process. The degree to which a client believes she can master a situation can have a significant impact on level of engagement in therapy and therapeutic outcome.

One factor that can contribute to a client's self-efficacy and therapeutic outcome is whether the client views her circumstances as controllable by herself or others. Having a sense of control over one's circumstances is known to be fundamental for emotional well-being and adaptive functioning (Thompson & Wierson, 2000). Whether a client believes she has control over a situation or not is often referred to as the client's *locus of control*, which can be internal ('I can be in control of this situation') or external ('I have no control over this situation').

To illustrate, a person who believes that her depressive symptoms are a result of external factors, such as financial stress, a husband with a difficult personality, or a chemical imbalance in the brain (external locus of control), would be likely to believe there is little she can do to foster a positive change in her symptoms (low self-efficacy). Conversely, a person who believes that his aggressive interpersonal style and tendency to spend money irresponsibly maintains depressive symptoms (an internal locus of control), would be more likely to believe that he could adapt his behaviour to foster positive change (high self-efficacy). These examples show that determining a client's personal beliefs about control is necessary to match the therapeutic approach.

Practice implications

Discuss with a client what his expectations are, and what his theory of change is. It is inappropriate to simply impose your view and treatment on a client without first finding out what he has tried to do to change, and his thoughts about his problem and what should be done about it. A lot of time can be wasted when a client will not go along with the treatment regime a therapist has embarked on without checking how it fits with the client's view of his issues.

Exercise 4.4

Watch Video 3, for an example of a therapist not fitting with a client, and what the consequences can be.

Client interpersonal factors

A central issue is the client's capacity to relate to and form relationships with others (Clarkin & Levy, 2004; Luborsky et al., 1993). Orlinsky and colleagues (1994) state that 'patients who are cooperative and open … are more willing to participate, can more readily absorb the experiences generated by effective therapeutic operations, [are] thus … more likely to benefit from therapy' (p. 363).

The client's ability to relate to others has been conceptualised from a number of theoretical perspectives, two of the most common being object relations theory and attachment theory.

Object relations theorists argue that influential interactions between children and their parents become internalised, and develop into schemas that determine how people establish relationships with others (Teyber, 2006; Teyber & McClure, 2010). They theorise that, even though early schemas evolve and increase in complexity, they provide basic structure for development of a sense of self, of an individual's internal organisation of the interpersonal world, and the shaping of subsequent relational patterns. In other words, our early childhood relational experiences influence the way we interpret and behave in social situations and relationships. Research has indicated that therapists' ratings of the quality of client object relations is directly related to effective therapeutic process, positive outcomes, and client retention, at least in short-term therapy (Piper et al., 1985; Horowitz et al., 1984; Piper et al., 1994); that is, individuals who have more mature, stable relational patterns are more likely to remain in and achieve more positive results from brief therapy.

Similarly, *attachment theorists* argue that early attachment patterns between infants and their parents form the basis for attachments in adult relationships. The seminal work of Bowlby (1960, 1980, 1988) and Ainsworth (1964) on attachment patterns between distressed infants and their mothers resulted in the identification of four primary attachment styles: secure, anxious ambivalent, anxious avoidant, and disorganised (Bowlby, 1988). Given the argument that an individual's early attachment style, and the quality of his or her attachments, influence later relationships, it is reasonable to expect that a client's attachment style would also have a significant influence on development of the therapeutic alliance, and the process and outcome of therapy. Research has offered support for this, indicating that individuals with a secure attachment style experience fewer pre-treatment symptoms and greater improvement post treatment than insecurely attached individuals (Meyer et al., 2001). Further, secure attachments are more strongly related to positive scores on the goals subscale of the working alliance inventory (Scatterfield & Lyddon, 1998), and securely attached individuals are better equipped to develop a positive therapeutic relationship in the early stages of therapy (Eames & Roth, 2000).

Research has indicated that object relations and attachment style also have indirect influences on therapeutic outcome through client expectancies and self-efficacy. For instance, attachment theory describes securely attached individuals as perceiving themselves to be competent in relationships, and to expect positive responses from other people (Bartholomew, 1997). Hence, it is likely that clients with secure attachments would be more likely to expect more positive things from their therapeutic relationship, which could have a positive impact on therapeutic outcome.

Parenting styles may also have an impact on clients. The construct of parenting style has been used to demonstrate variations in parents' ways of socialising and controlling their children (Baumrind, 1991), based on two main elements of parenting: how responsive parents are (how warm and supportive, and how well they foster self-regulation, self-assertion and differentiation in their children), and how controlling they are (Maccoby & Martin, 1983). Four main parenting styles are categorised based on these two dimensions: indulgent (high on responsive, low on control); authoritarian (high on control, low on responsiveness); authoritative (high on both, in the child's best interests, providing clear guidelines but also respectful and responsive to the children—the most effective style); and uninvolved (low on both). Parenting style can have quite considerable influences on children and their lives as adults.

Children of authoritative parents tend to do better on levels of competence, achievement, social development, self-esteem, and general mental health than children who have had other parenting styles. Children of uninvolved or disengaged parents tend to feel they are a liability to their parents; they feel insecure and unloved, and that they are largely responsible for their own care. To try to gain and maintain contact with parents, these children will often take on the 'adult' role themselves and look after the parent. In this way they get attention, but it is conditional on what the child can do for the parent, rather than how the parent can assist the child. A common term for such children is *parentified*; the conventional roles for parents and children are reversed (Boszormenyi-Nagy & Spark, 1973). Parentified children will sacrifice their own needs to get attention from their parents, who often are suffering from psychological problems, commonly depression, alcoholism, or bipolar disorder. Not surprisingly, such children suffer from feelings of inadequacy (a child can never fully take care of an adult), anxiety, worrying about not meeting the demands of others and their own expectations (Teyber, 2006; Teyber & McClure, 2010). As clients, they may try to take care of their therapist, often feel that they are a burden to the therapist, and try not to share too much so as not to be too much trouble.

Children of authoritarian parents who are firm disciplinarians receive unambiguous prescriptions for acceptable and unacceptable behaviour. Consequences for breaking rules are known by the children, who are not given reasons or explanations for the rules. There is lack of warmth or affection from authoritarian parents. Parental approval is obtained by being obedient and achieving the parents' goals. The children are often highly anxious that they will fail, and tend to be well behaved but insecure children, who have internalised their parents' harsh, critical, and demanding attitudes. Authoritarian parents often use discipline techniques based on love withdrawal. The beliefs that develop for children are, for example, 'It is my fault that they don't want me', or 'I should try harder and then they will love me'. Eventually, these children develop a shame-based sense of self. Adult clients who have had this type of parenting tend to present with guilt, depression, unassertiveness, anxiety, and low self-esteem. Low self-esteem, internalised anger, feelings of low self-efficacy, and lack of love, are a prescription for depression. Also, anxiety symptoms and control problems found in sufferers from eating disorders are often related to this type of parenting. Children often don't have a sense of their own internal experience, because their parents rigidly demanded conformity and obedience, and thus may not know what they like and dislike, and may even be confused about what feels good or not to them; they have not been allowed to 'have a mind of their own'.

Many parents, often if they had an authoritarian upbringing themselves, believe that being more permissive or indulgent will be best for their children. However, this style often results in children not knowing what is expected of them, or what the consequences will be of their actions. Although the parents may be more warm and expressive, the children are not given direction, which is what children need. These children are more likely to act out externalising problems, and are less likely to seek therapy as adults because they avoid taking responsibility for themselves, seeing problems as external to them. Their parents did not hold them accountable for their behaviour, and did not teach them appropriate behaviour by setting boundaries and providing rules. The children learned to avoid consequences by manipulating others, and learned that rules and limits do not apply to them. Consequently, they tend to be dependent, immature, demanding, and unhappy, with little self-control and low frustration tolerances, and lack empathy with others, thus tending to have poor long-term relationships with peers.

Related to the effect of parenting styles, clients often demonstrate a fixed interpersonal style adopted in childhood to reduce anxiety associated with unmet needs. Coping strategies become maladaptive if they are used inflexibly in all types of situations (Teyber, 2006; Teyber & McClure, 2010). The three identified styles are:

- *moving toward or pleasing people:* individuals relate to others by trying to please them; they do not assert their own needs

- *moving against others:* to reduce feelings of vulnerability from not having their needs met, and to seek to be in control of themselves and others, these individuals learn to respond to parental wishes with aggression and resistance
- *moving away from others:* individuals' defence against anxiety and unmet needs is by moving away from others through physical avoidance, emotional withdrawal, and self-sufficiency.

Therapists will experience clients engaging in the therapeutic alliance in a way which attempts to replay their experiences with significant caretakers. A client will attempt to elicit similar responses from the therapist that he or she had from significant others. This is discussed more fully in chapter 6.

Let's briefly consider the *eliciting manoeuvres* that clients with fixed interpersonal styles may adopt in therapy:

- the *moving toward style* will result in a client being helpful, trying to elicit approval, support, and liking from the therapist and others
- the *moving against style* is found in clients who are intimidating, competitive, and dominant; they tend to elicit self-doubt, fear, sense of competition, and aggression in others, including the therapist, if he or she doesn't pick up what is going on
- the *moving away style* presents as clients being avoidant, and tends to give the therapist the message that he or she needs to leave the client alone, not pursue difficult subjects, to treat the client very carefully. The therapist, if the client's eliciting attempt is successful, will avoid a range of issues.

It is suggested (e.g. by Teyber, 2006; Teyber & McClure, 2010) that the client is in some way testing the therapist, wanting to see whether the therapist will re-enact old patterns and behave as others have, or resolve maladaptive relationship patterns. When clients successfully elicit the same type of response from the therapist that they usually elicit from others, the therapist and client are re-enacting rather than resolving a problem. If the therapist recognises that they are re-enacting, when it is occurring in therapy, the therapist can use a process comment to make this interaction overt and a topic to discuss. If re-learning happens *in vivo*, in the therapeutic relationship, it is a powerful form of learning that allows clients to begin questioning, or even to let go of faulty beliefs and unrealistic expectations. This type of *corrective emotional experience* is discussed further in chapter 6.

Case study 4.1 (continued)

With **Joe** and **Andrew**, we can illustrate how clients' interpersonal relational styles can have an impact on the process and outcome of therapy. To do this, we need to make basic assumptions about their upbringing and subsequent quality of their object relations and attachment to others.

If you recall, Joe reports having numerous supportive relationships in his life and little difficulty in his relationships in the past. It may be assumed he has a positive, supportive relationship with his parents, given that they have moved closer to him in his time of distress. Based on this information, it is possible and probably likely that Joe would have a good quality of object relations and a secure attachment style. It appears that Joe's parents were closer to an authoritative style. Considering this, it is likely that Joe would possess a stable sense of self, and would view others in a positive light, enabling him to effectively interact with those around him.

Andrew was offered little stability in his relationships with adults when he was a child. He frequently moved between foster homes and reports that he has always struggled to maintain friendships and intimate relationships. From this information, we can fairly safely assume that Andrew has unstable object relations and difficulties with attachment to others. It would be important for Andrew's therapist to consider how his pattern of relating to others might play out in therapy, and the detriment this might have for outcome. By being aware of Andrew's relational style, his therapist will be better equipped to manage any difficulties that arise in the therapeutic relationship, and to use these difficulties to effect positive change.

The assumptions we have made about Joe and Andrew have been made on limited information. In practice, comprehensive assessments, via clinical interview, assessment tools, and the use of clinical judgment, would be beneficial in clarifying client relational patterns.

Practice implications

1   Clients will vary considerably in their interpersonal skills and ability to form a relationship with a therapist.
2   For best outcome, and of particular importance when working with more complex client presentations, the therapist needs to pay close attention to process and alliance issues.

DEMOGRAPHIC AND SOCIAL FACTORS

Various social factors have been suggested as predictors of therapeutic outcome. One of these, socioeconomic status, has gained extensive research attention (Falconnier, 2009). In her examination of the role of socioeconomic status in the treatment of depression, Falconnier (2009) found that lower socioeconomic status was associated with poorer outcomes across three different therapeutic interventions. Grilo and colleagues (1998) found that lower household income was an independent predictor of client attrition rate.

There is little evidence to suggest that age or gender is a significant determinant of outcome or therapy retention in general (Sledge et al., 1990). However, client age is receiving more attention as a determinant of the effectiveness of different types of intervention. To date, research examining the effects of various types of therapy for depressed elderly individuals indicates that various interventions, including those from a psychosocial (Scogin & McElreath, 1994), interpersonal (Reynolds et al., 1999), or cognitive behavioural perspective (Ladlaw et al., 2003), are equally effective (Gallagher-Thompson et al., 1990). Gender appears to have little influence on premature termination and therapy outcome (Petry et al., 2000).

Race has not been demonstrated to have any effect on outcome.

PRINCIPLES OF CHANGE APPLIED TO CLIENT FACTORS

Castonguay and Beutler (2006) summarise the principles, across various therapies, that tend to predict good outcome. This is an attempt to bridge the gap between approaches that highlight either specific or common factors, by focusing on principles of change that incorporate both. Building on the seminal work of Goldfried and colleagues (1980), Castonguay and Beutler (2006) argue that, in terms of abstraction, these principles lie between techniques and theoretical models. The authors define principles as 'general statements that identify patient characteristics, relational conditions, therapist behaviours, and classes of intervention that are likely to lead to change in psychotherapy' (p. 5). It is important to note, however, that these principles have not been empirically investigated as mediators of change within therapy, and may be more accurately viewed as 'hypotheses, rather than as established or factual processes of change' (Castonguay & Beutler, 2006, p. 8). Thus, although an invaluable contribution to the literature, empirically based principles of therapeutic change require significant empirical investigation.

Principles identified by these authors include:

Positive outcome is predicted for a client who:

- is psychologically minded
- has realistic expectations of therapy
- has contributed to the establishment of a strong alliance
- reports that he or she finds therapy helpful
- has a secure attachment style, no doubt based on authoritative parenting styles
- is willing and able to engage in the therapy process.

Poor outcome is predicted by a client who:

- has comorbidity
- has greater severity of disorder
- shows insecure attachment styles
- has significant interpersonal problems from early development.

Poor outcome will also be predicted by a therapist who:

- has unresolved countertransference issues
- shows negative reactions to the client and lacks empathy
- cannot tolerate negative feelings from the client.

We will discuss therapist factors in detail in chapter 5.

Client assets, resources, and interests

Our focus in treatment on problems often results in us overlooking assets that clients bring to therapy. We tend to focus on what Duncan and colleagues (2004) refer to as the 'Five Ds': diagnosis, disease, dysfunction, disorder, and deficit. These five Ds do tend to be the basis of thinking in clinical psychology. It is not an error for us to focus on these, as our clients come into therapy focusing on their problems rather than on their strengths. They want us to help them with their five Ds – although we can't imagine a client ever stating them as their presenting issue! However, we need to assist clients to see that they have more to offer than just problems—and we need also to remember this. It is clients' strengths that will help them to overcome problems, and we need to always consider these in our assessment.

Assets can include:

- resilience factors, including intelligence, social support, and motivation
- ability to extract their own meaning from therapy
- previous ability to solve problems
- ability to internalise the therapist
- insight
- ability to be rational
- ability to demonstrate affect regulation
- ability to work collaboratively
- character strengths (positive human traits).

A number of therapies focus on strengths, including the solution-focused approach, narrative therapies, the client-centred approach, and, of course, positive psychology (see chapter 7 for a further discussion).

Exercise 4.5

1 How often do you do an asset search on intake with a client?
2 Can you list the assets and strengths that each of your clients has?
3 Are you as aware of your clients' strengths as you are of their problems?
4 How frequently do you purposefully utilise your clients' strengths in their treatment?

The client's role in treatment

How do you view your client? As a blank slate, ready to receive your wisdom and theoretical knowledge and techniques? Or as an individual with a view of his or her problems, and of what should be done? As someone who should be assimilated into your way of working, or someone to whom you need to adapt? As a passive recipient or as an active participant? We know that the more willing clients are to be active in treatment, and the more they contribute to the alliance, the better their outcome (e.g. Bohart and Tallman, 2010). These authors suggest that therapists need to make use of and promote the strengths and resources a client has, and to see the client as the locus of change. The following points may be useful reminders of what factors are helpful to outcome:

- The client needs to own the process of change

- The therapist needs to encourage the client to shape his or her own agenda and to talk about issues that he or she feels are most salient
- There should not be a hierarchical relationship, where the client is compliant to the therapist, who tells the client what to do
- The therapist needs to co-create a relationship in which the client behaves assertively with the therapist, thus fostering independence
- The therapist needs to be engaging and active, but not directive, unless that is in the best interests of the client and appropriate
- The therapist needs to be able to tolerate ambiguity, and to refrain from subtly controlling the interaction; he or she should share control
- The therapist needs to look for opportunities to create immediacy by linking the client's problems to what is occurring between them, how they are interacting right now.

What do clients really want from therapy?

Clients routinely identify the therapy relationship as being of central importance in what helps them to change. In an early study, Sloane and colleagues (1975) suggested four main factors that matter:

- *therapist variables*, particularly positive behaviours, such as being warm and trustworthy
- *facilitative factors*, which help the client to feel cared for and understood: some examples: effective listening by the therapist; encouragement and direction from the therapist; therapy as a time and place for focus on self.
- *a conceptualisation that makes sense to the client*
- *actual change* in a range of areas, including behaviours, cognitions, fears, insight, meaning.

Norcross (2005) asked psychotherapists who had themselves been in therapy what they found useful. Most frequently, this group of clients also considered therapists' positive interpersonal qualities, such as warmth, empathy, humaneness, and patience, of central importance. This group of clients also suggested that harmful therapy was related to a therapist who was distant, rigid, and emotionally seductive, and where there were poor client–therapist matches.

CONCLUSION

We have discussed a range of client-related factors that may play a role in the nature and outcome of treatment. We have focused on the impact of client presenting problem and diagnosis, client beliefs and attitudes, client interpersonal factors, and social and demographic factors. We trust that the centrality of the client in therapy has been established, including taking the client's theory of change into consideration, and remembering that all clients have assets and strengths that may be engaged in treatment. Keep this in mind, that client factors are central to change in therapy, and let this knowledge drive your conceptualisation and treatment planning.

Recommended reading

Bohart, A. C. & Tallman, K. (1999). *How Clients Make Therapy Work: The Process of Active Self-Healing*. Washington DC: American Psychological Association.

Duncan, B. L. & Miller, S. D. (2000). The client's theory of change: consulting the client in the integrative process. *Journal of Psychotherapy Integration*, 10 (2), 169–87.

Duncan, B. L., Miller, S. D., & Sparks, J. A. (2004). *The Heroic Client: A Revolutionary Way to Improve Effectiveness Through Client-Directed, Outcome-Informed Therapy*. San Francisco: Jossey-Bass.

Duncan, B. L., Miller, S. D., Wampold, B. E., & Hubble, M. A. (eds). (2010). *The Heart and Soul of Change* (2nd edn). Washington, DC: American Psychological Association.

Irwin Yalom, who has written a number of novels about therapy, taking a client-centred approach. See website <www.yalom.com>.

Recommended websites

We also suggest that you look at the following websites for information about client factors:

<www.centerforclinicalexcellence.com>

<www.heartandsoulofchange.com>

<www.scottdmiller.com>

<www.whatsrigthwithyou.com>

Chapter 5

Therapist variables

INTRODUCTION

In this chapter we will examine therapist factors, and what it is about therapists that influences client outcome. First, we will consider therapist characteristics, and second, issues for therapists that are difficult to manage and potentially important to outcome. In examining some of the more common and perplexing therapist issues that have the potential to impede therapeutic effectiveness, we will provide guidelines to assist you to approach your work with clients in a way that will enhance outcomes. The intention is to assist you to recognise potential pitfalls, and to have strategies to deal with them.

THE IMPORTANCE OF THERAPIST FACTORS

Imagine being at a social event. Does it matter to you who you get to spend most of the time talking to? If so, are these the people your best friend or partner also wants to talk to, or do you like different people? Most individuals would respond to these questions by saying, 'Of course I would prefer certain people over others', and 'Yes, there are people I like who my partner doesn't like as much'. It seems obvious that you will connect better with some people than with others—especially if you are going to share intimate information with them, or talk about your problems and shortcomings. Strangely, however, outcome research until recently has paid limited attention to the individual therapist, as is captured by the following:

> It's as if treatment methods were like pills, in no way affected by the person adminis-
> tering them. Too often researchers regard the skills, personality and experience of the
> therapist as side issues, features to control to ensure that different groups receive com-
> parable interventions (Lebow, 2006, pp. 131–2).

From the beginnings of clinical psychology, it was argued that the 'right' sort of person was required to make an effective therapist (Hilgard et al., 1947). One of the earliest studies related to therapist characteristics influencing outcome was conducted by Ricks (1974). Based on data from only two therapists, Ricks found that therapists varied greatly in success rates in working with a group of adolescent boys who were more disturbed, whereas success rates did not differ with less disturbed boys. Descriptions of the differences between the therapists indicated that the more successful therapist was more positive and supportive of boys who were moving toward autonomy, and helped in everyday problem-solving. The less successful therapist focused on the boys' vulnerabilities, and appeared to withdraw from boys who were more distressed.

For a number of practical and theoretical reasons, early interest in the therapist began to dwindle from the 1970s (Bergin, 1997; Beutler, 1997; Garfield, 1997; Lambert & Okiishi, 1997; Luborsky et al., 1997). Research investigating therapist factors had been largely unsuccessful because of mixed results, poor methodology, and ambiguous outcome measurement (Rowe et al., 1975). During the 1990s, however, a new research paradigm came into vogue that involved focusing on each therapist's performance, as measured by caseload outcomes, and examining the therapist–therapy qualities that were related to that performance (Luborsky et al., 1997). This new paradigm led to a growing body of literature that demonstrated differential effectiveness between therapists; in turn, this has led to a resurgence of interest in the role the therapist plays in the success of therapy.

The recent findings of research on therapist effects perhaps gives us cause to question much of the outcome research that has been conducted in the past. After reviewing 140 studies, Crits-Cristoph and Mintz (1991) concluded that in 67.5 per cent of studies, the possibility of therapist effects had been ignored. The authors re-analysed data from these studies, found that therapist variables were indeed influential, and suggested that measures of therapist variables were vitally important in outcome research. It has also been argued that ignoring therapist effects in research has the effect of inflating technique effects (Wampold, 2001), and skews the differential impact of the four factors of therapeutic outcome, discussed in chapter 3.

Therapist effectiveness is generally measured as the degree to which a client's improvement can be attributed to the therapist only, not to factors such as the client's characteristics or type of treatment provided (Najavits & Weiss, 1994). Reviews and meta-analytic investigations estimate that an average of 6–10 per cent of the variance in client outcome is explained by therapist factors (e.g. Crits-Christoph & Mintz, 1991; Dinger et al., 2008; Kim et al., 2006; Wampold & Brown, 2005). Lutz and colleagues (2007) found that 8 per cent of client symptom reduction and 17 per cent of variance in rates of client improvement were attributable to the therapist. These findings appear to be robust, and hold up even in studies where attempts are made to minimise differences between therapists (Blatt et al., 1996; Huppert et al., 2001).

Another reliable finding is that different therapists have differential outcomes with clients (e.g., Lambert, 1989; Lafferty et al., 1989; Luborsky et al., 1982; Luborsky et al., 1986). Okiishi and colleagues (2003) demonstrated that the 1841 clients in their study varied in their recovery rate depending on which of the 91 therapists in a university counselling centre they were seeing for treatment. The authors found that the very effective therapists (called the 'supershrinks') had 10 times higher average ratings of change than the other therapists (referred to as 'pseudoshrinks'), whose clients just had a middling level of change. Okiishi and colleagues argued that 'something about these therapists and the way they work, independent of the amount of time spent with clients, has a significant impact' (p. 370).

There are important practical implications to research demonstrating therapist effects. Lambert (2007) summarised the findings of two research studies that investigated patient outcomes from specific therapists. Comparing the client outcomes of the top 10 per cent of therapists with those of the bottom 10 per cent, he found that 44 per cent of the more effective therapists' clients recovered, and just 5 per cent deteriorated. For the less effective therapists, the results were less flattering: 28 per cent recovered and 11 per cent deteriorated. Lambert (2004) argued that the research 'suggest[ed] that clients would be wise to pick a therapist as-a-person in parity with the selection of a therapeutic technique' (p. 181). Indeed, if a client were asked to decide between a therapist boasting a 44 per cent recovery rate and one with a 28 per cent recovery rate, the decision would seem clear.

It is also important to note that clients themselves frequently rate the person of the therapist as one of the most important aspects of treatment (Eugster & Wampold, 1996; Curtis et al., 2004; Littauer et al., 2005; Levitt et al., 2006). As clients are the most important variable in outcome, and remembering the rule of thumb from chapter 3 that clients always come first, such research cannot be ignored.

ARE EFFECTIVE THERAPISTS BORN OR TRAINED? THE NATURE–NURTURE DEBATE

If, as the research is suggesting, it is established that the therapist is an integral part of the therapeutic journey, and that some therapists are simply more effective than others, the logical next step would be to determine the characteristics of effective therapists. There has been ongoing debate about whether therapists are born or trained (Wheeler, 2002); that is, how much of a therapist's effectiveness is dependent on his or her training compared with personal characteristics?

The best position that can be taken, based on evidence to date, is that therapist effectiveness is most likely derived from a combination of personal characteristics and training.

Let us look at this research. For the sake of clarity, we first explore therapist characteristics from the 'nurture' perspective (experience and training), then consider the 'nature' perspective (demographics and personal characteristics). An attempt is then made to synthesise a balanced and realistic appreciation of the personality and training influences that constitute the person of an effective therapist.

Exercise 5.1

Keep your responses to these questions in mind as you read the next section, on the nature-versus-nurture characteristics of effective therapists.

1   Reflect on the kinds of knowledge and skills you would consider that a therapist needs to work effectively with a range of clients. Examples could include knowledge of psychological theories and psychopathology, ability to put people at ease, ability to recognise emotions in other people, or perhaps just good general people skills.

2   Thinking about each of these attributes, to what extent do you think these skills or knowledge areas can be learnt? Or do you think that some people are just born with them? To help you consider this, think of what your own skills may be, and how you came by them.

Nurture characteristics

The two most obvious *nurture characteristics* are (a) the type and extent of training the therapist undertakes, and (b) the therapist's level of experience in conducting psychotherapy. Although it would appear obvious that therapists with more training and greater experience would be more competent (and hence achieve better outcomes with clients), the research suggests a more complex picture.

Therapist training

It is generally assumed that more training will produce more effective therapists. Is this actually the case? Probably the most common method of investigating the benefit of training has been to compare professionally trained therapists with paraprofessional therapists who have had less, if any, formal training. You will note that many references in this section are older—this is because there was considerable research activity in this area three or four decades ago; research was relatively sparse during the 1990s and early 2000s. There has, however, been renewed interest in the area recently.

Early studies found no differences between postgraduate trained and untrained or paraprofessionals working with clients (e.g. Durlak, 1979; Nietzel & Fisher, 1981; Hattie et al., 1984; Berman & Norton, 1985). The most recent meta-analysis in this area concluded that a 'modest but fairly consistent treatment effect size is associated with training level from a number of measures of client improvement' (Stein & Lambert, 1995, p. 192). In this study, training led to improvements in clients' positive reports of satisfaction, lower premature dropout rates, and more effective therapy outcomes, when changes in client functioning and psychopathology were judged by independent judges or clinicians.

Some studies have found more specific differences between professionals and paraprofessionals, despite not finding an overall difference in 'global' effectiveness. Berman and Norton (1985) found that professionals tended to have better results in brief treatments with clients over the age of 21, whereas paraprofessionals tended to do well with younger clients over a longer period of time. A meta-analysis of the effectiveness of psychotherapy with children and adolescents provided further support for this, with professionals being effective with all age groups, whereas students and paraprofessionals were more effective with children and younger clients than with adult clients (Weisz et al., 1987).

Overall, the results suggest that paraprofessionals tend to have greater limitations regarding the types of clients they can achieve positive outcomes with, whereas professionals have success with a greater number of client groups. Burlingame and colleagues (1989) found that those with more training could achieve better results in a shorter time, although that advantage was lost if therapy was not time limited. Similarly, Callahan and Hynan (2005) found that, although novice therapists in a training clinic obtained equivalent outcomes to more experienced therapists, client response to treatment was not as rapid as might be expected, given previous research on the dose-effect model of psychotherapy outcome (Howard et al., 1986). Given the increasingly central role that economic factors play in service delivery, as well as the advantage to the client of earlier gains, greater time efficiency is an important advantage. These findings would seem to support the need for more training.

The difficulty in demonstrating empirically that training does produce more effective therapists may reflect the difficulty that postgraduate curricula have in addressing the various components of psychotherapy. Despite the fact that training is typically based on the scientist–practitioner model, few studies have looked at the relationship between academic knowledge and clinical competency. At stake here is a core assumption (albeit one rarely subjected to scrutiny) that is basic to clinical training and the scientist–practitioner model generally, that academic knowledge and clinical competency share a positive relationship. Of course, if this relationship exists, it is likely to be reciprocal, with competent clinical practice also leading to increased knowledge. One researcher who has examined this relationship (Tori, 1989) reported a moderate correlation (0.46) between knowledge and clinical competency, leading others (Robiner et al., 1994) to comment that psychological knowledge is likely to affect psychologists' clinical competence. Research in this area is important to clarify the relevance of training in psychotherapy.

Australia is the ideal setting in which to compare postgraduate training with the supervised practice model, as there have been two main routes to becoming a registered psychologist. O'Donovan and colleagues (2005) compared postgraduate-trained psychologists with those who followed the supervised practice (non-academic) pathway to full registration. They found that clinical trainees performed more effectively than non-trainees on measures assessing knowledge of psychological assessment, training, and evaluation and diagnosis. Individuals who obtain postgraduate clinical training, on average, demonstrated better clinical competence than those who were not in postgraduate clinical-training programs. This study also showed that trainees who started their courses below average on clinical competencies significantly improved as a result of training; non-trainees who started below average, and followed the supervision pathway, did not improve. For non-trainees who were above average at the end of their honours training, clinical competence actually became worse over the course of 12 months; they lost the advantages they had earlier. It would seem that postgraduate training improves competence or, at least, appears to maintain effective competence.

O'Donovan and colleagues (2005) found no evidence that training improved a trainee's ability to develop, or accurately judge, the working alliance. Given that the therapeutic alliance is one of the more robust indicators of successful psychotherapy outcomes (Horvath & Bedi, 2002), this raises the question of how successful postgraduate programs are at developing the interpersonal skills needed by therapists. Research into microskills training has perhaps provided most evidence of the effectiveness of training in practice skills. Two meta-analyses of microskills training (Baker & Daniels, 1989; Van Der Molen et al., 1995) respectively found mean effect sizes of 0.85 and 1.41, indicating large experimental effects for teaching in skills such as goal development, generating alternatives, and assertiveness training. Despite these results, it still has not been fully established that the capacity to establish a therapeutic relationship is trainable (Martin, 1990; Luborsky, 1990, O'Donovan et al., 2005, Crits-Christoph et al., 2006). But this finding may also just indicate that postgraduate training needs to focus more on this area.

Because the therapeutic alliance is known to be so important to client outcome, some researchers have attempted to devise interventions that target the alliance directly. In a preliminary study of five therapists, Crits-Christoph and colleagues (2006) examined the effectiveness of *alliance fostering therapy*. Results of this study were mixed (one of the therapists even showed decreased scores on the alliance after the intervention). In addition, while quality of life appeared to be positively affected by the training, only minimal improvements were made in clients' depressive symptoms. Thus, impact of the training on client outcome was marginal. While the authors suggested that these preliminary results warranted further investigation, they also noted that one possible explanation for the results might be that the relationship aspect of psychotherapy is not easily 'manualised', that 'patients may be able to pick up on the true "inner person" of the therapist, and that may not be trainable' (p. 277). If this is the case, it would argue heavily in favour of the *nature* side of this debate.

Therapist empathy is obviously an important component in the alliance. A recent study by Hassenstab and colleagues (2007) compared the ability of trainee therapists with non-therapists on a wide range of empathy measures. Although therapists were significantly better at demonstrating cognitive empathy—understanding what was going on for the other, based on verbal report (language)—they were not superior to non-therapists on measures of emotional empathy. Training, thus, appears to have an impact on cognitive empathy, but does not appear to influence emotional understanding of others. Interestingly, therapists' self-ratings indicated that they thought they were well able to manage their own emotions in challenging interpersonal situations, more so than non-therapists reported. These results may suggest that training generally tends to focus more on cognitive aspects of human behaviour than on emotional aspects. This is of concern, as emotions are central to the functioning of humans. Poor emotional regulation may well be one of the most common problems clients present with. It may also be that trainees are themselves less comfortable with emotions, and so do not pay much attention to the area. We would like to encourage all novice (and more experienced!) therapists to pay attention to emotions in working with clients, as well as to thoughts and behaviours.

What this debate highlights most is that we still don't know to what extent formal training increases a therapist's practical ability to engage and work effectively with clients. If, as many authors (such as Lambert, 1992) have suggested, factors associated with the therapeutic alliance are the 'active' ingredients in therapy, then ability in these areas is vital. If individual personality traits are of the greatest importance in fostering the alliance, this could provide an explanation for why many studies have found that individuals with little training, or without any university training at all, may be as effective as trained and experienced therapists (Andrews, 2000). There is clearly a need for further research on training for alliance skills, as well as on training generally (Ladany, 2007; Boswell & Castonguay, 2007).

Despite ambiguity on the impact of training, more recent findings, including those from O'Donovan and colleagues' (2005) study, indicate that, on average, an individual will have a wider range of skills and will be a more effective psychologist if he or she engages in postgraduate training.

Therapist experience

Therapist experience has also been examined for impact on effective outcome. Therapist experience is generally defined as the amount of experience the therapist has had working with clients. However, studies comparing therapists with varying amounts of experience have provided mixed findings. A surprising number of meta-analyses have concluded that the amount of client experience a therapist has does not have an impact on client outcome (e.g. Smith & Glass, 1977; Shapiro & Shapiro, 1982; Stein & Lambert, 1984; Crits-Christoph et al., 1991; Wierzbicki & Pekarik, 1993). Other, more recent, studies have also failed to demonstrate that increased experience predicts therapeutic efficacy (Blatt et al., 1996; Okiishi et al., 2003; Leon et al., 2005). Some studies have found a role for experience (Orlinsky & Howard, 1980; Lyons & Woods, 1991; Huppert et al., 2001).

How can we make sense of these findings? It is likely that some of the findings are a result of problems with research methodology, including the way in which experience is typically measured. Beutler (1997) has argued that time is a poor measure of true *experience* as, without consciously working at improving practice, simply doing something a lot will not necessarily lead to better practice. It cannot, therefore, be assumed that more experienced therapists (measured by time since graduation) will have superior clinical skills. Chapter 9 expands on this point, when we discuss the importance of using feedback to improve practice. It also appears that, in some instances, such as when using complex psychotherapeutic procedures, experience does matter. Last, it appears most likely that it is the therapist's capacity to use experience productively (Jennings & Skovholt, 1999) that is most relevant to practitioner competence.

Exercise 5.2

1 What have been the most important things you have learned in your academic training to date that will assist you to be an effective practitioner?
2 What has your training *not* focused on, and how can you achieve greater learning and experience in these areas (for example, by attending workshops)?

Therapist well-being

Therapist well-being, and how it is achieved and maintained, can arguably be a nature or a nurture factor. There is a cliché that therapists need to possess sound mental health to practise effectively with clients (and another, more cynical, adage that most psychologists have their own unresolved issues). In practice, it appears there may be some truth in the first statement. Although some studies have indicated that factors such as neuroticism and burnout do not appear to affect client outcomes (e.g. Antonuccio et al., 1982, Beck, 1988), many other studies have demonstrated that therapist adjustment is important. Lambert and Bergin (1983) suggested that therapists who are emotionally healthy facilitate positive outcomes, and therapists who lack emotional well-being are deleterious to outcome.

In a review by Beutler and colleagues (2004), effect sizes for therapist emotional well-being on treatment outcome ranged from 0 (Antonuccio et al., 1982) to .71 (McCarthy & Frieze, 1999). The mean effective size was small (.12) but statistically significant, indicating a positive relationship between psychotherapist well-being and outcome. This confirmed an earlier review by Beutler and colleagues (1986), where all but one of 10 studies pointed to the importance of therapist emotional health. Likewise, Luborsky and colleagues (1997) found that therapists' psychological health and skill correlated at .41 with outcome. Finally, the Australian study by O'Donovan and colleagues (2005) reported that trainees' emotional adjustment had an impact on their ability to engage effectively with clients at the beginning of clinical education, but ameliorated after one year of training. This research suggests that therapist well-being is an important factor for therapists to attend to from the beginning of their careers. Therapist burnout is discussed further in chapter 19.

Therapists in their own therapy
Bike and colleagues (2009) examined the rate and reasons for therapists seeking their own therapy in the USA. There appears to be a substantial increase in therapists getting their own therapy. In the 1970s and 1980s, between 52 and 62 per cent of therapists sought personal therapy. In the 1990s, there was an increase to between 72 and 75 per cent (Norcross, 2005). Bike and colleagues (2009) found that the number had increased to 84 per cent.

It is difficult to know to what extent the percentages are a reflection of self-selection of participants in the study, but these figures are supported by findings from other countries. Williams and colleagues (1999) found that, even by the late 1990s, up to 86 per cent of therapists in the UK had engaged in personal therapy. This trend should not come as a surprise, as mental-health professionals commonly recognise that having their own treatment is a central part of their professional development (Macran et al., 1999; Williams et al., 1999). In Bike and colleagues' study, male therapists were just as likely as female therapists to seek treatment.

Bike and colleagues (2009) and Norcross and colleagues (2008) suggest that trainers should encourage trainees to engage in personal therapy by discussing its benefits. The blocks to trainees seeing therapists include financial reasons (Holzman et al., 1996), but in Australia free services are available and most universities have a student counselling centre. Stigma is also a problem (Farber, 2000), often related to concerns about confidentiality and being judged by faculty (Dearing et al., 2005). Bike and colleagues (2009) report no change over time with the types of presenting problems that therapist have. The main ones include relationship issues, depression, and anxiety.

There have been mixed results for the effectiveness of practitioners seeking their own therapy, with some studies showing no correlation between practice and therapists attending therapy, whereas other studies have demonstrated positive relationships (Bike et al., 2009). However, therapist self-report indicates that personal therapy improves therapists' self-awareness, self-understanding, and self-esteem, increases their openness to and acceptance of feelings, and enhances their personal relationships (Pope & Tabachnick, 1994). In several studies, psychologists reported believing that personal therapy has made them better therapists (Macran et al., 1999; Williams et al., 1999). Fauth and Williams (2005) found that the more self-aware therapists were in session, when they could manage self-awareness, the more helpful clients experienced them to be. Personal work tends to enhance awareness and strategies to manage it.

Gold and Hilsenroth (2009) found that personal therapy was associated with therapists feeling more confident and having significantly better alliances with their clients than therapists who had not undertaken therapy. Linley and Joseph (2007, p. 392) found that 'therapists who had either received personal therapy previously, or were receiving personal therapy currently, reported more personal growth and positive changes, and less burnout'.

We encourage you to consider this option; clearly, it can be personally useful, as well as assist in your practice. Don't feel embarrassed about it—the majority of therapists endorse personal treatment (Orlinsky et al., 2004), even if they don't all talk about it.

Nature characteristics
The difficulty in demonstrating the superiority of nurture factors has been used to support the long-held belief, often expressed in the literature, that personal characteristics are immensely important for effective therapists (Luborsky et al., 1985; McConnaughy, 1987). Let's explore the research into 'innate' therapist characteristics.

Therapist demographics
There have been mixed results regarding the impact of therapist demographics, such as age and gender, on outcome. Some studies have indicated that therapist gender does not affect therapy outcome consistently (e.g. Atkinson & Schein, 1986; Okiishi et al., 2003), although one comprehensive review found a small but significant effect size favouring female therapists (Bowman et al., 2001). Similarly, some studies have found no effect for therapist age (e.g. Orlinsky & Howard, 1980), while others (e.g. Rosenberg et al., 1976) have found that older females were more effective than any other group at retaining clients in therapy. In a review of the literature, Beutler and colleagues (2004) reported little evidence that observable traits such as age, sex, or ethnicity have a significant impact on therapeutic outcome. Given that therapy is largely an interpersonal process between client and therapist, it is hardly surprising that this kind of research has failed to find clinically meaningful group differences.

These findings may come as a relief to many early-career practitioners, who are often concerned that clients may think them too young, or for some international students, who may be concerned there may be prejudice. Demographic factors are simply not important. However, in some cases, they can matter, as indicated in the video scene that is the subject of exercise 5.3. If demographic factors do seem to impede, an important issue is to discover how the therapist attempts to work with them. Further examples will be provided in chapter 15.

Exercise 5.3

Watch Video 9, which shows an interaction between a young therapist and an older client. Most new practitioners are young, often younger than their clients. Can this work? In this vignette, the client raises his concern that the therapist is too young to understand him and relate to his problems. The therapist attempts to allay the client's concerns.

1   Do you think the client really felt at the end of this segment that the therapist understood him, and that he really could relate to her?

2   What else could the therapist have done?

3   Now watch the two debriefs by the therapist and the client.

THERAPIST INTERPERSONAL AND RELATIONSHIP SKILLS, AND BUILDING THE ALLIANCE

There is evidence that a number of therapist relationship skills have a positive impact on client outcome. These skills include warmth, acceptance, positive regard, collaborating respectfully with clients, flexibility in adapting to client needs, openness, tolerance, honesty, trustworthiness, confidence, alertness, interest, friendliness, depth, willingness to explore issues, extent of reflectiveness, activity, ability to make accurate interpretations, being affirming of the client, attending to the client's experience, being supportive and creative, being able to manage anxiety, and being able to establish and maintain interpersonal emotional boundaries in therapy (Ackerman & Hilsenroth, 2001, 2003; Asay & Lambert, 1999; Beutler et al., 2004; Gelso et al., 2002). Anderson and colleagues (2009) also found that interpersonal skills, such as the therapists' ability to understand and communicate a range of messages of an interpersonal nature, an ability to persuade clients to desist from behaving in ways that are unhelpful, and an ability to try different ways to deal with their problems, are central to client outcome. In contrast, negative interpersonal behaviours, such as belittling, ignoring, blaming, attacking, rejecting, and neglecting, result in poor outcomes (Najavits & Strupp, 1994). Hostility directed at oneself as the therapist results in a poor alliance (Dunkle & Friedlander, 1996).

Many of these factors are related to the therapist's ability to build a strong alliance. In an Australian study, O'Donovan (2000) found that therapists who were non-collaborative, opinionated, overly anxious, rigid, controlling, disrespectful, lacking in empathy, provided little structure, had poor microskills, and were insensitive to feedback, did poorly in the alliance, as measured by the client and an observer. Ackerman & Hilsenroth (2001), in their review of therapist personal attributes, found that being distant, aloof, self-focused, tense, easily distracted, rigid, belittling, and critical were related to a negative alliance with clients. In addition, techniques that were superficial or inappropriate, such as inappropriate self-disclosure and inappropriate use of silence, as well as over-structuring or failing to structure the therapy session, had negative implications for the alliance.

As the focus of chapter 6 is the alliance, we will only briefly mention here that research suggests that the input of the therapist into the alliance, and how well he or she monitors it, is very important to client outcome (Baldwin et al., 2007). The therapist plays a central role in building the alliance, and there are many therapist characteristics, in addition to interpersonal skills, that assist, including therapist empathy.

Therapist empathy

We have suggested earlier that empathy is a core factor common to many effective forms of psychotherapy. This was emphasised by the early work of Rogers (1951, 1957), who suggested that outcome was very much in the hands of the therapist. According to Rogers, the therapist's ability to be empathic, congruent, and unconditionally accepting of the client, constitute necessary and sufficient conditions for positive change. Rogers (1980) described empathy as sensitively 'immersing' oneself in how the client experiences his or her world. To be empathic, he suggested:

> the therapist makes a maximum effort to get within and to live the attitudes expressed instead of observing them, diagnosing them, or thinking of ways to make the process go faster. Such understanding must be acquired through intense, continuous, and active attention to the feelings of others (p. 34).

Not surprisingly, many studies have found that therapists with high levels of Rogers' three factors, particularly empathy, were more successful than therapists without them (Barrett-Lennard, 1986; Rogers et al., 1967). The importance of empathy in therapeutic outcome has been well established (Greenberg et al., 2001); empathy is cited as an important characteristic of effective therapists by numerous authors (e.g., Castonguay & Beutler, 2006; Hassenstab et al., 2007; Orlinsky et al., 1994, 2004; Jorgensen, 2004; Curtis et al., 2004; Horvath & Bedi, 2002; Wheeler, 2000). In a meta-analytic review by Bohart and colleagues (2002), empathy had an effect size of .32, accounting for between 7 and 10 per cent of outcome variance.

Although this may seem self-evident, the research path for therapist empathy has been rocky (Bohart et al., 2002). Although Rogers' definition of empathy is often cited (Bohart et al., 2002), there has been a marked absence of consensus in the literature on the empathy construct, and, in particular, whether it should emphasise cognitive or affective components. Emphasis on the cognitive component suggests that empathy is an intellectual process that involves the capacity to understand and imagine others' thoughts, motives, and perspectives. Emphasis on the affective component suggests that empathy is triggered by emotions after perceiving another's experience of emotion. The current consensus is that both cognitions and emotions are central to the experience of empathy. In addition, therapist self-ratings of empathy have not been found to predict outcome, or to correlate with client- or observer-rated empathy (Barrett-Lennard, 1981; Gurman, 1977 cited in Greenberg et al., 2001). This finding led Greenberg and colleagues (2001) to conclude that empathy is 'probably better conceived as a mutually created climate variable, rather than as a variable unilaterally "provided" by the therapist' (p. 382).

What does all this mean for the novice therapist? First, it is important to bear in mind that clients who feel they are understood by their therapist have more effective outcomes (Bohart et al., 2002). Second, it is the client's perception of being understood that matters, which means that the therapist must regularly check in with the client that the therapist understands the client's situation accurately. Last, the meaning of being empathic is different with different clients. For example, some clients may need the therapist to modulate her or his level of empathy to suit the client's current level of distress (Duan & Hill, 1996).

It is not uncommon for beginning therapists to express concern that they have trouble being empathic with certain clients. While individuals differ in their ability to understand the internal world of others, almost everyone is capable of some empathy. As a therapist, you will constantly be presented with clients who have had radically different life experiences from yours. Even with these clients, however, aspects of their experience may be similar to yours. For example, every one of us has experienced fear, or to have lost something we really cared about; we all share the human condition. But it is vital to remember that our experience is unique to us, and not to make assumptions that someone else would experience, for example, loss in the same way we do. Therapists don't always differentiate fully; we think others are just like us. Through supervision, training, and checking in with clients, you are likely to find your own way of being empathic.

Therapist motivation

A therapist's motivation appears to be of immense importance. All therapists are encouraged to consider why they want to be therapists, as their reasons will have an impact on the way they practise therapy and their effectiveness. The research is quite clear on this point. Skovholt and Ronnestad (1995, cited in Skovholt & Jennings, 2004) have demonstrated that extent of professional growth hinges on type and intensity of motivation for the profession. Those who entered the profession for power or to avoid isolation were more at risk of stagnation than those who entered the profession for more altruistic reasons (to help others). Motivation appears to have a curvilinear relationship with therapeutic practice; too much altruism can lead one to become overwhelmed and to stagnate (Skovholt & Jennings, 2004). Such a suggestion is consistent with outcome research, which has shown that less effective therapists place greater emphasis on prosperity and stimulation as end states, and reduced value on intellect (Lafferty et al., 1989).

Because motivation is important, we often begin our clinical-training program by asking our new students to consider and discuss the following question: 'What are the events, and your personal characteristics, that you consider have most influenced you to be sitting in this room at this time?' Considering the diversity of individuals who undertake such training, it is striking to note the similarities in responses to this question. Almost all say things like: 'I was always the one my friends talked to about their problems'; 'I was often the linchpin in my family, making sure everyone got on well'; 'I've always wanted to help people'; 'I've always been fascinated by people'; 'I've always been intrigued by strange behaviours in others'; or 'I seem to be more sensitive to what is going on for others than many of my friends or family'. These types of comments were common too when Skovholt and Jennings (2004) interviewed a range of 'master therapists', to understand the motivations of individuals who excelled as psychotherapists. Consistent with these comments is Hill and associates' (2007) view that novice therapists who self-select into therapist training often have more natural helping ability than others, and that clinical training needs to shape that natural ability.

Exercise 5.4

1   What are your personal attributes, and the salient events that gave you an interest in psychotherapy, and have brought you this far in your training?
2   Read the article, 'Choosing psychotherapy as a career: why did we cross that road?' (Farber et al., 2005), to assist your reflections on why you became a psychotherapist.

Therapist personality

Despite the literature being replete with experts' opinions that therapist personality does play an important role in therapeutic outcome, research that has attempted to link personality characteristics to client outcome has so far been largely unsuccessful (Rowe et al., 1975; Beutler et al., 2004). The difficulty seems, in part, to have been a result of a tendency to measure global personality traits, rather than more specific (and perhaps more relevant) traits, and poor research designs. Given this lack of success, researchers have more recently attempted to identify therapists' effective in-session behaviours. Najavits and Strupp (1994) found that effective therapists demonstrated more 'positive' behaviours (demonstrations of warmth, affirmation, understanding, helping, and protecting) and fewer 'negative' behaviours (belittling, blaming, ignoring, neglecting, attacking, and rejecting). They were also more self-critical, and rated their sessions as less effective, suggesting perhaps that effective therapists may be overly critical of their own practice, perhaps missing when they are effective. The authors concluded by suggesting that least and most effective therapists were differentiated almost entirely by relationship variables, and that 'basic capacities of human relating—warmth, affirmation, and a minimum of attack and blame—may be at the centre of effective psychotherapeutic intervention' (p. 121).

What have a therapist's in-session behaviours to do with that therapist's personality? There is evidence to suggest that in-session behaviours are influenced by innate therapist characteristics such as personality traits. For example, researchers have discovered that therapists with negative introjects (i.e. where individuals have integrated the negative views of them held by significant other people in their lives, such as parents) were more likely to engage in hostile behaviours in therapy, with a negative impact on outcome (Henry et al., 1990). In a related study, Hersoug (2004) found that therapists who experienced good parental care had fewer negative introjects, which contributed to a positive impact on clients' levels of defensive functioning. Both studies suggest that treating in-session behaviours as a construct independent from the person of the therapist does not make empirical, or indeed logical, sense.

A promising area for research on innate characteristics may be a focus on therapist characteristics that are linked to mechanisms of change in the therapeutic process. We know that the working alliance is a robust indicator of outcome (Horvath
& Bedi, 2002). It would, therefore, make sense for researchers to focus on identifying
the specific characteristics that enable therapists to build such relationships, as this
could help guide the training and selection of therapists. Such a study was described
by Lambert and Ogles (2004), but has yet to be published. The 'Anderson study'
compared therapeutic outcomes achieved by graduate students in clinical psychology doctoral programs and graduate students from other disciplines. Differences in
outcome were predicted by the therapist's interpersonal skills, as measured through
responses on the Social Skills Inventory (Riggio, 1986) and observation of their
interpersonal skills during a therapy session. While this study requires replication,
it provides preliminary evidence that therapists' social skills are salient to outcome,
and provides a guide to specific therapist characteristics that have an impact on
mechanisms of change in the therapeutic process.

Therapist attachment style

There is a growing body of evidence to suggest that therapist attachment style may
have considerable impact on client outcome, primarily because of the impact it has
on the alliance. Not surprisingly, therapists with a secure attachment style tend to
have the best alliances with clients, whereas therapists with self-reported anxious
attachment styles tend to have poorer reported alliances with clients (Black et al.,
2005). Black and colleagues (2005) found that, specifically, a high need for approval,
common in anxious attachment styles, was associated with problems in therapy, as
those therapists may set targets that are perfectionistic, and may be less able to
manage difficulties when they arise. Anxious attachment-style therapists may also
not challenge their clients sufficiently, which reduces the possibility of change
(Dozier et al., 1994). Therapists with secure attachment styles tend to be perceived
as more open, receptive, and collaborative, characteristics more likely to facilitate a
good alliance.

RECENT DEVELOPMENTS

Master-therapists

A recent development in the examination of therapist variables comes from a focus
on *master-therapists*, therapists who are 'the best of the best' (Jennings & Skovholt,
1999). Having identified and interviewed ten peer-nominated master-therapists, the
authors identified characteristics common and important to them. These characteristics included: a voracious desire to learn; valuing of cognitive complexity and
ambiguity; a tendency to be self-aware, reflective, non-defensive, and open to feedback; and an ability to display mental health and maturity, and to attend to their
own emotional well-being. Master-therapists were also described as possessing
strong relationship skills, such as listening, observing, and caring for the well-being
of others. Master-therapists expressed the belief that the foundation for therapeutic
change is a strong working alliance, and were experts at using their exceptional

relationship skills in therapy. Also, they seemed to have sensitivity for the artistry in therapy, being skilled at timing and pacing.

Jennings and Skovholt's (1999) research has been criticised for including only ten 'master' therapists without a control group; the study did not provide empirical evidence that these 'master' therapists achieve better results with clients than do other, less esteemed, therapists. While these are valid criticisms, they should not detract from the potential usefulness of the study, especially given the authors' argument that their results should have an impact on the training of therapists. They argued that therapists-in-training should be encouraged to seek opportunities for continuous learning, feedback, and reflection, seek opportunities to attend to their own emotional well-being, seek their own therapy when necessary, and hone their relational skills. The authors also implied that therapy students should be selected on the basis of their emotional and relational skills as well as their cognitive skills, and that training programs should focus on fostering both sets of skills.

Therapist factors

Another fruitful area of research has been Castonguay and Beutler's (2006) delineation of 'empirically derived' therapist factors that influence client outcome. Some of these factors include:

- an ability to recognise the client's resistance, and to work effectively with it
- an ability to recognise the client's interactional style, and to base treatment on that style
- a tendency to be open and informed about and tolerant of various religious views
- an ability to be open-minded, flexible, and creative
- an ability to be comfortable with long-term emotionally intense relationships
- an ability to tolerate their own negative feelings regarding the patient and the treatment process
- patience
- an ability to establish and maintain a strong working relationship
- empathy
- a perceptible attitude of caring, warmth, and acceptance
- an attitude of congruence and authenticity
- an ability to use accurate relational interpretations appropriately.

New and novel research, such as this study and that of Jennings and Skovholt (1999), could help to unravel the mechanisms through which therapists facilitate change in their clients.

Authenticity

It is also important that a therapist finds a style that fits comfortably with him- or herself as a person. Kottler (2003, p. 35) captures this idea:

> All effective therapists intuitively find a way to capitalise on the strengths of their character. Freud's self-analytic skills, Rogers's genuineness, Ellis's capacity for rational thinking, Whitaker's playfulness, formed the nucleus for their respective theories. So, too, do clinicians translate their inner selves into a personal style of helping.

There is no prototype for the person a good therapist needs to be. Many different people, with their own personalities and interpersonal styles, can make great therapists. The key, suggested in the quote, seems to be authenticity. Therapists need to integrate their own personal styles into their therapeutic style. This idea has received support from a study by Eugster and Wampold (1996), who found that the client's experience of the therapist as a real or genuine individual seemed to contribute to a positive evaluation of a therapy session overall. If a therapist was perceived as acting in a manner that was natural, spontaneous, and not constricted by the frame of the therapeutic interaction, the client evaluated the session more positively.

Such research supports the need for you to find your own way of being a genuine therapist with your clients. Engaging in the supervisory relationship and in clinical training with openness, genuineness, and a commitment that parallels your engagement with your clients, is the most effective way for you to do this.

Practice implications

Our summary of the literature demonstrates that we are still some way from understanding therapist factors fully, and further research is clearly required. We can, however, draw some tentative conclusions from the current state of research into this area:

1 Therapists are neither completely born nor completely trained. There is evidence to suggest that pre-existing characteristics, and training and experience, influence the effectiveness of therapists.
2 Therapists who have been formally trained seem to achieve quicker gains with clients, and are effective with a greater range of clients, than those who have not.
3 Therapists who have been practising a long time are not necessarily more effective than less experienced therapists. It is the quality of the experience that seems to be important.
4 Demographic characteristics of therapists are largely unrelated to effectiveness. Effective therapists can be male or female, old or young.
5 Therapists motivated by genuine care for others may be more effective than those motivated by other factors, such as financial reward.
6 The ability to experience and demonstrate empathy appears to be important.
7 The emotional health of therapists appears to be important.
8 It seems that effective therapists need to have good interpersonal skills.

Exercise 5.5

1 Think of the person you are most likely to talk to about a very personal problem. Why would you pick this person? What characteristics make that person someone likely to assist?

2   Now think of the person you are least likely to talk to? What are their off-putting characteristics?

3   Would your preferred person fit your needs at any time of your life, or for any type of problem? If not, why not?

4   Are the characteristics of the preferred person the same for everyone? If not, why not?

5   What do your answers mean for yourself as a psychologist?

THERAPIST ISSUES THAT CAN IMPEDE CLIENT OUTCOME

As you realise by now, working with clients is not a straightforward task. People are complicated, and therapeutic work is characterised by complexity and ambiguity. In this section of the chapter, we discuss some of the more complex and difficult issues that beginning therapists typically need to navigate in their work.

Self-disclosure

Therapist self-disclosure has long been the subject of controversy and debate. Hill and Knox (2002) reviewed survey results in this area. They found that the following were cited as reasons for self-disclosure: to increase perceived similarity between therapist and client; to model appropriate behaviour; to foster the therapeutic relationship; to validate reality or to normalise client experiences; to offer alternative ways of thinking or feeling; or because the client wants the disclosure. They concluded that the available research suggested that therapist self-disclosure could be helpful to immediate outcome, but effects on ultimate outcome were uncertain. The authors recommended that self-disclosure be infrequent, and used only for the above reasons. They suggested that, when self-disclosure is used, the client's responses be monitored carefully. Of concern to the authors was that self-disclosure might be used to serve the therapist's own needs, as he or she struggled with unresolved conflicts.

A similar concern was raised by Kottler (2003), who cautioned that self-disclosure should never be used to meet the therapist's personal needs. Before engaging in self-disclosure, Kottler recommended that the therapist should ask him- or herself the following questions:

• What do I hope this will accomplish?
• Is there another way of making the same point?
• What do I risk by not sharing myself?
• To what extent am I attempting to meet my own needs?
• Is this the right time?
• How can I say this most concisely?
• How will the client personalise what I share about myself?
• What is the cultural context for the client's experience with personal disclosure?
• How can I put the focus back on the client?

We advise that you ask yourself similar questions before engaging in self-disclosure with your clients. For example, suppose that your client has recently experienced the death of a loved one, and you have struggled with this same issue at some point in your life. You may feel the urge to disclose to your client your own struggle. If your true motivation for doing this is that you like people to be impressed with you, and you like to compare yourself to other people, then disclosure is likely to be inappropriate. On the other hand, if after careful consideration, you believe that such self-disclosure will help to normalise the client's reaction, and to provide him or her with hope, then it may be appropriate. We advise therapists to self-disclose with caution, and only when it is in the client's best interests.

Therapists' personal problems

No doubt many of you will recall doing undergraduate abnormal psychology and concluding that you had a whole list of disorders! This iatrogenic response is common amongst novice therapists, and we all learn to not fret too much about what could be wrong with us. However, the reality is that we all do have problems from time to time, and we need to be professional in managing them. The most important issue to consider is whether personal issues are impairing our ability to practise competently and safely with clients. If this is the case, we need to consider a range of options, including taking leave from practice. Discuss your concerns with your supervisor, and take advice on the best possible action.

Commonly, considering a therapist as an impaired practitioner will be as a result of an acute issue, such as clinical depression. For many, however, there will be ongoing issues that can have an impact on effectiveness, but not sufficient impact to be seen as a major problem. In chapter 13, we discuss issues common to many disorders, and we'll alert you to how these may have an impact on client practice.

Emotional dysregulation, commonly seen as an excess of negative emotion, a lack of positive emotion, and an inability to effectively regulate negative emotion, is a common aspect of most disorders. From time to time, we all struggle to regulate our emotions; when a therapist struggles to regulate his or her emotions, there will be an impact on client practice. Related to an excess of negative emotions tends to be a lack of hope and excess of pessimism. What we need to provide our clients with is hope, positive regard, and a calm environment in which to work. Poor emotional regulation will get in the way of this, and an individual with poor emotional regulation is prone to becoming stuck in excessive rumination.

A second problem is avoiding issues rather than facing them and taking action. At times, we are all avoidant. The issue is how commonly we avoid action, and whether it has an impact on our practice. Teyber (2006, p. 190) warns that 'if therapists are not willing to work with their own emotional reactions to the material that clients present, they will tend to avoid client's feelings or to engage them on an intellectual level'. It is common for therapists to avoid not only client feelings, but many other aspects of client needs and information. If avoidance is one of your favourite coping strategies, consider the negative effects for your clients.

Therapists who are rigid, inflexible, or dogmatic (in thoughts, opinions, attitudes, or actions) will not just struggle generally, but will not adapt to client needs, and will be less effective. Also, many show a lack of mindfulness: low self-awareness, low self- and other-acceptance, failing to be present in the moment, and judgmental.

If you recognise some of these issues, or other concerns that could have a negative impact on your work with clients, spend time reflecting on them. You may also consider personal therapy to assist you to deal with them.

FACTORS PREVENTING THERAPISTS FROM RESPONDING TO CLIENTS' EMOTIONS

Being able to respond appropriately to your client's emotions is one of the most important aspects of being an effective therapist (Teyber, 2006; Teyber & McClure, 2010). But many therapists have difficulty responding in the most helpful way. Barriers that prevent therapists from responding to client emotions include countertransference, and other problems with differentiation and therapist needs.

The therapist's need to nurture or be liked

Frequently, therapists have described being the caretaker in their family of origin, which can lead to the conscious or unconscious 'need' to rescue others. This countertransference issue can interfere with therapy, as it can trigger the familiar need to 'fix' the caregiver. Because, in reality, this is an impossible task, the therapist can only feel that he or she is disappointing the other person, leading to feelings of inadequacy. It can also come as a shock to the therapist if a client responds negatively to these good intentions by being critical, competitive, and/or controlling. The risk is that the therapist will comply with the defensive side of the client's feelings, and stop approaching his or her conflicted emotions. For example, a therapist may collude with clients who are avoiding experiencing their own emotions, by focusing on cognitive aspects of their problems, allowing clients to avoid experiencing their emotions. This response is most likely from a therapist whose need to be liked or nurtured has been frustrated. Therapy is not about winning approval or being 'nice'; at the same time, we are not there to give clients an unnecessarily hard time. The key is understanding—if you try to understand the client, he or she will eventually feel safe enough to face his or her defences.

Therapists' misperceptions of their responsibility

Often, therapists believe that if they respond to a client's feelings, they are somehow responsible for causing those feelings, or for making them go away. They may feel that responding to a painful feeling is the same as causing it to exist. In reality, the client had feelings long before the therapist arrived on the scene. While it is possible for a therapist to distress a client, typically, the therapist will have responded in a manner which has revealed the feeling (just as watching a movie may), rather than causing it to exist. If a therapist mistakenly assumes responsibility for causing negative feelings that have been elicited in a therapy session, it makes sense to assume responsibility for 'fixing' them. Such beliefs are likely to lead to avoidance of clients' feelings, telling them what to do, reassuring them, or explaining and interpreting their feelings before they can experience them. Mostly, these responses are ineffective and counter-therapeutic.

A more effective approach is to help clients to identify and express their feelings while being empathic and emotionally responsive. In this way, clients can share their feelings with a concerned other rather than experience them alone. The therapist should also affirm the validity of clients' responses, by helping them to understand their feelings, and to make sense of why they are experiencing a feeling at a particular moment.

Family rules

The rules you learned in your family of origin will influence your ability to respond to your client's emotions. Suppose that in your family of origin, family members dealt with conflict by suppressing anger, and using passive-aggressive withdrawal. If your client becomes angry in a therapy session, you may struggle to know what to do. It is likely that you will become uncomfortable, or try to reassure your client, so the anger will go away, when what the client needs most is for the angry feelings to be validated and explored. In this instance, you will have failed to respond appropriately to your client's emotion. Often, clients will not be able to resolve longstanding conflicts unless the therapist can respond to each component of their affective constellation. Therapy often stops progressing at the point the therapist cannot respond to a feeling the client is experiencing.

Countertransference

With so much focus on the client, we sometimes forget that therapists are people too, with their own life circumstances, relationships, and problems. There are at least two circumstances in which a therapist's problems can be detrimental to therapy: when the therapist's problems demand much of the therapist's energy and time, and when the problems are similar to those of the client. When the therapist repeatedly fails to identify the client's feelings accurately, avoids rather than approaches the client's feelings, or becomes personally invested in the client's choices, the therapist's countertransference is operating.

Countertransference reactions are part of clinical practice. What is important is that countertransference is taken into account and managed, through insight, journaling, supervision, or personal therapy. Because change is predicated on the relationship the therapist creates with the client, therapists must commit to working with their own dynamics (Horvath, 2005). Without a willingness to work on their own reactions to a client, the help a therapist can provide will be limited. Therapists who are unwilling to work on persistent countertransference reactions, or are unaware of their countertransference, are more likely to act out and be reactive, and more likely to have a negative therapeutic impact on their clients (Friedman & Gelso, 2000; Kahn, 1997). Chapter 6 will provide more information on managing countertransference.

Poor boundaries and lack of differentiation

Bowen (1974) provided psychology with an important construct: *self-differentiation*. As Bowen was a family therapist, this concept primarily referred to an individual's ability to separate out his or her own functioning (intellectual and emotional) from that of the family. However, we can consider the concept in all our relations with others. Individuals with a low level of differentiation are more inclined to become 'fused' with others, think like them, confuse their own emotions with others', and depend on approval and acceptance by others. Lack of differentiation can result in trying to please others, or in trying to get others to see the world the way they do—both are attempts to achieve fusion with others.

But some individuals, to differentiate from their family, and then from others, will resist connection by emotional cutoff, another concept recognised by Bowen. They try to remain separate from their family by cutting off emotionally, to reduce the anxiety they experience by being in connection with their family. Neither fusion nor cutoff achieves a reduction in anxiety. This is only achieved when individuals manage a well-differentiated sense of self, in which they recognise their need for others, but don't have to depend on acceptance and approval. They neither fuse nor flee, can decide for themselves what their views are, and can identify and distinguish their own feeling in the moment. They are confident of who they are, and can be more reflective and less reactive. Achievement of a high level of self-differentiation is of much value, particularly to therapists.

As discussed in chapter 2, effective boundaries are essential for ethical practice. Many of the items on the 'At risk' measure in chapter 2 are related to boundary issues. Can you spot which ones?

The self-absorbed therapist

We use this heading to indicate issues that result in the therapist becoming more important in the session than the client. Therapy is about the client, and if therapist factors interfere, they need to be rectified. One of the most common causes of self-absorption in therapists is anxiety. Excessive anxiety is one of the biggest impediments to effective practice, in particular because the therapist becomes less present and available to his or her client (Gelso et al., 2002). Some anxiety is normal for the novice therapist (and for many of us with lots of experience).

If anxiety is interfering with your client practice, discuss this initially with your supervisor. The antidote to self-absorption is to focus on the other person in the room—your client. Accurate self-awareness is important to effective practice, but if self-awareness becomes self-indulgent, or excessive self-focus, it is likely lead to poor outcomes (Fauth & Williams, 2005). These authors suggest that a low-to-moderate level of self-focus may be useful in trainees, but the higher the level of self-focus, the more likely it is to become distracting and to reduce effectiveness. They also suggest that type of self-awareness may be important: awareness about in-session activity is helpful, but over-awareness of outside personal issues is not helpful. It may depend on how the trainee manages excessive levels of self-awareness. Wilson and Sperlinger (2004) provide a useful discussion of the value and limitations of self-knowledge. This paper is useful for understanding your own search for self-awareness, and that of your clients.

Therapist stress

A number of issues have been identified as contributing to stress in psychotherapists. Not surprisingly, being a novice therapist can be stressful, as the individual must learn many new skills, and rapidly expand his or her knowledge. In addition, novice therapists tend to worry more about their ability, and their effect on clients, than do more experienced therapists. Hill and colleagues (2007) found that the major challenges facing novice therapists were self-criticism, managing their reactions to clients, learning and using helping skills, and session management.

Beginning therapists may become overinvolved in the therapy process, and feel overwhelmed. Certain client behaviours and presenting problems can also be very stressful; clients who are at high risk of hurting themselves or others is an obvious one. Similarly, clients who are resistant to change, and/or hostile to the therapist's intervention, tend to be more stressful for therapists than clients who are eager to make use of treatment. The material that clients bring into therapy can also be stressful, with some authors (e.g. Pearlman & Ian, 1995) suggesting that therapists may be at risk of secondary or vicarious traumatisation.

Some factors may protect psychotherapists from excessive stress. Supportive personal relationships, within and outside the work setting, have been found to be important to a therapist's well-being (Mahoney, 1997). A positive work environment is an important factor in stress control, such as workplaces that encourage therapists and provide effective supervision (Savicki & Cooley, 1987), and those that create effective social systems and reduce administration and paperwork (Raquepaw & Miller, 1989). By recognising and building on protective factors, novice therapists can best help their clients. Chapter 19 provides more information on how to manage stress and prevent burnout.

Exercise 5.6

1   What are your positive characteristics in terms of being a good therapist?
2   What characteristics of yours could prevent effective work with clients?
3   Think about your own family when you were growing up. What rules were in place that governed how emotions were dealt with? Reflect on how you are most likely to bring your own familial rules and roles for emotional expression to your clinical work.
4   Assess your own motivation for becoming a clinician: what needs of your own are being fulfilled by doing therapy? Remember, the issue is not whether you have your own needs and countertransference propensities, but how you will deal with them.

CONCLUSION

Our aim in this chapter has been to debunk the myth of the prototypical therapist, and to provide novice therapists with rules of thumb to enhance clinical outcomes. The most important things to remember are that the client always comes first, and that the person of the therapist is integral to the change process. This second point implies that self-care and supervision are critical components of an effective therapist. Take a look at the points made below by Kahn (1997), a short list of the essential things we need to provide to our clients. Consider whether you are able to provide these to your clients. If your answer for any one is no, seek assistance from a supervisor or from your own therapist.

What we should give our clients (Kahn, 1997):

- our full attention and energy
- our best effort to understand them: to understand what they are experiencing at the present moment, and to understand the themes of their lives, both apparent and subtle, as they unfold
- let them know that they are indeed with someone who is trying hard to understand them
- give them the safety and freedom to reveal anything they wish, without fear of being judged
- give them certainty that they are with an ethical professional who knows the boundaries and will not cross them.

Practice implications

Although more research is needed to understand fully the role of therapist factors, we suggest that the following tenets guide your practice as a therapist:

1   The client must always come first in treatment
2   Each client is an individual, and you need to adapt your therapeutic style to suit each client for optimal outcome
3   You need to be accountable in using techniques or procedures that are based on the best available evidence from systematic research
4   You need to be mindful of all factors that have an impact on outcome, including your own skills and knowledge, theories and techniques, the alliance, and client factors
5   You must be aware of the therapeutic alliance, and be ready to address ruptures in that alliance (as discussed in chapter 6) with your client sooner rather than later
6   You need to monitor client progress, and address any lack of progress with your client in a collaborative manner
7   You must continually evaluate your practice, formally through reliable measures, and informally through reflection, to maintain the highest standards of client care
8   You need to be honest with your supervisor, and use the supervisory relationship effectively. If you feel you are holding back from your supervisor, have the ethical courage to raise this issue
9   You need to be constantly aware of your own emotional well-being, and of the impact of the 'tricky issues', raised above, on your therapeutic practice. These should be monitored through ongoing supervision and/or personal therapy.

Recommended reading
'Must-own' books for novices, and more experienced therapists, are Teyber (2006) and Teyber and McClure (2010). These books are written for beginning therapists.

Irwin Yalom has written many books about psychotherapy, largely for psychotherapists. All of his books are a great read, but for the novice we would recommend in particular:

Yalom, I. D. (2003). The Gift of Therapy: An Open Letter to a New Generation of
    Therapists and their Patients. New York: HarperCollins.
    Reading original texts by Carl Rogers is a wonderful experience for a therapist.
Two of his best-liked books are:
Rogers, C. R. (1961). *On Becoming a Person: A Therapist's View of Psychotherapy*. Boston:
    Houghton Mifflin.
Rogers, C. R. (1980). *A Way of Being*. Boston: Houghton Mifflin.
    Two books written specifically about therapist development and change are:
Goldfried, M. R. (ed.). (2001). *How Therapists Change: Personal And Professional Reflec-
    tions*. Washington, DC: American Psychological Association. A range of chap-
    ters by well-known therapists, sharing their personal journeys of development.
Orlinsky, D. E. & Ronnestad, M. H. (2005). *How Psychotherapists Develop: A Study of
    Therapeutic Work and Professional Growth*. Washington, DC: American Psycho-
    logical Association.

Chapter 6

The psychotherapy relationship

Introduction

The relationship between therapist and client has increasingly been recognised as an important factor in therapeutic change. Negotiating an effective therapeutic relationship to achieve desired outcomes is one of the most important and rewarding challenges for a psychologist. This chapter will address a range of issues related to the relationship, including types of therapeutic relationships (such as transference, countertransference, and the *real* relationship), empathy, issues of attachment, client needs regarding the relationship, how the relationship assists in client change, and measures used in assessing the effectiveness of the relationship.

Talking with another is a deceptively simple act. In our personal lives, we spend much time engaged in this way, and in pursuing, monitoring, and negotiating relationships that arise from this activity. In the professional context, however, there are both constraints and unique opportunities in the form of relationships that arise. In chapters 4 and 5 we discussed the variables that clients and therapists bring to this relationship, with the psychologist's ethical obligation to maintain a professional relationship, rather than one that fulfils his or her personal needs.

Gelso and Hayes (1998) have suggested that three related types of relationship may be present between a psychologist and his or her client. These are:

- the transference configuration
- the real relationship
- the working alliance.

Of these, the working alliance has received most empirical support. Consequently, we will focus on this. However, effective therapeutic work relies upon an understanding of all three types of relationship and the way they may influence each other.

The transference configuration

Transference has been variously defined. A useful way to understand transference is to regard it as a set of attitudes, expectations, and behaviours that may be present in the therapy relationship, and are the result of early experiences in significant interpersonal relationships. For example, a client—or therapist—who has experienced rejection from a significant other in his or her early life may be predisposed to perceive rejection from others in current relationships, and to act in pre-emptive and sometimes destructive ways because of that perception.

Transference has been regarded as critically informative in psychodynamic approaches, but with scepticism in some other approaches. In part, this scepticism may be related to rejection of therapeutic orientations that have elevated resolution of transference issues above all other hypothesised mechanisms of change, such as the development of self-efficacy, or the resolution of interpersonal difficulties. More recent work has helped to validate transference, and to reclaim understanding of the transference configuration as an important aspect of negotiating therapeutic relationships. In social psychology, Andersen and her colleagues have demonstrated that mental representations of significant others influence people in new interpersonal encounters, on the basis of the new person's resemblance to significant others (e.g., Andersen & Cole, 1990). Work in the area of attachment also supports the concept that people are influenced by *early working models* (EWM) of interpersonal relationships, and that these EWMs in turn may be activated in the therapeutic relationship (Dozier & Tyrrell, 1998). Understanding attachment patterns can provide valuable insight into the relational patterns of clients, and will be discussed in detail when we consider client characteristics.

It is important to note that the contemporary definition of transference is broader than the early psychoanalytic concept of transference. It refers to all the feelings, perceptions, and reactions the client has toward the therapist—both realistic and distorted. These reactions, which may be positive or negative, range from accurate and reality-based perceptions of the therapist to highly distorted responses that are based on past relationships. They do not necessarily suggest pathology; clients' reactions often hold at least a kernel of truth.

In managing problematic transference reactions, the goals are to:

- help the client to recognise repeated misperceptions about the therapist
- clarify how this pattern disrupts the therapeutic relationship and leads to problems with others
- work together to replace this pattern with a more flexible and reality-based relationship.

A psychologist has to be willing to explore, non-defensively, the basis of the client's responses towards him or her. One of the best ways a therapist can make sense of the client's conflicts and internal working models is to note how the client perceives and reacts to the therapist. Aspects of the client's maladaptive relational patterns that cause problems with others may be reenacted in the therapeutic relationship. Observation of these patterns can assist in conceptualisation of the client.

Countertransference

An important aspect of the transference configuration is that therapists may also experience transference-based reactions to clients. The key issue here is learning to manage countertransference, rather than preventing it. Maintaining awareness of countertransference reactions by the therapist is part of self-observational processes that are a necessary part of therapeutic work.

A small yet accumulating literature that links countertransference to negative client outcome (Gelso & Hayes, 2001) highlights the need for therapists of all orientations to manage countertransference. Most therapists anecdotally report that certain clients are more likely than others to 'push their buttons'. Being aware of this (and the types of clients who are most likely to elicit this reaction), and becoming familiar with strategies to manage potentially negative reactions, is an important part of therapeutic practice.

Exercise 6.1

Video 11 provides an example of a therapist experiencing countertransference, and illustrates the effects of unmanaged countertransference upon the working alliance. Then watch the client debrief to see the effect this can have on a client. Following this, the third part of the scene presents a discussion of the therapy event in supervision, and is a reminder that one of the most valuable aids to managing countertransference can be making good use of supervisory relationships.

To help identify countertransference, consider these questions:

1 Do you find yourself becoming impatient or irritable with certain clients?
2 Does your client remind you of someone from your past?
3 Do you want to be 'liked' by your clients?
4 Do you feel overly responsible for your clients' progress?
5 Do you prefer not to discuss particular issues in therapy?
6 Do you avoid certain discussions in supervision?

Not every negative reaction to a client is based on countertransference. Clients frequently present because they are experiencing difficulties in relating to others, and it is logical that these same interpersonal difficulties may be present in their dealings with their therapist. The importance of therapists learning to manage their own countertransference reactions is therefore threefold.

1 Evidence of the relationship between countertransference and poor client outcome suggests that the client's best interests are not served when the therapist fails to manage his or her countertransference reactions.
2 Effective recognition and management of countertransference reactions enables the therapist to more confidently make use of his or her observations of the client's behaviour in therapy, as a source of information regarding the client's behaviour in the 'real world'.
3 Confidence in these observations of client behaviour enables the therapist to intervene more effectively. Effective intervention often involves making skilful use of the therapeutic relationship to assist the client to understand his or her relationship patterns more fully, and, in some cases, to benefit from corrective emotional experiences.

Gelso and Hayes (2001) suggest five factors that may assist therapists to manage their desire to act out countertransference:

- *therapist self-insight:* the extent to which a therapist is aware of his or her feelings, and understands the basis of these feelings
- *therapist self-integration:* the extent to which a therapist possesses a healthy character structure, which will enable the maintenance of boundaries with the client, and clearly differentiate between therapist and client needs and desires; this is particularly important when ambivalence regarding process and/or outcomes exists
- *anxiety-management strategies:* to acknowledge the presence of anxiety, yet not allow it to influence responses to the client
- *empathic ability:* enables the therapist to remain attuned to the client's needs even at the most difficult points; the capacity to experience empathy is one of the most important skills a therapist brings to the work of therapy, and will be discussed in more detail below
- *conceptualising ability:* enables the therapist to go beyond a purely personal response to a client, and to understand potentially challenging behaviours in the context of an overarching theory or conceptualisation, which facilitates understanding of these behaviours in terms of client history.

As discussed in chapter 5, it may also be useful for you to consider entering into therapy yourself, to better understand experiences in your own life that may have an impact on the therapeutic relationships you form with clients.

THE *REAL* RELATIONSHIP

The *real* relationship falls at the opposite end of the spectrum to the transference configuration. Gelso and colleagues (2005) suggest there is a personal relationship between therapist and client that may influence both the transference configuration and the working alliance, yet goes beyond either of these relationships. Mutual liking is a key element. Both in brief therapy and often in work with more disturbed individuals, greater use of the real relationship is recommended. During the initial, and especially the latter stages of most therapies, the real relationship is most prominent; the transference tends to recede as the alliance develops. As the therapy relationship progresses, the real relationship deepens. Each participant holds a wider range of realistic perceptions of the other, and each is able to be more fully genuine. The emergence and deepening of the real relationship parallels and reflects client progress in psychotherapy.

This real relationship begins from the moment therapist and client meet, and encompasses two key elements:

- *realism:* the extent to which therapist and client can view and experience each other free from the distortions of the transference configuration
- *genuineness:* the extent to which therapist and client are authentic with each other in the here and now.

Realism and genuineness can be described in terms of their *magnitude* (how much they are present in the real relationship) and their *valence* (do client and therapist experience the genuineness and realism of each other in a positive or negative way?). One of the most important aspects of the real relationship is that it reminds us that the work we do calls on our innate human capacities for relating with others in a personal way. This real relationship is enhanced by a respectful and courteous stance towards our clients, who want a therapist who relates to them without pretence, and with genuineness and honesty.

Enhancing the real relationship
- Ensure that appointments begin at the agreed time
- Refrain from taking calls, or allowing interruptions
- Speak respectfully to the client
- Follow through on agreed actions
- Be willing to share personal reactions, if this seems appropriate
- At the end of a session, ask yourself, 'Do I feel I made contact with the client, and have a genuine feeling for who this person is?'

Note, however, that at all times this real relationship exists to serve the client, rather than therapist needs for relatedness. An example of this distinction is observed in self-disclosure. Although some therapeutic orientations have regarded any form of therapist self-disclosure as unacceptable, more recent investigations suggest that at times it may be helpful to clients. Some forms of self-disclosure, such as sharing certain of your reactions during sessions, can enhance the working alliance and will be discussed below. However, self-disclosure of your history or personal details may influence the real relationship, particularly when clients can already gain much information indirectly. Such information includes gender, age group, and issues of personal style and history (does the therapist dress casually or formally? does she wear a wedding ring? does she have an accent?). Beyond this is information that the psychologist may or may not choose to share with the client.

The guideline here is that psychologists should use personal disclosure only in the interests of the client. For example, disclosing that you used to feel anxious in certain situations may be helpful, whereas asking the client's advice about the ongoing difficulty you are experiencing in these situations is not. Therapy is about the client, not the psychologist, and self-disclosure should be used to assist the client. A strong desire to self-disclose may signal the beginnings of an inappropriate attachment to a client, or being overly self-focused, and should be discussed with a supervisor or respected colleague. We also discuss this in chapter 17.

THE WORKING ALLIANCE

The *working alliance* is the type of relationship that researchers and psychologists most frequently refer to when they use the term *therapeutic alliance* (Martin et al., 2000). Although much of the initial conceptualisation and research into the working alliance has come from psychodynamic literature (Raue & Goldfried, 1994), this relationship has received widespread attention from various therapeutic orientations. Current interest in this relationship owes much to Bordin's (1979) work. Bordin argued that the therapeutic relationship influenced outcome across a broad range of therapies. Describing the relationship between therapist and patient as 'the working alliance', Bordin conceptualised it as a collaborative relationship that comprised three components: goal, task, and bond.

Goals

- Short- and long-term targets of therapy that the therapist assists the client in identifying, and the extent to which therapist and client agree with and value change in these areas.
- Specific areas targeted for change, such as decrease in symptoms, improvement in interpersonal skills, or more global areas, such as development of new ways of thinking and behaving.

Goal agreement

Agreement on goals encompasses a shared understanding of the benefits of change, and confidence that change can be accomplished. In a working alliance where there is high agreement on goals, therapist and client view them as important, appropriate, and clear:

- *high agreement:* the client desires to have more friends, and the therapist supports attempts at increased social activity
- *low agreement:* the client desires a decrease in depressive symptoms, and the therapist focuses on origins of anxiety, or the therapist tries to change the behaviour of the client towards his or her spouse; the client wants the spouse to change.

Exercise 6.2

Video 3 is an example of the difficulties that can occur when there is low agreement on goals. How might the therapist proceed to get better agreement on goals?

Tasks

- Necessary therapeutic activities (practising skills) that are performed by client and therapist to attain goals agreed upon
- Global therapeutic strategies or methods, such as exploration, that help clients to increase their awareness of their own thoughts, feelings, values, and needs
- Specific therapeutic strategies, such as relaxation training or exposure work.

With the range of tasks available across therapeutic orientations, techniques associated with the 'task' element of the working alliance vary considerably, but may include support and reassurance, with a willingness to explore client feelings; reflection, to clarify feelings and facilitate experience; interpretation of meanings of underlying behaviour; or reformulation of client description, to clarify experience. These tasks may involve a degree of direction, with the therapist adopting the role of expert to guide the client's ways of thinking and behaving, using such techniques as information giving, homework assignments, and role-playing to rehearse new communication strategies.

Task agreement

The important aspect here is not so much the tasks themselves but the extent to which the tasks are negotiated between therapist and client, and the degree to which the tasks seem relevant and useful to the client:

- *high agreement:* tasks are seen as important, appropriate, and clearly defined by therapist and client
- *low agreement:* therapeutic interactions may be characterised by confusion or discomfort, as the therapist attempts to focus the client on areas or activities that the client perceives to be irrelevant, or as the client 'wanders off' from working on what the therapist perceives to be the main issue at hand; also evidenced by a lack of compliance with homework tasks.

Bond

- The development of a personal attachment between therapist and client, defined by the degree of mutual liking, respect, and trust.
- Characterised by therapist genuineness, warmth, and understanding, and client confidence in the therapist, as well as a sense of openness and comfort in the relationship.

Such a bond can be evidenced by a warm, relaxed tone of voice, the quantity and quality of client talk concerning intimate issues, and the degree of therapist comfort and accurate empathy.

Clearly, there is considerable interdependence between these working alliance components; that is, the bond between therapist and client develops out of both parties owning and being committed to the change goals, and they participate in tasks that are understood and perceived to be relevant to those goals. However, client and therapist views of the alliance may differ substantially (Horvath, 1994b). It is unclear why this difference exists. Therapists may simply be much less attuned to the state of the working alliance than they assume, or clients' pre-existing characteristics and expectations of helping relationships have an impact on their experience of the alliance. Horvath and Greenberg (1986) suggest that, while clients presumably rate alliance according to their direct experience, therapists may be influenced by their theoretical perspectives.

It is the client's rating of the working alliance that is most strongly linked to outcome. In part, this may reflect the fact that outcome is also most often gauged using client reports on standardised instruments, but the discrepancy between client and therapist ratings of alliance also signals the central importance of the therapist not simply trusting to her or his sense of 'how things are going' with clients. Instead, it is important that therapists regularly check in with clients, verbally and through use of standardised measures, and to use supervision to provide a more objective view.

Confident collaboration

Confident collaboration is a concept that has emerged out of recent factor-analytic research on the alliance, research that may also help to explain discrepancies in therapist–client perceptions (Clemence et al., 2005; Hatcher & Barends, 1996). Confident collaboration reflects the level of confidence and commitment a client feels towards therapy, and the degree to which therapy is experienced as worthwhile. Examining patient and therapist alliance ratings on the Combined Alliance Short Form (CASF), Clemence and colleagues (2005) demonstrated that while patients and therapists agree on the confident collaboration of alliance, therapists tended to rate bond more highly than do clients, but that this rating did not predict client improvement. This finding may reflect the philosophical commitment of many therapists to liking and respecting their clients regardless of outcome—and although these may be important facilitative conditions, a sense of purposefulness and expectation of improvement may be more central to prediction of outcome.

Working alliance: empirical findings

Psychotherapy research findings have supported the importance of the working alliance. In a meta-analysis of 24 studies, Horvath and Symonds (1991) found a moderate but reliable association, with an average effect size of 0.26, between working alliance and treatment outcome, independent of type of therapy practised and length of treatment. Martin and colleagues (2000) aggregated data from 78 published and unpublished studies, and similarly reported a consistent, although moderate, relationship (effect size = 0.22) between therapeutic alliance and various indices of therapeutic change. Similarly, a meta-analysis of 23 child and adolescent therapy studies found a moderate effect size between alliance and outcome of 0.20 (Shirk & Karver, 2003).

There is considerable diversity of opinion across therapeutic orientations about exactly how the alliance functions, and, in particular, the extent to which it is viewed as a central change mechanism (Gelso & Hayes, 1998; Zuroff & Blatt, 2006). Some researchers have even argued that a good working alliance may simply be an epiphenomenon of improvement (Feeley et al., 1999); that is, the client who is improving may simply rate his or her alliance more highly than the client who is not improving. A number of studies have examined this question, with mixed results (Barber et al., 2000; Feeley et al., 1999; Gaston et al., 1991; Klein et al., 2003; Zuroff & Blatt, 2006), and further research is warranted.

Collectively, however, the existing body of research suggests that, while there may well be a synergistic relationship between working alliance and symptom improvement that accounts, in part, for alliance–outcome correlations, there is sufficient evidence to warrant an assumption that the working alliance directly or indirectly contributes to treatment outcome, beyond the influence of early symptom improvement.

Moreover, as we noted in chapter 3, it is important to avoid the apparent schism that has opened up in many quarters regarding the relative contribution of various therapeutic factors. While it seems clear that simply applying the techniques of evidence-based therapies is unlikely to account for the complexity of client–therapeutic reactions, it seems equally limiting to assume that relationship factors by themselves can provide a comprehensive explanation for the process of change in all clients. As indicated by the model of psychotherapy that we have advanced in this book, a more useful perspective examines both alliance and technical factors to map principles of change (Castonguay & Beutler, 2006; Castonguay & Grosse Holtforth, 2005; Goldfried & Davila, 2005).

How does the alliance work?
Rogers (1957) famously asserted that a good working alliance was both the necessary and a sufficient condition for therapeutic change. A more recent trend is to suggest that the working alliance may exert its influence through facilitating the action of specific, technical factors (Casey et al., 2005; Rector et al., 1999), or by working with other important process variables to achieve outcome (Missirlian et al., 2005). Casey and colleagues (2005) demonstrated that a higher level of client-rated working alliance was associated with greater cognitive change in treatment of panic disorder. A broader perspective concerns the role of the alliance in providing a 'corrective emotional experience' that, depending on clients' needs and presenting problems, has been viewed as curative in its own right.

Alexander and French (1946) described *corrective emotional experience* as experiential relearning that allows clients to change rigid and unhelpful relationship patterns by experiencing more adaptive relationship patterns with their therapist. Clients will attempt to recreate the same types of relationships they have with others within the therapy relationship. However, if a therapist can behave in new and more effective ways with a client, the relational conflicts the client has experienced can be resolved, as the client experiences that at least some relationships can be more effective and healthy (Teyber, 2006; Teyber & McClure, 2010). The therapist, while joining with the client in his or her experience, behaves consistently in a manner that is helpful and constructive to the client. The experience is thus corrective, as it is different from what the client generally experiences in his or her relationships outside therapy.

Therapist contribution to positive working alliance
Given the evidence that a strong working alliance contributes to client improvement, it is useful to consider ways in which a therapist might build a positive alliance. In a review of the literature across a range of psychotherapy orientations, Ackerman and Hilsenroth (2003) concluded that there are two broad means by which therapists influence the development of a strong working alliance: therapist personal attributes, and therapist techniques (see table 6.1).

The alliance across different stages of therapy
We have discussed alliance as a static concept, but it would be a mistake to assume that the only challenge is alliance formation, or that, once formed, the alliance necessarily continues in an unchanging form. Research suggests that there are phases and important challenges to the alliance throughout therapy, and that these present both challenge and opportunity.

Table 6.1 Therapist's attributes and techniques

Attributes	Techniques
Flexibility	Exploration
Experience	Depth
Honesty	Reflection
Respectfulness	Supportive
Trustworthiness	Notes past therapy success
Confidence	Accurate information
Interest in client	Facilitates expression of affect
Alertness	Active
Friendliness	Affirming
Warmth	Understanding
Openness	Attends to client's experience

Early alliance

It is important to establish the therapeutic alliance early, as failure to do so may lead to dropout or poor outcomes. This phase is particularly important for brief treatments. Research has found that clients tend to rate the alliance as being more constant than therapists or observers do, and are more likely to perceive the alliance as positive at termination if their initial assessment was positive (Martin et al., 2000).

Mid-therapy alliance

This phase tends to be characterised by rupture and repair; the alliance is beginning to reflect the relational patterns of clients (and therapists). Kivlighan and Shaughnessy (2000) have identified three patterns of working-alliance development:

- *stable alliance:* moderate working alliance that does not change over the course of therapy
- *linear alliance growth:* characterised by positive incremental growth over the course of therapy
- *quadratic alliance growth:* a high–low–high pattern, characterised by tear-and-repair.

Quadratic alliance growth

Strains and ruptures

Some researchers have found that the quadratic growth pattern was related to greater client improvement (Kivlighan & Shaughnessy, 2000), although more research is required to establish if this finding holds true for different client categories. There is support for the concept that a psychologist's capacity to address strains and ruptures in the alliance is an important component in managing alliance across treatment.

Strains and ruptures are disagreements about tasks or goals of therapy, or problems in the therapeutic bond, that differ only in intensity—a strain is less intense, signifying less disruption to the alliance. Strains and ruptures are primarily caused by negative transference reactions or therapist error. Bordin (1994) has suggested that alliance rupture is inevitable with some clients, as the client's pathology creates relationship problems, and activities involved in repair are the essence of therapy. However, therapist error is also a potent source of strains and ruptures. Although errors can occur in a number of ways (such as poorly timed interventions or inappropriate homework assignments), a common reason is *empathic failure*; the therapist has failed to understand the client's state of mind or emotion arising from his or her internal world. A rupture can generally be healed if the therapist detects it quickly, and if the alliance has been strong enough to this time.

Healing of ruptures often serves to make the alliance stronger. A key issue is that therapists must remain vigilant to the possibility of strains and ruptures, and not simply depend on client verbal report to identify problems. Clients may find it difficult to voice their concerns about aspects of therapy, and it falls to the therapist to take a proactive role to monitor the state of the alliance and to facilitate client expression of concerns.

Cueing, shaping, and process comments
Useful principles to apply in facilitating expression of concerns by clients, and in generally promoting client collaboration in building the working alliance, are *cueing* and *shaping*. Cueing means providing a prompt to the client that his or her comment or response is desired ('How does that sound to you?'). Shaping refers to the process of reinforcing successive approximations to the desired behaviour. A client who raises a concern about some aspect of therapy might be thanked by the therapist for being willing to share that concern, whether or not the concern is perceived as 'valid' by the therapist. It is the client's behaviour of raising the concern that is desired, and is being reinforced, because it is behaviour likely to promote better collaboration and easier identification of potential strains and ruptures.

A third overarching principle concerns use of *process comments* in therapy. These typically involve making simple observations regarding the interaction between therapist and client occurring at the time. Although useful, these comments should be made tentatively, with attention to timing. If made in a clear and authentic way, such comments can provide a useful means of strengthening the alliance.

Managing ruptures
As Muran and Safran (2002) note, strains and ruptures can be dealt with in a number of ways. They can be dealt with directly or indirectly. If a client questions the relevance of discussing his or her emotional response to a situation, the therapist may provide the therapeutic rationale for doing so in a way that acknowledges the potential difficulty of the task, or thank the client for alerting the therapist to the difficulty, and change the task. Similarly, strains and ruptures can be dealt with at the surface level (again providing the therapeutic rationale), or more deeply (exploring the underlying meaning for the client). Decisions about how to deal with strains and ruptures are made by taking a number of factors into account, including client characteristics (does the client have the resources to do this work? does the client have difficulty expressing wants and needs?), and stage of therapy (has sufficient trust and rapport been built for the therapist to gently challenge the client, or will this be experienced at this stage as an overwhelming threat?).

The main steps in managing ruptures are:

- The therapist needs to be aware that a rupture has occurred. Having this awareness requires a range of skills, including a high level of empathy and observational skills. Impediments to recognising ruptures include therapist countertransference, excessive focus on technique or manualised treatment at the expense of paying attention to the individual client, and lack of empathy.
- The therapist needs to raise the issue as soon as possible. The longer a rupture is left, the more it will damage the alliance, and the more difficult it will be to raise the issue.
- Admit mistakes, and apologise if appropriate.
- Use process comments to manage the rupture.
- Encourage the client to discuss the rupture, and focus on trying to understand the client's point of view.

Managing strains and ruptures requires observation and skills in repair by the therapist, and a willingness by the client to work with the therapist to repair the alliance. The good news is that repaired ruptures strengthen the alliance, and can provide fertile ground for corrective experience and learning by the client (Safran et al., 1990; Teyber, 2006; Teyber & McClure, 2010). Explicit management of ruptures in the therapeutic alliance may then generalise to other relationships the client has, improving the quality of these relationships as well. Successful resolution of a rupture in the alliance can be a powerful means of achieving better outcome (Safran et al., 1990). In considering the importance of managing strains and ruptures in the alliance, it is useful to examine the concept of client resistance.

Client resistance

Primarily, resistance is the client's attempt to resist the impact of the therapist (Mitchell, 2007), and applies to any client behaviour that demonstrates a reluctance to collaborate or cooperate with a therapist's suggestions and agenda, and the therapeutic process (Bischoff & Tracey, 1995). Fundamentally, therapy is about a client interacting with a therapist. If the client resists the therapist, this resistance is likely to have an impact on treatment. Not surprisingly, client resistance can be challenging for all therapists, but it is often more so for novice therapists, who may not expect that this behaviour will be an issue. Often, novice therapists are mainly concerned with 'getting the information right'; to face a client who is resistant to much of their work can be confronting.

It is important to keep in mind that resistance is not simply 'bad' or always a problem. On some level, all humans are resistant, and such resistance is a necessary, adaptive, and often creative response. If we were not resistant, there would be no critical evaluation of the world, and we would be randomly affected by the latest influence in our life (Mitchell, 2007). Resistance in therapy can be a viewed as a positive sign, indicating that the client has a sense of self and his or her own views on issues.

Strong & Matross (1973) define resistance as 'psychological forces aroused in the client that restrain acceptance of influence and are generated by the way the suggestion is stated and by the characteristics of the counsellor stating it' (p. 26). This reminds us that resistance is not a one-sided situation in which the client resists treatment; the therapist also plays a role in the process.

Mitchell (2007) suggests there are a number of ways in which a therapist can try to influence a client, from non-forceful to forceful. The least forceful type of influence is being non-directive, followed by indirectly suggesting (such as mentioning that the therapist had read about a particular solution to a problem), directly suggesting (suggesting a particular solution directly), providing advice or educating, confronting, and finally, the most forceful way, through use of punitive force (for example, saying to a client that if he does not engage in a particular treatment, he will be reported to Child Services). The more resistant the client, the less directive the therapist should be, for optimal outcome (Castonguay & Beutler, 2006).

Signs of client resistance include:

- being regularly late for treatment, often rescheduling, or not making firm commitments to ongoing therapy
- being closed, not sharing much information
- demonstrating defences
- disagreeing with treatment options, or not wanting to do certain types of treatment, such as homework or exposure.

Exercise 6.3

1   Watch scene 1 of Video 3 for an example of a client resisting homework, and how the therapist attempts to respond to this resistance. What is unhelpful about the therapist's behaviour? What might be happening from the client's perspective?
2   Watch scene 2 of this video. Is the therapist's behaviour more helpful in this part? If so, what makes it better? Then watch the client's debrief.

Reasons for resistance
It is helpful to understand why clients may be resistant. Some reasons are:

- Clients may have experienced conflict regarding their decision to enter therapy, and are in two minds whether they really want to work on their problems, or they may feel that they have been forced to enter treatment (mandated clients).
- Clients do not feel they have the interpersonal safety needed to explore their conflicts. Therapy needs to be a safe place, otherwise clients will be resistant. Obviously, the therapist plays a significant role in whether therapy is safe for clients.
- Clients are reenacting rather than resolving some aspect of their problem.
- Clients experience shame and anxiety—feelings of worthlessness, inadequacy, or defectiveness—and may fear rejection or debasement, and cannot cope with readdressing issues, making it difficult for them to open up.
- Clients are avoiding conflicted emotions for fear that they will experience unwanted responses, such as being ridiculed, feeling invalidated, perceiving that their feelings have been discounted, ignored or unheard, or feeling that they may be a burden to or hurt others with their feelings.

- Clients refuse to let go of past events, which may, to some extent, define their identity. For some, the idea of 'letting go' equates to denying that they had negative and painful experiences; often clients will say something like, 'I can't let my past go, as it will be pretending nothing happened, or that it did not matter', or 'I owe it to my past to be screwed up now'. Clearly, we need to assist clients to conceptualise change in a positive manner.
- Clients may be achieving secondary gains from problems, such as receiving support, not having to take responsibility, controlling others, or having excuses for poor behaviour.

Fundamentally, resistance is about threat. Commonly, therapists become frustrated when clients demonstrate resistance. This response is not helpful, and will most likely increase the struggle between therapist and client. If you can keep in mind that resistance is about the client feeling threatened, resistance will be managed productively, as you find empathy for the client, and a way to decrease the threat and increase safety.

Teyber (2006) suggests three questions that therapists can ask to clarify what resistance is about:

- What does the client elicit from others?
- What is the threat? It may include attempts to manage unwanted feelings of, for example, shame, guilt, and anxiety, and fear that the therapist could hurt in ways similar to past experiences.
- How will the client express resistance?

We suggest you use these questions to try to understand client resistance.

Managing shame
Shame has been described as one of the most common sources of resistance (Teyber, 2006; Teyber & McClure, 2010). In fact, shame has been suggested to generate more opposition to working in therapy and obstructing change than any other emotion. Not only the client avoids shame; it is one of the feelings most avoided by therapists. Often, individuals experiencing significant shame try to defend against it by being controlling or intimidating, or by raging at the person they perceive to have demeaned them—who can just be a therapist trying to empathise with a client's vulnerability.

Inadequate therapist reactions
Teyber (2006) provides useful information regarding the poor responses therapists at times have to clients' difficult emotional experiences. Managing emotions—our own and those of clients—is often the most difficult task we face; not surprisingly, at times it is done ineffectively. Commonly, our own and others' emotions are seen as threatening, and we try to avoid them. Examples of therapists' poor responses to clients' emotions, which may increase resistance, include:

- interpreting what the client's feelings mean, and thus intellectually distancing from them
- becoming directive, telling the client what to do
- reassuring the client, explaining that everything will be all right

- changing the topic away from discussion centred on emotions
- falling silent and emotionally withdrawing, giving a clear message to the client that the therapist does not want to explore the issue further
- self-disclosing, or moving into his or her own feelings
- diminishing the client by trying to rescue him or her
- becoming over-identified with the client, and pressing him or her to make a decision or take some action.

Working with resistance

All therapists will recognise some of these manoeuvres, used to manage their own difficulties in dealing with client emotions. Unfortunately, all are unhelpful to clients and to the outcome of therapy. Teyber (2006) suggests a number of goals for the therapist in working with resistance, including:

- stay emotionally present and connected while clients experience painful feelings; reflect and affirm their experience of the feeling
- demonstrate to the client that you can tolerate intense feelings
- the client needs to see that the therapist is responding in new ways, different from how others respond to their emotions, but responsive in some of the ways described above
- debrief clients by asking how it was to share their feelings
- provide validation and care, which are helpful to restore dignity
- provide a 'good enough' holding environment
- learn to contain your own feelings—good affect management is important to being an effective practitioner.

We need to work on our 'stance' towards therapy. What actually is our role as a therapist? We suspect that a lot of the struggle between therapist and client (where the client ends up being labelled 'resistant') is based in the therapist's troublesome expectations of his or her own and the client's roles in treatment. Consider what Rogers said (1961): 'One brief way of describing the change which has taken place in me is to say that in my early professional years I was asking the question: "How can I treat, or care, or change this person?" Now I would phrase the question in this way: "How can I provide a relationship which this person may use for personal growth?"' This quote provides insight into how we may look at our roles, and reduce the risk of increasing client resistance and diminishing the potential benefits of treatment.

Therapists are often reluctant to address resistance. This is a problem because, if not addressed, resistance may continue to interfere with client improvement. There are a few ways that resistance can be directly addressed:

- give the client permission to be resistant; this often reduces resistance
- openly discuss with the client his or her reasons for being resistant, and show empathy and understanding
- educate the client about the role of resistance, including that we all need to be resistant to some degree to get through life
- explore the danger the client perceives in the proposed course of action, identifying the threat the client is experiencing that results in resistance

- use a direct interpretative stance as the last measure; interpretation is often more about the therapist's understanding than the client's.

Mitchell has a website <www.cliftonmitchell.com> that provides resources for recognising ways in which practitioners may play a role in the client's resistance.

Remember: never use the term 'resistant client' to blame the client for not getting better without considering what your contribution is to the problem. Very few clients are not suitable for therapy; the rest just take a bit more effort to engage. Don't distance yourself from a client by thinking, 'he is just resistant', and don't let others do so.

CLIENT PERSPECTIVES ON THE WORKING ALLIANCE

The working alliance is a shared relationship between therapist and client. Having discussed how a therapist can help to establish a good working alliance, it is important to examine client needs that must be met, and client characteristics that may influence the working alliance. We can do this from a general perspective by turning to research that has looked at client perspectives on alliance formation, and then look at specific client characteristics that may influence alliance formation.

Bedi and colleagues (2005) interviewed 40 clients, who were asked to recall critical incidents in therapy that they believed had contributed to the therapeutic alliance. Many of these incidents were simple gestures by the therapist, including non-verbal gestures (eye contact, smiling, personalised greetings, and farewells), basic counselling microskills (paraphrasing, identifying feelings, and encouraging the client), and references to previously mentioned material. By contrast, clients identified very few client-related factors, with only one-third acknowledging their role in the alliance. But more than 70 per cent of clients reported at least one technical activity as being important in the development of their alliance. Some clients also reported activities that may be seen to be inappropriate (such as providing home phone numbers, or walking the client to their car) as being positive events. This highlights the importance of therapist awareness of activities that may be meeting their own needs rather than those of the client.

Grounded theory analysis of interviews with 26 clients also emphasised the importance of care within the therapeutic relationship, beyond other factors (Levitt et al., 2006). While therapeutic interventions were considered helpful, clients, on average, recalled 1.6 significant events that they perceived to contribute to change or insight. Of the recalled activities, introspection on relationships, cognition, and emotion were considered most relevant. Clients were more likely to view global changes, such as improved relationships or feeling better about themselves, rather than symptom change, as important therapeutic outcomes (other than clients with eating disorders).

CLIENT CHARACTERISTICS AND THE WORKING ALLIANCE

Bowlby's (1969) seminal work in attachment theory has provided a useful framework for understanding relational patterns. His early experience in child development clinics led him to challenge the psychoanalytic focus on a child's fantasy life then in vogue, and to refocus on the events of childhood that shape an individual's interaction patterns with others. Bowlby argued that early experiences with parents and other caregivers led individuals to develop mental representations of relationships that persist into adulthood. These mental representations are of others and of oneself in relation to others, as well as relationships in general, and consist of conscious and unconscious memories, thoughts, and feelings, as well as strategies for affect regulation (Sable, 1997). These mental representations are typically elicited in close relationships, and the psychotherapy relationship is one that may activate attachment styles.

Research has found a relationship between aspects of clients' interpersonal functioning and outcomes in therapy. Muran and colleagues (1994) found a tendency for 'hostile-dominance' interpersonal problems (measured by the Inventory of Interpersonal Problems (IIP)) to have a negative impact on the alliance, that clients with 'non-assertive or submissive' interpersonal problems seem more inclined to agree with parameters of treatment, and a positive relationship between 'friendly-submission' and the alliance. However, scores on the Bond subscale of the Working Alliance Inventory were not significantly related to any interpersonal problem.

Hardy and colleagues (2001) measured the relative contribution of cognitive and interpersonal styles to treatment outcome, and the extent to which therapeutic alliance mediated these potential relationships. Client improvement on a measure of depression was significantly related to 'overinvolved' and 'underinvolved' interpersonal dimensions on the Inventory of Interpersonal Problems. Further analysis indicated that the 'underinvolved' interpersonal style (characterised by being highly avoidant of relationships) made the largest contribution to outcome variance, and the impact of this underinvolved interpersonal style was shown to be mediated in part by therapeutic alliance. This finding suggested that the alliance may play an important role in modifying the impact of client pre-treatment characteristics on outcome.

There may be client pre-treatment characteristics that are less amenable to modification through the alliance, and have a negative impact on the alliance. Rector and colleagues (1999) examined the extent to which pre-treatment depressogenic beliefs had an impact on client perception of the alliance. They found that higher Dysfunctional Attitude Scale scores were related to poorer ratings on Bond but not Goals or Tasks dimensions of the WAI, and that clients with perfectionistic standards and excessive need for approval had greater difficulty in forming trusting relationships.

MEASURING THE ALLIANCE

Horvath (1994b) has provided a comprehensive review of research into the working alliance. He noted that the vast majority of researchers have used one of five instruments to measure the alliance:

- California Psychotherapy Alliance Scales (Gaston & Marmar, 1994)
- Penn Helping Alliance Scales (Alexander & Luborsky, 1986)

- Therapeutic Alliance Scale (Marziali et al., 1981)
- Vanderbilt Psychotherapy Process Scale of Vanderbilt Therapeutic Alliance Scale (Hartley & Strupp, 1983)
- Working Alliance Inventory (Horvath & Greenberg, 1986).

Although Horvath (1994b) concluded that the considerable overlap between these measures at the global level suggests that they are measuring a similar basic concept, he noted that some instruments may be better predictors of outcome than others. Further, strength of prediction may vary according to the nature of the therapeutic approach under research and the varying sensitivity of the measures themselves. To date, the Working Alliance Inventory has been favoured by many researchers for measurement of alliance (Andrusyna et al., 2001; Raue et al., 1997; Rector et al., 1999; Soyguet et al., 2001), largely in recognition of its development as a pan-theoretical measure (Horvath, 1994a; Horvath & Greenberg, 1989). Safran and Wallner (1991) have found that the WAI can successfully predict client outcome, while Martin and colleagues (2000) found the WAI to be moderately related to outcome.

The strongest outcome-alliance correlations are found for client-reported outcome data (Horvath, 1994b). Further, evidence suggests that outcome may be best predicted by alliance measures taken early in therapy (Horvath, 1994b; but see Stiles et al., 1998 for findings that suggest the strength of this relationship may vary across time), and a majority of studies have examined the alliance during the second or third session (e.g. Andrusyna et al., 2001; Raue et al., 1997; Rector et al., 1999; Soyguet et al., 2001). In practice, it is advisable to measure the alliance throughout therapy, and in chapter 9 we discuss forms that can be used.

Practice implications

The therapeutic relationship can be viewed as a working alliance between therapist and client. A strong working alliance is characterised by mutual respect and liking, as well as agreement on the goals and tasks of therapy. Psychologists should take a proactive approach to managing strains and ruptures in the alliance; research indicates that successful management of these events is associated with better outcomes.

CONCLUSION

One of the most challenging yet rewarding tasks for a psychologist is establishing and maintaining a strong working alliance with a client. Substantial research can provide a useful guide to how you might create psychotherapy relationships that work. It is helpful to be aware that client differences can have an impact on the alliance, as well as therapist attributes and techniques. Maintaining a responsive therapeutic style that is flexible and reflective can enhance formation and management of the alliance. Strains and ruptures can occur, but if managed appropriately by the therapist, can enhance clinical outcomes.

Recommended reading

Gelso, C. J. & Hayes, J. A. (1998). *The Psychotherapy Relationship: Theory, Research and Practice*. New York: Wiley.

Gilbert, P. & Leahy, R. L. (eds) (2007). *The Therapeutic Relationship in the Cognitive Behavioral Psychotherapies*. East Sussex: Routledge.

Kahn, M. (1997). *Between Therapist and Client: The New Relationship* (2nd edn). New York: W. H. Freeman.

Norcross, J. C. (ed.) (2011). *Psychotherapy Relationships that Work: Evidence-Based Responsiveness* (2nd edn). New York: Oxford University Press.

Norcross, J. C. & Goldfried, R. (eds). (1992). *Handbook of Psychotherapy Integration*. New York: Basic Books.

Norcross, J. C. & Goldfried, M. R. (eds) (2005). *Handbook of Psychotherapy Integration* (2nd edn). Oxford: Oxford University Press.

Chapter 7

Theoretical frameworks: providing a rationale

INTRODUCTION

This chapter discusses the importance of using a theoretical framework in counselling practice, how to judge a good theoretical framework, the costs and benefits of eclecticism, and the difference between the practitioner's and the client's theoretical frameworks. This chapter also outlines common theoretical frameworks used in Australian counselling practice. There are over 360 forms of psychotherapy, with varying theoretical backgrounds; we will limit our discussion to the best-known and most fully investigated frameworks.

COMPONENTS OF A GOOD THEORETICAL FRAMEWORK

Imagine a friend coming to you in distress. What would you do to help? Now, consider why you responded in the way you did. If you chose to give advice on what to do, why did you do this? If you chose to simply sit and listen, why did you do that? In each case, your choice was most likely based on an idea of what your friend needed at the time to help her to feel better. If you gave advice, it was probably based on the idea that, if your friend were to follow your advice, she would be better off in dealing with the current crisis. If you chose to sit and listen, your decision was likely based on the idea that she would benefit just from talking about current problems.

What might you have done if you had not based your decision on some implicit theory of what your friend needed to feel better? What else would there be to base your decision on? You could simply have made your decision on a whim, but this is hardly a recipe for sound decision-making. You may have chosen to base your decision on what was best for you in that situation, trying to distract your friend so you didn't feel so anxious. Again, this is not the kind of decision that trained practitioners would applaud.

Without some concept of what might help someone such as a friend or client, there is little on which to base our decisions on what to do to help. This concept forms a component of what is referred to here as a *theoretical framework*.

A *theory* is an idea about the relationship between different observed phenomena that can be used to make predictions about future events. In counselling, theory guides the practitioner in understanding the client's presenting problems, and formulating a plan aimed at assisting the client to deal with them. In the absence of a theoretical framework, counselling becomes nothing more than a conversation. Even non-directive therapies such as person-centred therapy operate within a theoretical framework. These frameworks often specify that it is a certain element of the interaction (or *process*) with the therapist that leads to improvement in the client's situation. In some cases, it is suggested that it is simply the attitude of the therapist in the interaction with the client that is useful.

Good theoretical frameworks have common elements. It is the presence or absence of these elements that allows us to judge a sound theoretical framework from an unsound or poorly specified one.

Good theoretical frameworks

Good theoretical frameworks:
- are internally consistent
- are testable and falsifiable
- are logically consistent and sensible
- specify causal mechanisms for the client's problems
- specify corrective-change mechanisms
- suggest treatment methods
- are comprehensive
- allow predictions to be made about future events.

Internally consistent

Good theoretical frameworks are internally consistent. A good theoretical framework cannot contain ideas that are self-contradictory. Each element of the theory must be consistent with all other elements.

Testable and falsifiable

Good theoretical frameworks are testable and falsifiable. For a theoretical framework to be testable, its underlying premises must be open to evaluation. This does not necessarily mean open to evaluation in a laboratory setting, but there should be some means by which a sceptical observer could scrutinise information to judge that the theoretical framework was an accurate representation of reality. Similarly, the same sceptical observer should be able to test elements of a theoretical framework such that they can be shown to be untrue.

Assessment of elements of theoretical frameworks can come from peer-reviewed scientific literature. Recent researchers have defied previous critics of psychodynamic therapy by demonstrating experimentally the existence of unconscious processes and forgetting of distressing material (e.g. Anderson & Green, 2001). Sound theoretical frameworks, such as cognitive behavioural principles, are founded on a tradition of experimental investigation by which ideas are subjected to a hypothesis-testing approach that allows for testability and falsifiability.

Logical

Good theoretical frameworks are logical and sensible. Theories must rest within a perimeter that is bounded by scientific knowledge and understanding. Psychodynamic and solution-focused theories are logical and sensible, consistent with our current understanding of science and human psychology. Theories such as demonic possession and alien influence do not rest within what is described here as 'good' theory; these exist outside of what is usually defined as science.

Causally specific
Good theoretical frameworks specify causal mechanisms for the client's problem. Within a theoretical framework, there should be some explanation for why clients find themselves in their current situation. In interpersonal therapy, a client's problems are usually formulated in terms of key problem areas such as interpersonal deficits, role transitions, and grief. A practitioner operating from a cognitive-behavioural conceptualisation may formulate a client's depression as stemming from his or her deeply held beliefs about being a failure, beliefs that have been exacerbated by not having been promoted at work last month. From a psychodynamic viewpoint, an individual's overwhelming distress at the loss of an elderly friend may represent displacement of unresolved grief over a parent.

Corrective-change mechanisms
Good theoretical frameworks specify corrective mechanisms that would assist clients to deal with their problems. They suggest changes that need to occur for clients to resolve or better manage their difficulties. These changes are generally described in the same jargon and using the same principles as the causal mechanisms outlined above. In psychodynamic therapy, it may be thought that a client needs to experience a corrective emotional experience, in which the therapist displays ongoing positive regard for the client despite acknowledging difficulties in the relationship. From a cognitive-behavioural perspective, it may be thought that a socially anxious client needs to experience an increase in confidence in his or her ability (self-efficacy) to interact in social situations.

Treatment methods
Good theoretical frameworks suggest treatment methods. These may range from directive to non-directive, but are aimed at assisting clients with presenting problems and vulnerabilities that predispose them to future difficulties. All theoretical frameworks specify methods that may be used to assist clients, including humanistic schools. In the person-centred framework, change is thought to result from the experience of discussing problems with a genuine, empathic, interested therapist. In a cognitive framework clients may, in collaboration with the therapist, reflect on the nature and effect of their immediate automatic thoughts when they interact with a partner.

Comprehensive
A good theoretical framework is comprehensive. It does not need to explain all problems or challenges that clients may ever present with, but it must be amenable to use with more than a handful of clients. Of the theories reviewed here, the most comprehensive are the psychodynamic and cognitive-behavioural frameworks. Psychodynamic theory is founded upon an enormous body of theoretical literature specifying not only the causes and corrective-change mechanisms of severe psychopathology,

but most elements of human psychology and behaviour. The cognitive-behavioural framework has quickly grown to a rich body of conceptual and empirical literature, specifying etiological elements and treatment techniques for use with a wide array of presenting problems.

Predictive capacity

Good theoretical frameworks allow predictions to be made about a client's future behaviour, emotions, and experiences. Based on an understanding of how a problem has arisen and is maintained, therapist and client are able to speculate about likely future problems. The psychodynamic model allows the therapist to predict what sort of relationship is likely to develop between therapist and client. When such an interaction does develop, it can be highlighted to the client, and exposed to scrutiny.

Practitioners' theories and clients' theories

As we have shown in earlier chapters, it is not only the therapist who brings a theory of causation and a theory of corrective change to the consulting room. Clients come to therapy with an idea of how they arrived in their current situation, as well as how they might be assisted. In many cases, this theory will be consistent with that of the practitioner; at other times it will not. A client may attend a session with a person-centred therapist, for example, with the idea that discussing the problem with a neutral person may foster an understanding of his or her intense emotional experiences. In this case, client and therapist are likely to agree on what is needed for the client to benefit from counselling. Alternatively, the same therapist, seeing a client who demands clear advice on what to do about a problem, may experience difficulty.

Exercise 7.1

View Video 3, for an example of where a therapist adheres strongly to a theoretical approach.
1 What are the strengths and problems related to this adherence?
2 What would you do differently?

Eclecticism and theoretical purity

Some practitioners describe themselves as eclectic, meaning that they derive their counselling approach from a combination of several theoretical frameworks. Many practitioners use this to mean that they adopt different theoretical frameworks for different clients, and that this constitutes flexible treatment based on the individual needs of the client.

Another use of the term *eclectic* is where a practitioner combines concepts and ideas from different theoretical frameworks to work with a single client. Practitioners using such an approach may make the argument that this constitutes sound clinical judgment, and shows flexibility. Such eclecticism must be approached with caution.

In assisting a person to deal with anger problems, elements from cognitive-behavioural and psychodynamic frameworks may be incompatible. From a psychodynamic perspective, the cathartic release of anger may represent a valid strategy. A cognitive-behavioural view of anger would suggest that this is neither necessary nor desirable; instead, it focuses on releasing the physiological tension and ensuring that automatic thoughts do not inflate the anger response. Combining cognitive-behavioural and psychodynamic models results in a framework that is not internally consistent, having incompatible views about the same suggestion. Furthermore, choosing some elements and rejecting others from various frameworks may be difficult to justify beyond one's own preferences and prejudices.

Given this, it is important to address the ongoing dispute between using evidence-based treatment interventions and effective interventions. This dispute will be looked at in more detail later in this chapter. When discussing this point (and eclecticism in general), it is important to consider the evidence for common factors in psychotherapy, and how this might justify use of aspects of various forms of psychotherapy. See chapter 8 for a detailed discussion of this topic.

Theoretical frameworks used in Australia

In Australian practice, many theoretical frameworks are in common use. A comprehensive discussion of these is beyond the scope of this text. The dominant frameworks in Australian psychological practice are briefly outlined, with each theory examined with regard to its theory of causation and theory of corrective change. Each will also be examined in light of the components of a good theoretical framework. The benefits and drawbacks of each approach will be discussed, as well as the type of client for which each is suitable.

The theoretical frameworks we will outline are:

- Behaviour therapy
- Cognitive therapy
- Cognitive behavioural therapy
- Interpersonal therapy
- Psychodynamic therapy
- Systemic (family) therapy
- Person-centred therapy
- Motivational interviewing
- Solution-focused brief therapy
- Emotion-focused therapy
- Dialectical behaviour therapy
- Acceptance and commitment therapy
- Mindfulness and
- Positive psychology.

Behaviour therapy

Behaviour therapy focuses on changing undesirable behaviours. This type of therapy involves identifying problematic, maladaptive behaviours and replacing them with healthier types of behaviour. Behaviour therapy is also referred to as *behaviour modification*. Behaviour therapy is based on principles of behaviour that have been scientifically identified and established. Research has shown that as an individual practises new behaviours in response to familiar emotions or situations, the physical structure of the brain changes, developing new neural connections. Thus, with repetition, the new behaviour becomes an automatic response.

History and origin

Behaviour therapy is generally seen to have originated with three distinct groups: Wolpe's group in South Africa, Skinner's group in the United States, and Rachman and Eysenck in the United Kingdom. However, the first development may have been in a 1953 research project by Skinner and associates. Behaviour problems that are central to this type of therapy were viewed from different perspectives by each of these groups. Eysenck viewed interplay between personality, environment, and behaviour as the root of behaviour problems (Yates, 1970). Skinner's group focused on operant conditioning, which created a functional approach to assessment and interventions; this focused on contingency management (for example, token resistance and behavioural activation).

Theory

Classical conditioning and operant conditioning are the basic principles of behaviour therapy. *Classical conditioning*, or *respondent conditioning*, is a form of associative learning first demonstrated by Pavlov (1927; 1960). *Operant conditioning* is the use of consequences to modify the occurrence and form of behaviour, developed by Skinner. In terms of behaviour strategies used today, operant conditioning led to contingency management programs, which have been shown to be effective for a number of issues, even in adults suffering from schizophrenia (Paul & Lentz, 1977). Respondent conditioning led to the development of systematic desensitisation, as well as exposure and response prevention.

The behavioural framework specifies that behaviour is amenable to alteration through rewards. People attend work each day for many reasons: the reward of a challenging occupation, the reward of social contact, the reward of seeing the boss's smiling face, and maybe even the reward of financial remuneration. Children provide a clear example of the application of rewards to effecting a change in behaviour. The temptation of a chocolate can turn a child from monster to angel in the blink of an eye. Cognitive-behavioural practitioners refer to rewards as *reinforcers*, indicating that they reinforce, they increase the frequency of a target behaviour. *Positive reinforcement* occurs when a person's behaviour is rewarded through some positive consequence. *Negative reinforcement* occurs when a person's behaviour is rewarded through removal of an unpleasant state. In each case, according to the behavioural framework, the person would be more likely to behave similarly in future, under the same conditions.

Punishment occurs when a person is subjected to an aversive consequence, with the aim of reducing the likelihood of a behaviour being repeated. Punishment may occur through introduction of an aversive condition (positive punishment), or through removal of a pleasant condition (negative punishment). Punishment is less often used in adult counselling settings, although some behavioural practitioners may encourage a client to apply his or her own punishments (such as denying themselves dessert if they have not completed a certain task).

Application and techniques
Behavioural activation (BA) is a technique used in behaviour therapy. It focuses on introducing activities into a client's schedule to encourage the client to face situations the client may have been avoiding. This often results in a refocus on the client's goals in life. The technique involves exploring the person–environment interaction, and how it evolves, and identifying environmental triggers and maladaptive coping mechanisms responsible for maintaining depressive affect (Martell et al., 2001).

In this approach, depressive behaviour, such as social withdrawal and decreased motivation, is seen as a coping mechanism adopted to avoid situations that provide a decrease in positive reinforcement or an increase in control over unpleasant stimuli (Jacobson et al., 2001). *Avoidance strategies* are key in the BA treatment model; the first goal is to increase the client's awareness of events (either internal or external) that trigger a negative emotion or response and result in a pattern of avoidance (Cullen et al., 2006). The therapist can then help the client to reconnect with past healthy behaviours by developing alternative coping mechanisms.

On a basic level, teaching clients to *do* (take action), instead of thinking about doing, is the primary therapeutic technique in BA; therapists teach clients to consider the function of behaviours they engage in, and to make an informed choice about what to do next, whether to continue avoiding or engage in a different behaviour that improves mood. This should result in a decrease of avoidance behaviours.

Specific techniques used to accomplish a reduction in avoidance behaviours (Martell et al., 2001) include:

- rating mastery and pleasure of activities
- assigning activities to increase mastery and pleasure
- mental rehearsal of assigned activities
- role-playing behavioural assignments
- therapist modelling of behaviours
- periodic distraction from problems or unpleasant events
- mindfulness training or relaxation
- self-reinforcement
- skills training (such as sleep hygiene, assertiveness, communication, problem solving).

All these techniques can be used separately or in combination, depending on the client's needs. Keep in mind, however, that from a behavioural perspective, the ultimate aim of using any of these techniques is to reduce avoidance behaviours and reengage in healthy behaviours.

Interventions in behaviour therapy are based on functional analysis, and many problems have been functionally analysed, including intimacy in couples relationships (Cordova, 2003), forgiveness in couples (Cordova et al., 2006), chronic pain

(Sanders, 2006), substance abuse (Smith et al., 2004), depression (Kanter et al., 2005), anxiety (Hopko et al., 2006), and obesity (Stuart, 1967).

Benefits and limitations
The behaviourist perspective resulted in a number of effective techniques being used in psychotherapy. However, the behaviourist view of a person was completely objective. Behaviourists aspired to create a psychotherapy based exclusively on empirical grounds; the focus was on the observable behavioural response to a stimulus (Jacobsen et al., 2001). Thoughts and feelings, and how they are interpreted and experienced, were seen as irrelevant. Most modern psychologists agree that traditional behaviour therapy was not adequate, and that better methods of dealing with thoughts and feelings were needed.

Cognitive therapy
The goal of *cognitive therapy* is to help the client to overcome difficulties by identifying and changing dysfunctional thinking, behaviour, and emotional responses. This involves helping the client to develop skills for modifying beliefs, identifying distorted thinking, relating to others in different ways, and changing behaviours (Beck et al., 1979). Treatment is based on collaboration between client and therapist and on testing beliefs. Therapy may consist of testing assumptions made, and identifying how thoughts that are often unquestioned may be distorted, unrealistic, and unhelpful. Once thoughts have been challenged, feelings about the subject matter of these thoughts are more likely to change (Beck, 1991). Compared to other forms of psychotherapy, cognitive therapy is usually more focused on the present, more time limited, and more problem-solving orientated. Cognitive therapy has been scientifically tested, and found to be effective in clinical trials for a range of disorders (Butler et al. 2006).

Cognitive frameworks have added to the behavioural ideas discussed above, acknowledging the influence on behaviour of cognition. The cognitive framework specifies that early life experiences have a strong effect on later psychological development; practitioners are usually interested in how early experiences shape our beliefs about ourselves, others, and the world around us (that is, *core beliefs*, or *schemas*).

History and origin
Cognitive therapy was developed by Beck as a contrasting method to long-term psychodynamic approaches, which were based on gaining insight into unconscious emotions and drives. Beck concluded that the key to therapy was the way in which his clients perceived, interpreted, and attributed meaning in their daily lives (Beck, 1991), a process known as *cognition*. Similar ideas were developed by Ellis, but from a different perspective, which evolved into *rational emotive behaviour therapy (REBT)*.

The idea of an underlying schema about the self, the world, or the future was also introduced by Beck. A *schema* is a fundamental framework a person uses to process information. Taking depression as an example, Beck's theory proposes that a depressed individual acquires a negative schema of the world, either in childhood or adolescence. Schemas are acquired through loss of a parent, rejection by peers, criticism from teachers or parents, the depressive attitude of a parent, or other events. Negative schemas are activated when individuals encounter a situation that resembles the original conditions of the learned schema, even if it is only remotely similar (Neale & Davison, 2001).

Beck's theory also included a *negative triad*, which is made up of the negative schemas and cognitive biases of an individual. A cognitive bias is a view of the world, such as 'I never do a good job'. The triad is as follows: a negative schema helps give rise to the cognitive bias, and the cognitive bias helps fuel the negative schema (Neale & Davison, 2001).

Theory

Originally devised over three decades ago, the central idea of cognitive therapy is that a person's cognition is a mediator between stimuli (an event) and emotions (Beck, 1991); that is, a stimulus elicits a thought, belief, evaluation, or judgment, which gives rise to an emotion (as in Figure 7.1).

The importance of this is that an emotion is not caused directly by the stimulus itself; it is the person's evaluation or thought about the stimulus that elicits the emotional reaction (Ellis's ABC model is often used to describe the role of thoughts or attitudes that mediate events and emotional responses; Beck et al., 1979). There are two additional assumptions that underlie the cognitive approach to therapy: (a) the client has the capability to become aware of and change his or her thoughts; and (b) thoughts elicited by stimuli occasionally distort or otherwise fail to reflect reality. Thus, according to cognitive therapy, distorted thoughts about stimuli give rise to distressed emotions, which cause psychological distress (Beck, 1976/1979).

The theory is particularly well developed (and empirically supported) in depression. Depressed clients often experience a disproportionate number of automatic negative thoughts, even in response to stimuli that are intended as positive. For example, if a depressed client is told, 'Please stop talking in class', he might have the thought, 'Everything I do is wrong', or 'There is no point in trying'. Similarly, if the client is told he received top marks for an essay, the client might think, 'That was a fluke, I won't ever get a mark like that again'. Having these types of thoughts could lead to feelings of hopelessness or reduced self-esteem, which could maintain and even worsen the client's depression (Beck, 1976/1979).

Application and techniques

At the most basic level, the cognitive framework suggests that our current emotional state is influenced by our immediate thoughts and interpretations of current situations. These moment-to-moment cognitions are generally referred to as automatic thoughts, and much of the work done early in cognitive therapy attempts to help the

Figure 7.1 Beck's model of cognition as a mediator between stimulus and emotion

client to become more aware of these thoughts and the influence they have on feelings and behaviour.

The basic technique that is taught is *cognitive restructuring*, sometimes referred to as *cognitive reframing*. Clients are taught to become aware of their unconscious appraising and judging of events in their daily lives. The aim is to teach clients to consciously take charge of that appraisal process so they can draw unbiased conclusions (Beck et al., 1979). It is important to teach the steps outlined in the previous section (the ABC model) because: (a) the model sets the stage for interventions designed to help the client to identify and alter his or her interpretation process; and (b) it provides a sense of self-efficacy; it may be the first time the client has considered that he or she can have control over feelings.

The next step involves teaching the client how some core beliefs and automatic thoughts are biased and continue to create the same thought patterns in various situations (Trower et al., 1988). Examples of biased thinking patterns include *overgeneralisation* (mistakenly assuming that things are worse than they actually are), *selective attention* (paying attention to the single negative aspect of something, instead of concentrating on positive aspects), and *catastrophisation* (taking a small, usually insignificant negative event, and magnifying its importance tenfold, to believing it's 'horrible' and 'unbearable').

These errors in thinking are usually difficult to pinpoint because of their automatic nature. However, once they are written down, they become easier to recognise and analyse. The next step therefore involves a technique called *thought monitoring*, usually given to the client as homework (Trower et al., 1988). A thought-monitoring sheet is provided, on which the client is asked to record information relating to aspects of the ABC model:

1 *Write down the situation that triggered the negative thoughts.* The client make a brief note of the situation in the first column of the worksheet.
2 *Identify the moods and emotions felt in the situation.* In the second column, the client is asked to note the moods or emotions she felt. Moods can be explained as the emotions a person has about the situation, but are distinct from the thoughts that relate to the situation. Thoughts influence the client's mood, but are not the same as the client's mood.
3 *Write down automatic thoughts.* In the third column, the client writes down the thoughts that came into her mind when she felt the mood identified in column 2. The most distressing thoughts should be noted (*hot thoughts*).
4 *Identify the evidence* for *hot thoughts.* In the fourth column, the client writes down the objective evidence that supports the hot thoughts (the experiences and evidence that suggest the thoughts are true).
5 *Identify the evidence* against *hot thoughts.* In the next column, the client writes down the objective evidence that contradicts the hot thoughts. This is especially important, as it provides the client with the realisation that her thoughts may not necessarily be true, or that feared outcomes may not happen.
6 *Identify balanced thoughts about the situation.* At this point, the client should have gained clarity by taking both sides of the situation into consideration. It should

be possible for the client to take a more fair and realistic view of the situation. It may be necessary to discuss the situation further if uncertainty remains. This might be done through testing in some way, or by discussing it with other people to acquire their views. Then the client writes the more balanced view in column 6.

7 *Observe the current mood and decide what to do.* The client should have a clearer and less biased view of the situation, and should find that her mood has changed (and hopefully improved). The client then writes down the new mood in column 7. As a final step, the client decides what to do next; this could be doing nothing, or taking action to rectify the problem.

This is an example of *cognitive restructuring*. This exercise should be practiced repeatedly by a client, to increase awareness of cognitive errors and to reject them when they enter the mind. As the client makes fewer errors in thinking, the client should start to feel better.

Given that some people have difficulty learning to identify their automatic thoughts, and recognising the cognitive errors they make, or rewriting thoughts with the biases removed, implementing the thought monitor can be challenging. The therapist's main purpose is to help the client to practise recording thoughts, guiding the client through the process, to ensure the client is gaining the right perspective and restructuring cognitions in a helpful way.

Benefits and limitations

Cognitive therapy and cognitive restructuring have been shown to be beneficial for treating many psychological disorders. This technique empowers clients as they realise they can change the way they think, and change experiences, even though they do not actually change a situation. Furthermore, cognitive restructuring provides clients with a lifelong skill that they can draw on whenever emotional distress arises.

However, cognitive therapy has its limitations. The techniques in cognitive restructuring can be difficult to learn and utilise accurately for effective results; this creates further motivational problems for clients who wished to avoid therapy. There is also a question whether cognitive restructuring is in fact linked to change. In a comprehensive review of the benefits of challenging thoughts, Longmore and Worrell (2007) conclude that 'there is little empirical support for the role of cognitive change as causal in the symptomatic improvements achieved in CBT' (p. 173). This finding does not challenge the overall finding that cognitive therapy is helpful in many cases—it simply challenges the theory that claims that thought challenge is necessary. But, lending further weight to the possibility that cognitive therapy is not necessary to change cognitions is the finding that behavioural activation (BA), on its own, is just as effective as cognitive therapy in changing negative thinking (Jacobson et al., 1996).

In addition, learning how to use cognitive restructuring successfully takes practice, and given that therapy sessions usually occur only once a week, practice is assigned as homework. For clients to see gains from therapy, they need to fit this task into their schedule. Cognitive therapy is also limited to individuals who can grasp the connection between thoughts and emotions, and are able to identify thoughts that are involved in their distress. Thus, this technique may be difficult to implement with clients who have significant cognitive impairments, such as those with traumatic brain injury or organic brain disease. This is important to keep in mind when deciding on treatment options.

Cognitive behavioural therapy

The goal of *cognitive behavioural therapy (CBT)* is to help a client deal with problems concerning dysfunctional emotions, behaviours, and cognitions. The approach taken is goal orientated and systematic. CBT has been shown to be effective in treating a range of problems, including anxiety, mood, eating, substance abuse, personality, and psychotic disorders (Butler et al., 2006). Treatment for specific psychological disorders is often brief, direct, and time limited, incorporating specific techniques that are often manualised. CBT is used for individual clients and groups, and can be adapted for self-help. Within this framework, therapists can be more cognitive orientated (*cognitive restructuring*) or more behaviourally orientated (*in vivo exposure therapy*); some therapists choose to use interventions that combine both, such as *imaginal exposure therapy* (Foa et al., 2003).

History and origin

The contributions of Ellis and Beck from the 1950s to the 1970s, described previously, led to what can be classified as the first form of broad-spectrum CBT developed by Arnold Lazarus (Dobson & Dozois, 2001). Later, Lazarus expanded behavioural treatment to incorporate cognitive aspects (Lazarus, 1971); thus, cognitive and behavioural techniques were merged into CBT during the 1980s and 1990s. The development of treatment for panic disorder by Clark and Barlow was a major contribution to the success of combining these two frameworks (Rachman, 1997). Despite the theories having different foundations, common ground was found in their focus on the 'here and now', and on dealing with symptom management (Rachman, 1997).

Cognitive-behavioural practitioners have sought to validate experimentally its conceptual underpinnings and the effectiveness of its treatments. The health-care trend of evidence-based treatment is where specific treatments for symptom-based diagnoses are recommended, and CBT has been favoured over other approaches, such as psychodynamic treatments (Lambert, 2004).

Theory

A key feature of the cognitive-behavioural framework is how basic beliefs (core beliefs or schemas) influence how we perceive the world around us. For example, when Bob's partner asks for a divorce, he may observe this as evidence that he is completely unlovable, rather than making a more realistic assessment of his and his partner's contribution to their marital breakdown. Furthermore, the cognitive-behavioural framework specifies that clients may adopt compensatory behaviours in light of their core beliefs. For example, Bob may act in an overly submissive way towards his friends, with the unspoken idea that this will compensate for his unlovability.

The cognitive-behavioural framework meets all our criteria for what constitutes a good theory. It is an internally consistent, comprehensive, logical framework for understanding how clients arrived at their current situation, and specifies practical ideas for how to assist them.

Application and techniques

Although many techniques used in CBT are similar to those used in cognitive therapy and behavioural therapy, in CBT combinations of these techniques and additions are used. Techniques used to help a client to examine and change thoughts and behaviours include:

- *reality checking (testing cognitions):* the client is asked to provide support for certain thoughts or beliefs; often the client will be unable to produce objective evidence in support of assumptions, which leads to the client's beliefs and cognitions being exposed as invalid or faulty
- *cognitive rehearsal:* the client is asked to imagine a difficult situation from the past; the therapist then helps the client to cope with the problem so he or she can deal with a similar situation in future
- *relaxation techniques:* the therapist teaches the client a variety of methods to relax, to help lessen symptoms (for example, body sensations occurring from anxiety that mimic a heart attack and cause further anxiety)
- *modelling:* the therapist sets up role-plays in which the therapist models appropriate behaviour in a situation; the client can then reenact this behaviour in the problematic situation
- *in vivo exposure:* a basic concept in CBT treatment of anxiety disorders. The therapist sets up a hierarchy of anxiety-provoking situations that the client is gradually exposed to. This treatment is based on the theory that the fear response has been conditioned, and that avoidance reinforces and maintains that fear (Mowrer, 1960). Through exposure to the stimulus, the conditioned response can be unlearned, which is referred to as *extinction* and *habituation*.
- *journaling (or thought monitoring):* the client keeps a detailed diary of situations that arise in everyday life. The therapist informs the client of things to note, such as thoughts and emotions surrounding situations, and behaviours that accompany them. The therapist and client then review the journal together to discover maladaptive thought patterns and how these thoughts can have an impact on behaviour
- *homework:* in CBT, the therapist will often ask a client to do homework tasks, for the skills or insights obtained in session to be enhanced or practised and learned as a skill. These can include written tasks, relaxation techniques (often provided on a CD), or behavioural tasks that challenge biased expectations and assumptions.

Despite it being created as a brief intervention, CBT is generally not a speedy process. After a client eventually learns to recognise faults in his or her mental processes, and when they occur, it can still take considerable effort to exchange a maladaptive cognitive-affective-behavioural process for a more adaptive one.

Benefits and limitations

Cognitive behavioural therapy is most suitable for clients who are comfortable with introspection, who can easily use the method to explore their own psychology, and who have a belief in the basic theoretical approach. It may be less useful with a client who is not comfortable embracing these ideas, or who experiences distress of a more general interpersonal nature. If the distressing experience cannot easily be framed as interplay between thoughts, emotions, and behaviours within a given environment, then CBT may be more difficult.

CBT has been demonstrated to be an effective treatment method for many clinical disorders, personality conditions, and behavioural problems. It has been shown to be successful in treating generalised anxiety disorder, and possibly more effective than pharmacological treatments in the long term (Gould et al., 1997). There is evidence that CBT is effective in treating clinical depression (Cuijpers et al., 2008), schizophrenia (Wykes et al., 2008), in reducing use of benzodiazepine in treating insomnia (Morgan et al., 2004), and in treating a range of other conditions (Butler et al., 2006).

But, support for the hypothesised mediators of change in CBT is weak (e.g. Burns & Spangler, 2001; Morgenstern & Longabaugh, 2000), particularly in areas that are causal and explanatory rather than descriptive (Beck & Perkins, 2001; Bieling & Kuyken, 2003). As discussed earlier, this may be because the active ingredients in CT may not be effecting change after all (e.g. Longmore & Worrell, 2007). There can be little doubt about the effectiveness of BT, but there is some question about what cognitive therapy may add in CBT to the effects of behaviour therapy (e.g. Gortner et al., 1998).

Interpersonal therapy

Interpersonal psychotherapy (IPT) is a brief, time-limited form of psychotherapy, which can be delivered in a manualised form to individuals or groups. IPT posits that depression and other psychopathology results when clients are exposed to significant psychosocial stressors in the absence of sufficient psychosocial support (Parker et al., 2006).

History and theory

The origins of IPT are often traced to the work of Harry Stack Sullivan, although today's interpersonal therapy little resembles his method of therapy. A further key theoretical contribution to IPT comes from the attachment theory of John Bowlby (1960; 1980). At the heart of attachment theory is the idea that human beings have an inbuilt motive toward relating to others (Joyner & Coyne, 1999). While Bowlby and other attachment theorists emphasised the importance of early attachment experiences, the IPT model posits that need for attachment continues into our adult life. The current form of IPT, and the form used in the seminal NIMH study described below, was developed by Klerman and Weissman.

More recent use of the interpersonal process approach to psychotherapy was given impetus by inclusion of a manualised version of IPT in the large, multicentre trial of treatment of depression conducted by the US National Institute of Mental Health (NIMH) (Elkin et al., 1989). In this landmark research, treatments of depression with psychotherapy and pharmacotherapy were compared. Researchers were particularly interested in comparative effectiveness of pharmacological agents versus the fast-developing, increasingly popular cognitive therapies. Patients in the study were allocated to a pharmacological intervention (the antidepressant, imipramine) or to an active psychological intervention (cognitive therapy). The research team also included what they believed to be two placebos. The pharmacological placebo was a traditional inert tablet. Interpersonal therapy was chosen as the 'control' psychotherapy condition. To the surprise of the research team, there was little difference in effectiveness when cognitive therapy and interpersonal therapy were compared. This finding is often credited with providing the impetus for a wave of research that examined the effectiveness of interpersonal approaches for many different conditions.

Application in therapy

The client's problems are formulated in four major domains: interpersonal disputes, role transitions, grief, and interpersonal deficits and sensitivity. In its modern form, IPT has three phases: beginning phase, middle phase and focal problem areas, and final phase. These phases will be illustrated with treatment of depression.

The beginning phase (sessions 1–3) focuses on a psychological assessment of the client's interpersonal relationships, to assess suitability of IPT and to ascertain the focus of therapy. The client's problem (in this case, depression) is discussed as a medical condition in a social context. The focus of therapy is then established, depending on the client's interpersonal problems that seem most closely associated with the depressive symptoms presented (regarding both onset and maintenance). The goals of decreasing depressive symptoms and resolving interpersonal issues are explained to the client to provide positive expectations.

The middle phase and focal problem areas are dealt with in following sessions. Focal problem areas are obtained from research on determinants of health and disease, which have shown that interpersonal support has a protective function (Henderson et al., 1982). In addition, research has demonstrated the association between interpersonal adversity and depression (Brown & Harris, 1978).

The focal areas guide the therapeutic intervention in this phase of therapy by linking symptoms and affect to interpersonal events, changes, or isolation. Guidelines for the content of therapy have been provided by researchers (Klerman et al., 1984; Weissman et al., 2000) to frame life experiences into four main focal areas: personal disputes, role transitions, bereavement, and interpersonal deficits.

- *Interpersonal disputes* are situations in which the client and at least one other individual have incompatible expectations. When these incompatibilities are severe enough, they can cause significant emotional distress. The case of Sally (see case study 7.1) illustrates an interpersonal dispute where the client has felt increasingly isolated and despondent because of her partner's increasingly long working hours.
- *Role transitions* are situations where the client's life situation has changed significantly, and he or she is forced to adapt to these new circumstances. Such changes may include the start or end of a relationship, change in employment, or other major life events. When a client does not cope with the changes in her or his role, significant distress may result.
- In IPT, *grief* is defined as sense of loss experienced through bereavement.
- *Interpersonal deficits* describe a client's limited interpersonal relationships, in quantity or quality. These may arise out of problems with the client's interpersonal style, such as being aloof, or dependent.

The final phase of IPT, *termination*, aims to review and consolidate gains of therapy, as well as planning for possible future events to minimise relapse. At this stage, it is also important to discuss normal feelings of sadness compared with clinical depression. Ending therapy, and the inevitable feelings that follow, are openly discussed, and honest feedback is welcomed, enabling the therapist to extend treatment if it has failed to decrease depressive symptoms (Weissman et al., 2000).

Case study 7.1

Sally presented to a psychologist after becoming increasingly depressed. Over the previous six months she had grown increasingly dysphoric, since her move to a small town with her husband after his job transfer. Sally had given up her job to accompany her husband, and had not managed to find suitable work. She had become increasingly reliant on her husband for support, and had noticed that he had been spending increasingly long hours at work. She thought he seemed to find her depression difficult to deal with. Sally's frustration and isolation would often manifest as explosive arguments and outbursts.

Sally's therapist, working from the Interpersonal therapeutic model, conceptualised her problem using three of the four key components of IPT. First, he believed that Sally was in the midst of a significant interpersonal dispute with her husband. She believes he should support her through this difficult time, especially since she had given up her career to accompany him. The therapist assisted Sally in ways of communicating her distress to her husband, and ways of engaging with social activities in her new community. Sally's therapist saw that she was not effectively managing the role transition from full-time work in a large city to being an unemployed woman in a rural town. The therapist also saw that Sally's distress, and her increasing demand for support from her husband, was difficult for him, and Sally was assisted to learn different ways of interacting with him that would promote positive outcomes and make it more likely that he would reengage with her more fully.

Benefits and limitations
IPT attempts to address the four key areas outlined above. Clients may be taught communication and problem-solving skills to assist them in managing interpersonal disputes. They may be helped to develop skills to cope with changes brought about by role transitions. Bereaved, grieving clients are allowed to mourn their loss. Where clients have particular problem behaviours and interpersonal deficits, they are assisted to develop and enact different methods of interpersonal interaction.

IPT specifies causal mechanisms believed to underlie client problems, and corrective mechanisms that can be utilised by therapist and client. IPT is testable, and has been demonstrated to be effective for many psychological problems.

Psychodynamic therapy
The psychodynamic framework is the longest-utilised framework reviewed here, and has continued to evolve over more than a century. It emerged out of the psychoanalytic movement of the late nineteenth and early twentieth centuries, and was developed by Sigmund Freud and his contemporaries and followers. The long history of psychodynamic theoretical models has led to an ever-expanding number of different 'flavours' of psychodynamic thinking, with the generic term *psychodynamic*

used to refer to theoretical strands that are in some way associated with psychoanalysis (Leiper & Maltby, 2004). The models are diverse, with concepts changing over time. While each school has unique elements, they share key theoretical assumptions, outlined below. The psychodynamically-orientated reader may wish to consult with more specialist books that are aligned with their orientation (e.g. Malan, 1995; Luborsky & Crits-Christoph, 1998; McWilliams, 2004).

Theory

The term *psychodynamic* illustrates one of the main assumptions of this framework. It refers to the general perception that being human and living life is a difficult and demanding process; individuals are going to experience pain and internal conflicts. In response, individuals will develop strategies or defences (ways of behaving, perceiving, thinking, and feeling) to avoid suffering. An internal psyche is developed that helps to manage the struggles of life. The struggle is always dynamic and often unconscious—another key concept in psychodynamic theories.

Freud's conceptualisation of the psyche changed over the years. Initially, he devised a topographical model of the psyche, where the psyche consisted of *unconscious*, *preconscious*, and *conscious* elements (Robbins, 1989). He postulated that memories of traumatic events would be split off into the unconscious so that the individual would not have to experience the unpleasant affect associated with the memory. He went on to develop a structural-conflict model of the psyche, with the psyche consisting of three elements, the *id*, the *ego*, and the *superego*. Each element operates according to its own principles and goals. The *id* is the source of our drives and instincts, and operates according to the primary process, seeking instant gratification. The *superego* reflects moral and societal norms, often in conflict with the drive for instant gratification. The *ego* mediates between the two, capable of delaying gratification, and deploying a collection of defence mechanisms to help to manage conflicts between the drives of the id and the expectations of the superego.

It is the constant movement of these intrapsychic forces which is captured in the term *psychodynamic*. Building on this structural model, Freud went on to outline six stages of psychosexual development, oral, anal, urethral, phallic, latent, and genital (Kaplan & Sadock, 1988), that individuals need to resolve. He postulated that psychopathology emerged when a person did not resolve a developmental stage. Erik Erikson expanded this idea, incorporating intrapersonal and interpersonal stages of development across the life span (McWilliams, 2004; Sharf, 2004).

The models of understanding individuals' internal worlds that evolved from these early theories can be divided into *conflict models* (one-person psychology), *deficit models* (two-person psychology), *interpersonal models*, and *brief-therapy models*.

- Within *conflict models*, personality organisation and development, as well as psychopathology, result from conflicts between internal aspects of the psyche or different parts of the self. This would incorporate *drive* (Freud) and *ego psychology* (Erikson) theories.
- *Deficit models* focus on how the relational needs of a person may not have been met, with individuals developing internal representations of others and self within the context of their early relational experiences. *Object relations* and *self-psychology* are two of these models.

- The *interpersonal approach* (Sullivan) focuses on interpersonal relations, commencing between parent and child, whereby social interactions can result in faulty self-systems.
- *Brief-therapy models* tend to focus on techniques and processes for providing brief psychodynamic therapy, and may incorporate structural, object relations, or self-psychology theories to conceptualise an individual's difficulties (e.g. Strupp & Binder, 1984; Sifneos, 1979; Malan, 1963; Davanloo, 1980; de Jonghe, 1994).

Common to all these models is the idea that early environment and perceptions and experiences of others will have an impact on formation of a person's personality, strengths, and vulnerabilities. Difficulties, or psychopathology, arise when a person's (normally unconscious) attempts to avoid distress, anxiety, and pain prove ineffective, unhelpful, or self-limiting. Further, it is postulated that we are also, unconsciously, constantly influencing each other (Leiper & Maltby, 2004).

Application in therapy

Given the various theoretical approaches, there are numerous schools of treatment, and treatment methods can vary. A common aim, however, is to enhance clients' insights and understandings of their inner world, their (unconscious) patterns of thinking, feeling, and relating, and how these result in relationship difficulties and symptoms. The therapeutic relationship is considered to be the main tool of therapy, by providing a corrective emotional experience (learning new ways of relating, personality reorganisation, and personal growth) (Teyber, 2006; Teyber & McClure, 2010; McWilliams, 2004; Driessen et al., 2010). Some of the techniques used are free association, dream analysis, interpretation, interpretation of transference and/or countertransference, and projective identification.

Transference is the reemergence in the client of previous interpersonal feelings and behaviours, but focused on the therapist. A young male patient, for example, may begin to experience a sense of maternal reverence for an older female therapist, 'transference' of his feelings for his mother to the therapist. When such a transference emerges, it is often thought to reflect the nature of the client's current interpersonal problems. By examining these feelings and actions related to earlier, out-of-therapy relationships, therapist and client can 'work through' these feelings, allowing the client to resolve them, dealing with them quite differently from how he would have dealt with them in the past. When a client experiences a corrective emotional experience, the transference is played out with the therapist in a way that is new for the client.

Shedler (2010) notes there are seven types of interventions or processes specific to psychodynamic therapy that commonly occur in sessions:

- identification and expression of difficult emotions, with the aim of encouraging emotional insight
- exploration of behaviours related to the avoidance of painful emotions or cognitions; that is, identifying and exploring defence strategies and resistance
- identification and discussion of repeated themes and patterns
- linking current patterns of behaving and relating to early developmental experiences
- exploration of interpersonal and attachment experiences

- utilisation of the therapeutic relationship to create change and flexibility, through examining transference and countertransference, and creating a corrective emotional experience
- utilisation of all aspects of the client's experience, including dreams and fantasies, to help create insight and understanding of the client's experience and perceptions of the world.

Benefits and limitations

Psychodynamic models offer an internally consistent, logical, framework for understanding client problems and other forms of psychopathology. They are comprehensive, as evidenced by application of psychodynamic principles to fields such as literature, jokes, and the arts. They specify clear corrective-change mechanisms, with treatment methods that are theory-consistent.

Some have criticised psychodynamic models as being untestable and unfalsifiable. Recent developments in experimental research into unconscious processes, repression, and motivated forgetting (Anderson & Green, 2001) are challenging these critics. Also, much research shows that psychodynamic therapy is effective, but there may be 'biases in the dissemination of research findings' (Shedler, 2010, p. 98). The Psychodynamic Diagnostic Manual (PDM Task Force, 2006) provides a comprehensive section on the current research status and findings of psychodynamic psychotherapies.

Systemic (family) therapy

Family therapy, also referred to as *couple and family therapy* and *family-systems therapy*, is a form of psychotherapy in which therapists work with families and couples to nurture change and development. The main aim of family therapy is to improve communication between family members, and to help them solve family problems. Other goals include helping family members to understand and handle special situations (such as death, serious illness, or child and adolescent issues), and create a better functioning home environment. Where one member of a family has a serious illness, family therapy can educate families about the illness and work out problems associated with care of the family member. Family therapy may be chosen when a child or adolescent has a personality, anxiety, or mood disorder that impairs family and social functioning. Family therapy may also be used when there is a mix of races, cultures, or religions within a family, or when a family includes a same-sex couple (Heater, 2003). Forms of family therapy share a belief that, regardless of the origin of a problem and of whether the clients consider it an 'individual' or a 'family' issue, involving families in solutions is often beneficial.

History and theory

In the early years of family therapy, the family was defined by many clinicians in a traditional and narrow way: a family comprised parents and children. As the field evolved, 'family' became defined in terms of supportive, long-term roles and relationships between people who may or may not be related by blood. In the mid 1950s, the field was stimulated by anthropologist Gregory Bateson, and colleagues, who introduced ideas from cybernetics and general systems theory, with a strong focus on communications, into social psychology and psychotherapy (Guttman, 1991; Becvar & Becvar, 2008).

Several distinct forms of family therapy had emerged by the mid 1960s, with groups strongly influenced by cybernetics and systems theory developing into strategic therapy. *Structural family therapy* was developed soon after by Salvador Minuchin. The *Milan systems model* evolved as well. Subsequently, these would develop into *systemic therapy* (Sholevar, 2003). By the late 1970s, the original models had undergone a number of revisions, under the weight of clinical experience, such as treatment of serious mental disorders. This also led to a dilution of the theoretical purism that was previously maintained; that is, strict distinctions between various schools of family therapy began to soften, with a move towards integration and eclecticism (Sholevar, 2003; Barker, 2007; Nichols & Schwartz, 2006a).

From the mid 1980s until the present, family therapy has taken in diverse approaches that reflect parts of the original forms, while drawing on other theories and methods from individual psychotherapy. Some examples are brief therapy, structural therapy, solution-focused therapy, narrative therapy, a range of cognitive and behavioural approaches, psychodynamic approaches, and emotionally-focused therapy (e.g. Denborough, 2001; Dattilio, 1998). Many therapists use techniques from various areas, and claim to be 'eclectic'; their choices depend on personal inclinations, as well as on client needs. There is a movement toward a single 'generic' family therapy that seeks to incorporate the best of accumulated knowledge in the field, and can be adapted to many contexts (Lebow, 2005).

Application and techniques

Family therapy uses a range of approaches, including psycho-education, relationship education, systemic coaching, systems theory, and reality therapy. A family therapist usually meets several members of a family at the same time. This can be beneficial for both family and therapist, as it allows both to observe and to become aware of interaction patterns between family members. It can also provide awareness of the ways in which each family member perceives mutual relations.

Systemic therapy approaches problems practically rather than analytically; that is, it does not attempt to determine past causes, and it does not assign diagnosis (who is sick?; who is a victim?; Crago, 2006). Rather, systemic therapy seeks to identify stagnant patterns of behaviour in a family, and to address those patterns directly, irrespective of cause. In this way, systemic therapists are relational therapists; they are interested in what goes on between individuals rather than within one or more individuals. Depending on the conflicts at issue and progress of therapy, a therapist may focus on analysing previous instances of conflict, and reviewing a past incident, suggesting alternative ways in which family members might have responded to one another (Nichols & Schwartz, 2006b).

Problems are treated by changing the way the system works rather than by trying to fix a specific member. Family-systems theory is based on several major concepts (Barnes, 2004; Landau, 2004):

- *the identified patient (IP)*: the member of the family who presents with the symptoms that have given cause for treatment; often the IP is a child or adoles-

cent. Family therapists use this concept to stop the family from focusing all attention on that individual and avoiding problems in the rest of the family system

- *homeostasis (balance):* the concept of the family resisting change within therapy, as it seeks to maintain its organisation and functioning over time. This concept can be used by the therapist to explain why a certain symptom of the family has arisen, the reason for a member becoming the IP, and the likely results of the family starting to change
- *the extended family field:* the family inclusive of the immediate family, grandparents, and other relatives. The therapist uses this concept to explain the transmission of problems, attitudes, and behaviours between generations
- *differentiation:* the ability of each family member to stay emotionally connected to the family while maintaining a sense of self. Within a healthy family, members differentiate themselves, yet feel they are able to maintain support from the family
- *triangular relationships:* the concept that emotional relationships in families are usually triangular; that is, if there is a problem between two family members, a third family member will be brought into the conflict in an attempt to diffuse it. Triangular relationships often maintain homeostasis. Examples of triangles include a child and the parents, two children and one parent, or, husband, wife, and in-law (Barnes, 2004; Landau, 2004)

Benefits and limitations

A risk with family therapy is that individuals or relationships with rigid personality defences that were fragile before therapy can become unsettled and more fragile during therapy. Intensive family therapy may also be difficult for family members with psychological disorders; these might need to be addressed in individual therapy prior to family therapy. Family therapy may be especially difficult and stressful for children and adolescents, who may not fully understand interactions that occur.

Another limitation of this approach is its lack of suitability across disorders. Some families are not considered suitable for family therapy: families in which one, or both, of the parents is psychotic, or has been diagnosed with antisocial or paranoid personality disorder; families whose cultural or religious values are opposed to or suspicious of psychotherapy; and families with members who cannot participate in treatment sessions because of physical illness or similar limitations. However, in favourable circumstances, systemic therapy can induce greater insight, increased differentiation of individual family members, improved communication within the family, softening of previously automatic behaviour patterns, and resolution of the problem that led the family to seek treatment. Family therapy can also be helpful to stepfamilies, especially for children and adolescents who struggle to adjust.

Person-centred therapy

Person-centred therapy (PCT) is a psychotherapeutic approach where the therapist has a non-directive role, and most responsibility for the treatment process is placed on the client (Rogers, 1942). This therapy has two main goals, an increase in self-esteem and greater openness to experience. Person-centred therapy aims to foster a number of related changes: increased understanding of the self; a decrease in defensiveness, guilt, and insecurity; a decrease in the gap between the ideal and the actual self; more positive and comfortable relationships with others; and an increased capacity to experience and express feelings when they occur.

History and theory

PCT emerged from the humanistic–existential psychology movement of the mid twentieth century. It is most often associated with the work of Carl Rogers, and takes a positive view of an individual's ability to enact change in his or her own life (McLeod, 1993). The idea of a non-directive approach, however, appeared contradictory, given that a 'relationship' between client and therapist infers that influence is generated by both. Some evidence suggested that particular client statements may still have been subtly reinforced by therapists using this technique, while other statements were not given encouragement or approval (Traux, 1966); thus, the idea of non-directive therapy faced difficulties.

Despite these findings, there was research to suggest that change was initiated in clients by this therapy. The theory behind PCT evolved from there, incorporating ideas spawned from the inherent contradiction of a non-directive approach, which resulted in a new model of the therapeutic relationship. This included conditions that Rogers (1957) referred to as being 'necessary and sufficient'.

These conditions are:

- *empathy:* the client's 'inner world' must be understood by the therapist, as if it were his or her own, and the therapist must communicate this understanding to the client
- *congruence:* the therapist must be transparent and genuine with the client
- *acceptance (or unconditional positive regard):* despite any behaviours the client might engage in, the therapist should always accept or value the client as a person (Rogers, 1957).

The basis of PCT, formulated by Rogers, was trust in the client's humanity, as well as belief in self-actualisation in humans. It is this aspect, in particular, that is seen as a client's motivation for change. Given that the person-centred approach values the client's view, rather than that of an outside expert (Bozarth, 1990), clients determine the pace at which therapy moves, and are encouraged to pursue change by their own methods. The view of the external force (that is, the therapist) is irrelevant in therapy; the therapist is only there to facilitate the actualisation process of the client. The basic task of the therapist is to listen respectfully to and gain an understanding of the client's problems, to help clarify feelings and thoughts as they are expressed.

Application of theory to therapy

A key construct from the person-centred theoretical model is that of *genuineness and congruence*. For effective growth to occur, the client must experience the therapist as a genuine individual, expressing his or her honest feelings in reaction to the topic of discussion. Therapists working from the person-centred model attempt to maintain congruence between their inner feelings and their expression to the client. Emotional reactions, including negative ones, are often revealed to the client, in a timely, considered manner.

Unconditional positive regard is a second key construct of person-centred therapeutic approaches. Therapists believe that change occurs when clients experience the unconditional positive regard of the therapist. When individuals do not feel judged, despite exposure of their weaknesses and flaws to the therapist, it is possible for psychotherapeutic change to occur. Although they may find it difficult at times, person-centred therapists attempt to maintain this unconditional positive regard for their clients throughout therapy.

The therapist's ability to provide an interaction founded on accurate empathy is also a key element in person-centred approaches to counselling. The therapist maintains an effort to understand the client, and empathise with his or her experiences. An experience of accurate empathic contact with a person-centred therapist is thought to promote increased self-understanding. It allows constructive personality change to take place, as the client experiences increasing congruence between her or his self-perceptions and reality.

Unlike some other models of counselling practice, PCT focuses on the relationship between client and therapist as the agent of change. Whereas in other styles of therapy, such as cognitive behaviour therapy, emphasis is placed on the *content* of treatment (the material that is discussed and the skills that are learned), PCT asserts that the *process* is more important; what is discussed between therapist and client matters less than that the relationship between them has the key characteristics outlined above, accurate empathy, unconditional positive regard, and congruence and genuineness. Rogers and others from the person-centred school of counselling argue that, as long as these conditions are present, an individual will naturally move towards positive personality change. It is this strong belief in a person's ability to enact change in his or her own circumstances, and utilise his or her own resources, that colours the person-centred approach.

The person-centred approach to treatment focuses on experience of an equal relationship with a therapist who is genuine, and gives unconditional positive regard. Therapists assert that they do not need to arm themselves with an arsenal of therapeutic techniques and skills. Instead, the experience of such a relationship is sufficient to effect therapeutic change.

Benefits and limitations

The person-centred model has many of the characteristics of a good theoretical model. It is internally consistent, with the core concepts of congruence, unconditional positive regard, and accurate empathy all fitting with a belief in an individual's inherent ability to improve his or her situation. These key components are also consistent with a process-focused approach in which interaction between therapist and client is the vehicle for change. The tenets of the person-centred approach are amenable to testing, and there is considerable research evidence that attests to the importance of the therapeutic relationship in promoting change (e.g. Lambert, 2004). From the humanistic philosophical perspective, the concepts that underpin the person-centred approach to counselling are logical, rational, and sensible.

Person-centred approaches to therapy specify clear mechanisms that are thought to be associated with therapeutic effects. These mechanisms are process focused, in that the interaction and experience of the client in sessions is thought to promote use of their own resources to deal with their situation. From this perspective, the

person-centred approach specifies treatment methods, such as providing unconditional positive regard and genuineness.

Although Rogers asserted that the person-centred approach provided necessary
and sufficient conditions for positive change for all psychological problems, emerging research questions the comprehensiveness of this approach. A key factor that
limits comprehensiveness of the person-centred orientation is the belief that all clients have within themselves the resources to solve their problems. While this may
be the case for many individuals, there is considerable evidence that some presenting problems benefit from more specific, directive intervention. Some anxiety conditions, such as specific phobias and obsessive-compulsive disorder, are examples;
specific behavioural strategies are known to improve outcome beyond a non-directive person-centred method. Person-centred counselling approaches are also somewhat limited in their ability to make predictions about how an individual's problems
may recur in future.

Motivational interviewing

Motivational interviewing (MI) (Miller & Rollnick, 2002) refers to a collection of therapeutic techniques designed to move clients towards readiness to change. Rather
than specifying mechanisms of change, MI aims to increase motivation to change,
or to shift clients to a state of readiness to change. The MI approach is based on a
conceptualisation in which motivation, rather than being a permanent trait, is a
variable that changes over time and is open to influence. MI aims to increase an
individual's commitment to change by identifying and resolving ambivalence.

The MI approach was devised for working with individuals with problematic
alcohol use. It was developed as a precursor module run with clients prior to standard treatment of alcohol abuse, with the aim of reducing dropout and non-adherence.
MI has since been applied in a range of conditions, including smoking cessation,
eating disorders, exercise, and obsessive-compulsive disorder (Slagle & Gray, 2007).

MI is based on a transtheoretical model of change developed by Prochaska and
DiClemente (1982). In this model, a series of stages of change, from pre-contemplation to permanent change, are described. An individual's readiness to make change
is the result of movement along this pathway. An individual with an alcohol-use
problem, for example, may begin with no concern for or recognition of the problematic effects that drinking is having on his life (the *pre-contemplation stage*). The
contemplation stage follows, when the individual begins to recognise the problematic nature of his drinking, and to consider that he may wish to reduce his drinking. After a period of time, the problem drinker may make a decision that he needs
to reduce alcohol consumption (*determination*). When the individual begins a period
of abstinence, he is described as having entered the *action stage*. The *maintenance
stage* persists as long as the individual does not relapse, with hope of permanent
exit from the cycle. The *stages of change model* is depicted in figure 7.2.

MI utilises a number of approaches to facilitate a client's movement towards
action. These are listed in the first edition of *Motivational Interviewing* (Miller & Rollnick, 1991): giving advice, removing barriers, providing choice, decreasing desirability, practising empathy, providing feedback, clarifying goals, and active helping.

In the second edition of their text, Miller & Rollnick (2002) advocate 'less emphasis on techniques of motivational interviewing and ever greater emphasis on the

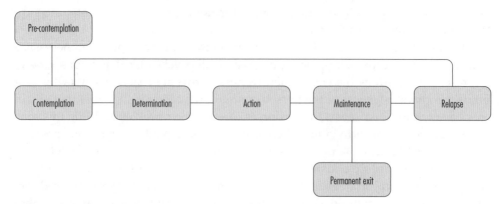

Figure 7.2   Prochaska and DiClemente's (1982) transtheoretical model of change

fundamental spirit that underlies it' (p. 33). The authors delineate three components of the 'spirit' of motivational interviewing: collaboration, evocation, and autonomy.

• The concept of *collaboration* in MI refers to the style of interaction between therapist and client; together they explore motivational factors, rather than the therapist providing directive instructions or information. The aim is to create interaction that is 'conducive but not coercive to change' (Miller & Rollnick, 2002, p. 34).
• *Evocation* in MI refers to the idea that the therapist's role is to draw motivation from the client, rather than the therapist 'causing' motivation to increase. The therapist aims to help the client to find his or her own reasons and motives, and enlist these to change behaviours.
• *Autonomy* refers to the principle that the client is free to decide to make whatever changes he or she wishes. Autonomy also means that clients are just as free to decide to not make changes in their behaviours. Decisions to make changes are made by the client, not imposed by the therapist.

Because of its transtheoretical nature, MI has been applied as an adjunct to other forms of psychological intervention. MI has been used to enhance motivation in clients to better enable them to participate in and benefit from the other intervention. One example of this has been Slagle & Gray's (2007) advocacy of MI to help manage the ambivalence that often characterises a client's feelings about exposure therapy for anxiety disorders. Motivational-interviewing principles, techniques, and skills have been increasingly adopted by therapists of many orientations.

Solution-focused brief therapy
Solution-focused brief therapy (SFBT) aims to assist clients to shift focus from genesis of their problems toward current therapy goals. A key difference between the solution-focused theoretical model and the other schools discussed here is that solution-focused work is exclusively orientated toward the present and future. Solution-focused therapists forego the extensive history-taking that is a key feature of all other schools discussed here. Solution-focused therapists see a major part of their role as assisting clients to move away from a focus on their problems towards a search for solutions. Like person-centred styles of counselling, the solution-focused model takes an optimistic view of human capacities.

Origin

The origin of solution-focused therapy lies in interest that researchers had in 'inconsistencies' within problem behaviour; the approach was subsequently developed by de Shazer and colleagues (1986). Practitioners believe that people have an inherent ability to work towards solutions to their problems. They also recognise there may be numerous ways to solve problems, some of which may be more suited to some clients than to others. Clients, it is thought, are the best judges of what is likely to be helpful to them. In addition, the more clarity a client has regarding his or her goals, the more likely it is that the client will achieve them (de Shazer, 1988, 1994; Berg, 1991).

History and theory

SFBT evolved theoretically from problem-focused therapy; however, it was based on the belief that the solution should be dealt with rather than the problem. The approach is generally interactional, where questions are typically asked in a way that provides answers about how key individuals interact. In this way, the therapist acquires an interactional perspective about the concerns and wishes of the client by seeing her in a context of her relationships with others (Saunders, 1998). The actual problem a client might have becomes ever less important in the interviewing process (George et al., 1999). Rather, all attention is focused on deriving a representation of the solution, as well as identifying the strengths and resources the client has to achieve the solution (Iveson, 2002). At times, a client is unable to imagine changing her life because of the degree of difficulty she is experiencing. A therapist can investigate how the client is coping with the difficulty, and how she is surviving despite the hardship (Letham, 2002).

Application and techniques

Solution-focused therapists encourage clients to examine areas of their current situation that are being effectively dealt with. Through focusing on positive elements, clients are assisted to use this knowledge to help resolve their difficulties. Where a client's current actions are not effective in managing problems, the therapist encourages the client to experiment with new solutions, and to see any positive consequences of these changes. Small steps towards a solution are the method by which larger, seemingly insurmountable, problems are solved.

Solution-focused therapists use many techniques to keep clients' attention on effective ways to manage their difficulty. A key strategy is to find exceptions to the current problem through asking *exception questions*. These questions are designed to demonstrate to clients that their problems are not omnipotent, by drawing their attention to situations where the problem has not occurred, or has been effectively managed.

Another specific questioning strategy used by solution-focused therapists is the *miracle question*. Clients are asked what they would be doing differently if their current core problem were instantly, miraculously, solved. Clients are hereby helped to examine actions that would be consistent with solving the problem, and to enact these now.

The solution-focused framework contains many of the elements of a good theoretical model. The theoretical underpinning of solution-focused brief therapy is internally consistent, being based on a particular set of ideas about how best to enact change. The theoretical model is not as elaborate or as comprehensive as some others, such as psychodynamic or cognitive-behavioural models, but it is logical and sensible. It specifies how clients become stuck in looking at the nature of their problem, rather than looking at solutions to it, and it specifies how change can be effected.

Emotion-focused therapy

Emotion-focused therapy (EFT) is based on the principles of attachment theory, and is used with individuals, couples, and, more recently, families. EFT proposes that emotions have an innately adaptive potential that, if activated, can help clients to change problematic emotional states or unwanted self-experiences. EFT advocates exploring the range of emotions associated with traumatic events, and begins a process whereby a negative feeling is exchanged for another, often an opposite emotion (Stiell et al., 2007). It involves managing the emotions aroused by a stressor, enabling the individual to maintain affective equilibrium (Johnson, 2002).

From the EFT perspective, emotional change occurs by means of four *stages* or *processes* (Greenberg & Watson, 2005).

- The first stage aims to increase the client's awareness and acceptance of feelings
- The second stage incorporates *regulation* into the process of healing, as the client must learn to tolerate emotions and control any self-destructive behaviours that seriously interfere with daily life. Thus, the aim is to learn healthy methods of coping with one's feelings, rather than allowing them to spin out of control. This stage allows the last two processes—*reflection* and *transformation*—to occur
- The third stage, *reflection*, helps clients to reflect on the emotions or feelings elicited, and to explore the journey they have gone through in order to accept these feelings and be able to control their self-destructive tendencies
- The fourth stage is *transformation of emotions*, which is achieved through creating a new adaptive emotional state that the client accesses within the session. EFT postulates that it is important for the client to really experience a maladaptive emotion (such as shame or guilt) in order to transform it.

Theory and origin

EFT is based on *attachment theory*, developed by Bowlby 50 years ago. Studies of babies and children who were orphaned in the Second World War led Bowlby to conclude that all humans innately yearn for trust and security, or attachment (Bowlby, 1988). It was argued that children have needs for attachment with at least one parent, and adults have these needs with a romantic partner.

It is postulated that in stressful situations an infant searches for closeness with an attachment figure. Adults who provide sensitivity and responsiveness to the infant in social interactions, and who are consistent caregivers for the infant between approximately six months and two years of age, are the persons with whom the infant will become attached. Within the later part of this period, *attachment figures*—familiar people—become a secure base for the child, which he or she can use to explore from and return to. It is the responses of parents, or attachment figures, that develop the patterns of attachment the child will form. In turn, these will lead to the child's internal working models—a mental representation of attachment relationships—that guide feelings, thoughts, and expectations in later relationships (Bretherton & Munholland, 1999).

A *secure attachment* is a close and trusting relationship, within which each person's valid dependency needs for contact and comfort, acceptance and safety, are fulfilled (Cassidy, 1999). In EFT, negative behaviours that occur between partners in conflict are viewed as justifiable and valid responses to frustration that occurs from the need for a secure attachment. Thus, if individuals are not able to get an attachment figure to respond to them and their needs, they will engage in whatever behaviours are necessary to solicit a response (even if it is a negative behaviour that leads to a negative response) (Cassidy, 1999). Similarly, a child who feels that his or her parents are not being protective may become defiant, clingy, or withdrawn.

It follows that, when there is a conflict between partners, the secure attachment is lost. If one partner is unsupportive or emotionally unavailable, the other partner might feel insecure. Any situation that might break attachment between partners is referred to in EFT as an *attachment injury*. If these injuries are unresolved, EFT postulates that the couple will move towards a distressed state that is characterised by a negative fight cycle, whereby one partner pursues while the other withdraws (Johnson & Sims, 2000). In the distressed state, partners often see each other as the cause of distress. EFT theory explains the negative fight cycle as a well-intentioned but misguided attempt by one partner to establish a secure attachment. EFT sees the negative cycle as the partners' stress reaction to fears of loss of intimacy and security. The goal is to aid the couple to regain the secure attachment.

Techniques and application
EFT can be used with individuals and, increasingly, with couples. The following section focuses on the goals of EFT specifically for work with couples. The goals are: to expand and reorganise key emotional responses; to create a shift in partners' interactional positions and develop new cycles of interaction; and to foster a secure bond between partners. EFT is collaborative, combining experiential and Rogerian techniques with structural systemic interventions. EFT focuses on experiential and systemic processes that encompass the following principles: present experience, primary emotions, process patterns, and positions.

- *Present experience:* it is important to deal with the past when it is re-experienced in the present, in order to validate how clients coped and survived. Subsequently, when emotion is re-experienced, it is in the present, and the focus shifts to current positions or patterns
- *Primary emotions:* it is essential to validate and move from secondary to primary emotions, to stay with emotions, and to create a safe haven. The therapist should then help organise the emotion associated with a past experience so that the client can engage in the 'here and now'
- *Process patterns:* the aim is for the therapist to explore individually how each person is processing emotions, thoughts, and past experiences in the moment: 'What happens…? Then what…? Then what?'

- *Positions*: exploring the position that each partner is taking in the relationship, then working towards creating new positions and patterns between them.

Key moves and moments in the change process have been delineated into nine steps within three stages-of-change events. Stage 1 focuses on de-escalation; stage 2 deals with restructuring the bond; stage 3 aims for consolidation.

Stage 1: De-escalation

In stage 1, the aim is to identify negative cycles and attachment issues, access underlying attachment emotions, and frame the problem cycle and attachment needs or fears. Thus, Stage 1 encompasses the first four steps of the change process:

- *Step 1:* Identify the relational conflict issues between partners. Create an alliance and delineate conflicts in the core struggle
- *Step 2:* Identify the negative interaction cycle
- *Step 3:* Access unacknowledged emotions underlying positions in the cycle
- *Step 4:* Reframe the problem in terms of the cycle, underlying emotions, and attachment needs.

Stage 2: Restructuring the bond

In stage 2, implicit needs, fears, and models of the self are accessed, and acceptance of others is promoted. In addition, the therapist structures emotional engagement, which is achieved through the client's expression of attachment needs. Stage 2 includes steps 5 to 7:

- *Step 5:* Promote the partner's identification with disowned attachment needs and aspects of the self; integrate them into relationship interactions
- *Step 6:* Promote acceptance by each partner of the other's experience
- *Step 7:* Facilitate expression of needs and wants to restructure interaction; create bonding events.

Stage 3: Consolidation

In stage 3, new positions or cycles are demonstrated through enactments, new stories are produced of the problems and how to repair them, and new solutions are developed to pragmatic issues. Stage 3 entails the last two steps for change:

- *Step 8:* Facilitate emergence of new solutions to old problems
- *Step 9:* Consolidate new positions and cycles of attachment behaviours.

Overall, the process involves developing an alliance, identifying cycles, identifying and accessing underlying emotions, and working to deescalate the problem. The withdrawer must be engaged and the pursuer or blamer softened. Subsequently, new emotional bonding events and new cycles of interaction should be created. Consolidation then occurs for new cycles of trust, and connection and safety.

Benefits and limitations

A potential strength of EFT is the emphasis on the role of adaptive emotion and the therapeutic relationship in psychotherapeutic change. Information from accessing previously-inhibited adaptive emotion is used to modify maladaptive meaning. In addition, EFT deals with a complex of disturbances by addressing core affective processes. However, short-term modalities with a circumscribed focus on past issues may be contraindicated for individuals with multiple ongoing problems. Evocative interventions that heighten arousal, such as those used in EFT, generally are inappropriate for severe anger problems or self-harm potential. Furthermore, using EFT to aid clients' ability to cope can be maladaptive if the stressors are controllable (Strentz & Auerbach, 1988; Vitaliano et al., 1990); in this situation, it may be more productive to use problem-focused coping mechanisms.

Dialectical behaviour therapy

Linehan (1993a) developed *dialectical behaviour therapy (DBT)* as an adaptation of CBT for treatment of borderline personality disorder. Although it was developed to aid suicidal clients primarily, it has evolved to treat individuals with borderline personality disorder (BPD) who also have a number of other problematic behavioural disorders where regulation of emotions is difficult. These include substance dependence (Linehan et al., 1999), depressed and suicidal adolescents (Miller et al., 1997), and binge eating (Telch et al., 2001). Controlled trials have provided evidence that this comprehensive treatment is effective in a number of ways: DBT improved social adjustment of clients, and led to a reduction in parasuicidal behaviours, inpatient hospitalisation days, and anger (Linehan et al., 1991; Linehan et al., 1993).

Theory

Generally, DBT is based on a transactional, or dialectical, model. The model recognises the importance of both the individual and the environment of the individual (Hoffman et al., 1999). There are other aetiological models, such as the diathesis-stress model, that recognise the importance of both of these, viewing biological and genetic factors as part of the individual, and viewing life experiences as part of the environment. The *diathesis-stress model* postulates that certain characteristics of the individual (especially a genetic predisposition to an abnormal behaviour), when combined with certain environmental stressors, are the cause of abnormal behaviour. But Linehan's *biosocial model* indicates that the individual and his or her environment influence each other in a reciprocal manner; the process is not interactional, but transactional (Hoffman et al., 1999).

Specifically, the dialectical basis of DBT originated from the 'combined capability deficit and motivational model of BPD' (Dimeff & Linehan, 2001, p. 10). DBT theory argues that emotion dysregulation, which is core to BPD, results from the transactional process between the individual and the environment in which the individual was raised or presently lives. For example, to be more vulnerable to and exhibit more dysregulation of emotion, a person's nature (the individual aspect of the transactional process) places demands on an already invalidating home life (the environment aspect of the transactional process) and *vice versa*. Central to DBT is the concept of the *invalidating environment*. When valid (true or effective) behaviours of an individual, such as thoughts, or emotional and sensory experiences, are criticised or punished, invalidation occurs (Hoffman, et al., 1999).

DBT is based on the major concepts of BPD: (a) a person with BPD lacks important interpersonal skills, self-regulation and emotional-regulation skills, and distress-tolerance skills; and (b) both individual and environmental factors hinder use of a person's existing behavioural skills, and reinforce dysfunctional behaviours (Dimeff & Linehan, 2001). The dialectical aspect of DBT is expected to be implemented in therapy with a client; see below.

Techniques and application
In DBT, 'dialectical' is also intended to suggest that, when working with suicidal clients with BPD, multiple forms of tension occur reciprocally between client and therapist. In addition, in DBT there is emphasis on replacing rigid, dichotomous thinking by enhancing dialectical thinking patterns. The essential dialectic aspect of DBT is between validation and acceptance of the client, since these two aspects aid client change simultaneously (Dimeff & Linehan, 2001). Acceptance procedures in DBT include mindfulness (such as attention to the present moment, assuming a non-judgmental stance, and focusing on effectiveness) and a variety of validation and acceptance-based stylistic strategies. These will be explored below. Change strategies in DBT include behavioural analysis of maladaptive behaviours and problem-solving techniques, including skills training, contingency management (reinforcers and punishment), cognitive modification, and exposure-based strategies (Dimeff & Linehan, 2001).

DBT is conceptualised in stages:

- *Stage 1* focuses on *stabilising the client* through behavioural targets that are organised hierarchically:
  1   decreasing life-threatening, suicidal behaviour
  2   reducing treatment-interfering behaviours
  3   decreasing quality-of-life threatening behaviours (such as substance abuse, depression, chronic unemployment, and homelessness)
  4   increasing behavioural skills (including mindfulness, emotion-regulation skills, distress tolerance, and self-management) (Linehan, 1993b).
- *Stage 2* focuses on *inhibited emotional range* (or experience), and aims to move the client from a state of silence or 'quiet desperation' to a non-traumatic emotional state. Disorders such as post-traumatic stress disorder are treated in this stage.
- *Stage 3* aims to identify and work through ongoing disorders and problems in living, while continuing to practise skills that increase awareness, tolerance, compassion, and confidence.
- *Stage 4* focuses on resolving a sense of being incomplete, achieving joy, and increasing overall well-being (Linehan et al., 1999).

Adding acceptance-based interventions and validation strategies to CBT, thereby forming DBT, communicates to clients that they are acceptable as they are, and that their behaviours, including self-harming, are meaningful. Furthermore, DBT helps clients to realise when they are having 'perfectly normal' thoughts, feelings, and behaviours. In turn, this helps them to discover that they have sound judgment and are capable of learning how and when to trust themselves. Acceptance strategies and change-based strategies, however, are not mutually exclusive;

each enhances use of the other, since clients must change to achieve changes that improve their lives.

Benefits and limitations

As noted above, one of the strengths of DBT is that it was designed as an adaptation of CBT for patients who are suicidal and/or practise self-harm. DBT is also useful for patients who acknowledge their illness, want to learn about it, and will work hard in therapy. However, DBT is demanding, intellectually and emotionally. Thus, DBT has been successful in addressing problems with an individual's emotional vulnerability (high sensitivity, high reactivity, and slow return to baseline) by intervening directly with the patient. Although interventions with family members are briefly noted in the original treatment manual, standard DBT does not attempt to directly affect the second component of the aetiological model for BPD and related disorders, the invalidating environment (Hoffman et al., 1999).

Acceptance and commitment therapy

Acceptance and commitment therapy (ACT) is a mindfulness-based behaviour therapy that has been shown to be effective with a diverse range of clinical conditions. ACT challenges the assumption of 'healthy normality', and assumes that psychological processes of a normal human mind are often destructive and create psychological suffering. ACT does not aim to reduce symptoms; it is based on a view that clinical disorders can be created by ongoing attempts to get rid of 'symptoms'. In ACT, there are two major goals: (a) acceptance of unwanted private experiences that are out of personal control; and (b) committed action towards living a life according to one's values. The aim of ACT is to create a rich, full, and meaningful life, while accepting the pain that inevitably goes with it (Harris, 2006).

Philosophical basis

Understanding ACT on a philosophical level makes the treatment's divergence from other cognitive and behavioural therapies clear. ACT is based on a philosophical position known as *functional contextualism* (Hayes, 1993), the goal of which is to predict and influence events, through precision, depth, and scope (Hayes, 1993). Functional contextualism contrasts with the assumption, upon which Western psychology was founded, that healthy normality and functioning is the absence of pathological thinking; psychological suffering is seen as abnormal; there is some 'part' to be fixed (such as replacing irrational cognitions with more rational ones) (Bach & Moran, 2008).

ACT, grounded in functional contextualism, assumes this is false. The subject matter of ACT is *behaviour-in-context*: thoughts are viewed as covert behaviours that are elicited by environmental events, taking the individual's unique history into account (Bach & Moran, 2008). Health is not defined by the absence of thoughts, feelings, or suffering; these are simply seen as normal or problematic. Thoughts and feelings do not cause other actions, except as regulated by context (Biglan & Hayes, 1996; Hayes & Brownstein, 1986). Therefore, to change overt behaviour, it is possible to go beyond attempting to change thoughts or feelings, and to change the context that causally links them.

Theory and origin

ACT is based on *relational frame theory (RFT)* (Hayes, 2001), a theory of human language and cognition. It argues that the learned ability to relate one event to another subjectively, and then to change the function of the events based on these relations, is at the core of human language and cognition. The following example demonstrates this concept. From the physical size difference between a one-dollar and a two-dollar coin, a child knows that the two-dollar coin is the smaller of the two; however, the child will not understand until later that the two-dollar coin is actually more valuable than the one-dollar coin through social attribution. According to RFT researchers, such relations can be trained as operant (Barnes-Holmes et al., 2004), and will alter the impact of other behavioural processes (Dymond & Barnes, 1995).

The primary applied implications of RFT, are that:

- underlying psychopathology are normal cognitive processes that are necessary for problem-solving and verbal reasoning, and cannot be eliminated
- distinct contextual features control the content and impact of cognitive networks
- cognitive networks are elaborated over time
- directly attempting to change key nodes within cognitive networks tends to expand that area of the network and increase its functional importance. From a therapeutic perspective, how language (covert behaviour) is 'related' to other stimuli is important, and would be functionally assessed to create treatment options.

Techniques and application in therapy

In ACT a primary source of psychopathology (as well as a process exacerbating the impact of other sources of psychopathology) is the way language and cognition interact with direct unforeseen acts to produce an inability to persist or change behaviour to achieve long-term valued ends. In ACT, this psychological inflexibility is argued to emerge from weak or unhelpful contextual control over language processes, and the model of psychopathology is thus linked point to point to the basic analysis provided by RFT. This yields an accessible and clinically useful middle-level theory bound tightly to more abstract basic principles. A model of the approach taken by ACT towards the emergence of psychopathology can be seen in figure 7.3.

Cognitive fusion refers to excessive or improper regulation of behaviour by verbal processes, such as rules and derived relational networks (see Hayes et al., 1999 for further details). In contexts that foster such fusion, human behaviour is guided more by relatively inflexible verbal networks than by contacted environmental contingencies. As a result, people may act in a way that is inconsistent with what the environment affords, relevant to chosen values and goals. From an ACT–RFT point of view, the form or content of cognition is not directly troublesome unless contextual features leads this cognitive content to regulate human action in unhelpful ways.

ACT targets the core problems shown in figure 7.3, with the goal of increasing psychological flexibility, 'the ability to contact the present moment more fully as a conscious human being, and to change or persist in behaviour when doing so serves valued ends' (Hayes et al., 2006). Psychological flexibility is established through six

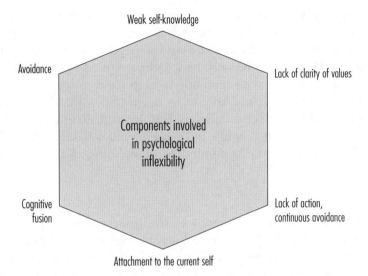

Figure 7.3 A model of ACT–RFT in psychopathology based on the model proposed by Hayes et al. (2006).

core ACT processes that derive from figure 7.3: being present, acceptance of private events, cognitive defusion, defining valued directions, committed action, and self as context (figure 7.4; Hayes et al., 2006). These processes are seen as positive psychological skills, not just methods of avoiding psychopathology.

Acceptance

Acceptance is taught as a skill to help overcome its counterpart core problem of *experiential avoidance*. Acceptance involves actively embracing private experiences and events from one's history that were seen as toxic, and include aspects of exposure.

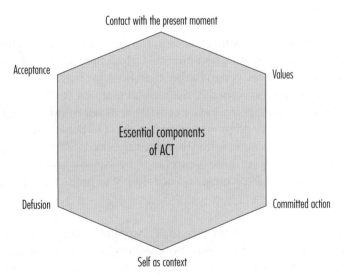

Figure 7.4 A model of the essential components of ACT based on the model by Hayes et al. (2006).

Rich, flexible interaction with the previously avoided experience, willingness, and flexibility are encouraged. This is done without attempts to change their frequency or form, especially if the result would be psychological harm. Clients with anxiety are taught to accept anxiety as a feeling, without defence; clients with chronic pain are provided with methods to help them to let go of the struggle against pain. Acceptance is not an end in itself; that would encourage simply living with the problem the client already had. Instead, acceptance is taught as a skill that fosters the client's ability to increase values-based action. The client learns to accept the anxiety, to be committed to pursuing and living according to his or her values.

Cognitive defusion

Cognitive-defusion techniques attempt to overcome cognitive fusion, which is when a thought and the thing it refers to (such as a story or event) become blended. Thus, cognitive defusion attempts to alter undesirable functions of thoughts and other private events, rather than trying to alter their form, frequency, or situational sensitivity. ACT attempts to change the way the client interacts with or relates to thoughts by creating contexts in which their unhelpful functions are diminished. For example, a negative thought could be repeated out loud until only its sound remains, or treated as an externally observed event by giving it a shape, size, colour, speed, or form. Other techniques include thanking the mind for an interesting thought, labelling the process of thinking ('I am having the thought that I am a failure'), or examining historical thoughts, feelings, and memories that occur while the person experiences that thought (Hayes & Strosahl, 2005; Harris, 2007). Such procedures attempt to reduce the literal quality of the thought, weakening the tendency to treat the thought according to what it refers to ('I am a failure'), rather than what it is directly experienced to be (the thought, 'I am a failure'). The result of defusion is usually a decrease in believability of the private events rather than an immediate change in their frequency.

Being present

Present-moment awareness counteracts dominance of the conceptualised past and future. ACT promotes ongoing non-judgmental contact with psychological and environmental events as they occur. Rather than having one's awareness focused on past or future, awareness is focused in the present moment. It is a mindfulness technique; it involves the client being aware of what is in her mind. The goal is to have the client experience the world more directly, so that her behaviour is more flexible, and her actions more consistent with the values she holds. This is accomplished by allowing workability to exert more control over behaviour, and by using language as a tool to note and describe events, and not simply to predict and judge them.

Self as context

Self as context counteracts attachment to the conceptualised self. As a result of relational frames, such as 'I versus you', 'now versus then', and 'here versus there', human language leads to a sense of self as a locus or perspective, and provides a transcendent, spiritual side to normal verbal humans. In ACT, a client is encouraged to see herself as the continuous and transcendent aspect of the central locus, the 'I' from which events are experienced, the observer–experience. A client can, therefore, be aware of her own flow of experiences without attachment to them or an investment in which particular experiences occur. Defusion and acceptance are fostered. In ACT, self as context is fostered by mindfulness exercises, metaphors, and experiential processes.

Values

Lack of clear values is seen as pathological. Clients are encouraged to discover and articulate their values. Values are seen as important in ACT, because they give direction to application of other aspects of ACT treatment. ACT uses a variety of exercises to help a client choose life directions in various domains (such as family, career, and spirituality), while undermining verbal processes that might lead to value choices based on avoidance, social compliance, or fusion (such as 'I should value X', or 'A good person would value Y', or 'My mother wants me to value Z').

Committed action

Once values have been determined, behaviours are planned that lead to achievable concrete goals that are consistent with these values. Larger and larger patterns of effective action are linked to chosen values. The behaviour is developed using standard behaviour-therapy techniques. In this regard, ACT looks very much like traditional behaviour therapy, and almost any behaviourally coherent behaviour-change method can be fitted into an ACT protocol, including exposure, skills acquisition, shaping methods, and goal setting. Efforts to change behaviours in turn lead to contact with psychological barriers that are addressed through other ACT processes, such as acceptance and defusion.

The core processes of ACT interrelate and overlap; each supports the other, and all aim for psychological flexibility. The processes can be placed in two groups. *Mindfulness and acceptance processes* involve acceptance, defusion, contact with the present moment, and self as context. *Commitment and behaviour-change processes* involve contact with the present moment, self as context, values, and committed action.

Contact with the present moment and self as context occur in both groups because all psychological activity involves the now as known. ACT can be defined as a psychological intervention based on modern behavioural psychology, including RFT, that applies mindfulness and acceptance processes, and commitment and behaviour-change processes, to the creation of psychological flexibility.

Benefits and limitations

A strength of ACT is its success across a broad range of problems, and for a range of severity, including psychosis, and for more ordinary situations, such as work-related stress (for a review, see Hayes et al., 2006). In addition, studies using ACT have been conducted on different ethnic groups, classes, and geographic regions, with no indication that outcomes or processes change. Furthermore, it appears that ACT targets processes that are in part responsible for desirable outcomes. It also appears that these processes are not targeted as efficiently by other interventions (such as cognitive therapy and CBT) that are supported empirically.

But many of the ACT interventions used in studies are brief and limited in scope. Another reason for caution is that ACT has similarities to mystical aspects of some of the major spiritual and religious traditions, such as Buddhism (Hayes, 2002). At times, there is controversy surrounding mechanisms of change proposed by ACT (Hofmann & Asmundson, 2008; Arch & Craske, 2008). There is also debate whether ACT takes a radically different approach to psychological experiences than do other forms of intervention. Evidence for ACT has been examined with a critical eye (Öst, 2008).

Mindfulness

Mindfulness is the practice of being aware in the present, in the 'here and now', moment to moment. Being mindful of the moment allows a person to be completely focused on what he or she is experiencing in that present moment. Kabat-Zinn (2003) defines mindfulness as: 'the awareness that emerges through paying attention on purpose, in the present moment, and non-judgmentally to the unfolding of experience moment by moment' (p. 145). Mindfulness also refers to open or receptive attention to and awareness of ongoing events and experience (Brown & Ryan, 2003; Kabat-Zinn, 1990; Segal et al., 2002). It is thought that mindfulness is inherent in all individuals to some extent (Kabat-Zinn, 1990). Mindfulness is consistent with Western concepts such as acceptance, exposure, and awareness (Baer, 2003), and the observing self and insight (Martin, 2002), yet within Western psychology there is no single construct that depicts the total meaning of mindfulness.

History and origin

Mindfulness originates in Buddhist philosophy, where rightmindfulness is considered the seventh aspect of the Noble Eightfold Path. This path is the way to the end of suffering, as described by Siddhartha Gautama, the historical Buddha. *Right-mindfulness* is considered an aspect of mental development; other aspects are *ethical development* and *development of wisdom*. But, it is not necessary to have a belief in or commitment to Buddhist teachings to practise mindfulness (Kabat-Zinn, 1990; Segal et al., 2002).

Theory

The concept of mindfulness, as described by Langer and Moldoveanu (2000), is the 'process of drawing novel distinctions regardless of whether or not the information is important or trivial—as long as it is new to the viewer' (p. 1). A person becomes situated in the present by focusing on these distinctions, and increases awareness of the context of the situation as well as his or her actions. That is, by being aware of novel distinctions, a person can achieve qualities of a mindful state.

According to Langer (1997), mindfulness includes the following attributes: openness to novelty, alertness to distinction, sensitivity to different contexts, awareness of multiple perspectives, and orientation in the present. *Mindlessness* involves relying on rigidly defined categories that have been created in the past, which lead to lack of attention being paid to context in any given moment; mindlessness is influenced by other factors, including repetition, practice, and premature cognitive commitment (Langer, 1989). Stated simply, those who perform tasks in a mindless state may do so in an automatic fashion, giving little or no consideration to the actions involved. General consequences of mindlessness may include limiting self-poten-tial, losing control, and learned helplessness.

Numerous studies, in a variety of settings, have provided evidence of the benefits of mindfulness. Mindfulness has been shown to improve health and longevity (Langer et al., 1984; Rodin & Langer, 1977), improve attention, learning, and recall in educational settings (Langer, 1997), and decrease addictions (Margolis & Langer, 1990; Wilson & Abrams, 1977). But, there have been calls for more research to draw definitive correlations between mindfulness and other areas of research (Demick, 2000; Sternberg, 2000).

Application and techniques
Mindfulness in therapy

Mindfulness was first applied in Western cultures in the *mindfulness-based stress reduction (MBSR)* program at the University of Massachusetts in 1979, which was aimed at hospital outpatients who had not had gains from traditional treatments for reducing stress, illness, and pain (Kabat-Zinn, 2003). This involved a major medita-tion component, where clients would take part in a half-day retreat, in addition to 8 weeks of sessions (2.5. hours each), and homework of 45 minutes of meditation per day (Kabat-Zinn, 1990).

Based on MBSR, *mindfulness-based cognitive therapy (MBCT)* aimed at assisting in relapse prevention of depressive symptoms (Segal et al., 2002). Although MBCT is similar to MBSR in session structure, three components distinguish them. MBCT involves psychoeducation on depression, the conceptualised relationship between thoughts and emotions, and enhancing awareness of relapse triggers through use of cognitive strategies (Segal et al., 2002).

Mindfulness is also utilised by other therapies as a technique within a treatment package that separates it from its meditative component. *Acceptance and commitment therapy (ACT)* employs mindfulness with informal exercises to help the client increase awareness, reduce experiential avoidance, and make a distinction between evaluative and descriptive thoughts (Hayes et al., 1999). *Dialectical behaviour therapy (DBT)* incorporates mindfulness as a core skill in a three-module treatment package. Clients learn to observe, describe, and participate in the moment with internal and external phenomena in a non-judgmental manner (Linehan, 2003). Mindfulness has also been used for eating disorders. *Mindfulness-based eating awareness training (MB-EAT)* is an integration of MBSR and CBT that has a specific application to eating, weight, and shape issues (Kristeller & Jones, 2006). Such mindfulness hybrids are continuously being created, and are often idiosyncratic treatments that are clini-cally inspired.

Mindfulness attitudes

Before teaching mindfulness to a client, it is important for the client to become familiar with the following attitudes, described by Kabat-Zinn (1990):

1 *Be non-judging:* this will challenge you to distance yourself from the thoughts that keep popping into your head and lead you astray. It allows you to realise

that there is no good or bad; these are just labels or notions; instead, you will realise that things simply 'are'. Thoughts will occur to you while you are trying to be mindful, such as 'this is boring', or 'this isn't working'. This is you judging the situation or yourself. When these thoughts occur, simply acknowledge them, and shift your focus back to your breath.

2 *Patience:* mindfulness is a skill that needs to be learned; it does not just happen. Just as any activity you performed as a child (your first experience of jumping into water, or playing on a swing) required patience to learn, so does mindfulness.

3 *Beginner's mind:* imagine what it must be like for a newborn baby, who is seeing everything for the first time; this is what is meant by a *beginner's mind*. Allow yourself to experience and to see everything as if for the first time. Through experiencing something more than once, people often miss a lot about the experience when it occurs again; they think they know everything about it. Try to perceive as if you were naïve.

4 *Trust:* as mindfulness skills develop, trusting yourself and your feeling will become easier. Becoming mindful will help you to fully become yourself. This allows you to learn that you can trust yourself to cope in whatever situation you find yourself in.

5 *Non-striving:* in being mindful, let go of the notion that you must strive to achieve. If you are constantly 'striving' to become mindful, and achieving the goals of being relaxed or reducing pain, you are thinking about the future rather than concentrating on the present. Pay attention to whatever is occurring right now; if you are having worries or feeling sad, simply pay attention to those feelings.

6 *Acceptance:* this involves taking things for what they are in the present moment. For example, frustration and impatience might arise when you are stuck in traffic; if you take the experience for what it is, instead of fighting against it, these feelings can be accepted and brought to awareness. This does not mean that you will like the experience; you will simply have the ability to take each moment as it comes, and be aware of every feeling or sensation. Fighting against a situation in which you have no control will only frustrate you further.

Once these attitudes are explained by the therapist and understood by the client, a mindfulness exercise should be practised in session. A good one to start with is *mindful breathing*; being aware of every breath keeps a person in the 'here and now', since each breath occurs in the present. Here is how you might prepare the client:

Mindfulness exercise

You say: 'In a moment, I will ask you to do a simple exercise of being mindful. This will give you the chance to notice the ease with which your mind is carried off and away from the present moment by other thoughts, feelings, or distractions. Before we start, it is important to note that most people will initially only focus on their breathing for a few seconds at a time, before their mind wanders off. The next exercises will hopefully give you an idea of the process of observing your body and mind deliberately, without judgment, and letting the experience occur from moment to moment. If your mind wanders, there is no need to worry and judge yourself with thoughts such as, "I shouldn't be thinking about this now" or "I'm feeling frustrated, am I doing this properly?" So, get comfortable in your chair, with your feet resting on the floor and your arms beside you, sitting in an upright position. Your back should be straight but not held tense. Now, close your eyes gently, and become aware of your breathing.'

The client can be guided through the breathing meditation by getting her to pay attention to various aspects of breathing (how the air feels coming in and out of the nostrils, the rise and fall of the ribcage or abdomen). While the client is paying attention to the breath, it is important to keep reminding her that her mind may wander, she might get distracted by thoughts, feelings, sensations, or urges, or start feeling impatient, anxious, or irritable. But the client should let these thoughts or feelings come and go, without judging them, and then return her attention to the breath. It is important to relay the message that mindfulness should be practised often; as with any skill, it takes time to learn.

Positive psychology

Positive psychology is the scientific study of positive experiences, positive individual traits, and the institutions that facilitate their development (Seligman, 2002). *Positive psychotherapy* is based on a positive image of humans, the view that all people are good by nature; humans are seen to have physical, mental, social, and spiritual capabilities. The goal of this therapy is to help the client to develop these inborn capabilities in everyday living. In addition, positive psychology aims to understand and promote the strengths that enable individuals and communities to thrive. Where most early forms of psychology focused on understanding problems and suffering, positive psychology looks at the positive side of life and what makes it worth living.

History and origin

Although Martin Seligman is at times considered the 'father of positive psychology' (Goldberg, 2006), the term comes from Maslow's, *Motivation and Personality* (1954). Seligman reiterated Maslow's view by stating that clinical psychology has been focused on mental illness and problems, rather than paying attention to strengths and positive aspects (Maslow, 1954; Seligman, 2002). It was his hope that psychologists would aim to improve normal life and to nurture the strengths of clients, as was once the mission of psychology (Compton, 2005).

The roots of positive psychology are in humanistic psychology from the twentieth century, where focus was on achieving happiness and fulfilment. Philosophical and religious sources were earlier influences on positive psychology. Two perspectives are taken by positive psychologists, hedonic and eudaimonic. In the *hedonic perspective*, pleasure is the main aspect being analysed, which is considered to be well-being purely related to an individual, regarding positive emotions and sensations (Kahneman et al., 1999). The focus of the *eudaimonic perspective* is analysing factors that facilitate an individual's development and fulfilment of potentials, as well as the individual's authentic human nature (Ryan & Deci, 2001). This perspective was developed from Aristotle's concept of *eudaimonia*: aspects that are useful for a person and factors that enrich a person's personality.

The term *eudaimonia* is often considered synonymous with the term *happiness*, as it describes individual satisfaction and development towards integration with the environment (Nussbaum, 1993). The idea, then, is to identify subjective indicators of well-being. Individuals may be asked to evaluate their health, degree of satisfaction in social, working, and personal domains, and achieved goals and future objectives. Studying subjective well-being gave rise to positive psychology (Seligman & Csikszentmihalyi, 2000).

Theoretical background

Seligman (2002) proposed that happiness embraced three scientifically manageable components: positive emotion (the pleasant life), engagement (the engaged life), and meaning (the meaningful life). Exercises used in positive psychology aim at enhancing these components:

1　*The pleasant life:* positive emotion about the past, present, and future, an idea endorsed by hedonic theories. The pleasant life also encompasses learning skills that help increase intensity and duration of positive emotions. Positive emotions about the past include satisfaction, contentment, fulfilment, pride, and serenity (e.g. Lyubomirsky et al., 2005; McCullough, 2000; Seligman et al., 2005). Positive emotions about the present include satisfaction derived from immediate pleasures. When considering the future, positive emotions include hope and optimism, faith, trust, and confidence (Seligman, 1991, 2002).

2　*The engaged life:* Seligman proposes that the engaged life is a second 'happy' life, in which engagement, involvement, and absorption in work, intimate relations, and leisure are pursued (Csikszentmihalyi, 1990). In the engaged life, all attention is placed on the activity at hand, with a loss of sense of self (Moneta & Csikszentmihalyi, 1996). It was proposed that getting people to identify their strengths and talents, then helping them to maximise their strengths when opportunities arise, is a way to enhance engagement in life (Seligman, 2002). This view dates to Aristotle, yet is in keeping with modern psychological notions; these include the ideal of the fully functioning person (Rogers, 1951), the concept of self-actualisation (Maslow, 1971), and self-determination theory (Ryan & Deci, 2000).

3　*The meaningful life:* the pursuit of meaning is Seligman's third 'happy' life, which is achieved through use of the person's main strengths and talents in a way that helps the person belong to something he or she believes is larger and more important than him- or herself. *Positive institutions* include religion, politics, family, and community. Establishing a meaningful life, regardless of which institution the person serves in order to do so, gives a sense of satisfaction and enhances the belief that the person has lived well (Myers, 1992; Nakamura & Csikszentmihalyi, 2002). Meaning-based research has a consistent theme: those who use meaning to transform perceptions of their circumstances from unfortunate to fortunate achieve the greatest benefits (McAdam et al., 1997; Pennebaker, 1993).

Application and techniques

The nature of humans is to be biased toward remembering, attending to, and expecting the negative (Baumeister et al., 2001); depressed individuals inflate this natural tendency. These individuals are inclined to remember the most negative aspects of their lives. Exercises in positive psychotherapy aim to shift the person from negative and catastrophic aspects of their life to positive and hopeful aspects. They aim to achieve this through re-educating memory, attention, and expectations.

Exercises in positive psychology are used to foster the three components of happiness proposed by Seligman (2002). Here are some examples of these exercises.

1 *Three good things:* the client writes down three good things that happened during the day and the reasons they may have happened.
2 *Obituary or biography:* the therapist asks the client to imagine that he passed away (or reached the age of 90) having lived a satisfying life; the client is then asked to write down what he would want an obituary or biography to say.
3 *Gratitude visit:* the client is asked to think of a person he feels gratitude towards yet has not properly thanked; the client should then write a letter that describes the gratitude he feels, after which he reads it to the person.
4 *Active or constructive responding:* reacting to a person's good news in an enthusiastic and visibly positive manner; the client should do this once a day.
5 *Savouring:* this technique is used to enable the client to enjoy something that is normally rushed through (such as eating or showering); the client is then asked to write down what he did, what was done differently, and how he felt, compared with rushing the same action.

Using the 'three good things' exercise can help the client to counteract the depressive bias toward the things that have gone wrong (Seligman et al., 2006). It then becomes more likely that the client will end the day with a positive memory of the day's events and achievements, rather than by remembering the difficulties and problems experienced.

During the 'gratitude visit', the client may have a shift in memory from the dysfunctional pattern in relationships in the past to the good things people have done.

Benefits and limitations

A number of benefits can be attributed to positive psychotherapy. It is concerned with the medical model in mental health and its insufficiencies. Its core focus is on positive outcome, and the belief that such an outcome is the most effective way to reduce psychological dysfunction (Cowen & Kilmer, 2002). For example, it has been shown that positive emotions counteract the detrimental effects of negative emotions on physiology, attention, and creativity (Fredrickson & Branigan, 2005; Fredrickson & Levenson, 1996; see Fredrickson, 2000, for a review), as well as contributing to resilience in crises (Fredrickson et al., 2003; Tugade & Fredrickson, 2004).

However, the approach has several major limitations. Well-being is best construed as a process that is multidimensional and dynamic; in positive psychology, it is viewed as a discrete end state (Ryff & Singer, 1998). Positive psychology does not have a well-integrated theoretical framework as its basis, and is somewhat detached from prior work that is closely related and aimed at wellness enhancement. Furthermore, positive psychology, which is mainly cross-sectional and with adults in mind, does not take into consideration important developmental pathways and factors facilitating positive outcome (Cowen & Kilmer, 2002).

Practice implications

Models of psychotherapy

The range of theoretical models and treatment methods presented in this chapter may seem bewildering to the novice therapist. Some models are supported by extensive bodies of clinical evidence, and grounding in psychological and cognitive science. Others are either emerging treatments or based on anecdotal reports of effectiveness.

- The major practice implication is that there is a range of therapeutic approaches available, and that a good scientist–practitioner will consider the evidence base of a treatment and its theoretical rationale in a decision about which style of treatment to use with a client.
- A second implication from our survey of schools of therapy is that there are many common elements. Be aware of the contributions of specific and non-specific elements in each school of therapy, and recognise common factors shared by all styles.

PSYCHOPHARMACOLOGICAL TREATMENT OF MENTAL ILLNESS

Many people in Australia are treated for psychological problems using medications prescribed by general practitioners or psychiatrists. There is an established evidence base for the treatment of many conditions with these medications; however, there are also limitations to the effectiveness of medications (e.g. Fournier et al., 2010). Some individuals may also take medications in conjunction with psychological interventions. The practising psychologist needs to have an understanding of the range of medications available in Australia, and the conditions for which they are prescribed. This section reviews the classes of medications available in Australia, as well as their most common uses.

Psychotropic medications available in Australia fall into five broad categories: antidepressants, anxiolytics, antipsychotics, mood stabilisers, and stimulants (MIMS, 2010). Each category has a mechanism of action, and is used for different purposes.

Antidepressants

Antidepressants are among the most widely prescribed drugs in Australia, with a dramatic rise in the rate of prescriptions beginning around 1990 (Mant et al., 2004). Despite the name, antidepressants are prescribed for a range of conditions other than depression, including anxiety disorders, eating disorders, and even enuresis (Ramakrishnan, 2008). In some cases, antidepressants are also prescribed for children and adolescents.

First-generation antidepressants

Antidepressants were first developed in the 1950s, with the drugs imipramine and iproniazid being released at around the same time. As has often been the case in the development of psychoactive medications, these drugs were developed for completely different purposes (for treatment of psychosis and tuberculosis, respectively) and serendipitously discovered to exert a different therapeutic effect (Healy, 1993). Discovery of the antidepressant effect of imipramine and iproniazid led to the development of a range of antidepressants with similar chemical properties and therapeutic effects.

Tricyclic antidepressants

Imipramine was the first drug from the class of agents that came to be called the *tricyclics antidepressants (TCAs),* so called because of their three-ring chemical structure. Tricyclics act to block the reuptake of noradrenaline and serotonin from the synapse, thereby increasing the availability of these two neurotransmitters (that is, they are noradrenaline and serotonin agonists). Other antidepressants from this class include trimipramine, amitriptyline, dothiepin, and nortriptyline.

TCAs have a range of side-effects, resulting from their action on other neurotransmitter systems. Their blocking of histamine receptors can lead to drowsiness and weight gain, while their actions on acetylcholine receptors can lead to constipation, blurred vision, and dry mouth. Each TCA has a different rate of each of these side-effects, and prescribers will often choose a medication with potential side-effects in mind (such as a drug that causes drowsiness for someone with insomnia with their depression).

Monoamine Oxidase inhibitors

Iproniazid was the prototype for a class of drugs called *monoamine oxidase inhibitors (MAOIs).* The MAOIs act to reduce the action of a key enzyme called monoamine oxidase (MAO), which is used by the body to break down certain chemicals, including serotonin and noradrenaline (both of which are *monoamines*). Similarly to the action of the TCAs, the act of inhibiting the MAO enzyme leads to an increase in the availability of these two neurotransmitters.

The MAOIs are less commonly prescribed today because of the potential for serious side-effects, the most noteworthy of which is the tyramine effect. Normally, MAO acts to break down tyramine and other compounds taken in with food. When MAO is inhibited by medication, it is not available to break down tyramine, which can lead to serious increases in blood pressure. As a result, individuals taking MAOIs are required to maintain a strict diet, avoiding tyramine-rich foods, such as red wine, processed meats, and spreads such as Vegemite. Currently in Australia, phenelzine and tranylcypromine are the only MAOIs available.

Clomipramine

The next major development in antidepressant medications came in the mid 1960s with the release of clomipramine. Although clomipramine is a TCA, it is significantly better at blocking the reuptake of serotonin than blocking the reuptake of noradrenaline. Clomipramine was the first medication found to be effective in the treatment of obsessive-compulsive disorder, and is still used in this role today.

Second-generation antidepressants

The TCAs and MAOIs are sometimes collectively referred to as *first-generation antidepressants* to distinguish them from newer compounds that have became available since the late 1980s. The most prominent of the new antidepressants is fluoxetine (more commonly referred to by its trade name, Prozac), which was the first of a new class of medications called the *serotonin specific reuptake inhibitors (SSRIs)*. The SSRIs work in a similar way to the TCAs, but are significantly more powerful at preventing serotonin reuptake than noradrenaline reuptake (they are serotonin specific). Additionally, the SSRIs are significantly less likely to bind with histamine and acetylcholine receptors, and therefore show a much-reduced level of side-effects. Reduced frequency of side-effects is seen as a key advantage of these medications; many more people can tolerate their use than earlier medications. Furthermore, the SSRIs are significantly safer in overdose than older medications, which is extremely important in use for depression, where overdose may be attempted as a means of suicide. Other SSRIs available in Australia include sertraline, flovoxamine, paroxetine, and citalopram.

Problems with the tyramine effect from use of MAOIs led to the development of a new class of medications without this effect. The reversible inhibitors of MAO (RIMAs) act similarly to the MAOIs: they inhibit the actions of the MAO enzyme. In contrast to the MAOIs, however, their effect is reversible, and when tyramine is present, MAO is still able to do its job in metabolising monoamines. Similarly to the SSRIs, then, RIMAs have the same therapeutic effect as the drugs that preceded them, but with a reduced side-effect profile. The only RIMA available for prescription in Australia is moclobemide. Other antidepressants are also available in Australia, such as venlafaxine, bupropion, desvenlanfaxine, duloxetine, mirtazepine, and mianserin.

Uses of antidepressants

Antidepressants are most commonly used in the treatment of depression or other conditions with a significant level of mood symptoms. Several large studies and meta-analyses attest to their effectiveness (e.g. Elkin et al., 1989). The Royal Australian and New Zealand College of Psychiatrists (RANZCP) recommends use of antidepressants as one option for treatment of depression, and prevention of its recurrence (RANZCP, 2004). It is important to note that some authors recently have questioned use of antidepressants in milder forms of mood disorder (e.g. Kirsch et al., 2008), and although the consensus in the psychiatric literature is still that these medications are more effective than placebo in more severe cases of depression, there is controversy about their effectiveness for mild to moderate depression.

Fournier and colleagues (2010) summarised their findings, based on data of 718 patients during the period 1980–2009, as:

> The magnitude of benefit of antidepressant medication compared with placebo increases with severity of depression symptoms and may be minimal or nonexistent, on average, in patients with mild or moderate symptoms. For patients with very severe depression, the benefit of medications over placebo is substantial (p. 47).

Antidepressants have become the pharmacological treatment of choice for management of anxiety disorders (e.g. RANZCP, 2003). The antidepressants are not associated with the same tolerance and dependence effects that are observed with some medications used to treat anxiety (see 'Anxiolytics' below), and also appear to have longer-lasting treatment effects, beyond period of use of the medication.

Anxiolytics

A range of medications, including barbiturates, benzodiazepines, and the non-benzodiazepine anxiolytics, has been developed for the management of anxiety and anxiety disorders. The earliest *anxiolytics drugs* (other than alcohol) were the *barbiturates* (such as phenobarbital), which have now been replaced in psychiatric use by newer medications. Barbiturates are significantly more dangerous in overdose than the drugs that followed them, and also have problematic interactions with many other compounds, including alcohol.

The most commonly prescribed anxiolytic in current use are the *benzodiazepines* (Nash & Nutt, 2007). These drugs include diazepam, oxazepam, and alprazolam. All benzodiazepines act in the same way, by increasing the effects of the neurotransmitter γ-amino butyric acid (GABA). As GABA acts in the central nervous system as an inhibitory neurotransmitter, all the benzodiazepines act to slow down (*depress*) activity. At low doses, this leads to reduced levels of anxiety and physiological arousal. At higher doses, benzodiazepines act as hypnotics, causing sleep.

The major difference between different benzodiazepines is duration of action. Some benzodiazepines, such as diazepam, have notoriously long durations of action, while others, such as midazolam, have very short-lived effects. Choice of which benzodiazepine to use is often based on duration of effect. Shorter-acting drugs, such as temazepam, are suitable for treatment of insomnia, as they are broken down quickly by the body, ensuring that the user does not remain drowsy in the morning. Alternatively, long-acting benzodiazepines, such as diazepam, are associated with less severe withdrawal symptoms, and require less frequent dosing.

All the benzodiazepines are associated with potential for tolerance and dependence. *Tolerance* refers to the phenomenon by which an individual requires more of the drug to achieve the same effect. *Dependence* refers to a psychological and physiological effect whereby the person experiences significant withdrawal symptoms when the drug is discontinued. In benzodiazepine dependence, withdrawal is associated with significant anxiety, tremor, perspiration, insomnia, and in extreme cases, seizures.

A new class of medications, known as the *non-benzodiazepine sedative-hypnotics*, is now available in Australia. The drugs have names beginning with the letter Z, such as zolpidem and zopiclone. Currently, these are used primarily for treatment of insomnia. The notably short duration of action of zolpidem makes it particularly suitable for use as a sleeping tablet.

Antipsychotics

The *antipsychotic medications* (also called *neuroleptics* or *major tranquillisers*) are the mainstay of treatment for schizophrenia and other psychotic illnesses. Antipsychotics are often divided into typical (or first-generation) and atypical (second-generation) drugs. Antipsychotics have revolutionised treatment of psychotic illnesses, and have allowed many individuals to live in the community who would otherwise have spent much of their life as psychiatric inpatients.

The first antipsychotic, chlorpromazine, became available in the 1950s. Chlorpromazine acts to block receptors for the neurotransmitter dopamine (it is a dopamine *antagonist*). The therapeutic effect is associated with its ability to block the D2-type dopamine receptor. Through this action, chlorpromazine causes a significant reduction in the positive symptoms of schizophrenia, such as delusions and hallucinations. Typical antipsychotics are generally observed to have much less effect on the negative symptoms of schizophrenia, such as withdrawal, amotivation, and flat affect. Other typical antipsychotics include haloperidol, fluphenazine, and thioridazine.

All the typical antipsychotics are associated with significant side-effects. A common constellation of side-effects are the *extrapyramidal side-effects (EPSs)*, sometimes also called *parkinsonian side-effects*. These arise from the blocking of D1 dopamine receptors. EPSs include stiffness and reduced movement (*akinesia*), abnormal involuntary movements such as tremors or severe shaking (*dyskinesia*), and restlessness and agitation (*akathisia*). The most problematic EPS is tardive dyskinesia, which includes symptoms such as involuntary movements of the face and mouth, and at its most extreme, writhing movements of the head, limbs, and torso (Sadock & Sadock, 2007). Other side-effects from antipsychotics include histaminic side-effects, such as sedation and weight gain, and cholinergic side-effects, such as dry mouth, constipation, and blurred vision.

The second generation of antipsychotics includes medications such as clozapine, risperidone, and olanzapine. These compounds have several advantages over typical antipsychotics, and have largely replaced the older medications in current use. One advantage is that some of the atypicals (such as clozapine) are effective in treatment-resistant schizophrenia where other medications have proven ineffective. Another advantage of the second-generation antipsychotics is that they are associated with a better therapeutic effect on negative symptoms of schizophrenia. A third advantage is that they cause significantly fewer side-effects, and so are much better tolerated than earlier medications.

Some antipsychotics (such as haloperidol, flupentixol, fluphenazine, and risperidone) are available in what are called *depot forms*. These preparations are designed to be injected every 2 to 4 weeks, thereby eliminating the need for the individual to take regular oral medication. In schizophrenia, this is designed to increase compliance with the prescription regime, which might be reduced because of disorganisation or lack of insight into the need for medication.

Mood stabilisers

While antidepressants are effective for the treatment of depressed mood, individuals with bipolar mood disorders may require medication that can also reduce clinically expansive mood and other symptoms of mania. The *mood stabilisers* are a small collection of medications that are effective in treatment of depressive and manic episodes of bipolar mood disorders, as well as in prophylaxis against future episodes.

The mood stabilisers used in Australia are lithium carbonate, carbemazepine, and sodium valproate. While lithium is used only in treatment of mania, carbemazapine and sodium valproate are also used in the treatment of epilepsy. The mechanism by which all three medications exert their mood-stabilising effects remains poorly understood (Stahl, 2006). It is noteworthy that use of lithium in the treatment of bipolar mood disorders was pioneered in Australia in the 1940s and 1950s by Dr John Cade. Lithium has also been associated with significant reductions in suicide rates when prescribed therapeutically (Cipriani et al., 2005), and when in higher natural concentrations in drinking water (Ohgami et al., 2009). Lithium can be extremely toxic in overdose, and individuals taking lithium are required to have regular blood tests to ensure that lithium levels do not become excessive.

Stimulants

Pharmacological management of attention-deficit disorders is usually conducted with *stimulant medications,* such as methylphenidate, dexamphetamine, and atomoxetine. These drugs work to reduce reuptake and facilitate release of noradrenaline and dopamine, with this action in the prefrontal cortex and basal ganglia being implicated in the treatment of attention-deficit and hyperactivity respectively (Stahl, 2006, 2008). Side-effects of stimulant medication include insomnia and appetite loss. In children with existing tics or nervousness, these can be increased by stimulants. Newer preparations of these medications include extended-release formulations and skin patches.

Generation of new medications

The field of psychopharmacology continues to generate new medications, with new purported mechanisms of action. While a complete review of all new developments in psychiatric treatment of mental disorders is beyond the scope of this chapter, several new, interesting, and surprising developments are worth mentioning briefly.

Treatment of anxiety disorders has gradually moved away from use of sedative-hypnotics, such as benzodiazepines, to use of serotonergic antidepressants, as the front-line pharmacological treatment. Recently, however, other novel agents have been used successfully in the treatment of some anxiety disorders. One example is the GABA analogue pregabalin. Pregabalin acts to bind with a subtype of GABA receptors, with the end product being a reduction in the release of stimulating neurotransmitters such as noradrenaline and glutamate (Boschen, 2011a). Pregabalin has now been investigated in eight controlled trials, and a meta-analysis demonstrating its efficacy in treatment of GAD, including in older adults (Boschen, 2011b, in press).

Another novel treatment for anxiety disorders is use of the partial NMDA agonist d-Cycloserine (DCS) in conjunction with exposure therapy. While DCS does not have direct anxiolytic effect, it is part of a new class of medications sometimes referred to as 'cognitive enhancers'. DCS has been proposed to improve learning when used during exposure therapy (e.g., Ressler, et al., 2004), although the impact may be merely to increase speed of response in exposure therapy, rather than final outcome (Norberg, Krystal, & Tolin, 2008). Despite the early promise, some subsequent research has failed to find significant effects of DCS in treating anxiety disorders (e.g., Guastella, et al., 2007).

Another example of adaptation of an existing medication for psychiatric treatment is use of the beta-blocker propranolol in the treatment of PTSD. Propranolol has been previously used in treatment of medical conditions such as hypertension and psychiatrically in treatment of performance-anxiety conditions such as social anxiety disorder. Over the last decade, several studies have been conducted in which propranolol has been administered soon after a traumatic event, with the aim of reducing incidence of PTSD. Some early reports suggested that propranolol may reduce subsequent risk of PTSD (e.g., Vaiva, et al., 2003). It is worth noting, however, that other research has failed to find a protective effect of propranolol in reducing PTSD in burn victims (McGhee, et al., 2009), and after physical injury (Stein, Kerridge, Dimsdale, & Hoyt, 2007). Research in children also suggests that the efficacy of propranolol may be limited (Sharp, et al., 2010), or that there may be different effects when propranolol is used in boys and girls (Nugent, et al., 2010).

Propranolol has also been used in individuals with existing PTSD as a means of reducing arousal associated with established traumatic memories. In this method, propranolol is given to patients during an exposure-type task where they are asked to describe (verbally or in written form) the traumatic event. Early preliminary research suggests that subsequent recall of the traumatic memory may be associated with less physiological arousal compared to patients given a placebo (e.g., Brunet, et al., 2008).

A more surprising example of use of existing agents in treatment of psychological illness is found in two trials using intravenous administration of the NMDA antagonist ketamine in the treatment of depression. While administration of ketamine has been associated with rapid reduction in depression symptoms, these antidepressant effects appear shortlived, which may reduce utility of the drug as a viable longer-term treatment for depressive disorders (Ibrahim et al., 2012, Zarate et al., in press).

PSYCHOTHERAPY AND PHARMACOTHERAPY: THE CASE OF DEPRESSION

A common question raised by patients, trainees, and therapists concerns the comparative effectiveness of psychological and psychiatric therapies for different conditions. This question is complex, and cannot be answered easily. Factors that must be considered are the nature of the condition being treated, and the type of drug or psychotherapy being compared. Furthermore, the methodology used for comparisons may have an impact on findings, with meta-analyses combining studies that are substantially different. While a detailed review of comparative studies is beyond the scope of this text, we have chosen depression as an example case where discordant findings in the literature make drawing definitive conclusions difficult or impossible.

The example of depression clearly demonstrates confusion and discord in the current literature around the comparative efficacy and effectiveness of psychological and pharmacological interventions. The only uncontroversial conclusion it is possible to make from current research is that both psychological and pharmacological approaches are effective in reducing depression severity. While some authors have questioned the role of the placebo response in antidepressant treatment (e.g. Kirsch et al., 2008; Rief et al., 2008), even these authors acknowledge that antidepressant medication is associated with reduction in symptom severity in major depressive disorders.

Some early research comparing treatment approaches such as cognitive behaviour therapy with antidepressants has been used to argue that antidepressants are more effective than psychotherapy, particularly in the case of severe depression. The influential National Institute of Mental Health Treatment of Depression Collaborative Research Program (Elkin et al., 1989) reported that, while both CBT and

Table 7.1 Common psychiatric medications in Australia

Drug type	Class	Drug name	Typical daily dose*
Antidepressants	MAOI	Phenelzine	15–60 mg
		Tranylcypromine	10–30 mg
	TCA	Amitriptyline	50–200 mg
		Clomipramine	25–100 mg
		Dothiepin	75–200 mg
		Doxepin	30–300 mg
		Imipramine	25–200 mg
		Nortriptyline	25–100 mg
		Trimipramine	50–300 mg
	RIMA	Moclobemide	300–600 mg
	SSRI	Citalopram	20–60 mg
		Escitalopram	10–20 mg
		Fluoxetine	20–80 mg
		Fluvoxamine	50–300 mg
		Paroxetine	20–60 mg
		Sertraline	50–200 mg
	Other	Duloxetine	40–120 mg
		Desvenlanfaxine	50–400 mg
		Mianserin	30–90 mg
		Mirtazepine	15–60 mg
		Venlafaxine	75–225 mg
Antipsychotics	Typical	Chlorpromazine	25–800 mg
		Droperidol	Injection
		Fluphenazine	Injection
		Flupentixol	Complex
		Haloperidol	1–15 mg
		Pericyazine	15–75 mg
		Pimozide	1–10 mg
		Thioridazine	50–800 mg
		Trifluoperazine	4–50 mg
		Zuclopenthixol	Injection
	Atypical	Amisulpride	5–16 mg
		Aripiprazole	15–30 mg
		Clozapine	150–900 mg

Table 7.1 Common psychiatric medications in Australia (cont.)

Drug type	Class	Drug name	Typical daily dose*
		Olanzapine	5–15 mg
		Quetiapine	150–750 mg
		Risperidone	4–16 mg
Anxiolytics and hypnotics	Benzodiazepine	Alprazolam	0.25–4 mg
		Bromazepam	5–60 mg
		Clobazam	10–30 mg
		Diazepam	4–40 mg
		Lorazepam	1–10 mg
		Oxazepam	30–120 mg
	Non-benzodiazepine	Buspirone	15–60 mg
		Zopiclone	7.5 mg
		Zolpidem	10 mg
Mood stabilisers	Lithium	Lithium	600–3000 mg
	Anticonvulsants	Carbemazepine	200–1200 mg
		Sodium valproate	1000–1500 mg
Stimulants		Atomexetine	40–100 mg
		Dexamphetamine	5–60 mg
		Methylphenidate	20–60 mg
		Modafinil	200–400 mg

* Doses are those prescribed orally for healthy adults, based on the recommended doses of MIMS (2009).

IPT were effective in treating depression, each was inferior to antidepressant medication. More recently, a meta-analysis by Cuijpers and colleagues (2008) also reported that antidepressants were associated with a superior treatment effect size, exceeding that of psychotherapy by 0.28, although the authors questioned the clinical meaningfulness of such a difference.

Other authors have asserted that CBT has specific advantages over antidepressants. A meta-analysis in 1998 (Gloaguen et al.) presented data from over 2700 individuals treated for depression, and concluded that CBT demonstrated superior treatment efficacy to wait-list controls, other psychotherapies, and antidepressant medication in treatment of unipolar mood disorder. The advantage of CBT over medication has been particularly strongly argued in comparisons between each treatment method's ability to reduce risk of relapse. Several authors have argued that psychotherapy may provide a prophylactic effect that exceeds that provided by medication treatment of acute depression (e.g. Gloaguen et al., 1998; Imel et al., 2008). However, considering the apparent lack of effect of pharmaceuticals in mild to moderate depression (Fournier et al., 2010), it seems that there is growing evidence for the effectiveness of psychotherapy.

Unsurprisingly, there also exists a body of evidence attesting to the equivalence of psychotherapy and pharmacotherapy for depression. When managed in primary-care settings, cognitive-behavioural interventions and antidepressant medication have been associated with equivalent outcomes, leading to suggestions that general practitioners should consider the use of psychological treatments in addition to antidepressant prescription (Bortolotti et al., 2008). Recent meta-analytic research by Australian authors has also attested to the equivalence of cognitive-behavioural treatments and antidepressants (Parker et al., 2008). Even for outpatient treatment of severe depression, some authors have argued that the best evidence supports the equivalence of medication and psychological treatments (De Rubeis et al., 1999).

However, where psychotherapy tends to excel is in longer-term outcome and maintenance of change. A recent meta-analysis of psychotherapy and medication in unipolar depression and dysthymia found that 'psychotherapy showed a significant advantage over medication at follow-up and this advantage was positively associated with length of follow-up' (Imel et al., 2008, p. 197). Thus, the longer the time between treatment and follow-up, the better the outcome for therapy.

An increasing number of questions are being raised about the robustness of some of the psychopharmacological outcomes. Kirsch and colleagues (2002) (cited in Sparks et al., 2006) reported that 57 per cent of drug studies funded by the pharmaceutical industry failed to show any difference between drug and placebos. This may mean that, for many individuals, the drugs they are taking are no more effective than sugar pills. Hollon and colleagues (2002) (cited in Sparks et al., 2006) have referred to this as the 'dirty little secret' that has been tightly kept by researchers working on drug trials. Considering the money involved in pharmaceuticals, there would be considerable pressure felt by researchers funded by these companies to demonstrate success.

Practice implications

Clearly, the debate around the comparative effectiveness of these two therapeutic approaches remains unresolved. As elsewhere in this text, we encourage you to familiarise yourself with this research literature, and consider the evidence with an open mind, refraining from dogmatically supporting one type of intervention based on personal preference or ideology.

FUTURE DIRECTIONS IN PSYCHOLOGY

New directions for psychotherapeutic interventions have recently emerged. Some 'new wave' therapies, such as ACT, have already been discussed. Internet-delivered therapy and neuroscience are others.

Internet-delivered therapy

An emerging trend that is likely to have a major impact on psychological practice is the use of the internet to provide psychological services. Use of information technology has developed at a phenomenal rate in our society. In 2008–09, 72 per cent of Australian households had home internet access, and 78 per cent of households had access to a computer (Australian Bureau of Statistics, 2010). Internet-delivered interventions offer the prospect of greater affordability and easier access for a larger number of clients to mental-health interventions (Casey & Halford, 2010; Ritterband et al., 2003; Ybarra & Eaton, 2005). Clients who are geographically isolated, physically disabled, or have excessive time constraints may more easily access internet-delivered treatments. Costs to the client associated with physically attending services (such lost time or wages for business hours appointments as well as transport or child-care costs (Cucciare & Weingardt, 2007)) can be reduced. Clients can remain anonymous, which can reduce feelings of anxiety, shame, or embarrassment associated with seeking treatment for some problems, and may serve to encourage more self-disclosure (Joinson, 1999; Lange et al., 2003).

Common types of internet-delivered interventions are web-based educational content sites with either no or very limited therapist support, web-based interventions that enable client-directed self-help with limited therapist contact, and direct *online counselling*, with active therapist monitoring of progress and regular contact between therapist and client (Barak et al., 2008; Andersson et al., 2005). Barak and colleagues (2008) conducted a meta-analysis of 92 studies of web-based interventions and direct online counselling that had been used to treat a wide variety of clinical conditions. They found a medium effect size (.53) across all internet interventions, therapeutic approaches, outcome measures, presenting problems, and communication modalities. Barak and colleagues (2008) also reviewed 14 studies that directly compared an internet-delivered versus face-to-face version of treatment for a number of clinical conditions. No significant difference was found between the average weighted effect size of the internet programs (0.39) and the weighted effect size of the face-to-face interventions (0.34).

However, there is some evidence to suggest that therapist-mediated online interventions may be more effective than interventions provided without therapist contact. Spek and colleagues (2007) conducted a meta-analysis of RCTs of web-based CBT interventions for depressive and anxiety symptoms, and found that effects on depression with therapist support (n = 5) had a large mean effect size, while interventions without therapist support (n = 6) had a small mean effect size. Similarly, it is important to note that internet-based programs may not be suitable for all clients, particularly for those presenting with severe psychopathology (Mallen et al., 2005; Laszlo et al., 1999).

The Australian Psychological Society has developed a set of guidelines regarding provision of services and products via the internet, and these should be consulted before offering psychological services using this new medium.

Neuroscience

The concept of applying biology to psychology has been around for a long time. William James, in one of the earliest textbooks in psychology (1890), argued that the scientific study of psychology should be grounded in an understanding of biology. For James, bodily experiences, and brain experiences in particular, needed to be part of the 'conditions of the mental life that should be accounted for by psychology'. Others have noted that some brain-psychology must be presupposed or included in psychology (Baxter, et al., 1992).

Success in all forms of psychotherapy, whether psychoanalysis or behavioural interventions, it has been argued, is limited by the extent to which the therapy can prompt change in relevant neural circuits (Cozolino, 2002). To gather evidence for theories about the way humans think, it is important to understand neurobiological constraints.

Neuroscience comprises neuroanatomy, neurophysiology, brain functions, and related psychological models. For many years, research on a neuronal level was distinct from research on a cognitive or psychological level. This was because of the complexity of the thinking process; there were too many possible solutions to the question of how cognitive operations might be accomplished.

Applications in psychotherapy
Dispenza (2007) argues for the importance to psychotherapy of neuroscience research. He suggests a neurochemical explanation for longstanding emotional states that may lead to resistance to change in many people. Chemicals that are produced by frequently-experienced emotions begin to become the basis of the brain's homeostatic balance. To maintain homeostasis, the brain seeks the constant release of these chemicals; the person is compelled to repeatedly create the emotions that produce the chemicals, whether the emotions are pleasant or unpleasant. An individual may constantly struggle with feelings of sadness, frustration, or anxiety; although these feelings are unpleasant, the individual is almost compelled to experience them, since they have become so familiar (Dispenza, 2007).

A client had been in a state of chronic negative mood for over 20 years and had been seeing a therapist for that time, with little success. The client explained his situation to the therapist by saying, 'It's like this, I'm like a bird who has sheltered from a storm in a pile of dung, and ended up staying; although it's a pile of dung, its warm, comfortable, and familiar'. Such a client remains unchanged for years, and can be a source of frustration and distress for the therapist who is trying hard to find ways to help.

A number of neuroscience methods analyse cognitive function; each has enhanced and facilitated understanding of normal and abnormal mental function. Such insights have helped to improve pharmacotherapy interventions for patients with mental illness (Ressler et al., 2004). Neuroscience research has also begun to provide an answer to the question of whether an understanding of mental function might also inform psychotherapeutic interventions.

Psychotherapy plays an important role in the treatment of a number of mental disorders. Studies of controlled clinical trials have shown that some forms of psychotherapy, especially cognitive behavioural therapy and interpersonal therapy, are therapeutically effective. Combined use of psychotherapy and medication has been shown to lead to improved treatment outcomes in certain circumstances, such as clinical depression (Ressler et al., 2004; Elkin et al., 1989; March et al., 2004). Certain forms of psychotherapy can even be helpful in severe disorders such as schizophrenia; psychoeducation and cognitive behaviour therapy, although having no direct effect on the course of the disease, have been shown to enhance a client's compliance with medication and reduce frequency of hospitalisation (Rector, 2005). But a biological perspective on psychotherapy mechanisms remains to be defined.

The ability to explore the biological consequences of psychotherapeutic interventions has started to become a reality because of advances in neuro-imaging techniques with high-spatial and temporal resolution, and it may be possible to document psychotherapy's effectiveness, to follow its course, and to refine appropriate applications for selected patients and disorders (Etkin et al., 2005).

Although the biological study of psychotherapy is in its infancy, it is clear that psychotherapy can result in detectable changes in the brain (Etkin et al., 2005). Neuro-imaging studies of psychotherapy have mostly focused on depression and obsessive-compulsive disorders, and have examined basal brain metabolism or basal cerebral blood flow in these disorders (Brody et al., 1998; Brody et al., 2001; Schwartz et al., 1996). It has been shown that, following psychotherapy, patients with these disorders demonstrate changes in brain activity, in comparison to healthy subjects. Frequently, treatment restored the brain to a state that superficially resembled that of comparison subjects (Martin et al., 2001; Brody et al., 2001). The findings also suggest that some changes associated with psychotherapy are similar to changes in brain activity seen with medication; in some instances, psychotherapy and pharmacology may act on a common set of brain targets.

In terms of clinical utility, much is to be gained by identifying the pre-therapeutic brain-marker predictors of treatment success. Activity of the anterior cingulate before treatment occurs has been shown to predict the degree to which a client will improve after pharmacological treatment of depression (Martin et al., 2001; Pizzagalli et al., 2001); in obsessive-compulsive disorder, activity in orbito-frontal cortices is similarly predictive (Brody et al., 1998; Saxena et al., 1999). There is potential for these two regions of the brain to be prognostic for outcome of psychotherapy, given their involvement in conflict detection and resolution, as well as behavioural inhibition (Horn et al., 2003; Lubman et al., 2004), and these are probable targets of psychotherapy. Future research will be important in determining which brain regions are predictive of outcome in specific disorders. It will also be important for research to explore whether predictions can be made regarding a differential response to medication versus psychotherapy (Etkin et al, 2005).

The links between psychological processes targeted in therapy and underlying neurobiological processes are captured by the expanded version of Beck's well-known cognitive model of depression. Advances in neurobiology allow for factors that are argued to influence depression, such as cognitive distortions and information-processing biases, to be understood in relation to genetic vulnerabilities, such as a hypersensitive amygdala (Beck, 2008).

The burgeoning new field of social neuroscience, which focuses on interplay between the social environment (e.g., early relationships, therapists) and brain functioning, is of particular interest. Social neuroscience can help us to understand many processes, such as empathy and self-reflection, that are critical to psychotherapy. A good overview of social neuroscience is provided by Lieberman (2007).

Practice implications

Psychologists need to have a basic understanding of the range of non-psychological interventions that are available to assist their clients. Clients will often present after a visit to a medical practitioner, and will often already have been prescribed medications to assist them with their presenting problem. Although psychologists do not prescribe in Australia, it is important that we recognise that treatments from other practitioners, such as psychiatrists, have an evidence base, and a role in treating a range of psychological conditions.

CONCLUSION

Psychologists need to be knowledgeable and skilled in at least one school of therapy that has an evidence base. In Australia, a wide range of theoretical orientations are used to guide practice. Psychologists should also be aware that effective interventions exist outside their areas of expertise, including psychopharmacological agents prescribed by medical practitioners.

Recommended reading
There is of course a huge range of excellent resources related to each of the theories reviewed in this chapter. The readings below are a few examples. Many of these readings are older and by the original authors—we recommend you read some of these; it is a rich experience to gather an understanding about theory from the source.

Bandura, A. (1977). *Social Learning Theory*. Englewood Cliffs: Prentice Hall.

Barlow, D. H. (ed.) (2008). *Clinical Handbook of Psychological Disorders: A Step-by-Step Treatment Manual* (4th edn). New York: Guildford Press.

Beck, A. T., Rush, A. J., Shaw, B. F., & Emery, G. (1979). *Cognitive Therapy of Depression*. New York: Guilford Press.

Carr, A. (2006). *The Handbook of Child and Adolescent Clinical Psychology: A Contextual Approach*. London, New York: Routledge.

Carr, A. & McNully, M. (eds) (2006). *The Handbook of Adult Clinical Psychology: An Evidence-Based Practice Approach*. London, New York: Routledge.

Freud, S. (1962). *Two Short Accounts of Psycho-analysis*. Harmondsworth: Penguin Books.

Greenberg, L. S. (2002). *Emotion-Focused Therapy. Coaching Clients to Work Through their Feelings*. Washington, DC: American Psychological Association.

Greenberg, L. S., Watson, J. C., & Lietaer, G. (1998). *Handbook of Experiential Psychotherapy*. New York: Guildford Press.

Hayes, S. C. & Strosahl, K. D. (eds) (2005). *A Practical Guide to Acceptance and Commitment Therapy*. New York: Springer-Verlag.

Kohut, H. & Strozier, C. (1985). *Self Psychology and the Humanities: Reflections on a New Psychoanalytic Approach*. New York & London: W. W. Norton.

Lambert, M. J. (ed.) (2004). *Bergin and Garfield's Handbook of Psychotherapy and Behavior Change* (5th edn). New York: Wiley.

Linehan. M. (2006). *Treating Borderline Personality Disorder: The Dialectical Approach*. New York: Guildford Press.

Linley, P. A. & Joseph, S. (eds) (2004). *Positive Psychology in Practice*. Hoboken, NJ: John Wiley.

Malan, D. H. (1995). *Individual Psychotherapy and the Science of Psychodynamics*: Oxford: Butterworth-Heinemann.

McKay, M., Wood, J. C., & Brantley, J. (2007). *Dialectical Behaviour Therapy Workbook: Practical DBT Exercises for Learning Mindfulness, Interpersonal Effectiveness, Emotion Regulation, and Distress Tolerance*. Oakland, CA: New Harbinger Publications.

Maslow, A. (1968). *Toward a Psychology of Being*. New York: Insight Books.

Mitchell, S. A. & Black, M. J. (1995). *Freud and Beyond: A History of Modern Psychoanalytic Thought*. New York: Basic Books.

Nichols, M. P. (2008). *Family Therapy: Concepts and Methods*. Boston, MA: Allyn & Bacon.

Peterson, C. & Seligman, M. E. P. (2004). *Character Strengths and Virtues. A Handbook and Classification*. Oxford: Oxford University Press.

Rogers, C. R. (1961). *On Becoming a Person: a Therapist's View of Psychotherapy*. Boston: Houghton Mifflin.

Rogers, C. R. (1980). *A Way of Being*. Boston: Houghton-Mifflin.

Skinner, B. F. (1976). *About Behaviorism*. New York: Vintage Books.

Snyder, C. R. & Lopez, S. J. (eds) (2002). *Handbook of Positive Psychology*. Oxford: Oxford University Press.

Recommended websites

In addition, here are a few websites that may be of interest:

<www.abct.org>

<www.heartandsoulofchange.com>

<www.scottdmiller.com>

Chapter 8

Common factors

INTRODUCTION

The idea that factors which are common across all therapies may be integral to thera-peutic change is not a new one, having been first proposed by Saul Rosenzweig in 1936. As noted in chapter 3, the argument that is most frequently cited in support of common factors as the agents of change in psychotherapy is the equivalence of psy-chotherapeutic outcomes across therapies. As argued by Greenberg (2002), the Dodo Bird Verdict (see chapter 3) was probably a reflection of 'understanding that human beings are nonlinear dynamic systems … in whom multiple processes interact con-tinuously in response to a constantly changing environment' (p. 154). In this chapter, we present an analysis of the common-factors argument, and explore the major models of common factors, and the most often identified common factors. We will also suggest ways in which use of common factors can enhance practice.

COMMON-FACTORS MODELS

Over the years, many factors have been argued to be common to all therapies. In this section we will provide you with an overview of these factors. The models will be presented temporally to provide a sense of the evolution of the common-factors field.

Grencavage and Norcross (1990) reviewed the literature and found that 89 common factors had been proposed in the 50 publications they reviewed. They identified four extant coding systems, and went on to define their own five-category coding system that included client characteristics, therapist qualities, change pro-cesses, treatment structure, and relationship elements. The therapeutic alliance, opportunity for catharsis, acquisition and practice of new behaviours, and clients' positive expectancies were the five factors most frequently endorsed as common across therapies.

Lampropoulos (2001) suggested that these 89 common factors could be distilled into eight: therapeutic relationship; catharsis and relief from distress; hope; self-exploration; awareness and insight into the problem; new rationale; problem con-frontation; acquisition and testing of new learning and control over and mastery of problem. In a recent analysis, utilising cluster analysis and dimensional scaling, the 89 common factors were divided into three clusters (therapeutic bond, therapeutic structure, and provision of a rationale) with two dimensions (thinking versus feeling and therapeutic activity) (Tracey et al., 2003).

At the time that Grancavage and Norcross (1990) put forward their common-factors framework, Frank and Frank (1991) proposed that effective therapy shared at least four features: an emotionally charged, confiding relationship with a helping person; a healing setting; a rationale or myth that provides an explanation for the client's difficulty; and a ritual or procedure that requires the active participation of therapist and client and is believed by both to be the means of restoring the client's health.

In a qualitative study of the experience of change, the most important common factors that underpinned change (Hanna & Ritchie, 1995) were seen as a new understanding, confronting the problem, a desire to change, a sense of necessity, and a willingness to experience anxiety or difficulty.

Further groupings of common factors hypothesised that catharsis, exposure, correctional emotional experiences, internalisation of the therapeutic interaction, affect regulation, development of mentalisation, and a new narrative about self are common active ingredients across therapies (Jorgensen, 2004). Jorgensen argued that all psychotherapeutic therapies and rationales were social constructions that helped therapist and client to generate meaningful and coherent narratives about psychotherapy and the client's difficulties.

Hubble and colleagues (1999) drew on Asay and Lambert's (1999) analysis of the outcome literature to conceptualise common factors within four domains: the client–extratherapeutic domain (such as severity of disturbance, motivation), relationship factors (such as the therapeutic alliance), placebo or hope and expectancy (credibility of rationale), and the model or technique (such as healing rituals).

As you can see, there has been no shortage of lists that attempt to capture the common factors that are implicated in therapeutic effectiveness, but with careful consideration, there is remarkable similarity between them. To enable a comparison, table 8.1 sets out the lists of common factors, with similar constructs set out in columns.

As table 8.1 shows, there is remarkable consistency across the conceptualisations. It can be seen that client expectation that therapy will help is highlighted across most models. The need for a strong therapeutic relationship or alliance is indicated by all models. Most models suggest some requirement for the client to have a new understanding (including insight, new narrative, and more adaptive explanation) of his or her difficulties. Most models suggest the requirement for some type of corrective experience. The notion that affective arousal is required for change is surprisingly absent from many of the taxonomies—this may well be an example of where a 'common' factor is not viewed as 'common' because it is 'specific' to a theory (as in emotionally focused therapy).

Table 8.1 reflects the complexity of the common-factors field, and the array of common factors that have been suggested as integral to therapeutic effectiveness. One limitation of the common-factors approach is confusion over the different ways in which the term 'common factor' is used (Lambert & Ogles, 2004). Different authors have focused on different domains, or levels of treatment, with the result that diverse conceptualisations of common factors have emerged. This has made it difficult to discuss common factors intelligibly or to apply them clinically (Greencavage & Norcross, 1990). Similarly, lists of common factors frequently involved all aspects of therapy—client, therapist, and process, plus interactions—which impeded valid and meaningful studies in this area (Lampropoulos, 2000). Common factors needed to be defined, operationalised, measured, researched, and analysed. Arkowitz (2009) also noted that progress in the common-factors field had been impeded by the absence of an effective way of conceptualising common factors: potentially trivial common factors, such as eye contact, were not differentiated from potentially more potent common factors, such as a corrective experience. Such limitations in the common-factors field presage a further criticism that is more relevant to you: specific clinical behaviours related to the common factors needed to be operationalised (Greencavage & Norcross, 1990). As these authors succinctly state, 'one cannot function nonspecifically in therapy or training' (p. 377).

Principles of change

An alternative to the confusing conceptualisations of common factors was the principles-of-change paradigm proposed by Goldfried in 1980 and developed by Goldfried and Padawer in 1982. In an exploration of different ways to approach the task of looking for commonalities across therapeutic orientations, Goldfried (1980) argued there were three levels of abstraction in the therapeutic enterprise. At the highest level was the theoretical framework for therapy, with its accompanying philosophical explanation for human suffering. At the lowest level of abstraction were therapeutic techniques. Goldfried (1980) argued that comparisons across therapies were unlikely to be useful at either of these levels, and suggested it was more likely that the field would achieve consensus through a mid level of abstraction, which he termed *principles of change*. Such principles, he argued, could function as clinical heuristics that implicitly guide therapist efforts through therapy.

Goldfried and Padawer (1982) argued that there were five general principles of change across different schools of therapy: the facilitation of client expectations that therapy would help (clients' positive expectancies); an optimal therapeutic alliance; increasing clients' awareness of what is contributing to their problems (new understanding); encouragement of corrective experiences; and continued reality testing (reiteration of awareness and corrective experiences).

Grencavage and Norcross (1990) found that change processes were the most frequently endorsed common factors as a level of potential convergence across the different orientations. They argued that this factor lent credence to Goldfried's (1980) hypothesis that the most useful level of abstraction for common factors was in the intermediate level above technique but below theory. Similarly, Lambert (2005) argued that focusing on empirically supported principles of change may enable a more collaborative exploration of mechanisms of change among the advocates of name brand psychotherapies.

Influenced by Goldfried's (1980) work, Castonguay and Beutler (2006) directly explored principles of therapeutic change. In their introduction to the book, Beutler

Table 8.1 Common-factors conceptualisations

Authors	Positive expectations	Therapeutic alliance	Viable explanation or rationale	Corrective experience	Therapist characteristics	Affective component	Other
Rosenzweig (1936)		Relationship between patient and therapist	Development of consistent schema		Therapist's personality		Catharsis
Strupp (1973)		Helping relationship	Interpretations of unconscious material		Therapist qualities		
Goldfried & Padawer (1982)	Expectation that therapy will help	Therapeutic relationship	External perspective on oneself and the world	Corrective experiences			Continued reality testing
Grencavage & Norcross (1990)*	Clients' positive expectancies	Therapeutic alliance	Provision of rationale	Acquisition and practice of new behaviours	Beneficial therapist qualities		Catharsis
Frank & Frank (1991)	Remoralisation	An intense and confiding relationship	Rationale or myth	Ritual or procedure		Facilitation of emotional arousal	Healing setting
Weinberger (1995)	Expectations of success	Therapeutic relationship		Confronting or facing the problem			Attribution of therapeutic outcome to own efforts
Hanna & Ritchie (1995)			New understanding	Confronting the problem			
Grawe (1997)			Clarification of meaning	Mastery and coping			Problem actuation and resource activation

Table 8.1 Common-factors conceptualisations (Continued)

Authors	Positive expectations	Therapeutic alliance	Viable explanation or rationale	Corrective experience	Therapist characteristics	Affective component	Other
Lampropoulos (2001)	Instillation of hope	Therapeutic relationship	Self-exploration, awareness and insight	Problem confrontation		Relief from distress	Catharsis
Tracey et al. (2003)		Therapeutic bond	Provision of rationale				Structure to therapy
Jorgensen (2004)		Therapeutic relationship	New narratives about self	Exposure, desensitisation		Affect regulation	Catharsis, mentalisation, self-reflexivity
Lambert & Ogles (2004)		Identification with therapist, positive relationship, therapeutic alliance, trust	Feedback, insight, rationale	Corrective emotional experience, encouragement to face risks, cognitive mastery, taking risks, mastery efforts, success experience	Therapist expertness, therapist warmth, respect, empathy, acceptance, genuineness	Release of tension, affective experiencing	Catharsis; mitigation of isolation; reassurance; structure; therapist–client active participation; advice; assimilating problematic experiences; cognitive learning; exploration of internal frame of reference; changing expectations of personal effectiveness; behavioural regulation; modelling; practice; reality testing; working through
Wampold (2007)	Remoralisation	Working alliance	New, more adaptive explanation	Activities consistent with explanation			

* Greencavage & Norcross (1989) identified 89 commonalities. Only those identified as 'most consensual' have been included in this table (i.e. cited by >24% of sample (N=50)).

and Castonguay (2006) explored the division between researchers who emphasised models and techniques and researchers who emphasised the interpersonal frame-work within therapy. They argued that each position was typically represented by people with very different beliefs and values who interpreted the same body of research in different ways. Thus, they aimed to 'think outside of the narrow view that simply distinguishes between "techniques" and "relationship" qualities, and of one variable versus another, and to begin to look for foundation principles that encompass a variety of therapeutic factors' (p. 5).

Beutler and Castonguay (2006) defined principles as 'general statements that identify patient characteristics, relational conditions, therapist behaviours, and classes of intervention that are likely to lead to change in psychotherapy' (p. 5). This is a broader definition of principles of change than that offered by Goldfried (1980). To extract the principles of change, 45 scholars reviewed extant literature on the treatment of affective disorders, anxiety disorders, chemical abuse, and per-sonality disorders, and compiled a list of consensually accepted and research-informed principles related to efficacy. As a result, lists of common principles (those that applied to many or most patients with varying disorders) and unique principles (those that predicted outcomes for only one of the patient-disorder groups) resulted in a total of 61 principles being identified, 26 of which were appli-cable to at least two of the four problem areas. The authors cautioned that the prin-ciples of change had not been measured directly or causally related to client improvement in definitive, experimental studies, with the result that they should be treated as hypotheses rather than established or factual processes of change. Despite this caution, this body of work is a significant step forward for the princi-ples-of-change movement.

Theoretical bases to common factors

Lambert and Ogles (2004) argued that there were three traditional views that attempted to explain the common-factors phenomenon. First, it was possible that all mental-health difficulties arose from 'learning processes', and that the mechanism of change involved 'unlearning' old response patterns and acquiring new patterns. Based primarily on learning theory, it was hypothesised that the two main mecha-nisms (desensitisation or extinction of anxiety responses, and learning of mastery behaviours) occurred in all therapies. Second, it was argued that the common factor was the therapeutic relationship that enabled the dropping of defences and reinte-gration of thought, feeling, and action that enables growth. A third view argued for psychotherapy as a special case of healing that included cathartic release, a rationale or belief system for one's difficulties, a set of rituals or procedures, and faith in the healer. Lambert and Ogles (2004) argued that all three explanations had merit, but none was a complete explanation for the process of psychotherapy.

However, Lambert and Ogles (2009) provide the following explanation for how their listing of sequential common factors play out in therapy:

> [Therapists] provide a cooperative working endeavour in which the patient's increased
> sense of trust, security, and safety, along with decreases in tension, threat and anxiety,

lead to changes in conceptualising ... problems and ultimately in acting differently by reframing fears, taking risks, and working through problems in interpersonal relationships (p. 173).

Frank and Frank (1991) argue that psychotherapy is a cultural-healing practice, and that demoralisation is the state of mind that characterises most people who seek psychotherapy. They described the demoralised person metaphorically as one who:

> cowers in a spatiotemporal corner ... he or she clings to a small round of habitual activities, avoids novelty and challenge, and fears making long-term plans. The state of demoralization ... is one of hopelessness, helplessness, and isolation in which the person is preoccupied with merely trying to survive (p. 35).

Effective therapy, Frank and Frank (1991) argue, combats demoralisation through an emotionally charged, confiding relationship with a socially-sanctioned helping person within a healing setting. Within that relationship, a rationale, conceptual scheme, or myth provided a plausible explanation for the patient's difficulties, which was followed by relevant rituals or procedures that are believed by both the helping and the demoralised person. Further, it is argued that those four common features reduce the patient's sense of alienation, strengthen the therapeutic relationship, inspire and maintain the patient's expectation of help, provide new learning experiences, arouse emotions, enhance the patient's sense of mastery or self-efficacy, and provide opportunities for practice.

This argument was largely taken up by Wampold (2007), as discussed in chapter 3. The earlier information is expanded upon in this chapter to provide an example of a theoretically-based model of common factors. Wampold (2007) proposed that a contextual model explained therapeutic change through provision of an alternative explanation for the client's difficulties that made sense to the client and led to explanation-consistent activities. Communication between therapist and client, he argued, is the basis of change. Wampold argued that the human brain has a number of characteristics that are unique: its capacity to interpret events, construct explanations, and attribute causality; its capacity to expand social networks and use language to manage those networks; its propensity to make inferences about the internal states of others, particularly goals, desires, motivations, and beliefs. Further, Wampold argued that the relative strengths of the human brain led to the development of psychotherapy as a cultural-healing practice that met the needs of those relative strengths. More specifically, Wampold (2007) argued that clients enter therapy as a result of persistent problems for which they have maladaptive explanations. Such explanations generally lead clients to perceive their difficulties as inevitable, with the result that they tend to feel demoralised and inactive in relation to the difficulties. Wampold (2007) argued that clients must acquire a new and more adaptive explanation for their problems through psychotherapy, with verbal communication between client and therapist providing the vehicle by which clients acquire that alternative explanation. Acquisition of such an explanation creates a positive expectation within clients that, if therapy is adhered to, their difficulties may be resolved. Wampold said that the therapist must be skilled at monitoring acceptance of the explanation, treatment, and outcome, and that the accepted explanation was both a cause of and a result of the working relationship (Wampold, 2007). Further, acceptance of the explanation is anticipated to change the client's response expectancy (thereby increasing hope) and self-efficacy (thereby leading to increased participation in the therapeutic process) (Wampold et al., 2007). It needs to be recognised that Wampold's work leans heavily on previous models of common factors.

SOME IMPORTANT COMMON FACTORS

By now you should be well acquainted with the arguments for the common-factors approach, and the limitations of the field as it currently stands. We now consider how this relates specifically to what is happening in the therapy room. We will look more closely at some of the common factors that have received most empirical attention, as well as the practice implications of each:

The alliance

The *alliance* is the common factor that has received most attention and, indeed, most empirical support for its role in therapeutic effectiveness. Indeed, it has been described as the 'quintessential common ground shared by most psychotherapies' (Horvath & Bedi, 2002). For this reason, the alliance is disucssed extensively in chapter 6.

Viable explanation or rationale

As noted in the model presented in chapter 3, a *viable explanation or rationale* is considered a factor common to all therapies. Chapter 7 provides models that are often utilised by therapists in their construction of an explanation for clients' difficulties; this chapter explores the reasons why such a viable explanation or rationale is so necessary to effective therapy. To obtain an overview of how this common factor is approached from various theoretical orientations, read a recent book devoted to the study of insight (Castonguay & Hill, 2007). In that book, Wampold and colleagues (2007) argue that a client requires an alternative understanding of her difficulties and that this alternative understanding enables her to engage in therapeutic tasks that lead to corrective experiences. The explanation needs to be proximal to the client's currently held explanation, and take into consideration client characteristics such as world view, culture, attitudes, and beliefs. Such an explanation, once accepted, demonstrates to the client that her therapist understands her, which facilitates the bond component of the working alliance, and facilitates the tasks or goals component of the working alliance.

Practice implications

1   The formulation of the client's difficulties must be sufficiently aligned with the client's current understanding to be acceptable, but sufficiently different to challenge the current understanding.

2   The therapist's role is to explore the client's acceptance of the explanation or ration-ale, and to monitor his or her acceptance through therapy.

3   If the client does not accept the rationale, then it is the therapist's job to find an expla-nation that sits more comfortably with the client's theory of change, or to refer the client to an alternative source of assistance.

Set of actions

Both common-factors models and specific-factor models (see chapter 7) argue for a rationale-consistent set of actions. It is often overlooked that common-factors advo-cates recognise the need for a therapeutic modality and techniques in therapy; it is merely the prioritisation they are given over common factors that is debated (Wam-pold, 2001; Frank & Frank, 1991; Lambert & Ogles, 2004). Wampold (2001) argued that a well-conceived mode of therapeutic action was necessary for a therapeutic relationship. Frank and Frank (1991) acknowledged that there had been a misinter-pretation of the common-factors field; if demoralisation were the core of a client's difficulties, and that all therapeutic schools and methods combated demoralisation, then training in a particular theory or technique would be superfluous. Taken to extremes, it was suggested that the common-factors approach could be interpreted as 'in psychotherapy anything goes' (Frank & Frank, 1991, p. xiv).

The authors were clear in addressing that misinterpretation. They argued it was possible that a client, for a variety of personal reasons, may be more amenable to one technique than to another. They noted that therapist mastery of at least one school of therapy heightened his or her sense of competence and consequently the client's confidence in the therapist. They suggested there might be certain tech-niques that were more effective for specific syndromes (such as exposure for pho-bias). Frank and Frank (1991) stated unequivocally that their position was 'not that technique is irrelevant to outcome' (p. xv), but that:

> ideally therapists should select for each patient the therapy that accords, or can be brought to accord, with the patient's personal characteristics and view of the problem. Also implied is that therapists should seek to learn as many approaches as they find congenial and convincing.

Beutler and Castonguay (2006) concluded that positive change was likely if the therapist could provide a structured treatment and remain focused in the applica-tion of his or her interventions. A strong predictor of negative outcome in therapy is lack of structure and focus in treatment (Duncan et al., 2010). It is important that psychologists are confident and knowledgeable in at least one school of therapy, to ensure that they are able to provide a credible rationale that is acceptable to the client and leads to a set of rationale-consistent actions.

Practice implications

1   Effective therapists must be confident and knowledgeable in at least one school of therapy.

2   Therapists must believe in the therapy they practice.
3   The techniques must be consistent with the rationale provided to and accepted by the client.
4   There must be a structure to therapy, balanced with flexibility, to ensure that the client's needs are met.

Positive expectations

Grencavage and Norcross (1990) identified positive expectations as the most commonly-cited client characteristic identified as a common factor. Facilitation of expectations that therapy will be helpful has also been postulated as a common principle of change (Beutler & Castonguay, 2006). Without such expectations, it is unlikely there will be a second session and a client willing to engage in therapy. Constantino and colleagues (2005) discovered that client expectations were positively associated with measures of the working alliance in the treatment of bulimia nervosa, and that the working alliance positively predicted outcome. Thus, it may be that the relationship between expectations and outcome is mediated by the working alliance. This question was explored directly by Joyce and colleagues (2003), who found that the working alliance accounted for approximately one-third of the direct effect of expectations on outcome. Thus, it appears that expectations will have both a direct relationship with outcome, and will be mediated by the working alliance. That dual role of expectations may account for some of the discrepancies in the literature to date.

The relationship between positive expectations and hope also needs to be discussed, as the two constructs are often discussed interchangeably. Snyder and colleagues (1999) argued that hope was a basic process through which people dealt with adversity in everyday life, and that successful therapy facilitated change through enhancement of hope. They argued that the therapeutic relationship and setting fostered clients' beliefs that they could change, whereas the particular rationale and ritual acted to enhance what they defined as *pathways* thoughts ('this is how I can change'). Hayes and colleagues (2007) suggested that the early response to therapy (prior to cognitive change) of 41 per cent of their sample was supportive of the role of hope in first-order change. Hope predicted lower levels of depression at the end of the study (independently of pretreatment levels of depression). This is consistent with the work of Howard and colleagues (1993), who saw installation of hope as the first phase of psychotherapy.

Goldfried (1991) cautioned that facilitation of expectations of the helpfulness of therapy must be the first step in the psychotherapy process. This is an important point, because it is logical that positive expectations at the beginning of therapy will be mediated by the process of therapy. Thus, the match between clients' expectations and experience of therapy must be monitored.

Practice implications

1   Effective therapists monitor clients' positive expectations of change throughout therapy.
2   Expectations should be explicitly elicited and discussed.

3   Overt scepticism on the part of the client should be discussed openly.

4   It may be helpful to include a non-technical review of the literature and provide realistic information about gradual change.

5   Clients' beliefs about the length and nature of treatment should be elicited, with any discrepancies addressed early in therapy, to prevent dropout because of incorrect assumptions about therapy.

Corrective experience, including exposure

The corrective experience is defined as a novel experience that involves changes in a client's thinking, feeling, desires, or behaviour (Goldfried & Davila, 2005). The notion of a *corrective emotional experience* came from Alexander and French (1946). In essence, *corrective emotional experiences* refers to situations where the client is able to alter his or her rigid relational patterns as a result of being exposed to new interpersonal experiences with the therapist (Bernier & Dozier, 2002).

While the construct of the corrective emotional experience may have initially been most prevalent in psychodynamic–psychoanalytic domains, more recent research in cognitive therapy has highlighted use of the therapeutic relationship to disconfirm maladaptive schema (Young et al., 2003), thereby providing a corrective experience. Research on therapeutic ruptures demonstrates use of a corrective interpersonal experience as a mechanism for change (Safran & Muran, 1996). Strauss and colleagues (2006) demonstrated that rupture-repair episodes were associated with pre-post treatment symptom reduction of 50 per cent or more on all measures in patients diagnosed with avoidant and obsessive-compulsive disorder. Thus, while initially in the psychodynamic domains, the corrective emotional experience attained through rupture-repair episodes has now extended to other therapies.

The construct of the corrective experience can also be broadened to domains other than the interpersonal domain (Grosse Holtforth et al., 2006). There is growing awareness that avoidance of negative experiences, whether behavioural, cognitive, interpersonal, or affective, is associated with psychopathology (Grosse Holforth, 2008; Hayes et al., 2005). Exposure to avoided material in the therapeutic setting is integral to effective therapeutic outcomes. Frequently thought of as a behavioural intervention, the effectiveness of exposure for anxiety disorders has been well documented (Emmelkamp, 2004).

More recently, the role of exposure in depression has been explored. Hayes and colleagues (2005) described vacillation between rumination and avoidance often found in depressed patients, and researched the effects of exposure to avoided material. Although preliminary, their results suggested that peak levels of processing avoided material were associated with higher levels of improvement in depression. It follows that the term *exposure* can be broadened to capture the confrontation by the client of difficult and anxiety-provoking behaviours, thoughts, emotions, or interpersonal situations. Such exposure, it is argued, is implicit in the very interaction between client and therapist, where they, together, explore the issues that brought the client to therapy. In the interpersonal interaction, through reliving memories, or engagement with difficult emotions, the client learns a sense of being able to cope with his or her problems (Jorgensen, 2004). In addition, difficult experiences become less anxiety provoking, and the client gains a greater sense of self-efficacy. In this way, exposure serves to change the way in which clients view themselves or their world, resulting in a corrective experience.

Practice implications

1   In therapy, monitor the ways in which behavioural, affective, cognitive, or interpersonal changes are assimilated into clients' views of themselves and/or their world.
2   When reviewing clients' progress, reflect on whether there has been a corrective experience during therapy and, if so, whether it was reinforced through therapy.

Affective arousal

All psychotherapies appear to engage with emotion to some extent (Whelton, 2004), with arguably the most profound changes for the client taking place when an alternative understanding occurs within the context of affective arousal (Hayes et al., 2007). However, affective arousal in the absence of an alternative understanding or a corrective experience is unlikely to effect therapeutic change (Greenberg & Pascual-Leone, 2006). According to Greenberg (2002), there are two types of knowing, 'knowledge by description (conceptual knowledge)' and 'knowledge by acquaintance (experiential knowing)', and that only by having an impact on both can change be effected.

Similarly, Samoilov and Goldfried (2000) suggest two modes of mental processing, an intellectual mode and an emotional mode, with the emotional mode most likely accessed through the presence of emotional arousal; thus, emotional arousal in-session is critical for change of implicit meaning structures. Supporting that argument, Missirlian and colleagues (2005) showed that outcome was predicted more effectively by emotional arousal in conjunction with perceptual processing than by either variable alone. Similarly, Hayes and colleagues (2007) found that at least one depressive spike (experienced by 62 per cent of their participants) during the emotional-processing phase of their study was predictive of lower levels of depression at the end of treatment. Taken together, these studies demonstrate the need for affective arousal (combined with processing) if therapeutic change is to be achieved.

Practice implications

1   Be aware that affective arousal without cognitive processing may not elicit effective outcomes for clients. And vice versa: focusing only on cognitions without emotional arousal may not elicit change.
2   Guiding or challenging interventions and long verbal interventions by the therapist are likely to lead clients away from affective arousal.

3   Likewise, highly controlling statements, close-ended questions, and interventions with minimal affective content will lead to lower affective experiencing by clients.
4   Try a friendly, non-controlling, interpersonal stance, reflections and acknowledgment, and minimal responses ('Hmmm; I see').

CONCLUSIONS

We hope that this chapter has provided you with a clear picture of the common-factors movement in psychotherapy-outcome research as it currently stands. Renewed focus on the role of common factors is likely to enrich how effective psychotherapy can be in improving client outcome, and it is hoped that a beginning therapist can 'combine all the different strategies and techniques into a unique approach that fits his or her philosophical worldview and personality' (Hill, 2009, p. 16). Such uniqueness, when practised ethically and with a focus always on client well-being and outcome, truly recognises the unique, dynamic and responsive practice that is psychotherapy. Remember Frank and Frank's (1991) point that a common-factors approach does not mean that anything goes in therapy. It merely means that the factors common across disparate theoretical orientations may well be the factors that work best among them (Norcross, 1999).

Recommended reading

Castonguay, L. G. & Beutler, L. E. (eds) (2006). *Principles of Therapeutic Change that Work.* Oxford: Oxford University Press.

Duncan, B. L., Miller, S. D., Wampold, B. E., & Hubble, M. A. (eds). (2010). *The Heart and Soul of Change* (2nd edn). Washington, DC: American Psychological Association.

Goldfried, M. R. (1980). Toward the delineation of therapeutic change principles. *American Psychologist*, 35, 991–9.

Wampold, B. E. (2007). Psychotherapy: the humanistic (and effective) treatment. *American Psychologist*, 62(8), 857–73.

Chapter 9

Client outcome

Introduction

'What treatment, by whom, is most effective for this individual with that specific problem under what set of circumstances?' (Paul, 1967, p. 111). This famous quote captures the complexity of measuring outcome in regard to the interplay of factors that influence therapeutic outcome. In the previous chapters of part B, we have covered each of those factors in detail. We have discussed both specific and common factors in therapy, we have discussed client and therapist characteristics, and we've had a good look at the therapeutic alliance. We've also introduced you to a range of issues about clients that can have an impact on the helpfulness of therapy.

In chapters 3 and 8 we also explored the debate about which factors matter the most to therapeutic outcome, and concluded that as yet there is no definitive answer to this question. Instead, it appears that all these aspects work together to assist with positive client outcome. Irrespective of orientation, all psychotherapies share a common aim, achieving optimal client outcomes. This chapter will cover a range of topics relevant to client outcome, including: what constitutes outcome in psychotherapy; client dropout and premature termination; preventing harm to clients, and insuring that therapy is not making clients worse; and using client feedback to improve outcome.

Monitoring client outcome

Consistent monitoring of client outcome is of vital importance. Lambert and colleagues have spent nearly 20 years in programmatic research focused on the importance of monitoring client progress and providing feedback to therapists about clients' progress. In summary, this is what they have found:

- Clinical trails in naturalistic settings show that 5 to 10 per cent of clients get worse as a result of treatment, and up to 60 per cent may not improve significantly (this does not mean they do not improve, but that the change is not clinically significant) (Hansen et al., 2002; Lambert & Ogles, 2004).
- Therapists, without the use of objective client feedback information, are very poor at recognising when their clients are deteriorating. Therapists working with 550 clients were asked to predict which clients would have a negative outcome. Therapists predicted that only three of the 550 clients would have a negative

outcome, when 26 did. Only one therapist correctly predicted outcome for a client, whereas the OQ45 algorithms predicted 20 of the 26 cases, in advance (Lambert, 2010). These findings can leave us in no doubt of how important it is to have objective feedback; we therapists tend to be overoptimistic, and mostly blind to when clients are deteriorating, and thus cannot trust our subjective judgment.

- Providing therapists with session-by-session feedback on how clients are progressing produces statistically significant improvements in client outcome (Lambert et al., 2002; Lambert et al., 2001; Whipple et al., 2003). In comparing therapists who received feedback on how their clients were progressing with therapists who did not receive feedback, feedback resulted in significant client outcome improvement (Lambert et al., 2005).
- Not only did outcome improve, but deterioration rates were reduced significantly (Lambert et al., 2005). Thus, feedback helped clients who would have continued to get worse as a result of treatment.
- Not satisfied with the remarkable gains made by simply informing therapists of client progress or lack of progress, Lambert and his team improved on previously enhanced client outcome by introducing a manual of *Clinical Support Tools (CSTs)* that could be used in a diagnostic manner by therapists to determine which factors were preventing improvement or resulting in deterioration. These tools will be discussed in the latter part of this chapter. Adding this enhanced feedback process resulted in improvements of 25 to 49 per cent for clients seeing therapists who received the tools, in comparison to no change for clients seen by therapists not receiving the tools. In addition, deterioration—or *not on track (NOT)*—in clients of therapists receiving the tools reduced from 19 to 8 per cent (Whipple et al., 2003). This study was replicated and results indicated that deterioration dropped from 21 to 7 per cent when the clinical support tools were used (Harmon et al., 2007).

Lambert (2007) makes the point succinctly: 'This means that in a client population of 1000 NOT (not on track) clients, recovered/improved clients would increase from 250 to 490 and clients that deteriorate would decrease from 190 to 80' (p. 51). Obtaining regular client feedback is essential in many cases to ensure positive outcome. A therapist would be considered negligent if he or she did not use a feedback method to try to combat client deterioration. We will expand further on the measure—*Outcome Questionnaire-45* (OQ45)—used in the above studies in the last section of this chapter, as well as on other measures used to obtain client feedback. But therapists cannot rely on their own 'opinion' or 'intuition', or the fact that a client returns for another session, to be confident they are accurately tracking the client and actually helping.

WHAT CONSTITUTES OUTCOME IN PSYCHOTHERAPY?

There is a surprising array of opinions regarding the purpose of therapy. A few very different views include:

- to help clients become more aware of their own internal reactions and interpersonal responses in problem situations (Teyber, 2006; Teyber & McClure, 2010).

- 'We have come to recognise that if we can provide understanding of the way the client seems to himself at this moment, he can do the rest. The therapist ... must concentrate on one purpose only; that of providing deep understanding and acceptance of the attitudes consciously held at this moment by the client as he explores step by step into the dangerous areas which he has been denying to consciousness' (Rogers, 1946, p. 412).
- 'We are not here to make people feel better, we are here to remove symptoms' (attributed to a well-known psychologist answering a question about the purpose of treatment during a presentation some years ago at a conference).

There can be little doubt that a therapist's view of client outcome will have an impact on how the therapist works with individuals, and to what the therapist pays attention. Clients, of course, also have a view on what they want from therapy. Clients sometimes come to therapy with a tremendous number of problems in their life, wanting a 'quick fix', expecting that things will change in a session or two. But, some clients don't think anyone can help them change; sometimes such clients have problems which are relatively easy to change.

One of this book's authors once had a client who, at the age of 40, while listening to a radio show on anxiety, for the first time realised that her 'turns' were in fact panic attacks, and that reliable and effective treatments were available. This client had suffered since adolescence, and had never thought anything could be done to help her—her suffering was simply the way she was. Many clients will not be fully cognisant of what can or cannot be achieved in therapy. Thus, we suggest that a good place to start is by enquiring about the client's goals in seeking treatment.

However, therapists may need to shape the client's desired outcome based on knowledge of the literature on outcome factors, including length of treatment and limitations. For example, no treatment can 'erase' memories of childhood abuse, but treatment can assist in overcoming the negative effects of such experiences.

Exercise 9.1

1   What do you think are the basic goals for treatment? What outcomes do you think you need to facilitate in clients?
2   What are your basic beliefs and assumptions about human nature? Do you believe that all people are fundamentally good? That all people can change for the better? That, if people were given the opportunity, they would choose to behave in a positive manner? Or do you think that people are fundamentally driven by self-interest? That some people are set in their ways and can't change? That some people enjoy behaving poorly and would not choose to behave positively even if given a chance to?
3   How do these beliefs and assumptions influence your work as a psychologist and what you focus on as goals in treatment?

Many types of outcome can be achieved through therapy, and clients will differ in what outcomes they want. One author learned this lesson while doing her postgraduate training, working with a client with severe OCD. The client had a particular obsession, that he would harm his family, which seemed completely out of character, as the client was a very mild-mannered person. In passing during therapy, he mentioned that, while growing up, his father would often threaten the family, and actually attack members of the family, with the client narrowly escaping with his life a few times. The author was delighted, as 'the mystery was solved', and harped on at length about how this 'insight' could assist in helping the client. The client, patiently and politely, let the author go on, and eventually said, 'Can we please continue with the exposure exercise?', showing no interest in making sense of the origins of his problem.

This is a good example of where a therapist's view of what will lead to positive outcome is quite different from the view held by the client. Fortunately, the author had the sense to stop trying to get the client to also relish the insight, and to get on with behavioural exposure—because, for therapy to be effective, the client's view of conceptualisation, treatment, purpose of treatment, and outcome focus must be respected and worked with. The client responded well to exposure, and the outcome was positive. The author is still frustrated that her brilliant detective work was of no interest to the client, but it was a valuable lesson. Of course, for other clients, insight about the link between their fear and their previous experience would've been important. And, as Paul's (1967) quote, at the beginning of the chapter, reminds us, it's what works for the client that matters.

Some clients will simply hope for symptom reduction; others will want insight into their presenting difficulties; still others aim for a greater quality of life. From the beginning of therapy, it is important to explore your client's desired outcome and determine whether it is consistent with the treatment you have in mind. A therapist must adapt to client needs and views, including about the purpose of treatment. If there is a rift between therapist and client goals, the therapist needs to work at shared treatment goals. In chapter 6, on the alliance, we discussed the importance of agreement on the tasks and goals of treatment to a strong alliance and a positive outcome.

It is important to then identify ways to measure whether your client is moving towards that desired outcome. For many clients, standardised psychometrically sound measures are available to capture outcome goals. The importance of monitoring client movement towards desired outcome goals cannot be overstated, and will be discussed in more detail later in this chapter.

How much therapy do clients need?

One of the most common questions a client will ask is, 'How long is this going to take?' This is also one of the big questions asked in the profession, often phrased as, 'How much treatment is required to assist a client in making significant changes?' Borrowing a term from medicine, some psychotherapy-outcome researchers have examined the concept of *dose-effect*, that is, how many 'doses' (psychotherapy sessions) does a particular client require to achieve a significant recovery after entering therapy at a dysfunctional range? This research allows us to compare how we are progressing with clients, in terms of number of sessions, with the generally expected rate of progress.

Dose-effect curve

It makes sense that there would be a need to adjust level of treatment (that is, number and frequency of sessions) to the treatment needs of a client, based on, for example, severity of impairment or risk of harm (Beutler et al., 2004). Howard and colleagues (1996) suggested that a curvilinear relationship, with a negatively accelerated curve of dose-effect, is the most common pattern of change for clients (Howard et al., 1996; Kopta et al., 1994; Sperry et al., 1996). This suggests that clients tend to improve more quickly early in treatment, and that treatment gains tend to flatten off over time. More recent findings are that 53 per cent of clients improved after only eight sessions, 75 per cent improved after 26 sessions, and most (83 per cent) improved after 52 sessions (Lambert & Ogles, 2004).

However, this 'curve' was identified through use of pre-post ratings rather than session-by-session improvements, making it impossible to pinpoint the exact time to recovery for individual patients (Lambert & Ogles, 2004). In a study that used sessional measures of outcome, Anderson and Lambert (2001) found that speed of recovery had been overestimated by Howard and colleagues (1996). In Anderson and Lambert's study, on average, clients required 13 sessions of therapy to achieve clinically significant change, with 75 per cent of clients achieving such change after 50 sessions. Extending this research paradigm to a national sample, Lambert and colleagues (2001) found that half of all clients (50 per cent) achieved clinically significant change within 21 sessions, but that session numbers had to double (up to 50 sessions) for 75 per cent of clients to change significantly.

Although it is tempting to use such figures to compare one's own clients' progress, more recent research is raising important questions about the dose-response model. Baldwin and colleagues (2009) set out to compare the dose-effect model, as construed by Howard and colleagues, which argues that therapy follows a negatively accelerating pattern, with the recently suggested *good-enough level (GEL)* model (Barkman et al., 2006). The GEL model suggests that clients change at different rates; there is not a pattern for all clients, as suggested by the dose-effect model; therapy is not more effective the longer it goes, because those who respond rapidly leave therapy early, with slow responders staying in therapy longer (Baldwin et al., 2009). Simply, those clients staying in therapy longer are not more likely to attain clinically significant change than those who stay for a shorter period, because those who stay longer respond more slowly. This does not mean that sessions become less potent over time—it is simply that some individuals need more sessions than others. Thus, as useful as the curvilinear model may be, researchers have observed that the model is not robust (e.g. Hilsenroth et al., 2001), and is not a one-size-fits-all model. As noted by Beutler and colleagues (2004), the shape or course of the relationship between treatment dose and outcome can be influenced by chronicity and reactivity of symptoms, type of client problem, type of treatment, and outcome evaluation.

In a recent Australian study, Harnett, O'Donovan & Lambert (2010) looked at dose response in two psychology clinics training postgraduate clinical students. Following the progress of 125 clients, results using survival analysis indicated that 50 per cent of the clients would require eight sessions to show reliable improvement, and by 21 sessions, 85 per cent of clients would have met criteria for reliable change (using the OQ45 as outcome measure). However, for clients to fully recover required on average 14 sessions for 50 per cent of the clients, and after 23 sessions, 70 per cent of clients had fully recovered. The authors concluded that the then Medicare (Better Access) policy of supporting six or 12 sessions per client per year is inadequate to achieve full recovery for the bulk of clients. Since this paper was published the number of sessions allowed has been reduced further to a maximum of 10.

In March 2008, the Australian Psychological Society (APS) conducted a survey of over 2000 psychologists who provide Medicare-funded services under the Better Access scheme, 649 being clinical psychologists. The survey results showed that the majority of clients complete between five and 12 sessions (approximately 70 per cent). However, therapists suggested that a substantial number of clients (14–17 per cent) required more than 12 sessions. This survey focused simply on number of sessions completed rather than outcomes—which means we don't know to what extent these clients improved. Thus, there can be no comment as to whether the number of sessions was sufficient to result in significant levels of change.

The take-home message from this is that there is no straightforward model that predicts the number of sessions required for effective client outcomes. The pressing question for future research is how to discriminate between clients who require more or less treatment (Baldwin et al., 2009). A clinical implication of these findings is that therapists cannot simply assume that 'more is better' for all, but need to discriminate between clients who require relatively few and those who require a considerable number of sessions. We discuss later a good way to assess this by using session-by-session outcome ratings.

Early responders
It is clear from the dose-effect curvilinear model that many clients who do well as a result of therapy tend to respond early on. These clients are commonly referred to as *early responders*. That there tends to be more benefit from treatment early in therapy rather than later is in general a useful guide (Lambert & Ogles, 2004). Thus, if you are working with a client who is responding well to treatment early on, you are likely to have greater success with this client than with a client who does not respond well early. Most of the clients in the study by Howard and colleagues (1986) had significantly improved, it seemed, before change could have been a result of type of treatment used, or before a strong alliance had been established (Bohart & Tallman, 2010). It seems that some clients need very little to change, and can even attend just one intake session of therapy.

Impact of problem severity
In contrast, some clients need a considerable amount of treatment. Severity of clients' problems has been shown to have an impact on dose-effect relations. Kopta and colleague (1994) clustered the symptoms clients presented with into three areas, acute distress, chronic distress, and characterological symptoms. Considerable difference in recovery rates was found across the three groups, with the least distressed group (acute) taking on average 10 sessions for 50 per cent of the clients to improve. In the characterological symptoms group (clients with symptoms of personality disorders), fewer than half recovered by the time they had had 52 sessions, and on average 104 sessions were required. Clearly, further research is needed to clarify impact of severity on dose-effect (Baldwin et al., 2009).

Practice implications for using rate of change in treatment

An important issue research on dose-effect raises is: how should rate of improvement of a client inform practice? Here are some suggestions:

1 Objectively monitor rate of change using outcome-evaluation measures. As we have already emphasised, it is imperative to effective practice to evaluate client outcomes— and not just pre or post, but more regularly, preferably session by session.

2 If your client is demonstrating a lot of change early in therapy, this is generally a sign predicting good outcomes. The one risk is that such a client may terminate prematurely, feeling that excellent gains have been made—which they have. Most of these clients could continue to make gains, and cement changes, if they remained in therapy a bit longer. A good way to manage this is to make follow-up appointments (such as a month or two from last session). This will act to maintain progress and provide relapse prevention.

3 Lambert and colleagues (2001) found that providing session-by-session feedback, using the OQ45, of clients who are progressing well resulted in a decreased therapy length for these clients. Without objective feedback that a client has reached an appropriate level of improvement, therapy may continue unnecessarily long, and cost more than it needs to.

4 If clients are slow to start making changes, there are a number of issues to consider, including: (a) how severe is their level of dysfunction? (if a personality problem, then it would not be unusual for treatment to take some time to start making a difference); and (b) is the treatment you are providing the right match for the client? (if the client is 'stuck', then it possibly means that what the therapist is doing is not suited to the client, and the therapist needs to consider changing tack).

How economic factors influence dose-effect

Although 70 per cent of clients receive only five to 12 sessions of psychotherapy in Australia, research suggests that for approximately 50 per cent of clients it may take more than 21 sessions to achieve significant change (Lambert et al., 2001). Medicare provides up to 6 sessions, or, with a GP's agreement, up to 10 sessions. The number of sessions provided by Medicare may be inadequate for a range of disorders (Harnett et al., 2010).

There is of course a cost to the government. The initial budget for psychological items covered by Medicare in the first five years of the new system (started in November 2006) was $538 million. By December 2009, three years later, $997 million had been paid out. However, a significant proportion of this amount was paid to GPs for referring clients to psychologists, rather than direct to psychologists.

Clearly, there are huge costs in providing mental health, and governments do not have unlimited funds. But are the costs worth it? There are savings for the health system as a whole by making psychological interventions more readily available. This is known as the *cost-offset effect*. Numerous studies have demonstrated that patients who receive psychological and medical services significantly reduce their use of medical services (e.g. Mumford et al., 1984; Gabbard et al, 1997). Most recently, Chiles and colleagues (1999) found that on average there was a 15.7 per cent reduction in use of medical services by individuals receiving psychotherapy, whereas there was a 12.3 per cent increase in use of medical services by those not in psychotherapy. Overall, this means a 25 per cent reduction in need for medical services for individuals receiving some form of therapy. As such, it seems that increased client access to psychological services reduces the burden on medical services and therefore cost to the health system as a whole. Economics and well-being are often not comfortable bedfellows. Our society needs to consider how important psychological well-being is, and how willing it is to support the role of psychological treatment in improving well-being.

CLIENT DROPOUT AND PREMATURE TERMINATION

An obvious predictor of poor outcome is premature dropout from treatment. Overall, studies indicate that the majority of clients terminate treatment before 10 sessions, with the median number of sessions being about six (Garfield, 1986; Kleinke, 1994). The Australian data discussed earlier appears to fit this international pattern quite closely, with 70 per cent of clients attending therapy for between five and 12 sessions. Further, international data suggest that about one-third of all clients who consult a mental-health professional attend only one session (Clarkin & Hull, 1991). In a meta-analysis of 125 studies, Wierzbicke & Pekarik (1993) found that 46.86 per cent of clients prematurely dropped out of treatment, when dropout was defined as therapist judgment that a client terminated treatment early. When failure to attend a scheduled session was used as the definition of dropout, the rate is lower. Bearing in mind our earlier discussion regarding dose-response, it is unclear whether some individuals considered to have dropped out of therapy may have reached significant change—and the therapist simply did not realise this, as he or she was not assessing client change regularly.

Why do many clients drop out of therapy before there has been an opportunity for therapy to have an effect? There have been a range of findings on this question. Some client factors may predict dropout. Socioeconomic status (SES) has been found to be associated with early dropout. Lower-SES clients tend to have a higher dropout rate than clients with higher SES, in particular when there was a difference between ethnic background of therapist and client (Bischoff & Sprenkle, 1993). Other demographic factors, such as age, have not been found to predict dropout (Sledge et al., 1990), but lower level of education does correlate with dropout.

Certain diagnoses have been found to be correlated with dropout, with obsessive-compulsive disorder (Hansen et al., 1992) and personality disorders, such as borderline personality disorder (Gunderson et al., 1989; Skodol et al., 1983), associated with higher dropout rates. Client expectations of treatment can correlate with dropout, as client expectations are strongly related to length of treatment or duration (Jenkins et al., 1986).

Most often, clients expect to be in treatment for shorter times than needed for treatment to have optimal outcome, and they leave prematurely. However, therapeutic factors also play a major role in dropout. Not surprisingly, studies have found that a poor early alliance will predict dropout (e.g. De La Pena et al., 2009).

Some clients drop out of therapy if they do not accept treatment rationale and/or related actions based on treatment type (Anderson et al., 2010), possibly through lack of fit with client expectations of treatment. A main conclusion of the study by Tracey (1986) regarding correlates of premature termination was that 'mutually agreeable definitions of what each is to do' (p. 787) is a major determinant of whether therapy continues past the first few sessions.

Practice implications:
What can therapists do to try to prevent premature dropout?

1. Possibly the main strategy is to focus on forming a strong alliance with a client from first contact. Not only does a good bond correlate with better outcome, it is a safeguard against premature termination. As Horvath (1995) has noted, 'The establishment of a good alliance early in therapy appears to be vital for a successful outcome' (p. 14).

2. Check what a client's theory of change is (see chapter 4), and check that the suggested rationale for treatment relates to the client's theory, at least to some extent, to assist the client to accept the rationale and associated interventions. If the rationale for treatment does not match the client's view, the likelihood of dropout is high.

3. Check regularly with the client that treatment is working for her, and enquire about any concerns. Encouraging the client to provide feedback is essential to improve treatment.

4. Create or encourage a sense of positive expectancy and hope that treatment will assist the client with her problems. An obvious way to do this is to give the client information on how her problem has been successfully treated with others. But most importantly, let the client know that you will be there to support her and have confidence that she will get better.

5. Use session-by-session ratings to check if indeed the client is prematurely leaving treatment, or whether the client actually has obtained significant or reliable change.

WHEN THERAPY LEADS TO DETERIORATION FOR CLIENTS

It is of concern that between 5 and 10 per cent of clients deteriorate while in treatment (Lambert & Ogles, 2004). A painful reality is that most psychotherapists, albeit unintentionally, at some point may have harmed some of their clients (Castonguay et al., 2010). What is meant by 'harming clients'? Harm can include providing treatment that results in slower than necessary change, using an ineffective treatment, or behaving in ways that are distressing for the client (Lilienfeld, 2007). Even the most experienced therapist has, most likely, taken unnecessarily long to help a client change (Castonguay et al., 2010).

However, we all need to take note of predictable sources of harm in treatment: *potentially harmful treatments (PHTs)*. A number of therapies have been highlighted by Lilienfeld (2007) as being potentially harmful for some individuals, including:

- critical incident stress debriefing, which may produce an increased risk for post-traumatic stress symptoms
- recovered-memory techniques, which can lead to the production of false memories of trauma
- dissociative identity disorder-oriented therapy, which can result in induction of 'alter' personalities
- grief counselling for individuals with normal bereavement reactions, which can increase depressive symptoms
- boot-camp interventions for conduct disorder, which can actually lead to exacerbation of conduct problems
- relaxation treatments for panic-prone clients, which may actually induce panic attacks.

The picture is complicated by the fact that not all of the treatments listed by Lilienfeld have arguably fetched sufficient data to suggest they are consistently harmful, and that some treatments (such as expressive-experiential therapies) are helpful for many clients. Castonguay and colleagues (2010), in discussing Lilienfeld's conclusions, remind us of Paul's (1967) quote with which we started this chapter: 'What treatment, by whom, is most effective for this individual with that specific problem under what set of circumstances?' However, some treatments listed by Lilienfeld probably have enough research to contraindicate use with any client. Critical incident stress debriefing, for example, has substantial evidence to warrant cessation—yet it continues to be used widely in Australia and across the world.

Castonguay and colleagues (2010) discussed the many technique factors that can cause problems in treatment. In an earlier study, Castonguay and colleagues (1996) found that rigid adherence to cognitive techniques interfered significantly with client outcome. Some specific techniques have also been found to commonly predict poor outcome, including overinterpretation by therapists, such as interpreting client frustration as transference, when it may be frustration at therapy (Piper et al., 1999). Such misinterpretations will lead to difficulties, as the therapist will not recognise the real rupture in the alliance, and the client is likely to become more resistant—and this too may be misinterpreted as transference.

Specific therapists may predict client deterioration to a much greater extent than type of therapy used (Lilienfield, 2007). This hypothesis is still to be fully tested, but research supports it. Lafferty and colleagues (1989) found that clients with therapists who lacked warmth and empathy tended to deteriorate, as do clients of therapists who are highly confrontational (Mohr, 1995). Other studies mentioned in chapter 5 also point to potential negative outcomes based on negative therapist behaviours. Henry and colleagues (1986; 1990) found that certain 'toxic' therapist behaviours, such as belittling or blaming clients, or ignoring and neglecting them, result in poor outcomes.

A number of studies have demonstrated that therapists vary considerably in their ability to enhance client outcome, and in their ability to manage at-risk clients. Brown and colleagues (2005) found that at-risk clients seen by the top quartile of therapists did much better in a shorter period than clients treated by therapists in the lowest quartile. In fact, clients seen by this last group of therapists, despite having many more sessions than clients seen by the better therapists, tended to continue deteriorating. More recently Okkishi and colleagues (2006) analysed data of 5000 clients treated by 149 therapists. Consistent with other studies (e.g. Beutler et al., 1994; Wampold & Brown, 2005), client outcome was not related to level or type of training, or to the theoretical orientation of the therapist; neither were there significant differences in size or type of case loads. There were significant differences between therapists in number of sessions they had with clients, and the speed and overall amount of change. Therapists were separated into bottom and top 10 per cent ranked, based on these factors. Twice as many clients deteriorated when they saw one of the bottom-ranked therapists compared to clients fortunate enough to see one of the top-ranked therapists (Okkishi et al., 2006). This type of data can leave little doubt that therapists vary considerably in their effectiveness, and in their risk of harm to clients.

Therapists appear remarkably poor at judging accurately how well treatment is going for a client. Hiatt and Hargreave (1995) found that the least helpful practitioners in their outcome study rated themselves as the most helpful. This indicates a clear lack of awareness of their practice—but it is very possible when practitioners fail to use objective measures of client outcome and rely on their own opinions. When comparing therapists' accuracy in determining which clients would deteriorate with actual deterioration data, Hannan and colleagues (2005) found that therapists were accurate in only one of 550 cases! Of the 40 clients who deteriorated in the study, only one client was identified by the therapist. Lambert (2010) argues that these types of findings are clear evidence of the necessity for therapists to use routine outcome measures to evaluate the progress of their clients.

Practice implication:
How to combat risk of doing harm to your clients

1   Be up to date with the literature about potentially-harmful treatments, and cognisant of the literature on evidence-based treatments, and apply these treatments as appropriate. However, no treatment is guaranteed to be successful with every client, and we need to monitor consistently what is happening for every client, even when using evidence-based treatments.

2   Keep in mind that a strong alliance is vitally important to outcome, and that client outcomes are likely to be hampered by poor alliances or collaborations between client and therapist (Horvath & Bedi, 2002; Martin et al., 2000). Work at establishing, monitoring, and maintaining strong alliances with all your clients.

3   Be open to feedback about your own behaviour and potential impact on clients. If your supervisor is not providing you with direct feedback on your personal style or behaviours (both your strengths and weaknesses), ask. Supervisors often shy away from commenting on personal attributes, which is a weakness in supervision, as it is vital to allow therapists to become aware of potential issues. Castonguay and colleagues (2010) state that:

> Clinical supervisors need to help trainees to know themselves, such as their strengths, limitations, interpersonal vulnerabilities, and countertransferential blind spots. Moreover, they need to develop the ability to monitor the impact of their internal experience, especially their hostile and negative feelings, on the therapeutic relationship (p. 40).

4   Blind spots and vulnerabilities: Castonguay and colleagues (2010) also recommend that attempts be made to match clients and therapists, in terms of what issues the therapist may not have dealt with, and are not yet ready to work with.

5   Watch as many videos as possible of yourself doing therapy to observe your actual behaviour and how this has an impact on clients. Consider personal therapy to deal with any issues that may have a negative impact on your practice.

6   Saptya and colleagues (2005) have pointed out that feedback is most effective when it provides information on actions that can be taken to improve performance, not just information about how far away you are from hoped-for goals. For example, it is more useful to know that you need to improve listening skills than just to be told that you have a long way to go to be an effective practitioner.

7   Routinely use outcome evaluations, alliance measures, and client satisfaction feedback to evaluate treatment and to monitor client progress session by session.

We recommend careful reading of the paper by Castonguay and colleagues (2010), and in particular of the table (p. 45) that lists recommendations for trainers who work with early-career therapists to minimise harm to clients.

Using client feedback to improve outcome

How does this information inform practice? We know that the trajectory of treatment is more complex than the dose-response model would imply. More treatment does not necessarily equate to more effective outcomes for clients. We know that dropout rates can be quite high, and that dropout is the ultimate impediment to good therapeutic outcomes. We know that there is a risk of deterioration for clients, and that therapists are not always able to predict accurately such deterioration. Lambert and colleagues' research (2004), discussed at the beginning of this chapter, provides us with a direction forward. The most important message concerns the need to track client progress through standardised outcome measures, and to use information from such tracking to elicit client feedback and inform treatment.

There are two primary ways to measure client outcome: client satisfaction with treatment, which is intended to assess client views of how helpful therapy was and what worked; and clinical-outcome measures, intended to measure the effectiveness of treatment through, for example, changes in symptoms (Saggese, 2005). Evaluation of client outcome is an integral and vital component of the professional and ethical practice of all psychotherapists (Ogles et al., 2002). Chapter 13 looks at types of outcome assessment, and related issues, such as clinical significance and reliable change. We will thus not focus on those aspects at this point; rather, we will continue to explore how using regular feedback can improve client outcome. In doing so, we will focus on two outcome methods that are used on a session-by-session basis, the *Outcome-Questionnaire 45 (OQ45)* (Lambert, et al., 1996; see <www.oqmeasures.com/site/> for information about this measure), and the *Outcome Rating Scale (ORS)* (Miller & Duncan, 2000; see <www.scottdmiller.com/>, <www.centerforclinicalexcellence.com>, <www.heartandsoulofchange.com/>, and <www.whatsrigthwithyou.com> for access to this measure and information on research and uses of the ORS and the alliance measure, the *Session Rating Scale* (SRS)).

We focus on these two instruments because they are readily available, and have a considerable body of literature to support their use. We have already provided the support for the OQ45. Support for the ORS is also quite substantial. Miller and colleagues (2003) found that over only one year of using outcome measures in treatment, therapists with 3000 client cases in one agency made a 150 per cent increase in client outcome. It is difficult to imagine what other practice in therapy could result in such impressive improvements. Not only does regular client outcome feedback provide the therapist with important information on how therapy is going, it enhances the sense of collaboration between therapist and client; it is another way of inviting the client to be an integral, proactive partner in the treatment process. More recent studies have further demonstrated excellent outcomes when the ORS has been used. Anker, Duncan, & Sparks (2009) investigated the effects of providing treatment progress and alliance information to both clients and therapists during couple therapy. 410 participants who were receiving couple treatment at a community family-counselling clinic were randomly assigned to one of two groups, treatment as usual (TAU) or session-by-session feedback. Couples in the feedback condition demonstrated significantly greater improvement (nearly four times) than those in the TAU condition at post-treatment, maintained a significant advantage on the primary measure at 6-month follow-up (47.6 per cent of couples in the feedback condition and 18.85 per cent in the TAU condition still reported reliable or significant change), and achieved a 46 per cent lower separation/divorce rate. Note that, although the OQ45 has superior psychometric properties to the ORS (Miller et al., 2003), the ORS has acceptable properties, and is free and brief.

We also strongly suggest using an alliance measure, as evidence for the importance of the alliance to outcome is overwhelming. A commonly used alliance measure, with good psychometric properties, and freely available on the web, is the *Working Alliance Inventory, Short Form* (Tracey & Kokotovic, 1989). Miller and colleagues also have an alliance measure, the *Session Rating Scale (SRS)*. In fact, the first step recommended in use of the *Clinical Support Tools (CST)*, mentioned earlier in relation to the OQ45 research, is to measure and review the strength of the therapeutic alliance. Based on the work of Safran and Muran (2000), the manual provides a number of suggestions for how the therapist can improve the alliance. Further areas of focus provided in the CST include extent of client support outside therapy, client readiness for change, and perhaps reassessment of the diagnostic formulation.

There is a range of outcome measures for children that track progress. One of the most common is the *Child Behaviour Checklist* (Achenbach & Rescorla (2001). Lambert and colleagues (Burlingame, Wells & Lambert, 1996) have developed an outcome measure for children and youth, called the *Youth Outcome Questionnaire-30*. There is also the *Child Outcome Rating Scale (CORS)* (Duncan, Sparks, Miller & Bohanske, 2003)), which, like the other measures, is free.

Practice implications: Managing client outcome

1   Collaborate with your clients on outcome goals to ensure you are working as a team. Therapy will be inefficient, and possibly ineffective, if there are fundamental differences between you on this issue.

2   Track client progress on a regular basis. The research suggests that this should be on a session-by-session basis. If in training or provisionally registered, you may need to suggest to your supervisor or employer that he or she support this practice by at least checking client outcome progress through use of measures in supervision, and perhaps even investing in some measures.

3   If a client is not progressing, or is deteriorating, consider what needs to change for the client to get on track. Do not just do more of the same thing—it is clearly not working. Ask for assistance from your supervisor, or from a peer. Discuss options. If the changes you make do not change the trajectory of the client, you need to consider referring the client to another practitioner.

HOW TO BECOME A 'SUPERSHRINK'

The concept of *supershrink*—the term commonly used for highly effective therapists—was introduced in chapter 5. We return to that concept, as it is argued that the secret to being an exceptional therapist is: 'As absurd as it sounds, the best of the best simply work harder at improving their performance than others' (Miller et al., 2009). And how do they work harder? By using feedback. Just doing something a lot will not necessarily improve competence; repetitive practice has to be accompanied by effective feedback.

Effective therapists can have hugely better outcomes than less effective ones. For example, highly effective therapists have 50 per cent fewer client dropouts than less effective therapists (Okiishi et al., 2006). Does this surprise you? It is uncomfortable to think that one may not be an effective therapist—but this is exactly the reason to work harder at improving one's performance.

The worrying issue is that, despite huge advances in research, the introduction of evidence-based practice, and increased years of training, 'no measurable improvement in the effectiveness of psychotherapy has occurred in the last 30 years' (Miller et al., 2009). How is this possible? The authors suggest this is the case because we have not focused on what might really make a difference to practice, unlike those engaged in other activities, such as sport, computers, and building, where there have been ongoing improvements in what humans can achieve. See Malcolm

Gladwell's 2008 book *Outliers: The Story of Success* for a fascinating insight into how individuals have obtained remarkable success in a variety of areas.

Psychotherapists can also be better. To improve therapist effectiveness, Miller and colleagues (2009) have suggested a three-part formula:

1 Determine your baseline of effectiveness (using a range of client-report measures, such as symptom change, strength of alliance, and dropout rate).
2 Engage in deliberate practice (to improve the baseline).
3 Get feedback (including ongoing supervision and watching videos of sessions).

In regular monitoring of progress, also referred to as 'Feedback Informed Therapy' (FIT), a client completes a brief measure of psychological function using standardised rating scales. This feedback is available to the client's therapist in 'real time', that is, in the session with the client. The process of obtaining feedback from a client in session is vital to how accurate the feedback is. To provide accurate rather than just complimentary feedback, a client may need good modelling from the therapist; some clients will find it difficult to be forthright in providing less-than-positive feedback. But, if the therapist is going to assist the client optimally, accurate feedback is essential. Feedback is collected session-by-session, and progress is graphed; the therapist has a systematic way of monitoring the client. If a client is not on track (NOT), the therapist needs to re-consider his or her approach (e.g., discuss with supervisor, change intervention, discuss outcomes with client). If a client continues to be NOT, further reconsideration, and decisions, will be necessary (e.g., refer the client).

For therapists-in-training (and their supervisors), a recent study by Reese and colleagues (2009) will be of particular interest. The authors found that a randomly-assigned group of postgraduate students who received session-by-session feedback from clients got significantly better outcomes than students who received training and supervision as usual. The clients of students who received feedback also improved significantly more quickly than clients of students who did not get session-by-session feedback, and students who received continuous feedback were consistently better at accurately rating their own effectiveness than students who did not receive continuous client feedback.

FIT has limitations, including the small number of studies to date (albeit with impressive outcomes), the small number of researchers who are currently involved in studies, and reliance on self-report measures (Lambert & Shimokawa, 2011). Other authors (Andrew, Nordberg, Kraus, & Castonguay, 2012; Sales & Alves, 2012) mention the risk of Type 2 error, and the possibility that change can be more complex than a general measure can detect, as potential limitations. There is enough evidence, though, to suggest that therapists need to be informed about research on FIT. A risk in not being informed is that therapists may assume that they are more effective than they are. In terms of effectiveness, most therapists rate themselves as A-grade, and the least effective tend to rate themselves as most effective. We have a duty to our clients to do what we can to increase positive outcomes, and FIT has already demonstrated considerable effectiveness. Such measures, of course, can't replace clinical judgement; they provide therapists with additional information about a client's progress (or lack of it) and can help inform treatment decisions.

We suspect that 'deliberate practice' is more likely to be applied by practitioners while in training—but what happens when they are fully trained and registered?

How many psychologists routinely measure client outcome? How many watch videos or DVDs of their own practice, closely examining their practice to see where they can improve? How many psychologists present case studies to other practitioners, having carefully considered their practice? How many, like the great therapists, such as Yalom, write about their practice, opening it to the scrutiny of others? How many get regular, honest feedback from someone who observes their actual practice—not just listening, as a supportive peer, about what the therapist thinks he or she has been doing? How many take a break between clients to contemplate how the session has gone, and prepare for the next client? How many busy practitioners gather data on client dropout, and contact clients, trying to work out why they left therapy, and how to decrease the dropout rate for their practice? We would venture to guess: very few. If 'deliberate practice' is important to effective practice, it is hardly surprising that there has been no major improvement in psychotherapy for decades.

With all this information on effective practice, we hope that you will make a commitment to working at being the most effective practitioner you can be. Follow the suggestions provided for improving your practice. Find further ways to improve. Try your best. Your clients will thank you for it.

CONCLUSION

Many variables can impact on client outcome. One factor that is always within the control of the therapist is the ability to monitor a client outcome and to use such information to elicit feedback from the client about the helpfulness of therapy and the strength of the therapeutic alliance. It is in your control to enhance the client's outcome, and it is your ethical imperative to do so to the best of your ability. Okiishi and colleagues (2003) suggest that therapist effectiveness falls within a normal curve. But would it not be great if we could work towards a skewed curve, where the majority of therapists are above the average? We should not settle for mediocrity—it is a privilege to help others make their lives better, and our clients deserve our best efforts in doing so. Monitoring outcomes provides a baseline for your own effectiveness, the first step in improving such effectiveness. We urge you to incorporate outcome measurement into your practice from the very beginning of your career.

Recommended reading

Brown, G. S., Lambert, M. J., Jones, E. R., & Minami, T. (2005). Identifying highly effective therapists in a managed care environment. *American Journal of Managed Care, 11*, 513–520.

Duncan, B. L. (2010). *On Becoming a Better Therapist*. Washington, DC: American Psychological. Association.

Duncan, B.L. (2012). The partners for change outcome management system (PCOMS): The heart and soul of change project. *Canadian Psychology, 52(2)*, 93–104.

Duncan, B. L., Miller, S. D., Wampold, B. E., & Hubble, M. A. (eds) (2010). *The Heart and Soul of Change* (2nd edn). Washington, DC: American Psychological Association.

Fitzpatrick, M. (2012). Blurring practice-research boundaries using progress monitoring: A personal introduction to this issue of Canadian Psychology. *Canadian
Psychology, 53(2)*, 75–81.

Lambert, M.J. (2010). *Prevention of Treatment Failure*. Washington: APA.

Lambert, M.J. (2010). *Prevention of Treatment Failure. The Use of Measuring, Monitoring,
and Feedback in Clinical Practice*. Washington, DC: American Psychological
Association.

Miller, S., Hubble, M.A., & Duncan, B. L. (2009). *Supershrinks: What is the Secret of Their
Success?* <http:// www.psychotherapy.net/article/Scott_Miller_Supershrinks>.

Miller, S.D., Duncan, B.L., Brown, J., Sorrell, R., & Chalk, B. (2006). Using outcome to
inform and improve treatment outcomes. *Journal of Brief Therapy, 5*, 5–22.

Okiishi J., Lambert M.J, Eggett D., Nielsen L., Dayton D., Vermeersch D.A. (2006). An
analysis of therapist treatment effects: Toward providing feedback to individual
therapists on their clients' psychotherapy outcome. *Journal of Clinical Psychology,
62(9)*, 1157–1172.

Okiishi, J. C., Lambert, M. J., Eggett, D., Nielsen, L., & Dayton, D. D. (2006). An analysis of therapist treatment effects: toward providing feedback to individual
therapists on their clients' psychotherapy outcome. *Journal of Clinical Psychology,
62(9)*, 1157–72.

Overington, L. & Ionita, G. (2012). Progress monitoring measures: A brief guide.
Canadian Psychology, 53(2), 82–92.

Reese, R.J., Norsworthy, L.A., & Rowlands, S.R. (2009). Does a continuous feedback
system improve psychotherapy outcome? *Psychotherapy: Theory, Research, Practice, Training, 46*, 418–431.

Slade, K., Lambert, M.J., Harmon, S.C., Smart, D.W., & Bailey, R. (2008). Improving
psychotherapy outcome: The use of immediate electronic feedback and revised
clinical support tools. *Clinical Psychology & Psychotherapy, 15*, 287–303.

Wampold, B.E. & Brown, G.S. (2005). Estimating Variability in Outcomes Attributable to Therapists: A Naturalistic Study of Outcomes in Managed Care. *Journal of
Consulting and Clinical Psychology, 73(5)*, 914–923.

Part C

Psychotherapy process and practice

Chapter 10

Common practical issues in therapy

INTRODUCTION

This chapter outlines common practical issues we are faced with when seeing clients. Our aim is to provide basic practical information on how to work with clients regardless of the theoretical approach you choose to use. The chapter will cover where to see clients (the setting); how to present; managing unexpected events; starting sessions; behaviours that can inhibit development of a good working relationship; session length and frequency; and payment and time issues. The chapter also addresses some tricky issues that may occur in therapy, such as clients crying and non-attendance. It is not meant to provide exhaustive coverage of all practical issues in therapy; it will provide a working base from which you can gain experience in conducting psychotherapy and develop your own style.

CREATING A SAFE PLACE

It is important to remember that when individuals present for psychotherapy they tend to feel vulnerable. They are usually experiencing some form of emotional difficulty, and may feel disempowered because they are stuck in some way in their life, feeling unable to solve their problem on their own. Consequently, clients enter the therapeutic relationship at a disadvantage. They are expected to talk about their problems, open up, and divulge intimate things about themselves—how they are feeling, what they are thinking, how they tend to behave and cope—that they have most likely never told anyone, even (or perhaps, especially) those they are closest to. Given clients' vulnerability, it is essential that the therapist behaves ethically and has the best interests of clients foremost in mind.

Exercise 10.1

Just for a moment, imagine what it would be like to be asked to divulge your deepest, darkest, best-kept secret to someone you have only just met. You don't know anything about this person except that he or she says, 'I am here to help you'. What would need to happen for you to share with this person the thing in your life you are most embarrassed about?

In responding to this exercise, it is likely that issues of safety and trust emerged. You would want to feel safe, and feel that you could trust this person enough to be able to talk about what is really going on. There are many practical ways by which you can create a safe physical space for clients, in addition to creating a safe therapeutic environment through the manner in which you communicate and how you present. As discussed in chapter 2, confidentiality is essential in therapy. To feel it is safe to open up to someone, you would want to be sure that what you divulge goes no further. Practical issues related to creating this safe place are discussed below, but here are some initial things to consider that can assist in promoting confidentiality and creating a safe place to talk:

- See the client in a place where it will not be possible for others to overhear what is being said; the room needs to be relatively soundproof and private.
- Ensure there will be no interruptions, by people at the door or by phone (be sure to turn off your mobile phone). Imagine trying to talk to someone about something really painful, when she or he answers the phone or opens the door to a knock. This is unlikely to make you feel safe or important, or foster a sense that you are being truly listened to.
- Dedicate a period of time to the client. Clients need to know that the agreed period, whether 45 minutes or an hour, is theirs, without interruption.
- In settings where it may be difficult to arrange a quiet room away from interruptions (for example, in a health setting, where clients are seen at their bedside), try as best you can to create a private space where you and the client can interact. It is important to keep in mind that limited privacy in some settings will have an impact on the extent of a client's disclosure.

The actual room or setting

What should a *therapy room* look like? You may not have much control over this if the room is determined by the organisation in which you work. Apart from the room being as soundproof as possible, it should have other aspects that may influence the process of therapy and the therapeutic relationship, and therefore outcome for clients. Some psychological theories more than others emphasise the importance of the setting. Some psychodynamic therapists believe that a safe working relationship involves seeing the client at the same time and place for each session (Langs, 1990). This is not so important when therapists see clients outside the therapy room; it is not uncommon for a therapist to be going up and down in a lift with a client who has an elevator phobia. Being flexible with settings may also be indicated when working with children or adolescents; some may find it easier to talk when going for a walk, or being in a familiar environment, where they feel safe.

Given that the processes that occur between client and therapist, such as 'transference', 'projection', 'projective identification', and 'countertransference', are critical factors in psychodynamic approaches, psychodynamic therapists place a lot of importance on what is in the room (Storr, 1990). They would argue that there be no personal objects, such as family photographs, in the room. If a client saw in a photograph that the therapist was married and had children, it might be more difficult for the client to project his or her need for a father figure onto the therapist. Whether or not you have items in the room that say something about your personal life may depend on your theoretical approach, but it is mostly a question of personal preference. A room devoid of any ornamentation may be overly clinical and impersonal. Also, if therapists spend most of their working day in the room, it is likely that they will want some objects that create a pleasant environment for themselves.

When deciding on personal objects in the therapy room, the ethical issue of dual relationships and appropriate boundaries (see chapter 2) needs to be taken into account. Therapists need to consider whether an object or picture could be taken in the wrong way or misunderstood. For example, numerous pictures of the therapist in different holiday destinations may convey the message that 'it is OK to talk about the therapist's life'. On rare occasions, a client may develop an inappropriate attachment to his therapist, and the therapist can protect her safety and privacy by carefully deciding what to have in the room. For instance, pictures of children in school uniforms may result in a client approaching the therapist when picking up her children from school.

Consider seating arrangement also. Having a comfortable place to sit is conducive to talking. It is useful to have comfortable chairs or settees that are movable and can accommodate a variety of client needs (for example, narrow or deep chairs may not be helpful for clients with weight problems or chronic pain). Having extra chairs available is also handy, as a client might unexpectedly bring someone else to the session. It is also important to think about where you place the chairs and the impact that this might have. Some clients like to sit near the door, but it might be wise for the therapist to sit near the door (as in forensic settings). Anything that creates a barrier between therapist and client, such as a desk, is not advisable. Having chairs at an angle, rather than directly facing each other, can be advantageous; this gives clients the opportunity to look at the therapist when they choose to, or to look away if they need to think or feel uncomfortable. Movable chairs are useful; clients can control how close to the therapist they sit. This can enhance their level of comfort, an issue influenced by culture. Direct eye contact, for example, with Indigenous or some Asian clients may be experienced as disrespectful; they may feel more comfortable sitting alongside the therapist; sitting opposite could be experienced as disempowering or threatening (Harlen, 2002).

An essential object to have in the room is a clock that both client and therapist can see (or having two). Clocks help both therapist and client to track how much time is left in the session, aid the therapist to decide whether to go into a topic in more depth, and guide the process of the session.

Another essential item is a box of tissues. Clients can cry as they talk about distressing and painful events or feelings. Having tissues within easy reach will be helpful to some clients. Having interesting pictures or artwork on the wall may also be useful, giving the client something to look at when contemplating what is going on for her or him.

First contact

First contact with a client can occur in a number of ways:

- A therapist's first contact with a client might be through a referral letter or a discussion with the person referring the client.
- A client might contact the therapist directly by phone or email.
- A therapist's first contact with a client might be when she or he greets the client in the waiting room, the appointment having been arranged through a secretary.
- In health settings, first contact may occur when a therapist visits the person in his or her room or at the bedside.
- First contact may occur when a client presents spontaneously, with no appointment (as in organisations where dropping in is possible).

In cases where client contact is preceded by a referral letter or discussion with the person referring, the therapist will have some impression of the client and her or his issues, and will be able to begin making hypotheses about what might be happening. Some therapists choose not to look at letters or files before seeing a client; they prefer to remain open to all possibilities without being influenced by previous opinions. Regardless of the way in which first contact takes place, whether by phone, email, through a secretary, or in person, it is important that rapport-building and conveying respect and positive regard begin from the first moment of interaction. The process of assessment also starts with the initial contact (see chapter 12). The therapeutic process has begun even before you have entered the therapy room.

Exercise 10.2

At which point would you consider that the process of therapy actually starts?

1   Is it when the client is in the contemplative stage of change (see 'Motivational interviewing', chapter 7) and realises that she has a problem she needs assistance with?

2   Is it when someone else suggests that the client needs help, and although the client may not agree, for whatever reason, decides to take the other person's advice?

3   Is it when the client first starts to consider who may help her and begins doing research (by, for example, going to the Yellow Pages, asking a friend who has had therapy, asking the HR manager if the organisation pays for therapy (Employee Assistance Program), asking a GP for a referral)?

4   Is it when the client first makes contact with the person she wants to see?

5   Is it when the client is thinking about what the therapist will be like, what the therapist will ask, what she will tell the therapist?

6   Is it when the client is thinking about what the therapist seemed like on the phone, what response was evoked by the therapist's photo or website, or what the client's friend or GP said about the therapist?

7   Is it when the client is considering what she knows about therapy through the media or perhaps previous experiences? Or is it only when the client is in the therapist's office?

In thinking through these issues, you will recognise that the therapy process, at least in terms of what is going on for the client, is likely to have begun quite some time before she actually enters the room in which therapy takes place. The therapist is thus well advised to be mindful of how to interact with the client, either directly on the phone, or indirectly through a website, business card, or referral source. Keep in mind that if there is initial phone contact, this should be subject to the same rules as any other first contact.

The process of informed consent also starts at this first contact, particularly with regard to fees. Clients should know how much they will be charged before they attend an appointment, and how long the session will be.

Meeting a client in a waiting room for the first time

When approaching a client in a waiting room, keep in mind that he is likely to be feeling anxious about being seen by a psychologist, worried about what it will be like, and wondering if he is doing the right thing. Factors to consider are whether or not you call out the person's full name (confidentiality), whether you shake hands with the client (the client may not like physical contact, or it could be culturally inappropriate), and how to introduce yourself. Do you give your first name, your full name, your title? Australia tends to be a fairly informal society, and it is rare for therapists to introduce themselves as 'Mr Smith' or 'Mrs Jones', or even as 'Dr Keen'. We suggest that, to the best of your ability, you match your introduction to what you know of the client, and rather err on the side of formality. Obviously, the age of the client will make a difference, with the therapist being more casual with children (using first names for both yourself and the client).

Each action associated with first introduction can make the person feel more comfortable and at ease or heighten his anxiety. Imagine what it would feel like if you didn't want anyone to know you were being seen, and then hearing your full name called out. Also, what would it be like if the therapist doesn't look at you, doesn't smile, but just turns and walks to the room after calling your name? Conversely, would it be appropriate to ask about or discuss personal information while walking to the consulting room? How would this ensure confidentiality?

Thinking through this is helpful when your aim is to establish a good working relationship. Although there is little formal research investigating the impact of therapist greetings and goodbyes on outcome, anecdotal evidence from administrative staff suggests a relationship between warmth and ease of therapist interaction with clients in the waiting room and whether clients return for a second session. Remember, first impressions are important. People often make decisions quickly about whether they like or dislike someone.

Personal presentation

Personal presentation is influenced by the types of clients you might see. For instance, wearing a tight business skirt that restricts your movement is not appropriate if you have a child client with whom you might want to sit on the floor and engage in play. The key question to consider is: 'What am I required to do, and what message do I want to give the client?'

The ethical principle of 'Respect for the rights and dignity of people and peoples' states, 'In the course of their *conduct, psychologists* communicate respect for other people through their actions and language' (Australian Psychological Society, 2007, p. 12). Dressing appropriately is a nonverbal way of conveying respect and being sensitive to cultural and gender issues. The client will be appraising the therapist, asking himself:

- 'Do I feel I can talk to this person?'
- 'Does this person seem to know what he is doing?'
- 'Could I trust this person?'

What the therapist wears will influence this appraisal. Because therapists are unlikely to know how sensitive a client is to dress standards, erring on the side of caution by wearing something as neutral as possible is the safest approach. Being too smartly dressed may intimidate clients, making it difficult for them to open up. Being too casually dressed (as in shorts and thongs) may give the impression that you don't see the interaction as important or worth the effort of dressing appropriately. Given the edict that there should be no sexual relationship between therapist and client, therapists need to avoid wearing anything that may be perceived as sexually provocative (such as low cut tops, hipsters, or short skirts). Our best advice is to dress smart–casual in something you feel comfortable in, ensuring that nothing is going to draw unnecessary attention.

Other aspects of appearance are worth considering. If the therapist is female, appropriate makeup can create a professional appearance and help a younger therapists to appear more mature. Wearing no makeup can make it seem as if little effort has been put in. Excessive makeup is a distraction, as is excessive jewellery, perfume, or aftershave (some clients may be allergic to perfumes), and unusual hair colours. Remember: therapists need to relate to a range of clients. If, through their appearance, therapists give a message that they belong, for example, to a particular subcultural group, they may appeal to one client but ostracise the rest.

Unexpected events

An issue that can pose a challenge in the first few moments of meeting a client is if the client unexpectedly brings someone else. Recall that the main aim of the first session is to establish rapport and some understanding of what brings a person to therapy. It is therefore not wise to refuse outright the inclusion of the other person in the session; you would not know why the other person has come along. Perhaps the client asked the person to come for moral support, or perhaps the other person insisted on coming along without the client wanting him or her? Perhaps the client thinks the other person might help explain to the therapist what is going on?

The following strategy may be of use in this situation: say that you would normally see people on their own, but they are welcome to bring the other person along if they feel this would be helpful. This gives clients the option of going in on their own, if they don't want the other person to be there (if they feel able to say so), or to bring the other person along, if this makes them feel safer.

Clients asking for reports or letters may be another unexpected event. Explaining what can and can't be done in a first session can be helpful here (see chapter 12), but you also need to find out what exactly is being asked for, to help you determine whether the request is appropriate. A client may, for example, ask for a report for court, and you, as the therapist, may not be in an appropriate position to provide this (it may be outside your expertise, or you may not be fully registered). Discussing expectations and being up front with the client is a helpful way of managing this, as well as referring the client on to someone who could possibly help.

There may be numerous other events (such as a fire alarm during the session) that are impossible to predict. A good rule of thumb is to give yourself a moment to think through the situation, ask for more information, seek assistance if appropriate, and keep what is in the best interests of the client in mind (do not continue the session if the fire alarm goes off; it is not safe for the client or for you).

BEGINNING FIRST (AND SUBSEQUENT) SESSIONS

Once you have made your introductions and accompanied the client to the therapy room, it is usually helpful to let the client choose where he or she wants to sit. Some therapists will subtly indicate which chair they usually sit on by putting something near or on their chair, thereby guiding the client to the other chair. This can have drawbacks. The main aim of the first session is to establish rapport, build an environment the client wants to return to if needed, and gather information about the client. Even seemingly minor touches, such as allowing the client to choose a seat, will assist. When entering the room the therapist could say, 'Please take a seat wherever you will feel comfortable.' Clients who prefer to sit near the door now have the option to do so. (Again, there may be situations where it is wise for the therapist to sit nearest the door).

Other therapists have furniture that clearly indicates which seat is for them, because it is the biggest and most comfortable seat in the room! Such subtle (sometimes less than subtle) shows of power can be acceptable to some clients, who are used to authority figures indicating their superiority. However, if we are serious about therapy being a collaborative and equal relationship, we might question our motives for elevating ourselves above our clients.

A session can be started in a number of ways; there are no fixed rules. Therapists usually develop their own style. In most cases, however, a session will begin with some basic tasks that are required to establish a therapeutic relationship, including:

- explaining the limits of confidentiality
- discussing payment, if required
- retrieving basic demographic details from the client
- explaining session length
- discussing procedures to contact the therapist in an emergency
- signing any administrative forms (such as consent forms) required by the organisation.

Finding out whether the client has seen a therapist before is useful; this will help the therapist to determine how much he or she should explain to the client about what the process involves. An example of beginning a first session might be:

Hi Bob. As I said, my name is Allan and I am a clinical psychologist. Did you have any trouble finding us? Have you seen a psychologist before? OK, let me explain what today's session is about, and please do ask any questions you may have. First, we will need to go through some consent forms, and then we will spend the rest of the session talking about what has brought you to see me. I may ask lots of questions today, so I can get a good picture of what is going on for you. This is also to help determine how therapy might be able to help. We will also talk about what you would like to get out of seeing me, and today's session is to give you a chance to ask any questions, and to see whether you would like to continue to work with me. How does that sound? Was there anything else that you were hoping to get out of today's session? Do you have any questions?

Some clients arrive at a first session in a state of distress, and start telling the therapist about their problem before the therapist has explained consent and/or the limitations of confidentiality. This is a tricky situation. On the one hand, it may be important to allow the person to talk freely; on the other hand, the person might not be aware of the consequences of this. The situation requires a judgment call. The therapist should use her micro-counselling skills to establish rapport and demonstrate that she is listening, but also bring the client's attention to consent and limitations of confidentiality as soon as possible. Other clients may feel so anxious that getting down to business immediately may not be helpful. In such cases, spending time talking about general, less personal topics (such as how their trip was, the weather) may help reduce their anxiety and to put them at ease. Good attending skills (see next chapter) are essential in this situation to assist the therapist to determine what approach might be most helpful to the client. Cultural differences will play a role in what is most appropriate. With Indigenous clients, too much professional distance is usually not helpful, making it difficult for the person to feel that she can share her story. Spending time talking about yourself can promote the relationship and assist the Indigenous person to feel non-threatened and able to share (Harlen, 2002).

Exercise 10.3

View Videos 5 and 1. What do you think went well and what would you do differently?

Second and subsequent sessions are simpler to begin, given that consent has already occurred. It is usually helpful to check in with clients about their thoughts, feelings, or concerns about the last session. It is also imperative to pay attention to homework if given in the previous session. Why ask clients to monitor their mood, for example, if you are not going to follow it up? Clients will not always produce homework spontaneously, and will wait for a cue from the therapist, so it is important to ask. A helpful way to start a second or subsequent session is to allow the client to tell you what has been going on for them, or what has happened, since the last session, and whether they have had any feelings or thoughts about the last session.

What *not* to do in session

Certain therapist in-session behaviours may cause damage to the working alliance. Here are some examples:

1 The therapist spends much of the time talking about him- or herself.
2 The therapist eats lunch or a snack during the session.
3 The therapist has coffee (especially without offering one to the client).
4 The therapist falls asleep during the session.
5 The therapist doesn't make appropriate eye contact with the client.
6 The therapist attends to phone calls or emails (unrelated to the client) during the session.
7 The therapist stops listening to the client (daydreaming) and appears uninterested.
8 The therapist is knowingly culturally inappropriate during the session.
9 The therapist has mannerisms that make the client uncomfortable; for example, sitting too close to the client, fiddling constantly with a pen, or moving a leg up and down.

Such behaviours can interfere with the therapist's ability to attend to the client's story and foster an environment of positive regard. Clients do not attend therapy to hear about the therapist's life. Although it is not unusual to eat and drink during meetings, this can be problematic during a therapy session. For the therapist not to offer the client coffee or something to eat can send a message to the client that the therapist is more powerful. Even if both have coffee, there is a danger that the session will be perceived as a social rather than a professional situation; more vulnerable clients can become confused about boundaries. Good attending is difficult, and requires that the therapist focuses all his or her attention on the client; drinking coffee or eating will inhibit this. It is reasonable, and possibly preferable, that water is available to both therapist and client. Points four to seven in the list above undoubtedly communicate that the client is not important. It is important to be aware of and steer clear of any behaviour that may unintentionally damage the most important therapeutic tool, the working alliance.

WHEN A CLIENT CRIES

Often, clients cry during a session. Being able to tolerate emotion, including expressions of sadness, is important in a therapist. One of the aims of therapy is to create a safe place where clients can express their thoughts and emotions without being judged. Being mindful of how you respond to expressions of emotion within sessions is essential. Having tissues at hand is useful, as is being mindful of the manner in which you offer them. Offering tissues to a client the moment she starts crying might convey the message that she needs to stop. Perhaps her mother used to give her a tissue immediately and say, 'Stop crying!' Alternatively, not offering tissues when they are available, may make the therapist appear indifferent to distress. Placing tissues where the client can easily reach them solves the problem. Remember that, even when they are crying or distressed, clients can still talk, and often want to.

Another question is, should the therapist shed a tear, or stoically stop her- or himself from showing emotion? As discussed in the chapter on therapist factors, therapists should not become more distressed than the client. Being genuine is an important micro-counselling skill, and showing some emotion, especially when faced with a very traumatic and/or distressing story, can be therapeutic for the client. Seeing that the therapist is moved by what they talk about may even give some clients permission to express emotions they had until that point repressed. It is not helpful if the therapist becomes so distressed that the client ends up feeling a need to take care of the therapist, or that their emotions are dangerous in some way.

Exercise 10.4

View Video 6. What would you do as a therapist if you had these experiences with clients?

SESSION DURATION AND FREQUENCY

Length of session

How long should a session be? Therapists see clients from anywhere between 30 minutes to many hours at a time. Since Freud, sessions of approximately an hour have been accepted as the norm. In reality, this means that individual sessions are about 50 minutes in length, to allow the therapist to take notes and to prepare for the next client. Family or couple sessions are often longer, with 80 minutes being usual (Plante, 2005). Many therapists set aside a longer period for initial intake sessions (such as 90 minutes for individual sessions), to allow time for administrative tasks and assessment. Session length is determined by a number of factors, in particular, the organisational context in which the client is seen, the needs of the client, the needs of the therapist, and financial considerations. It may be that the organisation in which the therapist works prescribes length of sessions. Some therapists may decide that they can only concentrate for 45 minutes, whereas others feel they work better in 60-minute sessions.

How the therapist is paid may determine session length. Since November 2006 Medicare has set the standard session length at 50 minutes, and pays a specified sum for sessions of 50 minutes or less, and a specified sum for sessions of more than 50 minutes. The therapist may determine length of the session according to how much he or she wants to ensure that the client is able to claim from Medicare.

Determining session length according to client need and cultural sensitivity, rather than therapist's personal choice, would be the most ethical approach, acting in the best interests of the client and likely to contribute to best outcomes. A client who has difficulty concentrating and engaging may benefit more from 30-minute sessions than if forced to sit for an hour. Other clients, with traumatic issues, or who require graded exposure, for example, might need longer than an hour. With Aboriginal people, time is perceived differently, and flexibility is essential; this gives them the option to tell their story in their own time, without feeling rushed or not respected (Dudgeon et al., 2000).

Accommodating client needs requires flexibility by the therapist and may not always be possible, but is worth striving for. Sticking to time once length of session has been determined can be important to both therapist and client. If doing therapy is your fulltime livelihood, sticking to time becomes an essential part of managing your business. If a therapist goes over time, there can be many consequences, such as keeping other clients waiting, or reducing the number of clients who can be seen.

Sticking to time

Sticking to time is also important for a healthy alliance. Effective therapy requires consistency and predictability. The therapist makes a contract with the client at the beginning of treatment about length of sessions. If the therapist allows session time to vary from the contract, there may be consequences.

The most concerning consequence is of loose boundaries being established, whereby the client may start to feel, for example, that the longer the therapist gives him, the more the therapist cares for or likes him. If the therapist then holds session times to an hour, the client may interpret this to mean that the therapist is cross with him or cares less. Changes in routine will be noticed and interpreted by clients, and can cause ruptures in the alliance. Consistency in time management in session is an essential skill that will benefit both therapist and client.

If you are consistently struggling to keep sessions to time, it may be helpful to ask yourself some of the following questions:

- Are there clients with whom I regularly go overtime? What do these clients have in common?
- Are there some topics or processes in therapy that I always go overtime with?
- What thoughts and feelings come to me when I'm aware that session time is up, but I don't attempt to conclude?
- If I regularly go overtime, is this a set length of time (say, 1.5 hours rather than 1 hour)? It may be that this time is more effective for some clients, but if so, this needs to be formally contracted, and, if paying, the client will have to pay for the extra time.

Discussing these issues in supervision will also be helpful; a plan can then be devised with the supervisor for how to manage time in future therapy sessions.

Time between clients

Usually, it is beneficial to have time between clients to reflect on work done, make notes, and take any toilet or lunch breaks. Having at least five to ten minutes between sessions can also prevent clients from bumping into each other. Some clients struggle with the notion that they are not the only client the therapist sees, and this may relate to specific (interpersonal) issues that would be important to address in therapy. Some therapists have clients leave by another door, rather than have them walk back through the waiting room, or ensure 10 to 15 minutes between clients. This is not always possible, and it can be less of an issue where a waiting room accommodates more than one therapist and/or other services.

Deciding on how much time a therapist needs between clients will be influenced by factors such as complexity of client presentations, organisational and service demand pressures, and therapist awareness of what works best for them. However, clinicians in training are unlikely to have a full load of clients, as the main goal of clinical placements is to learn how to do the work of a therapist, and this requires having time to prepare and reflect. Thus, while you are in training, we suggest that at least an hour between clients is set aside, where possible, to allow for reflection on the session held, make notes, and consider what needs to be discussed with supervisors.

All this will determine how many clients a therapist can see in a day. Ethically, a therapist always needs to be cognisant of striving to do his or her best work. So, a therapist needs to take into account how much time she or he needs between sessions to provide the best therapy, and to let this determine how much time is needed between clients.

Frequency of sessions

Outpatient or private-practice sessions commonly occur on a weekly basis. However, it is not unusual for clients to be seen more frequently if they are in hospital, or in crisis. Some types of therapy, notably psychoanalytic therapy, may require more than one session a week, but for most clients and organisations this is not financially viable.

At times, it is prudent for sessions to be more than a week apart, for example, when a client is getting close to termination. Fortnightly or monthly sessions can be useful to provide clients with more time to implement change and to help maintain change. Earlier in treatment, longer than a week between sessions may be less effective in keeping clients engaged or allowing for sufficient therapeutic momentum to build. An ideal balance is for sessions to be frequent enough for clients to maintain a heightened level of emotion, to motivate them to deal with issues, but not so frequent that they feel overwhelmed, or feel there is insufficient time between sessions to reflect on work being done. Naturally, the right balance will differ for each client, depending on individual needs and circumstances, and where she or he is in the therapeutic process.

Sometimes, frequency of sessions will be determined by a client's financial situation. Clients may, for example, be able to afford only fortnightly sessions. It is important to be aware of this when going through consent and contracting with a client. Sometimes, if there are financial constraints, the ethical thing to do will be to refer the client to another service.

PAYMENT

Payment is another issue to consider, depending on the context in which you work. In most government-funded clinics, clients are not charged. However, as psychologists increasingly work in private-practice settings, payment is a salient issue. It is commonly thought that therapists are not naturally good business people, given the possible conflict between wanting to help individuals who are suffering, but who may have financial constraints, and making a living by asking them to pay. A particularly difficult dilemma therapists can find themselves in is when the best interests of the client conflict with the best interests of the therapist; for example, a client requires further sessions but is unable to pay. Some therapists resolve this dilemma by doing some *pro bono* work, or ensuring that they do not take on clients who would not be able to afford their fees long term. Unfortunately, there is no straightforward answer to this dilemma.

Most therapists do psychotherapy to help people, and some therapists might find it difficult to 'demand' money, particularly beginning or student therapists. Not asking for payment, however, can lead to the service being undervalued or taken for granted by the client, and financial difficulties for the therapist or service. Providing good psychotherapy is a mentally and emotionally demanding task and can be exhausting. Contracting clearly about fees is a way of reinforcing that the work done is of value. There are no hard and fast rules about payment. Some therapists have secretaries accept payment, so it does not interfere with the therapeutic relationship. Some therapists will undertake the financial transaction before the session commences, while others will do so at the end. Being clear up front about the costs, when payment is due, and what will happen with non-payment, is essential, ethical, and important in ensuring that the financial transaction does not adversely affect the therapeutic process.

The Australian Psychological Society (2007) provides helpful guidelines and standards in the *Code of Ethics* for dealing financially with clients. For example:

> C.6.2. *Psychologists* make proper financial arrangements with *clients* and where relevant, third party payers. They:
> a)   make advance financial arrangements that safeguard the best interests of, and are clearly understood, by all parities to the *psychological service*; and
> b)   avoid financial arrangements which may adversely influence the *psychological services* provided, whether at the time of the provision of those services or subsequently (p. 30).

ENDING A SESSION

Ending a session in a timely manner is not easy, and is something that beginning therapists often struggle with. If clients are in the middle of telling the therapist something when it becomes time to end, does one stop them in mid flow and say, 'Sorry, time is up!'? This would be quite abrupt and invalidating. Managing time from the outset is the key to make a session end smoothly (this is why clocks in therapy rooms are handy). At the beginning of a session, it is useful to let the client know how much time you have together and what time the session will end. With some clients, it is also useful to alert them 10 minutes before the end of the session. At this point, rather than opening up a new topic, it can be helpful to summarise what has been covered in the session, and perhaps discuss what the client might work on in between sessions, There also needs to be enough time to organise the next appointment.

Sometimes, a client might say something important just as the session is about to finish. Although it can be tempting to sit down again and discuss it further, this is usually not helpful. The importance of the issue, however, does need to be acknowledged. Imagine being the client, and it has taken you the whole session to pluck up the courage to say what is really going on! It may feel safest to do this at the end, when you know you can leave, in case the therapist responds in a hurtful way. Acknowledge that what the client has said is helpful, then say something like, 'What you have just said sounds really important, and is something we will definitely talk about more in the next session.'

In some instances, clients may say something at the end of a session that indicates that they are at risk of harming themselves or others. Given the seriousness of such statements and psychologists' duty-of-care responsibilities, it is important to follow up with a risk assessment, even if it cuts into your next appointment. Let your next client know, either through the receptionist (especially if the client cannot be left alone) or in person, that there will be a delay, and ask if he or she would mind waiting or rescheduling, then continue with managing your client's risk. For some clients, however, raising a crisis at the end of a session can become typical, perhaps to test the therapist's care for them, or to get more time. This needs to be dealt with differently. The observed pattern needs to be discussed openly, and rules set in place to manage it, for example by doing a risk assessment at the beginning of most sessions.

We suggest you take the following steps with clients who find it difficult to end sessions:

- Inform the client when 10 minutes are left, and that it's time to summarise the session, and to consider work for next session.
- Do not get drawn into new topics, but gently and firmly remind the client that, 'We are now at the stage of summarising and winding up this session; let's keep those new topics in mind for next time'.
- Remind the client that there are five minutes left, and ask if there are any last questions.
- When it's time, stand up, maintain eye contact, and say, 'OK, our time for this week is up. Does the same time next week suit you? Good, let me walk you out.'
- It is always polite to stand up and walk the client to at least the door of the office and say goodbye formally.
- If the client is paying, then the last five minutes of the session may be spent with payment.
- It is difficult for a client to remain seated once the therapist has stood up and opened the door.
- Do not engage in any more therapy talk once the session is over. Remind the client that you can discuss any issues the following session.

Managing clients who have difficulty finishing sessions on time can be tricky. Often we feel that our behaviour is rude if we insist on ending a session on time when a client clearly does not want to leave. You may be tempted to give a client a few extra minutes if you don't have someone else waiting, but we would strongly advise you not to do so. As noted previously, unpredictable session lengths can cause problems for clients—particularly those with poor boundaries. Imagine that you give a client an extra 10 minutes one week, when you don't have another appointment, but the following week you insist on sticking to time, no matter what the client raises, because there is another client in the waiting room. What is the message you may be giving that client? 'Maybe she will only give me more time if I raise a crisis', or 'The other client matters more to her than I do'. Your gesture of intended kindness can be negatively construed. To prevent such misunderstandings, it is simpler for all parties if therapists consistently end sessions on time.

Exercise 10.5

1   Watch Video 13, scene 1. How well did the therapist manage ending the session on time? What would you have done differently?
2   Now watch scene 2 of Video 13. Is this an improvement, and if so, what were the factors that made this ending more effective?

MANAGING IRRELEVANT CHATTING IN SESSIONS

Some clients can talk excessively about trivial matters, may not respond readily to therapist cues to stop, and can make ending sessions difficult (they keep talking even when the therapist is standing at the door). First, try to assess (with the help of a supervisor) what is motivating the client to talk excessively, especially about trivial matters. Some clients are anxious about discussing difficult topics in therapy, and talking about superficial issues is an avoidance technique. Some clients use story-telling as a way of connecting with others. Other clients may be used to others not really listening to them; they have learned to talk a lot, expecting not really to be heard.

It is important to not reinforce a client using chat to avoid working in therapy or ending a session. The therapist can gently and respectfully interrupt, and move the client back to talking about issues she or he is in therapy for. When trying to end a session, a therapist may need to walk out of the room, or state clearly that the session has ended and that any issues can be discussed next time. Walking out or interrupting may feel rude, but avoidant chatting is not helpful to clients, and gently redirecting them to a more valuable topic of discussion is ethical and in their best interests. Our role is to ensure that clients get as much out of therapy as possible; in part, that means ensuring that superficial activity is limited.

One way of gently re-directing a client to key issues is to say:

You have been discussing in some detail the barbecue you had with your family on the weekend, and I'm trying to understand how this relates to our work in therapy. Are there specific issues related to this event which you think may be useful to discuss in therapy, that relate to your concerns and goals?

If the client continues to discuss superficial issues, the therapist may suggest:

It seems difficult for you to move away from the details of the weekend that are not apparently related to our work together. I wonder if you are finding it difficult today to discuss some issues that may have more impact for you.

Thus, the therapist needs to make process comments to remind the client of the purpose of therapy, and carefully assess what role the chat may serve for the client. Don't forget, however, that many individuals who have not been to therapy before (and some who have) don't fully understand the purpose of therapy, and may be chatting as they would to a friend. In this case, it would be important to revisit the client's perceptions and expectations of therapy, and come to a clear and mutual understanding of the purpose of therapy and the roles of therapist and client.

Exercise 10.6

1   Watch Video 2, scene 1. How effective was this interaction with the client? What would you have done differently?
2   Now watch scene 2 of Video 2. Is this more effective? If so, why?

MANAGING REPEATED MISSED OR CANCELLED APPOINTMENTS

This is a perennial problem in treatment. There are a variety of reasons for missed appointments; some we note below with possible responses.

Sometimes the problem is simply that times set for appointments are difficult for the client to keep regularly. In the first session, inform the client that there is an expectation that he or she will come to therapy on a weekly basis (unless there is another arrangement), and that appointments may be at set times and days. Check whether the client foresees any difficulty with this, and ask that you be told if this needs to change or what flexibility is needed.

Unless there are consequences, such as fees for missed sessions, or that therapy will cease after a certain number of missed sessions without reason, many clients may not put enough value on therapy, and simply not turn up to sessions regularly. Consider what is a reasonable consequence for the client. Usually, workplaces have established protocols for missed sessions, and it is important to be clear about these at the outset, as this raises the ethical issue of consent.

Missed sessions may be an indication that the client has not committed to therapy and change. Address the issue of missed sessions with the client, and enquire about reasons. Missed sessions may also be an indication that the client has not yet formed a bond with the therapist and is in two minds about the value of therapy. Again, addressing issues explicitly can identify the cause; you can then either work towards improving the alliance or referring the client on. Using specific measures of the alliance, such as the *Brief Rating Scale* (Duncan et al., 2003), will assist.

Some clients will have financial constraints and not be able to afford frequent sessions. Some clients are too embarrassed to acknowledge that they cannot afford treatment, or perhaps not regular sessions. Address this issue directly but sensitively with the client. You may need to arrange longer breaks between sessions. Alternatively, most therapists also provide some *pro bono* work for clients with cash flow problems, or reduced fees. Discussing fees and ability to pay at the beginning of therapy can prevent non-attendance because of financial difficulties. However, do keep in mind that individuals' circumstances can change, and be alert to the potential consequences of these changes; for example, a client could become unemployed while in therapy, resulting in financial constraints.

Some clients feel they have to hide aspects of their lives from others, and this can make regular therapy attendance problematic. For example, they may not have told family or friends that they are in treatment, and may not be able to explain their absence; as a result, they miss sessions. Some clients may have a drug or alcohol problem that interferes with functioning. For others, their lives may be so chaotic that they can't function well enough to keep regular appointments. Some clients may simply not have a diary. Again, carefully (and without blame) explore reasons for missed sessions, then problem-solve possible solutions with the client (a simple confirmation text message may prevent non-attendance). Such explorations can often reveal useful information that can assist in the overall treatment of the client.

Of course, it is more difficult to address non-attendance or cancellation if a client does not return to therapy. Of importance, however, is that the therapist always reflect on and address non-attendance with the client where possible, and when this is not possible, within supervision. Exploring reasons for non-attendance can provide valuable information about a client, but also about how the therapist is doing and what can be improved on. Alarm bells should ring for therapists if they, for instance, notice that they have a high percentage of non-attendance or cancellations after first sessions. Clearly, this would be an indication that reflection on how they do intake sessions is required.

Practice implications

The practical issues discussed in this chapter have highlighted the following issues that therapists need to be mindful of in their practice:

1   The setting in which therapists see clients can have an impact on client outcome and the process of psychotherapy, and needs to be carefully considered.
2   When deciding on a setting, issues such as confidentiality, privacy, and what is going to work best for clients need to be considered.
3   Therapists need to manage time well and be aware that how they present and communicate influences interactions and rapport with clients.

4   Therapists need to have thought through how they might respond to unexpected events.

5   Therapists need to consider how they respond to potentially tricky situations, such as non-attendance, crying, and chatty clients.

6   Therapists need to be flexible, and adjust to the differing needs of clients (such as financial constraints).

7   Therapists need to be aware of what helps them to provide the best psychotherapy they can (the number of sessions they do in a day, the time they need between sessions).

CONCLUSION

Managing these issues well will help build good working relationships with clients where appropriate boundaries are maintained. This chapter has highlighted the importance of providing a consistent framework for psychotherapy, which, when solid and well thought through, will help you provide the best therapy you can. To use an analogy: pictures without solid frames tend to fall off or damage the walls we try to hang them on.

Further reading

Australian Psychological Society (2002). *Guidelines Regarding Financial Dealings and Fair-trading.* Melbourne: Australian Psychological Society.

Australian Psychological Society (2007). *Code of Ethics.* Melbourne: Australian Psychological Society.

Hill, C. & O'Brien, K. (1999). *Helping Skills: Facilitating Exploration, Insight and Action.* Washington: American Psychological Society.

McWilliams, N. (1999). *Psychoanalytic Case Formulation.* New York: Guilford Press.

Schwartz, B. & Flowers, J. (2006). *How to Fail as a Therapist: 50 Ways to Lose or Damage Your Patients.* Atascedero: Impact Publishers.

Sommers-Flanagan, J. & Sommers-Flanagan, R. (2003). *Clinical Interviewing.* Hoboken, NJ: John Wiley & Sons.

Storr, A. (1990). *The Art of Psychotherapy* (2nd edn). Oxford: Butterworth Heinemann.

Chapter 11

Microskills

INTRODUCTION

As we have seen in previous chapters, the relationship between therapist and client is one of the most important factors predicting psychotherapy outcome. This chapter focuses on the fundamental communication skills needed to form positive therapeutic relationships.

To help clients in psychotherapy, you have to be able to hear and understand their stories: what is going on for them, how they think and feel about their story and life, where they have come from, and what they perceive will happen next. The essential skills involved, which are called *micro-counselling skills*, are common across all theoretical approaches. These are (a) skills related to listening; (b) skills related to encouraging further exploration; (c) skills related to communicating to clients that they are being understood; and (d) skills related to encouraging clients to develop a deeper understanding of what is going on for them:

a The *listening skills* are attending and observing.
b The *skills encouraging further exploration* are questioning, encouraging, paraphrasing, and reflection.
c The *skills relating to conveying understanding* are reflection, paraphrasing, and summarising.
d The *skills encouraging deeper understanding* include confrontation and challenging, and finding meaning.

The essential process of *empathy* enhances and utilises these skills, making them effective in building positive therapeutic relationships; without empathy, micro-counselling skills can be experienced by clients as empty, unhelpful, and meaningless. Accurate empathy has been shown to relate to enhanced rapport and positive client outcomes (Langs, 1990; Sommers-Flanagan & Sommers-Flanagan, 2003; Storr, 1990; Teyber & McClure, 2000). It is the central building block for building a strong working alliance with a client, and thus an essential component of any effective therapy (Teyber, 2006; Teyber & McClure, 2010). What follows is an overview of the micro-counselling skills, commencing with empathy; you are encouraged to refer to the further reading list at the end of this chapter for coverage of these skills in greater depth, and to view the videos to see these skills demonstrated.

EMPATHY

Empathy is a concept that involves cognitive, affective, and experiential processes (Sommers-Flanagan & Sommers-Flanagan, 2003). It refers to being able to understand the client's experience from the client's point of view, and being able to convey this understanding to the client. It involves imagining what it would be like to be this client at this point, and experiencing his or her life, but without getting lost in it. Clients need to know and feel that you have indeed had this empathic connection with their experience, and understand what it might be like to be them. It is *not* being sympathetic or feeling sorry for the client.

In his book, *The Gift of Therapy: Reflections On Being a Therapist*, Yalom (2001) describes empathy as 'looking out the patient's window. Try to see the world as your patient sees it' (p. 18). This conjures up a picture of the therapist and client, side by side, looking out of the same window. Yalom reminds us that clients gain much from feeling that they have been fully and accurately understood by the therapist. Sometimes even, accurate empathy is enough to allow the client to move on, without the therapist needing to assist with further problem-solving. In other words, empathy in and of itself can be curative.

Exercise 11.1

Recall the last time you told someone about something that really mattered to you and was causing you distress, and that person seemed to fully understand and 'get where you were coming from'. Remember what that felt like, and what the consequences were for you.

People vary in their capacity for empathy; for some it comes more naturally than for others. It requires you to be open and receptive to the other person's experience, while putting your own prejudices, beliefs, assumptions, and feelings aside. This can be particularly difficult when the client's experience is alien to, or close to, the therapist's own experience. There is probably greater risk of not being accurately empathic when the client's experience *seems* to be close to that of the therapist. The word *seems* is emphasised, because each individual's experience is unique. The therapist's conclusion that 'I know what she is feeling because I've been through that', is more likely to reflect the idea that, 'I know what I felt when that happened, and I'm assuming that it is the same for my client'. Clearly, the risk of not hearing the client accurately can be particularly great if the therapist over-relates to the client.

Exercise 11.2

Sometimes therapists-in-training may say something like: 'I can't work with parents; I don't have children'; 'I can't work with the bereaved; I've never lost someone'; or 'I'm a male and so I can't work with women who have been raped'. What advice would you give these trainees?

Empathy should not be confused with trying to merge with clients, or feeling exactly as they do; this could result in both therapist and client feeling overwhelmed. Boundaries are important in therapy, and the therapist does not want to lose his or her sense of separateness and objectivity by attempting to merge with the client. Empathy is understanding the client's experience without judgment and without becoming the client.

Naturally, understanding the client's experience and perspective requires well-developed listening and attending skills; often it is not the content of what clients say that is important but the way they say it, or the things they don't say, that informs you of their true experience. Empathy therefore also requires an element of deductive thinking, as *Webster's Dictionary* (1985) definition highlights:

> The action of understanding, being aware of, being sensitive to, and vicariously experiencing the feelings, thoughts and experiences of another of either the past or present without having the feelings, thoughts, and experience fully communicated in an objectively explicit manner (p. 407).

Empathy also requires being open to your own and others' emotions, and being relatively psychologically healthy; otherwise, the therapist may be defensive to what the client says and feels. Empathy requires genuine feelings of warmth and concern for others (Teyber, 2006; Teyber & McClure, 2010), and if the therapist is not in a functional place, he or she might find it difficult to feel this for others.

Empathy failures

Any interaction that leaves the client feeling misunderstood, alone, unimportant, or not respected is often the result of lack of empathy from the therapist. However, there can be instances when a client simply misunderstands the therapist's intentions or comments, and perceives the therapist to be lacking empathy, when the therapist does feel genuine concern and warmth for the client.

Most clients (and people generally) have experienced invalidation and denial of their feelings during their upbringing, captured in comments such as:

- 'Why do you feel that way? There is no reason for it.'
- 'You can't be hungry now. You've just eaten.'
- 'Why are you upset? It was nothing to get worked up about.'
- And this, from Teyber (2006), 'I'm cold. Put your sweater on' (p. 54).

These comments indicate a lack of empathy by the person making them—the judgments are based on one person's own view through the window, and not that of the other. Having survived such a world of (often unintentional) invalidation, receiving accurate empathy from another person can be a soothing and healing experience.

Strangely, however, some clients cannot tolerate empathy very well, especially in the early stages of therapy. Why may this be the case? We must first rule out the possibility that the therapist is showing sympathy or feeling sorry for the client. Treating a client like a poor victim may be offensive to clients who see themselves as resilient, and may encourage clients who perceive themselves at the mercy of the world and others to stay in a stuck and dependent position. If it is accurate empathy to which the client is reacting negatively, chances are that the client feels defensive about the content of the empathy. You might say, 'You seem to be really sad about the loss of your best friend all those years back', when the client wants to remain in denial that the loss mattered, to protect him- or herself from experiencing the pain of that loss. Clients may feel threatened that someone else may be able to understand them so well; perhaps, in their experience, people used knowledge about them to harm them, rather than to support them. Or perhaps, clients who have rarely received understanding and care, and long for it, find it too risky to accept it when it is offered? Most clients, however, will not have been so deeply damaged by others, and should respond well to accurate empathy. If they don't, and the therapist is relatively sure they have been accurate, then it is useful information. Reduce the amount of empathy, and gradually build up support, warmth, and understanding as the client's trust grows.

Exercise 11.3

1   View Videos 3, 5, 8, 12, 15, and 16 to consider the therapist's use of empathy.

LISTENING SKILLS

Accurately listening to someone is not easy. Just think about your day. How many times have you listened to someone talking to you while you have been thinking about something else? Our mind tends to hold a constant running commentary even when we are trying to listen, and will distract us from what is going on in the 'here and now'. This is even more pronounced if we are bored by what is being said, or think we have heard it all before. Conversely, we often know when someone is not listening to us. The other person may change the subject or appear distracted. Accurately hearing what a person has said is also not a given. Just think of any experience you may have had in telling someone a piece of news, and then hearing that piece of news after it has been retold by many people. Most likely the information changed. So let's explore what is required to listen accurately.

Attending
To attend you have to be present, and this presence needs to be communicated to the person you are listening to. This is done mostly nonverbally through body language and posture. A client is unlikely to feel comfortable talking to someone's back or talking to someone who is not able to keep eye contact. So having an open

relaxed body posture with good eye contact is important. Another way to show you are listening is to lean forward and to be aware of your facial expression. Nodding and smiling appropriately can encourage the client to discuss more. Sometimes, it may be helpful to lean forward toward the client, as this indicates to the client that attention is being paid, if it is done in a non-intimidating manner. It is important to be aware of cultural issues that may be pertinent to your client. For some clients, it might be rude to look them directly in the eye; others may not feel comfortable sitting too close (see chapter 15).

Another form of communicating your presence and attention is through the tone, pitch, and speed of your voice. If your client presents as very distressed, it may not be helpful to speak with a loud tone of voice. Appropriate tone is therefore important to think about.

An important skill in attending is to track and respond to the verbal content of what the client is saying and to follow his train of thought. A sure way to indicate that you are not listening is to ask a question completely unrelated to what the client has been talking about. If the client has been talking about a painful experience with his mother, and the therapist responds with, 'Tell me about your work', this would be an example of the therapist failing to track the client's verbal content, or avoiding certain issues.

It can be helpful to not immediately jump in and say something when the client pauses—he might be thinking or struggling with his emotions. Being appropriately quiet for a while can encourage such people to talk further and gather their thoughts. Again, silence should be used sensitively; silences that are too long can feel intimidating and punitive to some clients; they may be left feeling anxious or judged.

Thus, the skills of attending are:

- open relaxed posture
- tracking what is being said
- appropriate use of silence
- appropriate use of eye contact
- leaning forward
- using appropriate tone, pitch, and speed of voice
- facial expression.

Possible blocks to attending
A number of factors may hamper a therapist in attending to what the client is saying. These are:

- being preoccupied with yourself
- being worried about what the client is thinking about you
- comparing the client's problem to your problem
- being preoccupied with what you want to say next
- over-identifying with the problem of the client and thinking about your own past
- excessively judging your own performance in session ('Am I doing a good job?'; 'Am I saying the right thing?')

- making assumptions about what the client is going to say next and jumping in (a form of mind-reading)
- paying attention only to what you find comfortable or acceptable to listen to (for example, ignoring the topic of sex or strong emotions)
- daydreaming
- giving into the urge to jump in and give advice or solve the problem
- going off on a tangent (for example, when the client is talking about work difficulties, you ignore what is said, as you are more interested in the client's family)
- becoming preoccupied with feeling attracted to or repulsed by the client
- being affected by your own physical condition; for example, by feeling too tired, hungry, or ill to attend to the client
- having difficulty relating to the client's story or following his or her train of thought, especially if that story is unusual or different from your own experience; for example, if the client is disorganised in his or her speech or is experiencing psychotic symptoms.

Exercise 11.4

1   View Video 11. What may have interfered with the therapist's ability to attend?
2   Reflect on times when you did not feel listened to. Why do you think the other person was inattentive? (Refer to the above list.)

One way of addressing blocks to attending is to be self-aware, through tracking and monitoring of your ability to attend and of moments when your attention has drifted. Be careful, though, not to allow the self-monitoring to become another block (that is, an over-focus on one's self: the first factor). Some therapists like to take a few minutes before seeing a client to do some grounding or mindfulness practice, to be fully present and focused with the client for the next hour or so.

Observing

Another listening skill is observing the client's verbal and nonverbal behaviours. Part of this involves tracking the content of her speech and observing any themes, contradictions, or inconsistencies in what she talks about. Noticing how the client presents, what she is wearing, and whether her emotional expression is consistent with what she is talking about are all important pieces of information that can help you understand what is going on for her (see also chapter 12 on intake interviews). The main areas to focus on when observing are:

- the client's eye contact (for example, where does she tend to look?)
- the client's body language (does she sit comfortably or is she agitated?)
- changes in the client's body language (does she shift nervously when talking about certain topics?)
- the client's speech (is she softly spoken, does she speak rapidly, does her tone change when talking about different topics?)

These observations will provide rich information about what is going on for the client. For those familiar with the concept, mindfulness is what is being described: paying attention on purpose without judgment (Kabat-Zinn, 2003).

Exercise 11.5

Pick any of the scenarios on any of the videos and observe the client and therapist carefully. What can you determine from what you see?

SKILLS ENCOURAGING FURTHER EXPLORATION

Reflection

Letting a client know that you have understood what he is saying will usually result in him expanding on his story. A therapist can do this through the use of reflection of the content and/or affect of what the client is saying. *Affect* refers to what the client is observed to be feeling, through what he is saying, the tone of his voice, and/or his body language.

Reflection is usually a more helpful way of encouraging further exploration than questions. Questions can come across as interrogatory, and may take the client off topic; with reflection, the therapist stays with the client's story, and it is more difficult to lead and direct what is talked about. The client is allowed to discuss his own experience with minimal interference from the therapist's agenda.

Case study 11.1

Client: I don't know what is wrong with me. I get really frustrated when people keep asking me what is wrong with me, why I am not like my old self, when I can't answer them. All I know is that I can't seem to do anything. I find it really hard to motivate myself; I really can't be bothered.

Reflection of content

Therapist: You are finding it hard to motivate yourself, and you are unclear what is going on for you?

Reflection of affect

Therapist: You have been feeling frustrated, confused, and apathetic?

Reflection of feeling and content

Therapist: You are aware that you can't be bothered, but don't understand what this is about, which is leaving you feeling frustrated, especially when people ask you what is wrong?

A natural response by the client to the therapist's reflections in the scenario above would be to talk more about his experience. Reflections encourage further discussion and communicate to clients that the therapist is listening to them and has heard what they are saying. Sometimes it is useful for the therapist to use a 'checkout' at the end or beginning of a reflection, especially when the therapist is reflecting feelings, which are implied but have not been explicitly stated. This serves a twofold purpose: the therapist communicates that she is listening, but wants to make sure that she has accurately understand what the client has said. It also gives the client the opportunity to correct the therapist's understanding and expand further.

Case study 11.2

Reflection and checkout

Client: I just want to be left alone. People keep demanding things from me, and it is just too much. They don't understand. I wish someone would just help me!

Reflection of feeling and content with a checkout

Therapist: You seem to be feeling angry and frustrated that people don't seem to understand you or help you; am I understanding that right?

Exercise 11.6

Try to use reflections and checkouts in your day-to-day life when listening to others. What effect do they have on the conversation?

Questioning

Another way to encourage clients to tell you more about what is going on for them is through use of questions. There are two types of questions that are helpful in therapy: *closed questions* and *open questions*.

Closed questions

We all use questions when speaking to people, usually to obtain more information. Closed questions are useful in obtaining clarification, and can usually only be answered with one or two words, like 'yes' or 'no'. Examples of closed questions are:
- 'Where do you live?'
- 'How old are you?'
- 'Are you feeling depressed?'

Open questions

Open questions expand the range of information rather than hone detail, and usually require a longer, more expressive response than closed questions. Examples of open questions include:

- 'What has brought you to see me? How can I help?'
- 'What would you like to be different?'
- 'How have you been feeling?'
- 'Could you tell me a bit more about your family?'

Here is another way to think about open and closed questions: with closed questions, there is only one way of answering; with open questions, the client is free to decide how to answer. Using many closed questions is not usually helpful, as this can lead to the client feeling bombarded or interrogated. Closed questions can also be leading, which can give the client the impression of being judged. Examples of a *leading question* are: 'You are not very happy, are you?', and 'You want to leave him, don't you?' Such questions tend to force the client into making a certain response, and reduce options. It takes practice to know the type of question that will be most useful in helping the client to explore issues further, but a good rule of thumb is to use as few questions as you can.

A danger in using questions is that the therapist can use them to control the direction of the session, and lead the client away from topics that the client wants to talk about. Additionally, a therapist can sometimes jump to incorrect assumptions about a client and ask questions thinking that she already knows the answer. Such questions may lead the client to conclude that what the therapist thinks is right. A therapist may have a hypothesis that a client is depressed, because the client thinks that expressing anger toward his or her spouse is wrong. The hypothesis is that the client thinks that expressing anger is bad. The questions the therapist may then ask are:

Case study 11.3

Therapist: Can you tell me about your relationship with your spouse?
Client: Well, it is OK. We argue now and then.
Therapist: What happens when you argue?
Client: She tells me off about something, and then I usually keep quiet until she has calmed down.
Therapist: What makes you keep quiet?
Client: I don't really know. It is what I always do.
Therapist: Is it because you are angry?
Client: Maybe. I am not sure.
Therapist: Do you find anger difficult?
Client: Sometimes.

Therapist: Have you considered whether you may have difficulty with your spouse because you have difficulty expressing your anger?

The therapist is asking increasingly more closed questions, letting the hypothesis determine the questions, rather than letting herself be led by the client. This type of questioning sometimes gets mistaken for *Socratic questioning*, which involves using questioning to lead the client to discover more about him- or herself. Socratic questioning, also known as *guided discovery*, is about using appropriate questions to help clients discover more about themselves and their difficulties without there being any preconceived ideas about where you are going to end up (Wills & Sanders, 1997). Let's return to the above dialogue:

Therapist: Can you tell me about your relationship with your spouse?
Client: Well, it is OK. We argue now and then.
Therapist: Mmm … go on [nodding].
Client: She tells me off about something, and then I usually keep quiet until she has calmed down.
Therapist: So, you keep quiet when you feel told off by her?
Client: Yes.
Therapist: What makes you keep quiet?
Client: I don't really know. It is what I always do.
Therapist: You are saying that keeping quiet is what you always do. Has it always been like this, or has there been a time when it was different?
Client: Well, I remember, when we first met I used to say, 'You know that I don't like being told off'.
Therapist: What would happen then?
Client: We would end up in these big shouting matches that would be really upsetting, and once she ended up hitting me, so I decided it was better if I kept quiet.
Therapist: Can you tell me a bit more about how is it better if you keep quiet?

You can see how new information emerged, and that questions were aimed at helping the client to explore what makes him behave in a certain way. Exploring issues in more depth is an important aim of therapy, and questions can be helpful if used appropriately.

Cultural appropriateness should also be taken into account when using questions. Too many questions, particularly closed ones, could be perceived as disrespectful and impolite by Indigenous clients, who might also feel they can't trust the therapist, perceiving him or her as authoritarian, resulting in automatic agreement rather than a genuine response (Dudgeon et al., 2000; Harlen, 2002).

Exercise 11.7

As an experiment, try to hold a conversation with someone using only closed questions. What do you notice?

Encouraging

The above examples also use *minimal encouragers* to assist the client to explore and talk about his issues further. *Encouragers* are short utterances, body movements, and facial expressions that promote further discussion by clients. We use them in day-to-day conversation all the time (Ivey & Ivey, 2003). Just think about how often you smile or nod your head when listening, to encourage the other person to continue. Other encouragers are expressions such as 'mmmm', 'uhm', 'aha', 'right', or 'go on'. Encouragers can be used to let clients know you are listening without interrupting their flow of thought or injecting your agenda into the conversation.

Paraphrasing

Paraphrasing what a client has said is another way to encourage the client to continue and/or expand on what she or he is saying. This can be done by repeating a pertinent word the client has used. An example might be repeating the word 'hurt?', with your tone rising slightly to indicate that this is a question. Another form of paraphrasing is to summarise in one sentence what the client has just said, using the client's words; for example, 'You went to your sister's to discuss your relationship'. This type of paraphrasing communicates that you have heard what the client has said, and encourages further discussion. Do not be tempted to simply parrot what the client has said—most will find this irritating. Paraphrasing needs to add something of your own understanding of what is pertinent in what the client has said, not simply everything that has been said.

SKILLS CONVEYING UNDERSTANDING AND LISTENING

Summarising

Used appropriately, all these skills should convey that the therapist is following the client's story. Utilising summaries can help show clients that they are being heard, but are also useful in helping to focus the session (Egan, 2006). When summarising, the therapist usually provides a synopsis of what has been discussed so far. The summary includes reflections of content and affect. Summaries can be used at the beginning of sessions, to help remind both client and therapist of the main issues from the previous session, or at the end of sessions, to help conclude and to check that the therapist has understood what the client has been talking about. Therapists may also use summaries during sessions to convey that they have heard what has been said, and to highlight the main theme or issues. Utilising a summary can help keep sessions on track when clients provide a plethora of information. Ivey and Ivey (2003) state that it is often useful to check for accuracy at the end of summaries, to give the client the opportunity to confirm or disconfirm what the therapist has understood.

Client's frame of reference and multicultural competence

The object of micro-counselling skills is to assist in establishing rapport, to help clients to feel safe to talk through what has brought them to therapy, and to facilitate understanding of their issues. It is therefore important when using micro-counselling skills (such as summaries, reflections, and/or questions), to use language the client can relate to. One way of doing this is to use clients' terminology, understand their cultural background, and how they relate to their culture. Utilising words the client cannot relate to or understand is not going to make the client feel understood, and may exacerbate feelings of disempowerment, aloneness, and helplessness. Empathy is essential here, as it helps the therapist to respond according to the client's frame of reference.

This requires careful attending to how the client talks, what he talks about, and what he is familiar with. For example, a client may have grown up in a family in which domestic violence was an everyday occurrence. He may relate that in his family conflicts get resolved through hitting. Hitting a person may therefore be experienced as an appropriate behaviour in the face of conflict, and not hitting a person may be viewed as weak. If the therapist were to respond to this information by stating, 'Violence is the wrong way to resolve conflict', the client may feel judged and misunderstood; the therapist has failed to respond empathically or from the client's frame of reference. A more helpful way of responding is to explore further the client's experience, and how he views hitting, and the possibility of change, without the therapist conveying a sense that hitting is appropriate.

Every person is influenced by his or her individual history and cultural background. It is therefore important to be mindful of clients' culture, and how this may influence the therapeutic process, but not to make generalised assumptions about what culture means for how clients will behave or what is important to them (Egan, 2006). Also, it is important that you, the therapist, know your own biases, and how they may originate from your own culture and experiences, and to develop ways of sensitively assessing clients' 'cultural outlook' (Stuart, 2004, p. 6). Be open and curious when seeing clients, especially when seeing a client from a culture different from your own. A helpful process is to address possible differences between you and the client, and to explore with the client what is appropriate and not appropriate within his or her culture (Egan, 2006). Furthermore, it is important and ethical to support the client in achieving goals that are important to him or her, even when these goals may be inconsistent with your own culture. (See chapter 15 for more on cultural, religious and spiritual issues).

Exercise 11.8

View Videos 5 and 12. Which micro-counselling skills are used, and how do these skills assist in exploring the issues further?

CREATING A DEEPER UNDERSTANDING

The micro-counselling skills of *confrontation or challenging* and *reflecting on meaning* assist clients to obtain a deeper understanding of their issues, which can lead to change or action. Ivey and Ivey (2003) identify these as influencing skills.

Confrontation or challenging

According to Ivey and Ivey (2003), the aim of confrontation is to facilitate change, and requires use of all micro-counselling skills. *Confrontation* consists of:

- identifying inconsistencies or contradictions in what the client says, does, or feels
- being able to reflect these inconsistencies or contradictions back to the client in a supportive and nonjudgmental manner
- determining the outcome of the above in terms of the client activating change.

Case study 11.4
Challenging intervention

The therapist becomes aware that a depressed client says she wants to get better, but does none of the activities that might make her feel better.

Therapist: You tell me that you want to feel better, and you know that exercising, and not sitting in your chair watching television all day, will help you feel better, yet you find yourself sitting in your chair all day. I wonder what prevents you from doing what you say you know will help you?

This illustrates how a challenge, made in a supportive manner, might help a client to explore further her difficulty in changing the way she behaves. An example of an *unhelpful* challenge would be:

Therapist: You don't seem to want to do anything to help yourself.

This intervention comes across as judgmental and critical, and may put the client on the defensive and fearful of sharing anything further. Challenging must be done in such a way that the client is able to hear what you say. See Video 14, for an example of challenging.

Helping clients to find meaning

We can only really change what we understand. It is difficult to know what we need to change if we don't understand why we behave in a certain way or what the purpose of the behaviour(s) is. A way to facilitate change is to assist clients to understand the meaning or purpose of their behaviours, thoughts, and feelings. Interventions that can assist with this are:

- 'What does this mean to you?'
- 'How do you make sense of this?'
- 'How does this work for you?'
- 'How has this event lead to you feeling depressed?'
- 'What tends to go through your mind when you are in this situation?'

Naturally, the focus of questions that therapists may ask to facilitate indepth exploration might be determined by their theoretical orientation. A behavioural therapist might ask what the outcome of a behaviour is for a client. A cognitive therapist would focus on meaning for the client or what his or her thoughts and beliefs are about a situation. Usually, though, regardless of theoretical orientation, 'how?' and 'what?' questions encourage further exploration of issues by clients. Often, clients present with patterns of thinking, behaving, or feeling that may work in certain situations but not in others. For example, a client may respond in the same way regardless of the context. Facilitating further exploration is therefore helpful in encouraging greater understanding of issues presented, and may assist clients to experience their difficulties in a different way (seeing them from a different perspective), which may open up possibilities for change. Exploring meaning also helps the therapist to conceptualise the client's difficulties. For more on conceptualisation, see chapter 14.

Before you can delve deeper into a client's experience, a good working relationship and rapport does need to have been established. In addition to being empathetic, all the micro-counselling skills mentioned in this chapter will assist in establishing a good working alliance–therapeutic relationship.

Exercise 11.9

View Video 8. Try to identify how the therapist encourages the client to find a better understanding.

Practice implications

1 Therapists need to be practised and skilled in using micro-counselling skills to promote communication and exploration of clients' experiences regardless of their theoretical orientation.
2 Therapists need to have an ability to respond with accurate empathy.
3 Therapists need to be skilled in using a variety of micro-counselling skills flexibly and appropriately—not just to rely on one skill, as each skill leads to a different outcome.
4 Therapists need to be culturally sensitive and communicate using the client's frame of reference.

CONCLUSION

We trust that this chapter has shown how essential micro-counselling skills are in the process of psychotherapy, regardless of which theoretical approach is used. Psychotherapeutic treatment can only occur if the client feels she can open up, tell her story, and know she will be heard and understood. Micro-counselling skills, empathy in particular, are vital tools of any therapeutic approach. Practise them so you can use them flexibly. Utilising specific therapeutic techniques and interventions without these basic skills will be ineffective.

Recommended reading
Corey, G. (1996). *Theory and Practice of Counselling and Psychotherapy*. Pacific Grove, CA: Brooks Cole.
Egan, G. (2006). *Essentials of Skilled Helping: Managing Problems, Developing Opportunities*. Belmont, CA: Thomson Wadsworth.
Hill, C. & O'Brien, K. (1999). *Helping Skills: Facilitating Exploration, Insight and Action*. Washington: American Psychological Association.
Schwartz, B. & Flowers, J. (2006). *How to Fail as a Therapist: 50 Ways to Lose or Damage Your Patients*. Atascedero: Impact.

Chapter 12

Intake and outcome assessment

INTRODUCTION

Intake interviewing and outcome assessment are core skills required for psychologists in professional practice. This chapter describes the process of conducting an intake interview with a newly-presenting client, and the skills required to measure outcome of psychological interventions with individuals.

THE INTAKE INTERVIEW

The intake interview is one of the most important methods of assessment available to the practising psychologist. It is at the time of the intake interview that the psychologist and client gain their first impressions of each other, and it is usually the first substantial interaction between them. The intake interview also constitutes an assessment method that complements information from other sources, such as questionnaires, referral letters, and behavioural assessments.

Exercise 12.1

Imagine yourself as you arrive for your first session with your new psychologist. What thoughts are likely to be running through your mind? What concerns might you have? What are you hoping for? What are you worried about?

Goals

During the intake interview, the skilled psychologist is attempting to balance a number of diverse goals. While each of these goals may be of different importance at different times, and with different clients, the psychologist should be mindful of each throughout the intake session. Regardless of which theoretical orientation the therapist adheres to, each of these goals will be important in assessing the presenting problem, formulating the client's problem, and planning an intervention.

One of the most important goals of the intake interview is to establish rapport with the client. Depending on the therapist's theoretical orientation, this may be deemed to be the single most important goal of the intake-interview process. Development of rapport with the client provides a foundation on which all other interactions are based. Achievement of the other goals of the intake, such as information gathering and planning treatment, are likely to be difficult or impossible if the psychologist and the client have not been able to establish rapport. Attention to microskills (see chapter 11) is a key way to develop rapport, as is maintaining a positive attitude towards the client.

A second goal of the intake interview is to socialise clients into working within a particular therapeutic environment and framework (Beck, 1995). A client presenting for her first session with a new therapist may be unclear what her role will be in the therapeutic interaction. This may be because the client has no experience of therapy, or has an experience of therapy that is different from the style of the new therapist. A client who has previously worked with a nondirective, Rogerian therapist, for example, may be uncertain how therapy will operate with a therapist who utilises a more active, directive style, such as behaviour therapy. In these cases, it is the role of the therapist to help the client to understand what the client's role in therapy will be. Some authors have referred to this process as 'socialising the client into therapy' (e.g. Beck, 1995, p. 26). The way in which the therapist does this can take a number of forms, depending on style and orientation. Cognitive and cognitive behaviour therapists often make the role of clients explicit, informing them in the first session what will be expected of them during treatment. Other therapists, such as those from a psychodynamic orientation, may be less explicit, simply encouraging clients to talk about what first occurs to them. Regardless of the methods used, the therapist's behaviour helps shape the client's behaviour, and assists in communicating to the client what will be required of her as part of her treatment.

A third goal of the intake interview is to form a detailed understanding of the client's presenting problem. This information gathering is essential for the therapist to be able to formulate and plan an intervention to assist the client.

The information gained in the intake interview will often be used to assist with the diagnostic decision-making process. Different theoretical orientations place different amounts of emphasis on diagnosis. Many clinical psychologists and other nonmedical clinicians assert that generation of a diagnosis is less important than developing a clear understanding and formulation of a client's presenting problem. But, in many cases, a diagnosis will provide important information about what treatment is likely to be effective, and likely prognosis. It should be acknowledged, however, that clients may present with problems and difficulties that do not fit with or warrant a specific diagnosis (see chapter 13).

Almost all clinical psychologists and nonmedical counsellors and therapists would agree that generating a formulation of a client's presenting problem, according to an established theoretical framework, is a core goal of the first interaction with a client. This formulation guides the therapist's intervention. Case formulation is covered in detail in chapter 14.

Not all clients who present to a particular therapist will be suitable for her or his style of therapy. It is vitally important that psychologists are capable of recognising not only when they are able to assist clients, but also when clients are unlikely to benefit from their treatment; part of the intake interview is to assess the client's suitability for treatment. The characteristics that make a client suitable for treatment will vary depending on the nature of the treatment proposed. Short-term dynamic psychotherapy and cognitive behavioural therapy often require that a client has a clear, circumscribed problem. Behaviour therapists often require that a problem can be operationalised in terms of specific, observable behaviours.

Regardless of which orientation the therapist has, it is universal across treatment orientations that the client be able to participate in a collaborative, reflective process. It is also universal across styles of treatment that the client be willing to make or consider changes in behaviour and approach to critical events in his or her life. Client factors that are important in determining suitability for treatment are the focus of chapter 4.

Although a treatment plan may not be generated during the very first session, it is usually thought that another goal of the intake interview is to establish a plan for further assessment or treatment. In many cases, particularly for beginning therapists, it will be difficult to gather enough information in a single interview to prepare a formulation detailed enough to plan an intervention. In such cases, the therapist should work with the client to outline a plan for future assessment. This may be presented to the client at the conclusion of the first session, preparing him or her for the need for further information gathering:

> I think we have covered a lot of ground today. You've given me a lot of information about how you've been feeling depressed lately, as well as how you've had two panic attacks over the past fortnight. We've discussed some of the recent events in your life that have been causing you a large amount of stress. I am still interested in hearing about your history, as well as speaking to your wife about what happened during your last panic attack. I'd also like to get you to complete a couple of short questionnaires, just so that, together, we can keep track of your depression and anxiety symptoms over the next few weeks. Does this plan seem OK to you?

In some cases, there may be enough information gathered during the intake interview to present a tentative formulation and treatment plan to the client. In such cases, it should be made clear to the client that both formulation and treatment plan are preliminary, and are likely to be revised as treatment progresses.

A final goal of the intake interview is to obtain a commitment to further work from the client. In some cases, such as when further information gathering is needed, this will merely entail an agreement by the client to return for a second session. In other cases, where the therapist has worked with the client to develop a formulation and treatment plan, this may require a commitment by the client to actively work through, with the therapist, the agreed treatment plan.

To summarise, the goals of the intake interview are:

- to establish rapport with the client
- to socialise the client into working within a therapeutic environment or framework
- to form a detailed understanding of the presenting problem
- to assist the diagnostic decision-making process
- to assist the formulation process
- to understand factors that ameliorate or exacerbate the presenting problem

- to assess suitability for therapy
- to establish a plan for further assessment or treatment
- to obtain a commitment to further work from the client.

Basics of the intake interview

Many beginning therapists are unsure about even some of the most basic processes of the intake interview. How do I arrange the seats? How do I greet the client? Do I shake the client's hand? How do I address the client? Do I take notes during the session? It is easy for a novice therapist to become excessively concerned about protocol and doing things 'just right'.

Three general rules are:

- Treat the client as a fellow human being
- Treat the client in the way you would expect to be treated yourself
- Remember that your relationship with your client is a professional relationship, and not just a social interaction.

Most intake interviews move through a series of steps. Therapists will usually prepare by reading any material such as referral letters, chart entries, or assessment reports. After the client has been greeted in the waiting room and brought into the consulting room, the therapist will usually provide information about what will happen in the first session. This *agenda setting* is particularly important with clients who have not previously seen a psychologist, and who may not be sure what to expect. There is usually also some further preamble to the therapy interview in which the psychologist discusses fees (if not already arranged) and confidentiality. Discussion of the limits to confidentiality is also important to cover before entering into the intake. The intake interview then proceeds through information gathering and history taking. Usually, time is reserved at the end of the session for a summary, and for giving the client an opportunity to ask questions.

Information gathering

Exercise 12.2

View Video 10, for an example of engaging an adolescent in an intake interview, as well as the methods used to gain information about the family. What are your impressions?

In an intake interview, a delicate balance has to be struck between starting to build a relationship with a new client and gathering information about the presenting problem. Information gathered during the intake allows therapist and client to collaborate in developing a shared understanding of the aetiology and maintenance of the problem, as well as generating a tentative treatment plan. Therapists vary considerably in how they structure an intake interview. Most, however, would agree that the interview needs to possess structure to ensure that it achieves its goals. An unstructured interview runs the risk of gathering information inefficiently, confusing the client, and compromising the client's ability to convey details of the presenting problem.

There is a risk in imposing too much structure onto an intake interview. Too much structure may leave the client feeling disempowered, or not listened to. A balance must be struck between structure and flexibility.

One important component of the intake interview is *hypothesis testing*, the process by which the therapist uses information already gathered to develop ideas about the likely nature of the client's problem. These hypotheses can then be evaluated through further questioning. Such an approach allows the therapist to narrow the range of likely problems, and to proceed with the interview in a logical, efficient manner. This hypothesis-testing approach applies not only to attempts to establish a diagnosis but to assess other factors relevant to the formulation of the presenting problem. An example of this approach to diagnosis is given below.

Hypothesis testing for a diagnosis
Here are pieces of information from the client, and the hypothesis-testing logic of the therapist:

The client reports a sense of anxiousness: 'My initial hypothesis is of an anxiety or mood disorder.'

The client reports that anxiety is not episodic but chronic: 'I think I can rule out panic disorder. Maybe it is generalised anxiety disorder?'

The client states that his worry is mostly about doing harm to others through being 'dirty'. He reports few other worries: 'Hmmm. Perhaps this is not GAD. Maybe a mood disorder or inflated responsibility sometimes seen in OCD?'

The client denies any neurovegetative features of depression. He also reports engaging in very frequent cleaning rituals: 'OK. I think the OCD diagnosis is looking more likely, but I still need to check for psychotic symptoms.'

Another technique that assists in establishing a flexible structure in the intake interview is the use of *funnelling*, where the therapist guides the interaction with the client from a broad initial question, through a series of increasingly specific questions. Information gathered is then summarised for the client, checking for accurate understanding by the therapist. Often a transition statement is then made, and the therapist commences the funnelling again in the next area of discussion.

In funnelling, depicted in figure 12.1, the therapist assists the client to convey a sensible, coherent story by providing a structure designed to improve the efficiency of information gathering. Rather than imposing a rigid structure, or the therapist's agenda, on the client, funnelling is designed to ensure that the interview flows in a logical manner, giving the client the opportunity to discuss each aspect of his presenting problem, and then to correct any misunderstanding by the therapist. In funnelling, the therapist begins each area of discussion with *open questions* (see chapter 11) designed to allow the client to introduce new material and to define the area of discussion. As discussion of each aspect of the problem proceeds, the therapist's questions are more precisely targeted to elicit informa-

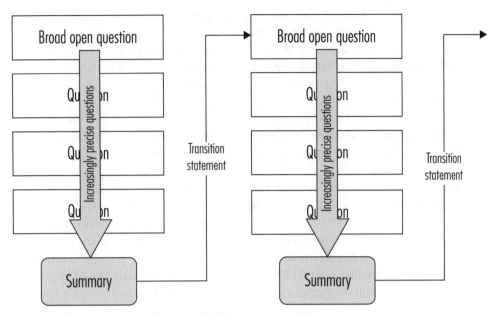

Figure 12.1   Improving efficiency of information gathering

tion not spontaneously offered by the client. Once an area of discussion is exhausted, or the client–therapist team is ready to move on, the therapist provides a summary of the theme, and makes a transition statement designed to open the next area of discussion.

Content of the intake interview

The information gathering that takes place during the intake interview allows the therapist to begin forming ideas about the nature of the client's problem, and interventions that may be useful. Information such as the specific nature of each presenting problem is crucial in generating a framework for further information gathering. Once the therapist has an idea of the array of problems, he or she can begin to assess specific information, such as frequency, duration, and intensity of the problems. Factors and events that make the problem worse or more manageable should also be investigated. In all cases, the therapist attempts to understand the factors that caused and maintain the client's problems.

Diagnosis can be useful in understanding likely prognosis, but therapists should be mindful of two points relating to diagnosis during the intake interview. First, not all clients who present for therapy have a specific diagnosis. Second, while diagnosis may assist with description of the client's presentation, it does little to guide the therapist's intervention. Most therapists would agree that it is formulation of the presenting problem, rather than diagnosis, that guides therapists in planning treatment strategy.

Concluding the intake interview

The conclusion to the interview plays a significant role in determining whether the client will return for further sessions. The conclusion of the initial interview should contain several key elements that aim to consolidate the gains of the session, and prepare client and therapist for future work.

Just as the therapist uses summaries throughout the interview to 'wrap up' each area of discussion and correct any misunderstandings, a similar process is used to begin drawing the interview to a close. The therapist provides a general summary of each of the areas discussed, including highlighting the most important aspects of the presenting problem, attempting to draw these themes into a meaningful whole. During this concluding summary, the client should be encouraged to correct any misunderstandings, to ensure that the plan for the future is based on accurate information.

A second key element to the conclusion of the first interview is the check for missed information. When a client presents with multiple difficulties, it can be difficult to cover all relevant information thoroughly in the first session. The client may have been reluctant to introduce certain presenting problems to the discussion (perhaps because of embarrassment). A simple question such as, 'Is there anything important that we haven't talked about today?', invites the client to flag aspects of his or her current situation that can be followed up immediately (if there is time) or covered in the next session.

The key elements in concluding the first interview are:

- Provide a summary of the session, checking for understanding and allowing the client to correct any misunderstandings
- Ask about any important themes not covered in the interview
- Provide an outline of the future, including (where relevant):
  - arrangements for the next session
  - further assessment requirements
  - referral to other treatment providers
  - treatment options and/or plan
- Allow time for the client to ask questions
- Provide hope and emphasise strengths.

Although active treatment rarely begins in a first session, it is important that the client leaves the first session with an understanding of the likely direction of subsequent visits. This direction will depend on the nature and complexity of the client's presenting problem. For clients who present with less severe and more circumscribed problems, the therapist may be able to provide an outline of how treatment will progress. In some cases (such as specific phobias), the therapist may be able to provide details on the nature of treatment, and even an estimate of how many sessions may be required. In other cases, the treatment outline may be tentative or even incomplete. Avoid discussing details of any treatment procedure until you have gained an adequate understanding of the nature of the client's presenting problem. Beginning therapists, in particular, are often eager to 'give something back' to the client, when they are yet to fully understand the nature and complexity of the client's challenges. It should also be remembered that, while some clients will be eager to commence active therapy, others will want the therapist to take time to fully develop a working relationship before attempting action.

In most cases, some sort of further assessment will be required. This may entail further assessment interviews, questionnaires, gathering of collateral information from significant others (such as spouse or family), medical investigations, or even behavioural tasks. When further information is required, the therapist should outline the reason for it, as well as what might be gained from such assessment. Some clients will require the therapist to explain the need for future assessment before moving into treatment.

In cases where a therapist believes that she is able to offer suitable treatment to a client, the therapist may begin providing details of her plan. Exact details will vary, depending on the nature of the therapy and the client's presenting problem. There is also considerable variation in the style used by therapists to provide an outline of treatment. Some will provide detailed descriptions of what is to be covered, while others will provide a general outline of what they think will be covered. Regardless of style, therapists should check with clients about their thoughts and feelings towards the suggested intervention, providing further information and clarification where required.

In some cases, it will become apparent during the intake that the client requires assessment or treatment from a different health professional. This can occur for many reasons. The therapist may not be adequately trained for or have specialist skills in treatment of the client's presentation, or the client may prefer treatment in a different therapy style. In some cases, treatment of choice will be pharmacological or medical. In all cases where it is clear that another professional needs to be involved, an explanation should be given to the client. Furthermore, the therapist should make every reasonable effort to facilitate referral to another treatment provider, including offering to write a letter of referral to assist the new provider to understand the reason for the referral.

Even in non-directive therapy, an outline for the future is crucial. While a therapist from a more directive school may provide specific details of treatment techniques that will be used, others may provide a less detailed description. In all cases, it is important that the client understands the roles of the therapist and him- or herself, so that he or she can participate adequately in whatever therapy or treatment is planned.

Outcome assessment

When starting work with a client, it is natural to focus on immediate interactions. The starting therapist is strongly motivated to work with a client on the client's immediate problem, either through active methods or more process-based interventions. Outcome assessment is easy to overlook when your primary concern is facilitating symptom relief or insight in a client (see chapter 1).

Thorough outcome assessment can also be seen as time-consuming. Even the shortest questionnaires take several minutes for the client to complete. When a battery of questionnaires is used, the time to complete them can be in excess of an hour, and may be perceived as placing a considerable burden on the client. Economy of assessment is an important principle to consider when devising your outcome-assessment methods. While following a client around for an entire week, observing every action he or she performs, may yield useful information, it would be seen as uneconomical (and intrusive) by client and psychologist alike. There are several ways to reduce impact of outcome assessment on session time. Many psychologists ask clients to complete short questionnaires in the waiting room. Others allow clients to take some questionnaires away to complete at home.

There are many benefits to assessing outcome in psychotherapy practice, for both therapist and client (Lambert et al., 1998). The use of assessment methods such as questionnaires gives results that are standardised and normed according to one or more reference groups. This allows a more objective evaluation of the construct in question, providing for a reliable, valid quantification. Questionnaires have usually been subjected to an assessment of their construct validity, one element of which is that the measure adequately covers the construct in question. The Depression scale of the Depression Anxiety and Stress Scales (DASS-D) (Lovibond & Lovibond, 1995), for example, has been deemed to cover adequately the construct of depression, including many of the major symptoms. Use of questionnaires can ensure that you consider all symptoms that may be important, rather than placing too much or too little emphasis on any one symptom area.

Another advantage of standardised questionnaires is that they allow for the quantification of a symptom or condition (Mellenbergh & van der Brink, 1998). Such quantification is useful when recording overall symptom severity in a client file, reporting it to another psychologist in a multidisciplinary team, or interpreting it for a client to demonstrate progress in treatment. Having such quantified data can be particularly useful in overcoming the cognitive distortions that accompany many psychological conditions. An individual with depression, for example, is likely to perceive his or her world in a negatively distorted fashion, attending to and recalling information that is congruent with the depressed mood. It may be difficult for such an individual to perceive changes in depression severity over time. A clear drop in score over several sessions on a measure of depression symptoms may be useful in showing progress to such a client.

Therapists are also subject to distortions in information processing. Having a quantified measure of an individual's problem may help to reduce the impact of them. For example, a therapist who has conducted many sessions with an individual may inadvertently attend to reports of symptoms that have reduced, while paying less attention to symptoms that are unchanged (or exacerbated).

Use of outcome assessment, particularly when it combines multiple assessment methods, allows the therapist to be much more confident in asserting that treatment has been effective. While a simple client verbal report of improvement is one source of outcome-assessment evidence, it is not nearly as compelling as a verbal report accompanied by congruent questionnaire and behavioural evidence of improvement. Such convergent information strengthens any claim of therapeutic effectiveness.

Through the routine use of outcome assessment, therapists can gain greater insight into the impact of their therapeutic interventions, and make use of this information in working with future clients. It also allows them to compare the effectiveness of their own treatment with reports in the research literature.

Exercise 12.3

View Video 14, for an example of feedback of assessment results to a client. What comments would you have on the content and process of this interaction?

_____

The advantages of outcome assessments include:

- they are standardised and normed according to reference groups
- they provide adequate coverage of the construct
- they provide quantification of the construct
- they overcome cognitive distortions in therapist and client
- they promote confidence in asserting effectiveness of treatment
- they contribute to professional learning and development.

METHODS OF OUTCOME ASSESSMENT

There are many methods by which outcome assessment can be conducted. The most routine method is the clinical interview with the client. Through the verbal report of the client, as well as observations by the therapist, a conclusion is reached about whether the client's presenting problem is improving. While this provides useful information about changes in the client's condition, further useful information can be gained from other sources. Behavioural assessment, self-report questionnaires, clinician-rated measures, and diary ratings are discussed below. Other useful sources of information regarding therapeutic outcome include collateral information from significant others, direct observation, and structured diagnostic interviews.

Behavioural assessment

In contrast to questionnaire-based assessment methods, behavioural assessments aim to gather information through having clients perform behaviours that are relevant to their presenting complaint. Behaviours used are determined by the nature of the client's presentation. When the task is selected appropriately, a behavioural assessment is ecologically valid, yielding direct information about the behaviour in question. Psychologists should be careful, however, in interpreting behavioural-assessment information, ensuring that it is a valid analogue of the client's problem.

One example of behavioural assessment is the *behavioural approach test (BAT)*. This method is used in assessment of anxiety-related avoidance behaviour. The client is asked to engage with a stimulus that he or she reports usually avoiding. For example, an individual with an elevator phobia is taken to an elevator in the therapist's building and asked to get as close to entering the elevator as possible. If the client was unable to approach the elevator to closer than two metres before treatment, but is able to ride the elevator through eight floors after treatment, this is indication of improvement. In some cases, clients may be able to engage the stimulus, but report less anxiety, after successful treatment.

To use the elevator phobia example again, pre-treatment, a client may only be able to ride the elevator with a subjective rating of 7/10 distress, whereas after treatment the client may be able to conduct the same task with 3/10 distress. During a BAT, the client may also be asked to articulate his or her current fears or automatic thoughts, which can be targeted in later sessions.

There are many other examples of behavioural assessments. Clients with social anxiety engage in a conversation with a stranger, or do something to draw attention to themselves deliberately. Individuals with contamination obsessions and cleaning rituals may be asked to touch a 'contaminated' surface and refrain from washing for as long as possible.

Self-report questionnaires

One of the single most common methods used by therapists in clinical practice to assess outcome are questionnaires. Self-report measures are an efficient, reliable, and valid way of measuring client symptoms and related constructs. Questionnaires exist for every conceivable construct, and are usually accompanied by detailed psychometric information (e.g. Antony et al., 2001; Nezu et al., 2000).

In choosing between questionnaires, the therapist must consider several factors. Among the most important are the psychometric qualities of the measure, such as reliability, validity, and appropriate normative data. Questionnaires must be able to measure the construct in question. When using questionnaires for outcome assessment, the measure must also be sensitive to change because of treatment effects. Personality measures are theoretically stable over time, and so may not be generally suitable for assessment in therapy. Some measures, such as the *Montgomery Åsberg Depression Rating Scale* (Montgomery & Åsberg, 1979), have been developed specifically to assess change in symptoms over course of treatment. Finally, the therapist must be satisfied that time invested in completion of the questionnaire is balanced against utility of the measure. There is little point asking a client to complete four hours of questionnaires if they yield little useful information.

When choosing between questionnaires, ask yourself:

- Is the questionnaire reliable?
- Is the questionnaire a valid measure of the construct?
- Does the questionnaire have suitable normative data?
- Is the questionnaire's item content suitable?
- Is the questionnaire sensitive to change over time?
- Is the questionnaire time-economical?

Questionnaires may also be used to measure constructs theoretically related to the symptoms being treated. Depending on the theoretical model underpinning therapy (see chapter 7), the therapist may decide to assess a construct that would also be expected to change in treatment. An individual being treated for panic disorder using cognitive therapy will likely be taught skills to help assess and restructure catastrophic cognitions. A skilled therapist may choose to measure not only a client's panic symptoms, but also the client's level of catastrophic cognitive content, using a measure such as the *Catastrophic Cognitions Questionnaire (CCQ)*

(Khawaja et al., 1994). If treatment is effective through reductions in catastrophic thought, then both the CCQ and panic symptoms should reduce.

Depression anxiety and stress scales

There are numerous questionnaires available for use by therapists, particularly for constructs such as depression and anxiety symptoms. One Australian instrument that has gained increasing prominence is the *Depression Anxiety and Stress Scale (DASS)* (Lovibond & Lovibond, 1995). The DASS consists of three subscales, designed to measure three different constructs of depression, anxiety and stress symptoms. As a self-report instrument for clinical practice, the DASS has many advantages:

- it is a reliable and valid measure of the constructs
- it is comparatively broad in coverage, covering three different symptom domains
- it is quick to administer and score, with a short form also available
- it is an Australian instrument with Australian normative data
- it is freely available.

Clinician-rated questionnaires

Some rating scales are designed to be completed by the therapist. These are usually completed following the interview, when the psychologist rates a number of symptoms according to a scale provided. One example of a clinician rating scale is the *Yale-Brown Obsessive Compulsive Scale (Y-BOCS)* (Goodman et al., 1989a; 1989b). This consists of a series of items that the psychologist rates on a given scale. These are then used to devise subscales for obsessions and compulsions. Other psychologist-rated instruments include the *Hamilton Rating Scale for Depression* and the *Hamilton Anxiety Rating Scale* (Hamilton, 1960; 1967).

Diary records

A common part of clinical outcome assessment, particularly for cognitive and behavioural therapists, are diary records completed by the client. In these diary records, also often called *self-monitoring*, the client is asked to record the occurrence of certain events or behaviours. The events recorded are determined by the nature of the client's presenting complaint. A client with an obsessive-compulsive cleaning problem may be asked to record the overall time spent in the shower each day, or the time spent cleaning the house each day. A client with panic disorder may be asked to monitor frequency and intensity of panic attacks over the course of a week. A client with depression may record his or her overall level of depression in the morning, afternoon, and evening on a simple 0–10 scale.

Multi-method assessment

Different assessment methods are not perfectly convergent. Different methods may yield different, unique information. By utilising multi-method assessment, the skilled therapist can look for converging information, comparing and contrasting data from different sources. Use of different assessment methods also allows the therapist to be more confident in concluding that change has occurred. If a client shows improvement on self-report, behavioural, and diary-based assessment, this provides strong evidence of significant symptom reduction.

Case study 12.1

Nina, a 23-year-old business manager, presented for treatment of a persistent, recurrent compulsion to check objects around her home and at work. She would routinely spend several hours per day, before leaving home and before retiring at night, checking that locks were closed, the stove and iron were off, and that no one had left a message on her answering machine. Her therapist conducted a thorough intake interview in which she gained a detailed understanding of Nina's presenting symptoms. The therapist asked Nina to complete a questionnaire designed to measure the frequency and severity of symptoms of obsessive-compulsive disorder (OCD), the *Obsessive Compulsive Inventory (OCI)* (Foa et al., 1998). Nina was also asked to record the amount of time spent checking in a 'checking diary' and to bring this in each week. After the first session, Nina's therapist completed a clinician-rated measure of OCD, the *Yale-Brown Obsessive Compulsive Scale* (Goodman et al., 1989a; 1989b). During the second session, the therapist asked Nina to turn several electrical items on and off in the consulting room, and to report on her desire to check again that these were off.

Nina's assessment was conducted again after completion of her treatment. Having such a broad, multi-method assessment allowed Nina and her therapist to gauge the effect of her treatment in several ways.

Assessing significance of change

The phrase *clinically significant change* refers to positive change in areas that are clinically relevant that is sufficiently large to be considered meaningful (Kazdin, 1999; Kendall et al., 1999). This is quite a different use of the term *significant* than that normally associated with scientific research. In a scientific context, *significant* refers to change in a group of scores that is unlikely to be a chance variation. However, a statistically significant change does not mean that the change is large enough to be clinically meaningful—merely that a consistent shift has occurred. Nor is a statistically significant change always in the right direction. It is possible that the statistically significant change went in the wrong direction (the client got worse). Clinicians and researchers needed a method that could be used with individual clients rather than with groups of clients. They also needed a method that offered a more useful and meaningful definition of 'significance', hence the concept of clinically significant change.

Clinically significant change has been defined in four ways:

• *Subjective improvement* is said to have occurred when positive changes in clients' lives are sufficiently meaningful for them to notice the change. The advantage of this definition is that it overcomes the fact that statistically small changes can be imperceptible to the client. It also overcomes the problem where the focus of therapeutic attention may be overly narrow, and change is more generalised. Subjective improvement can be assessed informally and formally. An informal assessment is binary. Does the client feel that his or her general functioning has improved meaningfully? If the answer is 'yes', then subjective improvement is said to have occurred.

A more formal assessment can focus on *particular areas of functioning or general functioning*. Clients are asked to rate their functioning on an arbitrary scale (say, 1 to 10, though it could be anything, really). In this variation, the client normally sets a goal score along an arbitrary scale devised by the therapist. Subjective improvement is said to have occurred when that goal is met. One limitation of using the subjective improvement definition of clinical significance is that the client might still be appreciably impaired despite subjective improvement. Another limitation is that there is no certainty that the apparent subjective improvement is anything more than a desire to please the therapist, or an attempt to appear better, for whatever reason.

- *Recovery* is said to have occurred when a client who was assessed as suffering from a formally diagnosed disorder fails to meet that diagnostic criteria. The recovery definition is therefore binary. Either clients still suffer from the diagnosed disorder or they do not. There is a compelling simplicity to this definition of clinically significant change that makes it appealing to third parties as a reporting method. But it is not without limitations.

  It is possible that a client makes marked improvements yet still meets diagnostic criteria. While the client has improved, recovery has not occurred. It is also possible that the client never met the diagnostic criteria for a formal disorder. In this case, no recovery (at least as it is defined here) can occur. In either case, the recovery definition may be less than helpful.

- The third and fourth definitions of clinically significant change are more widely used, and warrant the extended discussion offered in the sections that follow.

  The third definition of clinically significant change is the *normative definition*: the client would have moved from an abnormal level of symptoms to a level associated with a non-clinical population. In essence, the client crossed some norm-referenced threshold. The fourth and final definition is *reliable change*. Reliable change is said to have occurred when improvement is greater than can be accounted for by the measurement error inherent in the questionnaire used to assess the client (Beutler & Moleiro, 2001).

Normatively clinically significant change

This involves an assessment of whether a client's symptoms have crossed some particular threshold where it is deemed that the client is substantially less impaired by his or her symptoms. In each case, the individual's final level of symptom severity is compared with normative data to establish whether he or she is close enough to normal levels to have improved clinically. As is shown in figure 12.2, any clinical measure is expected to be distributed differently in the clinical and normative population. The anxiety subscale of the DASS (Lovibond & Lovibond, 1995), for example, is expected to show different distributions in those with and without anxiety disorders. Successful treatment involves movement of scores on an instrument from within the clinical range in a direction closer to the mean of the non-clinical population, as seen in figure 12.2.

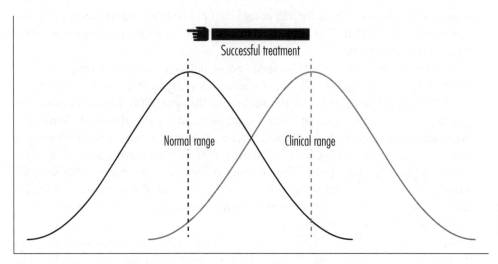

Figure 12.2 Clinical and normal distributions, and the effect of treatment

Several methods have been proposed to ascertain whether clinically significant change has occurred. Jacobson and colleagues (1999) discussed three different methods, and reported on the advantages and disadvantages of each. The first method discussed (Method A; see figure 12.3) involves comparison of the client's score against the distribution of the clinical population. If the client's score on the measure has fallen to more than two standard deviations below the clinical mean, then clinically significant change is said to have occurred.

The second method for assessing clinically significant change (Method B; see figure 12.4) involves comparison of the client's current score with the normal population. Clinically significant improvement is thought to have occurred when the

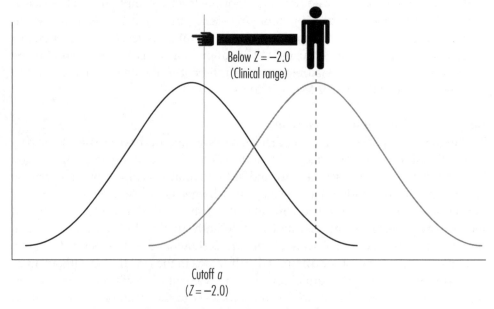

Figure 12.3 Method A for assessing clinically significant change

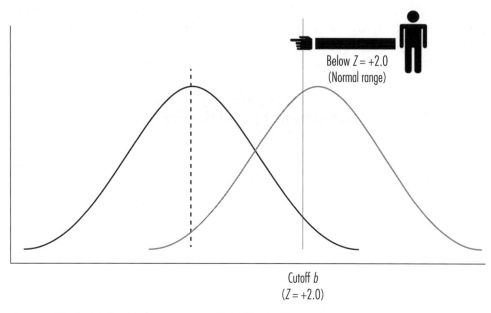

Below $Z = +2.0$
(Normal range)

Cutoff b
($Z = +2.0$)

Figure 12.4 Method B for assessing clinically significant change

client's score falls to within two standard deviations of the normal population mean.

While both Method A and Method B involve comparison with either the clinical or normative population, respectively, each only uses one distribution. Method C (Figure 12.5), the third of the methods discussed by Jacobson and colleagues (1999),

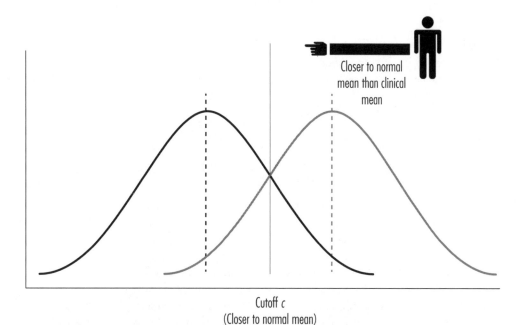

Closer to normal
mean than clinical
mean

Cutoff c
(Closer to normal mean)

Figure 12.5 Method C for assessing clinically significant change

involves comparison to both the clinical and normal distributions. To achieve clinically significant improvement, an individual must move closer to the normal mean than to the clinical mean.

Case study 12.2
Assessment of clinical significance

The Depression subscale of the DASS (DASS-D) has a mean of 6.34 and a standard deviation of 6.97 in the non-clinical population (Lovibond & Lovibond, 1995). For individuals with major depressive disorder, the distribution has a mean of 25.31 and a standard deviation of 10.24 (Brown et al., 1997).

Method A
Method A (equation 1, below) requires that an individual move to more than two standard deviations below the clinical mean for clinically significant change to have occurred.

$$
\begin{aligned}
\text{Cutoff}_A &= M_{Clin} - 2\,(SD_{Clin}) \\
&= 25.31 - 2\,(10.24) \\
&= 4.83
\end{aligned}
\tag{1}
$$

Method B
Method B (equation 2, below) requires that an individual move to within two standard deviations of the non-clinical mean.

$$
\begin{aligned}
\text{Cutoff}_B &= M_{Norm} + 2\,(SD_{Norm}) \\
&= 6.34 + 2\,(6.97) \\
&= 20.28
\end{aligned}
\tag{2}
$$

Method C
Method C (equation 3, below) requires that the individual's score be closer to the normal than to the clinical mean. The formula allows for unequal variances in the clinical and nonclinical distributions.

$$
\begin{aligned}
\text{Cutoff}_C &= \frac{(SD_{Norm}M_{Clin}) + (SD_{Clin}M_{Norm})}{SD_{Norm} + SD_{Clin}} \\
&= \frac{(6.97 \times 25.31) + (10.24 \times 6.34)}{6.97 + 10.24} \\
&= \frac{176.41 + 64.92}{17.21} \\
&= 14.02
\end{aligned}
\tag{3}
$$

Choice of Method A, Method B, or Method C requires the user to know about the effect of varying levels of overlap between the clinical and nonclinical distributions. As Figure 12.6 shows, the cutoff scores change considerably, depending on the distributions of the two samples. The example above, using the DASS, shows that cutoff A would be a very stringent criteria, requiring the person to be below the mean of the nonclinical population before being judged to have improved to a clinically significant level (see figure 12.6a). Jacobsen and colleagues (1999) recommend that Method C be used where possible, as this takes into account information about both the clinical and nonclinical populations in calculating a cutoff.

Reliable change

The final approach to determining the significance of change scores is to calculate the *Reliable Change Index (RCI)* (Jacobson & Truax, 1991). This involves examining change in a measure from pre-treatment to post-treatment, while taking into account the inherent unreliability of the instrument. Small variations in an individual's score on a questionnaire may reflect the fact that no particular measure is perfectly reliable, and that every test score is a combination of a true score and error.

Psychologists can calculate the change required in a particular measure (the RCI) using a series of equations, as illustrated in case study 12.3.

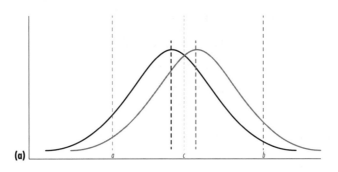

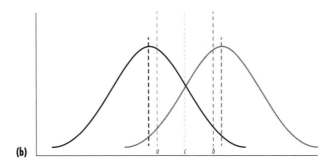

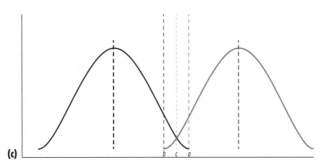

Figure 12.6 (a), (b), and (c) The effect of overlapping distributions on cutoff scores for clinical significance

Case study 12.3
Assessment of the reliable change index

Lily presented for treatment of depression, scoring 27 on the Depression subscale of the DASS. After 16 weeks of interpersonal therapy, her DASS-D score had fallen to 15. Has reliable change occurred?

Step 1
Calculate the *standard error of measurement (SEM)* for the DASS-D, using equation 4 below. From Brown and colleagues (1997) we know that the reliability of the DASS in a mood disorder population is 0.94, and that the standard deviation for the same population is 10.24.

$$SEM = SD_{Clin}\sqrt{1 - r_{xx}}$$
$$SEM = 10.24\sqrt{1 - 0.94}$$
$$SEM = 10.24\sqrt{0.06}$$
$$SEM = 2.51$$

(4)

Step 2
Calculate the *standard error of the difference*. From equation 4 above, we know that the SEM is 2.51.

$$S_{diff} = \sqrt{2(SEM)^2}$$
$$S_{diff} = \sqrt{2(2.51)^2}$$
$$S_{diff} = \sqrt{12.60}$$
$$S_{diff} = 3.55$$

(5)

Step 3
Calculate Lily's RCI. We know the *standard error of difference* is 3.55 from equation 5 above.

$$RC = \frac{x_{pre} - x_{post}}{S_{diff}}$$
$$RC = \frac{24 - 16}{3.55}$$
$$RC = 2.25$$

(6)

To say with 95 per cent confidence that a reliable change has occurred, Lily's DASS-D score must show an RCI score of 1.96 or more. In this case, with an RCI of 2.25 (see equation 6, above), we can say that Lily's depression symptoms have shown reliable change over the course of her treatment.

Practice implications

Working as a psychologist requires assessment of clients from start to end of treatment. Assessment begins with the intake interview, during which the skilled clinician must balance information gathering with rapport building. Intake assessment proceeds in a logical, systematic way, where the psychologist uses expert knowledge in a hypothesis-testing approach to attempt to gain an understanding of the client's presenting problem. The intake interview also aims to gather information which will allow psychologist and client to understand the genesis and evolution of the problem, and develop a shared treatment plan to attempt to assist the client. The impact of treatment is measured by psychologist and client, and this information is used to assess whether the intervention is successful or not.

CONCLUSIONS

This chapter reviewed the skills required of psychologists in professional practice in conducting initial intake assessments, and then measuring outcome of interventions. Outcome assessment is an important part of psychotherapy practice, and poor outcome assessment presents many potential dangers. While there are many methods of outcome assessment, a multi-method assessment often provides the most compelling evidence of therapeutic change.

Recommended reading

Jacobson, N. S., Roberts, L. J., Berns, S. B. & McGlinchey, J. B. (1999). Methods for defining and determining the clinical significance of treatment effects: description, application, and alternatives. *Journal of Consulting and Clinical Psychology, 67*, 300–7.

Jacobson, N. S. & Truax, P. (1991). Clinical significance: a statistical approach to defining meaningful change in psychotherapy research. *Journal of Consulting and Clinical Psychology, 59*, 12–19.

Kazdin, A. E. (1999). The meaning and measurement of clinical significance. *Journal of Consulting and Clinical Psychology, 67*, 332–9.

Chapter 13

Diagnosis

INTRODUCTION

This chapter discusses the role of diagnosis in psychotherapy. The construct of diagnostic classification, including definition and function of diagnosis, the history and evolution of diagnosis, including the relationship with the medical model, its limitations, and areas of controversy, are explored. Development of the Diagnostic and Statistical Manual of Mental Disorders (DSM) and the vision for DSM-5 are also discussed.

A HISTORY OF PSYCHOLOGICAL DIAGNOSIS

Ancient and premedical conceptualisations of mental illness

Descriptions of 'madness' and its causes reach at least as far back as the ancient Greeks. Prevailing theory from the advent of Western medicine until the 1800s ascribed mental disorder to moral or spiritual corruption. Treatment as we know it today did not exist; sufferers were exposed to 'curative' measures, ranging from exorcism, prayer, to privation, or were segregated from society in prison-like institutions that employed seemingly barbaric treatments, such as blistering, bleeding, and straightjacketing. As the popular labels 'madness' and 'insanity' suggest, a state of mental disturbance was considered permanent, pervasive, and associated with inevitable deterioration. Those suffering from mental disorder were frequently relegated to a status less than human. The severity of social degradation associated with 'insanity' is exemplified through records of European aristocrats taking 'sightseeing' tours through mental asylums, presumably for their entertainment and shock value.

Early psychiatric history and diagnostic classifications

Mental disorders came under the rubric of modern medical science only in the last 200 years (Kaplan et al., 1994), when medical science expanded to include psychological forms of disease, forming the branch of medicine known as psychiatry. Two broad categories of psychological disturbance were defined in the early days of psychiatry: *psychosis* and *neurosis* (Sadock & Sadock, 2007). From this rough distinction the psychiatric-diagnostic system grew. As psychiatry developed, so did demand for distinction between disorder presentations (Nathan, 1998). Labels afforded by distinctions served as heuristics, enabling doctors to organise their patients' symptoms into coherent themes, communicate patients' presentations, and formulate an approach to treatment.

The French psychiatrist Philipe Pinel furthered the classification of mental disorders, and is credited with 'liberating the insane from their chains' with his commitment to enrich the medical understanding of 'insanity' through an empirical approach. Pinel's classifications were based on his work with institutionalised patients from the 1780s to the early 1800s. Pinel strove to understand his patients through observation, interviewing, and detailed case histories. Pinel believed that the mentally ill could be better understood and managed, rather than imprisoned, abused, and degraded. Pinel did away with blistering, bleeding, purging, and the straightjacket as primary forms of treatment for mental illness. His observations and data collection resulted in the articulation of syndromes, or groups of identifying signs and symptoms. Some of Pinel's diagnostic classifications included *melancholia, mania, mania with delirium, dementia,* and *idiotism,* categories that are still in use today (although melancholia is now called depression, and the cruel term *idiotism* has been changed to intellectual disability). Pinel did not advocate the treatment of patients based on diagnosis; he urged treating doctors to consider each patient's unique characteristics, history, and perspective.

With the publication of his *Compendium of Psychiatry* in 1883, the German psychiatrist Emil Kraepelin is commonly credited with synthesising hundreds of identified mental disorders into a comprehensive diagnostic system. Kraepelin, like Pinel, developed diagnostic categories based on his direct observations of people living in mental institutions. Kraepelin's system organised disorders based on classification of syndromes. This system quickly usurped the previous practice of grouping disorders by similarity of major symptoms. Kraepelin's identified syndromes included *manic-depression* (now considered representative of recurrent major depression and/ or bipolar disorder) and *dementia praecox* (now schizophrenia). An enormously influential volume, Kraepelin's *Compendium* underwent eight revisions in his lifetime. Kraepelin's system marked the first major initiative to create diagnostic consistency across the field of psychiatry.

By the twentieth century, the burgeoning mental-health field spanned psychiatry and psychology, a scientific discipline distinct from medicine and focused exclusively on psychological phenomena. The development of official nomenclatures for the diagnosis of mental disorders was necessitated by the 'crippling confusion' caused by their absence (Widiger & Clark, 2000, p. 946); psychopathology was classified idiosyncratically by individual practitioners, and 'confusion reigned' (Kendell, 1975, p. 87). Demand for uniform nomenclature is a clear motivator behind the burgeoning *Diagnostic and Statistical Manual of Mental Disorders* (DSM), developed by the American Psychological Association (APA). In the foreword to the DSM-II, its authors expressed their hope that the diagnostic terms selected 'would facilitate maximum communication within the profession and reduce confusion and ambiguity to a minimum' (APA, 1968).

The DSM system is widely used in Australia and the United States, but alternatives are also used.

The leading competitor to the DSM system is the World Health Organization's *International Classification of Diseases* (ICD), currently undergoing a revision which will be published as the 11th edition (ICD-11); publication is expected in 2014. The current revision of the ICD has several methodological and practical strengths that should be considered in choosing between alternative taxonomies. The ICD is developed by the United Nations WHO in consultation with a wide range of professional groups; the DSM is developed solely by the American Psychiatric Association. The current edition of the ICD is provided free online, or at minimal cost, making the system more accessible, especially in poorer countries. Organisations that deal with both medical and psychological illnesses may also prefer the ICD, which covers the spectrum of mental and physical illness. Many health departments in Australia use the ICD system for record keeping of all patients.

Other tools are available to trained clinicians to assist with diagnostic processes in clinical practice and research. Some of these include:

- *Structured Clinical Interview for Diagnosis* (SCID) (Zanarini & Frankenburg, 2001)
- *Minnesota Multiphasic Personality Inventory* (MMPI and its revision MMPI-2) (Butcher et al., 1989)
- *Millon Clinical Multiaxial Inventory-111* (MCMI-111) (Millon et al., 2009)
- *Mental Status Examination* (MSE) (e.g., Patrick, 2000)
- *Personality and Psychological Disorders* (Claridge & Davis, 2003)
- *Psychodynamic Diagnostic Manual* (PDM) (PDM Taskforce, 2006).

An example (Patrick, 2000) of a Mental Status Examination (MSE), which assesses the way a person presents in session, is available for download from, www.nevdgp.org.au/files/programsupport/mentalhealth/Mental%20State%20Exam%20-%20form.pdf?PHPSESSID=aebebbe47bf4cfb4119bc939249f47aa

Some developing countries have their own diagnostic systems. Cuba uses the *Third Cuban Glossary of Psychiatry*; China uses the *Chinese Classification of Mental Disorders*; many countries in South America use the *Latin American Guide for Psychiatric Diagnosis*.

Although few psychologists in Australia need to be familiar with the range of diagnostic systems available, be aware that the DSM system is only one of many, and that many psychologists remain critical of its approach.

While the DSM and the ICD today comprise the officially accepted nomenclature of mental disorder diagnoses in the West, there is widespread debate surrounding the evidence or lack of evidence for the validity and reliability of these systems. As Widiger and Clark (2000) suggest, 'the science of psychopathology may not be sufficiently advanced at this time to develop an adequately conclusive or even authoritative nomenclature' (p. 946). This chapter will attempt to integrate discussion about the known, functional elements of our diagnostic system, with its criticisms and shortcomings, measured against the intention of facilitated understanding.

DEFINITION

The term *diagnosis* stems from the Greek word for knowledge, *gnosis*, which points to the potential for diagnostic classification to inform and deepen clinicians' understanding of clients' presenting problems. The current edition of the *Diagnostic and Statistical Manual* (DSM-IV-TR) (APA, 2000) conceptualises diagnosis as a systematic evaluation of the client along five axes spanning symptom disorders, personality disorders, general medical conditions, psychosocial and environmental problems, and overall functioning. A parallel diagnostic system exists in the World Health Organization's alternative, the *International Classification of Diseases* (ICD). However, this chapter will deal predominantly with the DSM, the most widely referenced diagnostic manual in Australia and the United States.

Diagnosis can be considered varying parts art, science, and investigation. Diagnosis is an art because equally experienced practitioners, using the same method, may diagnose the same person differently (e.g. Williams et al., 1992). While seemingly at odds, differing diagnostic labels can assist effective practitioners equally well. In this sense, diagnosis is a heuristic, a process of perception and informational organisation. By grouping clinically significant signs and symptoms into a manageable whole, practitioners can focus on the salient features of clients' presenting information, and then consult the research literature and their own expertise for similar features, their treatments, and outcomes.

Diagnosis is a science, as it is deeply rooted in the scientific method of phenomenological observation and descriptive classification. Diagnostic classification, as well as enabling communication, is intrinsic to psychology's adoption of the medical model, establishment of the scientist–practitioner model of psychotherapy, and the atheoretical framework of evidence-based practice.

Finally, diagnosis is an investigation; the process of diagnosing is a methodical exploration designed to broaden the clinical interview beyond a client's presenting narrative, and to elucidate clinical features that may not otherwise have been reported or observed. While it does not describe aetiology or directly inform treatment pathways, diagnosis functions to increase practitioners' knowledge about and potential for an informed response to clients' presenting problems.

The medical model and diagnosis

The process of diagnosis originates in the medical model, the predominant healing model of Western culture (Wampold, 2004). The medical model is essentially materialistic; it establishes the presence of disease based upon observable signs and symptoms of physical abnormality, and these observations support a diagnosis. Intervention is similarly materially based on the directly observable interaction between human physiology and disease. The medical model is also reductionist, or atomistic, in its assumption that symptoms can be reduced to a basic causal relationship between aetiology and pathology. This reductionist approach to healing harbours a basic distrust for anything that cannot be examined and verified.

The medical model and psychology

It is hardly surprising that this materialistic, reductionist model has struggled to satisfactorily explain human psychological phenomena. Foss (1994) argues that, given advances in knowledge, the medical model is no longer suitable even for medicine, and that a successor model is required. A consistent criticism of the medical model in psychology is that it precludes a biopsychosocial understanding of conditions and their treatment (Nathan, 1998). Furthermore, it is argued that, as most psychopathological processes have as yet no reliably identified physical substrates, psychological science is essentially at odds with the materialistic basis of the medical model. Students of statistics know that, to apply any model to the organisation and analysis of information, a set of assumptions must be met. When those assumptions are not fully met, data can become distorted, and the tradeoff for gaining access to interpretation of the data becomes this unknown amount of distortion. In this manner, the materialistic and reductionist assumptions of the medical model create an inherent tension when applied to psychology. This tension, and possible distortion to psychological understanding, is at the heart of the current controversy regarding the 'goodness of fit' between the medical model and psychotherapy, and the role of diagnosis within that 'fit'.

Transposition of the medical model to psychology answered a demand for evidence-based practice that followed the irresolvable theoretical debates that dominated psychology in the mid twentieth century. While divergent theories of personality and psychological development abounded, they violated a basic tenet of the scientific method; they were impossible to disprove or verify. Eysenck's (1952) incendiary critique of the unscientific basis of psychology, and, by implication, the unfounded assumption of psychotherapeutic effectiveness, helped to precipitate a new paradigm of evidence-based practice in psychology. The medical model, furthermore, offered a clear methodological distinction between psychology and traditional and/or popular faith-based healing practices, such as spiritual counselling, mysticism, and shamanism. The medical model was explicitly adopted by psychology at the pivotal Boulder Conference of 1949. It is worth noting that adoption of the medical model at Boulder was not unanimous, and many psychologists voiced concerns regarding possible negative implications and lack of fit between psychology and the medical model.

With the adoption of the medical model within psychology, emphasis moved away from theory-based and toward evidence-based practice. Medical language and concepts of *mental illness* and *mental disease* proliferated. Whereas the founding generations of psychotherapy tended to conceptualise psychological states along a continuum, with neurotic or psychotic states on one end and *self-integration* or *self-actualisation* on the other, the medical model of psychology was more binary, referring only to *pathological states* versus *symptom remission*.

Thus, mental health, like its counterpart, physical health, came to be defined by the absence of disease. *Randomised controlled trials (RCTs)*, the methodology used in drug research, became the gold standard for evaluating psychotherapeutic efficacy, legitimising treatment approaches found to be efficacious, and underpinning payment structures and treatment access. This system of reinforcement had profound implications for psychological research, promoting the search for quantitative, atomistic, causal relationships removed from social context. *Cognitive behavioural therapy (CBT)*, the form of psychotherapy perhaps most consistent with the medical model, tended to produce strong evidence for its efficacy and effectiveness.

Process-orientated therapies, an arguably poorer fit with the medical model, tended to produce ambivalent results or to simply defy RCT design methods. Application of the medical model and RCTs to psychological disorder also had profound implications for the medication of psychological problems; over the past 20 years, pharmacotherapy has come to be considered a frontline form of treatment for psychological disorders (Duncan et al., 2004).

CONTEMPORARY DIAGNOSTIC CONSTRUCTS

Unlike physical pathology, and contrary to the expectations of the early DSM authors, psychopathology does not reliably reduce to a single universally acknowledged pathogenesis. Thus, the effort to adopt a diagnostic system transmuted, over six incarnations of the DSM and a parallel process with the ICD, from aetiological references toward a descriptive, categorical-polythetic model of classification. As described in the foreword to the DSM-IV, this descriptive approach 'attempted to be neutral with respect to theories of aetiology' (APA, 1994; pp. xvii–xviii), instead utilising the conceptual structure of Kraepelin and Pinel's categorical classification and observational method. Contemporary diagnostic categories describe syndromes, or clusters of surface symptoms and conditions, that tend to co-occur and create functional impairment. These syndromes are considered discrete, either/or conditions, without exception or gradation (Krueger & Bezdjian, 2009). Classification is *polythetic* in that syndromes are defined by multiple symptoms, and not all symptoms are required to indicate the presence of a disorder—a combination of symptoms, less than the total number, must be observed to warrant diagnosis.

Contemporary diagnostic categories describe patterns of presentation, but do not directly inform aetiology, treatment pathways, or the essential nature of disorder. This categorical system represents an intention to remain congruent with the medical model. However, by transmutation to a descriptive rather than an aetiologically based form of classification, the function of diagnosis in psychology radically diverges from its function in medicine.

From its beginning to the present day, the DSM has been a focus of debate and research in psychology. While each edition of the manual has been roundly criticised, criticism has served as impetus for further research and knowledge development. Each revision of the manual therefore represents an evolving dialogue within the disciplines of psychology and psychiatry (American Psychiatric Association, 1968; 1980; 1987; 1994; 2000). The DSM-IV text revision (TR), published in 2000 (APA), represented the consensus of the American psychiatric community at that time. Many of the criticisms and acknowledged shortcomings of previous editions informed the 2000 manual; it was thus the best approximation at that time of an official nomenclature, with the effect that diagnosis became more reliable and consistent across settings, enabling better identification of clinical populations.

The DSM remains a work in progress, and must be utilised with a generous serving of common sense and critical thought. Even its authors acknowledge that its diagnoses and criterion sets are highly debatable (Frances et al., 1990; Spitzer et al., 1980).

The DSM should in no way be considered a 'bible', but a tool in the process of being fashioned by the collective voices and expertise of psychology and psychiatry.

As this textbook is published, the DSM-5 is about to be published; a number of work groups have examined matters such as the implications of diagnostic nomenclature and cross-cultural issues. Publication of DSM-5 is planned for May, 2013. The American Psychiatric Association's DSM-5 link, www.dsm5.org, should be checked regularly.

To enable you to use the tool wisely, some shortcomings and criticisms of the DSM-IV-TR are described below.

Limitations of the DSM approach

> Factually, it is quite uncertain that the clusters of symptoms that we bind together under discrete diagnostic labels really represent discrete conditions or disease processes at all. (Beutler, 2004, p. xii).

Low diagnostic reliability has plagued the DSM since its earliest psychometric evaluations. Williams and colleagues (1992) conducted extensive field investigations to determine the reliability of the DSM, and found only moderate correlations between the diagnoses of paired clinicians. To achieve diagnostic agreement in these trials, clinicians had only to identify the same class (rather than subtype) of disorder. This meant that two clinicians diagnosing panic disorder and OCD in a single individual was construed as supporting the reliability of the categories. Despite this loose definition of agreement, correlations among Axis I disorders ranged from .68 to .72, agreement for Axis II disorders ranged from .56 to .64, and individual reliability ratings on specific disorders were as low as .26. Since the publication of these findings, reliability standards have lowered rather than lifted. 'Good' diagnostic reliability is currently defined as between .60 and .74 agreement within a general diagnostic category, while above .75 is considered 'excellent' (Garb, 1998).

Nomenclature developed in early versions of the DSM was based on what the APA committee deemed to be 'generally agreed upon by well-informed psychiatrists' (APA, 1968). Thus, the DSM came to be based upon an assumption of discrete disorder categories developed from a 'top down', or expert-consensus, approach, rather than from a 'bottom up', or evidence-based, approach. A majority of research findings on the subject are at odds with this assumption, however, supporting a dimensional overcategorical model for psychopathology (First et al., 2002; Widiger & Clark, 2000). First (2003) states that, 'in the last 20 years, the categorical approach has been increasingly questioned as evidence has accumulated that the so-called categorical disorders like major depressive disorder and anxiety disorders, and schizophrenia and bipolar disorder seem to merge imperceptibly both into one another and into normality … with no demonstrable natural boundaries (p. 661)'. Lack of agreement between 'top down' and 'bottom up' approaches has created a number of gaps and aberrations in the DSM's ability to satisfactorily organise the burgeoning scholarship and clinical wisdom of the field. Perhaps explained by this tension, diagnostic categories have proliferated over the six versions of the DSM, from 66 identified disorders in 1952 to 397 in 1994, a proliferation far outpacing research required for its justification (Beutler, 2004).

Proliferation of polythetic categories has led to an awkward state of affairs, where diagnostic comorbidity rather than specificity is the norm (Clark et al., 1995; Krueger & Markon, 2006), and heterogeneity is rampant within diagnostic categories. As Krueger and Bezdjian (2009) suggest, this becomes highly problematic when 'persons of diverse symptomatology are considered exemplars of the same, putatively homogeneous, diagnostic category'. Krueger and Bezdjian (2009) point out that this conceptualisation is fundamentally 'incompatible with the data' (p. 4). Anomalous categories are prevalent; for example, eating disorder not otherwise specified (EDNOS) is the most common clinical eating-disorder presentation (Fairburn et al., 2007). Furthermore, in a categorical conceptualisation, cross-sectional symptoms are not accounted for; in typical clinical presentations, clients' symptoms usually do not observe the discrete boundaries of one syndrome, tending rather to cut across categories. Finally, categories don't account for the dimensional nature of disorders; most individuals function on a continuum of symptom severity, rather than on an either–or basis, as implied by the categorical system.

Categorical conceptualisation of disorder prompts clinicians to interpret clients' varied presentations in terms of discrete conditions that are qualitatively distinct from normal function and from one another (Widiger & Mullins-Sweatt, 2005). In reality, many pathology-generating and maintaining processes span diagnostic categories, differing only in their outward manifestation of psychopathology. All disorders appear to share fundamental components of dyscontrol, impairment, and pathology (Bergner, 1997; Spitzer & Williams, 1982; Widiger & Sankis, 2000). As an example, Fairburn and colleagues (2003) have shown that the same core psychological processes account for the full range of eating disorders; anorexia, bulimia, and atypical eating disorders share the same distinctive psychopathology, and are maintained by similar processes, with clinical populations showing frequent, non-random migration across diagnostic categories. Fairburn and colleagues theorised that common processes of perfectionism, low self-esteem, mood intolerance, and interpersonal difficulties drive the disorders. A transdiagnostic theory of eating disorder maintenance has been shown to directly inform effective treatments (Fairburn et al., 2003).

The same transdiagnostic theory may apply to many categories of disorder. Kendall and Jablensky (2003) suggest that, throughout the evolution of the diagnostic-classification system, its proponents have failed to consider the possibility that 'disorders might merge into one another with no natural boundary in between' (p. 5). These shortcomings in the categorical conceptualisation of disorder, now widely recognised in psychology (Widiger & Clark, 2000), speak to lack of fit between 'top down' order superimposed on phenomena by scientific constructs, and 'bottom up' expression of psychological disorder, as it occurs *in vivo*.

Despite this lack of fit, the DSM's categorical-polythetic diagnostic system has become intricately woven into multiple facets of the mental-health care system, including practitioner training, reimbursement, and research. Thus, the accumulated body of information on diagnosis is defined by the DSM conceptualisation of disorder syndromes (Clarkin & Levy, 2004), the DSM structure implicitly motivates diagnosing professionals to search for symptoms that match listed criteria (Ahn & Kim, 2008), and innovative research is at times restrained by the existing nomenclature (see

Clark et al., 1995; Pincus et al., 1992). These dynamics contribute to continuation of the diagnostic system, with an effect akin to a self-fulfilling prophecy.

Lack of cultural sensitivity in the DSM has also long been a source of contention. Ethnic and minority groups have had little input into development of the current classification system. As no firm guidelines for 'normal' psychological function or an accepted definition of psychological health exist, normality is largely culturally determined; a nomenclature that purports to be 'universal' is in fact based in the dominant Western culture.

Recently-published authors have been critical of how the DSM has been used to 'export' Western (and particularly American) ideas of psychopathology to different parts of the world. In his survey of the impact of the DSM diagnostic system, Watters (2010) argues that American systems of diagnosis have even, in some cases, 'introduced' these diagnoses or illnesses into societies where they did not previously exist. His opinion is controversial; you are referred to Watters' book, *Crazy Like Us: The Globalization of the American Psyche*, for detailed elaboration of his concerns about translation of Western psychiatric concepts into non-Western cultures.

DIAGNOSIS AND PSYCHOTHERAPY

While many psychologists would suggest that the medical model legitimises psychotherapy, distinguishing it from the practices of counsellors, priests, and shamen, an opposing body of psychologists would align themselves with Wampold's (2004) assertion that psychology must 'break free from the shackles of the medical model' to realise its potential. How then do the extremes of this dialectic interact within psychotherapy? Diagnosis is arguably the key process by which psychologists enact their affiliation with the medical model. While the functional elements of diagnosis help to explain why it has become a central feature of modern clinical psychology, the problematic implications of diagnosis are many. These include the potentially harmful impact of labelling and imposing categories on diverse expressions of humanity (do the labels serve to segregate misfits?), the power of diagnostic labels to both legitimise and stigmatise, the self-fulfilling nature of diagnostic constructs, and the coercive implications of embedding diagnostic labels in payment structures.

Psychology's effort to establish itself as evidence-based is frequently belied by the legacy of its diagnostic system. This leads to a frequently poor functional relationship between diagnosis, treatment, and outcomes. Although the 1970s saw the beginnings of a movement to base the DSM on research (Malik & Beulter, 2002), the consensus-based or 'top down' approach has remained. Tension between the utility of and the problematic implications of diagnosis and, by extension, the medical model, has long been a polarising force in psychology. Leading thinkers from both ends of the spectrum of debate hotly contest the merits and dangers of the current diagnostic classification system for psychology. However, many psychologists agree that the current diagnostic system can and should be improved upon. A discussion of proposed and projected directions for diagnosis in psychology will follow at the end of the chapter.

Diagnosis and social power

> Mental disorders are among life's most frightening vicissitudes, and the privilege to reduce their associated uncertainties by defining and naming the boundaries of 'illness' confers tremendous social power upon the diagnosing professions (Schacht, 1985, p. 514).

The old refrain about great power entailing great responsibility is highly relevant to any discussion of diagnosis and psychotherapy. It is important to acknowledge that political power and social control are embedded in mental-health diagnoses (Beutler, 1989). Schacht (1985) observed that the powerful appeal of the medical model derives in part from society's reliance on scientific experts to manage uncertainty. This social power may be a central attraction of the medical model, and for this reason many psychologists are reluctant to risk their expert status by engaging with alternative (such as client-centred) models of practice (Wampold, 2004). This form of social power raises the hackles of medical model critics. Szasz has long challenged the parallel drawn between physical and mental illness, suggesting that it disguises an agenda of social control. Szasz (1982) states that 'mental illness is a metaphor and a myth. The term mental illness is a label we attach to certain unwanted, undesirable, feared or prohibited acts' (p. 763). The loss of individual sovereignty is implicit in Gutheil and Applebaum's (1980) conceptualisation of the nature of psychiatric illness as such 'that the denial of a need for treatment is an inherent element of the disease itself' (p. 304). The paternalistic implications of imposed treatments, among them involuntary hospitalisation and medication, however well intentioned, are unavoidable.

A recent example of a social-control agenda infiltrating the diagnostic system is provided by the politics of sexual preference. Homosexuality was listed as a mental disorder in all versions of the DSM until 1973, when the APA voted to exclude it, following bitter political debates across the discipline, public media, and gay-rights organisations. Opposition to the inclusion of homosexuality was based on a lack of scientific support for the category. Rather than seeking evidence to justify inclusion, 'dyshomophilia' was proposed as a conciliatory replacement category. This process provides a stark example of 'official' language employed to obscure an absence of evidence, typifying the potential for DSM classification to confer legitimacy (Schacht, 1985).

DSM categories not only have the power to legitimise; they also delegitimise forms of disorder. For example, with the current multiaxial system, an Axis I diagnosis enables treatment access; the label is required for reimbursement through Medicare and comparable insurance systems in the US. Axis II diagnoses confer no such access, nor by implication, legitimacy. Personality disorders (PDs) can be attributed to early and severe social and environmental dysfunction, and people with PDs are grossly overrepresented in inpatient and prison populations (Linehan et al., 1999). What then might be the rationale for and implications of classifying personality disorders on Axis II?

Even if benevolence of the power of diagnosis could be assured, who is qualified to use it? The DSM makes no explicit statement regarding the skill level required to be a diagnostician, merely offering the disclaimer that, 'The proper use of these criteria requires specialized clinical training that provides both a body of knowledge and clinical skills' (APA, 1994, p. xxvii). This ambiguity has engendered yet another area of controversy in the field. Some psychiatrists assert that the DSM is derived mainly from the expertise of psychiatrists, and that diagnosis requires general medical knowledge; psychiatrists should therefore have exclusive rights to diagnose. Additional criticism of the relaxed qualification standards rests on anecdotal reports that many practising clinicians do not use the DSM in the way they are supposed to (Ahn & Kim, 2008). Consumer advocates report that abuses and inconsistency in the field are rampant, resulting in unscrupulous assignation of labels and 'up-coding' of diagnostic severity to prolong insurance payments. It has been suggested that, indeed, one intention of the 'cookbook' polythetic approach was to enable professionals and paraprofessionals from a variety of training levels and backgrounds to access the diagnostic system. It is even suggested that the APA broadened diagnosing rights in the interest of profit; and, indeed, the DSM-IV and DSM-IV-TR have sold millions of copies.

The role of diagnosis in psychotherapy

What is the role of diagnosis in therapy? Is diagnosis essential, or can therapy occur in its absence? How does diagnosis have an impact on the therapeutic relationship? As diagnosis is a central tool of the medical model, it is not surprising that lack of unison around use of the medical model in psychology is frequently expressed through the role of diagnosis in psychotherapy.

On one end of the spectrum, CBT-orientated practitioners would assert that the process of psychotherapy consists of four essential components: assessment, diagnosis, treatment, and evaluation. Diagnosis is an essential component, providing an external explanation for disorder located in expert scientific understanding; diagnosis informs a systematic focus on symptom remission, and treatment progress can be measured. At the polar opposite of this conceptualisation, Szasz (1978) fundamentally rejects the parallel between physical and mental illness, arguing by extension that if there are no mental diseases, there can be no treatments for them. Process-orientated practitioners occupy a middle ground in this debate, suggesting that diagnostic labels are merely data, neither more nor less significant than data offered through clients' body language, narrative, theory of change, and the responses they elicit in their therapist (Yalom, 2001). In Teyber's (2006) book-length description of the interpersonal-process approach to psychotherapy, he makes minimal reference to diagnosis, outlining instead a process of therapeutic change. This process consists of identifying maladaptive cognitive and interpersonal patterns, engaging with the client in the 'here and now', establishing a working alliance (consisting of Rogers' core conditions of genuineness, positive regard, and accurate empathy), offering a corrective emotional experience, and enabling the transfer of adaptive learning in therapy to life. Rather than assess, diagnose, treat, and evaluate, 'therapists are encouraged to join the client in a process of mutual exploration' (Teyber, 2006, p. 28). Similarly, client-centred approaches endeavour to harness clients' wisdom, experience, and self-understanding (Duncan et al., 2004).

Because an emphasis on collaboration between therapists' and clients' expertise can be at odds with the scientific expertise required for diagnosis, many psychotherapists do not diagnose as a matter of course. Opinions range from those who consider that diagnostic labels obscure more relevant material (Hillman, 2009) to those who acknowledge their potential for both utility and harm. Yalom (2001) makes this distinction: 'Though diagnosis is unquestionably critical in treatment considerations for many severe conditions with a biological substrate (for example, schizophrenia, bipolar disorders, major affective disorders, temporal lobe epilepsy, drug toxicity, organic or brain disease from toxins, degenerative causes, or infectious agents), diagnosis is often counterproductive in the everyday psychotherapy of less severely impaired patients' (p. 4). Whether diagnosis is considered essential to therapy appears to be determined by a therapist's theoretical orientation and experience, rather than evidence.

Is the role of diagnosis in determining disorder aetiology, course, or treatment type similarly optional? A consistent relationship between aetiology, course, and treatment has never been established with diagnosis (Beutler, 1989). By contrast, in medical diagnoses, 'clinically significant' symptoms are determined in part by the relationship between subsequent diagnosis, disease aetiology and course, and treatment options. In psychology, some diagnoses specify aetiology (such as organic brain syndromes), while others specify the expected course of disorder (such as bipolar disorder). In some categories, such as substance abuse disorders, diagnosis essentially describes the treatment targets. In other cases, such as mood disorders, diagnoses describe a pattern of complex and idiosyncratic behaviours that do not directly relate to mood or treatment pathways (Clarkin & Levy, 2004).

Furthermore, there is often a poor relationship between diagnosis and mode of intervention (Beutler, 1989). Therapists tend to base their choice of treatment modality on their training and preference, rather than on client diagnoses (Beutler & Crago, 1987). A diagnostic label may also miss out crucial therapeutic information—the conscious meanings of behaviours, while not considered in the DSM system, have been shown to be among the most relevant factors to treatment (Wakefield, 1998). Thus, while correlations between diagnosis, aetiology, and treatment exist, they are unsystematic, inconsistent, and incomplete.

The role of meaning in treatment, and the poor correlation between treatment type and diagnosis, may be a result of the way therapists think. Clinicians tend to rely on an intuitive rather than on an actuarial process when diagnosing (Dawes, 1994; Garb, 1998). Clinicians' conceptualisations of mental disorders have been shown to be theory based, rather than theory neutral; indeed, clinicians appear to be cognitively driven to form theories of disorder aetiology (Kim & Ahn, 2002). These theoretical representations of client presenting symptoms, while at odds with the explicitly atheoretical nomenclature of the DSM, may actually inform diagnosis, as clinician diagnoses tend to be consistent with their theory of aetiology and subsequent treatment plan (Kim & Ahn, 2002).

The poor relationship between diagnosis and treatment type raises questions about the functionality of nomenclature, rather than a need to increase treatment specificity. Extensive research has endeavoured to identify the 'active ingredients' of psychotherapy and their corresponding psychological changes, in keeping with the reductionist medical model. However, core causal relationships remain difficult to establish. While many RCTs have provided evidence of treatment efficacy (for example, CBT-based exposure therapy for PTSD has well-established empirical support), the parallel finding that all psychotherapies, when competently administered, are equally effective (Duncan et al., 2004) confounds any conclusion of treatment specificity. In fact, lack of treatment specificity appears to be the rule rather than the exception. CBT and interpersonal therapy (IPT) have been shown to work equally well in the treatment of bulimia, despite the fact that IPT does not address any of the maintaining mechanisms central to the CBT theory of bulimia, and it is not known how IPT achieves its beneficial effects (Fairburn, 1997b). Recent research that explores the implications of this phenomenon, instead of striving for distinction from traditional and faith-based healing practices, has explored the common active ingredients amongst a wide variety of therapies. This research demonstrates that psychological healing can be attributed to common factors such as explanation, remoralising rituals, the therapist–client relationship, therapist skill, the healing context, client expectation, and hope (Duncan et al., 2004).

Effective treatment approaches, therefore, appear to focus on processes rather than on diagnostic categories, with few diagnosis-specific differences between psychotherapies (Beutler, 1989). Dialectical behavioural therapy (DBT) teaches emotion regulation, distress tolerance, and interpersonal effectiveness—processes that have been shown to be effective in the treatment of disorders beyond borderline personality disorder, the original diagnostic target of DBT (Linehan et al., 1999). Fairburn and colleagues (2003) suggest, regarding the treatment of eating disorders, that 'the patient's specific eating-disorder diagnosis is not of relevance to the treatment. Rather, its content is dictated by the particular psychopathological features present and the processes that appear to be maintaining them' (pp. 522–3). Fairburn and colleagues suggest that, in any case, where diagnostic categories share distinctive clinical features, and patients commonly move between diagnostic states, common maintaining processes are likely, and a transdiagnostic approach to theory and treatment is supported.

There is an equally questionable functional relationship between diagnostic classification and therapeutic outcomes. Beutler (1989), in summarising the relationship, suggests that 'psychiatric diagnoses have proved to be of little value either to the development of individual psychotherapy plans or to the differential prediction of psychotherapy outcome' (p. 271). Wampold and Brown (2006), in a naturalistic study, found that diagnostic labels accounted for 1 per cent of outcome variance on average. Clearly, a diagnostic system with such a weak relationship with disorder aetiology, treatment choices, therapeutic processes, and outcomes has not realised its original potential as a tool for increasing knowledge. In the next section, some visions for an improved diagnostic system will be summarised.

FUTURE VISIONS

Resolution of key issues is seen as vital to the future of diagnosis in psychology. Incorporation of dimensional approaches (such as the quantification of extent of disorder or symptomatology) is seen as important. For Rounsaville (2002), the benefit of basing all or part of the DSM-5 on dimensions rather than on categories is the central consideration (Rounsaville, 2002). Maser & Cloninger (1990, p.12) argue that, 'It is clear that the classic Kraepelinian model in which all psychopathology is comprised of discrete and mutually exclusive diseases must be modified or rejected'. Regier (2007) sees a need for a unified international classification system for mental disorders, to be achieved by eliminating disparities between the DSM and ICD systems. Beutler (1989) sees a need for diagnosis to be seen as a dynamic rather than a static process; diagnosis has to be seen in context and needs to account for the unique individual encounter between client and therapist. To improve validity of the diagnostic system, Krueger & Bezdjian (2009) see a need for an integrated 'top down' (based on expertise and cumulative research findings) and 'bottom up' (driven by empirical analysis) approach.

Practice implications

1   Diagnosis in psychology rests on the assumption that psychology operates using the medical model; many psychologists are uncomfortable with this.
2   Although diagnosis may be useful in some circumstances, psychologists should be mindful of the theoretical and empirical limitations of current and future diagnostic systems.
3   Psychologists should endeavour to be familiar with both DSM and ICD diagnostic systems.
4   It is also worth investigating the PDM.
5   Clarifying a diagnosis can be crucial to effective treatment of a client. Often, this is the case with complex clients, with whom a novice clinician may be struggling to understand what the issues are. In such cases, it may be helpful to use a structured interview schedule such as the SCID or MMCI, to clarify diagnosis, and to investigate a range of symptoms as a basis for treatment.
6   However, carefully consider what is in your client's best interests.

Recommended reading
Central readings are the latest available versions of the DSM and ICD. In addition, the PDM provides an interesting view on diagnosis that may assist you to understand your clients.

Chapter 14

Case conceptualisation

INTRODUCTION

Case conceptualisation involves constructing a meaningful story by placing the client's current psychological difficulties in the context of his or her life. In developing a case conceptualisation, psychologists draw upon psychological principles in a way that is theoretically coherent and consistent with current knowledge, but which also makes sense to the client and communicates hope. Case conceptualisation is the foundation for treatment planning, and is a key process in psychological practice. In this chapter, we explain the purpose and advantages of case conceptualisation, and examine ways of developing and presenting a case conceptualisation to a client. We also examine difficulties that occur in case conceptualisation, and briefly review the research evidence for it.

DEVELOPMENT OF CASE CONCEPTUALISATION

The origins of case conceptualisation in its present form can be traced to the 1960s, when Kanfer and Saslow (1965, p. 407) described an approach to the assessment and treatment of psychosocial disorder that fundamentally transformed psychology. Their behaviour-analytic approach involved understanding and describing an individual's psychological difficulties in terms of environmental stimuli and response contingencies. They also argued that 'the patient takes the major responsibility for regulating his own environment and actions, according to a therapeutic plan worked out jointly with the therapist' (Kanfer & Phillips, 1970). As a result, early approaches to case conceptualisation focused on environmental factors in triggering and maintaining psychological difficulties. Reflecting the accumulation of knowledge about psychological health over the last 40 years, recent approaches to case conceptualisation have expanded to include the influence of private unobservable events. Thus, there has been a move away from examining environmental factors only to exploring the impact of factors internal to the individual, such as schemas, thoughts, and information processing.

What is case conceptualisation?

Good therapy depends on us being able to see our clients as individuals and not just as a diagnostic category (for example, as a bulimic, a social phobic, or a schizophrenic). A key aid in this process is case conceptualisation. Case conceptualisation is a method of organising case information into a 'map' that outlines the variables that influence, trigger, or maintain psychological difficulties (Eells, 2007). It combines a description of an individual's complaints and symptoms of distress with an understanding of how such complaints came into being, the variables that trigger them, and why such problems persist. It also applies research and theory to make sense of a client's concerns. In other words, a case formulation goes beyond diagnosis, and is a set of hypotheses about variables within the client's life that are involved in the emergence and maintenance of a psychological problem. Weerasekera (1996) breaks these hypotheses into four major domains: hypotheses about predisposing factors; hypotheses about precipitating factors; hypotheses about perpetuating factors; and hypotheses about protective factors (see table 14.1).

Complementary approaches might be useful for a psychologist in understanding what variables have influenced, triggered, or maintained the client's psychological difficulties. For instance, in addition to exploring hypotheses about predisposing, precipitating, perpetuating, and protective factors, Nurcombe and Fitzhenry-Coor (1987) suggested it is important to attend to hypotheses about pattern (the pattern of psychosocial and physiological phenomena in the client's presentation), presentation (why this client presents for treatment at this time), and prognosis (the outlook for this client with or without treatment).

Thus, case conceptualisation involves developing a set of hypotheses to explain how the client came to have psychological difficulties. The psychologist must review all potential contributors to the problem, and draw upon information from numerous broad information domains. Although the salience of specific areas will vary according to which theory of psychotherapy and psychopathology the psychologist applies, information domains typically include individual factors, including biological, behavioural, cognitive and/or psychodynamic components, systemic or environmental factors, including family, couple, school, occupational, and social factors, and early and recent life events. A comprehensive assessment should gather

Table 14.1 Four domains of case conceptualisation

Predisposing factors	All the antecedents or predating factors that may render a client vulnerable to developing a psychological problem
Precipitating factors	The stressors or triggers that activate or occur immediately before onset of the psychological problem
Perpetuating factors	The factors that reinforce, confirm, maintain, or worsen the psychological problem; that is, the factors that keep the psychological problem alive and prevent it from resolving naturally
Protective factors	The factors that protect against the development of the psychological problem, or protect against worsening of the current psychological problem

information from each of these domains to thoroughly inform hypotheses about predisposing, precipitating, perpetuating, and protective factors.

DEVELOPING A CASE CONCEPTUALISATION

The first step in developing a case conceptualisation is to develop a comprehensive list of the client's presenting problems (Persons & Davidson, 2002). It is useful to outline the problems by domain, including school or occupation, family and relationships, and psychological, medical, legal, and drug use. A number of assessment tools and information sources can be used to develop a problem list. The psychologist must then attempt to explain the client's difficulties in terms of the hypotheses outlined above, predisposing, precipitating, perpetuating, and protective factors.

For each client, some domains will contribute more to the problem than others. Meier (1999) recommends, in developing hypotheses about the client's difficulties, the rule of parsimony; that is, keep the conceptualisation 'as simple as possible' without being 'simplistic' (p. 857). As part of this process, the psychologist needs to apply knowledge and understanding of theories and models of psychopathology. Choice of theoretical approach will greatly influence the hypotheses developed and the overall conceptualisation. There are a number of case conceptualisation approaches, each informed by a theoretical framework (see Eells, 2007). Using a case study (see Tara, case study 14.1), we outline several of these approaches.

Case study 14.1
Tara

Tara is a 30-year-old single woman living alone and working as a nurse in a GP's office. She presented to treatment because she felt 'depressed' and 'her life was going nowhere'. The problem list developed by Tara's psychologist is as follows:

1   *Low mood: Thoughts:* 'I'll never marry and have children'; 'My life is going nowhere'. *Behaviours:* low motivation, poor initiation of activity.

2   *Social isolation:* Tara has several friends, however she feels that she is losing relationships. On weekends she will often be invited to social outings but will decline because of low motivation, fatigue, or self-consciousness. She often fails to return phone calls and rarely initiates contact. *Thoughts:* 'I bore people'; 'I'm too tired to go out'; 'People will judge me harshly'. *Behaviours:* social withdrawal (does not socialise anymore, fails to return phone calls, very little chatting while at work). *Mood:* sad and anxious.

3   *No relationship:* Tara reports, 'Everyone I know is in a relationship, I want to have a family, and I doubt that I ever will, as I will never meet anyone.' *Mood:* sad. *Behaviours:* no exploration of ways to meet potential partners, no dating, declines offers to be 'set up' by friends. *Thoughts:* 'As if anyone would be interested in me anyway; there is no point.'

4   *Occupational difficulties:* Tara reports that she has had several jobs over the past few years and describes leaving each job because of perceived exclusion and rejection by her co-workers. She described that she often felt 'on the outer' and that she was not accepted by

her peers. *Thoughts:* 'They don't like me'; 'I'm not good enough to be included'. *Behaviours:* increased isolation from colleagues, eventually resulting in leaving the position. *Mood:* sad.

Alternative case conceptualisations

Behavioural conceptualisation

Behavioural conceptualisations are based on an understanding of contingencies that may have been present during development of the client's difficulties, and on those that serve to maintain the difficulties. Martin and colleagues (1992) provide a useful guide to types of contingencies that govern behaviour, as well as procedures that have developed to alter these contingencies. A behavioural therapist may conceptualise Tara's difficulties as learned responses as a result of aversive antecedents. As a child, Tara recalls frequent criticism from her parents, and cannot recall praise. She also recalls victimisation from peers. Tara may have learnt at a young age that interactions with other people result in punishment in the form of feelings of rejection, sadness, and lowered esteem. She may have acquired socially avoidant behaviour to avoid negative experiences. This behaviour has been maintained through negative reinforcement for many years. Generalisation can account for expansion of this avoidant behaviour to social interactions with other individuals (colleagues, peers, and potential partners). As a child, Tara's socially avoidant behaviours were functional to the extent that they reduced negative experiences. As an adult, such behaviours are dysfunctional, in that social withdrawal and avoidance have prevented the extinction of the conditioned emotional response: social interaction = feeling bad. This has resulted in social isolation and loneliness, and has prevented her from achieving life goals, such as marriage and having children.

Cognitive conceptualisation

This conceptualises clients from the perspective of cognitive theory. The cognitive model, developed in the 1950s by Beck, has evolved into a comprehensive and evidence-based model of psychological disorder. Elements of a cognitive case conceptualisation may include core beliefs, automatic thoughts, information-processing biases, and/or schema. Significant contributors to the field of cognitive case conceptualisation include Judith Beck (1995), Muran and Segal (1992), and Persons (2008, 1997).

Beck (1985) developed an approach to cognitive case conceptualisation that has considerable clinical utility, and has received a great deal of empirical support. Beck's cognitive model states that external life events activate schemata to produce symptoms or problems. A conceptualisation based on Beck's model describes external life events and schemata that are relevant for a specific client. It describes the relationship between these components and the problems on the client's list. A cognitive conceptualisation also generates hypotheses about events or circumstances in the client's history that may have lead to development of these schemata. Beck emphasises the importance of examining the client's beliefs about self, others, the world, and the future.

A case conceptualisation of Tara based on Beck's cognitive model would propose that when Tara is confronted with other people achieving their goals and making life transitions (getting married, having a child), her schemata that she is unacceptable and damaged are activated. When these schemata are activated, she withdraws from other people and isolates herself. As a result, she becomes less likely to achieve her goals and feels even more hopeless. This pattern is occurring in both social and occupational settings, and has led to the difficulties she is currently experiencing. Withdrawal from others is maintaining her beliefs about herself, others, and the world.

Cognitive behavioural conceptualisation

Other approaches to cognitive case conceptualisation incorporate components from behavioural theory. The three-systems approach to cognitive behavioural case conceptualisation understands psychological difficulties in terms of three linked areas (Hawton et al., 1989). These areas are: (a) *behavioural:* what the person does; (b) *cognitive–affective:* how the person processes information, and how this influences mood; and (c) *physiological sensations:* bodily sensations that the individual experiences. Each area has an influence on the others. What people do when they are emotionally distressed will influence how they think about their situation, themselves, and others. How emotionally distressed people think and behave will influence the bodily sensations they experience. All of these consequences may be triggered by events and situations that are current or occurred in the past. *Triggering events* activate emotional distress and may include external events (such as social activities and anniversaries) or internal events (such as physical sensations). The three-systems case conceptualisation for Tara is shown diagrammatically in figure 14.1.

Interpersonal conceptualisation

Interpersonal psychotherapy, developed in the 1970s, was derived from a number of theoretical sources, including Meyer (1957), who viewed psychological disorders as an expression of an individual's attempt to adapt to his or her environment, Harry Stack Sullivan (1956), who explored the association between clinical psychology and sociology, and Bowlby (1969), whose theoretical emphasis was on attachment and bonding. *Interpersonal psychotherapy (IPT)* makes no assumptions about the cause of

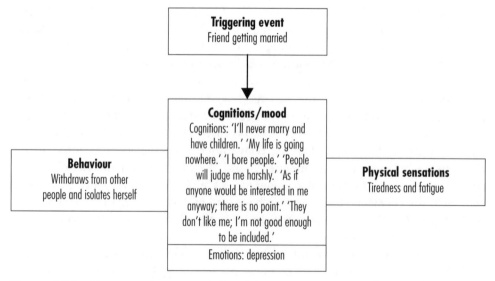

Figure 14.1   Diagrammatic representation of three-systems conceptualisation of Tara

psychological disorders, but simply characterises a disorder as an 'illness' and focuses attention on the factors that maintain this illness. In IPT, it is assumed that psychological difficulties occur in an interpersonal context, and that onset, response to treatment, and outcomes are influenced by relationships between the client and other people within his or her environment (Klerman et al., 1984). The role of the interpersonal conceptualisation is to elucidate the interpersonal events that are important in the onset and/or maintenance of psychological difficulties. Generally, one or sometimes two of the following problem areas are identified:

- *grief (complicated bereavement):* occurs when a significant other to the client has died. Other symbolic losses (such as job loss) are considered role transitions
- *role dispute:* involves significant struggles with a significant other in the client's interpersonal environment
- *role transition:* involves major life changes, such as getting married, divorce, becoming a parent, leaving home, or developing a serious illness
- *interpersonal deficits:* individuals with interpersonal deficits are chronically socially isolated; they have trouble making or sustaining relationships.

Thus, an interpersonal case conceptualisation helps clients to understand the connection between their psychological difficulties and their current interpersonal environment. The focus is on helping clients to learn that by altering their interpersonal environment they can improve their mood.

An IPT therapist would therefore conceptualise Tara's feelings of depression as a medical illness. Tara's illness would be seen to stem from a lack of social relationships. The IPT *focus* or *key domain* would be interpersonal deficits. An IPT conceptualisation would emphasise the impact that illness may have had on her social confidence and ability to interact socially, and the role her social isolation would have played in her becoming unwell. It would also note the connection between mood and recent life events. It would relate the impact that Tara observing others marrying and having children would have on her illness. The primary therapeutic objective would be to improve Tara's interpersonal functioning in her work and social environments.

Sharing case conceptualisations

An important element in case conceptualisation is involving the client in the process and then sharing the conceptualisation with her. During assessment, it is important for the psychologist to remember to continue to 'check in' with the client whether the psychologist understands the information the client is giving him. As we discussed in chapter 11, skilful use of microskills assists the client to feel understood, but also allows the psychologist to check that he is 'on track' in his understanding of the client's presenting problems and how these have developed. Further, use of reflections and summaries throughout assessment helps to shape a shared understanding of these problems; by the time the psychologist is discussing case conceptualisation with the client, many of the main elements will be apparent to the client.

However, it is also useful to provide the client with an explicit description of the way in which the psychologist is conceptualising the case. This should be put to the client in clear, non-technical language, and in a way that allows the client to feel able to comment on or correct aspects of it. Often, the use of a case conceptualisation diagram (for an example, see figure 14.1), on a sheet of paper or whiteboard, can assist the client to understand how the various elements within the conceptualisation 'fit'.

In discussing the case conceptualisation, the psychologist must remain alert to the possibility that (a) elements of the conceptualisation may need to be modified according to the client's input (for instance, that it is fear of closed spaces rather than of crowds that makes going to the cinema difficult); and (b) for some clients, seeing their difficulties laid out in these terms may initially prove confronting. Again, it is important that case conceptualisation occurs in the context of a warm, supportive therapeutic relationship, and that the psychologist ensures that he discusses the conceptualisation in an empathic and nonjudgmental manner. There must be a sense of collaboration in this process; psychologist and client are working together to arrive at an understanding of the difficulties; the psychologist is not simply playing 'the expert'. For most clients, the experience of the psychologist sharing with them an understanding of how their current difficulties have developed can provide enormous relief. Often, clients enter therapy feeling overwhelmed and confused by their difficulties. A good case conceptualisation, appropriately shared with them by the psychologist, can provide clarity about their difficulties. Case conceptualisation can also instil a sense of hope in clients about the possibility of change.

ADVANTAGES OF CASE CONCEPTUALISATION

Case conceptualisation offers benefits to psychologists, clients, and the therapeutic process. Case conceptualisation:

- provides a comprehensive understanding of the client's concerns
- assists in defining treatment objectives and goals
- assists in selecting treatment interventions
- provides a shared understanding of the client's difficulties
- assists in responding to difficulties in treatment
- assists in engaging the client.

A comprehensive understanding of clients' concerns

Case conceptualisation provides a structure for developing a dynamic, detailed, and individualised understanding of the development and maintenance of clients' difficulties. When working with clients, it is easy to 'drift' into therapy; that is, to operate on moment-to-moment intuition about clients and the cause of their difficulties. Case conceptualisation provides psychologists with an opportunity to think systematically at the outset of work with clients. When clients visit a psychologist they often feel overwhelmed, confused, and as though their life is in chaos. One way that psychologists can help to reduce these feelings is by outlining a clear understanding of their difficulties.

Defining treatment objectives and goals

Case conceptualisation can assist in selection of appropriate and individualised treatment goals. A clear and detailed case conceptualisation provides an understanding of the client's issues of concern, including how the problems developed, were maintained, and were possibly worsened. This understanding provides the psychologist with information that can assist in development of treatment objectives and goals to meet the particular needs of the client.

Selecting treatment interventions

A well-articulated case conceptualisation (see case study 14.2) serves as a guide for interventions that may be useful for a particular client. A thorough description of the client's problem provides an indication for how to change the salient contingencies to produce a different outcome. Furthermore, from a description of what produced the client's current difficulties, clues for treatment interventions that may be effective will be evident. This process may be particularly helpful for clients who have not had success with standardised treatments in the past, for clients with complex psychological programs, or for clients for whom there are few empirically supported treatments available (Eifert et al., 1997; Tarrier et al., 2000).

Case study 14.2
Sandra

Sandra is suffering from depression. Following a thorough assessment, Sandra's psychologist hypothesises that three factors are directly related to Sandra's depression:

1   heightened sensitivity to perceived negative evaluation
2   limited capacity to cope with everyday difficulties
3   withdrawal from social interactions.

   Based on these hypotheses, Sandra's psychologist develops a list of three treatment goals and potentially effective intervention strategies for each goal:

1   *Treatment target:* decrease dysfunctional beliefs
     Potential interventions: cognitive restructuring, problem-solving.
2   *Treatment target:* enhance coping skills
     Potential interventions: coping skills training, relaxation training.
3   *Treatment target:* reduce social withdrawal
     Potential interventions: activity scheduling.

These hypotheses can be evaluated by assessing the effectiveness of the interventions. If the interventions fail to alleviate Sandra's feelings of depression, the hypotheses can be revised to produce an alternate conceptualisation. In turn, this conceptualisation can be retested by exploring the success of interventions it proposes. Because of errors in assessment or biases in clinical judgment, hypotheses about a client and reasons for the client's current difficulties may be incorrect. The process enables identification and correction of errors. Meier (1999) describes this process as a *feedback loop*. As discussed in chapter 1, such a process is consistent with the scientist–practitioner model, which seeks to examine systematically the effects of psychological interventions in clinical practice.

A shared understanding of the client's difficulties

Case conceptualisation offers additional benefits to the therapeutic process. A vital ingredient for successful therapy is a 'rationale, conceptual scheme, or myth that provides a plausible explanation for the patient's symptoms and prescribes a ritual or procedure for resolving them' (Frank & Frank, 1991, p. 42). A case conceptualisation is an excellent tool for providing clients with a rationale for their difficulties. Sharing conceptualisation with clients can stop them feeling confused, overwhelmed, and thinking that their problems cannot be resolved. The process can help clients to realise that there are ways of reducing their difficulties. Like narrative therapy, case conceptualisation can assist clients to re-author or re-story the difficulties in their life (Freedman & Combs, 1996). In providing a rationale or narrative for a client's psychological difficulties, case conceptualisation can increase the likelihood of a positive therapeutic outcome.

Responding to difficulties in treatment

Psychologists who have developed a clear understanding of a client are better able to preserve a positive working alliance. Specifically, when problems arise in treatment, or when negative feelings are present within the therapeutic relationship, the case conceptualisation can be used to understand these difficulties (Eels, 2007). Rather than ignoring or managing these difficulties, the focus should be on learning more about them and incorporating them into the client's case conceptualisation (Lovett, 1996). This strategy will often elucidate the reasons for the difficulties, and may result in a more detailed understanding of the client's issues. By increasing the psychologist's understanding and awareness, the client feels better understood, the alliance is strengthened, and the psychologist may feel more confident in working with the client (Eells, 2007).

Case study 14.3
Tom

Tom is suffering from social anxiety. Tom fails to complete his homework task, which involved buying a newspaper from a local newsagent. This task was intended to expose Tom to social interactions. 'I just couldn't do it,' Tom informs his psychologist.

Tom's behaviour could be interpreted in different ways. The psychologist could interpret his behaviour as avoidance, forgetfulness, or a lack of motivation for treatment. But, given Tom's poor social skills, the psychologist views this as Tom not knowing how to interact with the newsagent cashier. Tom and the psychologist work on increasing Tom's social skills through psychoeducation, modelling, and role-plays.

Case study 14.4
Sharon

Sharon is suffering from depression. Sharon runs late for her weekly appointment two weeks in a row. She explains that her boyfriend's car has broken down and she has lent him her car. As a result, she has been catching the bus to sessions. 'The bus is always late,' she informs her psychologist.

Sharon's psychologist could interpret this situation in many ways, according to the conceptualisation. The most appropriate way to respond to this behaviour will vary accordingly. The psychologist could consider the behaviour as unimportant, as Sharon being disorganised, as Sharon displaying frustration regarding the need for treatment, or as low motivation. Given Sharon's history of submission, passivity, and unassertiveness in relationships, the psychologist opts to view this as Sharon submitting to her boyfriend and putting his needs before her own. The psychologist responds by stating, 'It seems like it is important for you to help your partner out, even if it means sacrificing some things for yourself.' This refocuses the session on Sharon's tendency to neglect her own needs in relationships, and its relationship to the current situation.

Engaging the client

Case conceptualisation helps to engage clients and build strong working alliances. Shared case conceptualisations strengthen working alliances by positively influencing clients' confidence in the psychologist and his or her ability to help. Shared conceptualisations can also strengthen alliances by helping clients to feel that they are understood by the psychologist.

DIFFICULTIES IN CASE CONCEPTUALISATION

Although case conceptualisation is highly desirable when treating individuals with psychological difficulties, psychologists should be aware that there are some pitfalls.

Inaccuracies in conceptualisations

By its nature, conceptualisation is fallible, and is best considered a working hypothesis; uncertainty and ambiguity are present within case conceptualisations. Failure to regard conceptualisations as working hypotheses can result in two common problems. Novice psychologists in particular may spend an inordinate amount of time gathering and making sense of client information to ensure that their conceptualisation of the client is 'perfect'. Alternatively, psychologists may form a premature conceptualisation and remain loyal to this despite contradictory evidence.

Regarding the conceptualisation process as a feedback loop, in which the psychologist generates a case conceptualisation and treatment plan, implements interventions, assesses success of interventions, then revises the conceptualisation as needed to develop a more effective treatment plan (Meier, 1999), will help prevent psychologists from making these mistakes. It is also vital to remember to remain open to the client, to view the client as an individual, and be willing to modify a conceptualisation when confronted with contradictory or disconfirming evidence.

Inaccuracies in client reporting

Psychologists should be aware that clients are not necessarily accurate in their report of difficulties. There may be a number of reasons for this, including, but not limited to, embarrassment, fear of stigma or shame, dishonesty, difficulties with memory recall, or resistance to treatment. Remember that, to an extent, every individual's description of events or situations is subject to bias or distortion (even psychologists'!). To minimise the likelihood of inaccuracies in client reporting, psychologists should attempt to corroborate information from other sources, including the client's family and/or friends. The psychologist can also gently address any perceived inaccuracies with the client, when clinically indicated, and remain aware that distortions and inaccuracies are a universal feature of human recall and experience.

Psychologists' misconceptions about case conceptualisation

Although most psychologists agree that case conceptualisation is important in producing positive client outcomes, a case conceptualisation is rarely offered to clients, and is almost never recorded in a client's record (Perry et al., 1987). Perry and colleagues outline the common 'misconceptions' provided by psychologists to explain why they do not routinely conceptualise cases:

- *Misconception:* Case conceptualisation is for beginning psychologists and not necessary for experienced psychologists. *Case conceptualisation is best used by all psychologists, regardless of experience.*
- *Misconception:* Case conceptualisation is too time-consuming. *Case conceptualisation does not need to be laborious or time-consuming. As noted earlier, viewing the conceptualisation as a working hypothesis can prevent the psychologist from spending an inordinate amount of time gathering and making sense of client information, to ensure that the conceptualisation of the client is perfect.*
- *Misconception:* A loosely constructed conceptualisation, stored in one's memory, is sufficient. *Conceptualisations are best stored in written form.*
- *Misconception:* Psychologists can become so invested in a conceptualisation that contradictory information is not considered. *Understanding the conceptualisation as a working hypothesis, and the conceptualisation process as a feedback loop, facilitates rather than hinders psychologists' understanding of client information that may not fit the original conceptualisation.*

RESEARCH EVIDENCE FOR CONCEPTUALISATION

Although there are compelling reasons for using case conceptualisations, research evidence of the usefulness of case conceptualisation is not so clear (Persons & Tompkins, 1997). Only a small amount of research has so far explored case conceptualisation, and results have been inconsistent and mixed. Several studies have demonstrated the positive impact of case conceptualisation on treatment outcome and therapeutic alliance (Crits-Christoph et al., 2001; Kuyken et al., 2005; Silberschatz & Curtis, 1993). Other studies have failed to find a positive impact of case conceptualisation on psychological treatment (Emmelkamp et al., 1994).

The limited amount of research may be a result of lack of consensus about what a case formulation should contain and what its goals should be. An early study (Seitz, 1966) found that psychologists demonstrate little agreement on the structure and content of conceptualisation constructed using the same clinical material. Recent developments in systemic approaches to developing case conceptualisation should assist in overcoming this difficulty.

Conclusion

Although more research is needed to explore outcomes associated with the use of case conceptualisation in clinical practice, case conceptualisation enables psychologists to step beyond the confines of diagnosis to provide a more individualised approach to work with clients. A good case conceptualisation is an important tool in building a strong working alliance, and can be informed by a number of theoretical orientations. The most useful way to regard case conceptualisation is as a set of working hypotheses about a client's presenting concerns which can be tested throughout the process of therapy.

Recommended reading
Eells, T. D. (ed.). (2007). *Handbook of Psychotherapy Case Formulation*. New York: Guildford Press, 314–39.

Chapter 15

Cultural and spiritual issues in treatment

INTRODUCTION

All individuals are influenced by their cultural, religious, and spiritual backgrounds and beliefs. People do not live in a vacuum. This chapter outlines some of the issues related to culture, religion, and spirituality that can have an impact on the process of therapy, and of which therapists need to be cognisant.

The section on cultural issues is intended to provide some ideas about what is required for therapists to develop an appropriate level of cultural competence, so they can work effectively with clients from other cultures. This section is written with the assumption that most of you will be from an individualistic Western culture, but acknowledges that if you are from a non-Western culture, living or studying in Australia, you may have already made considerable efforts to learn about the culture you are living in. You may be very aware of the need for cultural knowledge and skills. Various cultural differences will be outlined, followed by a section that focuses on working with Indigenous Australians. Although there are issues that are unique to Indigenous Australians, this section provides an example of adapting your therapeutic approach to cultural differences. The second half of the chapter focuses on religious and spiritual issues in psychotherapy, and how to work with these. Seventy-five per cent of Australians report having some religious affiliation (Australian Bureau of Statistics, 2002).

CULTURE AND PSYCHOLOGY

The purpose of the first part of this chapter is to alert you to issues that can arise when treating individuals or groups from a culture different from your own culture. Australia is a multicultural society, and cultural diversity is seen as a central part of Australian national identity (Australian Government, 2008). In 2009, over 22 million people were living in Australia, from over 200 countries. About 22 per cent of the population have immigrated to Australia. According to the 2006 census, the top ten countries from which immigrants have come are (in order) the United Kingdom, New Zealand, China, Italy, Vietnam, India, the Philippines, Greece, Germany, and South Africa. As Australia consists of so many diverse cultures, psychologists and counsellors will most likely be working with clients from a large range of different cultures.

Definition of culture

Helman (2000) suggests that culture can be understood as a set of guidelines – for how to view the world, how to experience it emotionally, how to behave in relation to other people – inherited by members of a particular society from previous generations. Helman (2000) suggests that culture is transmitted by symbol, art, ritual, and language. Cultural factors apply not only to clients from another country. Specific cultural factors can be relevant when seeing a client from a different race or from a particular sub-group (defined by class, sexual orientation, or ability) (Smeldy et al., 2006).

Individualistic versus collectivistic cultures

One of the most prominent cultural differences is whether someone has been acculturated in an *individualistic* (30 per cent of the world) or a *collectivistic* (70 per cent of the world) culture. Individualistic cultures focus on individuals' needs; there is a greater emphasis on group needs in collectivistic cultures. The difference in focus predicts how individuals perceive their sense of self (Markus et al., 1997). Those from individualistic cultures tend to be more self-focused than those from collectivistic cultures, and make sense of the world primarily in terms of their internal experience. A much more interdependent view of self is emphasised in collectivist cultures; individuals are more focused on and influenced by the thoughts, feelings, and behaviours of others with whom they have relationships. Keller (2002) summarised the main qualities of an individualistic conceptualisation of self: being competitive, efficient, self-sufficient, direct, assertive, and independent. A more collectivistic sense of self includes these qualities: being respectful, empathic, self-controlled, dutiful, self-sacrificing, conforming, cooperative, and attentive.

These cultural differences influence a wide range of issues, such as views of morality and what is considered appropriate behaviour. For example, in individualistic societies such as the UK, USA, and much of Australia, stopping to assist someone whose car has broken down on the side of the road would be considered a personal decision; not stopping would not necessarily be perceived negatively. In a collectivist culture, such as India, it would be considered immoral not to assist someone in need of help (Miller et al., 1990).

As individualistic cultures put more value on the person than on the collective, people from individualist cultures put greater value on romantic love, and finding the 'right person'. Highlighting these differences is a study by Levine and colleagues (1995) in which participants from the US and India were asked the question, 'If a man (woman) had all the other qualities you desired, would you marry this person if you were not in love with him (her)?' In the US, only 3.5 per cent of respondents said yes to the question; in India, 49 per cent said yes. Because there is so much more emphasis on personal fulfilment in intimate relationships, Western individuals tend to be more demanding of their partners (Hatfield & Sprecher, 1995).

In individualistic cultures, there is also a higher incidence of expressed aggression and violence. In contrast, individuals from collectivist cultures are less likely to be aggressive to others. For example, young children in the US have been found to be much more aggressive than their counterparts in Japan (Zahn-Waxler et al., 1996).

Cultural differences will also have an impact on how individuals conceptualise problems. In broad terms, those from an individualistic culture are more likely to understand individuals using dispositional characteristics (such as the person's temperament); someone from a collectivistic culture would be more likely to believe that the causes of problems are situational, contextual, or environmental (e.g. Menon et al., 1999).

Exercise 15.1

Western psychology is embedded in the principles and morals of an individualistic society. What impact do you think this has on how we conceptualise problems and how we assist those who are experiencing psychological problems?

Clients' cultural background

The importance of client cultural background in treatment depends on factors such as:

- how much the client identifies with his cultural background
- if the client has come from overseas, the length of time he has been in Australia and the extent to which he has become part of the Australian culture
- the client's language ability
- the extent of social support for the client and how much he mixes with individuals outside his own home culture
- the home culture's conceptualisation and view of psychological problems.

It is unlikely that cultural issues will be of no consequence to your clients. It is, thus, important to enquire about culture, what role culture plays in their life, and what the implications are for treatment.

Cultural differences can have a considerable impact on treatment process. How much a therapist should learn about other cultures will depend on the clients the therapist will see in practice, and how diverse the cultures of those clients are. At some stage, you will work with someone from a different culture to yours. You should be alert to and able to adjust to the differing needs of this client.

Cultural competence

Acknowledging the dynamic and developmental nature of the cultural-competency process, Wells (2000, p. 192) proposed a cultural-development model that placed cultural competency in health care on a continuum of six stages:

1 *Cultural incompetence:* a lack of awareness of the cultural implications of a person's behaviour

2 *Cultural knowledge:* learning the elements of culture and their role in shaping and defining health behaviour
3 *Cultural awareness:* recognising and understanding the cultural implications of behaviour
4 *Cultural sensitivity:* the integration of cultural knowledge and awareness into individual and institutional behaviour
5 *Cultural competence:* the routine application of culturally-appropriate health care interventions and practices
6 *Cultural proficiency:* the integration of cultural competence into one's repertoire for scholarship (such as practice, teaching, research).

Sue and Sue (2008) propose three components to cultural competence:

1 *Awareness of self:* being aware of one's own culture and cultural conditioning, as well as the beliefs, attitudes, and worldview that one holds. It is important to be aware of such issues, as the culture and beliefs of the therapist can explicitly and implicitly influence the therapeutic process.
2 *Knowledge of others:* relates to the clinician's understanding of the cultural values, beliefs, and worldviews of clients, and use of such information to inform case conceptualisation and treatment plans.
3 *Skills application:* the clinician's ability to develop and deliver interventions that are culturally sensitive and informed.

Sue and Sue (2008) is most helpful with suggestions for increasing cultural competence in the three identified areas.

Crosscultural differences

We will focus on how culture can have an impact on an individual's experience of mental disorders; there is much variation among and between cultures.

There are noticeable differences in the presenting symptoms of depression and how it is experienced between Western and Eastern cultures. There are much higher rates of depression in Western countries (Kawakami et al., 2004). There is also a much greater rate of relapse after one year in Western countries (33–44 per cent) than in Eastern countries (9 per cent) (Simon et al., 2002). There is evidence that the environment predicts risk of relapse, as the rate of depression in immigrants to Westernised countries is higher than in their home countries. Symptoms also vary across cultures. In Western countries, depression is recognised predominantly by changes in affect, such as feeling hopeless, sad, and even suicidal. Individuals suffering depression in Eastern countries are much more likely to experience and report somatic problems, such as a painful sensation in the heart (e.g. Krause, 1989).

Exercise 15.2

What are the possible reasons for the finding that there are higher rates of depression in Western countries?

Social phobia (another common Western disorder) also presents and is experienced differently in Western and Eastern cultures. Very few individuals suffer from social phobia in Eastern cultures (between 0.4–0.6 per cent). In contrast, 7–16 per cent of individuals in Western countries suffer from social phobia (Furmark, 2002). The experience of the disorder also differs. Western clients report worries such as embarrassing themselves or being viewed negatively. In Eastern cultures, concerns are more about what the effect will be on others, such as bringing shame to the family, rather than on the individual.

Some cultural differences in mental health are related to religious beliefs. In Muslim countries, there are considerably lower rates of alcohol abuse than in Western countries (World Health Organization, 2004); Islamic laws forbid use of intoxicants. However, even in Western societies, religion can have this impact. The Mormon religion also forbids use of intoxicants, including coffee and tea, and alcohol and drug abuse is considerably lower amongst members of this faith.

Some mental disorders appear unique to specific cultures. *Koro* is a culture-bound phenomenon, mainly found in Asian cultures, that is characterised by imagining the retraction or shrinkage of external genitals and an intense fear of death (Malinick et al., 1985; Garlipp, 2008). Another example is *latah*, a culture-bound syndrome found in Malaysia and Indonesia (Simons, 1980). Sufferers, when startled, exhibit an exaggerated startle response, often throwing objects, screaming, and shouting obscenities, and are prone to obeying commands given to them while in this state. These reactions are often considered amusing by friends and family, and sufferers of this syndrome are often provoked for entertainment (Simons, 1980).

What is viewed as healthy varies across cultures. Emotional expression and functioning provides a useful example of this. Emotions are central to psychological issues. In fact, problems with affect regulation are common across a range of psychological problems. It is, thus, important when considering crosscultural treatment to know whether emotions are universal. How humans express different emotions seems to be universal. No matter what culture someone comes from, their age or gender, there is a universal 'facial language' for expression of the seven emotions which are universally recognised: anger, surprise, fear, sadness, disgust, happiness, and contempt (Ekman, 1994). Note that these are only some of the emotions that exist. For a more comprehensive appreciation of the scope of emotions, consult Greenberg (2002), which provides a more expansive list.

Although all cultures express emotions in a similar way, there are differences in how cultures sanction how individuals manage emotions. There tends to be a range of social rules across cultures and across settings in regard to emotional behaviours. In Senegal, individuals who belong to a higher cast are expected to be restrained in emotional expression, whereas individuals from a lower cast are not only allowed to be more expressive, but are expected to more openly express a range of emotions (Irvine, 1990). Japanese are much less approving of individuals expressing pain than their US counterparts; in both cultures there are different rules for men and women, with more approval for women to openly express pain than for men.

In some Western European and American cultures, open emotional responding is considered a mark of psychological health (Wierzbicka, 1999). In Asian cultures, being emotionally controlled and only expressing moderate emotion is considered a sign of health (Bond, 1991). Hobara (2005) refers to the concept of *traditional stoicism* to explain greater restraint in Asian cultures. Individuals may pick up the cultural rules early. Camras and colleagues (1998) found that 11-month-old children in China were less expressive emotionally than same-aged children in the US and Japan. Interestingly, the English language contains many words to describe the intensity and context of a variety of emotions, whereas the Japanese language has fewer emotion words. Words that are used to describe an emotion are often language specific, and clients may feel they are not able to fully express how they feel (Altarriba et al., 2003).

Cultures also differ in what is considered attractive. In the US, white women rate larger women much lower in terms of preferred size, attractiveness, intelligence, and popularity than do black women (Hebl & Heatherton, 1998). Not surprisingly, eating disorders are much more prevalent among white women than among African-American women (Striegel-Moore et al., 2003).

Managing cultural differences

Below are some general suggestions for managing cultural differences. If you know in advance that you are seeing someone from a different culture, prepare for the first session by doing some reading and enquiry about the main aspects of the culture. If possible, also talk to colleagues and/or supervisors who may have knowledge of the client's culture.

- Be careful of misdiagnosis, as neither of the common tools, self-report measures or clinician-administered measures, may capture symptoms as experienced by the client. An example of this is the risk of overdiagnosis of depression in individuals from Asian cultures; they may not express well-being in the same way and as openly as their European counterparts (Diener et al., 1995). At the same time, there is the risk of underdiagnosis if, for example, depression is expressed largely as somatic rather than affective symptoms (e.g. Lin et al., 1985).
- Clients are the experts in their own culture, so ask them to give you an overview of important aspects of their culture, and how you may best fit in with them. It can be a good rapport-building exercise to have clients discuss aspects of their culture, and how these may have an impact on treatment. However, not all clients will be able to explain cultural differences, and consultation of other sources may be essential.
- Sometimes, it can be tricky to manage cultural biases. It may be difficult for a Western therapist to accept that his or her client is having her marriage arranged, or that a mother has been involved with her daughter's genital modification, or that a husband considers his wife's place to be in the home and to have limited outside contact. Of course, not only different cultural customs trigger discomfort; a range of other issues, such as child abuse, do too. When a therapist's values are challenged, supervision is particularly useful, to help determine the most appropriate therapeutic response.

Working with Indigenous clients

This section focuses specifically on working with Aboriginal and Torres Strait Islander clients, hereinafter referred to as Indigenous Australians. The Australian Bureau of Statistics (2006a) estimated the resident Indigenous population of

Australia as 517,000 people, or 2.5 per cent of the Australian population. Indigenous culture is primarily a collectivist culture. Social rules indicate how individuals should relate to others, and what obligations they have to maintain reciprocal relationships. There is a strong sense of group belonging, and identity comes primarily from being part of a collective rather than being an individual. Australian culture generally tends to be individualistic, with low expectations of reciprocity, high levels of personal freedom and choice, and few rules about types of relationships or interactions (Ranzijn et al., 2009).

The social and emotional well-being of Indigenous Australians is linked to the colonisation of Australia (Raphael & Swan, 1997). National inquiries into the removal of Indigenous children from their families (HROEC, 1997) and the human rights of people with a mental illness (HROEC, 1993) have highlighted the traumatic impact that past assimilation polices have had on the health and well-being of Indigenous Australians, and the failure of service providers to deliver culturally appropriate services to them. In turn, this has contributed to a health-status disparity between non-Indigenous and Indigenous Australians. Indigenous Australians are disadvantaged in a range of areas. Compared to the Australian population, they are more likely to be unemployed, have low life expectancies, be involved with the criminal justice system, and experience physical illness. Past government policies have resulted in what Ranzijn and colleagues (2009) refer to as 'a cycle of transgenerational trauma which leads to disadvantage in every area of Indigenous lives' (p. 147). It is acknowledged that the self-determination of Indigenous Australians is paramount in reducing the disparity. However, with respect to the process of reconciliation, psychologists may have a role to play in helping to address the legacy of past policies.

Cultural competence

The importance of the cultural-awareness component of cultural competence is made by Dudgeon (2000): 'There are no magical solutions, "best" methods or therapies for working with Indigenous people. However a critical starting point is for the practitioner to look inward—to take responsibility for gaining cultural awareness and sensitivity, not only toward people of another cultural group but also toward their own culture' (p. 249). Both knowledge and awareness are needed to develop skills for working effectively with Indigenous Australians. Having knowledge of Indigenous cultures, and the negative impact of Australia's sociopolitical history, is not enough to become culturally competent. A therapist may still unintentionally impose his or her worldview on the client, and have a negative impact on the therapeutic relationship.

A therapist who understands how his or her cultural values and beliefs (including Western-based assumptions inherent in a profession such as psychology) can have an impact on interactions with an Indigenous client will have an enhanced ability to interact in a respectful manner with the client, resulting in a more trusting relationship (Ranzijn et al., 2009). Ranzijin and colleagues (2009) describe a process of critical reflection for non-Indigenous clinicians to facilitate improved understanding of their own culture.

Model for working with Indigenous clients

Empowering the client, involving cultural consultants from referral to end of treatment, and using a flexible approach are the central processes recommended by Vicary and Andrews (2001) in their model of therapeutic intervention with Indigenous Australians. This model comprises eight stages:

1 *Referral:* cultural issues may make referral to a Western therapist inappropriate; cultural consultants should help ascertain the appropriateness of a referral.

2 *Examination of background and history:* background data collection can be extensive when working with an Indigenous client, including many sources other than the client. An understanding of the history of the area the client comes from is helpful. With client consent, practitioners may also consult with Indigenous co-workers about the client's background, including family and community histories, and any specific cultural issues. A holistic approach to gathering information is utilised; various resources may need be consulted.

3 *Potential limiting factors:* information gathered from research will help to identify and address any factors that might limit the treatment process, such as inappropriate location of therapy, inappropriate timeframe, or problems in choosing the person who should make initial contact.

4 *Contact and engagement:* flexibility of engagement and client input and choice seem to be the main themes in this stage. Initial engagement may be determined by numerous factors. For example, do established relationships exist with the client, family, or community? If relationships exist between co-workers and the community, introductions can be made. If relationships do not exist, the process needs time, for communication via correspondence, and needs to be conducted in a transparent manner. The therapist's role will be identified at this stage. Assessment or treatment is not started at this stage.

5 *Frequency of contact:* frequency of treatment and appropriate timeframes are negotiated with the client, taking into consideration cultural obligations and treatment issues. Being flexible is essential to the success of engagement.

6 *Therapeutic options:* providing a client with various Western treatment approaches, and outlining the strengths and weaknesses of each, can help the client to make an informed decision about each, while maintaining transparency, and therefore reducing anxiety for the client. Traditional approaches may be used with Western approaches. Consultants, workers, and family should still be involved, with the client, in providing feedback to the therapist at any time about treatment.

7 *Followup and evaluation:* client choice prevails in this stage as well. The evaluation process can be a formal meeting or a less formal catchup. The therapist can provide the client with progress reports and outline future options. The client can provide formal or informal feedback to the therapist about service provision.

8 *Closure:* although treatment and evaluation may have formally ended, a client may discuss issues when the therapist is seen in a different setting. The client may become a referral agent for other people in the community who are seeking

help; this can be viewed as positive feedback regarding the therapist's reputation in the community.

Effective practice with Indigenous clients

To investigate what therapists working with Indigenous clients need to know, Harlen (2002) conducted focus groups with Indigenous participants from an urban setting (Brisbane, Queensland). Issues and strategies for psychologists to consider and use when working with Indigenous clients were collated, based on feedback from participants. Participants were also asked what they would require from a non-Indigenous psychologist for the most distressing problem they had ever experienced, and how could the psychologist assist them. A number of strategies were indicated by participants. These are offered as suggestions, are not prescriptive, and are not necessarily appropriate for all Indigenous clients.

Interview style

Treatment is commonly conducted in a 'clinical' manner. However, this style does not work for most Indigenous Australians, who are sensitive to an arm's-length approach. In an Indigenous culture, people generally get to know one another well before sharing. There should be an emphasis on the personal rather than on the clinical. Take time to find out about the person, and where he or she comes from.

Self-disclosure by the psychologist may be important for rapport building. The process of therapy with an Indigenous client may involve a greater degree of self-disclosure than with other cultural groups. If the practitioner talks about his or her life, and develops a friendly relationship, the client will be enabled to talk more about his or her life, and there will be a greater cultural fit. Trust is developed by sharing of information and appropriate language use.

As part of Harlen's study, one of the authors of this book conducted an interview with an Indigenous client, and asked him to specify a preference for how to proceed. The client suggested they follow the convention of his culture, and discuss what group they each came from. He provided details of his tribe, its location, language (he was bilingual), and connection with other groups; he also described the effect of Australian government policies on himself and his group. He expected the therapist to share similar details. There was considerable overlap between the experiences and culture of a white South African woman and an Indigenous Australian man. Both were bilingual, having parents from different cultures. The Indigenous Australian man was a member of the 'stolen generation'. The grandparents of the author had been removed from their homes with their families, and put into a concentration camp, where they were forbidden to speak their primary language, Afrikaans, and where conditions were poor, with little food and sanitation, by a British Colonial government.

A therapeutic relationship with this beginning establishes a very different tone from the more power-orientated interrogative style that can occur in 'clinical' interviews. With a more reserved client, from another culture, this mutual story-telling approach would likely be offputting.

It seems timely at this point to remind you of a central message of this book: adapt to your clients and their preferred ways of interacting.

A base of Indigenous culture is sharing information. If information about experiences is not shared, some Indigenous clients will feel that they are on a different level, that the psychologist is 'looking down on them', and that they are being judged. Indigenous people are a communal people; they do not tend to relate in a hierarchical way. Thus, taking the role of 'expert', often favoured in Western culture, will not be effective in building rapport with Indigenous clients. Note that, in Indigenous culture, story-telling is of particular importance, and the therapist needs to allow time for Indigenous clients to tell their story. Build rapport by using an informal, conversational style, rather than direct questioning. Using open-ended questions will enable clients to share their stories (Haswell-Elkins et al., 2009).

Nonverbal communication, language, age, gender issues, and origin
The therapist should have an understanding of how to interpret nonverbal communication, such as reading facial features, sign language, and body language. Using Indigenous terminology is important. It would be useful to know and use some Aboriginal words. Language can be a barrier and can place people on different levels. Use simplistic language, with no jargon. Find out about the client's level of literacy. Do not assume your client will have a set literacy level. (This, of course, applies to all clients.)

It is important to attend to age and gender issues. It may be inappropriate for a client to speak to someone of the opposite sex, so a referral may be necessary. However, this is dependent on the client. Some may be happy to speak to a psychologist of the opposite sex about certain issues only, while others may feel comfortable talking about any issue. In Indigenous culture, older people are treated with respect; some older people will not open up to a younger psychologist.

It is important to find out what a client's specific cultural experiences have been. Was the client raised on a mission? In a white or black family? Validate early memories. Many clients will have experienced early abuse; always enquire about this issue.

The 'three worlds' and the concept of fatalism
The *three worlds* is a concept in Aboriginal culture. Indigenous people live in a holistic world: the spiritual, physical, and human worlds are all one. There is a strong belief that spirits are here, they are real, and they guide individuals. To work effectively, the therapist needs to be open-minded and accepting of Indigenous peoples' spiritual beliefs. The physical world is part of them.

The therapist needs to have an understanding of a fatalistic viewpoint. This can lead to individuals accepting negative experiences without questioning them, and without trying to change the situation or seeking help. If individuals believe there is nothing they can do, they may suffer from a passivity that is closely related to a fatalistic view. A helpful investigation of the effects of fatalism on health issues for Indigenous clients is provided by Shahid and colleagues (2009). Indigenous people experience a significantly higher mortality rate from cancer than non-Indigenous individuals. Some reasons for this are that Indigenous patients have lower participation in screening programs, are diagnosed later, have poor continuity of care, and poorer compliance with treatment. Shahid and colleagues (2009) found that fatalism, shame, fear of death, and beliefs, including that cancer is contagious, influenced patients accessing services, and resulted in poorer outcomes. It is important for therapists to be aware of such factors, which may also play a role in the outcome of psychological interventions.

Common mistakes made by non-Indigenous therapists

Participants in the Harlen (2002) study were asked what mistakes therapists who lack cultural awareness make that decrease therapeutic effectiveness. The two main points made were ignorance about Indigenous people and unintentional racism. Unintentional racism can be minimised with careful consideration of therapist prejudices. Ignorance about Indigenous people does not need to be an unsurpassable barrier. The therapist needs to be up front and honest about his or her lack of cultural awareness; this can lead to an opportunity for learning from the Indigenous client. Openly discuss the fact that therapist and client came from different groups, and talk about what this means for the client. Do not pretend that it's not an issue—it is.

Thus, make clear to the client from the beginning that you appreciate that you are from different cultures. Ask your client to excuse you if you break one of his or her social mores unintentionally. Dudgeon (2000, p. 258) provides a statement that may be used at the beginning of therapy:

> As you are aware, I am not an Aboriginal person, and I have little knowledge about your culture. It is important that our work here supports you and helps you. If during the work we do, I make any assumptions or statements about Aboriginal things that make you uncomfortable or angry, I would like you to tell me that, even if you think about it and tell me later.

Useful resources

All of these strategies are in keeping with what is suggested in various guidelines for working with Indigenous communities, including 'Protocols for the delivery of social and emotional wellbeing and mental health services in Indigenous communities: Guidelines for health workers, clinicians, consumers and carers' (Haswell-Elkins et al., 2009) and *Alcohol Treatment Guidelines for Indigenous Australians* (Department of Health and Ageing, 2007; see <www.alcohol.gov.au>.

Additional suggestions

The following are some additional guidelines commonly mentioned in these resources:

* *Setting:* it is important to determine an appropriate setting for treatment. For some Indigenous clients, seeing a psychologist in an office, however nicely it may be set up, will make them feel uncomfortable. A more appropriate setting may need to be negotiated, such as outside, under a tree, or by the river, a place where both client and practitioner feel comfortable (DHA, 2007; Haswell-Elkins et al., 2009; Vicary, 2000).
* *Client support:* clients should be given an option of having an Indigenous worker and/or support person present in the session, to help them feel more comfortable (Haswell-Elkins et al., 2009). Also, find out about Indigenous agencies or people to refer to.

- *Body language interpretation:* nonverbal behaviours can easily be misinterpreted by a therapist when talking with an Indigenous client. Psychologists are trained to observe and interpret nonverbal behaviours of clients; however, this training comes from a Westernised understanding of body language, which may not apply to an Indigenous client. With some Indigenous Australians, it is considered discourteous to make direct eye contact with an authority figure. It is also considered rude to disagree with or be assertive with an authority figure. Confusion can be created in a forensic setting, for example, when a naïve interviewer may interpret lack of eye contact as a sign of hiding the truth, or may assume that the client's agreement with suggestions made by the interviewer can be taken as fact. Powell (2000) provides insight into how to enhance understanding when working with Indigenous clients. This also highlights the importance of having cultural consultants involved. Westerman (2008) recommends that practitioners use cultural consultants to acquire cultural knowledge and skills.

Exercise 15.3

Watch Video 5, on working with a client who is from a non-mainstream Australian culture. The client is from India, and the therapist has very limited knowledge about this culture. How well does the therapist establish rapport, and if he does, how does he achieve this?

Cultural supervision

Therapists may find themselves working with Indigenous clients in various settings. These could include an inpatient setting in an urban hospital, a community health agency, rural or remote settings, clinical or forensic settings, in private or public sectors. The working environment will determine the level of cultural support or supervision to which a therapist might have access. Having access to both clinical and cultural supervision is ideal.

RELIGIOUS AND SPIRITUAL ISSUES IN THERAPY

Religious or spiritual beliefs and practices are an integral part of who your clients are and what they identify with. Religion and spirituality are expressed in many facets of a person's life (biological, psychological, relational, intimate, familial, and sociological), and each facet reveals a different dimension of a person's self (Chirban, 2001). There has been theoretical debate on definitions of religion and spirituality; there are guiding principles on the operationalisation of religion and spirituality in a therapeutic context. A content analysis of definitions of religiousness and spirituality found that all definitions were evenly distributed over nine content categories (Scott, 1997, cited in Zinnbauer et al., 1999). These categories were experiences of connectedness or relationship, processes leading to increased connectedness, behavioural responses to something sacred or secular, systems of thought or sets of beliefs, traditional institutional or organisational structures, pleasurable states of being, beliefs in the sacred and the transcendent, attempts at or capacities for transcendence, and concern with existential questions or issues. These categories will form the basis for our discussion of religion and spirituality in psychotherapy.

Spiritual and religious issues are considered important by most Australians. Seventy-five per cent of Australians in the 2001 Census reported having some religious affiliation (Australian Bureau of Statistics, 2002), and clients in therapy often report that these issues are important to them. In a survey of 79 psychiatric patients at Broken Hill Base Hospital, New South Wales, 79 per cent of patients rated religion and spirituality as very important to them. Eighty-two per cent of patients felt it necessary for their therapist to be aware of their spiritual and religious beliefs (D'Souza, 2002). Similarly, in a study of parents whose children were referred to a child mental-health service in Victoria, 74 per cent reported that spiritual and religious beliefs were important in terms of their child's problems (D'Souza & George, 2006). It is clear that clients consider religious and spiritual matters to be significant factors in therapy.

Religion and spirituality are not foreign concepts in Western psychotherapy. Many mainstream therapy techniques have some basis in formal religious traditions (Worthington et al., 1996). Forgiveness is one, used in, for example, couples therapy, mindfulness interventions, such as mindfulness-based cognitive therapy (MBCT), aspects of dialectical behavioural therapy (DBT), and religious integrated cognitive behavioural therapy (Thoresen et al., 1998).

Mental-health advantages

Numerous studies show a significant and important relationship between religion and spirituality and mental health (e.g. Hackney & Sanders, 2003; Koenig et al., 2001, Larson & Larson, 2003; Miller & Thoresen, 2003; Richards & Bergin, 1997, 2000; Sherman & Plante, 2001). This relationship may be explained, in part, because religion and spirituality: provide a sense of meaning or coherence; stimulate hope; give people a sense of control by a beneficent God, which compensates for reduced personal control; prescribe a healthier lifestyle, which yields positive health and mental-health outcomes; set positive norms that elicit approval, nurturance, and acceptance from others; provide a social-support network; and give a person a sense of the supernatural that is a psychological and spiritual boost.

There is also evidence that religion and spirituality are protective factors in a variety of areas. If a client has religious or spiritual beliefs, it may be beneficial for the client to utilise them. In a study of 850 men aged 65 or older, religious coping (that is, using behaviour related to religion, for example, prayer, to cope) was negatively related to symptoms of depression, and predicted lower depressive symptoms at six-month follow-up (Koenig et al., 1992). Similarly, spiritual beliefs have been shown to facilitate an adaptive form of coping in individuals who have faced personal hardships such as illness or loss (Pargament et al., 2006). Koenig (2004) reviewed the literature and found that religious and spiritual beliefs and practices were associated with lower rates of depression and suicide, lower rates of substance abuse, and increased levels of purpose and meaning. Religion and spirituality have been connected to post-traumatic growth (e.g. Shaw et al., 2005). Generally, if a client holds strong religious or spiritual beliefs, it is preferable to work with these beliefs than to ignore them.

Role of the therapist

There are advantages in a therapist having an understanding of a client's religious or spiritual beliefs. Research has demonstrated that if clients have a preference for religiously-orientated psychotherapy, treatment benefit is significantly enhanced if therapists accommodate this preference. If psychotherapists are open, informed, and tolerant of clients' religious views, treatment effects are likely to be enhanced (Castonguay & Beutler, 2006) because of increased empathic understanding. This enhanced empathy aids development of a good therapeutic alliance (Richards & Bergin, 1997). Similarly, it is essential that therapists have an understanding of how important religious and spiritual issues are to clients, given that client factors contribute significantly to therapy outcome. Open discussion of spiritual and religious issues may also assist the therapist to identify potential support networks for the client outside of therapy (Richards & Bergin, 1997). A focus on clients' spirituality in treatment can offer considerable benefits and resources for living, including hope, flow, compassion, wisdom, forgiveness, gratitude, truth, empathy and altruism, love, and living moral lives.

Despite this evidence, therapists often shy away from these areas. Some may not be religious themselves, may be atheist, and may think religious or spiritual issues irrelevant to the therapeutic process. Often, therapists feel they lack the skills or training to address such issues. Historically, there has been a separation between religious and spiritual beliefs and psychology; Freud (1961) pathologised religion, equating it to a form of neurosis. More recently, much work has been done on spiritual and religious awareness and integrating it into therapy (e.g. Worthington & Sandage, 2001; Koenig, 2004; Passmore, 2003). To gain a holistic and complete picture of your client, it is important that spiritual and religious issues be discussed (Passmore, 2003). As D'Souza and George (2002, p. 410) state, 'A whole person is someone who has physical, emotional, social and spiritual dimensions.'

Given that a majority of clients report that religious and spiritual matters are important to them, and that decades of research has consistently found that religion and spirituality are protective factors, it is necessary that clinicians have the knowledge and skills to work with clients from a variety of spiritual and religious backgrounds. It is also necessary that clinicians are able to facilitate spiritual and cultural exploration with clients who desire such support. In the sections that follow, we will discuss how spiritual and religious issues might arise in therapy, and how you, the clinician, can explore these issues with your client.

Religious and spiritual issues in therapy

Religious and spiritual issues can arise with many clients. At times, issues are directly related to a client's beliefs; for example, when a client comes from a strict religious or spiritual background and experiences guilt for not living up to the standards of the family and/or religious organisation. Waldfogel and Wolpe (1993) tell of a Jehovah's Witness who chose to get a heart transplant despite objection from his family and religious community. This client was highly distressed and required hospitalisation (Waldfogel & Wolpe, 1993). Such issues might also arise for a Catholic gay man or lesbian woman, whose sexuality may be objected to by family and religious community. Such clients can experience guilt or shame, as well as alienation from family and community. In such cases, it would be appropriate and important to address religious and spiritual issues.

Turner and colleagues (1995) tell of a patient who was hospitalised with depression and psychosis, and would talk only to request a priest for confession. After two months, the priest was called. After the client confessed what she felt she needed to confess, she recovered and was released from hospital within two weeks (Turner et al., 1995). This illustrates how important religious and spiritual matters can be for clients, and how vital it is that we are responsive to such needs.

Religious or spiritual issues can arise in therapy if you see a client who has been involved with a cult or sect. Such people have often given much time and money to such an institution, and can experience trauma and confusion when separating from it (Schreurs, 2002). A client may have left the sect, but retained his or her faith, and experiences significant distress as a result of this incongruence (Schreurs, 2002). Such clients may have lost contact with family and friends because of involvement with the sect, or have left family and friends by leaving it.

You may have a client who is functioning well in day-to-day life, has intimate relationships with others, and would not meet diagnostic criteria for depression, but is experiencing a vague desire for 'something more', or meaning, in life (Schreurs, 2002). An open discussion of the client's spiritual or religious beliefs can be helpful. You may have a client who is nearing the end of life, because of old age or terminal illness. Terminal illness often leads clients to think more about their own belief systems, and often results in a 'spiritual crisis' (Hay, 1989, p. 25).

Addressing spiritual and religious issues in therapy

Clients from religious backgrounds with strict beliefs and practices may feel uncomfortable seeing a therapist who does not share the same beliefs (Schreurs, 2002). However, there are ways of managing this situation. Clients are often concerned that their beliefs and values will not be respected by a therapist who does not share the same beliefs (Schreurs, 2002). Clearly, it is important that the therapist is not judgmental of the client's beliefs. The first step in working effectively with clients from a variety of spiritual and religious backgrounds is to acknowledge the importance of spiritual and religious issues (D'Souza & George, 2006). This does not mean that your religious or spiritual beliefs need to be the same as your client's, or that spirituality and religion are important to you. However, an understanding of the importance and impact of spiritual and religious issues in therapy is essential.

It is important that you know of your client's spiritual history (D'Souza, 2003). In a similar manner to how you might enquire about your client's cultural background, it is appropriate to ask about spiritual and religious beliefs (D'Souza, 2002, 2003; Schreurs, 2002), and vital if you want to gain a complete picture of your client. A commonly used spirituality-assessment tool is the *Spiritual Assessment Inventory (SAS)*, a 28-item scale with good reliability with total alpha coefficients of .92 (Hall &

Edwards, 2002). The inventory and scoring is attached to the publication, which is available on the web. The four main concepts of the SAS are unifying interconnectedness, purpose and meaning of life, inner resources, and transcendence. The SAS is not founded on any religion, making it useful for a wide range of people.

Richards and Bergin (1997) present a multi-level model for assessment of religious or spiritual beliefs. At the first, global assessment level, the therapist should ask the following questions:

1   What is the client's metaphysical worldview?
2   What were the client's childhood religious or spiritual affiliation and experiences?
3   What is the client's current religious and spiritual affiliation and level of devoutness?
4   Does the client believe her spiritual beliefs and lifestyle are contributing to her presenting problems and concerns in any way?
5   Does the client have any religious and spiritual concerns and needs?
6   Is the client willing to explore her religious and spiritual issues and to participate in spiritual interventions?
7   Does the client perceive that her religious and spiritual beliefs and community are a potential source of strength and assistance?

If religion and spirituality are important to a client, Richards and Bergin (1997) suggest further, more indepth assessment, exploring issues such as:

1   How orthodox is the client within her religious denomination?
2   What is the client's religious problem-solving style (deferring, collaborative, or self-directing)?
3   How does the client perceive God (such as loving and forgiving vs impersonal and wrathful)?
4   Does the client have a sound understanding of the important doctrines and teachings of her religious tradition?
5   Does the client have a spiritual assurance of her eternal spiritual identity and divine worth?
6   In what ways, if any, are the client's religious and spiritual background, beliefs, and lifestyle affecting her presenting problems and disturbance?
7   Are the client's lifestyle and behaviours congruent with her religious and spiritual beliefs and values?

For clients who are deeply religious, it may be appropriate to involve a respected member of their church or religious community in the treatment program. Worthington and Sandage (2001) also recommend that clinicians consider use of religious-accommodative therapies, which integrate religion and spirituality into treatment plans. In a meta-analysis that compared the efficacy of standard treatments of depression to religion-accommodative approaches, no difference was found (McCullough, 1999). It may be a matter of client preference; if clients prefer that religious or spiritual matters are incorporated into their treatment plan, it is likely that this is appropriate. Again, as we have said many times, type of treatment used depends on the client, and must be adapted to the client's needs.

Extra suggestions

Some clients will not want any religious or spiritual influence within therapy (Worthington & Sandage, 2001). Again, adapt your approach to your client.

Some forms of religion or spirituality are not adaptive. Having difficulty forgiving God, and having anger toward God, are associated with increased levels of depression and negative affect (Exline et al., 1999). Similarly, religious fear and guilt are associated with suicidality, particularly with regard to the belief that one has committed a sin that is unforgivable (Exline et al., 2000). If a client has such feelings, it is essential that you address them, as they have negative implications. These examples further highlight the importance of assessing spiritual and religious beliefs in clients; doing so allows you to become aware of beliefs or practices that are unhelpful to them.

Be mindful of the issue of competence. Although we have encouraged you to explore spiritual and religious issues with your clients, it is important that you do so within your level of competence. If a client requires specific religious knowledge, or wishes to engage in religious practices during therapy, unless you are qualified to provide these specialised services, you might best involve a member of the client's religious community (Miller, 2003). D'Souza and George (2006) warn clinicians against providing indepth religious counselling; they suggest that trained members of the particular religious community are best suited to such counselling (D'Souza & George, 2006).

Practice implications

1   Australia is a multicultural society; psychologists need to have knowledge and skills in working with individuals and groups from a range of cultures.
2   Therapists need to be aware of the differences between individualistic and collectivist cultures, and how this distinction can have an impact on clients' frames of reference and behaviour.
3   Therapists need to be aware of their own cultural background, and how this may influence how they do therapy.
4   Therapists need to be open to and cognisant of the importance of religious issues with clients.
5   Therapists need to be open and flexible, and to adjust their approach to the spiritual and cultural needs of clients.
6   Where appropriate, therapists should seek assistance from appropriate cultural and religious consultants, to gain knowledge of clients' cultural and religious background, or to help provide what is most helpful to clients.
7   Therapists need to ask about all aspects of a client's life, including cultural and religious/spiritual background.
8   Therapists should not make assumptions (generalisations) about clients' beliefs and culture; the client may not identify with his or her culture.

Conclusion

Clearly, culture and religious and spiritual belief systems have an impact on clients' mental health, and cannot be neglected or ignored in psychotherapy. To be competent, it is essential that therapists explore clients' frames of reference, both culturally and spiritually. Therapists also need to be openminded and flexible, and aware of their own culture, beliefs, morals, and values, and how these may have an impact on how they respond to clients who view things differently. Regular supervision and self-reflection are essential to promote continued awareness and ability to adapt. None of us lives in a vacuum; we are all influenced by our experiences and beliefs, which are unique to each of us.

Recommended reading

The following references may be particularly useful in understanding cultural differences, and enhancing efficacy when working with clients from different cultures:

Ranzijn, R., McConnochie, K., & Nolan, W. (2009). *Psychology and Indigenous Australians: Foundations of Cultural Competence.* South Yarra: Palgrave McMillan.

Sue, D. W. & Sue, D. (2008). *Counseling the Culturally Diverse: Theory and Practice* (5th edn). Hoboken, NJ: John Wiley.

Although a detailed description of how religion and spirituality can be integrated into therapy is beyond the scope of this chapter, the following references may be particularly useful:

Helmeke, K. B. & Sori, C. F. (2006). *The Therapist's Notebook for Integrating Spirituality in Counseling: Homework, Handouts, and Activities for Use in Psychotherapy.* Binghampton, NY: Haworth Press.

Miller, G. (2003). *Incorporating Spirituality in Counseling and Psychotherapy: Theory and Technique.* Hoboken, NJ: John Wiley.

Richards, P. S. & Bergin, A. E. (2004). *Casebook for a Spiritual Strategy in Counseling and Psychotherapy.* Washington, DC: American Psychological Association.

Schreurs, A. (2002). *Psychotherapy and Spirituality: Integrating the Spiritual Dimension into Therapeutic Practice.* London: Jessica Kingsley.

Chapter 16

Managing risk

INTRODUCTION

One of the most common issues clinicians who are newly qualified or currently in training express concern about is management of individuals in risk situations. There are some basic principles that relate to risk appraisal generally. However, there are also four distinct categories of risk that we will address in this chapter:

- the suicidal client
- the client at risk of harm (within a relationship, which is generally considered domestic violence, or the threat of violence from another person who is not cohabiting)
- a child who is at risk of harm through neglect or abuse
- the client who is a risk to others.

Exercise 16.1

Before you begin reading, spend some time noting your thoughts and emotions when you anticipate having to manage clients in crisis.

A significant problem in effective risk assessment occurs when a clinician who feels uncomfortable, anxious, or even angry avoids or fails to undertake a comprehensive risk assessment. Indeed, the clinician's emotional response to a potential risk situation has been described as potentially the greatest handicap to effective risk assessment (Motto, 1989). A reluctance to discuss risk may be detected by the client, with the result that the client becomes reluctant to provide sufficient information for a risk assessment to be conducted. It is imperative, then, that clinicians have insight into their own reactions before engaging in clinical work. The key is not to avoid feelings of anxiety but to manage such feelings so you can remain focused and clearheaded. Further, practitioners in training should ensure that they receive supervision when managing crisis situations.

Basic principles and practices of risk assessment

There are basic principles of risk assessment. First, it is essential that you anticipate and are prepared for a situation in which you will need to undertake a risk assessment. One of the authors of this book, when a trainee, asked her supervisor, 'What should I do if my client says he is suicidal?' The response was, 'Well, let's just hope that never happens'. But it did—two weeks later—and the author was left to her own devices to try to help the client. We take the view, 'It will happen at some point, so let's be prepared'.

There are preparatory steps that can be taken. Becoming familiar with the professional code of conduct or ethics of your discipline is essential. If you are a psychologist-in-training, this will be the Australian Psychological Society's *Code of Ethics* (reviewed in chapter 2). Also consult the APS *Guidelines Relating to Suicidal Clients* (2004).

Before you start to practise, make sure you are familiar with the specific procedures of your place of practice regarding risk of harm. All workplaces have health and safety procedures, and almost all will include guidelines on managing risk; make yourself familiar with them.

When you first find yourself in a situation that requires risk assessment, an initial response may be anxiety or even panic. Don't reprimand yourself for these feelings. Recognise the emotion and use strategies to become calmer and focused on the situation at hand. Whenever possible, consult with a colleague or supervisor before concluding a risk assessment. This is a sensible rule to follow for even experienced clinicians.

We recommend the following steps be taken by psychologists-in-training. While there will be some variability in settings—for example, community settings and homes do not have the same safeguards as clinical rooms or hospital wards—familiarisation with them will help you to determine your course of action.

1 Carefully assess the situation (see descriptions below for risk assessment).
2 If there is a possibility of risk, and you are uncertain what the best course of action may be, explain to your client that you need to contact your supervisor or line manager for advice.
3 If your client seems at imminent risk of harming him- or herself or others, do not leave the client alone unless you are at risk of being harmed by the client. Stay in the room with the client, and contact your supervisor. If your supervisor is in the same setting, he or she may be able to join you and your client, if the client agrees. Make sure you have an alternative contact for when your supervisor is not available.
4 If for any reason you need to leave the room—for example, you need to talk to the supervisor in private—try to ensure there is someone else to stay with the client.
5 In consultation with your supervisor, determine the best course of action.
6 As soon as possible afterwards, document in detail the sequence of events, the assessment you undertook, who you consulted with, and what decisions were made. Include in this the response of your client.

Process issues

Risk assessment typically arises in a discussion about difficult and/or emotional issues. Helping people give voice to sad, frightening, or highly distressing thoughts requires therapist attunement and sensitivity. Try not to rush clients—even if you are feeling anxious. Let clients use their own words, and help them develop a narrative that is their own. If you have another client waiting, ask administrative staff to inform the client there is a delay.

While it is important not to allow concerns around litigation to drive good practice, it is wise to remember that many of the words your client is using need to be noted verbatim, and may be part of court proceedings at some point. Make sure your clinical notes are written as you go or immediately after a session. The timing around note taking and progress notes may be discussed in court.

Perhaps the most difficult process issue that arises is *confidentiality*. A rule is to be clear and honest with your client. At the beginning of therapy, you would have explained the limitations of confidentiality (see chapter 2). If you need to break confidentiality, remind your client of this early discussion, and explain the reasons for doing so. If, for example, you believe there is reasonable cause for concern about child maltreatment that will require you to contact child-protection services, it is best to discuss this with the child's carers. However, clinical judgment is most important here. There are occasions when frank and open discussion of concerns regarding risk may place someone at increased risk of harm. Domestic violence discussions, for example, may expose a potential or current victim to retaliative action for having disclosed information. The only hard and fast rule is, consult whenever you can.

Keep in mind that the client who is suicidal, distressed, or angry may be making important decisions, and will have limited information-processing capacity. In such states, people are more inclined to act impulsively; be vigilant to this possibility. Conversely, it may be the case that your client appears emotionally flat. Do not assume that this person is less at risk because he or she appears less distressed.

Always take clients seriously if they indicate that they are thinking of suicide or of harming someone else. Never assume that it is just 'attention seeking', 'crying wolf', 'exaggerating', or 'letting off steam'. Thus, always err on the side of caution, and explore even the most obscure of comments suggestive of risk, as the client may be ambivalent about whether to tell you or not. Many individuals will change their mind about harming themselves or others if given some time. Part of your role is to provide this time, keeping them safe until they can look at their options more clearly.

Managing the suicidal client

Each year, approximately 2000 Australians die from suicide, about 1.7 per cent of deaths in Australia (ABS, 2010). The lowest number of deaths in a given year was 2098, recorded in 2004; the highest number was 2457 deaths, recorded in 2001. Over the 10-year period from 2001 to 2010, there was a 17 per cent decrease in the suicide rate, from 12.7 per cent to 10.5 per cent. For Australians between 15 and 34 years of age, however, suicide remains the main cause of death (ABS, 2010).

Suicide rates differ in relation to gender as well as age. Young men are a particularly high-risk group, with suicide accounting for 20 per cent of deaths for men between 20 and 34 years of age. Men are four times more likely to commit suicide than women, accounting for 80 per cent of deaths in Australia as a result of suicide. This gender difference is a worldwide phenomenon: men have a three-fold increase in suicide rates compared to women, approximately 24.5 of every 100 000 deaths for men, and 8.02 per 100,000 for women. Indigenous populations have relatively high rates of suicide (Hunter & Milroy, 2006), and Aboriginal and Torres Strait Islander peoples have close to twice the rate of suicide of non-Indigenous Australians (ABS, 2010).

The highest rate of suicide in Australia is in the Northern Territory, with 20.2 deaths per 100,000 people (ABS, 2010). Tasmania also has a relatively high rate of suicide; New South Wales has the lowest rate of suicide in Australia, with 8.5 deaths per 100,000 people. Although there has been a decline in deaths related to suicide across Australia, since 2000 there has been an increase in the Northern Territory and Tasmania (De Leo et al, 2006). It is suggested that areas with higher suicide rates are those with larger rural populations; risk of suicide is much higher in rural areas.

There is considerable variation in degree of lethality of methods to attempt suicide. Shooting results in mortality in 90 per cent of instances, attempted hanging in 83 per cent of instances, and jumping from a height in 60 per cent of instances. In contrast, self-poisoning or use of a sharp instrument has approximately 3 per cent risk of mortality (Large & Nielssen, 2010). Hanging, including strangulation and suffocation, is the leading cause of all suicides in Australia (45 per cent overall, 47 per cent for men, 40 per cent for women) (ABS, 2005). There has been a significant reduction in the use of firearms to commit suicide since ownership of firearms has been severely restricted in Australia (Large & Nielssen, 2010). Approximately 7 per cent of suicides are a result of use of firearms, compared to 60 per cent of deaths in the USA. Poisoning by drugs accounted for 12 per cent of deaths, and poisoning by other means, including motor vehicle exhaust, accounted for a further 16 per cent. The recent introduction of catalytic converters to cars has reduced mortality of exhaust fumes (Large & Nielssen, 2010). These authors also suggest that increased prescription of serotonin re-uptake inhibitors, and the relative decline in use of more toxic tricyclic antidepressants, has led to decreased mortality from use of pre-scribed medication. Other common methods of suicide include jumping from a high place, drowning, and bleeding; these, together, account for 14 per cent of deaths by suicide (ABS, 2005).

Mental and behavioural disorders are the most common linked causes for suicide in Australia (ABS, 2010). Bryan and Rudd (2006) summarise a number of factors related to an increase in suicide risk. These include: previous history of suicidal behaviour; previous history of psychiatric diagnosis; history of abuse; recent release from inpatient psychiatric care (the first year following is of particularly high risk); major mood disorder, especially depressive phases, with a sense of hopelessness being the most important predictor; alcohol or substance abuse (use of substances impairs judgment and reduces inhibition); high levels of impulsivity; trait rather than state anxiety; schizophrenia; and borderline personality disorder. Carr and McNulty (2006) point to other factors that are related to increased suicide risk: marital status, with individuals who are single, widowed, or divorced being at higher risk; losses early in life; personality traits such as a dichotomous thinking style, perfectionism, poor problem-solving skills, and aggression; and biological risk factors, such as a genetic vulnerability. For some, the presence of serious illness, such as cancer or AIDS, may increase suicide risk. But these lists are by no means exhaustive; any person is capable of self-harm.

Suicide risk assessment

There are a number of good suicide-assessment instruments, including:

Beck, A. & Steer, R. (1988). *Beck Hopelessness Scale*. San Antonio, TX: Harcourt Brace.

Beck, A. & Steer, R. (1991). *Beck Scale for Suicidal Ideation*. San Antonio, TX: Harcourt Brace. Available at <www.psycorp.com>

Linehan, M., Goodstein, J., Nielsen, S., & Chiles, J. (1983). Reasons for staying alive when you are thinking of killing yourself: the Reasons for Living inventory. *Journal of Consulting and Clinical Psychology, 54*, 880–1. Available at <http://depts. washington.edu/brtc/publications/assessment-instruments>.

Reynolds, W. (1991). *Adult Suicidal Ideation Questionnaire: Professional Manual*. Odessa, FL: Psychological Assessment Resources.

Reynolds, W. & Mazza, J. (1992). *Suicidal Behaviour History Form: Clinicians' Guide*. Odessa, FL: Psychological Assessment Resources.

A number of areas need to be assessed. Five of the main ones are: intent, means, mood or emotional state, previous attempts and/or threats, and protective factors. Each of these will be discussed.

Intent

The phrase *suicidal intent* is used to indicate that the individual has relatively advanced levels of planning to commit suicide (Carr & McNully, 2006). Inquire about the time frame: how immediate is the risk? Is the person still considering suicide? Will the person do so if something else happens in his or her life (say, if the partner leaves)? The more serious a client is, and the sooner he or she is planning to commit suicide, the greater the imminent risk.

The term *suicidal ideation* indicates a less immediate risk of self-harm. Someone with lower risk would have had periodic thoughts of not wanting to live, but the thoughts last only for a short time. In contrast, a person who has very intense and persistent thoughts of wanting to die is at much higher risk. Note that clients are usually relieved if someone asks them about suicidal ideation and intent; avoidance of the issue by the therapist just causes more anxiety for the client. Openly discussing issues with the client, even as clearly as, 'Would you actually like to die, or is it just that you would like the problem to go away?', is helpful.

The immediacy of plans is important. A client with no immediate plans, and with reasons to live, is less at risk than a client who wants to die, and has an imminent time frame. Sometimes a client who is at serious risk may say something like, 'I'm sure that I'll kill myself as soon as I leave here'. This client cannot leave the therapy setting on his or her own.

Means

Ask the client exactly how he or she intends to commit suicide. You require exact details, specifically about lethality of means. The more lethal the means, the more at risk the individual. When asking about means, be specific. If a client says, 'I'm going to drive over a bridge', you need to know what bridge, how long it would take the person to get there, and any other details. You also need to enquire about access to the means. If a client says, 'I'm going to shoot myself', ask where the client would obtain a gun and whether the client has used a gun before. Also, check knowledge of means. If a client says to you, 'I'm going to overdose', ask about the type of medication the client intends to use, and how much the client thinks will be needed. Clearly, the more a client knows about lethality of means and ease of access to means, the greater the imminent risk.

Mood or emotional state

This can be difficult to assess in terms of immediacy of risk, as people vary. Generally a person at reduced risk will be teary, cry easily, and perhaps be irritable. A person more at risk may have mood swings, or perhaps not express emotion. It is common for high-risk clients to show virtually no emotion, or be in turmoil. Levels of emotional distress may be easier to recognise, from mild distress, to feeling highly distressed, despairing, to feeling disconnected from others.

Previous attempts

Past suicide behaviour is a strong predictor of current risk. If the client has made a previous attempt that was serious (for example, she was found just in time and hospitalised, with means that could be lethal), this indicates increased risk and seriousness. If the client did not tell anyone when she made her previous attempt, and appeared to try and keep it secret, so that she could not be rescued, this is obviously another sign of seriousness. All previous attempts need to be taken seriously by the clinician.

Protective factors, including outside support

Explore any factors that would protect clients from self-harm. Ask if they have children and don't want to leave them orphaned. Ask if they have religious beliefs that indicate that suicide is inappropriate. That is, what are their reasons for staying alive? (Linehan et al., 1983). Discuss these reasons with clients in an attempt to have them reassess their decision. Obviously, someone who feels that they have the support and care of others will be at less risk, whereas those who have a lot of interpersonal conflict and are isolated are at much higher risk. Assess their support network, asking not just about who they like, but who is reliable and can be trusted to act maturely and responsibly. Finding a reason to live is one of the most protective factors. If clients feel completely helpless, have no hope, and feel powerless to influence their life, seeing it as meaningless, they are at much greater risk.

Areas for suicide risk assessment are summarised in table 16.1.

Carr and McNulty (2006) also provide a very helpful table you can use to assess risk.

Managing suicide risk

There are three levels of management, depending on the risk level:

1 *If the risk is low, and not imminent,* make a contract with the client that he will not not harm himself in a set period, and make another appointment for as soon as possible. Be aware that the evidence suggests that *no-harm contracts* do not guarantee that clients will not harm themselves. However, it is suggested that their

value is in demonstrating the strength of the therapeutic alliance, and thus provides a tool to work with (Bryan & Rudd, 2006). Also discuss *contacts* who can support the client during this period; obtain details of responsible friends and family, Lifeline numbers, and the client's GP and/or psychiatrist, if he has one. Refer to your list of telephone numbers for supervisors and staff and their after-hours numbers. Make sure you have access to these numbers at all times.

2 *If the risk is medium, but not imminent,* also make a contract and organise another session as soon as possible. In addition, make contact with someone who is trustworthy (the client's doctor, relative, or friend) and discuss the risks. Gain the agreement of this person to watch over the client in the short term. This negotiation should be done with the client present. Contact the responsible person after discussion with the client. Remain with the client until another person is taking responsibility for the client.

3 *If the risk is serious and imminent,* the client needs to be hospitalised. If the client has a psychiatrist, contact this person to assist with hospitalisation. If the client has previously been hospitalised, if possible refer to this base, which will have records of the client. You need to persuade the client to accompany you by taxi to the nearest Outpatients Department for immediate consultation and/or hospitalisation. If the client refuses to go, and the situation is deemed high risk, ask the police to escort the client.

Severe distress

In cases where a client is very distressed, but poses no threat of suicide or violence, you have a number of options.

- Most importantly, do not allow the client to drive.
- If possible, allow the client extra therapy time to reduce distress.
- If this is not possible, allow the client to stay in the therapy room until he feels better. The client will need to be checked before leaving.
- If he is not calming down, ask for the name and number of a person who might pick him up.
- You might arrange for the client to be escorted home (say, by taxi).

Suicide risk in children

Keep in mind that children may also be at risk of suicide, including the 5–14 age group. It is unclear if suicide can occur below this age. The vital point is that we must never discount risk of suicide in a child; children can, and do at times, commit suicide, whether they understand that it means 'an end to self' or not.

Clients who are frequently at high risk

Clients suffering from disorders such as borderline personality disorder (BPD) frequently present with high risk of suicide and/or self-harm. Never assume a client is 'just seeking attention' or 'acting out'. We must always carefully consider risk. However, with clients who are fairly regularly at high risk, managing the risk exactly as suggested above is not ideal. If you have such a client, find good supervision, and become familiar with the work of writers such as Marsha Linehan (1993a and 1993b). You will find a section on DBT (the treatment of choice) in chapter 7 of this book.

Table 16.1 Areas of risk assessment (Bryan & Rudd, 2006)

I	Predisposition to suicidal behaviour

- previous history of psychiatric diagnoses (increased risk with recurrent disorders, comorbidity, and chronicity)
- previous history of suicidal behaviour (increased risk with previous attempts, high lethality, and chronic disturbance)
- recent discharge from inpatient psychiatric treatment (increased risk within first year of release)
- same-sex sexual orientation (increased risk among homosexual men)
- male gender
- history of abuse

II	Identifiable precipitant or stressors

- significant loss (e.g. financial, interpersonal relationship(s), identity)
- acute or chronic health problems
- relationship instability

III	Symptomatic presentation

- depressive symptoms (e.g. anhedonia, low self-esteem, sadness, dyssomnia, fatigue (increased risk when combined with anxiety and substance abuse))
- bipolar disorder (increased risk early in disorder's course)
- anxiety (increased risk with trait anxiety)
- schizophrenia (increased risk after active phases)
- borderline and antisocial personality features

IV	Presence of hopelessness

- severity of hopelessness
- duration of hopelessness

V	The nature of suicidal thinking

- current ideation frequency, intensity, and duration
- presence of suicidal plan (increased risk with specificity)
- availability of means
- lethality of means
- active suicidal behaviours
- explicit suicidal intent

VI	Previous suicidal behaviour

- frequency and context of previously suicidal behaviours
- perceived lethality and outcome
- opportunity for rescue and help seeking
- preparatory behaviours

VII	Impulsivity and self-control

- subjective self-control
- objective control (e.g. substance abuse, impulsive behaviours, aggression)

VIII	Protective factors

- presence of social support
- problem-solving skills and history of coping skills
- active participation in treatment
- presence of hopefulness
- children present in the home
- pregnancy
- religious commitment
- life satisfaction
- intact reality testing
- fear of social disapproval
- fear of suicide or death

Table reproduced with permission. Source: Bryan, C. J. & Rudd, M. D. (2006). Advances in the assessment of suicide risk. Journal of Clinical Psychology: In Session, 62(2), 185–200. DOI: 10.1002/jclp.20222.

Self-harm, through cutting on arms, legs, or stomach, by ingesting dangerous substances (such as drain cleaner), or by overdosing on medications, can be a way for some clients to regulate their emotions or punish themselves. It can be upsetting for practitioners when first faced with a client who self-harms, but it is important to understand when behaviour has the intention of self-regulation rather than suicide. The risk, however, is that methods of self-harm can also be life threatening; thus, self-harm needs to be carefully monitored and managed. This behaviour is also covered by Linehan (1993a and 1993b), among others.

If a client does commit suicide ...

Some clients, despite our best efforts, will commit suicide. Risk assessments are only valid at the time they are undertaken, and events can push already vulnerable people to commit suicide. This occurs even when they have assured the therapist that they would not do so. Sometimes, clients who are aware of the duty of the practitioner to protect them from harm will underdisclose, so that their risk is not considered sufficiently high to require hospitalisation. Sometimes, clients leave hospital, then commit suicide. 'Suicide of a patient provokes not only professional questions, doubts and explanations, but also personal, basic human feelings, not entirely different from those experienced by the relatives and friends of the deceased' (Grad & Michael, 2005, p. 72). This quote captures some of the complex thoughts and emotions that practitioners may feel if they lose a client to suicide. Such a loss can result in considerable distress to the therapist, including shock, disbelief, anger, guilt, and shame. Sometimes, the therapist cuts off completely (Valente, 1994). If you ever lose a client, seek support from colleagues, a supervisor, or mentor, and perhaps undertake personal therapy.

Exercise 16.2

One of the biggest anxieties for early therapists (and experienced ones) is that a client may be suicidal. Video 15 shows a risk assessment with a depressed male client. The therapist initially picks up that the client may be at risk of suicide, and asks a range of questions necessary to do a risk assessment. It is not only the range of questions that are essential in a thorough risk assessment but the process between therapist and client. It is difficult for most clients to talk about their thoughts of committing suicide. The therapist has to provide a safe environment for the client to do so. In this vignette, the therapist is gentle, careful, and not pushy, but does not waver from the assessment until all risk factors are explored.

1   How well do you think the therapist managed each of these situations?
2   What is it that the therapist did (or did not do) that resulted in an effective or ineffective risk assessment in each case? Also, watch the second part where the therapist discusses her practice with this client. What are your views about the therapist's comments?

Useful contacts and sources of information
Kids Help Line: 1800 551 800 or <www.kidshelpline.com.au>.

Lifeline: 13 1114 or <www.lifeline.org.au>. Lifeline also puts out a manual that lists the resources available in the community—track down a copy for referral sources.

BeyondBlue: 1300 22 4636 or <www.beyondblue.org.au>.

Australian Psychological Society tip sheets on *Understanding and Preventing Suicide in Young People* and *Preventing Suicide*. Available from the APS website: <www.psychology.org.au>.

The client who is a risk to others

Clients can be a risk to others. Psychologists' Duty to Protect code of ethical practice stipulates that they need to ensure the safety of any person who may be at risk from a client. We will briefly consider how to deal with a potential or identified perpetrator of harm to others. Working with perpetrators requires specialist knowledge and training; a detailed discussion of this area of clinical practise falls outside the scope of this chapter.

If a client poses a threat to you or to anyone else in the vicinity, contact the security officers in your place of practice for assistance. If the threat is imminent, do not stay with the client. If you are uncertain about the risk the client may pose, inform the appropriate person in your practice, such as the director of the clinic, to ensure there is back-up close by and that someone is monitoring the session. Sit close to the door and leave the room if you feel in danger. Alternatively, request that someone, such as the clinic director or your supervisor, come into the session to assist you.

Do not underestimate risk to others. If there is even the slightest indication of such risk, explore it thoroughly. Follow the guidelines for suicide-risk assessment in regard to assessment of intent and likelihood of acting on threat, method and accessibility, history of violence towards others, and protective factors. If assessment indicates there is any potential risk toward another, and your supervisor concurs with this assessment, you must (a) inform your client that you will need to break confidentiality, and (b) inform the intended victim of the risk. In some situations, you will also need to inform the police. Issues regarding the alliance discussed earlier also apply here.

Some practice settings focus on work with clients who are a risk to others, as in Corrective Services. Individuals working in these areas need to obtain specialist training in working with clients who are a risk to others. Please also see the APS *Guidelines for Working with People who Pose a High Risk of Harm to Others* (2005).

The client who is at risk of harm from others

In clinical practice, working with victims of harm from others occurs more routinely.

The two main categories of clients who are at risk of harm from others are adults in domestic violence situations and children at risk of physical, emotional, or sexual abuse from parents or guardians.

Domestic violence

A domestic violence (DV) situation is often a complex situation to manage, as both adults and children living in the household are potentially at risk. Also, it is possible that a victim of abuse may also be perpetrating abuse towards his or her spouse and/or children. It is imperative that you not make presumptions about 'who is at fault'. Also, do not underestimate possible severe risk to the physical well-being of individuals in domestic violence situations; these can be the most volatile and dangerous situations therapists and police deal with.

Domestic violence is defined as 'an act of violence that occurs within intimate relationships in domestic settings'. The broader term *family violence* refers to violence between family members, as well as violence between intimate partners (Morgan & Chadwick, 2009). Domestic violence occurs when a partner or ex-partner attempts to dominate or harm the other partner physically or psychologically.

Domestic violence can be exhibited in many forms: (a) physical violence (including slapping, shaking, punching, kicking, damaging property, and hurting or killing pets); (b) sexual abuse (forcing the person to do sexual acts against his or her will); (c) emotional abuse (including making threats, or emotional blackmail, such as, 'I will kill myself if you leave me'; (d) calling the person names (belittling the other person); (e) intimidation (including throwing things or making threats); (f) economic deprivation (keeping the person financially dependent by preventing access to money and forcing the other person to ask for money); (g) spiritual domination (not allowing a person to have his or her own views about religion, cultural beliefs, and values); and (h) social domination (including insulting the person in front of others, controlling who the person can spend time with, and isolating the person). Control or power over others is often gained through fear and intimidation as well as by direct physical assault. Remember: domestic violence is a criminal offence, although most assaults go unreported.

The Australian Bureau of Statistics (2006b) *Personal Safety Survey* indicates that approximately one in three Australian women have experienced physical violence during their lifetime, and nearly one in five have experienced violence by a current or previous partner. Nearly one in five women in Australia has experienced some form of sexual violence, most commonly perpetrated by someone she knows. Although more women than men have been reported to have experienced violence from a partner, men are also at risk. The survey indicated that 2.1 per cent of women (160 100) and 0.9 per cent of men (68 100) aged 15 years and over have experienced violence from a current partner, and 15 per cent of women (1 135 500) and 4.9 per cent of men (367 300) have experienced violence from a former partner. Violence from a previous partner often poses a greater risk than violence by a current partner, and levels of severity also tend to be higher (Mouzos & Makkai, 2004). This fact should alert practitioners to ongoing risks, even if a client has left a violent relationship.

There is ongoing debate about rates of violence committed against men by women in intimate relationships. There is increasing evidence of abuse of men in homosexual relationships, as there is for women in lesbian relationships (Chan, 2005; Nicholas, 2005). Underreporting, particularly by men, limits the accuracy of statistics, but the consensus is that the majority of victims of DV are women. Violence perpetrated by men also tends to result in more serious injury (Tomison, 2000).

There are useful sources of information available for clients who want to understand more about domestic violence. <ReachOut.com> provides clear definitions and examples of inappropriate behaviour. Because they have been exposed to them for a long time, clients do not always realise that some behaviours by partners are not acceptable in the community. Educating clients about unacceptable behaviours can help them to ascertain what are appropriate or inappropriate actions in relationships. It is not uncommon for a client to state, 'I had no idea that was not OK!'

Shame is often associated with being a victim of domestic violence, and a client is unlikely to report that she or he is in a violent relationship. Surveys suggest that only 14–36 per cent of victims will report domestic violence to the police (Marcus & Braaf, 2007). Practitioners thus need to be alert to signs and symptoms that an adult may be a victim of domestic violence. These include anxiety and depression, PTSD, physical stress symptoms, suicide attempts, alcohol and drug use, sleep disturbance, reduced coping and problem-solving skills, loss of self-esteem and confidence, and social isolation.

Many victims of domestic violence are confused about their feelings toward the perpetrator. They may feel that not only should they hide the abuse because they are ashamed, but also because of fear of the perpetrator. They may even believe that they need to protect the perpetrator. Emotions and thoughts tend to become very confused when someone is in an abusive relationship. Be nonjudgmental about their choices to date and you will offer your clients something of value. This can be difficult for many therapists, as they struggle to understand why someone would stay in a harmful relationship—but it is essential that the practitioner works at having accurate empathy.

Domestic violence is associated with a range of problems, including health problems (Marcus & Braaf, 2007). In fact, domestic violence is the biggest health risk to Australian women aged 15 to 44 years (Access Economics, 2004). Problems include physical injury, depression, anxiety, trauma, impaired social skills, self-harm, and substance abuse. Further, more than half of all female homicide victims have been killed by their intimate partner (Dearden & Jones, 2008).

Risk factors for becoming a victim include being an Indigenous woman, living in a rural or remote area, being an older woman, and being a woman with disabilities (including intellectual disabilities). Mouzos and Makkai (2004) found that in 2002, 7 per cent of non-Indigenous women reported physical violence by partners, whereas 20 per cent of Indigenous women reported that they had been a victim of physical violence. Indigenous women are also approximately 35 times as likely as non-Indigenous women to sustain serious injury and require hospitalisation (Al-Yaman et al., 2006).

Women who have experienced violence commonly cite partner drinking habits, general levels of aggression, and controlling behaviours as risk factors for violence (Mouzos and Makkai, 2004). Alcohol is a significant risk factor in domestic violence, in particular when partners consume alcohol at high levels on a frequent basis (Marcus & Braaf, 2007). The problem with alcohol is even larger in Indigenous communities (Dearden & Payne, 2009).

Research has also demonstrated that traditional gender-role views and negative attitudes towards women increase risk of violence (Flood & Pease, 2006). Factors maintaining violence include societal views that domestic violence is 'private' business; people do not tend to intervene. In an attempt to break violent patterns, the

Australian Government has issued community advertisements encouraging citizens to report domestic violence.

Risk assessment

There are a number of steps suggested when undertaking a risk assessment in relation to domestic violence. First, be sensitive in assessing the situation, including risk of harm. Keep in mind that the client may be reluctant to tell the full story because of feelings of embarrassment, shame, and a desire to protect the perpetrator. Thus, you have to ask very specific questions related to possible harm being done: 'Have you been hit? kicked? threatened? emotionally abused? intimidated?' The Conflict Tactics Scale (Straus et al., 1996; Straus, 2007) may be used to assess specific behaviours of domestic violence towards both adults and children.

Check how imminent the risk is. Serious cases may involve a direct threat to harm or kill the client or children and a means to do so. Check whether police or other agencies have been involved. Discuss with your client the possibility of a protection order. However, be warned: although these orders may be useful in some instances, they are frequently broken, and may even serve to ignite a situation further. Victims of domestic violence who have a domestic violence order in place should not be lulled into a sense that they are at no further risk of harm.

If the client is at imminent risk and/or wants to leave the relationship, you need to explore possible places of safety. Remember: this is a risk situation, so you are advised to discuss the case with your supervisor, and not make any major decisions (for the client to leave the relationship) without seeking your supervisor's advice. Decisions about clients leaving a violent relationship need to be carefully considered and planned, as there is an increased risk of violence at this point.

Risk of retaliation from abusers can be the most serious problem. The risk of serious and lethal harm is most likely once the victim has left an abusive situation; as a result, safety plans have to be carefully put in place. A restraining order is not enough. Keep in mind that if your client has left an abusive situation, she will probably be under considerable pressure to return to it. Whether it is societal pressure to stay, the perpetrator promising to change, children missing their parent, or a romanticised memory of the relationship, you need to be prepared to support your client through a number of phases of leaving and returning. This will be stressful for you, and you will require support.

Agencies that can help

You can use the information included in the *Mental Health Act* of your State to get your client to a place of safety. There are potentially lots of further problems for victims if they leave a perpetrator, including the issue of child custody and economic dependency, and we strongly recommend that you assist your client to connect with agencies set up to offer support in DV situations. Examples of these agencies nationwide are:

- Violence Against Women, Australia Says No (specialises in domestic violence and sexual assault counselling and referrals): 1800 200 526

- Relationships Australia: 1300 364 277
- Mensline Australia: 1300 78 99 78.

Also, all states in Australia have help lines and organisations that specialise in DV.

Exercise 16.3

Watch Video 16+ debrief. In this vignette, the therapist explores the extent of aggressive behaviour in a relationship with a husband. The wife has threatened to leave the marriage unless her husband seeks treatment. The husband does not initially recognise that there is a problem, and uses minimisation and denial to play down the seriousness and consequences of his behaviour. The vignette demonstrates how the therapist nonjudgmentally but persistently remains focused on the alleged violence in the relationship. By doing this, the client begins to recognise the issues, and hopefully starts to take responsibility for his behaviour.

Children at risk of maltreatment

Child maltreatment is a general term encompassing four broad categories of harm, physical abuse, sexual abuse, physical neglect, and emotional maltreatment. These types of maltreatment do not occur in isolation from one other, and while it is possible for children to experience repeated occurrences of one type of maltreatment, they are also likely to be victims of other types of abuse and neglect as well, including the witnessing of domestic violence (Edwards et al., 2003).

Estimates of prevalence of child maltreatment vary widely. A conservative estimate can be undertaken by looking at the number of notifications made to child protective services. This information is collected by the Australian Institute of Health and Welfare (AIHW, 2010). There were 317 526 reports of child abuse or neglect made to statutory child protection departments in 2007–08. This is a twofold increase in 10 years. Of the reported cases, 55 120 were substantiated. These data are generally considered to be an underestimation of the extent of the problem, as they are based on notifications (Bromfield & Irenyi, 2009).

Risk factors

There are well-established risk factors for child maltreatment. One of the most important is poverty. Children with the greatest risk of adverse development, poor health, and compromised well-being live in families with financial disadvantage, social exclusion, and vulnerability. About half of the children who are disadvantaged live in single-parent families, predominantly headed by their mother. There is a relationship between social class and birth rates: for the least advantaged Australians, birth rates may be double those of the more affluent, and average age between generations is almost double for the more affluent than for the least (Hayes, 2008).

Families living with severe financial disadvantage have many other problems. Parental mental ill-health, parental substance abuse, and child-behaviour problems, including developmental delay, are but a few of the characteristics that increase risk of child maltreatment.

Child maltreatment does not occur only in 'poor families'. Maternal depression, especially in the postnatal period, may be associated with a restricted caregiving role that in its extreme falls into the category of child neglect. The longer the maltreatment continues, and the more types of abuse a child is exposed to, the greater the maladjustment and the poorer the outcomes for children (Lamont, 2008). Assessing risk of child maltreatment requires a comprehensive and multidisciplinary approach which is detailed in Carr (2006).

Identifying children at risk: whose responsibility?

In Australia, investigation and assessment of child maltreatment is the function of statutory child-protective services. However, all Australians—communities, organisations and individuals—have a responsibility to protect children. The importance of a concerted approach to child protection is reflected in the *National Framework for Protecting Australia's Children: Protecting Children is Everyone's Business (2009–2020)*. In this document, 'protecting children is not simply a response to possible child abuse or neglect but rather one of promoting the safety and wellbeing of children' (p. 7). The role of adult services or support services is highlighted: services addressing 'domestic violence, substance misuse, mental health, as well as housing, gambling, disability, employment and income support services, need to be more child-focused and responsive to the needs of families' (p. 21). It is contrary to the intention of the *National Framework* to argue that you do not enquire about children or refuse to assess family factors simply because, for example, a woman presents as a client in an adult service. The *National Framework* advocates a shift in thinking by all clinical staff, that a person is always considered within his or her social and family context. A clinician will then ask about family, relationships, and children and their welfare.

The *National Framework* is intended to provide an overarching framework to guide all Australians to help children and young people to remain safe and well. The goal is to make a substantial and sustained reduction in child abuse and neglect.

Confidentiality

Psychologists are also required to comply with the APS *Code of Ethics*. When considering child abuse and neglect, the *Code* gives clear directions regarding the importance of confidentiality, and stipulates that confidential information may be disclosed '(c) if there is an immediate and specified risk of harm to an identifiable person or persons that can be averted only by disclosing information'.

The APS has also produced *Guidelines on Reporting Abuse and Neglect, and Criminal Activity* (June 2010) for psychologists regarding disclosure of information about risk of harm to children and others (APS Guidelines 2.1; see <http://www.psychology. org.au/Assets/Files/EG-Reporting-child.pdf>). These Guidelines are subsidiary to the *Code*, and must be read and interpreted in conjunction with the *Code*. A psychologist may report abuse and neglect if he or she has a reasonable belief or suspicion that a child is in need of protection. Section 3.6 of the Guidelines states that such a belief may be formed when:

- a child states that he or she has been physically injured or sexually abused;
- a relative, friend, acquaintance, or sibling of the child states that the child has been physically injured or sexually abused; or
- professional observations of the child's behaviour or development lead the psychologist to form a belief that the child has been physically injured or sexually abused, or to form a belief that there has been a failure to provide for the shelter, safety, supervision, or nutritional needs of the child.

Mandatory reporting

There is considerable variability across jurisdictions whether psychologists are mandated to report suspected child abuse and neglect. Psychologists as an occupational group are mandated to report suspected child abuse and neglect in South Australia (*Children's Protection Act* 1993) and Tasmania (*Children, Young Persons and Their Families Act* 1997). All residents of Northern Territory, including psychologists, are mandated to report (*Community Welfare Act* 1983). Psychologists who are working in an occupational group that has mandated reporting requirements are also required to report suspected child abuse and neglect in certain states. For example, in New South Wales, school counsellors are mandated to report under the *Children and Young Persons (Care and Protection) Act* 1998. Even if reporting is not mandated, psychologists are required to comply with the *Code of Ethics*.

You should be familiar with the notification process for your jurisdiction. Each state government department overseeing child protection has information on its website about the process of making a Notification or Child Concern Report. Across all jurisdictions, the identity of the person making the notification is protected. There may be times when you do not discuss with your client that a notification is going to be made; for example, if you have a reasonable belief that a parent may leave the residence with a child if he or she is told that a notification is going to be made. However, there are many occasions when discussing child-protection concerns can be done sensitively and without a major disruption to the therapeutic relationship. Working collaboratively with child-protective services is possible, and in the best interests of the child.

PROCESS ISSUES IN RISK ASSESSMENT

- No matter what the risk situation, err on the side of caution, and carefully assess all potential risks.
- Always act within the *Code of Ethics* and other relevant professional guidelines, such as the *Psychology Board of Australia Guidelines on Mandatory Reporting*.
- Make all possible attempts to get support from a supervisor, mentor, or line manager in making decisions that could have serious implications for the safety of clients and others.

- Risk management is often stressful for the practitioner, so make sure you debrief and get support.

CONCLUSION

We have discussed a range of methods for the assessment and management of clients at risk of suicide, harming others, and harm from others, in domestic violence situations, and children at risk of maltreatment. Many adults and children are at risk of harm from others, and sometimes from themselves. If you are aware of such risk, it is your professional duty to protect clients and others to the best of your ability.

Recommended reading

Australian Psychological Society (2005). *Guidelines for Working with People Who Pose a High Risk of Harming Others*. Melbourne: Australian Psychological Society.

Australian Psychological Society (2004). *Guidelines Relating to Suicidal Clients*. Melbourne: Australian Psychological Society.

Australian Psychological Society (2010). *Guidelines on Reporting Abuse and Neglect, and Criminal Activity*. Melbourne: Australian Psychological Society.

Part D

Professional practice in the Australian context

Chapter 17

Professional training and development

INTRODUCTION

The purpose of this chapter is to provide you with an overview of topics relevant to your development as a practising professional in psychology. The work of the *Psychology Board of Australia (PsyBA)*, the *Australian Psychological Society (APS)*, and the *Australian Psychological Accreditation Society (APAC)* will be described. Medicare rebates for psychological services and the wide variety of positions available to psychologists are outlined. Because standards, codes, guidelines, requirements, etc., are often revised, we recommend that you visit the website of each key organisation regularly and 'phone as required.

KEY PROFESSIONAL BODIES

Currently, there are two main professional bodies for psychologists in Australia, the Psychology Board of Australia (PsyBA) and the Australian Psychological Society (APS). To work towards becoming a fully-registered psychologist, you have to become provisionally-registered with the Psychology Board of Australia (PsyBA). Although membership of the PsyBA is compulsory for psychologists, membership of the Australian Psychological Society (APS), and other professional bodies, is voluntary.

Psychology Board of Australia

From 1 July 2010, the *Australian Health Practitioner Regulation Agency (AHPRA)* began to oversee the nationwide registration and accreditation of numerous health professions, including psychology. Each profession is governed by a National Board, in psychology's case, the Psychology Board of Australia (PsyBA). The PsyBA is now responsible for the regulation and accreditation of all psychologists in Australia. Registration with the PsyBA is mandatory for psychologists.

National registration means that all psychologists across Australia are now subject to the same guidelines. Before July 2010, registration matters were managed on a state-by-state basis, at times resulting in quite different rules and procedures across states. The PsyBA has undertaken the difficult task of amalgamating the broad-ranging rules of the state boards, as well as the guidelines of the APS and the *Australian Psychology Accreditation Council (APAC)*. The PsyBA is now regularly providing important updates on codes and guidelines via its website <www.psychologyboard.gov.au>.

The main functions of the PsyBA are:

- registering psychologists
- developing standards, codes, and guidelines for the psychology profession
- handling notifications, complaints, investigations, and disciplinary hearings
- assessing overseas-trained practitioners who wish to practise in Australia
- approving accreditation standards and accredited courses of study.

If you are interested in registration as a psychologist, read carefully four sections of the PsyBA website:

- Registration
- Accreditation
- Standards and Guidelines
- Endorsement.

But we will summarise key points in the following sections.

PsyBA registration standards

For information on registration, go to the PsyBA website and read the sections, 'General Registration' and 'Provisional Registration', both of which are under the heading, 'Registration', and 'Registration Standards', which is under the heading, 'Standards and Guidelines'. The requirements that applicants need to meet are defined under 'Registration Standards'. These include:

- *Psychology Criminal History Registration Standard:* the PsyBA requires all applicants to undergo a criminal-history check as part of the registration process. In the event of an applicant or registrant having a criminal history, the PsyBA considers a range of factors in deciding the relevance of this history to his or her practice of the profession. Factors considered include the nature of the offence and likelihood of future threat to a patient.
- *Psychology English Language Skills:* applicants for registration who obtained their qualifications outside of Australia, or did not complete their secondary education in English, must demonstrate sufficient English language skills, as stipulated by the PsyBA.
- *Psychology General Registration Standard:* the qualifications required for full registration—that is, for the PsyBA to award a registrant the title of 'generalist psychologist'—are outlined in following sections.
- *Psychology Recency of Practice:* applicants for registration with the PsyBA, or renewal of registration, must demonstrate engagement in psychological practice in the five years preceding their application. For example, a practitioner returning from a leave of absence of up to five years must provide evidence that he or she has maintained sufficient connection with, and practised recently in, the profession since qualifying or obtaining registration. Individuals applying for provisional registration as higher education psychology students are generally exempt from meeting this standard.
- *Psychology Professional Indemnity Insurance:* the PsyBA requires all practising registered psychologists to hold Professional Indemnity Insurance that meets the Board's standards.

PsyBA codes and guidelines

The 'Codes, Guidelines and Policies' section of the PsyBA website, under the heading, 'Standards and Guidelines', provides guidance to both fully-registered and provisionally-registered psychologists on a range of issues. These include:

- *Psychology guidelines for mandatory notifications of other professionals:* the main purpose of this guideline is to protect the public and clients from practitioners who are behaving in ways that may cause harm. Under section 39 of the *Health Practitioner Regulation National Law Act* 2009 (National Law), there is an obligation on 'any practitioner or employer who forms a reasonable belief that another practitioner has engaged in a notifiable conduct to make a report to the National Agency as soon as practicable'. This Act covers all practitioners who are in one of the boards that are part of AHPRA, including psychologists. 'Notifiable conduct' by a practitioner includes placing the public at risk of harm by practising while intoxicated by alcohol or other drugs, engaging in sexual misconduct in connection with practice, practising with a physical or mental impairment that affects practice, and practising in a manner that is a significant departure from accepted professional standards. Section 237 of the National Law provides protection to those making a complaint if the complaint is made in a well-intentioned manner without malice.
- *Guidelines for Continuing Professional Development (CPD)*: to maintain registration, psychologists must participate in a range of professional-development activities, including active development and peer consultation. The rationale for CPD and specific requirements are outlined on the PsyBA website.
- *Guidelines on psychology area of practice endorsements:* psychologists who have completed postgraduate training, and thus have additional qualifications and advanced practice in an area of practice (including, if required, additional supervision after completing the postgraduate degree and becoming a registrar), can be granted an endorsement on their registration. These psychologists can then be identified as having qualifications and skills to practise in the endorsed area.

There are nine areas of endorsed practice for psychologists: clinical psychology, counselling psychology, forensic psychology, clinical neuropsychology, organisational psychology, sport and exercise psychology, health psychology, community psychology, and educational and developmental psychology. These areas reflect the nine specialist APS colleges. On the PsyBA website, under 'Endorsement', you will find information on how to obtain and maintain endorsement in one or more of the specialist areas.

All psychologists, whether fully- or provisionally-registered, need to be familiar with all the PsyBA guidelines and codes.

At this time, the Board has adopted the APS *Code of Ethics*, and this is also on the PsyBA website.

The 'News' section of the website will also be of interest. Posted there are various useful documents, among them Board communiqués, minutes of Board meetings, reminders of information sessions that are hosted by the Board, and consultation papers. The Board encourages feedback on consultation papers; this is an opportunity for you to participate in the decision-making for the professional practice of psychology in Australia.

Australian Psychological Society

Another well-established source of information for psychologists is the *Australian Psychological Society (APS)* website, which can be found at <www.psychology.org.au>. Like the PsyBA, the APS is a national organisation for psychologists, although membership with the APS is not compulsory for registration as a psychologist. The APS is Australia's largest professional association for psychologists, and, as stated on its website, aims to 'represent, promote and advance psychology within the context of improving community wellbeing and scientific knowledge'. It is possible to become a student member of the APS while still in training. The APS website contains many useful links for members and non-members.

Available to non-members are:

- Information about the *Australian Psychological Accreditation Council (APAC)*, which sets the standards for accreditation of Australian psychology programs, and provides information on undergraduate, Honours, and postgraduate courses at each university. Accreditation guidelines for all training courses are provided, so that prospective students are aware of what should be contained in courses.
- tip sheets on a variety of psychological problems
- position papers on a range of psychological topics.

Available to members only:

- *The APS Code of Ethics and Ethical Guidelines:* this provides greater detail on ethical practice, and includes papers on subjects such as supervision
- psychological publications and academic resources.

APS colleges

APS members with relevant specialist training and qualifications can join one of nine colleges. Each APS college is maintained and regulated by a national committee, and individuals can join at varying grades of membership. More information on the nine colleges is available on the APS website <www.groups.psychology.org.au/colleges>.

Australian Psychological Accreditation Council (APAC)

If you pursue postgraduate training in psychology, completing your studies in an accredited program is essential. APAC sets national standards for the education and training of psychologists, and regularly assesses courses to make sure they are meeting accreditation requirements. Their website is <www.psychologycouncil.org.au>.

Membership of voluntary professional bodies

There are other professional bodies specifically for clinical psychologists. The Australian College of Clinical Psychologists (ACCP) started in 1981; in 2010, the Australian Clinical Psychology Association (ACPA) was established (see <www.acpa.org.au>). Both organisations provide opportunities for students to become members.

MEDICARE FOR PSYCHOLOGICAL SERVICES

In November 2006, Medicare rebates became available for psychological services. This was a most important change for the profession of psychology, and has led to a dramatic increase in the number of psychologists in private practice. It has also offered access to psychological services to many more Australians. Psychologists need to be registered with Medicare and need to obtain a provider number for each place in which they see patients.

POSITIONS AVAILABLE TO PSYCHOLOGISTS

Psychologists have become sought after as their skills have increasingly been recognised in the workplace. The recent changes to Medicare put clinical psychology very much on the career map. A quick look at the latest APS *PsychXChange* (a jobseeking website for psychologists) revealed 68 psychology positions, including: Clinical or Counselling Psychologist–Private Practice; Program Senior Clinical Psychologist Grade 4; Senior Job Capacity Assessor; Aboriginal Child & Family Violence Counsellor (Specialising in Sexual Assault); Family Services Coordinator; Parentslink Coordinator; Psychology Lecturers; Mental Health Trainer; Research Psychologist; Director of Psychology Services; Psychologist, Family Planning Queensland Child & Family Sexual Assault Service; Psychologist (Child and Adolescent); Psychologist (Intensive Behaviour Support Team); Senior Clinical Psychologist; Grade 3 Clinical Neuro Psychologist; EAP Consultant; Student & Family Counsellor; Trauma Psychologist; Consultant Psychologist; and Manager, Counselling Services. This site is but one source of information about psychology positions; options are varied and plentiful.

Psychologists are paid at a varying rate, depending on level of training and experience, employer, position, private practice, area of specialty, sector, and, perhaps to a lesser extent, geographic location.

CONCLUSION

Since the advent of a national registration system, how an individual becomes a registered psychologist has changed significantly. Since the advent of the national registration board, PsyBA, the training and practice of psychologists has changed significantly. More than ever it is vital that psychologists maintain professional development and supervision throughout their careers.

Recommended websites
Psychology Board of Australia <www.psychologyboard.gov.au>
The Australian Psychological Society <www.psychology.org.au>
The Australian Psychology Accreditation Council <www.psychologycouncil.org.au>
Medicare related information <www.health.gov.au/epc/> <www.medicareaustralia.gov.au>

Chapter 18

Supervision

Introduction

There are a number of sources of learning you can access while in training. Although coursework may be the most obvious example, many if not most psychologists say, 'The two things I learnt the most from were my clients and my supervision'. Supervised practice of working with clients is a powerful learning tool as it links psychological knowledge, skills and experience, and actual practice. Many psychologists never forget the relationships they formed with effective supervisors (or, unfortunately, relationships with poor supervisors), while other aspects of training tend to become less salient with time. It is essential that you ensure optimal supervision. The following sections will assist you to understand the minimum to expect from supervision, your supervisor's role, and your responsibilities to ensure you receive the best possible supervision.

A collaborative relationship

For supervision to be effective, supervisor and supervisee must contribute toward the supervisory relationship and the progress of supervision. Michael Carroll (1996), one of the most influential contributors to the area, suggests that the relationship is best viewed as a collaborative one in which both parties take responsibility for a positive outcome. In this way, the supervisory relationship can be thought of as a 'learning partnership.'

There are numerous advantages for supervisees in a collaborative supervisory relationship, including:

- The adoption of a proactive attitude generally leads to more proactive learning styles, which tend to result in deeper learning. This is obviously an advantage for supervisees when working with clients.
- Such a relationship encourages autonomy and taking responsibility for learning. Supervisees who adopt a more dependent style are likely to view the supervisory relationship as one in which the supervisor has the main responsibility for their development as a clinician, and they risk achieving less competence.
- This relationship will probably increase the level of open communication, which will decrease problems in the supervisory alliance. Supervisees who feel

that the supervisory relationship is collaborative are likely to experience less anxiety about being assertive, or about disclosing difficulties they are having with clients.

- Such a relationship may decrease tension for the supervisee between being in the 'lead' role in therapy and then being in more of a 'follower' role in supervision. How you might integrate being a 'leader' in therapy and a 'follower' in supervision will be discussed more fully later in this chapter.

Advantages for supervisors of a collaborative relationship include the likelihood of a better supervisory alliance, more open disclosure from the supervisee, and a more rapid move toward independence and effective practice.

Intentional adult learners

Effective learning is best based on an *adult-learning model*. Adult learners choose to be learners, and most importantly, take responsibility for their own learning. Supervision requires discussion, sharing the journey, reflecting in safety, finding one's own voice to articulate views, being respected, recognising how much you actually know, and increasing autonomy.

Exercise 18.1

1   Before you started any supervision, how did you view your role and position as a supervisee? (If you have not yet started, how do you view your role when you become a supervisee?)
2   What did you imagine the supervisory relationship would be like? Did you think it would be collaborative or more directive?
3   Has this view changed? If so, what factors influenced the change?
4   To what extent do you think you are an adult learner?
5   How well does your current supervision arrangement encourage you as an adult learner? If not much, what can you do to improve this?

RESPONSIBILITIES OF SUPERVISORS AND SUPERVISEES

Here are some of the main responsibilities of each partner in supervision, based on APS documents and the literature on supervision, including Carroll and Gilbert (2006).

Supervisor responsibilities

Supervisors need to:

- make judgments about the supervisee's competency and be alert to issues as they arise. The supervisee is to be fully informed, in a timely manner, of the supervisor's views on his or her practice

- maintain supervisee confidentiality where possible, and inform supervisees if details of their practice and performance will be shared, with whom and when. Supervisors will refrain from making intemperate criticism of supervisees
- have competence in areas claimed as having competence, including knowledge and skills
- explain the process of supervision, including what processes or options are available to the supervisee if there are problems in supervision
- maintain professional boundaries. Part of this will be to explain the difference between therapy and supervision. Your supervisor needs to raise personal issues with you if such issues are affecting your practice, but it is not his or her role to provide ongoing therapy
- with the supervisee, establish a supervisory contract that may be updated during supervision
- be consistently available to the supervisee as arranged, and during times of client crises
- ensure that the supervisee has knowledge of the *Code of Ethics* and expected professional practice
- pitch supervision at a level appropriate to the supervisee's ability, and regularly revise input to ensure maximum learning
- regularly conduct formal evaluations of the supervisee's work, and request evaluation of the supervisor's own performance
- be vigilant regarding well-being of clients
- if secondary supervisors are involved, clarify roles and responsibilities
- if fees are to be paid, make arrangements before supervision starts
- check the supervisee's paperwork and sign supervisor notes if satisfied.

Castonguay and colleagues (2010) provide an interesting overview of what needs to be covered in supervision

> Clinical supervisors need to help trainees to know themselves, such as their strengths, limitations, interpersonal vulnerabilities, and countertransferential blind spots. Moreover, they need to develop the ability to monitor the impact of their internal experience, especially their hostile and negative feelings, on the therapeutic relationship (p. 40).

Supervisee responsibilities
Supervisees need to:

- have full knowledge of the APS *Code of Ethics*
- contribute toward the planning of supervision, which could include the initial contract, determining goals for each session, and organising other practical details, such as when, where, and how often to meet
- take responsibility for their own learning, and obtain set goals for supervision and professional development. This will include preparing for each supervision session by putting together case summaries to enable succinct presentations of the most essential information, setting agendas for what needs to be covered in a

supervision session, and bringing any documentation (including videos) for discussion and viewing

- reflect on their professional practice, and monitor and evaluate their own work
- seek assistance and advice from the supervisor where necessary, ensuring that they are supported in providing the most optimal service to clients
- openly disclose concerns about clients or other areas of clinical practice
- discuss with the supervisor what their supervisory needs are. If your supervisor is giving too little direction, for example, then raise the matter. Your supervisor cannot guess what you need—be assertive in expressing the assistance you would like
- in the event of problems occurring in supervision, refrain from making intemperate criticism that could cast doubt on the supervisor's professional competence. Attempts should be made to sort out problems with the supervisor first, using assertive and honest discussion. If this fails, you may need to contact another appropriate person, such as your course convener (if doing postgraduate training) or a colleague. Supervisees may also contact the Australian Psychology Board (PsyBA) for advice
- maintain records of supervision sessions that are clear, sufficiently detailed, and completed in a timely manner
- maintain appointments, and keep to time
- use supervision time effectively
- create ethical and professional environments for your work.

The supervisee as client

In the APS *Code of Ethics*, the definition of 'client' is broad and inclusive. The client is any 'party or parties to a psychological service involving teaching, supervision, research, and professional practice in psychology. Clients may be individuals, couples, dyads, families, groups of people, organisations, communities, facilitators, sponsors, or those commissioning or paying for the professional activity'. This definition clearly encompasses supervisees as well as those we have traditionally considered as clients.

While it may initially be a bit odd to think of yourself as a 'client' when you are a provisionally- or perhaps even fully-registered psychologist, it is useful to consider what this means. The ethical guidelines result in all psychologists at some point being a client, for at the very least, all psychologists will attend a training workshop. Being a client means that you have the right to competent professional services; if this does not eventuate, you have the right to complain and have your concerns carefully considered.

Specifically, as a client you have the right to be treated by your supervisor or trainer according to the three general ethical principles (see chapter 2):

- respect (the psychologist or supervisor has respect for the rights and dignity of people)
- propriety (the psychologist or supervisor is responsible and competent)

- integrity (the psychologist or supervisor must have good character and uphold the reputation and standing of the profession).

Carroll and Gilbert (2006), in their 'declaration of supervisee rights', suggest that supervisees have the right to:

- a safe, protected supervisory relationship
- fair and honest evaluations and reports that the supervisee can comment on
- clear and focused constructive feedback
- appeal decisions that the supervisor makes
- his or her own learning style
- negotiate the supervision contract
- mediation if the supervisory relationship breaks down
- respect as a learning professional.

So, how does the supervisee integrate being a *client* and a *psychologist* at the same time? The two roles may seem on the face of it to be incompatible. We suggest that this is not the case, and advise supervisees to be ever mindful of their dual status as both psychologist and client. As a psychologist, the supervisee should aspire to be the best psychologist he or she can be, while taking on board the responsibilities listed above. At the same time, supervisees should consider their rights as a client, and speak up when supervision or training, or any psychological service, is not adequate. Too often supervisees become stuck in the mindset that they cannot challenge their supervisor, express dissatisfaction with supervision, or in any way rock the boat. The common and understandable fear seems to be that the supervisor will fail to take this criticism on board in an appropriate manner. A supervisee may fear that the supervisor will abuse his or her power in some way, which could include giving the supervisee a poor evaluation or even failing them, or in some way negatively influencing their work prospects. These fears were highlighted by a study by O'Donovan and colleagues (2001), which asked provisionally-registered psychologists to state why they failed to report, challenge, or address concerns about supervisors. Typical quotes provided by supervisees were, 'Psychology is a small world', and 'It is too dangerous to cross a supervisor; he could have contacts'.

There is some truth in these statements; in all but the largest metropolitan areas, psychology is indeed a small world. However, this is one of the crucial challenges for the supervisee. Clients should not be treated poorly; psychologists should be made aware if their practice is inadequate or even harmful. Supervisees have the responsibility to ensure that they have adequate supervision to enable them to become an effective psychologist. In both roles, the supervisee must step forward and inform the supervisor of concerns, and if this does not bring positive results, further complaints need to be made. This is a difficult situation, but the responsibility of supervisees is clear: for their own sake and that of their clients, they must raise concerns about ineffective supervision as they arise. Good supervisors will address these concerns and take them seriously, to provide the best service to the supervisee and to the supervisee's clients.

Exercise 18.2

1 Do you agree with the list of responsibilities of supervisors and supervisees? If there are any items you disagree with, what is your view?
2 Are there any items you would add to the list for either supervisor or supervisee?
3 Have you ever received inadequate or harmful supervision? If so, did you challenge your supervisor and ensure that the situation changed? If not, what would you do now, having read the information provided in this section?

WHAT IS 'GOOD ENOUGH' SUPERVISION?

Without a reference point, supervisees may not realise when they are not receiving adequate supervision. 'Good enough' supervision can vary, but should include the following aspects:

- There is a supervisory contract in place that supervisor and supervisee have contributed towards and signed.
- The supervisor meets all the supervisor responsibilities listed above.
- The supervisee can discuss concerns and feelings about supervision with the supervisor without fear of retribution, and with hope that problems can be resolved.
- The supervisor has more of the characteristics of an effective supervisor than those of an ineffective supervisor (see table 18.1).
- The supervisor has greater knowledge and skill than the supervisee, at least in some areas of practice. However, it is impossible for any supervisor to have all the answers. You can't expect supervisors to be all knowing, only that they will tell you if they don't know and help you to find the answer or suggest that you source the answers yourself. This may involve input from an assistant supervisor. Keep in mind that a major purpose of supervision is to assist you to work autonomously once fully registered, and so learning how to solve problems, and to find answers independently, is an important skill.
- Keep in mind that there are relatively few *correct* answers in psychology, and we must all live with ambiguity. A supervisor who professes to know all the answers is providing too simplistic a view of the world.
- The supervisor has the best interests of the supervisee's clients in mind at all times.
- Feedback is constructive, useful, timely, and direct. Supervisees are not left guessing what supervisors think of their practice at any point, and should not be surprised at feedback given at formal evaluation times.
- The supervisee does not dread supervision.
- The supervisee feels respected.

- The supervisee does not consistently feel worse about her- or himself as a result of supervision.
- The supervisee should not feel supervision is unsafe and any need to defend her- or himself.
- The supervisee should not feel any need to manage the supervisor, by withholding the truth, having to compliment the supervisor, or take care not to upset the supervisor. If supervision feels like walking on eggshells, there is a problem.
- The supervisee does not continually second-guess him- or herself in terms of how they feel about supervision. Self-doubt is commonly a sign that there are power issues occurring in supervision.
- It is preferable that the supervisor has had training in being an effective supervisor. Although training in itself may not guarantee 'good enough' supervision, lack of training is likely to mean that the supervisor is simply doing what was done when he or she was a supervisee. A supervisor needs to have been exposed to the knowledge and skills required for adequate supervision.
- The supervisor demonstrates enough enthusiasm and curiosity about the supervisee's practices and clients to indicate to the supervisee that supervision is not simply a nuisance task. A negative attitude towards supervision will result in poor supervision.

Supervisees need to keep in mind that this list is intended to assist in judging how well supervision is going. However, supervision is a two-way street, and it is also the supervisee's responsibility to ensure a collaborative supervisory relationship.

O'Donovan and colleagues (2001) investigated supervisees' perceptions of supervisors, and asked supervisees to identify what they felt were supervisors' positive and negative characteristics. The results of this enquiry, with some typical quotes from supervisees, are summarised in table 18.1. Look at these characteristics and see if you agree with them.

THE SUPERVISION CONTRACT

At the beginning of supervision, a contract needs to be made. The following issues should be covered in the contract:

- expectations of supervision for both supervisee and supervisor
- shared disclosure provisions regarding such things as practice background, preferred working and learning styles, and theoretical orientations
- the supervisor's expertise, the areas he or she is competent to supervise in, and the areas the supervisee would like to focus on
- a prescribed process for when there are concerns regarding supervision, including conflict-resolution procedures
- the process of feedback regarding the supervisee's practice
- a description of any dual roles and how these will be managed. This is particularly pertinent when the supervisor is also the supervisee's line manager, or if at a university, if the supervisor is one of the training staff or the supervisee's research supervisor
- the responsibilities of both supervisor and supervisee in supervision

- when and where to meet
- method of supervision: individual or group?
- availability and contact details for supervision outside set supervision hours
- if the supervisee is paying for supervision, the cost and how payments are to be made; fees may vary
- the involvement of assistant supervisors if appropriate.

POTENTIALLY PROBLEMATIC ISSUES IN SUPERVISION

In an ideal world, supervision would meet all your greatest hopes and more. Unfortunately, we know that this is just not the case. In fact 10 per cent of all supervision has been found to be harmful (Ellis, 2001), and it is unknown how much supervision gives an indifferent result. A number of issues may detract from optimal effectiveness, and in this section we will consider some of the most common and potentially damaging ones. The steps the supervisee can take to try to resolve these problems will be addressed in a subsequent section.

Interpersonal relationship issues

It is a simple fact of life that not everyone gets along. A supervisory relationship in which there are interpersonal tensions is likely to cause stress, which may detract from the effectiveness of supervision. Sometimes, in supervision, people do not connect well because they hold different life values, have different working styles, have incompatible temperaments or personalities, hold different theoretical and/or practice views, and differ on how important they think supervision is.

Such differences can make the relationship difficult, but need not make supervision untenable if supervisor and supervisee recognise them and agree to try to find common ground. The supervisee needs to differentiate between supervisor views and characteristics that are simply not the supervisee's preferred working style, and those that would generally be viewed as deleterious to effective supervision. Supervisees commonly second-guess supervisors' attitudes and behaviours, and this may negatively affect their supervisory experience.

Often, the problem is simply misinterpretation of what is happening in the supervision relationship. The supervisee may become resigned and think, 'It's just me, I should adapt.' Sometimes, this is a good idea; we often learn most from those who are quite different to us. At other times, these differences are such that it is difficult or impossible to create a sound supervisory alliance.

Here are some behavioural indicators of interpersonal difficulties or incompatibility in supervision:

- Do you feel less than enthusiastic when the next session with a particular supervisor draws near?
- Do you think about how much longer you will have to stay in a particular supervisory relationship?
- Do you approach others for supervisory assistance because you prefer to avoid dealing with many issues with your current supervisor?
- Do you regret being in your current supervisory relationship?

Your answers to these questions may indicate that you are not satisfied in your current supervisory situation, and should examine it more closely. Ask these questions of your own supervision relationship, and consider whether any action needs to be taken.

Exercise 18.3

1   What interpersonal difficulties have you experienced with supervisors? Is there a pattern, or are difficulties specific to an individual supervisor?
2   If there is a pattern, is there anything about you that may be contributing to interpersonal difficulties? For example, are your expectations of supervision too high? How may your behaviour in supervision be contributing to problems?
3   Where would you go to get support if you experienced problems in supervision?

Conflict in supervision alliance

The literature suggests that 'the work of supervision may hinge on two fundamental supervisory competencies: the ability to establish strong alliances with trainees and the ability to manage interpersonal conflicts in supervision' (Nelson et al., 2001; p. 408). Problems which may result in conflicts in the alliance include:

* misunderstandings or disagreements about the goals or tasks of intervention
* difficult clients, which may result in both supervisor and supervisee feeling somewhat overwhelmed by the client's demands and perhaps unsure of how to proceed
* supervisor expectations that are not appropriate to the developmental level of the supervisee. Beginning trainees often lack the necessary clinical knowledge, spend a lot of time on individual clients, and tend to want more direction from a supervisor. More advanced trainees tend to have stronger personal views, and supervisor and supervisee may disagree about issues such as strategies for intervention and theoretical considerations
* evaluation may often be a source of rupture in the supervisory alliance, as fears and unresolved issues often become exacerbated during these periods.

If the supervisor is sensitive to the needs of the supervisee, the supervisor will often be the first to raise possible ruptures in the alliance. Repairing ruptures tends to strengthen the supervisory relationship (as it does in therapy). Thus, problems should not be avoided; if not raised by the supervisor, the supervisee should raise concerns.

Exercise 18.4

Have you experienced a rupture in supervision? If so, what happened, and what did you learn from the experience?

Table 18.1   Positive and negative characteristics of supervisors

Positive characteristics	Negative characteristics
Supportive and caring Includes being helpful; empathy; acknowledging the supervisee; providing a safe environment; attentive; concerned for supervisee's well-being personally and pedagogically; interested in the supervisee	**Lack of support and caring** Includes not caring about the supervisee; being cold and uninterested; discouraging and disparaging; inaccessible; not knowing where supervisee is up to; not giving guidance; 'he doesn't give a stuff about me'
Trust Arises from such factors as feeling liked and respected; feeling safe to disclose and explore; how comfortable the supervisee feels with the supervisor as a person; and the supervisor's perceived interest and care in the supervisee as a person	**Lack of trust** Supervisees did not trust supervisors who were seen as rigid, controlling, defensive, hostile, put the supervisee down, were uninterested, did not seem to care, discouraged exploration by the supervisee, and were unavailable. Some supervisees actually felt threatened by the supervisor in some way (through over-intrusiveness, or lack of certainty of being passed)
Availability Provision of additional time if needed; feeling welcomed and not as though they were 'interrupting' the supervisor; enough time to discuss issues to such a point that the supervisee feels confident and comfortable; the covert message that the supervisee matters to the supervisor	**Lack of availability** Failure to provide the full supervision time, and taking phone calls while in supervision. Consequences included feeling unimportant to the supervisor, lack of confidence and direction, and that the supervisor is not interested in the clients or the supervisee
Respect Supervisees felt respected when the supervision relationship was perceived as collegial and equal, their opinions were sought after and valued, and the supervisor was non-patronising. Supervisors who were seen as open and non-defensive, and gave supervisees autonomy, were perceived as more respectful	**Lack of respect** Did not value supervisees' opinions; were seen as controlling, rigid, and defensive; were not open to negotiation or discussion; the supervisor's agenda was central; the supervisees were of little importance
Breadth of experience and knowledge Supervisors who were perceived as having extensive knowledge and experience would be admired, and supervisees would trust their ability to provide useful advice. Going beyond the confines of particular theories was valued. Being viewed as professional was based on both knowledge and skills, and also on how effective they were as supervisors	**Lack of experience and knowledge** Supervisors who did not see clients themselves, had a poor reputation in the community, and were seen to be poor therapists and poor supervisors, were seen as unprofessional. Being out of date and failure to show a clear theoretical structure or conceptualisation skills (irrespective of what their theory was) were also perceived negatively
Personal connection Being comfortable with the supervisor as a person; 'clicking' as people; would like to be like the supervisor; working collaboratively; getting along well; developing a personal relationship	**Poor personal connection** A lack of connectedness; having no personal relationship, because of supervisors' apparent lack of interest in supervisees, supervisors' self-centeredness or defensiveness; simply not hitting it off
Effective challenging Challenge seen as positive but not necessarily liked, particularly regarding personal issues ('some challenges are very uncomfortable because you feel vulnerable'). Intellectual challenge is important and stimulating	**Negative challenging** Whether challenge was positive was dependent on how effective the supervisor was in terms of other issues, such as support and caring, and providing positive feedback and respect. Without these qualities, challenging was seen negatively, more threatening than stimulating

Table 18.1   Positive and negative characteristics of supervisors (continued)

Positive characteristics	Negative characteristics
Effective feedback and communication Good feedback was nonjudgmental, pitched at the right level ('not expecting too much from me'), finding alternative ways to explain until understood, mutual, empathic. Feedback was 'to help, not to put me down' and 'a two-way process'. If the feedback was good, supervisees would 'act on the feedback', 'internalise it', and 'work harder, put in more effort'	**Poor communication and negative feedback** Little or no feedback resulting in 'no sense of my own efficacy', no indication of supervisee's ability or what to work on. Destructive feedback resulted in poor self-esteem and self-efficacy. Excessively positive feedback (to the exclusion of critical feedback) was also disliked, as it did not help learning and was at times mistrusted
Clarity and consistency of communication Supervisors clarified expectations and were consistent regarding requests and directions. This was aided by keeping notes	**Lack of consistency** Contradictory messages are very frustrating for supervisees, particularly when asked why they did something suggested by the supervisor the week before!
Likable Characteristics of liked supervisors included being warm, caring, approachable, friendly, accepting, open, flexible, easygoing, honest, respectful, genuine, polite, humorous, encouraging, sensitive, thoughtful, enthusiastic, curious, and insightful	**Not likable** Characteristics of disliked supervisors included being self-interested, egocentric, arrogant, using people and lacking respect for others, passive-aggressive, defensive, insecure, not at ease with self, 'mentally sloppy', overly zealous, ineffectual ('lacks a backbone'), empty, inauthentic, deceptive, portraying a false image, image conscious, lacking self-awareness

Source: O'Donovan et al. (2001)

Concerns about disclosure in supervision

Difficulties and tensions with a supervisor can cause distress for a supervisee, and influence not only the extent of supervisory effectiveness, but ultimately the supervisee's professional practice. Of course, a poor supervisory relationship is likely to result in a lack of disclosure by supervisees, limiting the supervisor's ability to guide practice adequately.

There are several reasons why supervisees may not disclose fully in supervision, including:

• *Supervision does not seem 'safe':* the supervisee may feel denigrated or neglected, and/or afraid of further criticism
• *There is a lack of trust that the supervisor could help:* the supervisee may have concluded that the supervisor does not have the necessary knowledge or skills to adequately assist with client issues
• *There is a lack of awareness that some issues should be disclosed:* at times, supervisees lack the knowledge to judge which issues are important to effective treatment of the client, and may simply omit to mention these. Omissions could include important diagnostic information, or important historical data. It is also common for the supervisee not to pick up important process issues that are affecting treatment, particularly when there are ruptures in the treatment alliance

- *There can be embarrassment about mistakes:* supervisees may be reluctant to mention mistakes they have made because of the fear of appearing incompetent.

As this list shows, nondisclosure can occur for reasons besides the supervisee having some kind of negative reaction towards the supervisor (the most common cause). In most cases, it is up to the supervisee to identify and address the reason for nondisclosure: is it a problem with the supervisory relationship, or a result of the supervisee's own concerns? It is difficult for supervisors to pick up on nondisclosure unless they are directly observing therapy sessions. If the reason for nondisclosure is lack of awareness by the supervisee, direct observation is most likely the only way in which this will become apparent. Hopefully, such lack of awareness will become less of a problem with greater experience, although it should be noted that even experienced therapists miss important information in therapy.

A recent Australian study (O'Donovan et al., 2010) examined differences in disclosure by supervisees when providing feedback directly to supervisors, rather than providing feedback confidentially. As part of a program to train supervisors, supervisors had to provide feedback from a supervisee regarding satisfaction with supervision. Supervisors provided an eight-item *Supervisory Satisfaction Questionnaire (SSQ)* to their supervisees, who filled this in and returned it to the supervisor. At a later date, a random sample of supervisees was contacted by the program. Each supervisee was asked to re-rate his or her supervisor on the same eight items; supervisees were ensured confidentiality.

Five of the eight items were scored significantly differently when supervisees knew that their supervisor would not know what they had said. 95 per cent of supervisees told their supervisor they would definitely recommend him or her to someone else. However, when asked confidentially, only 63 per cent said they would definitely recommend the supervisor. None of the supervisees had told their supervisor that they would not recommend them, and yet over 8 per cent said they would not when asked confidentially. Similarly, none of the supervisees had indicated on the measure that they knew their supervisor would see that they would not return to the supervisor at the end of the contract, if given a chance. When asked confidentially, 22 per cent said they would not return to the supervisor, if given a chance!

The question is: are supervisees regularly not forthright with their supervisors on all issues, or is it simply too difficult to give supervisors directly honest answers to questions such as those asked on the SSQ? The issue of disclosure in supervision is a vexing one, as effective supervision and the strength of the supervisory alliance rest largely on open disclosure—and yet, this seems so difficult to achieve.

Exercise 18.5

1 Think about an example of where you chose not to disclose information about your client-related practice to your supervisor. Why did you not disclose?
2 What would have to have been different for you to disclose this information?

3   Do you think there are any important issues that you would generally be unlikely to disclose to your supervisor? If so, are there any factors about your supervisory relationship that would make it more or less likely that you do so?

4   Have any of your non-disclosures had negative consequences for your clients?

Supervisee anxiety

Supervision, no matter how supportive, will result in some anxiety for many supervisees. There are a number of reasons for this: the importance placed on being an effective clinician; fear of being inadequate; having one's work closely scrutinised and possibly receiving negative feedback; being unfamiliar with the process, the supervisor, and expectations; and individual differences in trait-anxiety levels.

Although it is hardly surprising that most neophyte supervisees will have some anxiety entering supervision, ongoing anxiety can be debilitating for supervision and for clinical practice. Most supervisors are happy to discuss supervisee anxiety; raise the issue. Remember, anxiety tends to reduce with exposure to the feared situation. If having your work closely scrutinised causes you anxiety, then consistently submitting your work for scrutiny should cause your anxiety to lessen. If you do not expose yourself to what is causing you anxiety in supervision, the anxiety will not diminish, and this will ultimately be detrimental to your clients.

Exercise 18.6

1   On a scale of 1 to 10, how anxious were you when you first started supervision?
2   What were you most anxious about?
3   On the same scale, how anxious are you now in supervision, on average?
4   Is this level of anxiety acceptable, or is it interfering with your well-being and/or practice?

Power differences

Power differences are inherent in the supervision relationship, largely because of the evaluatory role of the supervisor. Other factors, such as the relative status of supervisor to supervisee, may also contribute to power differences. By definition, supervisors need to have greater experience and knowledge than supervisees, and hold final control over supervisees' work. Although supervisees are encouraged to work independently, and to take responsibility for their practice, when there is any risk to a client, responsibility resides with the supervisor, particularly when supervisees are provisionally-registered.

Supervisees are the lynchpin between supervision and practice. As such, they experience frequent shifts in power and responsibility. When a therapist is dealing with a client, it is the therapist who is traditionally considered as holding the more powerful role (although there is debate about this issue in terms of treatment effectiveness). The therapist is expected to be responsible for designing and implementing treatment programs and for the overall process of client change. When that same therapist becomes a supervisee, a shift occurs, and he or she is now the less powerful member of a dyad. A supervisee, particularly a beginning supervisee, may be expected to defer to the supervisor's judgment regarding best practice. This constantly shifting power and responsibility dynamic can be difficult for supervisees to manage.

How difficult this dynamic can be to manage largely depends on the extent to which supervisee and supervisor have established a collaborative rather than a power-based relationship. Power differences become more salient when:

- there is disagreement between supervisor and supervisee about treatment of clients
- the supervisee's clinical practice is being evaluated
- there are dual relationships (when there is a friendship between supervisee and supervisor, or supervision becomes more therapeutic, or the supervisee is also a research assistant for the supervisor)
- the supervisor abuses his or her power by doing such things as intimidating the supervisee
- the supervisee wants more autonomy in decision-making and practice than the supervisor will allow. Sometimes, this problem is reversed, with the supervisee feeling that the supervisor allows too much autonomy when the supervisee wants greater direction.

The APS *Guidelines for Managing Professional Boundaries* (2008) provide useful information about risks of misuse of power by supervisors. The guidelines state: 'Psychologists [must] avoid therapy, intimate relationships and business ventures with supervisees.' In academic settings, where supervisees can also be research assistants, supervisors must be careful that the RA role does not interfere with the supervisee's training commitments by placing unreasonable demands on the student. In all cases of dual relationships, clarify expectations of all work relationships with supervisees in contracts.

Exercise 18.7

1   Are you aware of power differences in your current supervisory relationship?
2   Describe the nature of power differences, and how they affect you and your work.
3   Is the transition from therapist to supervisee facilitated comfortably in your supervision?

Dual relationships in supervision

Dual relationships include any type of relationship between supervisee and supervisor that is not strictly for the purpose of supervision. In this section, we will focus on the boundary between supervision and therapy, as this can be particularly problematic, and it is not always obvious when this boundary is crossed.

When it appears that personal issues may be interfering with competent practice, the supervisor needs to raise the issue with the supervisee, clearly explaining what the issue is and why it appears to be problematic. The next step is to deal with the issue, and this is where difficulties often arise. While the supervisor may be an experienced therapist, it is not the supervisor's role to provide therapy for the supervisee. The following steps are recommended to be followed by the supervisor:

- It must be made clear at the beginning of supervision, in the contract, that if the supervisee's personal issues or characteristics appear to have a negative impact on his or her professional practice, the supervisor has a responsibility to alert the supervisee.
- The supervisor must point out to the supervisee, in clear operationalised terms, how practice is being affected by his or her behaviour.
- The supervisor needs to state the issue in a neutral manner, without raising pejorative interpretations of the supervisee's behaviour.
- If the issue can be resolved without therapeutic intervention within supervision, this is done. It is appropriate for supervisors to deal directly with the blocks, defences, or emotional vulnerabilities of a supervisee by discussing how they are affecting intervention with clients.
- If it becomes evident to both supervisor and supervisee that more indepth discussion will be necessary, it is best to suggest that the supervisee seek the help of an external therapist. The supervisor may be able to suggest an appropriate therapist.
- At times, the process of treatment itself will result in issues, such as subclinical trauma from dealing with traumatic clinical cases. The supervisor needs to be alert to such professional hazards and raise them if they occur.

The role of the supervisee in such a situation is:

- To be open to the supervisor's feedback. It is not easy to hear that one's personal issues or characteristics may be affecting practice, but we cannot allow a personal issue to interfere with our practice.
- To seek professional support if issues require it.
- To assess potential effect on clients. In some cases, it may mean taking a break from practice until issues are resolved.

Exercise 18.8

1   Has a supervisor raised an issue personal to you? If so, what was the experience like?
2   How was the issue resolved?

FEEDBACK AND EVALUATION PROCESSES

In supervision, the process of feedback and evaluation is often tricky. There are a number of issues to keep in mind:

1 *What should be evaluated?* Supervisees need to know exactly what they need to do to pass a placement. Generally, it is clinical competencies that are assessed (for example, report writing, relationship skills, ethics, and knowledge). However, increasingly it is being recognised that the most important measure of effectiveness is client outcome.

2 *Sources of evaluation* include self-report by the supervisee, direct observation of practice by the supervisor or another observer (for example, by using videos), client feedback, and reports from other staff or the client's family. Written work is also used, reports, letters to third parties, and chart entries. It has been found that supervisee self-report tends to be the least accurate method of evaluation, followed by supervisor subjective opinion. Direct client feedback and direct observation of practice have been found to be more accurate sources of information about clinician effectiveness (Bernard & Goodyear, 2004, 2009).

3 Many supervisees struggle with the *different hats* a supervisor has to wear, particularly being a support and mentor and, at the same time, an evaluator. While the supervisor's role is to be supportive and assist the supervisee to work through practice issues, the supervisor also needs to evaluate the supervisee's competence. Understandably, supervisees may perceive a risk in disclosing information that could put their ability in a negative light. However, in a collaborative supervisory relationship, these issues can be discussed and need not be a problem if supervisees' views are respected, there is sufficient trust, and both parties listen well and are assertive and open.

Exercise 18.9

1 How do you think your effectiveness should be evaluated?
2 Have you experienced difficulties in relation to different roles played by your supervisor, in particular, supportive encourager versus evaluator?

HOW TO KNOW WHETHER YOU HAVE A MAJOR PROBLEM IN SUPERVISION

In the previous section, we discussed a number of potential problems in supervision, including conflict over certain issues, supervisee anxiety, lack of disclosure by the supervisee, the possible effects of power differences, and the impact of dual relationships. In our experience, relationship problems are most often managed through avoidance by one party or both. Avoidance may bring short-term relief (reduced anxiety and effort) but, as supervisory relationships tend to be long term, it is rarely a sustainable option.

Remember: supervisory problems will reflect in your practice with clients, and for their sake as well as your own professional development, it is your responsibility to deal with problems in supervision that impact on your learning. If you manage interpersonal conflicts in supervision through avoidance, imagine the counter-transference you will experience when working with an avoidant client!

Because they often lack adequate reference points for what constitutes good or bad supervision, beginning supervisees often doubt their own feelings regarding supervision, and may wonder whether bad supervision is really as bad as it seems. If you are experiencing difficulties in your relationship with your supervisor, we recommend that you check your reactions with the facts:

• Is your supervisor meeting the responsibilities outlined earlier in this chapter?
• Does your supervisor exhibit characteristics that mainly fall in those listed as effective in table 18.1?
• Does your supervision meet most of the criteria listed above for 'good enough' supervision?
• Do you feel safe to discuss your concerns with your supervisor?

If you have answered 'no' to any of these questions, action is most likely required.

Managing supervision problems

In many cases, the problem is lack of a collaborative relationship between supervisee and supervisor. If you find yourself with problems in supervision, here are some strategies that have been found to be helpful:

1 *Self-awareness by the supervisee regarding what the problem is.* Sometimes it is obvious what the problem is, for example, if the supervisor or supervisee consistently turns up late for supervision or misses sessions. Some equally damaging problems may not be obvious, such as the supervisor's consistent but subtle undermining of the supervisee's confidence. The supervisee may feel insecure during supervision, and start to dread going to supervision, but is not sure exactly what the problem is. The first step is for the supervisee to consider the issues, and to get some idea about what the problem is.

2 If the supervisee considers the problem is having an impact, or might have an impact, on the effectiveness of supervision, and is not purely personal, then he or she has several choices:

a An option commonly taken is to not address the issue with the supervisor. Instead, the supervisee can take full responsibility for the problem and blame himself, simmer quietly, having hostile fantasies about the supervisor, or complain to fellow supervisees about his bad luck. This is unlikely to resolve the issue, and could result in an even poorer supervisory relationship.

b Discussion with fellow supervisees can be productive if the person is able to clarify the issue. Sometimes this type of clarification and even debriefing will be sufficient to assist the supervisee to overcome the impasse, and to get a new perspective. The risk is that the supervisee feels better for a short time, having talked about the problem, but that this respite will not result in a change in the situation.

c   The supervisee needs to assess objectively his role in the identified problem. Although it is possible that the problem is one-sided (solely the responsibility of the supervisor), few are. The supervisee needs to consider to what extent he is contributing to the problem and whether he is exaggerating the issue. The supervisee needs to be able to consider what is reasonable to expect from the supervisor.

d   The obvious solution is to raise the concern with the supervisor. The more collaborative the relationship, the easier this will be to do. Some supervision relationships discourage open discussion of concerns. The supervisee does not feel safe to address a problem. The supervisee may fear that the supervisor will become angry, be dismissive of his concern, or inflict greater negative consequences, such as interfering in potential work opportunities. Dual relationships can also limit disclosure. If the supervisee is also a friend of the supervisor, he may withhold feedback for fear of offending someone he likes and putting strain on the friendship. The best outcome from raising an issue is that the supervisor will take on board the feedback, and cooperate in finding a solution.

3   What to do if supervisee and supervisor are unable to work out the issue together:

a   If the supervisee has attempted to discuss the issue with the supervisor and there has been no resolution, the matter would generally be taken to the person who oversees supervision arrangements. This could be the clinic manager or director of the training program. In most cases, it is reasonable that the supervisor is aware that the supervisee is taking this action.

b   While making your supervisor aware of any action you plan to take is considered good professional practice, there are some circumstances in which this is not necessary. In cases of alleged threatening behaviour or sexual harassment, the supervisee will be advised by the convener on how to proceed.

c   If the issue between supervisee and supervisor cannot be resolved, the supervisee may need to be assigned a new supervisor.

Exercise 18.10

1   Have you ever been involved with managing a problem in supervision? If so, describe the issue, and what happened. Was the issue resolved?

2   Do you presently have an issue in supervision you would like to address? If so, how will you go about it? What would an ideal outcome be?

3   What has prevented you from dealing with problems in supervision in the past? What sort of things are likely to prevent you from dealing with problems in the future?

As difficult as it may be, it is your responsibility, as a supervisee, to ensure that you receive effective supervision. If, for whatever reason, your supervision is ineffective, it is your ethical duty to take action.

Exercise 18.11

Watch Video 11, the third part on supervision. You have already been invited to watch the first part of this video, illustrating the consequences of the therapist becoming emotionally reactive to material a client raises in therapy (see chapter 5). Now, please consider the third part of this vignette, in which the therapist receives supervision that explores the therapist's reaction, and encourages insight into the issue and the consequences in therapy, including a loss of empathy.

1   To what extent do you think your own issues interfere in the therapy you do?
2   How well would you manage if your supervisor were to raise these issues?

Practice implications

1   Be familiar with the responsibilities of both supervisors and supervisees, and ensure that you fulfil your responsibilities as a supervisee.
2   Think of yourself as an adult learner, and work with your supervisor to establish a collaborative supervisory alliance.
3   If you have an issue in supervision, discuss it with your supervisor as soon as you recognise it. If this does not work, then discuss it with an appropriate person. Supervision is essential to your effective practice.
4   Use supervision to its full extent: prepare for supervision sessions, disclose openly to your supervisor, ask questions, learn as much as possible.
5   Once fully registered, continue supervision, whether formal or peer supervision.

CONCLUSION

Most early-career trainees indicate that supervision is the most valuable form of learning. Supervisees are advised to participate fully in making the supervision relationship as collaborative and productive as possible. Be aware of what 'good enough supervision' consists of, and what role you can play to enhance supervision. Take responsibility: if supervision is not going as well as it needs to for you to learn and provide the best service to your clients, discuss any issue with your supervisor. Consider supervision a lifelong professional practice—there is never a point at which a practitioner no longer requires supervision.

Recommended reading
Bambling, M. (2000). The effect of clinical supervision on the development of counsellor competency. *Psychotherapy in Australia, 6*(4), 58–63.

Bernard, J. M. & Goodyear, R. K. (2009). *Fundamentals of Clinical Supervision* (4th edn). New Jersey: Pearson Education.

Bradley, L. J. & Ladany, N. (2010). *Counselor Supervision*. Ann Arbor: Brunner-Routledge.

Campbell, J. M. (2000). *Becoming an Effective Supervisor. A Workbook for Counselors and Psychotherapists.* Ann Arbor: Sheridan Books.

Carroll, M. (1996). *Counseling Supervision: Theory, Skills, and Practice.* London: Cassell.

Carroll, M. & Gilbert, M. C. (2006). *On Being a Supervisee. Creating Learning Partnerships.* Melbourne: PsychOz Publications.

Hawkins, P. & Shohet, R. (2012). *Supervision in the Helping Professions.* Milton Keynes: Open University Press.

Piper, M. (2003). *Letters to a Young Therapist.* New York: Basic Books. A delightful book, written by a supervisor for her supervisee, which is a must-read to appreciate the supervisory relationship at its best.

Shohet, R. (2008). *Passionate Supervision.* London: Jessica Kingsley Publishers.

Chapter 19

Self-care

INTRODUCTION

This last chapter will focus on how to maintain your passion for practice and prevent burnout by having good self-care practices.

BURNOUT

Psychology, regardless of specialisation, can be a highly satisfying career. As with any profession, however, there is always the risk of becoming 'burnt out'. This section provides information regarding burnout, its causes, how to identify it, and suggestions for staying satisfied and competent.

What is burnout?

Maslach (1982) defines burnout as 'a response to the chronic emotional strain of dealing extensively with other human beings, particularly when they are troubled or having problems' (p. 8). Baker (2003) has described it as 'the terminal phase of therapist distress' (p. 21). The main components of burnout are emotional exhaustion, depersonalisation, and a reduction of personal accomplishment (Jenaro et al., 2007; Rupert & Morgan, 2005).

Burnout has also been referred to as 'emotional fatigue' or 'emotional overload', which suggests feeling drained, depleted, as if you have nothing left to give others (e.g. Smith & Moss, 2009). *Depersonalisation* can be recognised when psychologists experience a general dislike of others, and even a detached or callous attitude towards people they are supposed to be helping. Clients can become dehumanised in the view of the burnt-out therapist (Jenaro et al., 2007). The therapist tends to have low energy levels, and experiences decreased interest and markedly reduced satisfaction in his or her work. Not surprisingly, many burnt-out therapists come to dread going to work, and may well feel quite ineffectual (Rupert & Morgan, 2005). The reality is that this sense of reduced efficacy is probably accurate; an emotionally fatigued practitioner is unlikely to perform as effectively as a colleague who is not experiencing burnout. Of even greater concern is the burnt-out practitioner who lacks an awareness of his or her reduced functioning; such a practitioner risks doing harm in therapy because the unrealistically favourable self-evaluation reduces his or her perceived need to seek help (Smith & Moss, 2009).

Burnout results not only in reduced work satisfaction and poorer performance, but is related to high rates of depression, drug and alcohol use, relationship problems, and in the worst cases, possibly suicide (Smith & Moss, 2009). And while burnout is a risk in any profession, psychologists and therapists appear to be particularly at risk. As several authors (e.g., Barnett et al., 2007; O'Connor, 2001) have pointed out, there seem to be two major reasons for this. First, psychologists are more likely than the general population to have histories that place them at risk for developing emotional problems. Specifically, psychotherapists are more likely to have experienced a history of childhood abuse, and many also report being *parentified*: having assumed a primary role of parenting in their family of origin (Pope & Feldman-Summers, 1992). Second, it is widely acknowledged that there are factors specific to the role of psychologists that place them at risk for developing problems. Psychotherapists face a higher than average risk of burnout (Weiss, 2004) in part because of their chronic exposure to clients' emotionally arousing material (Canfield, 2005). Psychotherapy is an emotionally demanding profession, and this can take its toll on the helping professional. The interaction between these two risk factors (developmental predisposition plus emotionally demanding job) can be a recipe for burnout.

Such emotionally taxing work all too readily leads to maladaptive coping, exemplified by the finding that 1 in 10 psychologists, including those in master's- and doctorate-level training programs, describe their alcohol use as problematic (Deutsch, 1985; Thoreson et al., 1989). The temptation to self-medicate is understandable, as psychologists rate emotional exhaustion, work-related stress, fatigue, and disillusionment among their greatest personal-distress concerns (Mahoney, 1997). Deutsch found in 1985 that an alarming 57 per cent of master's- and doctorate-level psychotherapists reportedly considered themselves to be depressed; in 2002, Gilroy and colleagues reported that 62 per cent of a sample of counsellors identified themselves as depressed.

These grim statistics underscore the need for psychologists to 'know thy enemy'—by confronting the reality of burnout, and familiarising themselves with its signs, maintaining factors, and prevention. Whether by conducting therapy under the influence of substances, enabling harmful boundary violations with clients, or simply by attempting client work when too distressed to be effective, psychologists are likely to face the end-state of burnout, which is professional impairment (Smith & Moss, 2009).

Identifying burnout
Burnout has significant potential to compromise psychologists, personally and professionally, impeding capacity to function effectively across several important domains. It is of vital importance, and in your clients' best interests, that you familiarise yourself with the risk factors and warning signs of burnout. It is sobering to realise how often psychologists practise when they should take time out. Some studies have found that as many as 60 per cent of practising psychologists have

worked when they thought they may have been too distressed to be really effective (Pope et al., 1987).

Factors commonly linked to heightened burnout risk include:

- younger psychologists are at higher risk (Rupert & Morgan, 2005)
- vicarious traumatisation and secondary traumatic stress (Baird & Kracen, 2006; Canfield, 2005):
  - are most likely for therapists treating PTSD (Baird & Kracen, 2006)
  - are more common in female psychologists who have greater contact with sexual abuse survivors and greater exposure to graphic details of abuse (Brady et al., 1999)
  - are more likely if a therapist has a personal trauma history (Pearlman & Ian, 1995)
  - are likely if a therapist has a personal history and motivations for entering the profession (O'Connor, 2001).
- poor client outcomes (Barnett & Cooper, 2009)
- high work load (Demerouti et al., 2001)
- inadequate professional resources (Demerouti et al., 2001).

Even therapists who do not have these risk factors remain vulnerable to compassion fatigue, because of the nature of psychological work. All therapists should therefore familiarise themselves with the common signs of burnout:

- irritability, decreased patience (Mahoney, 1997)
- doubting one's own therapeutic success, decreased confidence (Mahoney, 1997)
- reduced energy, fatigue (Gilroy et al., 2002), and exhaustion (Demerouti et al., 2001)
- impaired concentration (Gilroy et al., 2002)
- feelings of grief, anger, sorrow, hypervigilance, or numbing (symptoms associated with vicarious traumatisation) (Baird & Kracen, 2006; Canfield, 2005)
- increased substance use
- job detachment, disengagement (Demerouti et al., 2001)
- reduced quantity and quality of work (Boisaubin & Levine, 2001)
- disillusionment (Mahoney, 1997).

Research has also shed light on factors that are most likely to maintain burnout:

- the culture of the discipline: from training onward, psychotherapists are not encouraged to express self-doubt, but to maintain a competent façade (O'Connor, 2001)
- fear of the negative consequences of confrontation to oneself and one's colleagues (Floyd et al., 1998)
- lack of knowledge about how to deal with a colleague's impairment (Sherman, 1996)
- isolation as a result of professional independence
- avoidant coping, such as substance use (Deutsch, 1985; Thoreson et al., 1989), burying oneself in work, and hoping the problem will go away (Sherman, 1996)
- feelings of personal invulnerability: a professional blind spot (Barnett, 2008)

- self-neglect, which can be facilitated by a stance of attending to others (Barnett et al., 2006)
- self-censure: feelings of shame around expressing personal vulnerability along-side fear of damage to one's professional reputation (Barnett & Hillard, 2001)
- impairment that is often slow and insidious at the outset, thus easily overlooked (Smith & Moss, 2009).

The debilitating effects of burnout can be difficult to identify in oneself, especially with the associated increases in substance misuse, depression, and disengagement. A practitioner's awareness of his or her burnout may in fact be prompted by a concerned colleague. Recognising the signs of burnout in others is therefore important:

- they may become withdrawn and isolated (Gilroy et al., 2002)
- their relationships with colleagues deteriorate (Gilroy et al., 2002)
- their substance abuse can be difficult to observe directly, but indirect signs include:
    - marked changes in behaviour
    - arriving late to appointments and meetings
    - poor self-care or hygiene
    - frequent, unexplained absences
    - complaints from colleagues or supervisees (Thoreson et al., 1986).

Practice implications

1   Burnout is probably the issue furthest from the mind of a novice practitioner. However, it is important to be aware of the risks and indicators, and to take steps to prevent yourself from becoming overly stressed. Your clients will not thank you if you become impaired because you did not take sufficient care of your own well-being.

2   Be supportive towards colleagues, who may not be aware that they are becoming overly stressed. Provide them with thoughtful feedback. As discussed in chapter 17, the Psychology Board of Australia has guidelines for mandatory notifications, which you may have to act on if a colleague is impaired and putting clients at risk of harm. Do consult with a trusted supervisor or colleague if you are concerned about another health professional.

SELF-CARE IN PSYCHOLOGY

The danger and deleterious effects of burnout are compounded by the fact that psychologists have proven quite poor at looking after themselves, and may be unlikely to seek help even if available (Barnett & Hillard, 2001). It is every psychologist's ethical responsibility to prevent burnout, and to deal with the problem if it arises. This is what Barnett and colleagues (2007) term 'the self-care imperative'.

Defining self-care

The concept of self-care consists of a number of related domains, each of which plays an essential role in the sustainability of optimal psychological practice. It is an essential component in the prevention of distress, burnout, and impairment (Barnett et al., 2006). Psychologists can enlist self-care strategies to promote psychological wellness and ensure they are functioning well (Coster & Schwebel, 1997, p. 5). One is regularly engaging in self-reflection to maintain high levels of self-awareness. Self-care can also be defined or identified by patterns that commonly emerge in psychological practice when it is lacking. These clues of inadequate self-care include loss of objectivity in relation to work, boundary violations with clients, emotional dysregulation, such as becoming easily angered or overwhelmed, and feelings or symptoms of depression or anxiety.

Self-care should not be thought of as an indulgence, an added extra, or 'bonus' to which you pay attention when time permits. Rather, it is a fundamental aspect of professional practice that, if neglected, can lead to burnout and a shortened length of service in the profession. It warrants equal, if not greater, attention to that given to the facets of sound psychological practice, such as a broad clinical knowledge base.

Self-care should not be attended to only after exams, dissertation, internship, and licensure, as the sequence of challenges never ends (Barnett & Cooper, 2009). All registrants have a responsibility to themselves, the profession, and to clients to build self-care into their framework from the outset. If self-care is an aspect of psychological practice you have not thought about before, consider how you may find ways to contribute to, support, and cultivate a culture of self-care in your graduate-training program.

Developing your self-care practice

It is easy to fall foul of the myth of caregiver invulnerability: psychotherapists are susceptible to burnout. The good news is that the risk can be reduced by paying close attention to self-care. There are a number of ways of doing this:

1 *Scrupulously self-monitor for symptoms and behaviours that may increase risk of burnout* (Floyd et al., 1998). Perhaps most obviously, do what you tell your clients to do: pay attention to your own general self-care. Actively confront signs of distress, burnout, and impaired professional competence (Smith & Moss, 2009). Ensure that you are eating well and getting as much sleep as your body needs. Limit your work hours to what feels comfortable, and take adequate time off and holidays. Try to maintain an active social life and interests outside of your work. If you are working 12 hours a day, skipping meals, and neglecting interpersonal relationships, you are placing yourself at increased risk of burnout. It is not uncommon for psychologists to increasingly have a social group comprised of other psychologists! Try to enlarge and diversify your social group. Do not spend excessive time with friends who leave you feeling that you are their therapist.

2 *Seek consultation and supervision* (APA, 2002). Ensure that you have ongoing supervision. One of the biggest mistakes you can make is to presume that when your

training is complete, or you are fully registered, you no longer need supervision. In the UK, recognition of the vital nature of ongoing supervision is incorporated into the professional rules for psychologists. Although this is not a clearcut rule in Australia, we strongly suggest that ongoing peer supervision is part of ethical professional practice.

3 *Assertively place realistic limits around the scope of work duties* (Norcross & Guy, 2007). Remember that practising at a high standard today includes working in such a way that you can perform at this standard throughout your career.

4 *Avoid maladaptive coping strategies* such as compartmentalisation, avoidance, and denial (Barnett & Cooper, 2009).

5 *Check your level of self-compassion.* Go to the website <www.self-compassion.org> for a measure of your self-compassion (Raes et al., 2010). Self-compassion is comprised of factors such as self-kindness, self-judgment, sense of isolation, and degree of mindfulness. It is useful to measure how kind we are to ourselves in considering whether we may need support.

6 *Seek personal therapy as needed* (APA, 2002). If you really believe that psychological interventions are useful in treating psychological problems, you will have no difficulty becoming involved in therapy for yourself. If your attitude is, 'Therapy is only for people who are not strong enough to deal with their own problems', or, 'It would be so embarrassing to see a therapist', you may wish to consider what your attitudes to your clients are when they come in for therapy. Granted, we all want to have privacy in choosing to do therapy ourselves, and communities of psychologists even in capital cities can be quite small, so you may feel more comfortable seeing someone outside your profession, such as a social worker or psychiatrist.

7 *Continue learning and attending workshops and talks.* Sometimes burnout can result from feeling out of touch or simply jaded. New ideas are refreshing and can broaden our horizons.

8 *Join your professional organisation.* Members will ensure that you are in contact with other professionals and keep abreast of what is going on in your profession. It will also mean that there is greater accountability for you to keep your skills and knowledge up to date.

9 *Get insurance if not covered already by your training institution.* One of the most stressful aspects of working as a psychotherapist is the risk of harm to your clients or from them to others (and your responsibility in preventing this). Make sure you are well insured, know the steps of risk management, and have others you can trust who can give you good advice if needed.

10 *Stay up to date with paperwork.* Ensure that your records are up to date, consent forms are signed, and billing is maintained.

11 *Pay attention when others suggest* you seem a bit tired, anxious, flat, worried, out of sorts, withdrawn, unhappy, or cranky. Most often, it will be others who will first notice that you are burning out. Encourage friends, family, and co-workers to provide feedback.

12 We know it is often said, but it's true—*have a balanced lifestyle.* For psychotherapists, that can mean balancing how much you give with how much you receive in emotional care. Make sure you get sufficient time on your own to regroup. Take breaks, weekends, and holidays.

13 *Acknowledge personal vulnerabilities* and seek assistance.

14 *Practise what you preach:* challenge cognitive distortions, negative self-evaluation, and psychological rigidity (Norcross & Guy, 2007).

15 *Challenge patterns of martyrdom:* do you care for yourself as well as you advocate for your clients to care for themselves? Are you as forgiving and accepting of yourself as you are of your clients?

16 *Practise mindfulness:* nonjudgmental, present-moment awareness of sitting, walking, breathing, and being.

17 *Enhance the mind-body connection* through tai chi, yoga, meditation, or dance.

18 *Exercise regularly and maintain a healthy diet.*

19 *Practise unconditional self-acceptance* as a psychotherapist and a person (Norcross & Guy, 2007).

SELF-CARE: AN ETHICAL IMPERATIVE

When is a psychologist 'off duty'? The realisation tends to dawn among psychologists-in-training that the answer is, essentially, never. By committing to uphold our professional code of ethics, psychologists not only commit to a mode of professional practice but to one of personal comportment. This personal comportment not only proscribes external, public behaviours (including quasi-public settings such as online social-networking sites), but necessitates an internal orientation toward those practices and attitudes that will maintain our primary therapeutic tool—the self. As outlined in the previous section, self-care is intricately connected with professional competence. To neglect oneself as a psychotherapist is to risk professional impairment, thereby placing oneself, one's clients, and the profession at risk (Barnett & Cooper, 2009). Thus, while one's inner orientation before becoming a psychotherapist may not have been particularly self-nurturing, by officially pledging to abide by the APS's professional code of ethics, self-care is reframed as an essential part of our professional identities (Barnett et al., 2006).

Recommended reading

Baker, E. K. (2003). *Caring for Ourselves: A Therapist's Guide to Personal and Professional Well-being.* Washington, DC: American Psychological Association.

Barnett, J. E., Baker, E. K., Elman, N. S., & Schoner, G. R. (2007). In pursuit of wellness: the self-care imperative. *Professional Psychology: Research and Practice, 38*(6), 603–12.

Ellis, A. (1984). How to deal with your most difficult client—you. *Psychotherapy in Private Practice, 2,* 25–35.

Elman, N. S., Illfelder-Kaye, J., & Robiner, W. N. (2005). Professional development: Training for professionalism as a foundation for competent practice in psychology, *Professional Psychology: Research and Practice, 36*(4), 367–75.

Epstein, R. M. & Hundert, E. M. (2002). Defining and assessing professional competence. *Journal of American Medical Association (JAMA), 287*(9), 226–35.

Goldfried, M. R. (ed.). (2005). *How Therapists Change: Personal and Professional Reflections.* Washington DC: Americal Psychological Association.

Krishnamurthy, R., VandeCreek, L., Kaslow, N. J., Tazeau, Y. N., Miville, M. L., Kerns, R., Stegman, R., Suzuki, L., & Benton, S. A. (2004). Achieving competence in psychological assessment: directions for education and training. *Journal of Clinical Psychology, 60*(7), 725–39.

Norcross, J. C. & Guy, J. D. (2007). *Leaving It at the Office: A Guide to Psychotherapist Self-care.* New York: Guilford.

Roe, R. A. (2002). What makes a competent psychologist? *European Psychologist, 7*(3), 192–202.

Spruil, J., Rozensky, R. H., Stigall, T. T., Vasquez, M., Bingham, R. P., & De Vaney Olvey, C. (2004). Becoming a competent clinician: basic competencies in intervention. *Journal of Clinical Psychology, 60*(7), 741–54.

Wolfe, J. L. (2000). A vacation from musterbation. *Professional Psychology: Research and Practice, 31,* 581–3.

FINAL THOUGHTS

We have reached the end of our discussion about aspects central to practice as a psychologist in Australia. It seemed appropriate to end with a section on self-care for practitioners. Working with clients is a privilege and highly rewarding, but at times, also very taxing. Do take care of yourself. You will be a much better professional and a happier person! We hope that you have found the ideas shared in this text stimulating and that you will continue to work towards being the most effective practitioner you can be.

References

Achenbach, T. M. & Rescorla, L. A. (2001). *Manual for the ASEBA School-Age Forms and Profiles*. Burlington, VT: University of Vermont, Research Center for Children, Youth, and Families.

Ackerman, S. J. & Hilsenroth, M. J. (2001). A review of therapist characteristics and techniques positively impacting the therapeutic alliance. *Clinical Psychology Review, 23*, 1–33.

Ahn, H. N. & Wampold, B. E. (2001). Where oh where are the specific ingredients? A meta-analysis of component studies in counseling and psychotherapy. *Journal of Counseling Psychology, 48*(3), 251–7.

Ahn, W. & Kim, N. S. (2008). Causal theories of mental disorder concepts. *Psychological Science Agenda, Science Briefs*, web archive, June.

Ahn, W., Novick, L., & Kim, N. S. (2003). 'Understanding makes it normal': Causal explanations influence person perception. *Psychonomic Bulletin and Review, 10*, 746–52.

Ainsworth, M. (1964). Patterns of attachment behaviour shown by the infant in interaction with his mother. *Merrill-Palmer Quarterly, 10*, 51–8.

Alexander, F. & French, T. (1946). *The Corrective Emotional Experience*. New York: Ronald Press.

Alexander, L. B. & Luborsky, L. (1986). The Penn Helping Alliance Scales. In Greenberg, L. S. & Pinsof, W. M. (eds.). *The Psychotherapeutic Process: A Research Handbook*. New York: Guilford Press, 325–66.

Altarriba, J., Basnight, D. M., & Canary, T. M. (2003). Emotion representation and perception across cultures. In Lonner, W. J., Dinnel, D. L., Hayes, S. A., & Sattler, D. N. (eds.). *Online Readings in Psychology and Culture*. Bellingham, WA: Western Washington University Center for Cross-Cultural Research.

Al-Yaman, F., Van Doeland, M., & Wallis, M. (2006). *Family Violence among Aboriginal and Torres Strait Islander Peoples*. Canberra: Australian Institute of Health and Welfare.

American Psychiatric Association (1968). *Diagnostic and Statistical Manual of Mental Disorders* (2nd edn). Washington, DC: American Psychiatric Association.

American Psychiatric Association (1980). *Diagnostic and Statistical Manual of Mental Disorders* (3rd edn). Washington, DC: American Psychiatric Association.

American Psychiatric Association (1988). *Diagnostic and Statistical Manual of Mental Disorders* (3rd rev. edn). Washington, DC: American Psychiatric Association.

American Psychiatric Association (1994). *Diagnostic and Statistical Manual of Mental Disorders* (4th edn). Washington, DC: American Psychiatric Association.

American Psychiatric Association (2000). *Diagnostic and Statistical Manual of Mental Disorders* (4th edn Revised-Trade). Washington, DC: American Psychiatric Association.

American Psychological Association. (2002). Ethical principles of psychologists and code of conduct. *American Psychologist, 57*, 1060–73.

American Psychological Association (2010). *Ethical Principals of Psychologists and Code of Conduct*. Washington, DC: American Psychiatric Association.

Andersen, S. M. & Cole, S. W. (1990). 'Do I know you?': The role of significant others in general social perception. *Journal of Personality and Social Psychology, 59*(3), 384–99.

Anderson, E. M. & Lambert. M. J. (2001). A survival analysis of clinically significant change in outpatient psychotherapy. *Journal of Clinical Psychology, 57*, 875–88.

Anderson, M. C. & Green, C. (2001). Suppressing unwanted memories by executive control. *Nature, 410*, 366–9.

Anderson, T., Lunnen, K. M., & Ogles, B. M. (2010). Putting models and techniques in context. In Duncan, B. L., Miller, S. D., Wampold, B. E. & Hubble, M. A. (eds). *The Heart and Soul of Change* (2nd edn). Washington, DC: American Psychological Association.

Anderson, T., Ogles, B. M., Patterson, C. L., Lambert, M. J., & Vermeersch, D. A. (2009). Therapist effects: Facilitative interpersonal skills as a predictor of therapist success. *Journal of Clinical Psychology, 65*, 755–68.

Andersson, G., Bergstrom, J., Carlbring, P., & Lindefors, N. (2005). The use of the Internet in the treatment of anxiety disorders. *Current Opinion in Psychiatry, 18*(1).

Andrew, A. M., Nordberg, S. S., Kraus, D., & Castonguay, L. G. (2012). Errors in treatment outcome monitoring: Implications for real-world psychotherapy. *Canadian Psychology, 53(2)*, 105–114.

Andrews, H. B. (2000). The myth of the scientist-practitioner: A reply to R. King (1998) and Ollendick (1998). *Australian Psychologist, 35*, 60–3.

Andrusyna, T. P., Tang, T. Z., DeRubeis, R. J., & Luborsky, L. (2001). The factor structure of the Working Alliance Inventory in cognitive-behavioral therapy. *Journal of Psychotherapy Practice and Research, 10*(3), 173–8.

Anker, M. G., Duncan, B. L., & Sparks, J. A. (2009). Using client feedback to improve couple therapy outcomes: A randomized clinical trial in a naturalistic setting. *Journal of Consulting and Clinical Psychology, 77*, 693–704.

Antonuccio, D. O., Lewinsohn, P. M., & Steinmetz, J. L. (1982). Identification of therapist differences in a group treatment for depression. *Journal of Consulting and Clinical Psychology, 50*(3), 433–5.

Antony, M. M., Orsillo, S. M., & Roemer, L. (2001). *Practitioner's Guide to Empirically Based Measures of Anxiety*. New York: Kluwer Academic/Plenum Publishers.

Arch, J. J. & Craske, M. G. (2008). Acceptance and commitment therapy and cognitive behavioral therapy for anxiety disorders: Different treatments, similar mechanisms? *Clinical Psychology: Science and Practice, 5*, 263–79.

Arkowitz, H. (2009). Principles of change vs therapy techniques or principles of change and therapy techniques: A commentary on Goldfried's 1980 paper. *Applied and Preventive Psychology, 13*, 5–7.

Armitage, C. J. (2009). Is there utility on the transtheoretical model?, *British Journal of Health Psychology, 14*, 195–210.

Arnkoff, D. B., Glass, C. R., & Shapiro, S. J. (2002). Expectations and preferences. In Norcross, J. C. (ed.). *Psychotherapy Relationships That Work*. New York: Oxford University Press, 335–56.

Asay, T. P. & Lambert, M. J. (1999). The empirical case for the common factors in therapy: Quantitative findings. In Hubble, M. A., Duncan, B. L., & Miller, S. D. (eds). *The Heart and Soul of Change: What Works in Therapy*. Washington, DC: American Psychological Association, 33–56.

Atkinson, D. R. & Schein, S. (1986). Similarity in counseling. *Counseling Psychologist*, 14(2), 319–54.

Australian Bureau of Statistics (ABS) (2002). Population religion, 2002 <http://www.abs.gov.au/ausstats/abs>.

Australian Bureau of Statistics (ABS) (2006). *Experimental Estimates of Aboriginal and Torres Strait Islander Australians* <http://www.abs.gov.au/ausstats/abs>.

Australian Bureau of Statistics (ABS) (2006). *Personal Safety Survey, Australia 2005*. ABS cat. no. 4906.0. Canberra: Australian Bureau of Statistics.

Australian Bureau of Statisitics (ABS) (2008–09). *Household Use of Information Technology*. ABS cat. no.. 8146.0. Canberra: Australian Bureau of Statistics.

Australian Bureau of Statistics (2010). *Household Use of Information Technology, Australia*. Canberra: Australian Bureau of Statistics.

Australian Bureau of Statistics (ABS) 2010. *Suicides, Australia 2010*. Canberra: Australian Bureau of Statistics.

Australian Government (2008). *About Australia* series. Canberra: Department of Foreign Affairs and Trade.

Australian Institute of Health and Welfare (2010). *Child Protection, Australia 2008–09*. Canberra: Australian Institute of Health and Welfare. <http://www.aihw.gov.au/publications/index.cfm/title/10859>.

Australian Psychological Society (2002). *Guidelines Regarding Financial Dealings and Fair-trading*. Melbourne: Australian Psychological Society.

Australian Psychological Society. (2003). *Guidelines for the Provision of Psychological Services for, and the Conduct of Psychological Research*. Melbourne: Australian Psychological Society.

Australian Psychological Society (2004). *Guidelines on Record Keeping*. Melbourne: Australian Psychological Society.

Australian Psychological Society (2004). *Guidelines Relating to Suicidal Clients*. Melbourne: Australian Psychological Society.

Australian Psychological Society (2005). *Guidelines for Working with People Who Pose a High Risk of Harming Others*. Melbourne: Australian Psychological Society.

Australian Psychological Society (2007). *Code of Ethics*. Melbourne: Australian Psychological Society.

Australian Psychological Society (2008). *Guidelines on Confidentiality*. Melbourne: Australian Psychological Society.

Australian Psychological Society. (2008). *Guidelines for Managing Professional Boundaries and Multiple Relationships*. Melbourne: Australian Psychological Society.

Australian Psychological Society (2008). *Guidelines for the Provision of Psychological Services for, and the Conduct of Psychological Research with, Aboriginal and Torres Strait Islander People of Australia*. Melbourne: Australian Psychological Society.

Australian Psychological Society (2009). *Guidelines for Working With Young People*. Melbourne: Australian Psychological Society.

Australian Psychological Society (2010). *Guidelines on Reporting Abuse and Neglect and Criminal Activity*. Melbourne: Australian Psychological Society.

Bach, P. A. & Moran, D. J. (2008). *ACT in Practice: Case Conceptualizations in Acceptance and Commitment Therapy*. Oakland, CA: New Harbinger.

Baer, R. A. (2003). Mindfulness training as a clinical intervention: A conceptual and empirical review. *Clinical Psychology: Science and Practice, 10*(2), 125–43.

Baird, K. &Kracen, A. D. (2006). Vicarious traumatization and secondary traumatic stress: A research synthesis. *Counselling Psychology Quarterly, 19*, 181–8.

Baker, E. K. (2003). *Caring for Ourselves: A Therapist's Guide to Personal and Professional Well-Being*. Washington, DC: American Psychological Association.

Baker, S. B., & Daniels, T. G. (1989). Integrating research on the microcounseling program: A meta-analysis. *Journal of Counseling Psychology, 36*(2), 213–22.

Baldwin, S. A., Berkeljon, A., Atkins, D. C., Olsen, J. A., and Nielsen, S. L. (2009). Rates of change in naturalistic psychotherapy: Contrasting dose-effect and good-enough level models of change. *Journal of Consulting and Clinical Psychology, 77*(2), 203–11.

Baldwin, S. A., Wampold, B. E., & Imel, Z. E. (2007). Untangling the alliance–outcome correlation: Exploring the relative importance of therapist and patient variability in the alliance. *Journal of Consulting and Clinical Psychology, 75*, 842–52.

Bambling, M. (2000). The effect of clinical supervision on the development of counsellor competency. *Psychotherapy in Australia, 6*(4), 58–63.

Bandura, A. (1977). *Social Learning Theory*. Englewood Cliffs: Prentice Hall.

Barak, A., Hen, L., Boniel-Nissim, M., & Shapira, N. A. (2008). A comprehensive review and a meta-analysis of the effectiveness of Internet-based psychotherapeutic interventions. *Journal of Technology in Human Services, 26*(2–4), 109–60.

Barber, J. P., Connolly, M. B., Crits Christoph, P., Gladis, L., & Siqueland, L. (2000). Alliance predicts patients' outcome beyond in-treatment change in symptoms. *Journal of Consulting and Clinical Psychology, 68*(6), 1027–32.

Barker, P. (2007). *Basic Family Therapy* (5th edn). New York: Wiley-Blackwell.

Barkman, M., Connell, J., Stiels, W., Miles, J. N., Margison, F., Evans, C., & Mellor-Clark, J. (2006). Dose-effect relations and responsive regulation of treatment duration: The good enough level. *Journal of Consulting and Clinical Psychology, 74*, 160–7.

Barlow, D. H. (ed.) (2008). *Clinical Handbook of Psychological Disorders: A Step-by-Step Treatment Manual* (4th edn). New York: Guildford Press.

Barnes, G. G. (2004). *Family Therapy in Changing Times*. Gordonville, VA: Palgrave Macmillan.

Barnes-Holmes, Y., Barnes-Holmes, D., Smeets, P. M., Strand, P., & Friman, P. (2004). Establishing relational responding in accordance with more-than and less-than as generalized operant behavior in young children. *International Journal of Psychology and Psychological Therapy, 4*, 531-558.

Barnett, J. E. (2008). Impaired professionals: Distress, professional impairment, self-care, and psychological wellness. In Herson, M. & Gross, A. M. (eds). *Handbook of Clinical Psychology* (Vol. 1). New York: John Wiley, 857–84.

Barnett, J. E., Baker, E. K., Elman, N. S., & Schoener, G. R. (2007). In pursuit of wellness: The self-care imperative. *Professional Psychology: Research and Practice, 38*, 603–12.

Barnett, J. E. & Cooper, N. (2009). Creating a culture of self-care. *Clinical Psychology: Science and Practice, 16*(1), 16–20.

Barnett, J. E. & Hillard, D. (2001). Psychologist distress and impairment: The availability, nature, and use of colleague assistance programs for psychologist. *Professional Psychology: Research and Practice, 32*, 205–10.

Barnett, J. E., Johnston, L. C., & Hillard, D. (2006). Psychotherapist wellness as an ethical imperative. In VandeCreek, L. & Allen, J. B. (eds). *Innovations in Clinical Practice: Focus on Health and Wellness*. Sarasota, FL: Professional Resources Press, 257–71.

Barrett-Lennard, G. T. (1981). The empathy cycle: refinement of a nuclear concept. *Journal of Counseling Psychology, 28*, 9–100.

Barrett-Lennard, G. T. (1986). The Relationship Inventory now: Issues and advances in theory, method, and use. In Greenberg, L. & Pinsof, W. (eds). *The Psychotherapeutic Process*. New York: Guildford Press, 439–76.

Bartholomew, K. (1997). Adult attachment processes: individual and couple perspectives. *British Journal of Medical Psychology, 70*, 249–63.

Baumeister, R. F., Bratslavsky, E., Finkenauer, C., & Vohs, K. D. (2001). Bad is stronger than good. *Review of General Psychology, 5*, 323–70.

Baumrind, D. (1991). The influences of parenting style on adolescent competence and substance use. *Journal of Early Adolescence, 11*, 56–95.

Baxter, Jr., L. R., Schwartz, J. M., Bergman, K. S., & Szuba, M. P. (1992). Caudate glucose metabolic rate changes with both drug and behavior therapy for obsessive-compulsive disorder. *Archives of General Psychiatry, 49*(9), 681–9.

Beck, A. T. (1976/1979). *Cognitive Therapy and the Emotional Disorders*. New York: Penguin.

Beck, A. T. (1991). Cognitive therapy: A 30-year retrospective. *American Psychologist, 46*(4), 368–75.

Beck, A. T., Emery, G., & Greenberg, R. L. (1985). *Anxiety Disorders and Phobias: A Cognitive Perspective*. New York: Basic Books.

Beck, A. T., Rush, A. J., Shaw, B. F., & Emery, G. (1979). *Cognitive Therapy of Depression*. New York: Guilford Press.

Beck, A. & Steer, R. (1988). *Beck Hopelessness Scale*. San Antonio, TX: Harcourt Brace.

Beck, A. & Steer, R. (1991). *Beck Scale for Suicidal Ideation*. San Antonio, TX: Harcourt Brace <www.psycorp.com>.

Beck, D. F. (1988). *Counselor Characteristics: How They Affect Outcomes*. Milwaukee, WI: Family Service America.

Beck, J. S. (1995). *Cognitive Therapy: Basics and Beyond*. New York: Guilford Press.

Beck, R. & Perkins, T. S. (2001). Cognitive content specificity for anxiety and depression: A meta-analysis. *Cognitive Therapy and Research, 25*, 651–63.

Becvar, D. S. & Becvar, R. J. (2008). *Family Therapy: A Systemic Integration* (7th edn). Boston: Allyn & Bacon.

Bedi, R. P., Davis, M. D., & Williams, M. (2005). Critical incidents in the formation of the therapeutic alliance from the client's perspective. *Psychotherapy: Theory, Research, Training, 42*(3), 311–23.

Berg, I. K. (1991). *Family Preservation: A Brief Therapy Workbook*. London: BT Press.

Bergin, A. E. (1997). Neglect of the therapist and the human dimension of change: A commentary. *Clinical Psychology: Science and Practice, 4*, 83–9.

Bergner, R. M. (1997). What is psychopathology? And so what? *Clinical Psychology: Science and Practice, 4*, 235–48.

Berman, J. S. & Norton, N. C. (1985). Does professional training make a therapist more effective? *Psychological Bulletin, 98*(2), 401–7.

Bernard, J. M. & Goodyear, R. K. (2004). *Fundamentals of Clinical Supervision* (3rd edn). Boston: Pearson.

Bernard, J. M. & Goodyear, R. K. (2009). *Fundamentals of Clinical Supervision* (4th edn). New Jersey: Pearson.

Bernier, A. & Dozier, M. (2002). The client-counselor match and the corrective emotional experience: Evidence from interpersonal and attachment research. *Psychotherapy: Theory, Research and Practice, 39*(1), 32–43.

Bersoff, D. (2008). *Ethical Conflicts In Psychology* (4th edn).Washington, DC: America Psychological Association.

Beutler, L. E. (1989). Differential treatment selection: The role of diagnosis in psychotherapy. *Psychotherapy, 26*(3), 271–81.

Beutler, L. E. (1991). Have all won and must all have prizes? Revisiting Luborsky et al.'s verdict. *Journal of Consulting and Clinical Psychology, 59*(2), 226–32.

Beutler, L. E. (1997). The psychotherapist as a neglected variable in psychotherapy: An illustration by reference to the role of therapist experience and training. *Clinical Psychology: Science and Practice, 4*(1), 44–52.

Beutler, L. E. (2004). In Duncan, B. L., Miller, S. D., & Sparks, J. *The Heroic Client: A Revolutionary Way to Improve Effectiveness through Client-Directed, Outcome-Informed Therapy* (foreword to first edition). San Francisco: Jossey-Bass.

Beutler, L. E. & L. G. Castonguay (2006). The task force on empirically based principles of therapeutic change. In Castonguay, L. G. and Beutler, L. E. (eds). *Principles of Therapeutic Change that Work*. Oxford: Oxford University Press, 3–10.

Beutler, L. E. & Crago, M. (1987). Strategies and techniques of psychotherapeutic intervention. In Hales, R. E. & Frances, A. J. (eds). *Annual Review, 6*, 378–97.

Beutler, L. E., Crago, M., & Arizmendi, T. G. (1986). Therapist variables in psychotherapy process and outcome. In Garfield, S. L. & Bergin, A. E. (eds). *Handbook of Psychotherapy and Behavior Change* (3rd rev. edn). New York: Wiley, 257–310.

Beutler, L. E., Machado, P. P., & Neufeldt, S. A. (1994). Therapist variables. In Bergin, A. E. & Garfield, S. L. (eds). *Handbook of Psychotherapy and Behaviour Change* (4th edn). New York: John Wiley, 229–69.

Beutler, L. E., Malik, M., Alimohamed, S., Harwood, T. M., Talebi, H., Noble, S., &Wong, E. (2004). Therapist effects. In Lambert, M. J. (ed.). *Bergin and Garfield's Handbook of Psychotherapy and Behavior Change* (5th edn). New York: John Wiley, 227–306.

Beutler, L. E. & Moleiro, C. (2001). Clinical versus reliable and significant change. *Clinical Psychology Science and Practice, 8*, 441–5.

Bieling, P. J. & Kuyken,W. (2003). Is cognitive case formulation science or science fiction? *Clinical Psychology: Science and Practice, 10*, 52–69.

Biglan, A. & Hayes, S. C. (1996). Should the behavioural sciences become more pragmatic? The case for functional contextualism in research on human behavior. *Applied and Preventive Psychology: Current Scientific Perspectives, 5*, 47–57.

Bike, D. H., Norcross, J. C., & Schatz, D. M. (2009). Processes and outcomes of psychotherapists' personal therapy: Replication and extension 20 years later. *Psychotherapy, 46*, 19–31.

Bischoff, M. M. & Tracey, T. J. G. (1995). Client resistance as predicted by therapist behavior: A study of sequential dependence. *Journal of Counseling Psychology,* 42(4), 487–95.

Bischoff, R. J. & Sprenkle, D. H. (1993). Dropping out of marriage and family therapy: A critical review of research. *Family Process, 32,* 353–75.

Black, S., Hardy, G., Turpin, G., & Parry, G. (2005). Self-reported attachment styles and therapeutic orientation of therapists and their relationship with reported general alliance quality and problems in therapy. *Psychology and Psychotherapy: Theory, Research, and Practice, 78*(3), 363–77.

Blatt, S. J., Sanislow III, C. A., Zuroff, D. C., & Pilkonis, P. A. (1996). Characteristics of effective therapists: Further analyses of data from the National Institute of Mental Health Treatment of Depression Collaborative Research Program. *Journal of Consulting and Clinical Psychology, 64*(6), 1276–84.

Blatt, S. J. & Zuroff, D. C. (2005). Empirical evaluation of the assumptions in identifying evidence based treatments in mental health. *Clinical Psychology Review, 25,* 459–86.

Bohart, A. C., Elliott, R., Greenberg, L., & Watson, J. (2002). Empathy. In Norcross, J. C. (ed.). *Psychotherapy Relationships That Work.* New York, Oxford University Press, 89–108.

Bohart, A. C. & Tallman, K. (1999). *How Clients Make Therapy Work: The Process of Active Self-Healing.* Washington, DC: American Psychological Association.

Bohart, A. C. & Tallman, K. (2010). Clients: The neglected common factor in psychotherapy. In Duncan, B. L., Miller S. D., Wampold, B. E., and Hubble, M. A. (eds). *The Heart and Soul of Change* (2nd edn). Washington, DC: American Psychological Association, 83–112.

Boisaubin, E. V. & Levine, R. E. (2001). Identifying and assisting the impaired physician. *American Journal of Medical Sciences, 322,* 31–6.

Bond, M. H. (1991). *Beyond the Chinese Face: Insights from Psychology.* Oxford: Oxford University Press.

Bordin, E. S. (1979). The generalizability of the psychoanalytic concept of the working alliance. *Psychotherapy Theory, Research and Practice, 16,* 252–60.

Bordin, E. S. (1994). Theory and research on the therapeutic working alliance: New directions. In Horvath, A. O. & Greenberg, L. S. (eds). *The Working Alliance: Theory, Research, and Practice.).* New York: John Wiley, 13–37.

Bortolotti, B., Menchetti, M., Bellini, F., Montaguti, M. B., & Berardi, D. (2008). Psychological interventions for major depression in primary care: A meta-analytic review of randomized controlled trials. *General Hospital Psychiatry, 30,* 293–302.

Boschen, M. J. (2011a). Generalized anxiety disorder: Focus on pregabalin. *Clinical Medicine Insights: Psychiatry, 4,* 17–35.

Boschen, M. J. (2011b). A meta-analysis of the efficacy of pregabalin in the treatment of generalized anxiety disorder. *Canadian Journal of Psychiatry, 56,* 558–566.

Boschen, M. J. (in press). Pregabalin: Dose-response relationship in generalized anxiety disorder. *Pharmacopsychiatry.*

Boswell, J. F. & Castonguay, L. G. (2007). Psychotherapy training: Suggestions for core ingredients and future research. *Psychotherapy: Theory, Research, Practice, Training 44*(4), 378–83.

Boszormenyi-Nagy, I. & Spark, G. (1973). *Invisible Loyalties: Reciprocity in Intergenerational Family Therapy*. New York: Harper & Row.

Bowen, M. D. (1974). *Toward the Differentiation of Self in One's Family of Origin*. New York: Jason Aronson.

Bowlby, J. (1969). *Attachment*. New York: Basic Books.

Bowlby, J. (1969). Disruption of affectional bonds and its effects on behaviour. Canada's *Mental Health* (Canadian supplement), *59*, 12.

Bowlby, J. (1980). *Attachment and Loss. III: Loss: Sadness and Depression. International Psycho-Analytical Library*, *109*, 1–462.

Bowlby, J. (1980). By ethology out of psycho-analysis: An experiment in interbreeding. *Animal Behaviour*, *28*, 649–56.

Bowlby, J. (1988). *A Secure Base: Parent-child Attachment and Healthy Human Development*. New York: Basic Books.

Bowman, D., Scogin, F., Flowd, M., & McKendree-Smith, N. (2001). Psychotherapy length of stay and outcome: A meta-analysis of the effect of therapist sex. *Psychotherapy*, *38*(2), 142–8.

Bozarth, J. D. (1990). The essence of client-centered/person-centered therapy. In Lietaer, G., Rombauts, J., & Van Balen, R. (eds). *Client-Centered and Experiential Psychotherapy: Toward the Nineties*. Leuven: Katholieke Universiteit te Leuven, 59–64.

Bradley, L. J. & Ladany, N. (2001). *Counselor Supervision: Principles, Process, and Practice*. Ann Arbor: Brunner-Routledge.

Brady, J. L., Guy, J. D., Poelstra, P. L., & Brokaw, B. F. (1999). Vicarious traumatization, spirituality, and the treatment of sexual abuse survivors: A national survey of women psychotherapists. *Professional Psychology: Research and Practice*, *30*, 386–93.

Bretherton, I. & Munholland, K. A. (1999). Internal working models in attachment relationships: A construct revisited. In Cassidy, J. & Shaver, P. R. (eds). *Handbook of Attachment: Theory, Research and Clinical Applications*. New York: Guilford Press, 89–114.

British Psychological Society (2009). *Code of Ethics and Conduct*. Leicester: British Psychological Society.

Brody, A. L., Saxena, S., Schwartz, J. M., Stoessel, P. W., Maidment, K., Phelps, M., & Baxter Jr., L. R. (1998). FDG-PET predictors of response to behavioral therapy and pharmacotherapy in obsessive compulsive disorder. *Psychiatry Research*, *84*(1), 1–6.

Brody, A. L., Saxena, S., Stoessel, P., Gillies, L., Fairbanks, L. A., Alborzian, S., Phelps, M. E., Huang, S.-C., Wu, H.-M., Ho, M. L., Ho, M. K., Au, S. C., Maidment, K., & Baxter Jr, L. R. (2001). Regional brain metabolic changes in patients with major depression treated with either paroxetine or interpersonal therapy: Preliminary findings. *Archives of General Psychiatry*, *58*, 631–40.

Bromfield, M. & Irenyi, L. (2009). *Child Abuse and Neglect Statistics*. Melbourne: Australian Institute of Family Studies.

Brown, G. S., Lambert, M. J., Jones, E. R., & Minami, T. (2005). Identifying highly effective therapists in a managed care environment. *American Journal of Managed Care*, *11*, 513–20.

Brown, G. W. & Harris, T. O. (1978). *Social Origins of Depression*. London: Tavistock.

Brown, K. W. & Ryan, R. M. (2003). The benefits of being present: mindfulness and its role in psychology. *Journal of Personality and Psychological Well-being: Social Psychology*, *84*(4), 822–48.

Brown, T. A., Chorpita, B. F., Korotitsch, W., & Barlow, D. H. (1997). Psychometric properties of the Depression Anxiety Stress Scales (DASS) in clinical samples. *Behaviour Research and Therapy, 35,* 79–89.

Brunet, A., Orr, S. P., Tremblay, J., Robertson, K., Nader, K., & Pitman, R. K. (2008). Effect of post-retrieval propranolol on psychophysiologic responding during subsequent script-driven traumatic imagery in post-traumatic stress disorder. *Journal of Psychiatric Research, 42,* 503–506.

Bryan, C. J. & Rudd, M. D. (2006). Advances in the assessment of suicide risk. *Journal of Clinical Psychology: In Session, 62*(2), 185–200. DOI: 10.1002/jclp.20222.

Burlingame, G. M., Fuhriman, A., Paul, S., & Ogles, B. M. (1989). Implementing a time-limited therapy program: Differential effects of training and experience. *Psychotherapy, 26*(3), 303–13.

Burlingame, G. M., Wells, M. G., & Lambert, M. J. (1996). Youth Outcome Questionnaire. American Professional Credentialing Services: Stevenson, MD.

Burns, D. D. & Nolen-Hoeksema, S. (1992). Therapeutic empathy and recovery from depression in cognitive-behavioural therapy: A structural equation model. *Journal of Consulting and Clinical Psychology, 60,* 441–9.

Burns, D. D. & Spangler, D. L. (2001). Does psychotherapy homework lead to improvements in depression in cognitive-behavioral therapy or does improvement lead to increased homework compliance. *Journal of Consulting and Clinical Psychology, 68,* 46–56.

Butcher, J. N., Dahlstrom, W. G., Graham, J. R., Tellegen, A., & Kaemmer, B. (1989). *Minnesota Multiphasic Personality Inventory (MMPI-2): Manual for Administration and Scoring.* Minneapolis: University of Minnesota Press.

Butler, A. C., Chapman, J. E., Forman, E. M., & Beck, A. T. (2006). The empirical status of cognitive-behavioral therapy: A review of meta-analyses. *Clinical Psychology Review, 30,* 194–202.

Callahan, J. L., & Hynan, M. T. (2005). Models of psychotherapy outcome: Are they applicable in training clinics? *Psychological Services, 2*(1), 65–9.

Campbell, J. (2000). *Essentials of Clinical Supervision.* Hoboken, NJ: John Wiley.

Campbell, J. M. (2000). *Becoming an Effective Supervisor. A Workbook for Counselors and Psychotherapists.* Ann Arbor: Sheridan Books.

Camras, L. A., Oster, H., Campos, J. Campos, R., Ujiie, T., Miyake, K., Wang, L, & Meng, Z. (1998). Production of emotional facial expressions in European American, Japanese, and Chinese infants. *Developmental Psychologist, 34,* 616–28.

Canfield, J. (2005). Secondary traumatization, burnout, and vicarious traumatization: A review of the literature as it relates to therapists who treat trauma. *Smith College Studies in Social Work, 75,* 81–101.

Carkhuff, R. R., Kratochvil, D., & Friel, T. (1968). Effects of professional training: communication and discrimination of facilitative conditions. *Journal of Counseling Psychology, 15*(1), 68–74.

Carr, A. (2006). *The Handbook of Child and Adolescent Clinical Psychology: A Contextual Approach.* London, New York: Routledge.

Carr, A. & McNully, M. (eds) (2006). *The Handbook of Adult Clinical Psychology: An Evidence-based Practice Approach.* London, New York: Routledge.

Carroll, M. (1996). *Counseling Supervision: Theory, Skills, and Practice.* London: Cassell.

Carroll, M. & Gilbert, M. C. (2006). *On Being a Supervisee: Creating Learning Partnerships*. Melbourne: PsychOz Publications.

Casey, L. M. & Halford, W. K. (2010). Couples and the silicon chip: Applying technology to couple relationship services. In Hahlweg, K., Grawe, M., & Baucom, D. (eds). *Enhancing Couples: The Shape of Couple Therapy to Come*. Gottingen: Hogrefe, 216–30.

Casey, L. M., Oei, T. P., & Newcombe, P. A. (2005). Looking beyond the negatives: A time period analysis of positive cognitions, negative cognitions, and working alliance in cognitive-behaviour therapy for panic disorder. *Psychotherapy Research*, 15(1–2), 55–68.

Cassidy, J. (1999). The nature of a child's ties. In Cassidy, J. & Shaver, P. R. (eds). *Handbook of Attachment: Theory, Research and Clinical Applications*. New York: Guilford Press, 3–20.

Castonguay, L. G. & Beutler, L. E. (eds.) (2006). *Principles of Therapeutic Change that Work*. New York: Oxford University Press.

Castonguay, L. G. & Beutler, L. E. (2006). Principles of therapeutic change: A task force on participants, relationships, and techniques factors. *Journal of Clinical Psychology*, 62(6), 631–8.

Castonguay, L. G., Boswell, J. F., Constantino, M. J., Goldfried, M. R., & Hill, C. E. (2010). Training implications of harmful effects of psychological treatments. *American Psychologist*, 65(1) 34–40.

Castonguay, L. G., Constantino, M. J., & Grosse Holtforth, M. (2006). The working alliance: Where are we and where should we go? *Psychotherapy: Theory, Research, Practice, Training*, 43(3), 271–9.

Castonguay, L. G., Goldfried, M. R., Wiser, S., Raue, P. J., & Hayes, A. M. (1996). Predicting the effect of cognitive therapy for depression: A study of unique and common factors. *Journal of Consulting and Clinical Psychology*, 64(3), 497–504.

Castonguay, L. G. & Grosse Holtforth, M. (2005). Change in psychotherapy: A plea for no more 'nonspecific' and false dichotomies. *Clinical Psychology: Science and Practice*, 12(2), 198–201.

Castonguay, L. G. & Hill, C. E. (eds) (2007). *Insight in Psychotherapy*. Washington, DC: American Psychological Association.

Chambless, D. L. (2001). Empirically supported psychological interventions: Controversies and evidence. *Annual Review of Psychology*, 52, 685–716.

Chambless, D. L. (2002). Beware the dodo bird: The dangers of overgeneralization. *Clinical Psychology: Science and Practice*, 9(1), 13–16.

Chambless, D. L., Baker, M. J., Baucom, D. H., Beutler, L. E., Calhoun, K. S., Crits-Christoph, P., Daiuto, A., DeRubeis, R., Detweiler, J., Haaga, D. A. F., Bennett Johnson, S., McCurry, S., Mueser, K. T., Pope, K. S., Sanderson, W. C., Shoham, V., Stickle, T., Williams, D. A., & Woody, S. R. (1998). Update on empirically validated therapies, II. *Clinical Psychologist*, 51(1), 3–16.

Chambless, D. L., & Crits-Christoph, P. (2006). What should be validated? The treatment method. In Norcross, J. C., Beutler, L. E., & Levant, R. F. (eds). *Evidence-based Practice in Mental Health: Debate and Dialogue on the Fundamental Questions*. Washington, DC: American Psychological Association, 191–200.

Chan, C. (2005). *Domestic Violence In Gay And Lesbian Relationships*. Sydney: Australian Family and Domestic Violence Clearing House.

Chiles, J. A., Lambert, M. J., & Hatch, A. L. (1999). The impact of psychological interventions on medical cost offset: A meta-analytic review. *Clinical Psychology: Science and Practice, 6*, 204–20.

Chirban, J. T. (2001). Assessing religious and spiritual concerns in psychotherapy. In Plante, T.G. & Sherman, A. C. (eds). *Faith and Health: Perspectives on the Relationship between Religious Faith and Health Outcomes*. New York: Guildford Press.

Cipriani, A., Pretty, H., Hawton, K., & Geddes, J. R. (2005). Lithium in the prevention of suicidal behavior and all-cause mortality in patients with mood disorders: A systematic review of randomized trials. *American Journal of Psychiatry, 162*, 1805–19.

Claridge, G. & Davis, C. (2003). *Personality and Psychological Disorders*. London: Arnold.

Clark, L. A., Watson, D., & Reynolds, S. (1995). Diagnosis and classification of psychopathology: challenges to the current system and future directions. *Annual Review of Psychology, 46*, 121–53.

Clarkin, J. F. & Hull, J. W. (1991). The brief psychotherapies. In Hersen, M., Kazdin, A. E., et al. (eds). *The Clinical Psychology Handbook* (2nd edn). Pergamon General Psychology Series, *120*, 780–96. New York: Pergamon.

Clarkin, J. F. & Levy, K. N. (2004). The influence of client variables on psychotherapy. In Lambert, M. J. (ed.), *Bergin and Garfield's Handbook of Psychotherapy and Behavior Change* (5th edn). New York: Wiley, 194–226.

Clemence, A., Hilsenroth, M., Ackerman, S., Strassle, C., & Handler, L. (2005). Facets of the therapeutic alliance and perceived progress in psychotherapy: Relationship between patient and therapist perspectives. *Clinical Psychology and Psychotherapy, 12*(6), 443.

Compton, W. C. (2005). *An Introduction to Positive Psychology*. New York: Wadsworth.

Connolly Gibbons, M. B., Crits-Christoph, P., Barber, J.-P., & Schamberger, M. (2007). Insight in psychotherapy: A review of empirical literature. In Castonguay, L. G. & Hill, C. E. (eds). *Insight in Psychotherapy*. Washington, DC: American Psychological Association, 143–65.

Constantine, M. G. & Sue, D. W. (2005). *Strategies for Building Multicultural Competence in Mental Health and Educational Settings*. Hoboken, NJ: John Wiley.

Constantino, M. J., Arnow, B. A., Blasey, C., & Agras, W. S. (2005). The association between patient characteristics and the therapeutic alliance in cognitive-behavioral and interpersonal therapy for bulimia nervosa. *Journal of Consulting and Clinical Psychology, 73*(2), 203–11.

Cordova, J. (2003). Behavior analysis and the scientific study of couples. *Behavioural Analyst Today, 3*, 412–15.

Cordova, J., Cautilli, J. D., Simon, C., & Axelrod-Sabtig, R. (2006). Behavior analysis of forgiveness in couples therapy. *International Journal of Behavioral Consultation and Therapy, 7*, 192–207.

Corey, G. (1996). *Theory and Practice of Counselling and Psychotherapy*. Pacific Grove, CA: Brooks Cole.

Coster J. S. & Schwebel, M. (1997). Well-functioning in professional psychologists. *Professional Psychology: Research and Practice, 28*, 5–13.

Cowen, E. L. & Kilmer, R. P. (2002). 'Positive psychology': Some plusses and some open issues. *Journal of Community Psychology, 30* (4), 449–60.

Cozolino, L. J. (2002). *The Neuroscience of Psychotherapy: Building and Rebuilding the Human Brain*. New York: Norton.

Crago, H. (2006). *Couple, Family and Group Work: First Steps in Interpersonal Intervention*. Maidenhead, Berkshire; New York: Open University Press.

Craighead, W. E., Sheets, E. S., & Bjornsson, A. S. (2005). Specificity and nonspecificity in psychotherapy. *Clinical Psychology: Science and Practice, 12*(2), 189–93.

Crits-Christoph, P. (1997). Limitations of the Dodo Bird Verdict and the role of clinical trials in psychotherapy research: Comment on Wampold et al. (1997). *Psychological Bulletin, 122*(3), 216–20.

Crits-Christoph, P., Baranackie, K., Kurcias, J., Beck, A. T., Carroll, K., Perry, K., Luborsky, L., McLellan, A., Woody, G., Thompson, L., Gallagher, D., & Zitrin, C. (1991). Meta-analysis of therapist effects in psychotherapy outcome studies. *Psychotherapy Research, 1*(2), 81–91.

Crits-Christoph, P., Cooper, A., & Luborsky, L. (2001). *The accuracy of Therapists' Interpretations and the Outcome of Dynamic Psychotherapy Helping Skills: The Empirical Foundation*. Washington, DC: American Psychological Association, 297–307.

Crits-Christoph, P., Gibbons, M. B., & Hearon, B. (2006). Does the Alliance cause good outcomes? Recommendations for future research on the Alliance. *Psychotherapy: Theory, Research and Practice, 43*(3), 280–5.

Crits-Christoph, P. & Mintz, J. (1991). Implications of therapist effects for the design and analysis of comparative studies of psychotherapies. *Journal of Consulting and Clinical Psychology, 59*(1), 20–6.

Crits-Christoph, P., Siqueland, L. Blaine, J., Frank, A., Luborsky, L., Onken, L. S., Muenz, L. R., Thase, M. E., Weiss, R. D., Gastfriend, D. R., Woody, G. E., Barber, J. P., Butler, S. F., Daley, D., Salloum, I., Bishop, S., Najavits, L. M., Lis, J., Mercer, D., Griffin, M. L., Moras, K., & Beck, A. T. (1999). Psychosocial treatments for cocaine dependence: National Institute on Drug Abuse collaborative cocaine treatment study. *Archives of General Psychiatry, 56*, 493–502.

Csikszentmihalyi, M. (1990). *Flow: The Psychology of Optimal Experience*. New York: HarperCollins.

Cucciare, M. A. & Weingardt, K. R. (2007). Integrating information technology into the evidence-based practice of psychology. *Clinical Psychologist, 11*(2), 1–10.

Cuijpers, P., Dekker, J., Hollon, S.D., & Andersson, G. (2009). Adding psychotherapy to pharmacotherapy in the treatment of depressive disorders in adults: A meta-analysis. *Journal of Clinical Psychiatry, 70*, 1219–29.

Cuijpers, P., van Straten, A., Andersson, G., & van Oppen, P. (2008). Psychotherapy for depression in adults: A meta-analysis of comparative outcome studies. *Journal of Consulting and Clinical Psychology, 76*, 909–22.

Cuijpers, P., van Straten, A., van Oppen, P., & Andersson, G. (2008). Are psychological and pharmacological interventions equally effective in the treatment of adult depressive disorders? A meta-analysis of comparative studies. *Journal of Clinical Psychiatry, 69*, 1675–85.

Cullen, J. M., Spates, C. R., Pagoto, S. & Doran, N. (2006). Behavioral activation treatment for major depressive disorder: A pilot investigation. *Behavior Analyst Today, 7*, 151–64.

Curtis, R., Field, C., Knaan-Kotsman, I., & Mannix, K. (2004). What 75 psychoanalysts found helpful and hurtful in their own analyses. *Psychoanalytic Psychology, 21*(2), 183–202.

Dattilio, F. R. (ed.) (1998). *Case Studies in Couple and Family Therapy: Systemic and Cognitive Perspectives*. New York: Guildford Press.

Davanloo, H. (1980). *Short-term Dynamic Psychotherapy*. New York: Jason Aronson.

Davidson, G. (2002). Dealing with subpoenas: advice for APS psychologists. *Inpsych, 24*, 31, 33, 35.

Dawes, R. M. (1994). *House of Cards: Psychology and Psychotherapy Built on Myth*. New York: Free Press.

Dearden, J. & Jones, W. (2008). *Homicide in Australia: 2006–07 National Homicide Monitoring Program Annual Report. Monitoring Report No 1*. Canberra: Australian Institute of Criminology.

Dearden, J. & Payne, J. (2009). Alcohol and homicide in Australia. *Trends and Issues in Crime and Criminal Justice, 372*. Canberra: Australian Institute of Criminology.

Dearing, R. L., Maddux, J. E., & Tangney, J. P. (2005). Predictors of help seeking in clinical and counselling psychology graduate students. *Professional Psychology: Research and Practice, 36*, 323–9.

de Jonghe, F. (1994). Psychoanalytic supportive psychotherapy. *Journal of the American Psychoanalytic Association, 42*, 421–46.

De La Pena, C. M., Freidlander, M., & Escudero, V. (2009). Frequency, severity, and evolution of split family alliances: How observable are they? *Psychotherapy Research, 19*(2), 133–42.

Demerouti, E., Bakker, A. B., Nachreiner, F., & Schaufeli, W. B. (2001). The job demands-resources model of burnout. *Journal of Applied Psychology, 86*, 499–512.

Demick, J. (2000). Toward a mindful psychological science: Theory and application. *Journal of Social Issues, 56*(1), 141–59.

Denborough, D. (2001). *Family Therapy: Exploring the Field's Past, Present and Possible Futures*. Adelaide: Dulwich Centre.

Department of Health and Ageing (2007). *Alcohol Treatment Guidelines for Indigenous Australians*. Canberra: Department of Health and Ageing, <www.alcohol.gov.au>.

DeRubeis, R. J., Brotman, M. A., & Gibbons, C. J. (2005). A conceptual and methodological analysis of the nonspecifics argument. *Clinical Psychology: Science and Practice, 12*(2), 174–83.

DeRubeis, R. J., Gelfand, L. A., Tang, T. Z., & Simons, A.D. (1999). Medications versus cognitive behavior therapy for severely depressed outpatients: Mega-analysis of four randomized comparisons. *American Journal of Psychiatry, 156*, 1007–13.

de Shazer, S. (1988). *Clues: Investigating Solutions in Brief Therapy*. New York: Norton.

de Shazer, S. (1994). *Words Were Originally Magic*. New York: Norton.

de Shazer, S., Berg, I. K., Lipchik, E., Nunnally, E., Molnar, A., Gingerich, W., & Weiner-Davis, M. (1986). Brief Therapy: Focused solution development. *Family Process, 25*, 207–22.

Deutsch, C. J. (1985). A survey of therapists' personal problems and treatment. *Professional Psychology: Research and Practice, 16*, 305–15.

Devilly, G. J. & Cotton, P. (2004). Caveat emptor, caveat venditor, and critical incident stress debriefing/management. *Australian Psychologist, 39*, 35–40.

Diener, E., Diener, M., & Diener, C. (1995). Factors predicting the subjective well-being of nations. *Journal of Personality and Social Psychology, 69*(5), 851–64.

Dimeff, L. & Linehan, M. M. (2001). Dialectical behaviour therapy in a nutshell. *California Psychologist, 34*, 10–13.

Dinger, U. M., Strack, M., Leichsenring, F., Wilmers, F., & Schauenburg, H. (2008). Therapist effects on outcome and alliance in inpatient psychotherapy. *Journal of Clinical Psychology, 64*(3), 344–54.

Dispenza, J. (2007). *Evolve your Brain: The Science of Changing Your Mind*. New York: HCI.

Dobson, K. S., & Dozois, D. J. A. (2001). Historical and philosophical bases of the cognitive-behavioral therapies. In Dobson, K. S. (ed.). *Handbook of Cognitive-behavioral Therapies*. New York: Guilford.

Dozier, M., Cue, K. L., & Barnett, L. (1994). Clinicians as caregivers: Role of attachment organisation and treatment. *Journal of Consulting and Clinical Psychology, 62*, 793–800.

Dozier, M. & Tyrrell, C. (1998). The role of attachment in therapeutic relationships. Attachment theory and close relationships. In Simpson, J. A. & Rhodes, W. S. (eds). *Attachment Theory and Close Relationships*. New York: Guildford Press, 221–48.

Driessen, E, Cuijpers, P., de Maat, S. C. M., Abbass, A. A., de Jonghe, F., & Dekker, J. J. M. (2010). The efficacy of short-term psychodynamic psychotherapy for depression: A meta-analysis. *Clinical Psychology Review, 30*, 25–36.

Drozd, J. F. & Goldfried, M. R. (1996). A critical evaluation of the state-of-the-art in psychotherapy outcome research. *Psychotherapy, 33*(2), 171–80.

D'Souza, R. (2002). Do patients expect psychiatrists to be interested in spiritual issues? *Australasian Psychiatry, 10*(1), 44–7.

D'Souza, R. (2003). Incorporating a spiritual history into psychiatric assessment. *Australasian Psychiatry, 11*, 12–15.

D'Souza, R. D. & George, K. (2006). Spirituality, religion and psychiatry: Its application to clinical practice. *Australasian Psychiatry, 14*(4), 408–12.

Duan, C. & Hill, C. (1996). The current state of empathy research. *Journal of Counselling Psychology, 43*(3), 261–74.

Dudgeon, P. (2000). Counseling with Indigenous people. In Dudgeon, P., Garvey, D. & Pickett, H. (eds). *Working with Indigenous Australians: A Handbook for Psychologists*. Perth: Gunada Press, 249–70.

Dudgeon, P., Garvey, D., & Pickett, H. (eds) (2000). *Working with Indigenous Australians. A Handbook for Psychologists*. Perth: Gunada Press.

Duncan, B. L. (2010). *On Becoming a Better Therapist*. Washington, DC: American Psychological. Association.

Duncan, B. L. (2012). The partners for change outcome management system (PCOMS): The heart and soul of change project. *Canadian Psychology, 52*(2), 93–104.

Duncan, B. L. & Miller, S. D. (2000). The client's theory of change: Consulting the client in the integrative process. *Journal of Psychotherapy Integration, 10*(2), 169–87.

Duncan, B. L., Sparks, J. A., Miller, S.D., & Bohanske, R. T. (2006). Giving youth a voice: A preliminary study of the reliability and validity of a brief outcome measure for children, adolescents, and caretakers. *Journal of Brief Therapy, 5*, 71–88.

Duncan, B. L., Miller, S. D., & Sparks, J. A. (2004). *The Heroic Client: A Revolutionary Way to Improve Effectiveness through Client-Directed, Outcome-Informed Therapy* (rev. edn). San Francisco: Jossey-Bass.

Duncan, B. L., Miller, S. D, Sparks, J. A., Claude, D. A., Reynaulds, L. R, Brown, J., & Johnson, L. D. (2003). The Session Rating Scale: Preliminary psychometric properties of a 'Working' Alliance measure. *Journal of Brief Therapy, 3*(1), 3–12.

Duncan, B. L., Miller, S. D., Wampold, B. E., & Hubble, M. A. (eds) (2010). *The Heart and Soul of Change* (2nd edn). Washington, DC: American Psychological Association.

Duncan, B. L. & Monyihan, D. (1994). Applying outcome research: Intentional utilization of the client's frame of reference. *Psychotherapy, 31,* 294–301.

Dunkle, J. H. & Friedlander, M. L, (1996). Contribution of therapist experience and personal characteristics to the working alliance. *Journal of Counseling Psychology, 43,* 456–60.

Durlak, J. A. (1979). Comparative effectiveness of paraprofessional and professional helpers. *Psychological Bulletin, 86*(1), 80–92.

Dymond, S. & Barnes, D. (1995). A transformation of self-discrimination response functions in accordance with the arbitrarily applicable relations of sameness, more-than, and less-than. *Journal of the Experimental Analysis of Behavior, 64,* 163–84.

Eames, V. & Roth, A. (2000). Patient attachment orientation and the early working alliance: A study of patient and therapist reports of alliance quality and ruptures. *Psychotherapy Research, 10,* 421–34.

Edwards, V. J., Holden, G. W., Felitti, V. J., & Anda, R. F. (2003). Relationship between multiple forms of childhood maltreatment and adult mental health in community respondents: Results from the adverse childhood experience study. *American Journal of Psychiatry, 160,* 1453–60.

Eells, T. D. (ed.) (2007). *Handbook of Psychotherapy Case Formulation.* New York: Guilford Press.

Egan, G. (2006). *Essentials of Skilled Helping: Managing Problems, Developing Opportunities.* Belmont: Thomson Wadsworth.

Eifert, G. H., Schulte, D., Zvolensky, M. J., Lejuez, C. W., & Lau, A. W. (1997). Manualized behavior therapy: Merits and challenges. *Behavior Therapy, 28*(4), 499–509.

Ekman, P. (1994). Strong evidence for universals in facial expressions: A reply to Russell's mistaken critique. *Psychological Bulletin, 115,* 268–87.

Elkin, I., Gibbons, R., Tracie, S., Stosky, S, Watkins, J., Pilkonis, P., & Hedeker, D. (1995). Initial severity and differential treatment outcome in the National Institute of Mental Health treatment of depression collaborative research program. *Journal of Consulting and Clinical Psychology, 63*(5), 841–7.

Elkin, I., Shea, M. T., Watkins, J. T., Imber, S. D., Sotsky, S. M., Collins, J. F., Glass, D. R., Pilkonis, P. A., Leber, W. R., Docherty, J. P., et al. (1989). National Institute of Mental Health Treatment of Depression Collaborative Research Program: General effectiveness of treatments. *Archives of General Psychiatry, 46*(11), 971–82.

Ellis, A. (1984). How to deal with your most difficult client—you. *Psychotherapy in Private Practice, 2,* 25–35.

Ellis, M. V. (2001). Harmful supervision, a cause for alarm: Comment on Gray et al. (2001) and Nelson and Friedlander (2001). *Journal of Counseling Psychology, 48*(4), 410–16.

Elliott, R. (1985). Helpful and nonhelpful events in brief counseling interviews: An empirical taxonomy. *Journal of Counseling Psychology, 32*(3), 307–22.

Elman, N. S., Illfelder-Kaye, J., & Robiner, W. N. (2005). Professional development: Training for professionalism as a foundation for competent practice in psychology, *Professional Psychology: Research and Practice, 36*(4), 367–75.

Emmelkamp, P. M. G. (2004). Behaviour therapy with adults. In Lambert, M. J. (ed.). *Bergin and Garfield's Handbook of Psychotherapy and Behaviour Change*. New York: John Wiley, 139–93.

Emmelkamp, P. M. G., Bouman, T. K., & Blaauw, E. (1994). Individualized versus standardized therapy: A comparative evaluation with obsessive -compulsive patients. *Clinical Psychology and Psychotherapy, 1,* 95–100.

Epstein, R. M. & Hundert, E. M. (2002). Defining and assessing professional competence. *Journal of American Medical Association (JAMA), 287*(9), 226–35.

Etkin, A., Pittenger, C., Polan, J., & Kandel, E. R. (2005). Toward a neurobiology of psychotherapy: Basic science and clinical applications. *Journal of Neuropsychiatry and Clinical Neuroscience, 17,* 145–58.

Eugster, S. L. & Wampold, B. E. (1996). Systematic effects of participant role on evaluation of the psychotherapy session. *Journal of Consulting and Clinical Psychology, 64*(5), 1020–8.

Exline, J. J., Yali, A. M., & Lobel, M. (1999). When God disappoints: Difficulty forgiving God and its role in negative emotion. *Journal of Health Psychology, 4*(3), 365–79.

Exline, J. J., Yali, A. M., & Sanderson, W. C. (2000). Guilt, discord, and alienation: The role of religious strain in depression and suicidality. *Journal of Clinical Psychology, 56,* 1481–96.

Eysenck, H. J. (1952). The effects of psychotherapy: An evaluation. *Journal of Consulting Psychology, 16,* 319–24.

Fairburn, C. G. (1997). Interpersonal psychotherapy for bulimia nervosa. In Garner, D. M. & Garfinkel, P. E. (eds). *Handbook of Treatment for Eating Disorders*. New York: Guilford Press, 278–94.

Fairburn, C. G., Cooper, Z., Bohn, K., O'Connor, M. E., Doll, H. A., & Palmer, R. L. (2007). The severity and status of eating disorder NOS: Implications for DSM-V. *Behavioral Research and Therapy, 45*(8), 1705–15.

Fairburn, C. G., Cooper, Z., & Shafran, R. (2003). Cognitive behaviour therapy for eating disorders: a 'transdiagnostic' theory and treatment. *Behaviour Research and Therapy, 41,* 509–28.

Falconnier, L. (2009). Socioeconomic status in the treatment of depression. *American Journal of Orthopsychiatry, 79,* 148–58.

Farber, B., Manevich, I., Metzger, J., & Saypol, E. (2005). Choosing psychotherapy as a career: Why did we cross that road? *Journal of Clinical Psychology, 61,* 1009–31.

Farber, N. K. (2000). Trainees' attitudes toward seeking psychotherapy scale: Development and validation of a research instrument. *Psychotherapy, 37,* 341–53.

Fauth, J. & Williams, E. N. (2005). The in-session self-awareness of therapist-trainees: Hindering or helpful? *Journal of Counseling Psychology, 52,* 443–7.

Feeley, M., De Rubeis, R. J., & Gelfand, L. A. (1999). The temporal relation of adherence and alliance to symptom change in cognitive therapy for depression. *Journal of Consulting and Clinical Psychology, 67*(4), 578–82.

First, M. B., Bell, C. B., Cuthbert, B., Krystal, J. H., Malisson, R., Offord, D. R., Reiss, D., Shea, M. T., Widiger, T. A., & Wisner, K. L. (2002). Personality disorders and relational disorder: A research agenda for addressing critical gaps in DSM. In Kupefer, D. J., First, M. B., & Regier, D. A. (eds). *A Research Agenda for DSM-V*. Washington, DC: American Psychiatric Association, 123–99.

First, M. B. (2003). Psychiatric classification. In Tasman, A., Kay, J., & Lieberman, J. (eds). *Psychiatry, Vol. 1* (2nd edn). New York: Wiley, 659–76.

Fitzpatrick, M. (2012). Blurring practice-research boundaries using progress monitoring: A personal introduction to this issue of Canadian Psychology. *Canadian Psychology, 53(2)*, 75–81.

Fletcher, J., Bassilios, B., King, K., Kohn, K., Blashki, G., Burgess, P., & Pirkis, J. (2009). *Evaluating the Access to Allied Psychological Services Component of the Better Outcomes in Mental Health Care Program: Fourteenth Interim Evaluation Report.* Melbourne: Centre for Health Policy, Programs and Economics, University of Melbourne.

Flood, M. & Pease, B. (2006). *The Factors Influencing Community Attitudes in Relation to Violence Against Women: A Critical Review of the Literature.* Melbourne: VicHealth.

Floyd, M. Y., Myszka, M. T., & Orr, P. (1998). Licensed psychologists' knowledge and utilization of a state association colleague assistance committee. *Professional Psychology: Research and Practice, 29*, 594–8.

Foa, E. B., Kozak, M. J., Salkovskis, P. M., Coles, M. E., & Amir, N. (1998). The validation of a new obsessive compulsive disorder scale: The Obsessive-Compulsive Inventory. *Psychological Assessment, 10*, 206–14.

Foa, E. B., Rothbaum, B. O., & Furr, J. M. (2003). Augmenting exposure therapy with other CBT procedures. *Psychiatric Annals, 33*, 47–53.

Foss, L. (1994). Putting the mind back into the body: A successor scientific medical model. *Theoretical Medicine and Bioethics, 15(3)*, 291–313.

Fournier, J. C., De Rubeis, R. J., Hollon, S. D., Dimidjian, S., Amsterdam, J. D., Shelton, R. C., & Fawcett, J. (2010). Antidepressant drug effects and depression severity. A patient-level meta-analysis. *Journal of American Medical Association, 303(1)*, 47–53.

Frances, A. J., Pincus, H. A., Widiger, T. A., Davis, W. W., & First, M. B. (1990). DSM-IV: Work in progress. *American Journal of Psychiatry, 147*, 1439–48; c.f. Widiger & Clark, 2000, p. 946.

Frank, J. D. & Frank, J. B. (1991). *Persuasion and Healing: A Comparative Study of Psychotherapy.* Baltimore: John Hopkins University Press.

Fredrickson, B. L. (2000). Cultivating positive emotions to optimize health and well-being. *Prevention and Treatment, 3.* Available from <http://journals.apa.org/prevention/>.

Fredrickson, B. L. & Branigan, C. (2005). Positive emotions broaden the scope of attention and thought–action repertoires. *Cognition and Emotion, 19*, 313–32.

Fredrickson, B. L. & Levenson, R. W. (1996). Positive emotions speed recovery from the cardiovascular sequelae of negative emotions. *Cognition and Emotion, 12*, 191–220.

Fredrickson, B. L., Tugade, M. M., Waugh, C. E., & Larkin, G. R. (2003). What good are positive emotions in crises? A prospective study of resilience and emotions following the terrorist attacks on the United States on September 11, 2001. *Journal of Personality and Social Psychology, 84*, 365–76.

Freedman, J. & Combs, G. (1996). *Narrative Therapy: The Social Construction of Preferred Realities.* New York: Norton.

Freud, S. (1961). *The Future of an Illusion.* New York: Norton. (Original publication 1927).

Freud, S. (1962). *Two Short Accounts of Psycho-analysis.* Harmondsworth: Penguin Books.

Friedman, S. M. & Gelso, C.J. (2000). The development of the Inventory of Counter-transference Behaviour. *Journal of Clinical Psychology, 56*(9), 1221–35.

Furmark, T. (2002). Social phobia: Overview of community surveys. *Acta Psychiatrica Scandinavica, 105,* 84–93.

Gabbard, G. L., Lazar, S. G., Hornberger, J., & Spiegel, D. (1997). The economic impact of psychotherapy: A review. *American Journal of Psychiatry, 154,* 147–55.

Gallagher-Thompson, D., Hanley-Peterson, P., & Thompson, L. W. (1990). Mainte-nance of gains versus relapse following brief psychotherapy for depression. *Journal of Consulting and Clinical Psychology, 58,* 371–4.

Garb, H. N. (1998). *Studying the Clinician: Judgment Research and Psychological Assess-ment.* Washington, DC: American Psychological Association.

Garfield, S. L. (1981). Psychotherapy: A 40-year appraisal. *American Psychologist, 36*(2), 174–83.

Garfield, S. L. (1986). Some comments on a revolution in the training of professional psychologists. *American Psychologist, 41*(10), 1175–6.

Garfield, S. L. (1997). The therapist as a neglected variable in psychotherapy research. *Clinical Psychology: Science and Practice, 4*(1), 40–3.

Garlipp P. (2008). Koro: a culture-bound phenomenon: intercultural psychiatric implications. *German Journal of Psychiatry, 11,* 21–8.

Gaston, L., & Marmar, C. R. (1994). The California Psychotherapy Alliance Scales. In Horvath, A. O. & Greenberg, L. S. (eds). *The Working Alliance: Theory, Research, and Practice.).* New York: John Wiley, 85–108.

Gaston, L., Marmar, C. R., Gallagher, D., & Thompson, L. W. (1991). Alliance predic-tion of outcome beyond in-treatment symptomatic change as psychotherapy processes. *Psychotherapy Research, 1,* 104–12.

Gelso, C. J. (1993). On the making of a scientist-practitioner: A theory of research training in professional psychology. *Professional Psychology: Research and Prac-tice, 24,* 468–76.

Gelso, C. J. & Hayes, J. A. (1998). *The Psychotherapy Relationship: Theory, Research, and Practice.* New York: John Wiley.

Gelso, C. J., & Hayes, J. A. (2001). Countertransference management. *Psychotherapy: Theory, Research, Practice, Training, 38*(4), 418–22.

Gelso, C. J., Kelley, F. A., Fuertes, J. N., Marmarosh, C., Holmes, S. E., Costa, C., & Hancock, G. (2005). Measuring the real relationship in psychotherapy: Initial validation of the therapist form. *Journal of Counseling Psychology, 52*(4), 640–9.

Gelso, C. J., Latts, M. G., Gomez, M. J., & Fassinger, R. E. (2002). Countertransference management and therapy outcome: An initial evaluation. *Journal of Clinical Psy-chology, 58,* 861–7.

George, E., Iveson, C., & Ratner, H. (1999). *Problem to Solution.* London: BT Press.

Gilbert, P. & Leahy, R. L. (eds) (2007). *The Therapeutic Relationship in the Cognitive Behavioral Psychotherapies.* Hove, East Sussex: Routledge.

Gilroy, P. J., Carroll, L., & Murray, J. (2002). A preliminary survey of counseling psy-chologists' personal experiences with depression and treatment. *Professional Psychology: Research and Practice, 33,* 402–7.

Gitlin, M. J., Swendsen, J., Heller, T. L., & Hammen, C. (1995). Relapse and impair-ment in bipolar disorder. *American Journal of Psychiatry, 152,* 1635–40.

Gladwell, M. (2008). *Outliers: The Story of Success.* London: Little, Brown.

Glass, L. L. (2003). The gray areas of boundary crossing and violations. *American Journal of Psychotherapy, 57*(4), 429–44.

Gloaguen, V., Cottraux, J., Cucherat, M., & Blackburn, I. (1998). A meta-analysis of the effects of cognitive therapy in depressed patients. *Journal of Affective Disorders, 49,* 59–72.

Goddard, A., Murray, C. D., & Simpson, J. (2008). Informed consent and psychotherapy: An interpretative phenomenological analysis of therapists' views. *Psychology and Psychotherapy: Theory, Research and Practice, 81*(2), 177–91.

Gold, S. & Hilsenroth, M. (2009). Effects of graduate clinicians' personal therapy on therapeutic alliance. *Clinical Psychology and Psychotherapy, 16,* 159–71.

Goldberg, C. (2006). Harvard's crowded course to happiness: 'Positive psychology' draws students in droves, *Boston Globe,* 10 March.

Goldfried, M. R. (1980). Toward the delineation of therapeutic change principles. *American Psychologist, 35,* 991–9.

Goldfried, M. R. (1991). Transtheoretical ingredients in therapeutic change. In Curtis, R. C. & Stricker, G. (eds). *How People Change Inside and Outside Therapy.* New York: Plenum Press, 29–38.

Goldfreid, M. R. (ed.). (2001). *How Therapists Change: Personal And Professional Reflections.* Washington, DC: American Psychological Association.

Goldfried, M. R. (ed.). (2005). *How Therapists Change: Personal and Professional Reflections.* Washington DC: Americal Psychological Association.

Goldfried, M. R. & Davila, J. (2005). The role of relationship and technique in therapeutic change. *Psychotherapy: Theory, Research, Practice, Training, 42*(4), 421–30.

Goldfried, M. R. & Padawer, W. (1982). Current status and future directions in psychotherapy. In Goldfried, M. R. (ed.). *Converging Themes in Psychotherapy.* New York: Springer, 3–49.

Gollwitzer, P. M. (1993). Goal achievement: The role of intentions. *European Review of Social Psychology, 4,* 141–85.

Goodman, W. K., Price, L. H., Rasmussen, S. A., Mazure, C., Fleischmann, R. L., Hill, C. L., Heninger, G. R., Charney, D. S., et al. (1989a). The Yale-Brown Obsessive Compulsive Scale: I. Development, use, and reliability. *Archives of General Psychiatry, 46,* 1006–11.

Goodman, W. K., Price, L. H., Rasmussen, S. A., Mazure, C., Delgado, P., Heninger, G. R., & Chaney, D. S. (1989b). The Yale-Brown Obsessive Compulsive Scale: II. Validity. *Archives of General Psychiatry, 46,* 1012–16.

Gortner, E. T., Gollan, J. K., Dobson, K. S., & Jacobson, N. S. (1998). Cognitive behavioral treatment for depression: Relapse prevention. *Journal of Consulting and Clinical Psychology, 66*(2), 377–84.

Gould, R. A., Otto, M. W., Pollack, M. P., & Yap, L. (1997). Cogntive-behavioral and pharmacological treatment of generalized anxiety disorder: A preliminary meta-analysis. *Behavior Therapy, 28,* 285–305.

Grad, O. T. & Michel, K. (2005). Therapists as client suicide survivors. *Women and Therapy, 28*(1), 71–81.

Grawe, K. (1997). Research-informed psychotherapy. *Psychotherapy Research, 7*(1), 1–19.

Greenberg, L. S. (2002). *Emotion-Focused Therpay. Coaching Clients to Work through Their Feelings.* Washington, DC: American Psychological Association.

Greenberg, L. S. (2002). Integrating an emotion-focused approach to treatment into psychotherapy integration. *Journal of Psychotherapy Integration, 12*(2), 154–89.

Greenberg, L. S., Elliott, R., Watson, J., & Bohart, A. (2001). Empathy. *Psychotherapy, 38*(4), 380–4.

Greenberg, L. S. & Pascual-Leone, A. (2006). Emotion in psychotherapy: A practice-friendly research review. *Journal of Clinical Psychology: In Session, 62*(5), 611–30.

Greenberg, L. S., Watson, J. C., & Lietaer, G. (1998). *Handbook of Experiential Psychotherapy.* New York: Guildford Press.

Greenberg, L. S. & Watson, J. C. (2005). *Emotion-Focused Therapy for Depression.* Washington, DC: American Psychological Association Press

Greenberg, M. D., Craighead, W. E., Evans, D. D., & Craighead, L. W. (1995). An investigation into the effects of comorbid Axis II pathology on outcome of inpatient treatment for unipolar depression. *Journal of Psychopathology and Behavioural Assessment, 17*, 305–21.

Greenberg, R. P., Constantino, M. J., & Bruce, N. (2005). Are patient expectations still relevant for psychotherapy process and outcome? *Clinical Psychology Review, 26*, 657–78.

Grencavage, L. M. & Norcross, J. C. (1990). Where are the commonalities among the therapeutic common factors? *Professional Psychology: Research and Practice, 21*(5), 372–8.

Grilo, C. M., Mondy, R., Barolow, D. H., Goddard, A. W., Gorman, J. M., Hofmann, S. G., Papp, L. A., Shear, M. K., & Woods, S. W. (1998). Pre-treatment client factors predicting attrition from a multicentre randomized controlled treatment study for panic disorder. *Comprehensive Psychiatry, 39*(6), 323–31.

Grosse Holforth, M. (2008). Avoidance motivation in psychological problems and psychotherapy. *Psychotherapy Research, 18*(2), 147–59.

Grosse Holtforth, M., Grawe, K., & Castonguay, L.G. (2006). Predicting a reduction of avoidance motivation in psychotherapy: Toward the delineation of differential processes of change operating at different phases of treatment. *Psychotherapy Research, 16*(5), 639–44.

Guastella, A. J., Lovibond, P.F., Dadds, M. R., Mitchell, P., & Richardson, R. (2007). A randomised controlled trial of the effect of d-cycloserine on extinction and fear conditioning in humans. *Behaviour Research and Therapy, 45*(4), 663–72.

Gunderson, J. G., Frank, A. F., Ronningstam, E. F., Wachter, S., Lynch, V. J., & Wolf, P. J. (1989). Early discontinuance of borderline clients from psychotherapy. *Journal of Mental and Nervous Disease, 177*(1), 38–42.

Gutheil, T. G. & Applebaum, P. S. (1980). Substituted judgment and the physician's ethical dilemma: With special reference to the problem of the psychiatric patient. *Journal of Clinical Psychiatry, 41*, 303–5.

Guttman, H. A. (1991). Systems theory, cybernetics, and epistemology. In Gurman, A. S. & Kniskern, D. P. (eds). *Handbook of Family Therapy, Vol. 2.* New York: Brunner/Mazel.

Haas, E., Hill, R. D., Lambert, M., & Morrell, B. (2002). Do early responders to psychotherapy maintain treatment gains? *Journal of Clinical Psychology, 58*(9), 1157–72.

Hackney, C. H. & Sanders, G. S. (2003). Religiosity and mental health: A meta-analysis of recent studies. *Journal of the Scientific Study of Religion, 42*(1), 43–55.

Hall, T. W. & Edwards, K. J. (2002). The Spiritual Assessment Inventory: A theistic model and measure for assessing spiritual development. *Journal for the Scientific Study of Religion, 41*(2), 341–57.

Hamilton, M. (1960). A rating scale for depression. *Journal of Neurology, Neurosurgery and Psychiatry, 23,* 56–62.

Hamilton, M. (1967). Development of a rating scale for primary depressive illness. *British Journal of Social and Clinical Psychology, 6,* 278–96.

Hanna, F. J. & Ritchie, M.H. (1995). Seeking the active ingredients of psychotherapeutic change: Within and outside the context of therapy. *Professional Psychology: Research and Practice, 26*(2), 176–83.

Hannan, C., Lambert, M. J., Harmon, C., Nielsen, S. L., Smart, D. M., Shimokawa, K., & Sutton, S. W. (2005). A lab test and algorithms for identifying patients at risk for treatment failure. *Journal of Clinical Psychology: In Session, 61*(2), 155–63.

Hansen, A. M., Hoogduin, C. A., Schaap, C., & de Haan, E. (1992). Do drop-outs differ from successfully treated obsessive-compulsives? *Behavior Research Therapy, 30*(5), 547–50.

Hansen, N. B., Lambert, M. J., & Forman, E. M. (2002). The psychotherapy dose-response effect and its implications for treatment delivery services. *Clinical Psychology: Science and Practice, 9,* 329–43.

Hardy, G. E., Cahill, J., Shapiro, D. A., Barkham, M., Rees, A., & Macaskill, N. (2001). Client interpersonal and cognitive styles as predictors of response to time-limited cognitive therapy for depression. *Journal of Consulting and Clinical Psychology, 69*(5), 841–5.

Harlen, M. (2002). *The Effect of a Brief Indigenous Workshop on the Cultural Competence of Psychology Students: A Pilot Study.* Brisbane: Griffith University.

Harmon, S. C., Lambert, M. J., Smart, D. W., Hawkins, E. J., Nielsen, S. L., Slade, K., & Lutz, W. (2007). Enhancing outcome for potential treatment failures: Therapist/client feedback and clinical support tools. *Psychotherapy Research, 17,* 379–92.

Harris, R. (2006). Embracing your demons: An overview of acceptance and commitment therapy. *Psychotherapy in Australia, 12,* 2–-8.

Harris, R. (2008). *The Happiness Trap: Stop Struggling, Start Living.* Wollombi: Exisle Publishing Limited.

Hartley, D. E. & Strupp, H. H. (1983). The therapeutic alliance: Its relationship to outcome in brief psychotherapy. In Masling, J. (ed.). *Empirical studies of psychoanalytical theories, Vol. 1.* Hillsdale, NJ: Analytical Press, 1–38.

Harnett, P., O'Donovan, A., & Lambert, M. J. (2010). The dose response relationship in psychotherapy: Implications for social policy. *Clinical Psychologist, 14*(2), 39–44.

Hassenstab, J., Dziobek, I., Rogers, K., Wolf, O., & Convit, A. (2007). Knowing what others know, feeling what others feel: A controlled study of empathy in psychotherapists. *Journal of Nervous and Mental Disease, 195*(4), 277–81.

Haswell-Elkins, M., Hunter, E., Wargent, R., Hall, B., et al. (2009). *Protocols for the Delivery of Social and Emotional Well-being and Mental Health Services in Indigenous Communities: Guidelines for Health Workers, Clinicians, Consumers and Carers.* Cairns: University of Queensland and Queensland Health.

Hatcher, R. L. & Barends, A. W. (1996). Patients' view of the alliance in psychotherapy: Exploratory factor analysis of three alliance measures. *Journal of Consulting and Clinical Psychology, 64,* 1326–36.

Hatfield, E. & Sprecher, S. (1995). Men's and women's preferences in marital partners in the United States, Russia and Japan. *Journal of Cross-cultural Psychology, 26,* 278–750.

Hattie, J. A., Sharpley, C. F., & Rogers, H. J. (1984). Comparative effectiveness of professional and paraprofessional helpers. *Psychological Bulletin, 95*(3), 534–41.

Hawkins, P. & Shohet, R. (2012). *Supervision in the Helping Professions.* Milton Keynes: Open University Press.

Hawton, K., Salkovskis, P. M., & Kirk, D. B. (eds). (1989). *Cognitive BehaviourTherapy for Psychiatric Problems.* Oxford: Oxford Medical Press.

Hay, M. W. (1989). Principles in building spiritual assessment tools. *American Journal of Hospice Care, 6,* 25–31.

Hayes, A. (2008). Are family changes, social trends and unanticipated policy consequences making children's lives more challenging? *Family Matters, 78,* 60–3.

Hayes, A. M., Beevers, C. G., Feldman, G. C., Laurenceau, J., & Perlman, C. (2005). Avoidance and processing as predictors of symptom change and positive growth in an integrative therapy for depression. *International Journal of Behavioral Medicine, 12*(2), 111–22.

Hayes, S. C. & Brownstein, A. J. (1986). Mentalism, behavior-behavior relations, and a behavior analytic view of the purposes of science. *Behavior Analyst, 9,* 175–90.

Hayes, A. M., Feldman, C. G., Beevers, C. G., Laurenceau, J., Cardaciotto, L., & Lewis-Smith, J. (2007). Discontinuities and cognitive changes in an exposure-based cognitive therapy for depression. *Journal of Consulting and Clinical Psychology, 75*(3), 409–21.

Hayes, A. M., Feldman G. C., & Goldfried, M. R. (2007). The Change and Growth Experiences Scale: A measure of insight and emotional processing, In Castonguay, L.G. & Hill, C. E. (eds.). *Insight in Psychotherapy.* Washington, DC: American Psychological Association, 231–53.

Hayes, J., Riker, J., & Ingram, K. (1997). Countertransference behavior and management in brief counseling: A field study. *Psychotherapy Research, 7,* 145–53.

Hayes, J. & Wall, T. (1998). What influences clinicians' responsibility attributions? The role of problem type, theoretical orientation, and client attribution. *Journal of Social and Clinical Psychology, 17,* 69–74.

Hayes, S. C. (1993). Analytic goals and the varieties of scientific contextualism. In Hayes, S. C., Hayes, L. J., Reese, H. W., & Sarbin, T. R. (eds) *Varieties of Scientific Contextualism.* Reno, NV: Context Press, 11–27.

Hayes, S. C. (2002). Buddhism and acceptance and commitment therapy. *Cognitive and Behavioral Practice, 9,* 58–66.

Hayes, S. C., Barlow, D. H., & Nelson-Gray, R. O. (1999). *The Scientist Practitioner: Research and Accountability in the Age of Managed Care* (2nd edn). Boston: Allyn & Bacon.

Hayes, S.C., Barnes-Holmes, D., & Roche, B. (eds). (2001). *Relational Frame Theory: A Post-Skinnerian Account of Human Language and Cognition.* New York: Plenum Press.

Hayes, S. C. & Brownstein, A. J. (1986). Mentalism, behavior-behavior relations, and a behavior-analytic view of the purposes of science. *Behavior Analyst, 9,* 175–90.

Hayes, S. C., Luoma, J. B., Bond, F. W., Masuda, A., & Lillis, J. (2006). Acceptance and commitment therapy: Model, processes and outcomes. *Behavior Research and Therapy, 44*(1), 1–25.

Hayes, S. C. & Strosahl, K. D. (eds) (2005). *A Practical Guide to Acceptance and Commitment Therapy.* New York: Springer-Verlag.

Hayes, S. C., Strosahl, K. D., & Wilson, K. G. (1999). *Acceptance and Commitment Therapy: An Experiential Approach to Behaviour Change.* New York: Guilford Press.

Healy, D. (1993). *Psychiatric Drugs Explained.* London: Mosby.

Heater, M. L. (2003). Ethnocultural considerations in family therapy. *Journal of the American Psychiatric Nurses Association, 9,* 46–54.

Hebl, M. R. & Heatherton, T. F. (1998). The stigma of obesity in women: The difference is black and white. *Personality and Social Psychology Bulletin, 24,* 417–26.

Heckhausen, H. (1991). *Motivation and Action.* New York: Springer-Verlag.

Helbok, C. M. Mrinelli, R. P., & Walls, R. T. (2006). National survey of ethical practices across rural an urban communities. *Professional Psychology: Research and Practice, 37*(1), 36–44.

Held, B. S. (1991). The process/content distinction in psychotherapy revisited. *Journal of Social and Clinical Psychology, 28,* 207–17.

Helman, C. (2000). *Culture, Health and Illness.* Oxford: Butterworth Heinemann.

Helmeke, K. B. & Sori, C. F. (2006). *The Therapist's Notebook for Integrating Spirituality in Counseling: Homework, Handouts, and Activities for Use in Psychotherapy.* Binghampton, NY: Haworth Press.

Henderson, S., Byrne, D. G., & Duncan-Jones, P. (1982). *Neurosis and the Social Environment.* Sydney: Academic Press.

Henrink, R. (ed.) (1980). *The Psychotherapy Handbook: The A to Z Guide to More than 250 Different Therapies in Use Today.* New York: New American Library.

Henry, W. P., Schacht, T. E., & Strupp, H. H. (1986). Structural analysis of social behavior: Application to a study of interpersonal process in differential psychotherapeutic outcome. *Journal of Consulting and Clinical Psychology, 54,* 27–31.

Henry, W. P., Schacht, T. E., & Strupp, H. H. (1990). Patient and therapist introject, interpersonal process, and differential psychotherapy outcome. *Journal of Consulting and Clinical Psychology, 58,* 768–74.

Hersoug, A. G. (2004). Assessment of therapists' and patients' personality: Relationship to therapeutic technique and outcome in Brief Dynamic Psychotherapy. *Journal of Personality Assessment, 83*(3), 191–200.

Hiatt, D. & Hargrave, G. E. (1995). The characteristics of highly effective therapists in managed behavioural provider networks. *Behavioral Healthcare Tomorrow,* 19–22.

Hickie, I. B., Davenport, T., & Luscombe, G. M. (2007). Mental health expenditure in Australia: Time for affirmative action. *Australian and New Zealand Journal of Public Health, 30*(2), 119–22.

Hickie, I. B. & McGorry, P. D. (2007). Increased access to evidence-based primary mental health care: will the implementation match the rhetoric? *Medical Journal of Australia, 187*(2), 100.

Hilgard, E. R., Kelly, E. L., Luckey, B., Sanford, R. N., Shaffer, L. F., & Shakow, D. (1947). Recommended graduate training program in clinical psychology. *American Psychologist*, 2, 539–58.

Hill, C. E. (1995). What are the mechanisms of change in the common factors? A reaction to Weinberger. *Clinical Psychology: Science and Practice*, 2(1), 87–9.

Hill, C. E. (2009). Reaction to Goldfried (1980): What about therapist techniques? *Applied and Preventive Psychology*, 13, 16–18.

Hill, C. E. & Knox, S. (2002). Self-disclosure. In Norcross, J. C. (ed.). *Psychotherapy Relationships that Work*. New York: Oxford University Press, 249–59.

Hill, C. & O'Brien, K. (1999). *Helping Skills: Facilitating Exploration, Insight and Action*. Washington: American Psychological Society.

Hill, C. E., Stahl, J., & Roffman, M. (2007). Training novice psychotherapists: Helping skills and beyond. *Psychotherapy: Theory, Research, Practice, Training*, 44(4), 364–70.

Hill, C. E., Sullivan, C., Knox, S., & Schlosser, L. (2007). Becoming psychotherapists: Experiences of novice trainees in a beginning graduate class. *Psychotherapy: Theory, Research, Practice, Training*, 44(4), 434–49.

Hillman, J. (2009). Clinical demonstration: Case history/soul history. Anaheim, CA: Evolution of Psychotherapy Conference, 11 December 2009.

Hilsenroth, M. J., Ackerman, S. J., & Blagys, M. D. (2001). Evaluating the phase model of change during short-term psychodynamic psychotherapy. *Psychotherapy Research*, 11, 29–47.

Hobara, M. (2005). Beliefs about appropriate pain behaviour: Cross-cultural and sex differences between Japanese and EuroAmericans. *European Journal of Pain*, 9, 389–93.

Hoffman, P. D., Fruzetti, A. E., & Swenson, C. R. (1999). Dialectical Behavior Therapy: Family skills training. *Family Process*, 38(4), 399–414.

Hofmann, S. G. & Asmundson, G. J. (2008). Acceptance and mindfulness-based therapy: New wave or old hat? *Clinical Psychology Review*, 28(1), 1–16.

Holub, E. A. & Lee, S. S. (1990). Therapists' use of non-erotic physical contact. *Professional Psychology: Research and Practice*, 21(2), 115–23.

Holzman, L. A., Searight, H. R., & Hughes, H. M. (1996). Clinical psychology graduate students and personal psychotherapy: Results of an exploratory survey. *Professional Psychology: Research and Practice*, 27, 98–101.

Hopko, D. R., Robertson, S., & Lejuez, C. W. (2006). Behavioural activation for anxiety disorders. *Behavior Analyst Today*, 7, 212–32.

Horn, N. R., Dolan, M., Elliott, R., Deakin, J. F. W., & Woodruff, P. W. R. (2003). Response inhibition and impulsivity: an fMRI study. *Neuropsychologia*, 41(14), 1959–66.

Horowitz, M. J., Marmar, C. M., Weiss, D. S., DeWitt, K. N., & Rosenbaum, R. (1984). Brief psychotherapy of bereavement reactions. *Archives of General Psychiatry*, 41, 438–48.

Horvath, A. O. (1994a). Empirical validation of Bordin's pantheoretical model of the alliance: The Working Alliance Inventory perspective. In Horvath, A. O. & Greenberg, L. S. (eds.). *The Working Alliance: Theory, Research, and Practice*. New York: John Wiley, 109–28.

Horvath, A. O. (1994b). Research on the alliance. In Horvath, A. O. & Greenberg, L. S. (eds.). *The Working Alliance: Theory, Research, and Practice*. New York: John Wiley, 259–87.

Horvath, A. O. (1995). The therapeutic relationship: From transference to alliance. *Psychotherapy in Practice*, *1*(1), 7–17.

Horvath, A. O. (2005). The therapeutic relationship: Research and theory. An introduction to the Special Issue. *Psychotherapy Research*, *15*(1–2), 3–7.

Horvath, A. O. & Bedi, R. P. (2002). The Alliance. In Norcross, J. C. (ed.). *Psychotherapy Relationships that Work: Therapist Contributions and Responsiveness to Patients*. New York: Oxford University Press, 37–69.

Horvath, A. O. & Greenberg, L. S. (1986). The development of the Working Alliance Inventory. In Greenberg, L. S. & Pinsof, W. M. (eds). *The Psychotherapeutic Process: A Research Handbook*. New York: Guilford Press, 529–56.

Horvath, A. O. & Greenberg, L. S. (1989). Development and validation of the Working Alliance Inventory. *Journal of Counseling Psychology*, *36*, 223–33.

Horvath, A. O. & Symonds, B. D. (1991). Relation between working alliance and outcome in psychotherapy: A meta-analysis. *Journal of Counseling Psychology*, *38*, 139–49.

Howard, K. I., Kopta, S. M., Krause, M. S., & Orlinsky, D. E. (1986). The dose-effect relationship in psychotherapy. *American Psychologist*, *41*(2), 159–64.

Howard, K. I., Lueger, R.J., Maling, M.S., & Martinovich, Z. (1993). A phase model of psychotherapy outcome: Causal mediation of change. *Journal of Consulting and Clinical Psychology*, *61*(4), 678–85.

Howard, K. I., Moras, K., Brill, P. L., Martinovich, Z., & Lutz, W. (1996). Evaluation of psychotherapy: Efficacy, effectiveness and patient progress. *American Psychologist*, *51*(10), 1059–64.

Hubble, M. A., Duncan, B. L., & Miller, S.D. (1999). Introduction. In Hubble, M. A., Duncan, B. L. & Miller, S. D. (eds). *The Heart and Soul of Change: What Works in Therapy*. Washington, DC: American Psychological Association, 1–19.

Hubble, M. A., Duncan, B. L., and Miller, S. D. (1999). *The Heart and Soul of Change: What Works in Therapy*. Washington, DC: American Psychological Association.

Hubble, M. A., Duncan, B. L., Miller, S. D., & Wampold, B. E. (2010). In Duncan, B. L., Miller, S. D., Wampold, B. E. & Hubble, M. A. (eds). *The Heart and Soul of Change* (2nd edn). Washington, DC: American Psychological Association, 23–46.

Human Rights and Equal Opportunity Commission (HROEC) (1993). *Report of the National Inquiry into the Human Rights of People with Mental Illness*. Sydney: Human Rights and Equal Opportunity Commission <www.humanrights.gov.au>.

Human Rights and Equal Opportunity Commission (HROEC) (1997). *Bringing Them Home: National Inquiry into the Separation of Aboriginal and Torres Strait Islander Children from their Families*. Sydney: Human Rights and Equal Opportunity Commission <www.humanrights.gov.au>.

Hunter, E. & Milroy, H. (2006). Aboriginal and Torres Strait Islander Suicide in context. *Archives of Suicide Research*, *10*, 141–57.

Huppert, J. D., Bufka, L. F., Barlow, D., Gorman, J., Shear, M., & Woods, S. (2001). Therapists, therapist variables, and cognitive-behavioral therapy outcomes in a multicenter trial for panic disorder. *Journal of Consulting and Clinical Psychology*, *69*(5), 747–55.

Ibrahim, L., DiazGranados, N., Franco-Chaves, J., Brutsche, N., Henter, I. D., Kronstein, P., et al. (2012). Course of improvement in depressive symptoms to a single intravenous infusion of ketamine vs add-on riluzole: Results from a 4-week, double-blind, placebo-controlled study. *Neuropsychopharmacology, 2012,* 1–8.

Ilardi, S. S. & Craighead, W.E. (1994). The role of nonspecific factors in cognitive-behavior therapy for depression. *Clinical Psychology: Science and Practice, 1*(2), 138–56.

Imel, Z. E., Malterer, M. B., McKay, K. M., & Wampold, B. E. (2008). A meta-analysis of psychotherapy and medication in unipolar depression and dysthymia. *Journal of Affective Disorders, 110,* 197–206.

Irvine, J. T. (1990). Registering affect: Heteroglossia in the Linguistic expression of emotion. In Lutz, C. A. & Abu-Lughod, L. (eds). *Language and the Politics of Emotions.* Cambridge, UK: Cambridge University Press, 126–61.

Iveson, C. (2002). Solution-focused brief therapy. *Advances in Psychiatric Treatment, 8,* 149–57.

Ivey, A. E. & Ivey, M. B. (2003). *Intentional Interviewing and Counselling: Facilitating Client Development in a Multicultural Society* (5th edn). Melbourne: Thomson.

Jacobson, N. S., Dobson, K. S., Traux, P. A., Addis, M. E., Koerner, K., Gollan, J. K., Gortner, E., & Prince, S. (1996). A component analysis of cognitive-behavioural treatment for depression. *Journal of Consulting and Clinical Psychology, 64*(2), 295–304.

Jacobson, N. S., Martell, C. R., & Dimidjian, S. (2001). Behavioral activation therapy for depression: Returning to contextual roots. *Clinical Psychology: Science and Practice, 8,* 255-270.

Jacobson, N. S., Roberts, L. J., Berns, S. B. & McGlinchey, J. B. (1999). Methods for defining and determining the clinical significance of treatment effects: Description, application, and alternatives. *Journal of Consulting and Clinical Psychology, 67,* 300–7.

Jacobson, N. S. & Truax, P. (1991). Clinical significance: A statistical approach to defining meaningful change in psychotherapy research. *Journal of Consulting and Clinical Psychology, 59,* 12–19.

James, W. (1890). *The Principles of Psychology.* Boston: Harvard University Press.

Jenaro, C., Flores, N., & Arias, B. (2007). Burnout and coping in human service practitioners. *Professional Psychology: Research and Practice, 38,* 80–7.

Jenkins, S. J., Fuqua, D. R., & Blum, C. R. (1986). Factors related to duration of counselling in a university counselling center. *Psychological Reports, 58,* 467–72.

Jennings, L., & Skovholt, T. M. (1999). The cognitive, emotional, and relational characteristics of master therapists. *Journal of Counseling Psychology, 46*(1), 3–11.

Johnson, S. M. (2002). *Emotionally Focused Couple Therapy with Trauma Survivors: Strengthening Attachment Bonds.* New York: Guilford Press.

Johnson, S. M. & Sims, A. (2000). Attachment theory: A map for couples therapy. In Levy, T. (ed.). *Handbook of Attachment Interventions.* San Diego: Academic Press, 167–91.

Joinson, A. (1999). Social desirability, anonymity and Internet based questions. *Behavior Research Methods, 31,* 433–8.

Jones, E. E., Cumming, J. D., & Horowitz, M. J. (1988). Another look at the nonspecific hypothesis of therapeutic effectiveness. *Journal of Consulting and Clinical Psychology, 56*(1), 48–55.

Jones, E. E. & Zoppel, C. L. (1982). Impact of client and therapist gender on psycho-therapy process and outcome. *Journal of Consulting and Clinical Psychology, 50*(2), 259–72.

Jorgensen, C. R. (2004). Active ingredients in individual psychotherapy. *Psychoanalytic Psychology, 21*(4), 516–40.

Joyce, A. S., Ogrodniczuk, J. S., Piper, W. E., & McCallum, M. (2003). The alliance as mediator of expectancy effects in short-term individual therapy. *Journal of Consulting and Clinical Psychology, 71*(4), 672–9.

Joyner, T. & Coyne, J. C. (1999). *The Interactional Nature of Depression.* Washington, DC: American Psychological Association.

Kabat-Zinn, J. (1990). *Full Catastrophe Living: Using the Wisdom of your Body and Mind to Face Stress, Pain and Illness.* New York: Delacorte.

Kabat-Zinn, J. (2003). Mindfulness-based interventions in context: Past, present and future. *Clinical Psychology: Science and Practice, 10*(2), 144–56.

Kadera, S. W., Lambert, M. J., & Andrews, A. A. (1996). A session-by-session analysis of the psychotherapy dose-effect relationship. *Journal of Psychotherapy Practice and Research, 5,* 132–51.

Kahn, M. (1997). *Between Therapist and Client.* New York: Freeman.

Kahneman, D., Diener, E., & Schwarz, N. (eds) (1999). *Well-Being: The Foundations of Hedonic Psychology.* New York: Russel Sage Foundation.

Kampf, A., McSherry, B., Thomas, S., & Abrahams, H. (2008). Psychologists' perceptions of legal and ethical requirements for breaching confidentiality. *Australian Psychologist, 43*(3): 194–204.

Kanfer, F. & Phillips, J. S. (1970). *Learning Foundations of Behavior Therapy.* New York: Wiley.

Kanfer, F. & Saslow, G. (1965). Behavioral analysis: An alternative to diagnostic classification. *Archives of General Psychiatry, 12,* 529–38.

Kanter, J. W., Cautilli, J. D., Busch, A. M., & Baruch, D. E. (2005). Toward a comprehensive functional analysis of depressive behavior: Five environmental factors and a possible sixth and seventh. *Behavior Analyst Today, 6,* 65–78.

Kaplan. H. I. & Sadock, B.J. (1988). *Synopsis of Psychiatry. Behavioral Sciences, Clinical Psychiatry* (5th edn). London: Williams & Wilkins.

Kaplan, H. I., Sadock, B. J., & Grebb, J. A. (1994). *Synopsis of Psychiatry* (7th edn). London: Williams &Wilkens.

Kawakami, N., Shimizu, H., Haratani, T., & Iwata, N. (2004). Lifetime and 6-month prevalence of DSM-III-R psychiatric disorders in an urban community in Japan. *Psychiatry Research, 121,* 293–301.

Kazdin, A. E. (1986). Comparative outcome studies of psychotherapy: Methodological issues and strategies. *Journal of Consulting and Clinical Psychology, 54*(1), 95–105.

Kazdin, A. E. (1999). The meaning and measurement of clinical significance. *Journal of Consulting and Clinical Psychology, 67,* 332–9.

Kazdin, A. E. (2003). *Research Design in Clinical Psychology.* Needham Heights, MA: Allyn & Bacon.

Kazdin, A. E. (2005). Treatment outcomes, common factors and continued neglect of mechanisms of change. *Clinical Psychology: Science and Practice, 12*(2), 184–8.

Kazdin, A. E. (2006). Mechanisms of change in psychotherapy: Advances, break-throughs and cutting-edge research (do not yet exist). In Bootzin, R. R. & McKnight, P. E. (eds). *Strengthening Research Methodology: Psychological Measurement and Evaluation*. Washington, DC: American Psychological Association, 77–101.

Kazdin, A. E. (2007). Mediators and mechanisms of change in psychotherapy research. *Annual Review of Clinical Psychology, 3*, 1–27.

Kazdin, A. E. (2008). Evidence-based treatment and practice: New opportunities to bridge clinical research and practice, enhance the knowledge base, and improve patient care. *American Psychologist, 63*, 146–59.

Keller, H. (2002). Culture and development: developmental pathways to individualism and interrelatedness. In Lonner, W. J., Dinnel, D. L., Hayes, S. A., & Sattler, D. N. (eds). *Online Readings in Psychology and Culture*. Bellingham, WA: Center for Cross-Cultural Research, Western Washington University, unit 11, chapter 11.

Kendall, P. C., Marrs-Garcia, A., Nath, S. R. & Sheldrick, R. C. (1999). Normative comparisons for the evaluation of clinical significance. *Journal of Consulting and Clinical Psychology, 67*, 285–99.

Kendall, R. & Jablensky, A. (2003). Distinguishing between the validity and utility of psychiatric diagnoses. *American Journal of Psychiatry, 160*, 2–12.

Kendell, R. E. (1975). *The Role of Diagnosis in Psychiatry*. London: Basil Blackwell.

Kenneth, R. M. & Montgomery, R. B. (1977). The first national conference on training in professional psychology. *Australian Psychologist, 12*(3), 319–26.

Khawaja, N. G., Oei, T. P. S., & Baglioni, A. J. (1994). Modification of the Catastrophic Cognitions Questionnaire (CCQ-M) for normals and psychiatric patients: Exploratory and LISREL analysis. *Journal of Psychopathology and Behavioral Assessment, 16*, 325-342.

Kim, D.-M., Wampold, B. E., & Bolt, D. M. (2006). Therapist effects in psychotherapy: A random-effects modelling of the National Institute of Mental Health Treatment of Depression Collaborative Research data. *Psychotherapy Research, 16*(2), 161–72.

Kim, N. S., & Ahn, W. (2002). Clinical psychologists' theory-based representations of mental disorders predict their diagnostic reasoning and memory. *Journal of Experimental Psychology: General, 131*, 451–76.

Kirsch, I., Deacon, B. J., Huedo-Medina, T. B., Scoboria, A., Moore, T. J., & Johnson, B. T. (2008). Initial severity and antidepressant benefits: A meta-analysis of data submitted to the Food and Drug Administration. *PLoS Medicine, 5*, 260–8.

Kivlighan, D. M. & Shaughnessy, P. (2000). Patterns of working alliance development: A typology of clients working alliance ratings. *Journal of Counseling Psychology, 47*(3), 362 71.

Klein, D. N., Schwartz, J. E., Santiago, N. J., Vivian, D., Vocisano, C., Castonguay, L. G., Arnow, B., Blalock, J. A., Manber, R., Markowitz, J. C., Riso, L. P., Rothbaum, B., McCullough, J. P., Thase, M. E., Borian, F. E., Miller, J. W., & Keller, M. B. (2003). Therapeutic alliance in depression treatment: Controlling for prior change and patient characteristics. *Journal of Consulting and Clinical Psychology, 71*(6), 997–1006.

Kleinke, C. L. (1994). *Common Principles of Psychotherapy*. Pacific Grove, CA: Brooks Cole.

Klerman, G. L., Weissman, M. M., Rounsaville, B. J., & Chevron, E. S. (1984). *Interpersonal Psychotherapy of Depression*. New York: Basic Books.

Koenig, H. G. (2004). Religion, spirituality, and medicine: Research findings and implications for clinical practice. *Southern Medical Journal, 97*(12), 1194–1200.

Koenig, H. G., Cohen, H. J., Blazer, D. G., Pieper, C., Meador, K. G., Shelp, F., Goli, V., & DiPasquiale, B. (1992). Religious coping and depression among elderly hospitalized medically ill men. *American Journal of Psychiatry, 149*(12), 1693–1700.

Koenig, H. G., McCullough, M. E., & Larson, D. B. (2001). *Handbook of Religion and Health.* New York: Oxford University Press.

Kohut, H. & Strozier, C. (1985). *Self Psychology and the Humanities: Reflections on a New Psychoanalytic Approach.* New York & London: Norton.

Kopta, S. M., Howard, K. I., Lowry, J. L., & Beutler, L. E. (1994). Patterns of symptomatic recovery in psychotherapy. *Journal of Consulting and Clinical Psychology, 62,* 1009–16.

Kottler, J. A. (2003). *On Being a Therapist.* San Francisco: John Wiley.

Krause, I. (1989). Sinking heart: A Punjabi communication of distress. *Social Science and Medicine, 29,* 563–75.

Krishnamurthy, R., VandeCreek, L., Kaslow, N. J., Tazeau, Y. N., Miville, M. L., Kerns, R., Stegman, R., Suzuki, L., & Benton, S. A. (2004). Achieving competence in psychological assessment: directions for education and training. *Journal of Clinical Psychology, 60*(7), 725–39.

Kroeber, A. L. & Kluckhohn, C. (1952). *Culture: A Critical Review of Concepts and Definitions.* Cambridge, MA: Peabody Museum.

Krueger, R. F. & Bezdjian, S. (2009). Enhancing research and treatment for mental disorders with dimensional concepts: toward DSM-V and ICD-11. *World Psychiatry, 8,* 3–6.

Krueger, R. F., & Markon, K. E. (2006). Reinterpreting comorbidity: A model-based approach to understanding and classifying psychopathology research. *Annual Review of Clinical Psychology, 2,* 111–33.

Kristeller, J. & Jones, J. (2006). A middle way: Meditation in the treatment of compulsive eating. In Kwee, M. G. T., Gergen, K. J., & Koshikawa, F. (eds). *Horizons in Buddhist Psychology: Practice, Research and Theory.* Ohio: Taos Institute of Publications, 85–100.

Krupnick, J. L., Sotsky, S. M., Simmens, S., & Moyer, J. (1996). The role of the therapeutic alliance in psychotherapy and pharmacotherapy outcome: Findings in the National Institute of Mental Health Treatment of Depression Collaborative Research Program. *Journal of Consulting and Clinical Psychology, 64,* 532-539.

Kuyken, W., Fothergill, C., Musa, M., & Chadwick, P. (2005). The reliability and quality of cognitive case formulation. *Behaviour Research and Therapy, 49*(3), 1187–1201.

Ladany, N. (2007). Does psychotherapy training matter? Maybe not. *Psychotherapy: Theory, Research, Practice, Training, 44*(4), 392–6.

Lafferty, P., Beutler, L. E., & Crago, M. (1989). Differences between more and less effective psychotherapists: A study of select therapist variables. *Journal of Consulting and Clinical Psychology, 57*(1), 76–80.

Laidlaw, K., Thompson, L. W., Dick-Siskin, L., et al (2003). *Cognitive-Behavioural Therapy with Older People.* New York: John Wiley & Sons.

Lambert, M. J. (1989). The individual therapist's contribution to psychotherapy process and outcome. *Clinical Psychology Review, 9*(4), 469–85.

Lambert, M. J. (1992). Psychotherapy outcome research: Implications for integrative and eclectic therapists. In Norcross, J. C. & Goldfried, M. R. (eds). *Handbook of Psychotherapy Integration*. New York: Basic Books.

Lambert, M. J. (ed.) (2004). *Bergin and Garfield's Handbook of Psychotherapy and Behavior Change* (5th edn). New York: John Wiley.

Lambert, M. J. (2005). Early response in psychotherapy: Further evidence for the importance of common factors rather than 'placebo effects'. *Journal of Clinical Psychology, 61*(7), 855–69.

Lambert, M. J. (2007). Outcome oriented supervision: Advantages of adding systematic client tracking to supportive consultations. *Counselling and Psychotherapy Research, 7*(1), 48-53.

Lambert, M. J. (2007). Presidential address: A program of research aimed at improving psychotherapy outcome in routine care: What we have learned from a decade of research. *Psychotherapy Research, 17*, 1–14.

Lambert, M. J. (2010). Yes, it is time for clinicians to routinely monitor treatment outcome. In Duncan, B. L., Miller, S. D., Wampold, B. E., & Hubble, M. A. (eds). *The Heart and Soul of Change* (2nd edn). Washington, DC: American Psychological Association.

Lambert, M. J. (2010). *Prevention of Treatment Failure. The Use of Measuring, Monitoring, and Feedback in Clinical Practice*. Washington, DC: American Psychological Association.

Lambert, M. J. (2010). *Prevention of Treatment Failure*. Washington: APA.

Lambert, M. J. & Asay, T. A. (2004). Clinically significant change. In Charman, D. P. (ed.). *Core Processes in Brief Psychodynamic Psychotherapy: Advancing Effective Practice*. New York: Routledge.

Lambert, M. J. & Barley, D. E. (2001). Research summary on the therapeutic relationship and psychotherapy outcome. *Psychotherapy: Theory, Research, Training, 38*(4), 357–61.

Lambert, M. J., & Bergin, A. E. (1983). Therapist characteristics and their contribution to psychotherapy outcome. In Walker, C. E. (ed.). *The Handbook of Clinical Psychology, Vol. 1*, Homewood, IL: Dow Jones-Irwin, 205–41.

Lambert, M. J. & Bergin, A. E. (1994). The effectiveness of psychotherapy. In Bergin, A. E. & Garfield, S. L. (eds). *The Handbook of Psychotherapy and Behaviour Change* (4th edn). New York: John Wiley.

Lambert, M. J., Burlingame, G. M., Umphress, V., Hansen, N. B., Yancher, S. C., Vermeersch, D., & Clouse, G. C. (1996). The reliability and validity of a new psychotherapy outcome questionnaire. *Clinical Psychology and Psychotherapy, 3*(4), 249–58.

Lambert, M. J., Hansen, N. B., & Finch, A. E. (2001). Patient-focused research: Using patient outcome data to enhance treatment effects. *Journal of Consulting and Clinical Psychology, 69*, 159–72.

Lambert, M. J., Harmon, C., Slade, K., Whipple, J. L., & Hawkins, E. J. (2005). Providing feedback to psychotherapists on their patients' progress: Clinical results and practice suggestions. *Journal of Clinical Psychology: In Session, 61*(2), 165–74.

Lambert, M. J. & Ogles, B. M. (2004). The efficacy and effectiveness of psychotherapy. In Lambert, M. J. (ed.). *Bergin and Garfield's Handbook of Psychotherapy and Behavior Change* (5th edn). New York: Wiley, 139–93.

Lambert, M. J., & Okiishi, J. C. (1997). The effects of the individual psychotherapist and implications for future research. *Clinical Psychology: Science and Practice*, 4(1), 66–75.

Lambert, M. J., Okiishi, J. C., Finch, A. E. & Johnson, L. D. (1998). Outcome assessment: From conceptualization to implementation. *Professional Psychology: Research and Practice, 29*, 63–70.

Lambert, M. J. & Shimokawa, K. (2011). Collecting client feedback. *Psychotherapy, 48(1)*, 72–79.

Lambert, M. J., Whipple, J. L., Smart, D. W., Vermeersch, D., Nielsen, S. L., & Hawkins, E. J. (2001). The effects of providing therapists with feedback on client progress during psychotherapy: Are outcomes enhanced? *Psychotherapy Research, 11*, 49–68.

Lambert, M. J., Whipple, J. L., Vermeersch, D., Smart, D. W., Hawkins, E. J., Nielsen, S. L., & Goates, M. K. (2002). Enhancing psychotherapy outcomes via providing feedback on client progress: A replication. *Clinical Psychology and Psychotherapy, 9*, 91–103.

Lamont, A. (2010). *Effects of Child Abuse and Neglect for Children and Adolescents.* Canberra: National Child Protection Clearinghouse, Australian Institute of Family Studies.

Lampropoulos, G. K. (2000). Definitional and research issues in the common factors approach to psychotherapy integration: Misconceptions, clarifications and proposals. *Journal of Psychotherapy Integration, 10*(4), 415–38.

Lampropoulos, G. K. (2001). Common processes of change in psychotherapy and seven other social interactions. *British Journal of Guidance and Counselling, 29*(1), 29–33.

Landau, E. (2004). *Family Therapy.* Danbury, CT: Scholastic Library Publishing.

Lange, A., van de Ven, J.-P., & Schrieken, B. (2003). Interpay: Treatment of posttraumatic stress via the internet. *Cognitive Behaviour Therapy, 32*(3), 110–24.

Langer, E. (1989). *Mindfulness.* Cambridge: Perseus Books:

Langer, E. (1997). *The Power of Mindful Learning.* Reading: Addison Wesley.

Langer, E., Beck, P., Janoff-Bulman, R., & Timko, C. (1984). The relationship between cognitive deprivation and longevity in senile and non-senile elderly populations. *Academic Psychology Bulletin*, 6211–26.

Langer, E. & Moldoveanu, M. (2000). The construct of mindfulness. *Journal of Social Issues, 56*(1), 1–9.

Langs, R. (1990). *Psychotherapy. A Basic Text.* London: Jason Aronson.

Large, M. M. & Nielssen, O. B. (2010). Suicide in Australia: meta-analysis of rates and methods of suicide between 1988 and 2007. *Medical Journal of Australia, 192*(8), 432–437.

Larson, B. D., & Larson, S. S. (2003). Spirituality's potential relevance to physical and emotional health: A brief review of quantitative research. *Journal of Psychology and Theology, 31*(1), 37–51.

Laszlo, J. V., Esterman, G., & Zabko, S. (1999). Therapy over the Internet? Theory, research and finances. *CyberPsychology & Behavior, 2*(4), 293–307.

Lazarus, A. (1971). *Behavior Therapy and Beyond.* New York: McGraw-Hill.

Leon, S. C., Matinovich, Z., Lutz, W., & Lyons, J. (2005). The effect of therapist experience on psychotherapy outcomes. *Clinical Psychology and Psychotherapy, 12*, 417–29.

Lebow, J. (2005). *Handbook of Clinical Family Therapy.* Hoboken, NJ: John Wiley.

Lebow, J. (2006). *Research for the Psychotherapist: From Science to Practice.* New York: Routledge.

Leiper, R., & Maltby, M. (2004). *The Psychodynamic Approach to Therapeutic Change.* London: Sage.

Letham, J. (2002). Brief solution focused therapy. *Child and Adolescent Mental Health, 7,* 189–92.

Levine, R., Sato, S., Hashimoto, T., & Verma, J. (1995). Love and marriage in eleven cultures. *Journal of Cross-cultural Psychology, 26,* 544–71.

Levitt, H., Butler, M., & Hill, T. (2006). What clients find helpful in psychotherapy: Developing principles for facilitating moment-to-moment change. *Journal of Counseling Psychology, 53*(3), 314–24.

Lilienfeld, S. O. (2007). Psychological treatments that cause harm. *Perspectives on Psychological Science, 2,* 53–70.

Lilienfeld, S. O., Lynn, S. J., & Lohr, J. M. (2003). *Science and Pseudoscience in Clinical Psychology.* New York: Guilford Press.

Lin, E. H. B., Ihle, L. J., & Tazuma, L. (1985). Depression among Vietnamese refugees in a primary care clinic. *American Journal of Medicine, 78*(1), 41–4.

Linehan, M. M. (1993a). *Cognitive-Behavioral Treatment of Borderline Personality Disorder.* New York: Guilford Press.

Linehan, M. M. (1993b). *Skills Training Manual for Treating Borderline Personality Disorder.* New York: Guilford Press.

Linehan, M. M. (2003). *Skills Training Manual for Treating Borderline Personality Disorder.* New York: Guilford Press.

Linehan. M. (2006). *Treating Borderline Personality Disorder: The Dialectical Approach.* New York: Guildford Press.

Linehan, M. M., Armstrong, H. E., Suarez, A., Allman, D., & Heard, H. L. (1991). Cognitive- behavioral treatment of chronically parasuicidal borderline patients. *Archives of General Psychiatry, 48,* 1060–4.

Linehan, M., Goodstein, J., Nielsen, S., & Chiles, J. (1983). Reasons for staying alive when you are thinking of killing yourself. The reasons for Living inventory. *Journal of Consulting and Clinical Psychology, 54,* 880–1.

Linehan, M. M., Heard, H. L., & Armstrong, H. E. (1993). Naturalistic follow-up of a behavioral treatment for chronically parasuicidal borderline patients. *Archives of General Psychiatry, 50*(12), 971–4.

Linehan, M. M., Kanter, J. W., & Comtois, K. A. (1999). Dialectical behavior therapy for borderline personality disorder. In Janowsky, D. (ed.). *Psychotherapy Indications and Outcomes.* Washington, DC: American Psychiatric Press, 93–118).

Linehan, M. M., Schmidt, H., Dimeff, L. A., Kanter, J. W., Craft, J. C., Comtois, K. A., & Recknor, K. L. (1999). Dialectical behavior therapy for patients with borderline personality disorder and drug-dependence. *American Journal on Addiction, 8,* 279–92.

Linley, P. A. & Joseph, S. (eds) (2004). *Positive Psychology in Practice*. Hoboken, NJ: John Wiley.

Linley, P. A. & Joseph, S. (2007). Therapy work and therapists' positive and negative well-being. *Journal of Social and Clinical Psychology, 26*, 385–403.

Littauer, H., Sexton, H., & Wynn, R. (2005). Qualities clients wish for in their therapists. *Scandinavian Journal of Caring Science, 19*, 28–31.

Longmore, R. J. & Worrell, M. (2007). Do we need to challenge thoughts in cognitive behaviour therapy? *Clinical Psychology Review, 27*, 173–87.

Lovett, H. (1996). *Learning to Listen: Positive Approaches and People with Difficult Behaviour*. Baltimore: Brookes.

Lovibond, P. F. & Lovibond, S. H. (1995). The structure of negative emotional states: Comparison of the Depression Anxiety and Stress Scales with the Beck Depression and Anxiety Inventories. *Behaviour Research and Therapy, 33*, 335–43.

Lubman, D. I., Yucel, M., & Pantelis, C. (2004). Addiction, a condition of compulsive behaviour? Neuroimaging and neuropsychological evidence of inhibitory dysregulation. *Addiction, 99*(12), 1491–1502.

Luborsky, L. (1990). Theory and technique in dynamic psychotherapy: Curative factors and training therapists to maximize them. *Psychotherapy and Psychosomatics, 53*(1–4), 50–7.

Luborsky, L. (1995). Are common factors across different psychotherapies the main explanation for the Dodo Bird verdict that 'Everyone has won so all shall have prizes'? *Clinical Psychology: Science and Practice, 2*(1), 106–9.

Luborsky, L., Barber, J. P., & Beutler, L. (1993). Introduction to special section: a briefing on curative factors in dynamic psychotherapy. *Journal of Consulting and Clinical Psychology, 61*(4), 539–41.

Luborsky L. & Crits-Christoph, P. (Eds.). (1998). Understanding Transference: The CCRT Method (2nd edn). Washington, DC: American Psychiatric Association.

Luborsky, L., Crits-Christoph, P., Alexander, L., Margolis, M., & Cohen, M. (1986). Do therapists vary much in their success? Findings from four outcome studies. *American Journal of Orthopsychiatry, 56*(4), 501-512.

Luborsky, L., McLellan, A. T., Diguer, L., Woody, G., & Seligman, D. A. (1997). The psychotherapist matters: Comparison of outcomes across twenty-two therapists and seven patient samples. *Clinical Psychology: Science and Practice, 4*, 53–65.

Luborsky, L., McLellan, T., Woody, G. W., O'Brien, C. P., & Auerback, A. (1985). Therapist success and its determinants. *Archives of General Psychiatry, 42*, 602–11.

Luborsky, L., Mintz, J., Auerbach, A., Christoph, P., Bachrach, H., Todd, T., Johnson, M., Cohen, N., & O'Brien, C. (1980). Predicting the outcome of psychotherapy. *Archives of General Psychiatry, 37*, 471–81.

Luborsky, L., Rosenthal, R., Diguer, L., Andrusyna, T. P., Berman, J. S., Levitt, J. T., Seligman, D. A., & Krause, E. D. (2002). The Dodo Bird verdict is alive and well—mostly. *Clinical Psychology: Science and Practice, 9*(1), 2–12.

Luborsky, L., Singer, B., & Luborsky, L. (1975). Comparative studies of psychotherapies: Is it true that 'everyone has won and all must have prizes'? *Archives of General Psychiatry, 32*, 995–1008.

Luborsky, L., Woody, G., McLellan, A., O'Brien, C., & Rosenzweig, J. (1982). Can independent judges recognise different psychotherapies? An experience with manual-guided therapies. *Journal of Consulting and Clinical Psychology, 50*(1), 49–62.

Lutz, W., Leon, S. C., Martinovich, Z., Lyons, J. S., & Stiles, W. B. (2007). Therapist effects in outpatient psychotherapy: A three-level growth curve approach. *Journal of Counseling Psychology, 54*(1), 32–9.

Lutz, W., Stulz, N., Martinovich, Z., Leon, S., & Saunders, S. M. (2007). Methodological background of decision rules and feedback tools for outcomes management in psychotherapy. *Psychotherapy Research, 19*(4–5), 502–10.

Lyons, L. C. & Woods, P. J. (1991). The efficacy of rational-emotive therapy: A quantitative review of the outcome research. *Clinical Psychology Review, 11*(4), 357–69.

Lyubomirsky, S., Sheldon, K. M., & Schkade, D. (2005). Pursuing happiness: The architecture of sustainable change. *Review of General Psychology, 9*, 111–31.

McAdam, D. P., Diamond, A., de St. Aubin, E., & Mansfield, E. (1997). Stories of commitment: The psychological construction of generative lives. *Journal of Personality and Social Psychology, 72*, 678–94.

McCarthy, W. C. & Frieze, I. H. (1999). Negative aspects of therapy: Client perceptions of therapists' social influence, burnout and quality of care. *Journal of Social Issues, 55*(1), 33–50.

Maccoby, E. & Martin, J. (1983). Socialization in the context of family: Parent-child interactions. In Hetherington, E. M. (ed.) & Mussen, R. H. (series ed.). *Handbook of child psychology, Vol. 4.* New York: Wiley, 1–101.

McConnaughy, E. A. (1987). The person of the therapist in psychotherapeutic practice. *Psychotherapy, 24*, 303–14.

McCullough, M. E. (1999). Research on religion-accommodative counseling: Review and meta-analysis. *Journal of Counseling Psychology, 46*(1), 92–8.

McCullough, M. E. (2000). Forgiveness as a human strength: Conceptualization, measurement, and links to well-being. *Journal of Social and Clinical Psychology, 19*, 43–55.

McDermut, W. & Zimmerman, M. (1998). The effect of personality disorders on outcome in the treatment of depression. In Rush, A. J. (ed.). *Mood and Anxiety Disorders* Philadelphia: Williams & Wilkins, 321–8.

McGhee, L. L., Maani, C. V., Garza, T. H., DeSocio, P. A., Gaylord, K. M., & Black, I. H. (2009). The effect of propranolol on posttraumatc stress disorder in burned service members. *Journal of Burn Care and Research, 30*, 92–97.

McKay, K. M., Imel, Z. E., & Wampold, B. E. (2006). Psychiatrist effects in the psychopharmacological treatment of depression. *Journal of Affective Disorders, 92*, 287–90.

McKay, M., Wood, J. C., & Brantley, J. (2007). *Dialectical Behaviour Therapy Workbook: Practical DBT Exercises for Learning Mindfulness, Interpersonal Effectiveness, Emotion Regulation, and Distress Tolerance.* Oakland, CA: New Harbinger Publications.

McLellan, A. T., Woody, G. E., Luborsky, L., O'Brien, C. P., & Druley, K. A. (1983). Increased effectiveness of substance abuse treatment: A prospective study of patient-treatment 'matching'. *Journal of Nervous and Mental Disease, 171*, 597–605.

McLeod, J. (1993). *An Introduction to Counselling.* Buckingham: Open University Press.

McMahon, M. (2006). Confidentiality, privacy and privilege: protecting and disclosing information about clients. In Morrissey, S. & Reddy, P. (eds). *Ethics and Professional Practice for Psychologists.* Sydney: Thomson, 74–88.

Macran, S., Stiles, W. B., & Smith, J. A. (1999). How does personal therapy affect therapists' practice? *Journal of Counseling Psychology, 46,* 419–31.

McWilliams, N. (1999). *Psychoanalytic Case Formulation.* New York: Guilford Press.

McWilliams, N. (2004). *Psychoanalytic Psychotherapy: A Practitioner's Guide.* New York: Guilford Press.

Mahoney, M. J. (1997). Psychotherapists' personal problems and self-care patterns. *Professional Psychology: Research and Practice, 28,* 14–16.

Malan, D.H. (1963). *A Study of Brief Psychotherapy.* London: Plenum.

Malan, D. H.(1995). *Individual Psychotherapy and the Science of Psychodynamics.* Oxford: Butterworth Heinemann.

Malik, M. L., & Beulter, L. E. (2002). The emergence of dissatisfaction with the DSM. In Malik, M. L. & Beutler, L. E. (eds). *Rethinking the DSM: A Psychological Perspective.* Washington, DC: American Psychological Association, 3–15.

Malinick, C., Flaherty, J. A., & Jobe, T. (1985). Koro: How culturally specific? *International Journal of Social Psychiatry, 31*(1), 67–73.

Mallen, M. J., Vogel, D. L., Rochlen, A. B., & Day, S. X. (2005). Online counseling: Reviewing the literature from a counseling psychology framework. *Counseling Psychologist, 33*(6), 819–70.

Mant, A., Rendle, V.A., Hall, W.D., Mitchell, P.B., Montgomery, W.S., McManus, P.R., & Hickie, I. B. (2004). Making new choices about antidepressants in Australia: The long view 1975–2002. *Medical Journal of Australia, 181,* s21–s24.

March, J., Silva, S., Petrycki, S., Curry, J., Wells, K., Fairbank, J., Bunns, B., Domino, M., McNulty, S., Vitiello, B., & Severe, J. (2004). Fluoxetine, cognitive-behavioral therapy, and their combination for adolescents with depression: Treatment for Adolescents with Depression Study (TADS) randomized controlled trial. *Journal of the American Medical Association, 292*(7), 807–20.

Marcus, G. & Braaf, R. 2007. *Domestic and Family Violence Studies, Surveys and Statistics: Pointers to Policy and Practice.* Sydney: Australian Domestic and Family Violence Clearinghouse.

Markus, H. R., Mullally, P. R., & Kitayama, S. (1997). Selfways: Diversity in models of cultural participation. In Neisser, U. & Jopling, D. A. (eds). *The Conceptual Self in Context.* Cambridge, UK: Cambridge University Press, 13–61.

Margolis, M. & Langer, E. J. (1990). An analysis of addictions from a mindful/mindless perspective, *Psychology of Addictive Behavior, 4*(2), 107–15.

Marmar, C. R., Weiss, D. S., & Gaston, L. (1989). Toward the validation of the California Therapeutic Alliance Rating System. *Psychological Assessment, 1*(1), 46–52.

Martell, C. R., Addis, M. E., & Jacobson, N. S. (2001). *Depression in Context: Strategies for Guided Action.* New York: Norton.

Martin, D. J., Garske, J. P., & Davis, M. K. (2000). Relation of the therapeutic alliance with outcome and other variables: A meta-analytic review. *Journal of Consulting and Clinical Psychology, 68*(3), 438–50.

Martin, D. W. (1989). Research methods used in applied settings. In Gregory, W. L. & Burroughs, W. J. (eds). *Introduction to Applied Psychology*. Glenview, IL: Scott, Foresman.

Martin, G., Pear, J., & Garry, M. (1992). *Behavior Modification: What It Is and How to Do It*. Upper Saddle River, NJ: Prentice Hall.

Martin, J. M. (1990). Confusions in psychological skills training. *Journal of Counselling and Development, 68*, 402–7.

Martin, J. R. (2002). The common factor of mindfulness: An expanding discourse: Comment on Horowitz. *Journal of Psychotherapy Integration, 12*(2), 139–42.

Martin, P. R. & Birnbrauer, J. S. (eds). (1996). *Clinical Psychology: Profession And Practice in Australia*. Melbourne: Macmillan Education Australia.

Martin, S. D., Martin, E., Rai, S. S., Richardson, M., & Royall, R. (2001). Brain blood flow changes in depressed patients treated with interpersonal psychotherapy or venlafaxine hydrochloride: preliminary findings. *Archives of General Psychiatry, 58*(7), 641–8.

Marziali, E., Marmar, C. R., & Krupnick, J. L. (1981). Therapeutic alliance scales: Development and relationship to psychotherapy outcome. *American Journal of Psychiatry, 138*, 361–4.

Maser, J. & Cloninger, C. R. (1990). *Comorbidity in Anxiety and Mood Disorders*. Washington, DC: American Psychiatric Press.

Maslach, C. (1982). *Burnout: The Cost of Caring*. Englewood Cliffs, NJ: Prentice Hall.

Maslow, A. H. (1954). *Motivation and Personality*. New York: Harper.

Maslow, A. H. (1968). *Toward a Psychology of Being*. New York: Insight Books.

Maslow, A. H. (1971). *The Farther Reaches of Human Nature*. New York: Penguin.

Meier, S. (1999). Training the practitioner-scientist. *Counseling Psychologist, 27*(6), 846–69.

Mellenbergh, G. J. & van der Brink, W. P. (1998). The measurement of individual change. *Psychological Methods, 3*, 470–85.

Menon, T, Morris, M. W., Chiu, C., & Hong, Y. (1999). Culture and construal of agency: Attribution to individual versus group dispositions. *Journal of Personality and social Psychology, 76*, 701–17.

Meyer, A. (1957). *Psychobiology: a Science of Man*. Springfield, IL: Thomas.

Meyer, B., Pilkonis, P A., Proietti, J. M., Heape, C. L., & Egan, M. (2001). Adult attachment styles, personality disorders, and response to treatment. *Journal of Personality Disorders, 15*, 371–89.

Miller, A., Rathus, J. H., Linehan, M. M., Wetxler, S., & Leight, E. (1997). Dialectical behavior therapy adapted for suicidal adolescents. *Journal of Practical Psychiatry and Behavioral Health, 3*, 78–86.

Miller, G. (2003). *Incorporating Spirituality in Counseling and Psychotherapy: Theory and Technique*. Hoboken, NJ: John Wiley.

Miller, J. G., Bersoff, D. M., & Harwood, R. L. (1990). Perceptions of social responsibilities in India and in the United States. Moral imperatives or personal decisions? *Journal of Personality and Social Psychology, 58*, 33–47.

Miller, S. D. & Duncan, B. L. (2000). *The Outcome Rating Scale*. Chicago: Miller & Duncan.

Miller, S. D., Duncan, B. L., Brown, J., Sorrell, R., & Chalk, M. (2003). The Outcome Rating Scale and the improvement of effectiveness in a telephonic EAP setting. Unpublished manuscript.

Miller, S. D., Duncan, B. L., Brown, J., Sorrell, R., & Chalk, B. (2006). Using outcome to inform and improve treatment outcomes. *Journal of Brief Therapy, 5*, 5–22.

Miller, S. D., Duncan, B. L., Brown, J., Sparks, J., & Claud, D. (2003). The outcome rating scale: A preliminary study of the reliability, validity, and feasibility of a brief visual analog measure. *Journal of Brief Therapy, 2*(2), 91–100.

Miller, S. D., Duncan, B. L., & Hubble, M. A. (1997). *Escape from Babel* (1st edn). New York: Norton.

Miller, S., Hubble, M. A., & Duncan, B. L. (2009). *Supershrinks: What is the secret of their success?* <http://www.psychotherapy.net/article/Scott_Miller_Supershrinks>.

Miller, W.R. & Rollnick, S. (1991). *Motivational Interviewing: Preparing People to Change Addictive Behavior*. New York: Guilford Press.

Miller, W.R. & Rollnick, S. (2002). *Motivational Interviewing: Preparing People to Change Addictive Behavior* (2nd edn). New York: Guilford Press.

Miller, W.R. & Thoresen, C.E. (2003). Spirituality, religion, and health. *American Psychologist, 58*(1), 24–35.

Millon, T., David, R., Millon, C., & Grossman, S. (2009). *The Millon Clinical Multiaxial Inventory-III, Third Edition (MCMI-III)*. Upper Saddle Creek, NJ: Pearson.

MIMS (2009). *MIMS Annual 2009*. St Leonards: CMPMedica Australia.

MIMS (2010). *MIMS Annual 2010*. St Leonards: CMPMedica Australia.

Missirlian, T. M., Toukmanian, S. G., Warwar, S. H., & Greenberg, L. S. (2005). Emotional arousal, client perceptual processing, and the working alliance in experiential psychotherapy for depression. *Journal of Consulting and Clinical Psychology, 73*(5), 861–71.

Mitchell, C. (2007). *Effective Techniques for Dealing with Highly Resistant Clients*. Johnson City, TN: Clifton Mitchell Publishing.

Mitchell, S. A. & Black, M. J. (1995). *Freud and Beyond: A History of Modern Psychoanalytic Thought*. New York: Basic Books.

Mohr, D. E. (1995). Negative outcome in psychotherapy: A critical review. *Clinical Psychology, Science and Practice, 2*, 1–27.

Moneta, G. B. & Csikszentmihalyi, M. (1996). The effect of perceived challenges and skills on the quality of subjective experience. *Journal of Personality, 64*, 275–310.

Montgomery, S. A. & Åsberg, M. (1979). A new depression scale designed to be sensitive to change. *British Journal of Psychiatry, 134*, 382–9.

Morgan, A. & Chadwick, H. (2009). Key issues in domestic violence. *Research in Practice, 7*. Canberra: Australian Institute of Criminology.

Morgan, K., Dixon, S., Mathers, N., Thompson, J., & Tomeny, M. (2004). Psychological treatment for insomnia in the management of long-term hypnotic drug use: A pragmatic randomised controlled trial. *British Journal of General Practice, 53*, 923–8.

Morgenstern, J. & Longabaugh, R. (2000). Cognitive-behavioral treatment of alcohol dependence: A review of evidence for its hypothesized mechanisms of action. *Addiction, 95*, 1475–90.

Morrisey, S. & Reddy, P. (2006). *Ethics and Professional Practice for Psychologists*. Sydney: Thomson.

Motto, J. A. (1989). Problems in suicide risk assessment. In Jacobs, D. & Brown, H. N. (eds.). *Suicide: Understanding and Responding*. Madison, WI: International Universities Press, 129–42.

Mouzos, J. & Makkai, T. (2004). *Women's Experiences of Male Violence: Findings from the Australian Component of the International Violence Against Women Survey (IVAWS)*. Research and Public Policy Series No 56. Canberra: Australian Institute of Criminology.

Mowrer, O. H. (1960). *Learning Theory and Behavior*. New York: Wiley.

Mumford, E., Schlesinger, H. J., Glass, G. V., Patrick, C., & Cuerdon, T. (1984). A new look at evidence about reduced cost of medical utilization following mental health treatment. *Journal of Psychotherapy Practice and Research, 7*, 68–86.

Muran, J. C. & Safran, J. D. (2002). A relational approach to psychotherapy: Resolving ruptures in the therapeutic alliance. In Kaslow, F. W. (ed.). *Comprehensive Handbook of Psychotherapy*. New York: John Wiley.

Muran. J. C. & Segal, Z. V. (1992). The development of an idiographic measure of self-schemas: An illustration of the construction and use of self-scenarios. *Psychotherapy, 29*, 524–35.

Muran, J. C., Segal, Z. V., Samstag, L. W., & Crawford, C. (1994). Patient pretreatment interpersonal problems and therapeutic alliance in short-term cognitive therapy. *Journal of Consulting and Clinical Psychology, 62*, 185–90.

Myers, D. G. (1992). *The Pursuit of Happiness: Who Is Happy—And Why*. New York: Morrow.

Najavits, L. M. & Strupp, H. H. (1994). Differences in the effectiveness of psychodynamic therapists: A process-outcome study. *Psychotherapy, 31*(1), 114–23.

Najavits, L. M. & Weiss, R. D. (1994). Variations in therapist effectiveness in the treatment of patients with substance use disorders: An empirical review. *Addiction, 89*(6), 679–88.

Nakamura, J. & Csikszentmihalyi, M. (2002). The concept of flow. In Snyder, C. R. & Lopez, S. J. (eds). *Handbook of Positive Psychology*. New York: Oxford University Press, 89–105.

Nash, J., & Nutt, D. (2007). Psychopharmacology of anxiety. *Psychiatry, 6*, 143–8.

Nathan, P. E. (1998). The DSM-IV and its antecedents: Enhancing syndromal diagnosis. In Barron, J. W. (ed.). *Making Diagnosis Meaningful*. Washington, DC: American Psychological Association.

Nathan, P. E. & Gorman, J. M. (eds) (2002). *A Guide to Treatments that Work* (2nd edn). New York: Oxford University Press.

Nathan, P. E. & Gorman, J. M. (2007). *A Guide to Treatments that Work* (3rd edn). New York: Oxford University Press.

National Framework for Protecting Australia's Children (2009). *Protecting Children is Everyone's Business (2009–2020)*. Canberra: Department of Families, Housing, Community Services and Indigenous Affairs.

Neale, J. M. & Davison, G. C. (2001). *Abnormal Psychology* (8th edn). New York: John Wiley, 247–50.

Nelson, M. L., Gray, L. A., Friedlander, M. L., Ladany, N., & Walker, J. A. (2001). Toward relationship-centered supervision: Reply to Veach (2001) and Ellis (2001). *Journal of Counseling Psychology, 48*(4), 407–9.

Nezu, A. M., Ronan, G. F., Meadows, E. A., & McClure, K. S. (2000). *Practitioner's Guide to Empirically Based Measures of Depression*. New York: Kluwer Academic/Plenum Publishers.

Nicholas, R. (2005). *The Role of Alcohol in Family Violence.* Adelaide: Australasian Centre for Policing Research.

Nichols, M. P. (2008). *Family Therapy: Concepts And Methods.* Boston, MA: Allyn & Bacon.

Nichols, M. P. & Schwartz, R. C. (2006). *Family Therapy: Concepts and Methods* (7th edn). Boston: Pearson/Allyn & Bacon.

Nietzel, M. T. & Fisher, S. G. (1981). Effectiveness of professional and paraprofessional helpers: A comment on Durlak. *Psychological Bulletin, 89*(3), 555–65.

Norberg, M. M., Krystal, J. H., & Tolin D. F. (2008) A meta-analysis of d-Cycloserine in the facilitation of fear extinction and exposure therapy. *Biological Psychiatry, 63,* 1118–1126.

Norcross, J. C. (1999). Foreword. In Hubble, M., Duncan, B. L. & Miller, S. D. (eds). *The Heart and Soul of Change What Works in Therapy.* Washington, DC: American Psychological Association, xvii–xix.

Norcross, J. C. (ed.) (2002). *Psychotherapy Relationships that Work. Therapist Contributions and Responsiveness to Patients.* Oxford: Oxford University Press.

Norcross, J. C. (2005). The psychotherapist's own psychotherapy: Educating and developing psychologists. *American Psychologist, 60,* 840–50.

Norcross, J. C., Beutler, L. E., & Levant, R. F. (eds). (2006). *Evidence-Based Practices in Mental Health: Debate and Dialogue on the Fundamental Questions.* Washington, DC: American Psychological Association.

Norcross, J. C., Bike, D. H., Evans, K. L., & Schatz, D. M. (2008). Psychotherapists who abstain from personal therapy: Do they practice what they preach? *Journal of Clinical Psychology, 64,* 136–76.

Norcross, J. C. & Goldfried, M. R. (eds). (1992). *Handbook of Psychotherapy Integration.* New York: Basic Books.

Norcross, J. C. & Goldfried, M. R. (eds) (2005). *Handbook of Psychotherapy Integration* (2nd edn). New York: Oxford University Press.

Norcross, J. C. & Guy, J. D. (2007). *Leaving It at the Office: A Guide to Psychotherapist Self-care.* New York: Guilford Press.

Norcross, J. & Lambert, M. J. (2005). EBP in mental health: Debate and dialogue on the fundamental questions. In Norcross, J., Beutler, L. E., & Levant, R. F. (eds). *Evidence-based Practices in Mental Health.* Washington, DC: American Psychological Association Press, 38–42.

Nugent, N. R., Christopher, N. C., Crow, J. P., Browne, L., Ostrowski, S., & Delahunty, D. L. (2010). The efficacy of early propranolol administration at reducing PTSD symptoms in pediatric injury patients: A pilot study. *Journal of Traumatic Stress, 23,* 282–287.

Nurcombe, B. & Fitzhenry-Coor, I. (1987). Diagnostic reasoning and treatment planning: I Diagnosis. *Australian and New Zealand Journal of Psychiatry, 21,* 477–99.

Nussbaum, M. (1993). Non-relative virtues: An Aristotelian approach. In Nussbaum, A. & Sen, A. (eds). *The Quality of Life.* Helsinki: United Nation University and WIDER, 242–69.

O'Connor, M. F. (2001). On the etiology and effective management of professional distress and impairment among psychologists. *Professional Psychology: Research and Practice, 32,* 345–50.

O'Donovan, A. (2000). The impact of postgraduate training on the competency and satisfaction of clinical psychology trainees. Unpublished PhD thesis, Brisbane: Griffith University.

O'Donovan, A., Bain, J. D., & Dyck, M. J. (2005). Does clinical psychology education enhance the clinical competence of practitioners? *Professional Psychology: Research and Practice, 36*(1), 104–11.

O'Donovan, A., Dooley, R., & Kavanagh, D. (2010). *Supervisee Feedback on the Effectiveness of Supervisor Training.* Melbourne: ICAP Conference.

O'Donovan, A., Dyck, M., & Bain, J. (2001). Supervisees' experience of postgraduate clinical training. *Australian Psychologist, 36*(2), 149–56.

Ogles, B. M., Lambert, M. J., & Fields, S. A. (2002). *Essentials of Outcome Assessment.* New York: John Wiley.

O'Gorman, J. G. (2001). The scientist-practitioner model and its critics. *Australian Psychologist, 36*(2), 164–9.

Ohgami, H., Terao, T., Shiotsuki, I., Ishii, N., & Iwata, N.(2009). Lithium levels in drinking water and risk of suicide. *British Journal of Psychiatry, 194,* 464–5.

Okiishi, J. C., Lambert, M. J., Eggett, D., Nielsen, L., Dayton, D. D., & Vermeersch, D. A. (2006). An analysis of therapist treatment effects: Toward providing feedback to individual therapists on their clients' psychotherapy outcome. *Journal of Clinical Psychology, 62*(9), 1157–72.

Okiishi, J. C., Lambert, M. J., Nielsen, S. L., & Ogles, B. M. (2003). Waiting for Supershrink: An empirical analysis of therapist effects. *Clinical Psychology and Psychotherapy, 10,* 361–73.

Orlinsky, D. E., Grawe, K., & Parks, B. K. (1994). Process and outcome in psychotherapy: Noch einmal. In Bergin, A. E. & Garfield, S. L. (eds). *Handbook of Pychotherapy and Behavior Change* (4th edn). New York: John Wiley, 270–376.

Orlinsky, D. E. & Howard, K. (1980). Gender and psychotherapeutic outcome. In Brodsky, A. M. & Hare-Mustin, R. T. (eds). *Women and Psychotherapy.* New York: Guildford Press, 3–34.

Orlinsky, D. E. & Ronnestad, M. H. (2005). *How Psychotherapists Develop: A Study of Therapeutic Work and Professional Growth.* Washington, DC: American Psychological Association.

Orlinsky, D. E., Ronnestad, M. H., & Willutzki, U. (2004). Fifty years of psychotherapy process-outcome research: Continuity and change. In Lambert, M. J. (ed.). *Handbook of Psychotherapy and Behaviour Change.* New York: John Wiley.

Öst, L. (2008). Efficacy of the third wave of behavioral therapies: A systematic review and meta-analysis. *Behaviour Research and Therapy, 46*(3), 296–321.

Overington, L. & Ionita, G. (2012). Progress monitoring measures: A brief guide. *Canadian Psychology, 53*(2), 82–92.

Paris, J. & Zweig-Frank, H. (2001). A 27-year follow-up of patients with borderline personality disorder. *Comprehensive Psychiatry, 42*(6), 482–7.

Pargament, K. I., Desai, K. M., & McConnell, K. M. (2006). Spirituality: A pathway to posttraumatic growth or decline. In Calhoun, L. G. & Tedeschi, R. G. (eds). *Handbook of Posttraumatic Growth: Research and Practice.* Mahwah, NJ: Lawrence Erlbaum.

Parker, G. B., Crawford, J., & Hadzi-Pavlovic, D. (2008). Quantified superiority of cognitive behaviour therapy to antidepressant drugs: A challenge to an earlier meta-analysis. *Acta Psychiatrica Scandinavica, 118*, 91–7.

Parker, G., Parker, I., Brotchie, H., & Stuart, S. (2006). Interpersonal psychotherapy for depression? The need to define its ecological niche. *Journal of Affective Disorders, 95*, 1–11.

Passmore, N. (2003). Religious issues in counselling: Are Australian psychologists 'dragging the chain'? *Australian Psychologist, 38*(3), 183–92.

Patrick, J. (2000). *Mental Status Exam. Rapid Record Form* <http://www.nevdgp.org.au/files/programsupport/mentalhealth/Mental%20State%20Exam%20-%20form.pdf>.

Paul, G. L. (1967). Strategies of outcome research in psychotherapy. *Journal of Consulting and Clinical Psychology, 31*, 109–18.

Paul, G. L. & Lentz, R.J. (1977). *Psychosocial Treatment of Chronic Mental Patients: Milieu Versus Social Learning Programs*. Cambridge, MA: Harvard University Press.

Pavlov, I. P & Anrep, G. V.. (1927/1960). *Conditional Reflexes*. New York: Dover Publications. (The 1960 edition is an unaltered republication of the 1927 translation by Oxford University Press <http://psychclassics.yorku.ca/Pavlov/>).

PDM Task Force (2006). *Psychodynamic Diagnostic Manual*. Silver Spring, MD: Alliance of Psychoanalytic Organizations.

Pearlman, L. A. & Ian, P. S. M. (1995). Vicarious traumatization: An empirical study of the effects of trauma work on trauma therapists. *Professional Psychology: Research and Practice, 26*, 558–65.

Pennebaker, J. W. (1993). Putting stress into words: Health, linguistic, and therapeutic implications. *Behaviour Research and Therapy, 31*, 539–48.

Perry, S., Cooper, A. M., & Michaels, R. (1987). The psychodynamic formulation: Its purpose, structure, and clinical application. *American Journal of Psychiatry, 144*, 43–550.

Persons, J. B. (2008). *Case Formulation-driven Cognitive-behavior Therapy*. New York: Guilford Press.

Persons, J. B. & Davidson, J. (2002). Cognitive-behavioral case formulation. In Dobson, K. S. (ed.). *Handbook of Cognitive Behavioral Therapies*. New York: Guilford Press.

Persons, J. B. & Tompkins, M. A. (1997). Cognitive-behavioral case formulation. In Eells, T. D. (ed.). *Handbook of Psychotherapy Case Formulation*. New York: Guilford.

Peterson, C. & Seligman, M. E. P. (2004). *Character Strengths and Virtues. A Handbook and Classification*. Oxford: Oxford University Press.

Peterson, C. & Stunkard, A. J. (1992). Cognates of personal control: Locus of control, self-efficacy, and explanatory style. *Applied and Preventive Psychology, 1*, 111–17.

Petry, N. M., Tennen, H., & Affleck, G. (2000). In Snyder, C. R. & Ingram, R. E. (eds.). *Handbook of Psychological Change. Psychotherapy Process and Practices for the 21st Century*. New York: John Wiley, 88–108.

Pincus, H. A., Frances, A. J., Davis, W. W., First, M. B., & Widiger, T. A. (1992). DSM-IV and new diagnostic categories: Holding the line on proliferation. *American Journal of Psychiatry, 149*, 112–17.

Piper, M. (2003). *Letters to a Young Therapist.* New York: Basic Books.

Piper, W. E., de Carufel, F. L., & Szkrumelak, N. (1985). Patient predictors of process and outcome in short-term individual psychotherapy. *Journal of Nervous Mental Disorder, 173,* 726–73.

Piper, W. E., Joyce, A. S., Azim, H. F. A., & Rosie, J. S. (1994). Patient characteristics and success in day treatment. *Journal of Nervous Mental Disorder, 182,* 382–6.

Piper, W. E., Ogrodniczuk, J. S., Joyce, A. S., McCallum, M., Rosie, J. S., O'Kelly, J. G., & Steinberg, P. I. (1999). Prediction of dropping out in time-limited, interpretive individual psychotherapy. *Psychotherapy: Theory, Research, Practice, Training, 36,* 114–122.

Pizzagalli, D., Pascual-Marqui, R. D., Nitschke, J. B., Oakes, T. R., Larson, C. L., Abercrombis, H. C., Schaefer, S. M., Koger, J. V., Benca, R. M., & Davidson, R. J. (2001). Anterior cingulate activity as a predictor of degree of treatment response in major depression: Evidence from brain electrical tomography analysis. *American Journal of Psychiatry, 158*(3), 405–15.

Plante, T. G. (2005). *Contemporary Clinical Psychology* (2nd edn). Hoboken, NJ: John Wiley.

Pope, K. S. & Feldman-Summers, S. (1992). National survey of psychologists' sexual and physical abuse history and their evaluation of training and competence in these areas. *Professional Psychology: Research and Practice, 23,* 353–61.

Pope, K. S. & Tabachnick, B. G. (1994). Therapists as patients: A national survey of psychologists' experiences, problems, and beliefs. *Professional Psychology: Research and Practice, 25,* 247–58.

Pope, K. S., Tabachnick, B. G., & Keith-Speigal, P. (1987). Ethics of practice: The beliefs and behaviours of psychologists as therapists. *American Psychologist, 42,* 993–1006.

Pope, K. S. & Vetter, V. A. (1992). Ethical dilemmas encountered by members of the American Psychological Association: A national survey. *American Psychologist, 47,* 397–411.

Powell, M. B. (2000). PRIDE: The essential elements of forensic interview with an Aboriginal person. *Australian Psychologist, 35*(3), 186–92.

Prochaska, J. O. & DiClemente, C. C. (1982). Transthcoretcial therapy: Toward a more integrative model of change. *Psychotherapy: Theory, Research, and Practice, 19,* 276–88.

Prochaska, J. O. & DiClemente, C. C. (1983). Stages and processes of self-change of smoking: Toward and integrative model of change. *Journal of Consulting and Clinical Psychology, 51,* 390–5.

Prochaska, J. O., DiClemente, C. C., Velicer, W. F., & Rossi, J. S. (1993). Standardized, individualized, interactive and personalized self-help programs for smoking cessation. *Health Psychology, 12,* 399–405.

Project Match Research Group. (1998). Therapist effects in three treatments for alcohol problems. *Psychotherapy Research, 84*(4), 455–74.

Psychologists Board of Queensland (2006). *Registrants Update, April 2006.* Brisbane: Psychologists Board of Queensland.

Psychologists Board of Queensland (2008). *Annual Report 2007–2008.* Brisbane: Psychologists Board of Queensland.

Psychology Board of Australia (2010). *Guidelines for Mandatory Notifications*. Canberra: Psychology Board of Australia.

Rachman, S. (1997). Cognitive theory of obsessions. *Behaviour Research and Therapy*, *35*, 793–802.

Raes, F., Prommier, E., Neff, K. D., & Van Guckht, D. (2010). Construction and factorial validation of a short form of the Self-Compassion Scale. *Clinical Psychology and Psychotherapy*, 18(3): 250–5.

Raimy, V. C. (ed.) (1950). *Training in Clinical Psychology*. New York: Prentice Hall.

Ramakrishnan, K. (2008). Evaluation and treatment of enuresis. *American Family Physician*, *78*, 489–96.

RANZCP (2003). Australian and New Zealand clinical practice guidelines for the treatment of panic disorder and agoraphobia. *Australian and New Zealand Journal of Psychiatry*, *37*, 661–6.

RANZCP (2004). Australian and New Zealand Clinical Practice Guidelines for the treatment of depression. Australian and New Zealand Journal of Psychiatry, *38*, 389–407.

Ranzijn, R., McConnochie, K., & Nolan, W. (2009). *Psychology and Indigenous Australians: Foundation of Cultural Competence*. South Yarra: Palgrave Macmillan.

Raphael, B. & Swan, P. (1997). The mental health of Aboriginal and Torres Strait Islander people. *International Journal of Mental Health*, 26(3), 9–22.

Raquepaw, J. W. & Miller, R. S. (1989). Psychotherapist burnout: A componential analysis. *Professional Psychology: Research and Practice*, 20(1), 32–6.

Raue, P. J. & Goldfried, M. R. (1994). The therapeutic alliance in cognitive-behavior therapy. In Horvath, A. O. & Greenberg, L. S. (eds). *The Working Alliance: Theory, Research, and Practice*. New York: John Wiley, 131–52.

Raue, P. J., Goldfried, M. R., & Barkham, M. (1997). The therapeutic alliance in psychodynamic-interpersonal and cognitive-behavioral therapy. *Journal of Consulting and Clinical Psychology*, *65*, 582–7.

Rector, N. A. (2005). Cognitive behavioural therapy reduces short term rehospitalisation compared with psychoeducation in inpatients with schizophrenia. *Evidence Based Mental Health*, 8(1), 8.

Rector, N. A., Zuroff, D. C. & Segal, Z. V. (1999). Cognitive change and the therapeutic alliance: The role of technical and nontechnical factors in cognitive therapy. *Psychotherapy: Theory, Research, Practice, Training*, 36(4), 320–8.

Reese, R. J., Norsworthy, L. A., & Rowlands, S. R. (2009). Does a continuous feedback system improve psychotherapy outcome? *Psychotherapy: Theory, Research, Practice, Training*, *46*, 418–431.

Reese, R. J., Usher, E. L., Bowman, D. C., Norsworthy, L. A., Halstead, J. L., Rowlands, S. R., & Chisholm, R. R. (2009). Using client feedback in psychotherapy training: An analysis of its influence on supervision and counselor self-efficacy. *Training and Education in Professional Psychology*, 3(3), 157–168.

Regier, D. A. (2007). Dimensional approaches to psychiatric classification: Refining the research agenda for DSM-V: An introduction. *International Journal of Methods in Psychiatric Research*, 16(S1): S1–S5.

Ressler, K. J., Rothbaum, B. O., Tannenbaum, L., Anderson, P., Grapp, K., Zimand, E. et al. (2004). Cognitive enhancers as adjuncts to psychotherapy: Use of D-cycloserine in phobic individuals to facilitate extinction of fear. *Archives of General Psychiatry, 61*(11), 1136–44.

Reynolds, C. F., Frank, E., Perel, J., Imber, S., Cornes, C. Miller, M. Mazmdar, S., Houck, P. R., Dew, M. A., Stack, J. A., Pollock, B. G., & Kupfer, D. J. (1999) . Nortriptyline and interpersonal psychotherapy as maintenance therapies for recurrent major depression. *Journal of the American Medical Association, 281*, 39–45.

Reynolds, W. (1991). *Adult Suicidal Ideation Questionnaire: Professional Manual.* Odessa, FL: Psychological Assessment Resources.

Reynolds, W. & Mazza, J. (1992). *Suicidal Behaviour History Form: Clinicians' Guide.* Odessa, FL: Psychological Assessment Resources.

Richards, P. S. & Bergin, A. E. (1997). *A Spiritual Strategy for Counseling and Psychotherapy.* Washington, DC: American Psychological Association.

Richards, P. S., & Bergin, A. E. (eds). (2000). *Handbook of Psychotherapy and Religious Diversity.* Washington, DC: American Psychological Association.

Richards, P. S. & Bergin, A. E. (2004). *Casebook for a Spiritual Strategy in Counseling and Psychotherapy.* Washington, DC: American Psychological Association.

Ricks, D. (1974). Supershrink: Methods of a therapist judged successful on the basis of adult outcome of adolescent patients. In Ricks, D., Roff, M. & Thomas, A. (eds). *Life History Research in Psychopathology*, Vol. III. Minneapolis: University of Minnesota Press.

Rief, W., Nestoriuc, Y., Weiss, S., Welzel, E., Barsky, A. J., & Hofmann, S. G. (2008). Meta-analysis of the placebo response in antidepressant trials. *Journal of Affective Disorders, 118*, 1–8.

Riggio, R. E. (1986). Assessment of basic social skills. *Journal of Personality and Social Psychology, 51*(3), 649–60.

Ritterband, L. M., Gonder-Frederick, L. A., Cox, D. J., Clifton, A. D., West, R. W., & Borowitz, S. M. (2003). Internet interventions: In review in use and into the future. *Professional Psychology: Research & Practice, 34*(5), 527–34.

Robbins, S. B. (1989). Role of contemporary psychoanalysis in counseling psychology. *Journal of Counseling Psychology, 36*(3), 267–78.

Robiner, W. N., Arbisi, P. A., & Edwall, G. E. (1994). The basis for the doctoral degree for psychology licensure. *Clinical Psychology Review, 14*(4), 227–54.

Rodin, J. & Langer, E. (1977). Long term effects of a control-relevant intervention with the institutionalized aged. *Journal of Personality and Social Psychology, 35*(12), 35897–902.

Roe, R. A. (2002). What makes a competent psychologist? *European Psychologist, 7*(3), 192–202.

Rogers, C. R. (1942). *Counseling and Psychotherapy: Newer Concepts in Practice.* Boston: Houghton Mifflin.

Rogers, C. R. (1946). Significant aspects of client-centered therapy. *American Psychologist, 1*, 415–22.

Rogers, C. R. (1951). *Client-Centred Therapy: Its Current Practice, Implications, and Theory.* Boston: Houghton Mifflin

Rogers, C. R. (1957). The necessary and sufficient conditions of therapeutic personality change. *Journal of Consulting Psychology, 21*, 95–103.

Rogers, C. R. (1961). *On Becoming a Person: A Therapist's View of Psychotherapy.* Boston: Houghton Mifflin.

Rogers, C. R. (1980). *A Way of Being*. Boston: Houghton Mifflin.

Rogers, C. R., Gendlin, G. T., Kiesler, D. V., & Truax, L. B. (1967). *The Therapeutic Relationship and its Impact: A study of Psychotherapy with Schizophrenics*. Madison: University of Wisconsin Press.

Rosenberg, C. M., Gerrein, J. R., Manohar, V., & Liftik, J. (1976). Evaluation of training of alcoholism counselors. *Journal of Studies on Alcohol, 37*(9), 1236–46.

Rosenzweig, S. (1936). Some implicit common factors in diverse methods of psychotherapy. *American Journal of Orthopsychiatry, 6*, 412–14.

Roth, A. & Fonagy, P. (2005). *What Works for Whom? A Critical Review of Psychotherapy Research* (2ndedn). New York: Guildford Press.

Rounsaville, B. J. (2002). Experience with ICD-10/DSM-IV substance use disorders. *Psychopathology, 35*(2–3), 82–8.

Rowe, W., Murphy, H. B., & Csipkes, R. A. (1975). The relationship of counselor characteristics and counseling effectiveness. *Review of Educational Research, 45*(2), 231–46.

Rupert, P. A. & Morgan, D. J. (2005). Work setting and burnout among professional psychologists. *Professional Psychology: Research and Practice, 36*, 544–50.

Ryan, R. M. & Deci, E. L. (2000). Self-determination theory and the facilitation of intrinsic motivation, social development, and well-being. *American Psychologist, 55*, 68–78.

Ryan, R. M. & Deci, E. L. (2001). On happiness and human potentials: a review of research on hedonic and eudaimonic well-being. *Annual Review of Psychology, 52*, 141–66.

Ryff, C. D. & Singer, B. (1998). Contours of positive human health. *Psychological Inquiry, 9*, 1–28.

Sable, P. (1997). Disorders of adult attachment. *Psychotherapy: Theory, Research, Practice, Training, 34*(3), 286–96.

Sadock, B. J. & Sadock, V. A. (2007). *Kaplan and Sadock's Synopsis of Psychiatry: Behavioral Sciences/Clinical Psychiatry* (10th edn). Philadelphia: Wolters Kluwer.

Safran, J. D., Crocker, P., McMain, S., & Murray, P. (1990). Therapeutic alliance rupture as a therapy event for empirical investigation. *Psychotherapy, 27*(2), 154–65.

Safran, J. D. & Muran, J. C. (1996). The resolution of ruptures in the therapeutic alliance. *Journal of Consulting and Clinical Psychology, 64*(3), 447–58.

Safran, J. D., & Wallner, L. K. (1991). The relative predictive validity of two therapeutic alliance measures in cognitive therapy. *Psychological Assessment, 3*, 188–95.

Saggese, M. L. (2005). Maximising treatment effectiveness in clinical practice: An outcome-informed, collaborative approach. *Families in Society: The Journal of Contemporary Social Services, 86*, 558–64.

Sales, C. M. D., & Alves, P. C. G. (2012). Individualized patient-progress systems: Why we need to move towards a personalized evaluation of psychological treatments. *Canadian Psychology, 53*(2), 115–121.

Samoilov, A. & Goldfried, M. R. (2000). Role of emotion in cognitive-behavior therapy. *Clinical Psychology: Science and Practice, 7*(4), 373–85.

Samstag, L. W. (2002). The common versus unique factors hypothesis in psychotherapy research: Did we misinterpret Rosenzweig? *Journal of Psychotherapy Integration, 12*(1), 58–66.

Sanders, S. H. (2006). Behavioral conceptualization and treatment for chronic pain. *Behavior Analyst Today, 7,* 253–75.

Sapyta, J., Riemer, M., & Bickman, L. (2005). Feedback to clinicians: Theory, research, and practice. *Journal of Clinical Psychology, 61,* 145–53.

Saunders, C. (1998). Solution focused therapy: What works? *Counselling, 9,* 45–8.

Savicki, V. & Cooley, E. J. (1987). The relationship of work environment and client contact to burnout in mental health professionals. *Journal of Counseling and Development, 1,* 249–52.

Saxena, S., Brody, A. L., Maidment, K. M., Dunkin, J. J., Colgan, M., Alborzian, S., Phelps, M. E., Baxter Jr, L. R. (1999). Localized orbitofrontal and subcortical metabolic changes and predictors of response to paroxetine treatment in obsessive-compulsive disorder. *Neuropsychopharmacology, 21*(6), 683–93.

Scatterfield, W. A. & Lyddon, W. J. (1998). Client attachment and the working alliance. *Counseling Psychology Quarterly, 11,* 407–15.

Schacht, T. E. (1985). DSM-III and the politics of truth. *American Psychologist, 40*(5), 513–21.

Schank, J. A. & Skovholt, T. M. (2006). Ethical practice in small communities: Challenges and rewards for psychologists. *Washington DC: American Psychological Association.*

Schmidt, L. D. & Strong, S. R. (1970). 'Expert' and 'inexpert' counselors. *Journal of Counseling Psychology, 17*(2), 115–18.

Schreurs, A. (2002). *Psychotherapy and Spirituality: Integrating the Spiritual Dimension into Therapeutic Practice.* London: Jessica Kingsley.

Schulte, D. (2008). Patients' outcome expectancies and their impression of suitability as predictors of treatment outcome. *Psychotherapy Research, 18*(4), 481–94.

Schwartz, B. & Flowers, J. (2006). *How to Fail as a Therapist: 50 Ways to Lose or Damage Your Patients.* Atascedero: Impact Publishers.

Schwartz, J. M., Stoessel, P. W., Baxter Jr., L. R., Martin, K., & Phelps, M. (1996). Systematic changes in cerebral glucose metabolic rate after successful behavior modification treatment of obsessive-compulsive disorder. *Archives of General Psychiatry, 53*(2), 109–13.

Scogin, F. & McElreath, L. (1994). Efficacy of psychosocial treatments for geriatric depression: A quantitative review. *Journal of Consulting and Clinical Psychology, 62,* 69–74.

Segal, Z. V., Williams, J. M. G., & Teasdale, J. D. (2002). *Mindfulness-Based Cognitive Therapy for Depression: A New Approach to Preventing Relapse.* New York: Guilford Press.

Seitz, P. (1966). The consensus problem in psychoanalytic research. In Gottschalk, L. A. & Auerbach, A. H. (eds). *Methods of Research in Psychotherapy.* New York: Appleton-Century Crofts, 209–25.

Seligman, M. (2002). *Authentic Happiness: Using the New Positive Psychology to Realize Your Potential for Lasting Fulfillment.* New York: Simon & Schuster.

Seligman, M. E. (1991). *Learned Optimism.* New York: Knopf.

Seligman, M. E. & Csikszentmihalyi, M. (2000). Positive psychology: An introduction. *American Psychologist, 55,* 5–14.

Seligman, M. E., Rashid, T., & Parks, A.C. (2006). Positive psychotherapy. *American Psychologist, 61,* 774–88.

Seligman, M. E., Steen, T. A., Park, N., & Peterson, C. (2005). Positive psychology progress: Empirical validation of interventions. *American Psychologist, 60*, 410–21.

Shahid, S., Finn, L., Bessarab. D., & Thompson, S. C. (2009). Understanding, beliefs and perspectives of Aboriginal people in Western Australia about cancer and its impact on access to cancer services. *Biomed Central Health Services Research, 9*, 132.

Shapiro, D. A., Barkham, M., Rees, A., Hardy, G. E., Reynolds, S., & Starup, M. (1994). Effects of treatment duration and severity of depression on the effectiveness of cognitive-behavioural and psychodynamic-interpersonal psychotherapy. *Journal of Consulting and Clinical Psychology, 62*, 522–34.

Shapiro, D. A. & Shapiro, D. (1982). Meta-analysis of comparative therapy outcome research: A critical appraisal. *Behavioural Psychotherapy, 10*(4–25).

Sharf, R. S. (2004). *Theories of Psychotherapy and Counselling: Concepts and Cases* (3rd edn). Pacific Grove: Thomson, Brooks/Cole.

Sharp, S., Thomas, C., Rosenberg, L., Rosenberg, M., & Meyer, W. (2010). Propranolol does not reduce risk for acute stress disorder in pediatric burn trauma. *Journal of Trauma, 68*, 193–197.

Shaw, A., Joseph, S., & Linley, P. A. (2005). Religion, spirituality, and posttraumatic growth: A systematic review. *Mental Health, Religion, and Culture, 8*, 1–11.

Shedler, J. (2010). The efficacy of psychodynamic psychotherapy. *American Psychologist, 65*(2), 98–109.

Sherman, M. D. (1996). Distress and professional impairment due to mental health problems among psychotherapists. *Clinical Psychology Review, 16* (4), 299–315.

Sherman, A. C. & Plante, T. G. (2001). Conclusions and future directions for research on faith and health. In Plante, T. G. & Sherman, A. C. (eds). *Faith and Health: Psychological Perspectives*. New York: Guildford Press, 389–402.

Shirk, S. R., & Karver, M. (2003). Prediction of treatment outcome from relationship variables in child and adolescent therapy: A meta-analytic review. *Journal of Consulting and Clinical Psychology, 71*(3), 452–64.

Shohet, R. (2008). *Passionate Supervision*. London: Jessica Kingsley Publishers.

Sholevar, G.P. (2003). Family theory and therapy. In Sholevar, G. P. & Schwoeri, L.D. (eds). *Textbook of Family and Couples Therapy: Clinical Applications*. Washington, DC: American Psychiatric Publishing, 3–28.

Sifneos, P.E. (1979). *Short-Term Dynamic Psychotherapy*. New York: Plenum Medical.

Silberschatz, G. & Curtis, J. T. (1993). Measuring the therapist's impact on the patient's therapeutic process. *Journal of Consulting & Clinical Psychology, 3*, 403–11.

Simon, G. E., Goldberg, D. T., Von Korff, M., & Ustun, T. B. (2002). Understanding cross-national differences in depression prevalence. *Psychological Medicine, 32*, 585–94.

Simons, R. C. (1980). The resolution of the Latah paradox. *Journal of Nervous and Mental Disease, 168*(4), 195–206.

Skinner, B. F. (1976). *About Behaviorism*. New York: Vintage Books.

Skodol, A. E., Buckley, P., & Charles, E. (1983). Is there a characteristic pattern to the treatment history of clinic outpatients with borderline personality? *Journal of Nervous and Mental Disease, 171*(7), 405–10.

Skovholt, T. M. & Jennings, L. (2004). *Master Therapists: Exploring Expertise in Therapy and Counselling.* Boston: Pearson.

Slade, L., Lambert, M. J., Harmon, S. C., Smart, D. W., & Bailey, R. (2008). Improving psychotherapy outcome: The use of immediate electronic feedback and revised clinical support tools. *Clinical Psychology & Psychotherapy, 15,* 287–303.

Slagle, D. M. & Gray, M. J. (2007). The utility of motivational interviewing as an adjunct to exposure therapy in the treatment of anxiety disorders. *Professional Psychology: Research and Practice, 38,* 329–37.

Sledge, W. H., Moras, K., Hartley, D., & Levine, M. (1990). Effect of time-limited psychotherapy on client dropout rates. *American Journal of Psychiatry, 147,* 1341–7.

Sloane, R. B., Staples, F. R., Cristol, A. H., Yorkston, N. J., & Whipple, K. (1975). Short-term analytically oriented psychotherapy versus behavior therapy. *American Journal of Psychiatry, 132*(4), 373–7.

Smedley, B. D., Stith, A. Y., & Nelson, A. R. (2003). *Unequal Treatment: Confronting Racial and Ethnic Disparities in Health Care.* Washington, DC: National Academies Press.

Smith, J. E., Milford, J. L., & Meyers, R. J. (2004). CRA and CRAFT: Behavioral approaches to treating substance-abusing individuals. *Behavior Analyst Today, 5,* 391–403.

Smith, M. L. & Glass, G. V. (1977). Meta-analysis of psychotherapy outcome studies. *American Psychologist, 32,* 752–60.

Smith, M. L., Glass, G. V., & Miller, T. I. (1980). *The Benefits of Psychotherapy.* Baltimore: John Hopkins University Press.

Smith, P. L. & Moss, S. B. (2009). Psychologist impairment: What is it, how can it be prevented, and what can be done to address it? *Clinical Psychology: Science and Practice, 16*(1), 1–15.

Snyder, C. R. & Lopez, S. J. (eds) (2002). *Handbook of Positive Psychology.* Oxford: Oxford University Press.

Snyder, C. R., Michael, S. T., & Cheavens, J. S. (1999). Hope as a psychotherapeutic foundation of common factors, placebos and expectancies. In Hubble, M. A., Duncan B. L., & Miller, S. D. (eds) *The Heart and Soul of Change: What Works in Therapy.* Washington, DC: American Psychological Association, 179–200.

Spitzer, R. L. & Williams, J. B. W. (1982). The definition and diagnosis of mental disorder. In Gove, W. R. (ed.). *Deviance and Mental Illness* Beverly Hills, CA: Sage, 15–32.

Spitzer, R. L., Williams, J. B. W., & Skodol, A. E. (1980). DSM-III: The major achievements and an overview. *American Journal of Psychiatry, 137,* 151–64.

Somberg, D. R., Stone,G. L., & Claiborn,C. D. (1993). Informed consent: Therapists' beliefs and practices. *Professional Psychology: Research and Practice, 24,* 153–9.

Sommers-Flanagan, J. & Sommers-Flanagan, R. (2003). *Clinical Interviewing.* Hoboken, NJ: John Wiley.

Soyguet, G., Nelson, L., & Safran, J. D. (2001). The relationship between patient pretreatment interpersonal schemas and therapeutic alliance in short-term cognitive therapy. *Journal of Cognitive Psychotherapy, 15*(1), 59–66.

Sparks, J. A., Duncan, B. L., & Miller, S. D. (2006). Integrating psychotherapy and pharmacotherapy: Myths and the missing link. *Journal of Family Psychotherapy, 17*(3–4), 83–107.

Spek, V., Cuijpers, P., Nyklicek, I., Riper, H., Keyzer, J., & Pop, V. (2007). Internet-based cognitive behaviour therapy for symptoms of depression and anxiety: A meta-analysis. *Psychological Medicine, 37*, 319–28.

Sperry, L., Brill, P. L., Howard, K. I., & Grissom, G. R. (1996). Treatment outcomes in psychotherapy and psychiatric interventions. New York: Brunner/Mazel.

Spruil, J., Rozensky, R. H., Stigall, T. T., Vasquez, M., Bingham, R. P., & De Vaney Olvey, C. (2004). Becoming a competent clinician: basic competencies in intervention. *Journal of Clinical Psychology, 60*(7), 741–54.

Stahl, S. M. (2006). *Essential Psychopharmacology: The Prescriber's Guide* (rev. edn). Cambridge: Cambridge University Press.

Stahl, S. M. (2008). *Essential Psychopharmacology: Neuroscientific Basis and Practical Applications* (3rd edn). Cambridge: Cambridge University Press.

Stein, D. M. & Lambert, M. J. (1984). On the relationship between therapist experience and psychotherapy outcome. *Clinical Psychology Review, 4*(2), 127–42.

Stein, D. M. & Lambert, M. J. (1995). Graduate training in psychotherapy: Are therapy outcomes enhanced? *Journal of Consulting and Clinical Psychology, 63*(2), 182–96.

Stein, M. B., Kerridge, C., Dimsdale, J. E., & Hoyt, D. B. (2007) Pharmacotherapy to prevent PTSD: Results from a randomized controlled proof-of-concept trial in physically injured patients. *Journal of Traumatic Stress, 20*, 923–932.

Sternberg, R. J. (2000). Images of mindfulness. *Journal of Social Issues, 56*(1), 11–26.

Stiell, K., Naaman, S. C., & Lee, A. (2007). Emotion-focused therapy: Pioneering new treatment for emotional trauma and depression. *Journal of Systemic Therapies, 26*(4), 59–75.

Stiles, W. B., Honos Webb, L., & Surka, M. (1998). Responsiveness in psychotherapy. *Clinical Psychology: Science and Practice, 5*(4), 439–58.

Stiles, W. B., Shapiro, D. A., & Elliot, R. (1986). Are all psychotherapies equivalent? *American Psychologist, 41*(2), 165–80.

Storr, A. (1990). *The Art of Psychotherapy* (2nd edn). Oxford: Butterworth Heinemann.

Strauss, J. L., Johnson, S. L., Laurenceau, J.-P., Hayes, A. M., Newman, C. F., Brown, G. K., Barker, J. P., & Beck, A. T. (2006). Early alliance, alliance ruptures, and symptom change in a nonrandomised trial of cognitive therapy for avoidant and obsessive-compulsive personality disorders. *Journal of Consulting and Clinical Psychology, 74*(2), 337–45.

Straus, M. A. (2007). Conflict tactics scales. In Jackson, N. A. (ed.). *Encyclopedia of Domestic Violence*. New York: Routledge/Taylor & Francis, 190–7.

Straus, M. A., Hamby, S. L., Boney-McCoy, S., Sugarman, D. B. (1996). The Revised Conflict Tactics Scales (CTSZ): Development and preliminary psychometric data. *Journal of Family Issues, 17*(3), 283–316.

Strentz, T., & Auerbach, S. M. (1988). Adjustment to the stress of simulated captivity: Effects of emotion-focused versus problem-focused preparation on hostages differing in locus of control. *Journal of Personality and Social Psychology, 55*(4), 652–60.

Striegel-Moore, R. H., Dohm, F. A., Kraemer, H. C., Taylor, C. B., Daniels, S., Crawford, P. B., & Schreiber, G. B. (2003). Eating disorders in white and black women. *American Journal of Psychiatry, 160*, 1326–31.

Strong, S. R. & Matross, R. P. (1973). Change process in counseling and psychotherapy. *Journal of Counseling Psychology, 20*(1), 25–37.

Strupp, H. H. (1973). On the basic ingredients of psychotherapy. *Journal of Consulting and Clinical Psychology, 41*(1), 1–8.

Strupp, H. & Binder, J. (1984). *Psychotherapy in a New Key: A Guide to Time-Limited Dynamic Psychotherapy.* New York: Basic Books.

Stuart, R. B. (1967). Behavioral control of overeating. *Behavior Research and Therapy, 6,* 357–65.

Stuart, R. B. (2004). Twelve practical suggestions for achieving multicultural competence. *Professional Psychology: Research and Practice, 35*(1), 3–9.

Sue, D. W. & Sue, D. (2008). *Counseling the Culturally Diverse: Theory and Practice* (5th edn). Hoboken, NJ: John Wiley.

Sue, S. & Dhindsa, M. (2006). Ethnic and racial health disparities research: Issues and problems. *Health Education and Behavior, 33*(4), 459–69.

Sullivan, H. A. (1956). *Clinical Studies in Psychology.* New York: Norton.

Symons, M. (2009). Legal and ethical aspects of working with young people. *Inpsych, 31*(4), 28–9.

Szasz, T. S. (1972). *The Myth of Mental Illness: Foundations of a Theory of Personal Conduct.* London: Paladin.

Szasz, T. S. (1974). *The Myth of Mental Illness: Foundations of a Theory of Personal Conduct* (rev. edn). New York: Harper & Row.

Szasz, T. S. (1978). *The Myth of Psychotherapy: Mental Healing as Rhetoric, Religion, and Repression.* Garden City, NY: Doubleday.

Szasz, T. S. (1982). The psychiatric will: A new mechanism for protecting persons against 'psychosis' and psychiatry. *American Psychologist, 37,* 762–70.

Tarrier, N., Wells, A., Haddock, G., & Davidson, J. (2000). Treating complex cases: The cognitive behavioural approach. *Journal of Cognitive Psychotherapy, 14*(4), 410–13.

Telch, C. F., Agra, W. S., & Linehan, M. M. (2001). Dialectical behavior therapy for binge eating disorder. *Journal of Consulting and Clinical Psychology, 69,* 1016–69.

Teyber, E. (2006). *Interpersonal Process in Therapy: An Integrative Model* (5th ed). Belmont, CA: Thomson Brooks/Cole.

Teyber, E. & McClure, F. (2000). Therapist variables. In Snyder, C. R. & Ingram, R. E. (eds). *Handbook of Psychological Change: Psychotherapy Processes and Practices for the 21st Century.* New York: John Wiley, 62–87.

Teyber, E. & McClure, F. H. (2010). *Interpersonal Process in Therapy: An Integrative Model* (6th edn). Florence, KY: Brooks/Cole.

Thackwray, D. E., Smith, M. C., Bodfish, J. W., & Meyers, A. W. (1993). A comparison of behavioral and cognitive-behavioral interventions for bulimia nervosa. *Journal of Consulting and Clinical Psychology, 61,* 639–45.

Thompson, S. C. & Wierson, M. (2000). Enhancing perceived control in psychotherapy. In Snyder, C. R. & Ingram, R. E. (eds). *Handbook of Psychological Change: Psychotherapy Processes and Practices for the 21st Century.* New York: John Wiley, 177–97.

Thoreson, R. W., Budd, F. C., & Krauskopf, C. J. (1986). Alcoholism among psychologists: Factors in relapse and recovery. *Professional Psychology: Research and Practice, 17,* 497–503.

Thoresen, C., Luskin, F., & Harris, A. (1998). Science and forgiveness interventions: Reflections and recommendations. In Worthington. E. (ed.). *Dimensions of For-*

giveness: Psychological Research and Theological Perspectives. Philadelphia: Temple-ton Foundation, 163–92.

Thoreson, R. W., Miller, M., & Krauskopf, C. J. (1989). The distressed psychologist: Prevalence and treatment considerations. *Professional Psychology: Research and Practice, 20,* 153–8.

Tomison, A. (2000). *Exploring Family Violence: Links between Child Maltreatment and Domestic Violence.* Issues in Child Abuse Prevention, No 13. Sydney: Australian Domestic and Family Violence Clearing House.

Tori, C. D. (1989). Quality assurance standards in the education of psychologists: Reliability and validity of objective comprehensive examinations developed at a freestanding professional school. *Professional Psychology: Research and Practice, 20*(4), 203–8.

Tracey, T. J. (1986). Interactional correlates of premature termination. *Journal of Consulting and Clinical Psychology, 54*(6), 784–8.

Tracey, T. J. (1988). Relationship of responsibility attribution congruence to psychotherapy outcome. *Journal of Social and Clinical Psychology, 7,* 131–46.

Tracey, T. J., & Kokotovic, A. M. (1989). Factor structure of the Working Alliance Inventory. *Psychological Assessment: A Journal of Consulting and Clinical Psychology, 1*(3), 207–10.

Tracey, T. J. G., Litchenberg, J. W., Goodyear, R. K., Claiborn, C. D., & Wampold, B. E. (2003). Concept mapping of therapeutic common factors. *Psychotherapy Research, 13*(4), 401–13.

Tracey, T. J. G. & Rounds, J. (1999). Inference and attribution errors in test interpretation. In Goodyear, R. K. & Lichtenberg, J. W. (eds). *Test Interpretation: Integrating Science and Practice.* Boston: Allyn & Bacon, 113–31.

Traux, C.B. (1966). Therapist empathy, warmth and genuineness and patient personality change in groups psychotherapy: A comparison between unit measures, time sample measures, patient perception mesurens. *Journal of Clinical Psychology, 22,* 225–9.

Trower, P., Casey, A., & Dryden, W. (1988). *Cognitive-Behavioural Counselling in Action.* London: Sage.

Tugade, M. M. & Fredrickson, B. L. (2004). Resilient individuals use positive emotion to bounce back from negative emotional experiences. *Journal of Personality and Social Psychology, 86,* 320–33.

Turner, R., Lukoff, D., Barnhouse, R. T., & Lu, F. G. (1995). Religious or spiritual problem: A culturally sensitive diagnostic category in the DSM-IV. *Journal of Nervous and Mental Disease, 183,* 435–44.

Tversky, A. & Kahneman, D. (2005). Judgment under uncertainty: Heuristics and biases. In Hamilton, D. L. (ed.). *Social Cognition: Key Readings.* New York: Psychology Press.

Vaiva, G., Ducrocq, F., Jezequel, K., Averland, B., Lestavel, P., Brunet, A., & Marmar, C. R. (2003). Immediate treatment with propranolol decreases posttraumatic stress disorder two months after trauma. *Biological Psychiatry, 54,* 947–949.

Valente, S. M. (1994). Psychotherapists reactions to the suicide of a patient. *Journal of Orthopsychiatry, 64,* 614–21.

Van Der Molen, H., Smit, G. N., Hommes, M. A., & Lang, G. (1995). Two decades of microtraining in the Netherlands: Narrative and meta-analysis. *Educational Research and Evolution*, *1*, 347–78.

Vicary, D. (2000). A model of intervention. In Dudgeon, P., Garvey, D., & Pickett, H. (eds). *Working with Indigenous Australians: A Handbook for Psychologists*. Perth: Gunada Press, 425–30.

Vicary, D. & Andrews, H. (2001). A model of therapeutic intervention with Indigenous Australians. *Australian and New Zealand Journal of Public Health*, *25*, 349–51.

Vitaliano, P. P., DeWolfe, D. J., Maiuro, R. D., Russo, J., & Katon, W. (1990). Appraised changeability of a stressor as a modifier of the relationship between coping and depression: A test of the hypothesis of fit. *Journal of Personality and Social Psychology*, *59*, 582–92.

Wakefield, J. C. (1998). Meaning and melancholia: Why the DSM-IV cannot (entirely) ignore the patient's intentional system. In Barron, J. W. (ed.). *Making Diagnosis Meaningful*. Washington, DC: American Psychological Association, 29–72.

Waldfogel, S. & Wolpe, P. R. (1993). Using awareness of religious factors to enhance interventions in consultation-liaison psychiatry. *Hospital and Community Psychiatry*, *44*, 473–7.

Wampold, B. E. (2001). *The Great Psychotherapy Debate: Models, Methods and Findings*. Mahwah, NJ: Lawrence Erlbaum.

Wampold, B. E. (2004). Foreword. In Duncan, B. L., Miller, S. D., & Sparks, J. *The Heroic Client: A Revolutionary Way to Improve Effectiveness through Client-Directed, Outcome-Informed Therapy* (rev. edn). San Francisco: Jossey-Bass.

Wampold, B. E. (2007). Psychotherapy: The humanistic (and effective) treatment. *American Psychologist*, *62*(8), 857–73.

Wampold, B. E., & Brown, J. (2005). Estimating variability in outcomes attributable to therapists: A naturalistic study of outcomes in managed care. *Journal of Consulting and Clinical Psychology*, *73*(5), 914–23.

Wampold, B. E. & Hubble, M. A. (eds). (2010). *The Heart and Soul of Change* (2nd edn). Washington, DC: American Psychological Association.

Wampold, B. E., Imel, Z. E., Bhati, K. S., & Johnson-Jennings, M. D. (2007). Insight as a common factor. In Castonguay, L. G. & Hill, C. E. (eds). *Insight in Psychotherapy*. Washington, DC: American Psychological Association, 119–39.

Wampold, B. E., Minami, T., Baskin, T. W., & Callen Tierney, S. (2002). A meta-re(analysis) of the effects of cognitive therapy versus 'other therapies' for depression. *Journal of Affective Disorders*, *68*, 159–65.

Wampold, B. E., Mondin, G. W., Moody, M., Stich, F., Benson, K., & Ahn, H. (1997). A meta-analysis of outcome studies comparing bona fide psychotherapies: Empirically, 'all must have prizes'. *Psychological Bulletin*, *122*(3), 203–15.

Watters, E. (2010). *Crazy Like Us: The Globalization of the American Psyche*. Carlton North: Scribe.

Webster's Ninth New Collegiate Dictionary. (1985). Springfield, MA: Webster's.

Weerasekera, P. (1996). *Multiperspective Case Formulation: A Step Towards Treatment Integration*. Melbourne: Krieger Publishing.

Weinberger, J. (1995). Common factors aren't so common: The common factors dilemma. *Clinical Psychology: Science and Practice, 2*(1), 45–69.

Weiss, L. (2004). *Therapist's Guide to Self-care.* New York: Brunner-Routledge.

Weissman, M. M., Markowitz, J. C., & Klerman, G. L. (2000). *Comprehensive Guide to Interpersonal Psychotherapy.* New York: Basic Books.

Weisz, J. R., Weiss, B., Alicke, M. D., & Klotz, M. L. (1987). Effectiveness of psychotherapy with children and adolescents: A meta-analysis for clinicians. *Journal of Consulting and Clinical Psychology, 55*(4), 542–9.

Wells, K. B., Burnam, A., Rogers, W., Hays, R., & Camp, P. (1992). The course of depression in adult outpatients. *Archives of General Psychiatry, 49,* 788–94.

Wells, M.I. (2000). Beyond cultural competence: A model for individual and institutional cultural development. *Journal of Community Health Nursing, 17*(4), 189–99.

Westerman, T. (2008). The value of unique service provision for Aboriginal Australians: The benefits of starting from scratch. In Ranzijn, R., McConnocie, K., & Nolan, W. (eds). *Psychology and Indigenous Australians: Foundation of Cultural Competence.* South Yarra: Palgrave Macmillan.

Wheeler, S. (2000). What makes a good counsellor? An analysis of ways in which counsellor trainers construe good and bad counselling trainees. *Counselling Psychology Quarterly, 13*(1), 65–83.

Wheeler, S. (2002). Nature or nurture: Are therapists born or trained? *Psychodynamic Practice, 9*(4), 427–41.

Whelton, W. J. (2004). Emotional processes in psychotherapy: Evidence across therapeutic modalities. *Clinical Psychology and Psychotherapy, 11,* 58–71.

Whisman, M. A. (1993). Mediators and moderators of change in cognitive therapy of depression. *Psychological Bulletin, 114*(2), 248–65.

Whipple, J. L., Lambert, M. J., Vermeersch, D. A., Smart, D. W., Nielsen, S. L., & Hawkins, E. J. (2003). Improving the effects of psychotherapy: The use of early identification of treatment failure and problem solving strategies in routine practice. *Journal of Counselling Psychology, 58,* 59–68.

Widiger, T. A. & Clark, L. A. (2000). Toward DSM-V and the classification of psychopathology. *Psychological Bulletin, 126*(6), 946–63).

Widiger, T. A. & Mullins-Sweatt, S. (2005). Categorical and dimensional models of personality disorder. InOldham, J., Skodol, A., & Bender, D. (eds). *Textbook of Personality Disorders.* Washington, DC: American Psychiatric Press, 35–53.

Widiger, T. A. & Sankis, L. (2000). Adult psychopathology: Issues and controversies. *Annual Review of Psychology, 51,* 377–404.

Wignenfield Hammond, S. & Freckelton, I. (2006). Being the subject of a complaint to a regulatory board. In Morrissey, S. & Reddy, P. *Ethics and Professional Practice for Psychologists.* Sydney: Thomson, 150–62.

Wierzbicka, A. (1999). *Emotions Across Languages and Cultures: Diversity and Universals.* Cambridge: Cambridge University Press.

Wierzbicki, M. & Pekarik, G. (1993). A meta-analysis of psychotherapy dropout. *Professional Psychology: Research and Practice, 24*(2), 190–95.

Wig, N. N. (1999). Mental health and spiritual values. A view from the east. *International Review of Psychiatry, 11,* 92–6.

Williams, E. N. & Fauth, J. (2005). A psychotherapy process study of therapist in session self-awareness. *Psychotherapy Research, 15*(4), 374–81.

Williams, F., Coyle, A., & Lyons, E. (1999). How counselling psychologists view their personal therapy. *British Journal of Medical Psychology, 72*, 545–55.

Williams, J. B. W., Gibbon, M. G., First, M. B., Spitzer, R. L., Davies, M., Borus, J., Howes, M. J., Kane, J., Pope, H. G., Rounsaville, B., & Wittchen, H. (1992). The Structured Clinical Interview for DSM-III-R (SCID): II. Multisite test-retest reliability. *Archives of General Psychiatry, 49*, 630–6.

Wills, F. & Sanders, D. (1997). *Cognitive Therapy.* London: Sage.

Wilson, G. & Abrams, D. (1977). Effects of alcohol on social anxiety and physiological arousal: Cognitive versus pharmacological procedures. *Cognitive Therapy and Research*, 1195–1210.

Wilson, M., & Sperlinger, D. (2004). Dropping out or dropping in? A Re-examination of the concept of dropouts using qualitative methodology. *Psychoanalytic Psychology, 18*(2), 220–37.

Wolfe, J. L. (2000). A vacation from musterbation. *Professional Psychology: Research and Practice, 31*, 581–3.

World Health Organization (2004). *The World Health Report, 2004.* Geneva: World Health Organization.

Worthington, E. L. & Sandage, S. J. (2001). Religion and spirituality. *Psychotherapy, 38*(4), 473–8.

Worthington, R. & & Atkinson, D. (1996). Effects of perceived etiology attribution similarity on client ratings of counselor credibility. *Journal of Counseling Psychology, 43*, 423–9.

Wykes, T., Steel, C., Everitt, B., & Tarrier, N. (2008). Cognitive behavior therapy for schizophrenia: Effect sizes, clinical models, and methodological rigor. *Schizophrenia Bulletin, 34*, 523–37.

Yalom, I. D. (1989). *Love's Executioner and Other Tales of Psychotherapy.* New York: Basic Books.

Yalom, I. D. (2001). *The Gift of Therapy. Reflections on Being a Therapist.* London: Judy Piatkus.

Yapko, M. D. (2003). *Trancework* (3rd edn). New York: Brunner-Routledge.

Yates, A. J. (1970). *Behavior Therapy.* New York: Wiley.

Ybarra, M. L., & Eaton, W. W. (2005). Internet-based mental health interventions. *Mental Health Services Research, 7*(2), 75–87.

Young, J. E., Klosko, J. S., & Weishaar, M. E. (2003). *Schema Therapy: The Practitioner's Guide.* London: Guilford Press.

Zahn-Waxler, C., Friedman, R.J., Cole, P. M., Mizuta, I., & Hiruma, N. (1996). Japanese and United States preschool children's responses to conflict and distress. *Child Development, 67*, 2462–77.

Zanarini, M. C. & Frankenburg, F. R. (2001). Attainment and maintenance of reliability of Axis I and II disorders over the course of a longitudinal study. *Comprehensive Psychiatry, 42*, 369–74.

Zarate, C. A., Brutsche, N. E., Ibrahim, L., Franco-Chaves, J., Diazgranados, N., Cravchik, A., et al. (in press). Replication of ketamine's antidepressant efficacy in bipolar depression: A randomized controlled add-on trial. *Biological Psychiatry.*

Zinnbauer, B. J., Pargament, K. I., and Scott, A. B. (1999). The emerging meanings of religiousness and spirituality: Problems and prospects. *Journal of Personality, 67*(6), 889–919.

Zuroff, D. C. & Blatt, S. J. (2006). The therapeutic relationship in the brief treatment of depression: Contributions to clinical improvement and enhanced adaptive capacities. *Journal of Consulting and Clinical Psychology, 74*(1), 130–40.

Zuroff, D. C., Blatt, S. J., Sotsky, S. M., Krupnick, J. L., Martin, D. J., Sanislow, C. A., & Simmens, S. (2000). Relation of therapeutic alliance and perfectionism to outcome in brief outpatient treatmet of depression. *Journal of Consulting and Clinical Psychology, 68*(1), 114–24.

Index

and depression 166
history and origin 129–130
interpersonal skills of therapists 82–86
interpersonal styles 66–67
interventions
    and case conceptualisation 279–280
    challenging 234–235
    and diagnosis 269–270
    explanation-consistent 49–50
    and informed consent 18
    responding to difficulties 280
interviews
    and Indigenous clients 292–293
    see also intake interviews
iproniazid 159

jobs available 325
journaling 125–126, 128

ketamine 164
knowledge and supervisors 335

language and Indigenous clients 293
legitimatisation of disorders 267–268
life
    engaged 156
    meaningful 156
    pleasant 156
lifestyle balance 351
likeableness and supervisors 336
limitations and self-care 351
listening skills 226–234
lithium 166
lithium carbonate 162–163
lorazepam 166

maltreatment, children at risk of 315–317
mandatory notifications 17, 33–34, 317, 323
mania 162
martyrdom 352
master-therapists 86–87
meaning, clients finding 235–236
medical model
    and diagnosis 261
    and psychology 261–263
Medicare Benefits Schedule (MBS)
    and dose-effect 191, 192–193
    and empirically supported treatments
        (ESTs) 41
    and ethics 33
    rebates 324–325
    and session length 214
    and session numbers 192–193
medications, psychiatric 165–166

mental health
    history of diagnosis 258–260
    psychopharmacological treatment
        158–164
    and religious beliefs 296–297
    and spiritual beliefs 296–297
methylphenidate 163, 166
mianserin 160, 165
midazolam 161
mind-body connection 352
mindful breathing 154
mindfulness 152, 352
    application and techniques 153–155
    attitudes 153–154
    exercise 154–155
    history and origin 152
    theory 152–153
    in therapy 153
mindfulness-based cognitive therapy
    (MBCT) 153
mindfulness-based eating awareness training
    (MB-EAT) 153
mindfulness-based stress reduction
    (MBSR) 153
miracle questions 141
mirtazpine 160
misunderstandings 333
    and empathy 225–226
moclobemide 160, 165
modafinil 166
modelling 128
monoamine oxidase inhibitors (MOIs) 159
    typical daily doses 166
mood 8, 307
mood stabilisers 162–163
    typical daily doses 166
motivation
    of clients 58
    of therapists 84–85
motivational interviewing (MI) 139–140
multi-method assessments 249–250

nature-nurture debate
    nature characteristics 81–82
    nurture characteristics 76–81
negative reinforcement 121
neuroscience 168–169
    application in psychotherapy 169–170
nomenclature 264
non-benzodiazepines
    sedative-hypnotics 161
    typical daily doses 166
non-judging 153–154
non-striving 154